The Well-Crafted Argument

A Guide and Reader

Third Edition

Fred D. White   *Santa Clara University*

Simone J. Billings   *Santa Clara University*

Houghton Mifflin Company

Boston   New York

Executive Publisher: Patricia Coryell
Editor in Chief: Carrie Brandon
Senior Sponsoring Editor: Lisa Kimball
Senior Marketing Manager: Tom Ziolkowski
Senior Project Editor: Samantha Ross
Art and Design Manager: Jill Haber
Cover Design Director: Tony Saizon
Senior Photo Editor: Jennifer Meyer Dare
Senior Composition Buyer: Chuck Dutton
New Title Project Manager: Susan Brooks-Peltier
Editorial Associate: Sarah Truax
Marketing Assistant: Bettina Chiu

Cover image: © Ralph Mercer, Ralph Mercer Photography.

Credits are on page xxvi, which constitutes an extension of the copyright page.

Printed in the U.S.A.

Library of Congress Control Number: 2007925597

ISBN-10: 0-618-83207-6
ISBN-13: 978-0-618-83207-1

3 4 5 6 7 8 9 – CRW– 11 10 09 08 07

Brief Contents

Contents

7 Researching Your Argument   194

8 Documenting Your Sources: MLA and APA Styles   221

3   Media Regulation: What Are the Issues?   354

6 Science and Religion: If Common Ground Exists, Where Does It Lie?   531

7 Biomedical Research: What Role Should Ethics Play?   586

8   Masterpieces of Argument: What Do They Teach Us About the Art of Persuasion?   648

Introduction   648

Preface

The ability to plan and write a well-crafted argument has always been highly prized, but never more so than in these times of rapid scientific and technological development and social change. Mastery of argumentative writing brings tremendous advantages in academia, in the workplace, and in life generally. It can also provide the satisfaction that comes with thoughtful self-expression and effective, responsible communication. For these reasons, we wrote *The Well-Crafted Argument: A Guide and Reader*. A textbook was clearly needed that could equip students with a comprehensive set of skills necessary for writing argumentative essays in a wide variety of contemporary social contexts. *The Well-Crafted Argument* is based on a process pedagogy that encourages individual voice and vision. At the same time, it introduces models of good writing that provide grounding for inexperienced writers.

Features

Over the years we have used a number of argumentation textbooks in our courses. Time after time, we found that these books left out too much—or put in too much that was not essential in helping students to master argumentative writing. This textbook is distinctive because it contains the following:

- **A thorough discussion of critical reading strategies**. Critical reading skills help students to understand and evaluate arguments, perform successful peer critiquing, and draft and revise their own arguments.

- **An introduction to the three principal methods of argument**. Separate chapters are devoted to instruction in Classical, Toulmin, and Rogerian methods of constructing arguments. Similarities and differences among the three methods are also discussed.

- **Extensive use of student essays to represent the full range of argumentative writing**. Both in Part I, The Rhetoric of Argument, and Part II, Reading Clusters, student argumentative essays are included to illustrate different topics and strategies and form the basis for discussions, exercises, and writing projects. No other textbook on argument contains so many student-written argumentative essays covering so many different topics and strategies.

- **A focus on the writing process as it applies to argumentative writing.** Chapter 1, The Nature and Process of Argument, and other chapters within Part I, The Rhetoric of Argument, consider the writing process—gathering ideas, drafting, and revising—in the context of structuring and writing effective arguments.

- **Comprehensive instruction in conducting research for purposes of argument.** Chapter 7, Researching Your Argument, helps students to locate and use print, database, and Internet resources, to use effective search strategies, and to avoid plagiarism. This chapter also introduces students to interviewing, conducting surveys, and designing questionnaires as ways of obtaining information. Chapter 8, Documenting Your Sources, presents MLA and APA citation styles, with examples.

Divided into two parts, a rhetoric and a reader, *The Well-Crafted Argument* provides instructors and students with a wealth of materials and tools for effective argumentative writing, thinking, and reading.

Part I: The Rhetoric of Argument

- **Practical Coverage.** Eight thorough and readable skills-building chapters cover (1) planning, drafting, and revising strategies for argumentative essay writing; (2) critical reading strategies, including strategies for reading and evaluating visual arguments, using (3) Classical, (4) Toulmin, and (5) Rogerian models to develop an argument; (6) reasoning effectively and recognizing pitfalls in reasoning; (7) researching arguments, and locating and integrating outside information using print, electronic, and interpersonal resources; and (8) documenting sources (both print and electronic), following the formats of the Modern Language Association (MLA) and the American Psychological Association (APA).

- **Reasoning skills covered in context.** This book combines methods of effective reasoning with instruction in identification and avoidance of *errors* of reasoning. Most argument texts present only an out-of-context discussion of the latter.

- **Thorough and pedagogically sound apparatus.** Exercises appear throughout each chapter to help students reinforce for themselves what they have just learned in a particular section. Each chapter concludes with a summary, a checklist of protocols relevant to each chapter, and a set of writing projects.

Part II: Reading Clusters

- **Fresh topics.** Part II presents 85 readings, many new to this edition, organized thematically into eight clusters. Popular debate topics such as freedom of speech and multicultural learning appear along with newer, and we hope, stimulating topics seldom represented in argument texts. These include intellectual property, intersections of science and religion, biomedical research, and national security issues. Each cluster includes a wide range of contrasting (not just opposing) views on issues that students will find intriguing and challenging, as well as refreshing.

- **Readings drawn from a wide range of sources.** Each cluster of readings includes essays from both mainstream periodicals and academic journals. Each cluster includes at least one student essay on that topic.

- **Famous essays well represented.** A separate cluster contains masterpieces of argument, including Plato's "Allegory of the Cave," Jonathan Swift's "A Modest Proposal," Frederick Douglass's "I Hear the Mournful Wail of Millions," Rachel Carson's "The Obligation to Endure," and Stanley Milgram's "The Perils of Obedience." We include this cluster so students can become acquainted with historically important arguments and consider ways of incorporating masterful argumentative techniques into their own arguments.

- **Readings from many disciplines.** Readings come from many academic disciplines: political science, international relations, biology and biotechnology, earth science, psychology, athletics, education, literature, law, communication, philosophy, religious studies, and cultural studies. Students thus are made dramatically aware of the fact that argumentative writing is vital to all fields.

- **Effective and interesting apparatus.** Each cluster begins with a brief introduction to the cluster topic and ends with Connections Among the Clusters questions, Writing Projects, and Suggestions for Further Reading. Each reading selection has a contextualizing headnote and is followed by Reflections and Inquiries questions and Reading to Write assignments.

New to the Third Edition

We have reinforced the strengths of the first and second editions by updating, enhancing, and adding new features.

- *New:* Expanded coverage of visual argument throughout the text, with special attention to reading visual arguments and applying the Aristotelian appeals to visual arguments.

- *New:* Two new cluster topics: argumentative essays, investigative and lively, in the area of Athletics and Academics and in the rapidly evolving, controversial field of Biomedical Research.

- *New:* Updated argumentative essays added to the existing clusters of Intellectual Property, and Religion and Science (including a new "Issues for Further Research" group of essays on the Intelligent Design controversy).

- **Expanded commentary on models of argument.** This new edition of *The Well-Crafted Argument* offers fuller commentary on the different models of argument, especially the Toulmin model. Toulmin's concepts of claims, qualifiers, grounds, backing, and warrants are presented in a way that students can more readily understand and apply. Essays illustrating these different methods are more fully annotated.

- **Expanded commentary on errors in reasoning.** Additional logical fallacies are introduced and illustrated. Also, additional exercises have been added throughout the chapter.

- **Updated information on search engines, databases, and Internet resources.**

- **More commentary on ways of avoiding plagiarism.** In addition, two essays on the subject of plagiarism appear in the Intellectual Property cluster.

- **Expanded discussion of the Aristotelian appeals.**

The Well-Crafted Argument Website

The Well-Crafted Argument has its own website at <college.hmco.com/PIC/white3e>. For instructors, the website contains sample syllabi; answer keys to selected exercises in the text; discussion launches for the reading clusters; handouts and transparency masters for peer critiquing guidelines; a sample essay evaluation sheet; information on other modes of argument such as satiric, evaluative (review), and motivational (with links); and information about where to look for help in teaching students for whom English is a second language. The Instructors Resource Manual is available in PDF on this site, for use in either electronic or print form. For students, the website provides resources to supplement topics covered in the text chapters and related topics. The website contains additional details on the Rhetorical Rhombus and on the Toulmin model; an interview with student writers, such as Daniela Gibson; additional sample student essays; additional examples of logical fallacies; grammar exercises; and an annotation exercise (containing an article to annotate). *The Well-Crafted Argument* website also provides links for Aristotle and Aristotelian (Classical) argument, Stephen Toulmin and Toulmin argument, Carl Rogers and Rogerian argument, logic, and the eight thematically organized reading clusters comprising Part II of the textbook. In addition, the site links students and instructors to the Houghton Mifflin Research Guide and the Library of Exercises.

Acknowledgments

We wish to thank Santa Clara University and our current and former department chairs John Hawley, Phyllis Brown, and Richard Osberg for their ongoing support of this project. We are also grateful to our colleagues Terry Malik, Jeff Zorn, and

Aparajita Nanda for their feedback. To our spouses, Terry M. Weyna and William R. Billings, we express our deepest gratitude for their inspiration, patience, understanding, and caring. We extend a special thank you to Devorah Harris, who expressed enthusiasm for the book from the very beginning.

Throughout the development of this text, many of our colleagues have been extremely helpful with their suggestions and generous with their time. We gratefully acknowledge the assistance of the following reviewers for the first, second, and third editions:

Edmund August, McKendree College; Joseph E. Becker, University of Maine at Fort Kent; Lynette Beers, Santiago Canyon College; Marck L. Beggs, Henderson State University; L. Bensel-Meyers, University of Denver; Ellen Bernabei, Grossmont College, Mirimar College; Nancy Blattner, Southeast Missouri State University; Arnold J. Bradford, Northern Virginia Community College; Sydney Darby, Chemeketa Community College; Christy Desmet, University of Georgia; Bonnie L. Ehmann, Gateway Community College; Tom Ghering, Ivy Tech Community College of Indiana; Emily Golson, University of Northern Colorado; Lorien J. Goodman, Pepperdine University; Keith Gumery, Temple University; Robert W. Hamblin, Southeast Missouri State University; Susan Hanson, Southwest Texas State University; William A. Harrison, III, Northern Virginia Community College; Karen Holleran, Kaplan College; Tom Howerton, Johnston Community College; J. Allston James, Monterey Peninsula College; Alex M. Joncas, Estrella Mountain Community College; Karen J. Jones, St. Charles Community College; Erin Karper, Purdue University; Eleanor Latham, Central Oregon Community College; Cathy Leaker, Empire State College; Debbie Mael, Newbury College; Rita Malenczyk, Eastern Connecticut State University; Linda McHenry, University of Oklahoma; JoAnna Stephens Mink, Minnesota State University; Bryan Moore, Arkansas State University, William Pierce, Prince George's Community College; Marcia Ribble, University of Cincinnati; Barbara Richter, Nova University; Libby Roeger, Shawnee College; Peter Burton Ross, University of the District of Columbia; Vicki Santiesteban, Broward Community College; Wayne Stein, University of Central Oklahoma; Daphne Swabey, University of Michigan; Jim Wallace, University of Akron; Kathleen Walsh, Central Oregon Community College; Taryn R. Williams, Johnston Community College.

We also wish to thank our students at Santa Clara University and at other academic institutions. Their help has been essential to the creation of this text, and we have learned a great deal from them. We owe a special debt of gratitude to the talented student writers who have given us permission to include their work: Nikolay Balbyshev, Gaby Caceras, Quentin Clark, Andrea De Anda, Powell Fraser, Chris Garber, Alicia Garcia, Daniela Gibson, Jarrett Green, Patrick

Green, Justine Hearn, Daniel Jackson, Scott Klausner, Michelle Lei, Daniel Neal, Alex Nickel, Regina Patzelt, Kareem Raad, Kelly Ryan, Nathan Salha, Elspeth Simpson, Kiley Strong, Mohammed Surve, and Gina Takasugi.

Finally, we thank the remarkable staff of Houghton Mifflin editors, in particular Carrie Brandon, Editor in Chief; Tom Ziolkowski, Senior Marketing Manager; Bess Deck, Development Manager; Lisa Kimball, Senior Sponsoring Editor; Judith Fifer, Senior Development Editor; Jane Acheson, Development Editor; Samantha Ross, Senior Project Editor; Sarah Truax, Editorial Associate; and Bettina Chiu, Marketing Assistant; and we are deeply grateful for the superb job of copyediting and book production of the third edition, coordinated by Merrill Peterson and his staff at Matrix Productions; many thanks to Sara Planck at Matrix for her shrewd assistance with last-minute copyediting.

We have made a special effort to present this challenging and complex material in an engaging, stimulating fashion, and we welcome all feedback on how this book can continue to be improved in the future. As supporters of well-crafted arguments in all their forms, we also invite users of this book to send in examples of argumentative writing to us, in care of Houghton Mifflin College English, 222 Berkeley Street, Boston, MA 02116, for consideration in subsequent editions. We also invite you to email us with any questions or suggestions you might have.

Fred D. White <fwhite@scu.edu>
Simone J. Billings <sbillings@scu>
Santa Clara University

Additional Text Credits

p. 35: Reprinted by permission of Steven Waldman, the editor-in-chief and CEO of beliefnet.com and John C. Green, Senior Fellow at the Pew Forum on Religion.

p. 327: Reproduced with permission of San Francisco Chronicle in the format textbook via Copyright Clearance Center.

p. 347: Reprinted by permission of Deborah R. Gerhardt, Copyright and Scholarly Communications Director, University Libraries, University of North Carolina at Chapel Hill, Director of Intellectual Property Initiative and Adjunct Professor of Law, UNC School of Law.

p. 443: The Association for Supervision and Curriculum Development is a worldwide community of educators advocating sounds policies and sharing best practices to achieve the success of each learner. To learn more, visit ASCD at www.ascd.org.

Photo Credits

Insert A: Courtesy Promax & Black Box Studio; insert B: Courtesy Florida's Natural Growers; insert C: PORSCHE, CARRERA, the Porsche Crest and the shape of the PORSCHE 911 are registered trademarks of Dr. Ing. h. c. F. Porsche AG. Used with permission of Porsche Cars North America, Inc. Copyrighted by Porsche Cars North America, Inc.; insert D: Courtesy Toyota Motor Sales/Saatchi & Saatchi LA; p. 22: Courtesy Catholic Charities, Chicago; p. 23: Courtesy The New Republic; p. 34: © The New Yorker Collection 1993 Mike Twohy from cartoonbank.com. All Rights Reserved; p. 37: © Stocko Inc.; p. 38: Data courtesy Ray. C.Bliss Institute and Pew Forum on Religion & Public Life/The Atlantic Monthly; p. 46: © Tony Auth; p. 46–51: Courtesy the Herb Block Foundation; p. 66: © David Plowden; p. 77: © Bettmann/CORBIS; p. 85: Erich Lessing/Art Resource, NY; p. 91: Courtesy UNICEF.org; p. 92 (top): Courtesy Joe Torre Safe At Home Foundation; (bottom): Digital Vision/Getty Images; p. 93: U.S. Army materials courtesy of the U.S. Government, as represented by the Secretary of the Army; p. 94: © Ed Quinn/Corbis; p. 97: Courtesy Americans for the Arts; p. 112: © Sijmen Hendriks; p. 136: Department of Special Collections, University of California. Reproduced, permission of Natalie Rogers; p. 265: © The New Yorker Collection 2002 Edward Koren from cartoonbank.com. All Rights Reserved; p. 302 (top left) : © Mike Segar/ Reuters/Corbis; p. 302 (top right) : © HO/Reuters/Corbis; p. 302 (middle left and right): © Randy Faris/Corbis; p. 302 (center): © Reuters/Corbis; p. 302 (bottom left): © Jessica Rinaldi/Stringer/Reuters/Corbis; p. 302 (bottom middle): © John Sommers/Reuters/Corbis; p. 302 (bottom right): © Comstock Select/Corbis; p. 312: © Lloyd Dangel Comics and Illustration; p. 355: © Chappatte in International Herald Tribune–www.globecartoons.com; p. 384: © Lionel Delevingne/Stock Boston; p. 389: © Gordon Parks/Corbis; p. 407: © Jim Huber/www.conservativecartoons. com; p. 436: © John Darkow/Cagle Cartoons; p. 437: © Monte Wolverton/Cagle Cartoons; p. 481: © Jim Harrison/Stock Boston; p. 490: © Slane Cartoons Limited; p. 500: © Darrin Bell/Bellcartoons.com; p. 532: Creators Syndicate; p. 576: © 2006 by the Council for Secular Humanism (CSH). This cartoon originally appeared in *Free Inquiry* magazine. Volume 26, number 3 (April/May 2006), published by the CSH in Amherst, New York; p. 578: © Bettmann/Corbis; p. 587: Speed Bump © 2004 Dave Coverly. All rights reserved. Used with the permission of Dave Coverly and the Cartoonist Group; p. 589: © Jonathon Rosen; p. 604: Peter MacDiarmid/Reuters; p. 649: AP Images/Nick Ut; p. 680: © Bettmann/Corbis; p. 685: © Bettmann/Corbis.

Part I

The Rhetoric of Argument

1 The Nature and Process of Argument

Give me the liberty to know, to utter, and to argue freely according to conscience, above all liberties.

—John Milton

The freedom to think for ourselves and the freedom to present and defend our views rank among the most precious rights that we as individuals possess, as the great poet and essayist John Milton knew. The more we know about argument—what it involves, how a strong argument is constructed, and what a weak argument lacks—the more likely we are to benefit from this liberty.

Why Argue?

All of us find occasions to argue every day. Sometimes we argue just to make conversation. We argue casually with friends about which restaurant serves the best food, which movies are the most entertaining, or which automobile performs the best or most reliably for the money. Sometimes we engage in arguments presented in the media, taking positions on topics debated in newspapers and magazines and on television, radio, and the Internet. And sometimes we argue in a more analytical manner on issues we have thought a lot about, such as which political party is most sympathetic to education reform, whether the Internet is a reliable research tool, or how we might solve a particular problem. When more is at stake, as in this last type of argument, the chances are greater that we will fail to be persuaded by what we hear or read or become frustrated by our own failure to persuade. We often fail to persuade because we lack evidence to back up our claims or because the evidence we do have is inadequate.

In other words, while casual arguments often consist of little more than exchanges of opinions or unsupported generalizations, more formal arguments are expected to include evidence in support of generalizations if they are to succeed in making strong points, solving real problems, or changing minds.

What Is an Argument?

People sometimes say that *everything* is an argument. That is quite true in the sense that whatever is communicated represents an individual point of view, one compelling enough to be accepted by the audience. Thus, if you're writing on a seemingly neutral *topic*, such as a day in the life of an emergency room nurse, you are implicitly arguing that your portrayal of the nurse is accurate and that nurses play a vital role in emergency rooms.

But *argument* as we use the term in this textbook is more explicitly an effort to change readers' minds about an issue. Thus, we would generally call a day-in-the-life article mainly explanatory or reportorial writing. However, if your aim is to show that people often have the wrong idea about the role or importance of hospital nurses, then you would be engaged in argumentative writing.

An argument must possess three basic ingredients to be successful. First, it must contain as much *relevant information* about the issue as possible. Second, it must present *convincing evidence* that enables the audience to accept the writer's or speaker's claim. The more controversial the claim, the more compelling the evidence must be. Third, it must lay out a *pattern of reasoning*. That is, it must logically progress from thesis to support of thesis to conclusion. Before we examine these three elements, though, let us consider a formal definition of argument.

A Formal Definition of Argument

An argument is *a form of discourse in which the writer or speaker tries to persuade an audience to accept, reject, or think a certain way about a problem that cannot be solved by scientific or mathematical reasoning alone.* The assertion that the circumference of a circle is a product of its diameter times *pi* is not arguable because the assertion cannot be disputed; it is a universally accepted mathematical fact. At the other extreme, asserting an unsubstantiated opinion is not stating an argument; it is only announcing a stance on a particular issue. For example, someone in a casual conversation who asserts that public flogging of robbers would be a more effective deterrent than jailing them is voicing an opinion, not presenting an argument. If you respond by saying "Yeah, probably," or "No way—that would contribute to a culture of violence," you are also stating an opinion. If you respond instead by requesting evidence, such as statistics that show a correlation between public punishment and crime rate, you are helping to shape the conversation into a true argument. It is useful to keep in mind that the word *argument* is derived from the Latin word *arguere*, to clarify or *prove*.

A good argument is not casual. It takes considerable time and effort to prepare. It not only presents evidence to back up its claim but also acknowledges the existence of other claims about the issue before committing to the claim that corresponds most closely to the arguer's convictions. A good argument also guides the audience through a logical, step-by-step line of reasoning from thesis to conclusion. In short, a good argument uses an argumentative *structure.*

Amplifying the Definition

Let us now amplify our definition of argument: An argument is *a form of discourse in which the writer or speaker presents a pattern of reasoning, reinforced by detailed evidence and refutation of challenging claims, that tries to persuade the audience to accept the claim.* Let us take a close look at each of the elements in this definition.

". . . a pattern of reasoning"   This element requires that a good argument disclose its train of thought in a logical progression that leads the reader or listener from thesis to support of thesis to conclusion. It also implies that any unfamiliar terms or concepts are carefully defined or explained, and that enough background information is provided to enable readers or listeners to understand the larger *context* (interacting background elements) contributing to the argument. For example, to make the claim that gas-guzzling sports utility vehicles (SUVs) are selling better than fuel-efficient subcompacts does not qualify as an argument because no context for the claim is given. Readers or listeners would ask, "So what?" But if the assertion is placed in the context of an urgent problem— for example, that the enormous popularity of SUVs is rapidly increasing gasoline consumption nationally, which in turn is leading to greater dependence on foreign oil—then a valid argument is established.

". . . reinforced by detailed evidence"   In a formal argument, any assertion must be backed up with specific, compelling evidence that is accurate, timely, relevant, and sufficient. Such evidence can be data derived from surveys, experiments, observations, and firsthand field investigations (statistical evidence), or from expert opinion (authoritative evidence).

". . . that tries to persuade the audience to accept the claim"   This last element of the definition brings to mind the ultimate aim of any argument: to convince the audience that the arguer's point of view is a sensible one, worthy of serious consideration if not outright acceptance. To accomplish this aim, arguers often reinforce their evidence with what are known as *appeals*—appeals to authority and traditional values, to feelings, and to reason. In an ideal world, evidence (the hard facts) alone would be enough to persuade audiences to accept the truth of a claim; but in reality, more persuasive force often is needed and appeals are drawn in.

Using Evidence in Argument

Argumentative writing uses two kinds of evidence: indisputable (or factual) and disputable. The first kind refers to matters of public record that anyone can verify. No one is going to dispute the fact that the earth revolves around the sun every 365.25 days, say, or that the state of California was admitted to the Union on September 9, 1850. How such facts are applied is another matter, but the facts themselves are beyond dispute.

But what about disputable evidence? Imagine that a friend's room is filled with art books and reproductions of paintings. If someone asks about this friend's interests, you would reply, "Art!" without hesitation, and cite as evidence the books and paintings. But that evidence is disputable: The books and paintings could belong to a roommate, could be a mere inheritance, or could represent a former interest only recently abandoned.

Just the fact that evidence is disputable, however, does not mean it is unreliable. Such evidence often represents the closest one can get to the truth. Will banning handguns prevent tragedies like the Columbine school shootings? One researcher might discover statistical evidence of a correlation between banning guns and reduced crime; yet another researcher could find evidence of a contrary correlation. Different parts of the country or the world, different years, different times of year, different age groups, all represent constantly changing variables that can affect such a correlation. The more aware you are of the possible ways in which evidence may be disputed, the less likely you are to reach facile or premature conclusions.

 Exercise 1.1

1. Consulting an unabridged dictionary, prepare a critical summary of the terms *argument, debate, dispute,* and *quarrel.* In what ways do the definitions differ? Where do they overlap, and how do you account for the overlap? Supplement these definitions with examples, drawing from your own experiences.

2. Which of the following assertions could be developed into a formal argument, and which could not? Explain your reasons.

   a. A clear link has been established between secondhand cigarette smoke and lung cancer.

   b. The Surgeon General has determined that smoking is a health hazard.

   c. Studying a foreign language gives children a greater command of their native language.

   d. The more video games children play, the less likely their abstract reasoning skills are to develop properly.

3. List the topics of recent disputes you have had with friends or family. Under each topic, note the claims asserted by each side, followed by any support that had been attempted for each. Next, go back over these topics and list additional support you would give to one or more of these claims if you had been asked to elaborate on them in a more formal manner.

4. Discuss the kinds of evidence writers would want to use to resolve the following controversial assumptions. What problems with definitions might arise in some of these claims?

   a. Adults are safer drivers than teenagers.

   b. The many species of birds that still inhabit the Everglades suggest that this ecosystem is not as endangered as environmentalists say it is.

    c. The greater number of violent shows you watch, the more likely you are to commit acts of violence.

    d. Male smokers are three times more likely to become impotent than male nonsmokers.

    e. Obscene books should be banned from public school libraries.

Communicating with a Purpose

Before we turn to the writing of effective arguments, consider the elements in an act of communication. Any communication act consists of the *writer* or *speaker,* an *audience,* and the *subject* being communicated. This is known as the *Aristotelian* or *Communication Triangle,* as shown in Figure 1.1.

The Aristotelian Triangle reminds us that the act of writing, virtually by definition, involves writing about something to someone—that writing never occurs in a vacuum.

Any act of communication involves a writer or speaker conveying a particular viewpoint to a particular audience in a particular way. We have all had the experience of describing something one way to one person and quite another way to someone else. For example, we might discuss a romantic relationship one way with a friend, quite another way with a parent, and yet another way with a minister, rabbi, or psychologist. The writer or speaker, subject, and audience all shape the communication.

A fourth major element that shapes communication is *purpose.* There are three basic kinds of communication, each with a different purpose:

1. *Referential* or *expository:* communication that primarily aims to inform and explain;

2. *Expressive:* communication that primarily aims to stimulate the imagination, create mood or "atmosphere," and evoke feelings; and

3. *Argumentative:* communication that primarily aims to help skeptical readers or listeners make up their minds about a debatable issue.

FIGURE 1.1

The Aristotelian or
Communication
Triangle

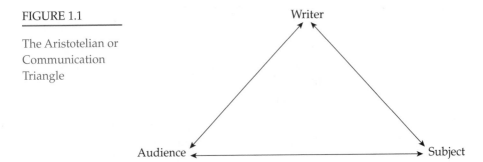

FIGURE 1.2

Rhetorical
Rhombus

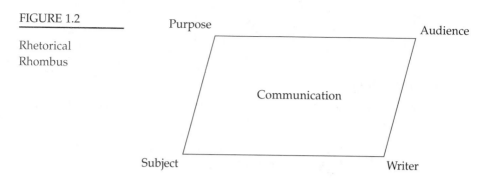

These three modes of communication are not mutually exclusive. For instance, writers of arguments must take time to inform readers about the facts underlying a problem. They also must try to make such explanations interesting—perhaps by dramatically re-creating a moment of discovery or by describing the beauty of an observed phenomenon. But argumentative writing does have a distinct purpose, which is to present, support, or challenge a debatable proposition (such as a conflict in ethical behavior or policymaking). Such views cannot be proven with experiments or made compelling through descriptive writing alone.

To incorporate this element of purpose, we can transform Aristotle's triangle into a square or, to be a bit more alliterative (to help remember it better), into a *rhetorical rhombus* (see Figure 1.2). Simple as this diagram may seem, it calls to mind a subtle interconnection among the elements; that is, any one element is indispensable to the other three. Thus, the writer's way of seeing the world is made significant by the fact that he or she has a particular purpose for writing; a subject is enriched by the way in which it is made relevant to a particular audience; and so on.

Let us examine each element of the rhetorical rhombus separately, in depth, as it pertains to the writing of effective arguments.

Once you establish that your primary purpose is not expository (to inform) or expressive (to evoke feelings) but argumentative (to persuade your audience to agree with your claim), you will want to consider purpose in that context.

Purpose in an Argumentative Context

The purpose of your argument is the reason *why* you want your audience to agree with your claim and take whatever action is necessary to carry it out. Often, the purpose for wanting to communicate anything is complex. For example, if your claim is that wolf hunting must be stopped (say, by passing laws that prohibit wolf hunting), your purpose might consist of the following:

- The facts make it clear to you that wolves are rapidly becoming an endangered species.

- You are convinced that such species endangerment poses a serious threat to the environment.

- You love wolves, and it distresses you to see these beautiful, intelligent animals slaughtered by those who cannot appreciate them.

Purpose, then, is the motivational force that imbues the mere potential for communication with the desire to communicate. In a required writing course, however, purpose becomes even more complicated. Unlike working writers whose purpose for writing a given piece is intrinsically related to the subject, student writers are often motivated by extrinsic matters, such as getting a good grade on the assignment or in the course. While there is nothing wrong with this kind of motivation, it does not quite constitute a bona fide purpose for writing about a given topic.

It is preferable, however, to adopt a professional sense of purpose toward your subject matter. The best way to accomplish this involved, engaged stance is to role-play. *Become* the writer you would like to be. Instead of thinking of yourself as a student in a composition course, think of yourself as an expert in the field you are writing about—one who genuinely cares about the topics at hand enough to want your audience to understand them and appreciate them the way you do.

Audience in an Argumentative Context

The people to whom you aim your argument can significantly influence the way you present that argument. For example, two arguments supporting the prohibition of wolf hunting, one aimed at legislators and the other aimed at hunters, would differ greatly from each other. If you were addressing an audience of legislators, you would want to focus on the need for laws that would better protect the environment. If you were addressing an audience of hunters, you would want to explain why it is in the hunters' best interest to stop hunting wolves. You could argue that damage to the habitat would ultimately cause the wolves to die out.

Audience also affects the writing and reading of arguments, in that some arguments may be classified as academic (or scholarly) and others as nonacademic (or popular). Academic arguments are written for fellow scholars affiliated with higher education, although some scholars are "independent"—that is, they are not employed by a college or university yet pursue similar research projects. The purpose of such writing is knowledge-sharing or idea-sharing; academic arguers say, in effect, "Here is what fellow researchers have determined thus far about the issue at hand; now, here are my views on the matter." A research paper is the student version of the professional scholarly article, in which the scholar carefully and explicitly articulates a claim and provides support for that claim.

Types of Academic Arguments   As college students, you are probably experiencing several different audiences for arguments. In a literature course, you are asked to write papers in which you argue for what you consider to be an important theme in a poem, work of fiction, or play. This type of argumentation is known as *literary criticism*. The evidence you would gather for such an argument would consist of specific passages from the literary work in question (and possibly other works by the same author as well), relevant information about the author's life and times, and commentary from other scholars.

In a science course you learn to write *scientific papers* in which you analyze, say, the properties of newly observed phenomena; or *laboratory reports* in which you accurately describe and interpret the results of physics, chemistry, or psychology experiments. "The Perils of Obedience" (Cluster 8, Masterpieces of Argument, pages 691–703), is Stanley Milgram's reworking of his original psychological experiment into an article for lay readers.

Another type of academic argument is the *ethnographic study*, common to sociology and anthropology. The ethnographer closely observes the behavior of individuals of a particular community or group, and derives inferences from what has been observed.

One of the most common types of academic writing is the *position paper*, in which you take a stance on a debatable issue, making sure that you represent each challenging view as fairly as possible before demonstrating the limitations of those views and proceeding to support your own view. "Two Languages Are Better Than One," by Wayne Thomas and Virginia Collier (pages 443–448), is one of several position papers that appear in this textbook.

Your history courses present you with the opportunity to conduct a *historical inquiry* into a particular period or event. New archaeological discoveries or lost documents brought to light can profoundly change the way a historical event or even an entire period is interpreted.

Students as well as professionals in the fields of engineering, business administration (management, finance, marketing), and law all must produce documents that have an argumentative component: A *proposal* describes a work in progress, often to receive approval for its completion; a *feasibility study* demonstrates the need for a new program or facility; and a *progress report* chronicles, as the name implies, the progress that has been made on a given project. Of course, many of these forms of academic writing exist outside the academy. Magazines publish literary criticism, specialized companies submit proposals to large manufacturers or agencies, and so on.

Nonacademic Arguments   On the other hand, nonacademic arguments focus more on reporting the "gist" of new developments or controversies. While academic arguments examine issues in depth and use specialized language to ensure

TABLE 1.1   **Distinction Between Academic and Nonacademic Arguments**

Academic Arguments	Nonacademic Arguments
Specialized (i.e., discipline-specific), precise language	Nonspecialized, less precise but more accessible language
Formal or semiformal tone	Less formal, more personal tone
All primary and secondary sources explicitly cited and documented, using standard formats (MLA, APA, etc.)	Sources are acknowledged informally, without footnoting
Contributions by other scholars in the field are discussed formally and in detail	Contributions by other writers in the field are discussed briefly
Scholarly audience	General audience

precision, nonacademic arguments tend to gloss over the technicalities and use nonspecialized language, which is less accurate but more accessible to the general public. The chief distinguishing features between academic and nonacademic arguments are outlined in Table 1.1.

The more aware you are of your target audience's needs and existing biases, the greater the likelihood that you will address their particular concerns about the topic and, in turn, persuade them to accept your *thesis*. To heighten your audience awareness, ask yourself these questions:

1. What do my readers most likely already know about the issue? Most likely do not know?

2. How might the issue affect my readers personally?

3. What would happen to my argument if my conclusions or recommendations are accepted? If they are not accepted?

4. Why might readers not accept my conclusions or recommendations?

Note that this last question leads you to think about counterarguments and how you might respond to them. See "Refutation" in Chapter 3, pages 98–99.

Writer in an Argumentative Context

How, you may wonder, is the writer a variable in the communication, aside from the obvious fact that the writer is the one who presents the argument (the "Communication" that lies at the center of the rhetorical rhombus and is its very reason for being)? Actually, the writer can assume one of many roles, depending on the target audience. Say, for example, that you are trying to convince a friend to lend you $500 to use as a down payment for a summer trip to Europe. Your role here is that of trustworthy friend. If instead you are trying to convince your bank to lend you that same $500, your role becomes that of client or applicant. You are likely to use different language and different support in making your argument to the bank's loan officer than you are to your friend. Similarly, writers often are obliged to play different roles, depending on the particular needs of different audiences.

Subject in an Argumentative Context

The subject refers to what the argument (the text) is about. Although the subject remains identifiably constant, a writer might shift the *focus* of a subject to accommodate a particular audience or situation. For example, to convince your friend to lend you $500 for the down payment on that European trip (your argument's subject), you might focus on how the friend could come with you to make for an even more rewarding trip. To convince the bank, you might shift the focus to emphasize future job security and the likelihood of your paying back the loan.

As you study the Classical, Toulmin, and Rogerian models of argument in the chapters that follow, think about how the rhetorical rhombus applies to each and about how different models place different emphasis on **p**urpose, **a**udience, **w**riter, or **s**ubject (PAWS).

The Process of Composing an Argument

Unlike cooking, which follows a rather fixed sequence of steps, writing arguments (or essays of any kind) is mainly a dynamic, recursive process rather than a linear one. That is, you can start anywhere and return to any stage at any time. You can *brainstorm* for additional ideas, rework the organizational scheme, wad up and rewrite part of the existing draft, or walk over to the library or log onto the Internet to conduct additional research—and you can do any of these activities whenever you feel the need. Some writers simply do not feel comfortable composing in a linear fashion; some like to compose their endings first, or "flesh out" particular points of an argument as they leap to mind, and then organize them into a coherent sequence later on. Some writers need to map out their ideas in clusters, write outlines, or simply let loose their spontaneous flow of associations via freewriting.

Freewriting to Generate Ideas Rapidly

As you may recall from your earlier composition studies, freewriting is a good way to generate material for an argument. Start writing without any advance planning. Your goal is to let your thoughts run loose on the page; do not concern yourself with organization, sentence structure, word choice, or relevancy to the topic of your argument. You might surprise yourself with how much you already know!

There are two kinds of freewriting: unfocused and focused. In *unfocused freewriting,* let your pen move across the page, recording whatever comes to mind. Try not to pause. In the following example a student, Janis, engages in some unfocused freewriting to stir up ideas about a subject for her argument. She is thinking spontaneously with a pencil, you might say, making no effort to develop a thesis.

Let's see, I'm supposed to write an argument that would persuade first-year college students what would be the best major in preparation for a particular career. Well, I'm undeclared myself, but want to study law after I graduate, so maybe I could do a comparative analysis of three or four majors that would seem to offer the best preparation for law school (hey, this could help me make up my own mind). Poli sci seems like an obvious possibility, since lawyers need to have a basic knowledge of the way governments work, the nature of public policy, how laws are passed. . . . Also, English, because lawyers need strong communication skills and need to acquire the kind of deep insight into the human heart that great works of literature offer . . . Then I might talk to law students as well as professors in the four different majors—and maybe even practicing attorneys to find out what they majored in as undergraduates, and why. Hey, my aunt is a lawyer! I could talk to her.

Janis knows that she likely will discard most, if not all, of her freewriting; her goal was not to whip out a rough draft or even test out a topic, but to help her mind tease out ideas and associations that otherwise might have remained buried. The goal of freewriting is greater than overcoming not knowing what to say; it includes becoming more receptive to what is possible.

In *focused freewriting*, you write spontaneously as well, but attempt something resembling an actual draft of the essay. Your goal is to generate as much as you know about the topic. It is an excellent way of discovering gaps in knowledge.

Immersing Yourself in the Subject

Imagine spending twenty minutes or so freewriting and getting down on paper everything that comes to mind; you produce several scraggly pages in longhand, or neater ones on a computer. You read them over, highlighting with a marker or with your computer's highlighting tool what seems most relevant and useful. Then you ask yourself these questions: What seems to be the dominant or recurrent trend? What more do I need to know about my topic to write persuasively about it? What kinds of evidence do I need to back up my thesis, however tentative it may be at this stage? In taking these steps, you are preparing to immerse yourself in your subject.

Having relevant information available is important to all writers. Once you know what more you need, you can start looking for information. On the Internet, an enormous quantity of information can be accessed quickly, so it is a good place to begin your research. A strong search engine like Google, Dogpile, or Yahoo! can bring material from any subject onto your screen in seconds. On the other hand, a large percentage of Internet sources are superficial, dated, or not very relevant to your needs. Balance your Internet research by examining a variety of reliable print sources, such as books, articles, encyclopedias (general as well as subject-specific), handbooks, and specialized dictionaries. For more information about using sources, see Chapter 7, Researching Your Argument.

Your goal in reading and researching should be to learn all you possibly can about your topic. Familiarize yourself with the differing views experts have about it. Talk to experts. As a college student you are surrounded by them; get in the habit of contacting professors who can give you timely and in-depth information about your topic or suggest material to read. Read and explore as many sources as possible. In other words, immerse yourself in the subject matter of your argument. This involvement will show in your writing and will give the finished paper added depth and vigor.

Using Listing and Clustering

Like freewriting, listing and clustering tap into writers' natural inclination to take a mental inventory of what they already know about a topic as well as to discover what they do not know about it. To list, jot down as quickly as you can ideas (or idea fragments) or names of people, places, events, or objects. One student prepared the following list as a prelude to writing about the increasing problem of childhood obesity:

> Fast-food chains aggressively target their products to preteen kids.
>
> TV commercials give wrong impressions.
>
> Parents too busy to cook.
>
> Hamburgers often loaded with mayonnaise.
>
> Burgers, fries, milk shakes, ice cream loaded with fat.
>
> Parents not paying close enough attention to their kids' diets.

You can use lists to make notes to yourself or to ask questions the moment they occur to you:

> Check how many calories are in a typical fast-food burger.
>
> How much fat content in a bag of fries?
>
> What do nutritionists and pediatricians say about the increasing obesity problem?
>
> Find out how often kids eat fast food, on the average.
>
> How can kids learn more about this problem in school?

Clustering helps writers take an inventory of what they know, but it also helps them discover relationships among the ideas they list by seeing how the cluster bubbles connect. This discovery helps writers organize their ideas more efficiently when they begin outlining or drafting their arguments.

To cluster an idea for an argumentative essay, take a sheet of paper and write down words or phrases; at the same time, keep similar words and phrases close together and draw large circles around them to form "clusters." Next, draw lines between bubbles that seem to go together. Figure 1.3 shows how one student clustered her thoughts for an argumentative essay on why teenagers should spend more time reading books.

Exercise 1.2

1. Your science instructor asks you to evaluate the benefits and dangers of vitamin C. Using the Internet, locate information that both supports and challenges claims about the benefits and dangers of this vitamin. Keep a record of the websites that you visit.

2. List things you might say in a paper arguing for or against the benefits or dangers of vitamin C.

3. Having gathered potentially useful information about vitamin C and listed things you might want to include in your argument, do a focused freewrite. Do not pause or organize your thoughts or choice of words and phrases. Write rapidly until you have filled at least two handwritten pages.

Using Appeals in Argument

To argue successfully, a person does not rely solely on facts; facts need to be explained, placed into a particular context (that is, related to the problem being argued), or have their importance validated. Successful writers of argument often demonstrate the importance of these facts so as to persuade their audience that the facts are important. For such demonstration, these arguers turn to strategies of *persuasion* known as appeals.

The ancient Greek philosopher Aristotle in his *Rhetoric* identifies three kinds of appeals:

1. *Ethical:* the appeal to tradition, authority, ethical and moral behavior, which Aristotle terms *ethos;*

2. *Emotional:* the appeal to feelings and basic human needs such as security, love, belonging, health and well-being, which Aristotle terms *pathos;* and

3. *Rational:* the appeal to reason and logic, which Aristotle terms *logos.*

FIGURE 1.3   Student Cluster Diagram

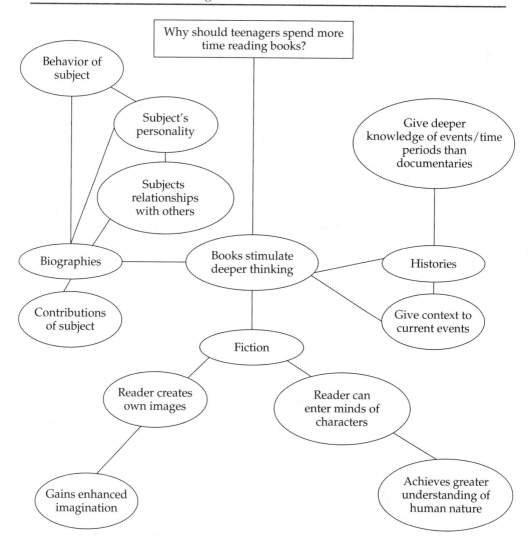

As Figure 1.4 shows, these three appeals correspond to Aristotle's three modes of communication, Writer, Audience, and Subject (see Figure 1.1). In other words, Ethos (character, values, trusted authority) is the attribute of a responsible Writer. Similarly, Pathos (emotion, compassion) suggests appealing to the needs and desires of the public; that is, of the Audience. Finally Logos (reason) corresponds to the factual, rational truth-content of the Subject.

How do appeals reinforce evidence? Say that a writer wishes to argue that if acid rain fallout continues to increase, agriculture in a certain region will be threatened. To argue this claim convincingly, a writer first needs to bring in indisputable facts—those derived from scientific experiments. These facts would

FIGURE 1.4

Aristotelian Appeals,
in Correspondence
with the Elements of
Communication

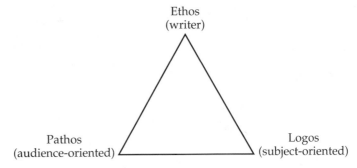

Ethos
(writer)

Pathos
(audience-oriented)

Logos
(subject-oriented)

suggest a correlation between increased acidity and rainfall and decreased crop yield. Note that the correlation may be disputable, but it still constitutes valid evidence.

Use of appeals can enhance the persuasive force of the thesis. The writer above, for example, might use one or more of the following appeals:

- An ethical appeal that introduces the testimony of an expert, such as a farmer whose crops have been affected or an industrial chemist who has a professional understanding of the way in which acidity in rainfall reacts with soil nutrients.

- An emotional appeal that discusses the basic human need for uncontaminated food or justifies the fear of cancer many people will have if the situation is not corrected.

- A rational appeal that emphasizes the logical and inevitable consequences of what happens to soil and crops when acid rainfall goes untreated.

Appeals such as these go a long way toward reinforcing the evidence and strengthening the writer's argument.

Combining appeals in a given argument can be especially effective. In the following excerpt from *The Souls of Black Folk* (1903), the educator and pioneer sociologist W. E. B. Du Bois (1868–1963)—the first African American to earn a Ph.D. from Harvard University—calls attention to the living conditions of black people in the post–Civil War South, specifically in Dougherty County, Georgia. Note how Du Bois appeals to both reason and emotion in order to convince readers of the injustice of such living conditions.

> Above all, the cabins are crowded. We have come to associate crowding with homes in cities almost exclusively. This is primarily because we have so little accurate knowledge of country life. Here in Dougherty County one may find families of eight and ten occupying one or two rooms, and for every ten rooms of house accommodation for the Negroes there are twenty-five persons. The worst tenement abominations of New York do not have

above twenty-two persons for every ten rooms. Of course, one small, close room in a city, without a yard, is in many respects worse than the larger single country room. In other respects it is better; it has glass windows, a decent chimney, and a trustworthy floor. The single great advantage of the Negro peasant is that he may spend most of his life outside his hovel, in the open fields.

There are four chief causes of these wretched homes: First, long custom born of slavery has assigned such homes to Negroes; white laborers would be offered better accommodations, and might, for that and similar reasons, give better work. Secondly, the Negroes, used to such accommodations, do not as a rule demand better; they do not know what better houses mean. Thirdly, the landlords as a class have not yet come to realize that it is a good business investment to raise the standard of living among labor by slow and judicious methods; that a Negro laborer who demands three rooms and fifty cents a day would give more efficient work and leave a larger profit than a discouraged toiler herding his family in one room and working for thirty cents. Lastly, among such conditions of life there are few incentives to make the laborer become a better farmer. If he is ambitious, he moves to town or tries other labor; as a tenant-farmer his outlook is almost hopeless, and following it as a makeshift, he takes the house that is given him without protest.

First, Du Bois appeals to reason by providing "accurate" information about country life to reverse the assumption that crowding occurs only in city life; he also appeals to reason by examining the "four chief causes" of such housing. But appealing to reason is not enough: It is important to address the heart as well as the mind. Hence, Du Bois appeals to emotion by referring to the urban tenements as "abominations," adding that they are less extreme than the country housing situation, and by calling the prospects for tenant-farmers "almost hopeless."

In the following passage, from "Civil Disobedience" (originally delivered as a lecture to his fellow townspeople in 1848), we see Henry David Thoreau using all three appeals—ethical, emotional, and rational—in his effort to convince his audience, although the ethical appeal dominates.

Under a government which imprisons any unjustly, the true place for a just man is also a prison. The proper place to-day, the only place which Massachusetts has provided for her freer and less desponding spirits, is in her prisons, to be put out and locked out of the State by her own act, as they have already put themselves out by their principles. It is there that the fugitive slave, and the Mexican prisoner on parole, and the Indian come to plead the wrongs of his race, should find them; on that separate, but more free and honorable ground, where the State places those who are not *with* her but *against* her,—the only house in a slave-state in which a free man can abide with honor. If any think that their influence would be lost there, and their voices no longer afflict the ear of the State, that they would not be as an enemy within its walls, they do not know by how much truth is stronger than error, nor how much more eloquently and effectively he can combat injustice who has experienced a little in his own person. Cast your whole vote, not a strip of paper merely, but your whole influence. A minority is powerless while it conforms to the majority; it is not even a minority then; but it is irresistible when it clogs by its whole weight. If the alternative is to keep all just men in prison, or give up war and slavery, the State will not hesitate which to choose. If a thousand men were not to pay their tax-bills this year, that would not be a violent and bloody measure, as it would be to pay them, and enable the State to commit violence and shed innocent blood. This is, in fact, the definition of a peaceable revolution, if any such is possible. If the tax-gatherer, or any other public officer, asks me, as one has done, "But what shall I do?" my answer is, "If you really wish to do any thing, resign your office." When the subject has refused allegiance, and the officer has resigned his office, then the revolution is accomplished. But even suppose blood should flow. Is there not a sort of blood shed when the conscience is wounded? Through this wound a man's real manhood and immortality flow out, and he bleeds to an everlasting death. I see this blood flowing now.

I have contemplated the imprisonment of the offender, rather than the seizure of his goods,—though both will serve the same purpose,—because they who assert the purest right, and consequently are most dangerous to a corrupt State, commonly have not spent much time in accumulating property. To such the State renders comparatively small service, and a slight tax is wont to appear exorbitant, particularly if they are obliged to earn it by special labor with their hands. If there were one who lived wholly without the use of money, the State itself would hesitate to demand it of him. But the rich man—not to make any invidious comparison—is always sold to the institution which makes him rich. Absolutely speaking, the more money, the less virtue; for money comes between a man and his objects, and obtains them for him; and it was certainly no great virtue to obtain it. It puts to rest many questions which he would otherwise be taxed to answer; while the only new question which it puts is the hard but superfluous one, how to spend it. Thus his moral ground is taken from under his feet. The opportunities of living are diminished in proportion as what are called the "means" are increased. The best thing a man can do for his culture when he is rich is to endeavour to carry out those schemes which he entertained when he was poor. Christ answered the Herodians according to their condition. "Show me the tribute-money," said he;—and one took a penny out of his pocket;—If you use money which has the image of Caesar on it, and which he has made current and valuable, that is, *if you are men of the State,* and gladly enjoy the advantages of Caesar's government, then pay him back some of his own when he demands it; "Render therefore to Caesar that which is Caesar's, and to God those things which are God's,"— leaving them no wiser than before as to which was which; for they did not wish to know.

When I converse with the freest of my neighbors, I perceive that, whatever they may say about the magnitude and seriousness of the question, and their regard for the public tranquility, the long and the short of the matter is, that they cannot spare the protection of the existing government, and they dread the consequences of disobedience to it to their property and families. For my own part, I should not like to think that I ever rely on the protection of the State. But, if I deny the authority of the State when it presents its tax-bill, it will soon take and waste all my property, and so harass me and my children without end. This is hard. This makes it impossible for a man to live honestly and at the same time comfortably in outward respects. It will not be worth the while to accumulate property; that would be sure to go again. You must hire or squat somewhere, and raise but a small crop, and eat that soon. You must live within yourself, and depend upon yourself, always tucked up and ready for a start, and not have many affairs. A man may grow rich in Turkey even, if he will be in all respects a good subject of the Turkish government. Confucius said,—"If a State is governed by the principles of reason, poverty and misery are subjects of shame; if a State is not governed by the principles of reason, riches and honors are the subjects of shame." No: until I want the protection of Massachusetts to be extended to me in some distant southern port, where my liberty is endangered, or until I am bent solely on building up an estate at home by peaceful enterprise, I can afford to refuse allegiance to Massachusetts, and her right to my property and life. It costs me less in every sense to incur the penalty of disobedience to the State, than it would to obey. I should feel as if I were worth less in that case.

Thoreau's appeal to ethics is revealed in his allusions to the injustice of the State, to what constitutes proper and honorable behavior when the State has exercised unethical judgment. He also appeals to ethics by invoking Christ's example regarding Roman tribute-money.

We can detect Thoreau's subtle appeal to emotion in at least two ways: by presenting seemingly nonviolent acts such as taxation as acts of violence that can "shed innocent blood" as easily as cannons and by presenting the State as harassing its citizens rather than protecting them whenever those citizens dare to challenge the State's authority.

Finally, Thoreau appeals to reason by tracing the logical consequences of a tax-bill: "it will . . . waste all my property and so harass me and my children, which in turn makes it no longer worth the while to accumulate property."

◎/◎   **Exercise 1.3**

1. What types of appeals would be most appropriate for persuading readers of the following assumptions?

    a. Reading stories to children greatly enhances their mental skills as well as their emotional stability.

    b. All work and no play makes Jill a dull girl.

    c. Severer penalties should be imposed on those who abuse animals.

    d. Safety should be anyone's top priority when purchasing a family car.

    e. This painting is definitely a Picasso because an art historian from Yale authenticated it as such.

2. Determine the appeals at work in each of the following passages. What words or images show the appeals at work?

    a. My mistress was . . . a kind and tender-hearted woman, and in the simplicity of her soul she commenced, when I first went to live with her, to treat me as she supposed one human being ought to treat another. In entering upon the duties of a slaveholder, she did not seem to perceive that I [was] mere chattel, and that for her to treat me as a human being was not only wrong, but dangerously so. Slavery proved as injurious to her as it did to me. When I went there, she was a pious, warm, and tender-hearted woman. There was no sorrow or suffering for which she had not a tear. She had bread for the hungry, clothes for the naked, and comfort for every mourner that came within her reach. Slavery soon proved its ability to divest her of these heavenly qualities. Under its influence, the tender heart became stone, and the lamb-like disposition gave way to one of tiger-like fierceness. The first step in her downward course was in her ceasing to instruct me. . . . Nothing seemed to make her more angry than to see me with a newspaper. —Frederick Douglass, *The Narrative of the Life of Frederick Douglass, an American Slave* (1845) ch. 7.

    b. Most films and television shows are produced by men for men. Their main purposes are to show white males triumphant, to teach gender roles, and to cater to men's delight in male predation and victimization, especially young, pretty, near-naked women with highly developed breasts and buttocks (parts that are usually the locus of attack). Like the men of the proto-Nazi German Freikorps that waged between the wars, shooting women between the legs because they carried grenades there (!), American men's most satisfying target is women's sexuality, the area of men's greatest fear. Pornography is a systemic abuse of women because the establishment colludes in this male sadism toward women, which fits its purposes. Case in point: the Indian government, which does censor films for political content, *forbids scenes of lovemaking or kissing but allows rape;* indeed, a rape scene has been "all but requisite" in Indian films for some years, writes Anita Pratap. —Marilyn French, *The War Against Women* (New York: Ballantine, 1992) 175.

c. There is no single way to read well, though there is a prime reason why we should read. Information is endlessly available to us; where shall wisdom be found? If you are fortunate, you encounter a particular teacher who can help, yet finally you are alone, going on without further *mediation*. Reading well is one of the great pleasures that solitude can afford you, because it is, at least in my experience, the most healing of pleasures. It returns you to otherness, whether in yourself or in friends, or in those who may become friends. Imaginative literature is otherness, and as such alleviates loneliness. We read not only because we cannot know enough people, but because friendship is so vulnerable, so likely to diminish or disappear, overcome by space, time, imperfect sympathies, and all the sorrows of familial and passional life. — Harold Bloom, *How to Read and Why* (New York: Scribner, 2000) 19.

3. Read the magazine ads on pages 22–23, plus those in the color pages, and consider the images they use. Then answer these questions:

a. What are the basic arguments of the magazine ads?

b. What appeals can you identify in them?

c. Is there more than one appeal in a given ad?

Organizing the Argument

All writing must be organized or structured. Whether you are relating an experience (*narration*), or explaining an idea or process (*exposition* or *explanation*), or defending a thesis (*argumentation*), you must structure your writing to communicate best with an audience.

Organizing your writing means that you do the following:

1. Introduce the topic (the situation in a narrative; the subject matter to be explained in an exposition or explanation; the problem in an argument)

2. Present the particulars of the situation (the sequencing of incidents in a narrative; elements of a phenomenon in an exposition or explanation; the nature of the problem, followed by the body of evidence, in an argument)

3. Conclude (the outcome in a narrative; the "whole picture" in an explanation; the interpretation, assessment, and recommendations, if appropriate, in an argument)

How you meet these three organizational requirements in an argument depends on the type of model you adopt: the Classical (or Aristotelian/Ciceronian), the

Toulmin, or the Rogerian. The chapters that follow examine each model in depth, but for now you merely need to be aware of each one's distinguishing organizational features.

In the *Classical model*, the organizational scheme is predetermined. One begins with an introduction that establishes the problem and states the thesis; next, one analyzes the evidence and refutes opposing views in light of the evidence collected; finally, one draws conclusions and provides recommendations.

In the *Toulmin model* (named for the philosopher Steven Toulmin), truth is not absolute but value-dependent. Accordingly, the logic content of the arguments is scrutinized for its underlying values. Evidence does not operate in a

vacuum, but must be tested according to the values (called *warrants*) of the arguer. These values always come into play during the argument, meaning that no one argues for timeless, eternal truths.

In the *Rogerian model* (named for the psychologist Carl Rogers), one shifts emphasis to the social act of negotiating difference through argument. Truth is not only value-based but it must be negotiated cooperatively if argument is to have any constructive social function.

Drafting the Argument

There are several ways to compose a draft. One way of drafting (and, alas, too common) is to put off the task until the day or night before it is due and then to dash off a single draft and proofread it hastily. In general, this is the least productive way of writing. The best writers tend to revise *most* often, not least often.

Another way of drafting is to use an outline as a template. By elaborating on each section of the outline, the drafter takes an important step toward substantive *development* of the essay. The subsequent rethinking of the argument and the additional research that results becomes more apparent using this method.

A third way is to produce a *discovery draft,* which is like freewriting in its spontaneity and in its goal of getting down on paper as much as possible about the topic. However, discovery drafters do have a rudimentary sense of structure and purpose in mind. They believe that, to some extent at least, the things they want to say will fall into place through the very act of writing, and if not, they can rearrange, revise, and edit once they have a rough draft in hand.

Whichever drafting method you choose, allow yourself enough time to reread the draft two or three times and to make marginal notations about possible changes. Mark up a printout of your draft with reminders of what else to include, questions that might help you identify and gather additional evidence, and ideas for changes that will strengthen your argument.

Composing Openings

Openings can be difficult to write because they usually lay out the terrain for the whole argument. Nobody likes to spend a lot of time writing an introduction, only to realize later that it has to be scrapped because the claim or approach has shifted during drafting. But no rule says that you must write your opening first. You can postpone writing the full opening until you have written part of the body of the paper or until you have a firm sense of your paper's shape.

Openings serve two purposes: to introduce the topic and the background information needed to understand or appreciate the topic's seriousness, and to state the thesis.

Consider the following types of openings. Keep in mind that one type can overlap the other (for example, startling openings can be partly anecdotal).

- **Occasional Opening.** An occasional opening refers to a current event or local incident and uses it as the occasion for writing the essay. "In light of the current crisis in Addis Abbaba . . ."

- **Startling Opening.** A startling opening grabs the attention of readers with unexpected information. "While you are reading this sentence, fifty people will die of cigarette-related illnesses in this country."

- **Anecdotal Opening.** An anecdotal opening uses a brief story to engage the reader's attention quickly. An article arguing that some of the most dangerous toxins are found in the home might begin with an anecdote about a toddler lifting an opened bottle of nail polish remover to his lips just as his mother enters the room.

- **Analytical Opening.** An analytical opening launches immediately into a critical discussion of the issue. An argument on the effects of alcohol on the body might open with an explanation of how alcohol damages certain bodily functions.

What makes an opening more appropriate than another? When choosing, consider the four interconnected elements of communication discussed earlier in the rhetorical rhombus. You may find that your subject lends itself more to an analytical opening. Or perhaps the writer's personal experience with the issue leads to an anecdotal opening. Or your purpose to shock readers into accepting the urgency of the matter suggests a startling opening. Maybe the kind of audience you are targeting (impatient to learn the facts? uncertain about the relevance of the topic?) justifies the use of an occasional opening.

Therefore, weigh the purpose of your argument, the kinds of readers you are targeting, and the nature of the subject matter.

◎/◎ Exercise 1.4

Discuss the rhetorical techniques used in each of the following openings:

1. The opening to an argument about the potential significance of discovering life elsewhere in the universe, by a professor of natural history.

   The recent discovery of abundant water on Mars, albeit in the form of permafrost, has raised hopes for finding traces of life there. The Red Planet has long been a favorite location for those speculating about extraterrestrial life, especially since the 1890s, when H. G. Wells wrote *The War of the Worlds* and the American astronomer Percival Lowell claimed that he could see artificial canals etched into the planet's parched surface. Today, of course, scientists expect to find no more than simple bacteria dwelling deep underground, if even that. Still, the discovery of just a single bacterium somewhere beyond Earth would force us to revise our understanding of who we are and where we fit into the cosmic scheme of things, throwing us into a deep spiritual identity crisis that would be every bit as dramatic as the one Copernicus brought about in the early 1500s, when he asserted that Earth was not at the center of the universe. —Paul Davies, "E.T. and God," *Atlantic Monthly* Sept. 2003:112.

2. The opening to an argument about the merits of urban public schools, by a newspaper columnist.

   I was terrified. It felt as if I were shoving my precious 4-year-old into a leaky canoe and pushing him off into croc-infested waters. My friends acted as if they thought I was crazy. I was enrolling my little boy in a mob scene, sending him off to a place as dangerous as it was crowded. Didn't I see the newspaper that showed students crammed into shower-stall study halls or watch the television report where box-cutter-wielding delinquents were barely contained by exhausted security guards? Hadn't I read Jonathan Kozol? My tow-headed treasure was poised at the edge of the blackboard jungle, a place where the stairwells were as dangerous as the banks of the Amazon. It was 10 years ago, and I was sending my son off to kindergarten in the infamous New York City public school system. —Susan Cheever, "Thriving in City's Schools—Until 9th Grade?" *Newsday* 12 Nov. 2003:32.

3. The opening to an argument about how best to curtail obsesity among young people, by two medical researchers.

Obesity in children has tripled in the past 20 years. A staggering 50 percent of adolescents in some minority populations are overweight. There is an epidemic of type 2 (formerly "adult onset") diabetes in children. Heart attacks may become a disease of young adults. In response to this public health crisis, federal and state officials are seeking ways to protect children from the ravages of poor diet and physical inactivity. National legislation on the prevention and treatment of obesity is being considered. California and Texas are working to remove snack foods from schools. There are proposals for the regulation of food advertising to children. —Kelly D. Brownell and David S. Ludwig, "Fighting Obesity and the Food Lobby," *Washington Post* 9 June 2002.

Composing the Body of the Argument

If you think of your argument's opening as the promise you make to your readers about what you are going to do, then the body of the argument is the fulfillment of that promise. Here you deliver the goods that comprise the subject node of the rhetorical rhombus: the detailed support—facts, examples, illustrations—as well as the emotional, logical, and ethical appeals that collectively demonstrate to your readers that the claim you set forth in your introduction is valid.

Let's consider the development strategy of a famous argument, "Allegory of the Cave." In this famous allegory from *The Republic,* Plato aims to convince his audience of the difference between appearance (or illusion) and reality. (You may wish to read the allegory on pages 650–657 before continuing.) After introducing his statement of purpose to his pupil Glaucon—"Let me show in a figure how far our nature is enlightened or unenlightened"—Plato first describes the setting of the cave (or underground den) and the condition of the prisoners: They are chained so that they see only the shadows that are cast on the walls, and they can hear voices but are unable to determine who is speaking because they cannot turn their heads toward the actual source. Plato is now ready to elaborate on his thesis, which is in two parts: (1) Even though, when released, the prisoners would be temporarily blinded by the actual light (from the fire in the cave and then, even more so, after being dragged against their will outside the cave, from the light of the sun), their eyes would eventually grow accustomed to the true reality of things; that is, "the journey upwards [represents] the ascent of the soul into the intellectual world." (2) It is not enough to take the journey upwards; once accomplished, one should return to the cave to acquire a clearer judgment of the quality of life down there and to persuade the prisoners that a better life exists above.

How should you proceed in writing out the body of your argument? First, check that the sequence you developed in your outline includes everything you want to say about the issue. Jot down additional notes in the margins if necessary. If you have completed a freewrite or rough draft, now is the time to retrieve those pages and decide what to keep. You may already have more of the draft of your argument completed than you realize!

Many writers find it productive to move back and forth from draft to outline. The outline gives a bird's-eye view of the whole scheme; the draft concentrates on the minutiae of point-by-point discussion and exemplification.

Composing Conclusions

A good conclusion enables readers to grasp the full impact of the argument. If the introduction states the claim and the body argues for the validity of the claim by citing evidence for it, then the conclusion encapsulates all those points of evidence, leaving readers with a renewed sense of the argument's validity.

To write an effective conclusion, then, aim for conciseness: capture in just one or two paragraphs the gist of your argument. Conclusions of short papers need not be long but could be just three to four sentences.

What might you do in a conclusion? Here are three possibilities:

1. Reflect back on the paper.
   - Return to the image or analogy or anecdote you discussed in the introduction and provide a frame for the piece.
   - Restate the thesis to underscore the argument of your essay.
   - Summarize your main points if the argument is complex or the paper is longer than six pages.
2. Broaden the scope beyond your paper.
   - Forecast the future if your main points should prove to be true.
   - Point out the implications of the ideas presented.
   - Exhort your readers to action.

3. Reinforce your readers' emotional involvement in the matter at hand. Keep in mind that "emotional involvement" can refer to feelings of security, hope, happiness, self-confidence, optimism, or overall well-being.

   • Introduce or reintroduce in a different way appropriate rational, ethical, or emotional appeals.

   • Aim for conciseness. Less is more when it comes to striking an emotional chord with readers.

◎/◎   Exercise 1.5

Discuss the strengths and/or weaknesses in the body and conclusion of the following essay in which the author argues that video games are doing a better job than schools with teaching kids to think.

High Score Education | James Paul Gee

The US spends almost $50 billion each year on education, so why aren't kids learning? Forty percent of students lack basic reading skills, and their academic performance is dismal compared with that of their foreign counterparts. In response to this crisis, schools are skilling-and-drilling their way "back to basics," moving toward mechanical instruction methods that rely on line-by-line scripting for teachers and endless multiple-choice testing. Consequently, kids aren't learning how to think anymore—they're learning how to memorize. This might be an ideal recipe for the future Babbitts of the world, but it won't produce the kind of agile, analytical minds that will lead the high tech global age. Fortunately, we've got *Grand Theft Auto: Vice City* and *Deus Ex* for that.

After school, kids are devouring new information, concepts, and skills every day, and, like it or not, they're doing it controller in hand, plastered to the TV. The fact is, when kids play videogames they can experience a much more powerful form of learning than when they're in the classroom. Learning isn't about memorizing isolated facts. It's about connecting and manipulating them. Doubt it? Just ask anyone who's beaten *Legend of Zelda* or solved *Morrowind*.

The phenomenon of the videogame as an agent of mental training is largely unstudied; more often, games are denigrated for being violent or they're just plain ignored. They shouldn't be. Young gamers today aren't training to be gun-toting carjackers. They're learning how to learn. In *Pikmin*, children manage an army of plantlike aliens and strategize to solve problems. In *Metal Gear Solid 2*, players move stealthily through virtual

Source: James Paul Gee, "High Score Education: Games, Not School, Are Teaching Kids to Think," *Wired* 05 2003 pp. 91–92. Reprinted by permission of the author.

environments and carry out intricate missions. Even in the notorious *Vice City*, players craft a persona, build a history, and shape a virtual world. In strategy games like *WarCraft III* and *Age of Mythology*, they learn to micromanage an array of elements while simultaneously balancing short- and long-term goals. That sounds like something for their résumés.

The secret of a videogame as a teaching machine isn't its immersive 3-D graphics, but its underlying architecture. Each level dances around the outer limits of the player's abilities, seeking at every point to be hard enough to be just doable. In cognitive science, this is referred to as the regime of competence principle, which results in a feeling of simultaneous pleasure and frustration—a sensation as familiar to gamers as sore thumbs. Cognitive scientist Andy diSessa has argued that the best instruction hovers at the boundary of a student's competence. Most schools, however, seek to avoid invoking feelings of both pleasure and frustration, blind to the fact that these emotions can be extremely useful when it comes to teaching kids.

Also, good videogames incorporate the principle of expertise. They tend to encourage players to achieve total mastery of one level, only to challenge and undo that mastery in the next, forcing kids to adapt and evolve. This carefully choreographed dialectic has been identified by learning theorists as the best way to achieve expertise in any field. This doesn't happen much in our routine-driven schools, where "good" students are often just good at "doing school."

How did videogames become such successful models of effective learning? Game coders aren't trained as cognitive scientists. It's a simple case of free-market economics: If a title doesn't teach players how to play it well, it won't sell well. Game companies don't rake in $6.9 billion a year by dumbing down the material—aficionados condemn short and easy games like *Half Life: Blue Shift* and *Devil May Cry 2*. Designers respond by making harder and more complex games that require mastery of sophisticated worlds and as many as 50 to 100 hours to complete. Schools, meanwhile, respond with more tests, more drills, and more rigidity. They're in the cognitive-science dark ages.

We don't often think about videogames as relevant to education reform, but maybe we should. Game designers don't often think of themselves as learning theorists. Maybe they should. Kids often say it doesn't feel like learning when they're gaming—they're much too focused on playing. If kids were to say that about a science lesson, our country's education problems would be solved. ◎/◎

Revising the Argument: A Form of Reevaluation

You have written a draft of your argument, using one of the above methods. Now it is time to revise. "I love the flowers of afterthought," the novelist Bernard Malamud once said. The wonderful thing about writing is that you do not need "to get it right the first time." In fact, you can try as many times as you wish, which is not the case with speaking. Malamud, you will notice, is commenting on the opportunity that revision provides writers with: the opportunity to say it better—more clearly, effectively, or convincingly. And for most writers the very best "flowers" of thought occur only *after* they have written something down.

In revising argumentative essays, attend closely to the ways you have presented the problem, stated your claims, reported the evidence and testimony, represented the challenging views, drawn inferences, and reached reasonable conclusions. What follows is a closer look at each of these steps.

- **Presenting the problem.** Unless you capture the exact nature and full complexity of the problem you are examining, your entire argument is built on a shaky foundation. To determine whether the problem is represented well, question whether the introduction suits the audience and subject (recall the PAWS rhombus) and whether you establish sufficient ethos and pathos for readers to care to read on and to trust you, the writer.

- **Stating the claim.** Just as the problem must be stated clearly, so must the assertions that presumably solve the problem. Ask yourself whether your claim is realistic, practical, and sensible in light of the nature of the problem and the circumstances underlying it.

- **Reporting the evidence.** Facts and statistics—the raw data that comprise evidence—do not carry much meaning outside of a context of discussion. In presenting evidence in support of a thesis, the writer aims to communicate the significance of those facts and figures, not simply to drop them on the page. The writer also aims to present facts and figures in a way that readers can easily absorb, ideally in a visual configuration of some kind, such as an attractively designed chart or graph. When revising your discussion of evidence, ask yourself whether you interpret the data accurately, relate one cluster of data to another clearly enough (through visual representation of the data), and establish your ethos as a careful researcher and thinker on the issue.

- **Refuting challenging views.** When revising refutations, make sure that your writing represents the claims and evidence of the other side as fairly as possible. If you argue from a Rogerian perspective, think of establishing common ground with the audience in terms of shared values (warrants) or of cooperating to reach shared goals. Resist the temptation to omit parts of a challenging perspective because you are not sure about how to refute it. Also, double-check the reliability of your refutation: Does it reveal the limitations or falsity of the challenging view?

- **Drawing inferences and conclusions.** How do you interpret your findings? How clearly do your underlying warrants emerge? Should you give more attention to them? How willing will your readers be to cooperate with you, based on your interpretation of the findings? What else can you say to ensure their cooperation—assuming that you would find such cooperation desirable?

The Pulitzer Prize winning journalist and teacher of writing Donald Murray, in *The Craft of Revision*, 5th ed. (2004), identifies three cardinal virtues of revision:

1. Revision allows one to identify problems to be solved.

2. Revision enables writers to explore the topic more deeply to arrive at new insights into the topic.

3. Revision enhances the brain's capacity for recall and patterning.

Reading to Revise

Reading well, especially in the context of writing, provides you with a wider perspective of your subject and of the many divergent views that give it depth and richness. As a well-read writer, you are in the position of integrating the ideas of different authors into your own views on the subject. Reading and reflecting critically on what you have read also help you to revise more successfully because they force you to get into the habit of reading your own writing as if it were someone else's. The advantage to beginning your project well in advance of the due date is that you will have the time to do such a critical reading of your drafts.

Using Your Reading Skills in Peer-Critiquing Workshops

You may be given the opportunity to respond critically to other students' drafts. Always read the draft as carefully as you would any published argument. Consider the following criteria as you read the first draft of a peer.

- **Purpose-related issues.** Is the purpose of the draft apparent? Stated clearly enough? Is the thesis (claim) well stated? Directly related to the purpose?

- **Content-related issues.** Is the scope of the topic sufficiently limited? Does the writer provide enough background information? Provide enough evidence in support of the claim? Provide enough examples and illustrations to support the evidence? Represent challenging views fully and fairly before pointing out their flaws? Are the writer's interpretive and concluding remarks thorough? Does the writer offer clear recommendations, if appropriate?

- **Issues relating to style and format.** Is the writing concise? Easy to read? Are the sentences coherent, well constructed, varied? Is the level of usage consistent and appropriate for the intended audience? Is the word choice accurate? Are unfamiliar terms defined? Does the writer use subheadings and visual aids where appropriate? Follow proper documentation format?

For a discussion of the way incorporating visuals can enhance your argument, see "Visual Aids as Tools for Argumentative Writing," beginning on page 33.

Types of Revision Tasks

Revising an argument involves a lot more than just "fixing things up"; it also involves re-*seeing* the entire draft from a fresh perspective, checking to make sure that each assertion is fully discussed and that the discussion follows a logical sequence. Here are some different types of revision strategies:

Holistic Revision   F. Scott Fitzgerald liked to speak of "revising from spirit"— that is, revising from scratch after realizing that the first draft is on the wrong track or just does not seem to "click" in your mind. This kind of holistic revision— of revision as re-seeing—makes it more likely that new energy and insights will be infused into the argument. For this kind of revision to work best, you often need to set aside (though not necessarily "scrap") the original draft and start afresh.

Content Revision   When revising for content, you examine your ideas in greater depth than you did during the earlier draft. Typically, you gather more information or return to the original information to process it more efficiently. You may discover that you have underdeveloped an idea, so you would need to provide specific detail to support your claim. Usually, such revisions can be "pasted into" the original draft.

Organizational Revision   Writers often revise to strengthen the structure of their argument. When you revise for organization, pay close attention to the logical progression of your ideas. An argument can be more effective, for example, by saving the most compelling point for last. As for moving coherently and smoothly from one point to the next, make sure you include transitional markers such as "on the other hand," "nevertheless," "in spite of," "according to," "however," and so on.

Strive for the best possible order of ideas, not just the order in which the ideas occurred to you. When an argument unfolds logically, you create what is casually referred to as *flow*. The smoother the flow, the more likely your readers are to follow along and comprehend your argument.

Stylistic Revision   When revising to improve your style, pay attention to the way you sound on paper—to the manner in which you convey your ideas. Stylistic problems include inconsistency in tone of voice (too informal here, excessively formal there), lack of sentence and paragraph variety and emphasis, and use of jargon.

One of the pleasures of writing is projecting something of your individual personality and your own manner of emphasizing ideas, of relating one point to another, and of making colorful or dramatic comparisons. As Sidney Cox writes, "What you mean is never what anyone else means, exactly. And the only thing that makes you more than a drop in the common bucket, a particle in the universal hourglass, is the interplay of your specialness with your commonness" (*Indirections,* 1981:19).

One way to become more adept at constructing sentences and paragraphs is to play around with them. Take any paragraph, your own or someone else's from a magazine article, and rewrite it in different ways, discovering what is possible. You can sense a personality behind Cox's tone of voice, can you not? Look at his syntax, his peculiar word choice. But the point is, if *you* were the one asserting Cox's point, you would have done so in your own manner. For example, you might have expressed the point like this:

> People communicate ideas differently because each person sees the world differently. Each person uses language differently. At the same time, all of us who belong to the same culture share a common language. It is a writer's special blending of his or her individual voice with a commonplace voice that makes for a memorable writing style.

In this "revised" passage, the voice has become less conversational and more impersonal. The syntax and word choice seem more formal, which create the impression that the author is speaking to a large audience rather than to a single person.

Proofreading   One of our students once referred to proofreading as *prof*-reading—making sure the essay is ready for the prof's critical eye. Some students mistakenly equate proofreading with copyediting or even with revision in general; but proofreading refers to a very careful line-by-line scrutiny of the semifinal draft to make sure that no errors of any kind are present. The term *proofreading* comes from the profession of printing; a proof is an initial printing of a document that is used for correcting any mistakes. Most desk dictionaries list common standardized proofreaders' marks: symbols and abbreviations that professional compositors use to indicate changes. You already know some of them: the caret (^) to indicate insertion of a word or letter; the abbreviation *lc*, which means change to lowercase (a diagonal line drawn through a capital letter means the same thing). Proofreading is not reading in the usual sense. If you try to proofread by reading normally, you will miss things. An ideal way to proofread is slowly and orally.

Visual Aids as Tools for Argumentative Writing

Our eyes "are the monopolists of our senses," asserts the poet-naturalist Diane Ackerman in *A Natural History of the Senses* (Random House, 1990), so it's no surprise, as she also points out, that "our language is steeped in visual imagery" (229, 230). Visual elements—photographs, drawings, charts, and diagrams—contribute much to the comprehension of ideas by stimulating the audience's imagination— "imagination" in the sense of being able to see, to image, in the mind's eye, a concrete representation of the ideas being discussed in the text. Keep in mind, however, that abstract ideas are not automatically "improved" by translating them into visuals. Visuals need to be selected with care. It is perfectly all right, often preferable—even in this visual age—to write text-only documents. Most books and articles (even in popular magazines, aside from an introductory visual) continue to be written that way.

That said, images used judiciously help assimilate information and add persuasive force to an argument. It isn't just that "seeing is believing," as the cliché goes, but that a good visual serves as a kind of near-instantaneous summary of the verbal argument being made. Consider how quickly the following cartoon conveys its premise: that digitizing texts will become so commonplace it will be necessary to distinguish between them and "old-fashioned" books, much the way "snail mail" is used to distinguish old-fashioned mail from email.

In the following article, "Tribal Relations," Steven Waldman and John C. Green argue that instead of religion versus secularism being the major determining factor for the way Americans vote, many more factors are involved. As you read the article, consider the role that the visual elements play in conveying the author's premise.

Tribal Relations

How Americans really sort out on
cultural and religious issues—
and what it means for our politics

By Steven Waldman
and John C. Green

Many Americans, when they think about values and politics, focus on the "religious right"—conservatives led by James Dobson, Jerry Falwell, and Pat Robertson, and interested mostly in cultural issues, such as abortion and same-sex marriage. So on election night in 2004, when exit polls found that the No. 1 priority cited by voters was "moral values," many jumped to the conclusion that these voters and their agenda had propelled George W. Bush back into the White House.

Soon it became clear that the "values vote" had been exaggerated. Only one fifth of the respondents listed moral values as the primary basis for their vote. Nearly four out of five listed one of several foreign-policy, economic, or other domestic concerns. And the same polls showed Americans to have social views that would make conservative Christians weep: 60 percent said gays should be allowed either to legally marry or to form civil unions, and 55 percent believed that abortion should be legal in all or most cases.

Religion and values undoubtedly play a large role in our politics. But their impact is often misunderstood. In the most simplistic renderings values come in only two varieties: those held by the religious right and those held by everybody else. During the 2004 campaign we began to map out a very different topology of religion, values, and politics in America, based on survey data gathered by the Ray C. Bliss Institute at the University of Akron in collaboration with the Pew Forum on Religion & Public Life. We combined measures of religious affiliation, behavior, and belief to see how values cluster within the voting public. The resulting picture—which we initially described on the faith-and-spirituality Web site Beliefnet.com and have continued to refine—reveals not two monolithic and mutually antagonistic camps but, rather, twelve coherent blocs with overlapping interests and values. We call these groups the twelve tribes of American politics.

The chart on page 38 shows the twelve tribes and their politics in 2004— Republican tribes in [black], Democratic in [gray], and swing in [dark gray]. The tribes have been placed on a two-way grid that reflects their positions on cultural and economic issues. The cultural issues include abortion, stem-cell research, and gay rights. The economic issues include social-welfare programs and the scope of the federal government. Foreign-policy issues are left off the grid for simplicity's sake, but we will mention them where relevant.

Source: "Tribal Relations" by Steven Waldman and John C. Green, from *The Atlantic Monthly,* January-February 2006.

A brief review of the political habits and migratory patterns of the twelve tribes shows both the complex relationship between values and voting in the United States and the striking degree of compatibility in the values of most Americans. It reveals the role actually played by moral values in the 2004 election, and helps illuminate how the clash of values is likely to influence politics and law in the future.

The Republican Tribes

The fervor and coherence of the Republican base, especially the base of social conservatives, attracted a lot of attention in 2004—and compared with the Democratic base, it is cohesive on moral issues. But it's not monolithic. The Republican base sorts into three related tribes that agree on many issues but place different emphasis on each.

The **religious right**, consisting of traditional evangelical Protestants, accounted for 12.6 percent of the electorate and the core of the moral-values voters in 2004. Almost 90 percent of these voted for Bush. This cohort is as Republican as Republican gets: no group is more conservative on moral values, economic issues, or foreign policy. Contrary to popular belief, the religious right is not growing quickly; its size barely changed from 2000 to 2004.

Heartland culture warriors stand arm-in-arm with the religious right on most moral issues and are nearly as numerous (11.4 percent of the electorate). They are traditional Christians outside the evangelical community, the most prominent being Bush (a traditional United Methodist). Culture warriors are neither as religiously orthodox nor as politically conservative as the religious right, but they were nonetheless energized by same-sex marriage and other high-profile moral issues in 2004. Seventy-two percent voted for Bush in that election.

Heartland culture warriors did not exist as a distinct political group twenty years ago. They are the product of a convulsive theological restructuring—one that has pushed moral values further into the political limelight. Whereas denomination used to predict political affiliation (Catholics were Democrats; Episcopalians were Republicans), religious beliefs and practices are now more important. Congregations and denominations have split over issues such as the inerrancy of the Bible, the role of women, and sexual morality. In recent decades theological conservatives from different denominations—Catholic, Protestant, Mormon—have found one another. In some cases they've formed caucuses within their churches. In others they've switched to more-congenial congregations. One consequence is that they've coalesced on Election Day, voting for candidates who fit their beliefs rather than their churches' historic loyalties.

Moderate evangelicals (10.8 percent of the electorate) make up the final solidly Republican tribe. The less traditional members of evangelical churches, they are culturally conservative but moderate on economic issues, favoring a larger government and aid to the poor. Bush received 64 percent of this tribe's vote, up from 60 percent in 2000.

Moderate evangelicals are much less absolutist than their religious-right cousins: for example, they favor restricting rather than banning abortion, and support some gay rights but not same-sex marriage. As much as anything, they like Bush's personal faith. If you want a Rosetta stone for Bush's evangelical appeal, watch *George Bush: Faith in the White House,* a 2004 documentary that was shown at many church-based Republican campaign events and barely mentions gays or abortion. Rather, it emphasizes that Bush once was lost—a drunk and a ne'er-do-well—but found his faith and was saved; that he was persecuted (by the media) for his faith; that his faith gave him strength and moral clarity; and, most controversial, that he was called by God to the office. These themes resonated deeply among evangelicals.

The three red tribes make up about 35 percent of the electorate, and although their members don't vote exclusively on the basis of cultural issues, values are certainly a key ingredient in the glue that holds the three together. Most of these voters desire a measure of religious expression in public life and a person of faith in the White House. But their positions on such hot-button issues as abortion, gay rights, and stem-cell research are not uniform. Should a future presidential election offer two obviously pious candidates, the Republican "values" base may show itself to be less cohesive than it now appears—and moderate evangelicals in particular could conceivably begin to defect.

The Democratic Tribes

While much hay was made of the "religion gap" in 2004—the tendency of weekly worship attendees to vote Republican—Democrats have religious constituencies too. Indeed, though Democrats may attend church less frequently, many have rich devotional lives, and a surprising number hold conservative cultural views.

A deep-blue **religious left** is almost exactly the same size as the religious right but receives much less attention. John Kerry is perhaps one representative of this group, which draws members from many Christian denominations and is a product of the same theological restructuring that created the heartland culture warriors. Members of the religious left espouse a progressive theology (agreeing, for instance, that "all the world's great religions are equally true") and are very liberal on cultural issues such as abortion and gay marriage. About a quarter attend church weekly. The religious left is somewhat liberal on economic policy and decidedly to the left on foreign policy. Its stances on both moral values and the Iraq War—but especially the latter—have

pushed it further into the Democratic camp. Seventy percent backed Kerry in 2004; 51 percent had backed Gore in 2000. The religious left was the largest—and the fastest-growing—single tribe in the Kerry coalition.

Spiritual but not religious voters, who made up 5.3 percent of the electorate in 2004, are also increasing in number. These are people with no religious affiliation who nonetheless believe in God or the soul. It might be tempting to imagine the members of this tribe as aging flower children or their cultural heirs—and indeed, these voters are liberal on both economic issues and foreign policy. But they actually lean slightly to the right on abortion and gay rights. In 2004 their votes were based on economics and the war, so Kerry won more than three fifths of them.

Black Protestants (9.6 percent of the electorate) are the most traditionally religious of the Democratic tribes, and the most culturally conservative as well—in fact, on moral-values issues they are remarkably similar to the hard-right heartland culture warriors. Whereas many Democrats worried about the intermingling of Bush's faith and his politics, 50 percent of African-Americans said his faith had too little impact on his policymaking. Bush made modest gains among black Protestants in Ohio and other battleground states, and those gains contributed to his re-election. But this tribe was also the most liberal on economic and foreign-policy issues, and more than four fifths voted for Kerry.

Jews and **Muslims and Others** make up a small part of the electorate—1.9 percent and 2.7 percent, respectively—but the latter group is growing. Members of non-Christian faiths tend to be liberal on cultural issues, and moral values may have helped Kerry a bit with these constituencies, but like many of the blue tribes, they favor the Democratic Party mostly because of its economic and foreign-policy stances.

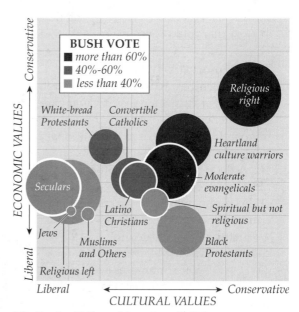

The Twelve Tribes of American Politics
This chart breaks the 2004 electorate into twelve politically relevant "tribes" based on their values, behaviors, and religious affiliation. Each circle corresponds in relative size to the group it represents. The chart reveals some polarization of the electorate. But it also shows that voting preferences do not sort as neatly by cultural values or religious affiliation as people might expect.

Color Advertisement A

Color Advertisement B

You could spend a lifetime gazing at the Carrera 4. That would be a pity. So much more awaits inside. The fluid all-wheel drive. A race-bred 300 horsepower engine. Drive it, and every promise made by that famous shape will be fulfilled. Contact us at 1-800-PORSCHE or porsche.com

Looks fast standing still.
That's called truth in packaging.

 PORSCHE

Color Advertisement C

Color Advertisement D

Non-religious Americans, or **seculars** (10.7 percent of the electorate), are largely responsible for the common view that Democrats are less religious than Republicans—and deeply divided from them on most cultural issues. Seculars are the most culturally liberal of the twelve tribes, and also liberal on economics and foreign policy. Many seculars are especially irritated by Bush's religious expression, and most dislike any commingling of religion and public life. Seculars pose a political dilemma for the Democratic Party: Attempts to energize them based on moral issues would antagonize not only the red tribes and many swing voters but also many blue tribes. Yet attempts to play to more-mainstream American views may turn them off, depressing their turnout.

Indeed, while the blue tribes are fairly well united on economic and foreign-policy issues, they're all over the map on cultural issues. Because the Democratic coalition includes highly religious tribes, non-religious tribes, and everything in between, talking about values can be perilous. Go strongly pro-gay, and one will alienate black Protestants and the spiritual but not religious. Go anti-abortion, and one will lose seculars and the religious left. So Democrats tend to elevate one particular moral value—tolerance—above all others. The merits of tolerance aside, it is part of what keeps the coalition together. But it leaves the Democrats open to attack for lacking a strong moral identity.

The Swing Tribes

Three tribes were up for grabs in 2004 and are still on the move politically. Bush won two of them, and could not have been re-elected without them.

White-bread Protestants (8.1 percent of the electorate) are the most Republican of the purple tribes. They come from the once dominant mainstream Protestant churches that were the backbone of the Republican coalition from William McKinley to Gerald Ford. By now their more traditional co-religionists have joined the heartland culture warriors, and their most liberal brethren the religious left.

In 2004 Bush won just under three fifths of this tribe. He held those voters because of his views on tax cuts (they tend to be affluent and laissez-faire) and terrorism. But white-bread Protestants are closer to the Democrats on moral issues: for instance, a majority are pro-choice. From a historical perspective Kerry did well among this group—perhaps a harbinger of further Democratic gains.

Convertible Catholics (seven percent of the electorate) are the moderate remnant of the non-Latino Catholic vote. Bush won 55 percent of them in 2004. If Kerry, who is Catholic, had done as well with them as the Southern Baptist Al Gore did in 2000, he probably would have won Ohio and the national election.

Convertible Catholics are true moderates. Both the Democrat Maria Shriver and her Republican husband Arnold Schwarzenegger are good examples.

Few believe in papal infallibility, but they are less likely than liberals to say that "all the world's great religions are equally true." They are conflicted on abortion and the scope of government, but strongly favor increased spending to help the poor. Many favor a multilateral foreign policy—except when it comes to the war on terrorism, about which they agree with the president. Scholars describe them as "cross-pressured"—in other words, squishy. They feel that neither party represents them well.

Bush pursued convertible Catholics aggressively in 2004 with shrewd appeals to social stability (backing traditional marriage), concern for the poor (faith-based initiatives), and toughness on terrorism. Al-Qaeda was more important than abortion to his success with this tribe.

Latino Christians are the final swing tribe. They went 55 percent for Kerry in 2004, but Bush made large inroads: he'd won only 28 percent of them in 2000. Values played a large part in this swing—but not primarily because of any Latino Catholic affinity for Republican stances on hot-button cultural issues. Latino Catholics, although they tend to be pro-life, voted for Kerry by more than two to one, largely because of their liberal economic views. Bush did best among Latino Protestants, many of whom come from a Pentecostal tradition that stresses conservative values and an emotional, spirit-filled worship experience. Bush's personal history was appealing to them, as were his efforts to reach out to evangelical churches and religious voters.

As one might expect, the purple tribes lean in different directions on different issues. But where they lean least—or, more precisely, where they vote their leanings least—is on moral issues. They are generally religious, but care little for the culture wars. Their values are largely in line with the legal status quo, and they usually vote based on economic and foreign-policy concerns—at least so long as they don't see either party as seeking a revolution (one way or the other) in personal freedom or the separation of church and state.

Given the beliefs and attitudes of the twelve tribes, what can we say about the future of moral values in politics?

Perhaps the most important lesson is that the size and beliefs of the moderate tribes—the "moral middle," comprising the swing tribes and even a few of the tribes within each party's base—strictly limit how much public policy can actually change after an election. Nothing illustrates that better than the behavior of the Bush administration in the White House. Republican control of all three branches of the federal government is the realization of a religious-right dream. Yet Bush, whatever he said on the campaign trail, has done little to advance the religious right's agenda.

In the 2004 election the official Republican policy, as stated in the party's platform, was to support a constitutional amendment banning abortion. The Republicans also championed Bush's support for an amendment banning gay marriage. Since the election, however, Bush has been silent on both issues. He has not proposed any major restrictions on abortion—nor have the Republican leaders who control both houses of Congress—and has limited his public remarks to criticisms of "partial-birth" abortion and general comments about the "culture of life." He has given not one major speech advocating an amendment to ban gay marriage; in fact, he has dramatically reduced his emphasis on this issue. Bush made a few well-publicized comments expressing openness to the teaching of intelligent design in public schools, but he subsequently pushed no legislation to encourage that goal.

In the past when we've asked religious conservatives privately why they tolerated Bush's doing so little on the cultural issues that were so important during the election, they have responded, in effect, "We need to keep our eye on the ball." The "ball" is the Supreme Court. Religious conservatives believe that permissive judges are the root of much evil in America, and consequently they have allowed Bush enormous latitude as long as they thought he would deliver on judicial nominees.

But he hasn't really—at least not obviously. Conservatives reacted so harshly to the Harriet Miers nomination because neither Miers nor John Roberts was prepared to side with them openly on crucial sexual and moral issues. Had Roberts and Miers replaced Rehnquist and O'Connor, the Court would probably not have shifted much to the right; in fact, it might have shifted a bit to the *left*.

Even the Samuel Alito nomination is telling on this point. Religious conservatives were thrilled with the choice and yet went along with the White House strategy of obscuring rather than clarifying Alito's views on abortion. Alito may yet turn out to be a hero to religious conservatives, but surely it pained them to see him courting Democrats and moderate Republicans by asserting his respect for *Roe* v. *Wade*.

President Bush and his political tacticians are fully aware that they won the election in part by appealing to convertible Catholics, Latinos, moderate evangelicals, and white-bread Protestants. These tribes simply do not support most of the agenda of the religious right. Of course, this is not to say that our laws and cultural norms are forever frozen—far from it. For instance, polls suggest public support for some blurring of the church-state divide: many Americans think that God has been ejected too forcefully from the public square. And to judge from the slow drift of public opinion since the 1980s toward expanding gay rights, it's quite possible that government at all levels will eventually become more supportive of gay unions and even gay marriage. But such changes depend on support from the center—and for the most part our nation's current laws and policies on issues of moral values reflect majority opinion quite well.

None of this means, however, that our elections are likely to become any less fractious. In fact, we believe that the culture wars will increase in intensity during the next few election campaigns, even as the government continues to serve the broad cultural center.

There are two reasons for this view. First, although the poles are not demographically dominant, they have grown somewhat as heartland culture warriors and the religious left have each coalesced into a coherent voting bloc that can be cultivated politically. The secular and moderate-evangelical blocs are also growing. Second, both parties have strong tactical incentives to turn up the rhetorical volume in soliciting support from these tribes during campaigns.

This is especially true for the Republicans. Using moral values to rally the base has become a central tenet of Republican strategy. Because of the investments the party has made in building social-conservative networks and cultivating relationships with them, it would be extremely difficult to abandon this strategy in the short term.

Instead the Republicans may be compelled to intensify their strategy. The personal nature of George Bush's connection to evangelicals is unusual. Someone who lacks that "I once was lost but now am found" narrative may need a harder-edged stand on cultural issues to connect with social conservatives. And the state of other issues behind the Bush coalition, such as foreign policy and the economy, may also necessitate further emphasis on values.

Perhaps this is why Senate Majority Leader Bill Frist took on the Terri Schiavo case, and why the would-be presidential nominee Mitt Romney—who starts with the double disadvantage of being a Mormon and a resident of Massachusetts—has taken the lead in opposing gay marriage. It may also explain why the Republican Senator Sam Brownback so publicly questioned the nomination of Harriet Miers.

But most of the specific issues emphasized by the Republicans are likely to be symbolic, and much of their language carefully coded so as not to alienate the swing tribes. Above all, the Republicans will try to paint themselves as the party of faith. One of the most striking outcomes of the 2004 election is that the Democrats were tagged as "anti-religion." A Pew Forum poll last summer showed that only 29 percent of the public—compared with 40 percent in the summer of 2004—saw the Democrats as "friendly" toward religion. It is hard to appeal even to blue tribes if one is perceived as hostile to faith in general. Surely the Republicans, having opened this wound, will want to make it bleed some more.

Yet if the conservative values agenda is advanced too far, Democrats and liberal interest groups may go on the attack, and Republicans will find themselves at a distinct electoral disadvantage. For instance, if religious conservatives prevail in their efforts to allow teaching of intelligent design in public schools, we can expect that liberals will push hard for reversals. And the center—including convertible Catholics, Latinos, and especially white-bread Protestants—may start to get twitchy if Republicans are perceived as "anti-progress." God is popular, but so is education, because most voters consider it crucial to the future economic prospects of their children.

In politics as in physics, every action produces a reaction, so continued pushing by conservatives will no doubt lead to pushing back by liberals.

Cultural conflict will remain a staple of American politics for the foreseeable future. But concerns that the nation may become subject to the cultural views of either party's poles are alarmist—as is the view that at any one time half the nation is oppressed by the federal government's cultural agenda. The gap between the rhetoric and the reality of American cultural division is unlikely to shrink anytime soon. And it's that gap that is perhaps the most fundamental feature of our cultural politics today.

Before discussing the two visuals (a drawing and a chart) that accompany the article, let's consider its typography. Instead of unbroken, uniform type (tedious to readers of articles and book-length nonfiction, although not a problem for fiction readers), the writers divide their text into sections and subsections to allow for more efficient assimilation of the material.

In "Tribal Relations," consider the use of the bold-faced headings and subheadings that, respectively, divide the article into three main components, each representing the major-party tribes plus the swing tribes, and then subdivide each of these into segments based on individual tribes (for example, the "heartland culture warriors" and the "moderate evangelicals" that constitute the Republican tribes). Note how segmenting the article this way serves a dual purpose: (1) It enables the reader to know at a glance what facet of the subject matter is going to be examined in detail, and (2) it reinforces the overall coherence of the article—in this case, the way the authors have classified the "tribes" of American politics. These simple forms of document design do much to help organize the article and make it visually attractive.

Turning now to the two visuals: what do they contribute to the piece? Let's start with the fanciful drawing of a man wearing a maze of religious symbols around his neck. Is this just a bit of frivolity, or does the illustration reinforce the authors' views on the subject? Notice the particular icons dangling from the man's neck. Some of them reflect particular religions; others, like the Mercedes-Benz icon, do not. But then, why are they even depicted? Perhaps the artist and/or author wants to create an image of "values complexity"—that American voters possibly bring a great deal more than what they themselves are consciously aware of to the polls.

The second image appears to be more explicitly purposeful. It is a chart consisting of circles of varying sizes depicting the degree of influence of particular criteria on the Bush vote of 2004. The bigger the circle, the greater the influence. One might speculate on the choice of a field of circles rather than, say, a bar graph. Perhaps it serves to allude wryly to the election-year party conventions during which balloons are dropped from the ceiling—a bit of playfulness that may not contribute to the argument other than to suggest the spiritedness of the voters, regardless of political affiliation.

Chapter Summary

An argument is a form of discourse in which a writer or speaker tries to persuade an audience to accept, reject, or think a certain way about a problem that cannot be solved by scientific or mathematical reasoning alone. To argue well, a writer uses the three appeals of ethos, pathos, and logos—personal values and ethics, feelings, and logical reasoning—to supplement the facts themselves. The rhetorical rhombus reminds us that every communication act involves targeting a particular audience, whose particular needs and expectations regarding the subject must be met by the writer, and that every act of communication must have a clear, often urgent purpose for establishing communication in the first place.

Good argumentative writing is carefully structured. The three models of argumentative structure—Classical, Toulmin, and Rogerian—represent three different views about the nature and purpose of argument. *Classical argument* follows a predetermined structure consisting of an introduction and statement of the problem, presentation of evidence, refutation of opposing views, and a conclusion derived from the evidence presented. *Toulmin argument,* growing out of the practicalities of political and legal debate, emphasizes the context-dependency of argument and the arguer's underlying values associated with the data the arguer brings forth to support a claim. *Rogerian argument,* growing out of modern humanistic psychology, emphasizes the need for human cooperation when viewpoints differ; hence, a basic assumption underlying the Rogerian argument is that a common ground can be found between the arguing parties, no matter how irreconcilable their differences may seem to be.

Composing arguments is a dynamic process that involves generating ideas, organizing the argument, drafting, revising, editing, and proofreading. These phases of composing overlap and are recursive. Understanding the composing process also means being aware of using different strategies for different parts of the argument, such as openings and conclusions. One final vitally important phase in the composing process is acquiring feedback from peers. Feedback on first drafts is usually immensely valuable in helping writers think more deeply about the purpose, audience, and subject of their arguments.

Checklist

1. Do I clearly understand the four elements of the rhetorical rhombus that comprise the communication act? How each element interacts with the others?

2. Do I understand how the three appeals of ethos, pathos, and logos function in argumentative writing?

3. Do I understand the nature of evidence? Of refutation?

4. Am I familiar with the strategies that comprise the composing process?

5. Have I prepared an outline to prompt me in my drafting?

6. Am I familiar with the different kinds of revision?

7. Have I learned to proofread my drafts carefully?

8. Do I know the definitions of Classical, Toulmin, and Rogerian arguments?

Writing Projects

1. Conduct an informal survey of students' study habits by talking to your fellow students. How many of them "cram" for exams or write their papers immediately before the assignment is due? What specific strategies do students use when they study? (For example, do they make marginal glosses in their books? Write notes on index cards? Make flash cards? Get together with other students in regular study groups?) Can you correlate methods or habits of study to levels of academic success? Write an essay in which you argue for or against such a correlation, using the responses you have gathered.

2. Write an essay on the role that argumentative writing can play in helping people who disagree about a given issue to arrive at better understanding—or at least at a greater willingness to cooperate. What likely obstacles must initially be overcome?

3. Keep a "writing process log" the next time you write an argument. Describe in detail everything you do when prewriting, composing each draft, revising, and proofreading. Next, evaluate the log. Which facets of the composing process were most useful? Which were least useful?

4. Compose four possible openings, each a different type (occasional, anecdotal, startling, analytical) for your next argument writing assignment. Which opening seems most appropriate for your essay, and why?

5. Prepare an outline (Classical, Toulmin, or Rogerian) for an essay taking a position on one of the following topics:

   a. All bicyclists should (should not) be required by law to wear helmets.

   b. This college should (should not) sponsor formal skateboarding competitions.

   c. More courses or programs in multicultural awareness need (do not need) to be offered at this college.

6. Locate four or five editorial cartoons on a single, timely subject. Write an essay in which you analyze their different strategies for satirizing the subject.

7. Read the following essay on editorial cartoons by Herb Block, himself an editorial cartoonist for *The Washington Post*. Write an essay of your own in which you agree or disagree with Block's assertion that "I don't believe there should be any sacred cows." In your support or rebuttal, consider the case in early 2006 in which a series of Danish editorial cartoons satirizing the prophet Mohammed generated outrage among Islamic communities worldwide.

The Cartoon | Herb Block

In one of Charles Schulz's *Peanuts* strips, Lucy announces that she's going to be a political cartoonist "lashing out with my crayon." Just as Charlie Brown asks the subject of her work, she strikes the paper with such a bold stroke that it snaps her crayon in half. "I'm lashing out," she says, "at the people who make these stupid crayons."

Herblock painting McCarthy, Nixon, Reagan, and Clinton. "The Cartoon," copyright 1977, 2000 by Herbert Block. Cartoons appear courtesy of the Herb Block Foundation.

I don't believe in the Lucy method of deciding first to "lash out" and then picking a convenient target. But as a person with definite opinions, she might have done well to stick with cartooning anyhow.

A wide range of work comes under the heading of editorial or political cartooning today, including gag cartoons on current topics. I enjoy many of these and usually put some fun into my work. But I still feel that the political cartoon should have a view to express, that it should have some purpose beyond the chuckle. So what I'm talking about here is the cartoon as an opinion medium.

The political cartoon is not a news story and not an oil portrait. It's essentially a means for poking fun, for puncturing pomposity.

Cartooning is an irreverent form of expression, and one particularly suited to scoffing at the high and the mighty. If the prime role of a free press is to serve as critic of government, cartooning is often the cutting edge of that criticism.

We seldom do cartoons about public officials that say: "Congratulations on keeping your hands out of the public till," or "It was awfully nice of you to tell the truth yesterday." Public officials are *supposed* to keep their hands out of the till and to tell the truth. With only

"What—us tell fibs of some kind?" "The Cartoon," copyright 1977, 2000 by Herbert Block. Cartoons appear courtesy of the Herb Block Foundation.

one shot a day, cartoons are generally drawn about officials we feel are *not* serving the public interest. And we usually support the "good guys" by directing our efforts at their opponents.

For people who think political cartoons are inclined to be negative, a good explanation is in the story of the school teacher who asked the children in her class to give examples of their kindness to birds and animals. One boy told of how he had taken in a kitten on a cold night and fed it. A girl told of how she had found an injured bird and cared for it. When the teacher asked the next boy if he could give an example of his kindness to nature's creatures, he said, "Yes ma'am. One time I kicked a boy for kicking a dog."

In our line of work, we frequently show our love for our fellow men by kicking big boys who kick underdogs. In opposing corruption, suppression of rights and abuse of government office, the political cartoon has always served as a special prod—a reminder to public servants that they ARE public servants.

That is the relationship of the cartoonist to government, and I think the job is best performed by judging officials on their public records and not on the basis of their cozy confidences.

As for the cartoonist's relationship to the rest of the newspaper, that depends on the individual cartoonist and the paper. The editorial page cartoon in the *Washington Post* is a signed expression of personal opinion. In this respect, it is like a column or other signed article—as distinguished from the editorials, which express the policy of the newspaper itself.

Other newspapers operate differently. On some, the cartoon is drawn to accompany an editorial. The cartoonist may sit in on a daily conference, where the content of editorials and cartoons is worked out. Or he may be given copies of the editorials before publication.

A completely different arrangement is followed when the cartoonist simply sends in his work, sometimes from another city. Still other variations include cartoonists submitting sketches (one or several) for editorial approval.

I draw my cartoons at the *Washington Post*, but don't submit sketches or sit in on editorial conferences. And I don't see the editorials in advance. This is for much the same reason that I don't read "idea letters."

Fiddler. "The Cartoon," copyright 1977, 2000 by Herbert Block. Cartoons appear courtesy of the Herb Block Foundation.

I like to start from scratch, thinking about what to say, without having to "unthink" other ideas first. That's something like the old business of trying *not* to think of an elephant for five minutes. It's easier if nobody has mentioned an elephant at all.

In my case, the actual work process is more methodical than inspirational —despite the apparent aimlessness of strolls out of the office, chats with friends, shuffling papers, lining up drawing materials and other diversions that may or may not have to do with creativity. It's methodical compared to the popular impression that "getting an idea" consists of waiting for a cartoon light bulb to flash on overhead.

The day's work begins with reading the newspapers, usually starting the night before with the first edition of the *Washington Post*, and making notes on possible subjects. I also flip on the radio or TV for late news developments. This practice began when I was just about to turn in a finished cartoon one day, only to learn that a major story had broken and kept the newsroom people too busy to tell me about it. The quick return to the drawing board to produce a new cartoon in minutes was an experience I wouldn't want to repeat. And with broadcast reports on the hour or even the half hour, I now occasionally pass along late-breaking news to others.

Unless there is one subject of overriding importance or timeliness on a particular day, or some special outrage, I generally try to narrow down the list of subjects to two or three. Next comes the business of thinking about what it is that needs to be said—and then getting the comment into graphic form, which involves drawing several rough sketches.

It is hard to say just when a thought turns into a cartoon. In writing or speaking, we all use phrases that lend themselves to visual images. Where you might say that a politician is in trouble up to his neck, a drawing might show him as a plumber in a flooded basement or a boy at the dike with his chin just above the water line. On one occasion when a public figure obviously was not telling the truth, I did a sketch of him speaking, with a tongue that was shaped exactly like a table fork. These are pretty simple examples, but they may provide some clue to how concepts develop into drawings.

"Speak softly and carry a big stick." "The Cartoon," copyright 1977, 2000 by Herbert Block. Cartoons appear courtesy of the Herb Block Foundation.

It may not sound very exciting or "cartoony," but to me the basic idea is the same as it ought to be with a written opinion—to try to say the right thing. Putting the thought into a picture comes second. Caricature also figures in the cartoons. But the total cartoon is more important than just fun with faces and figures.

I mention this because it is a common conversational gambit to ask cartoonists if they're having a good time with some well-known face. And when media people are doing articles on a new political personality, they often phone cartoonists to ask what it is about the politician's features that grabs them. Some even ask which candidate you would like to see elected on the basis of "drawability." That's like asking a writer what person he wants elected on the basis of whether the candidate's name lends itself to puns.

I have not yet yielded to the temptation to answer such questions by saying I liked Ronald Reagan's right ear lobe or Jimmy Carter's left nostril. Actually, anyone can be caricatured. And if a cartoonist needed a public figure with Dumbo-the-Elephant ears or a Jimmy Durante nose, he'd have to be pretty hard up for ideas *and* drawing.

From time to time the question of cartoon fairness comes up—with some practitioners asserting that they are not supposed to be fair. This is a view I don't share. Caricature itself is sometimes cited as being unfair because it plays on physical characteristics. But like any form of satire, caricature employs exaggeration—clearly recognized as such. Also the portrayal of a person is often part of the opinion. For example, President George Bush was associated with words like "Read my lips" and "The vision thing." Emphasizing his overhanging upper lip and squinty eyes expressed a view identifying him with his words. I think fairness depends on the cartoon—on whether the view is based on actual statements, actions or inactions.

Questions of fairness are not confined to pictures. Some broadcasters and columnists regularly earn championship belts for fighting straw men. (Those "liberals" want the government to take all your money and run your lives in Washington. Those "conservatives" want to see your kids starve to death.) Incidentally I would like to see a better word than "conservative" for some who are not eager to conserve basic rights or the environment.

Arms payoff for hostage release. "The Cartoon," copyright 1977, 2000 by Herbert Block. Cartoons appear courtesy of the Herb Block Foundation.

A columnist who opposes political campaign funding reform—based on his interpretation of the First Amendment—wrote a piece in which he pointed out that we spend more on potato chips than on political campaigns. But if true, the purchase and consumption of potato chips, whatever they do to our diets, can hardly be compared to the purchase and corruption of public offices. I'd guess the columnist who reached for that statistical irrelevance probably regards cartoons for campaign funding reform as "gross caricatures."

But back to the drawing board and the sketches—a series of "roughs" may approach a subject from different angles or may be variations on a theme. This is where other people come into the picture—or, more accurately, where I bring the pictures to other people. By showing sketches to a few colleagues on the paper, I often find out which sketch expresses a thought most clearly. The purpose of these trial runs is not only to get individual reactions, but also to get out any bugs that might be in the cartoon ideas.

One of the advantages of working at the *Washington Post* is the access to information about government and assorted news items. Reporters, researchers and other staff members are available—with special knowledge about subjects they have dealt with. They also know where to find answers to questions about who said what or exactly what happened when. And computers now make it possible to recall statements and records of all kinds.

A sketch on arms programs or military costs, for example, is one I'd particularly want to discuss with the Pentagon correspondent. A writer covering the courts can tell me if I've missed anything in a decision. Capitol Hill writers, familiar with the exact status of congressional bills, can tell if a sketch on a piece of legislation is well-timed. Staff members may also have information that helps me decide which cartoon is the best bet for that day. Such help—not "ideas for cartoons," but background information and relevant facts—is of enormous value.

I'm a deadline pusher, and one reason the finished cartoon is usually a last-gasp down-to-the-wire effort is because of the time spent on sketches. I work on them as long as possible. And after deciding on one, I send a Xerox copy of it to the editor's office.

Impeachment parade. "The Cartoon," copyright 1977, 2000 by Herbert Block. Cartoons appear courtesy of the Herb Block Foundation.

Other cartoonists—as well as other papers—prefer different arrangements. One cartoonist told me he had tried for years to get the kind of freedom I have on the *Post*. When he finally got it, he found the decision-making to be a burden. He went back to asking an editor to make the daily choice.

I enjoy the freedom to express my own ideas in my own way. And this is also consistent with the *Washington Post* policy expressed by the late publisher, Eugene Meyer, who said he believed in getting people who knew what they were doing and then letting them do it.

One of the things that has made the *Washington Post* great is the fact that it *does* provide for differing views instead of offering a set of written and drawn opinions all bearing the stamp of a single person. Over the years, there have been differences between the cartoons and the editorials on issues, on emphasis and on performances of individual public figures.

In 1952, for example, the *Washington Post* endorsed Gen. Dwight Eisenhower for president before either major party had made nominations. The cartoons expressed my unhappiness with the campaign conducted by Eisenhower and his choice for vice president, Richard Nixon—and expressed my clear preference for candidate Adlai Stevenson.

About 1965, with a different editor and a different publisher, the cartoons focused more and more on President Johnson's "credibility gap" and his escalation of the war in Vietnam, while the editorials generally supported the president and his Vietnam policy. Even on this extremely divisive issue, the editor and I respected each other's views.

Later, the cartoons and editorials diverged on other subjects. For example, in the 1970s I did a series of cartoons opposing the confirmation of Clement Haynsworth to the Supreme Court—a view not shared in the editorials. But we were in agreement in opposing the next nominee—G. Harold Carswell.

During the Clinton administration I did not share in the *Post*'s approval of the expansion of the North American Treaty Organization (NATO) after the collapse of the Soviet Union. And the cartoons hardly matched the editorials on Independent Counsel Kenneth Starr—which acknowledged that he had made mistakes in the probe of President Clinton's relationships but saw him as a victim of a vicious organized attack.

On important issues involving civil rights and civil liberties the editorials and cartoons have been in general agreement. There was no possible doubt about the stands they shared on the attempted censorship involved in the publication of the Pentagon Papers on Vietnam or the culmination of the Nixon scandals in Watergate. And they have both been involved in the long continuous battles for campaign finance reform and gun controls and tobacco industry curbs.

But even where the general viewpoints have been the same, there have been times when I knew a publisher or editor would have preferred my using a different approach. During the Watergate disclosures, I did a "naked Nixon." This might have seemed like *lèse majesté* to an editor but was *au naturel* for a cartoonist.

I've often summed up the role of the cartoonist as that of the boy in the Hans Christian Andersen story who says the emperor has no clothes on. And that seemed to be just what was called for during this phase of the "imperial presidency."

What a written piece can do more easily than a cartoon is to comment on a subject that requires giving background information. Wordiness can be awkward in a cartoon— though sometimes needed to explain an issue or provide dialogue. But a cartoon at times can say something that might be harder to put into words. The one of Nixon hanging between the tapes comments not only on his situation at the time, but on his veracity and honesty— without using any words other than his own.

Nixon hanging between the tapes."The Cartoon," copyright 1977, 2000 by Herbert Block. Cartoons appear courtesy of the Herb Block Foundation.

As for a comparison of words and pictures—each has its role. Each is capable of saying something necessary or something irrelevant—of reaching a right conclusion or a wrong one.

A cartoon does not tell everything about a subject. It's not supposed to. No written piece tells everything either. As far as words are concerned, there is no safety in numbers. The test of a written or drawn commentary is whether it gets at an essential truth.

As for subject matter, I don't believe there should be any sacred cows. But there's no obligation for the cartoonist to deal with a topic unless he feels there is a point that needs to be made. Regardless of Lucy's view, the object is not to "lash out" just because the means is at hand.

There is no shortage of subjects for opinions. I don't long for public misfortunes or official crooks to provide "material for cartoons." Hard as it may be for some people to believe—I don't miss malefactors when they are gone from public life. There are more things amiss than you can shake a crayon at.

If the time should come when political figures and all the rest of us sprout angel wings, there will still be different views on the proper whiteness and fluffiness of the wings, as well as flaps over their flapping, speed and altitude. And there will still be something funny about a halo that's worn slightly askew.

When that happy heaven-on-earth day comes, I'd still like to be drawing cartoons. I wouldn't want to see any head angel throwing his weight around. ◎/◎

2 | Methods of Critical Reading

A reader must learn to read.
—Alberto Manguel

Reading and writing are intimately related modes of thinking—so intertwined that you really cannot do one without doing the other. Just as writers determine how to approach their subjects by considering their purpose and their readers, so too do readers determine how to approach *their* purpose for reading by considering how to approach the subject, often working along similar lines to those intended by the author.

Reading as the Construction of Meaning

Some researchers refer to the symbolic relationship between reading and writing as the *construction of meaning.* That is, readers must process meaning from those symbols on the page that, by themselves, possess no intrinsic meaning.

As readers we also construct meaning beyond what we see on the page before us. For example, when we read through a draft of an argument to revise and edit it, we monitor our sense of direction, the development of the ideas, the coherence (that is, the logical progression of ideas), the clarity, and the larger concerns of persuasiveness and originality.

All of these activities are context-dependent. As the example in Table 2.1 reveals, reading strategies that work well, say, in drafting an essay that objectively analyzes the strengths and weakness of a high school exit test may not work when drafting a more subjective essay on why the school should retain or abandon such tests. In the first essay, you need to read for such elements as logical progression of ideas, thorough support of assertions, and fair representation of challenging or alternative views. In the second essay, aware that you are presenting an individual preference, you need to keep an eye out for sufficiently clear (if not always logical) reasons behind your preferences.

Thus, whenever we read, we do a great deal more than simply absorb words like a sponge. In reading others' work, we sometimes think to ourselves, "If I had written this essay, I'd have made this introduction much shorter and put in more examples in the third paragraph—I barely understood it, after all!" Such

TABLE 2.1   **Sample Perspectives from Which We Read**

Topic	Perspective 1 (neutral outsider)	Perspective 2 (offensive)	Perspective 3 (defensive)
Value of Exit Tests	To weigh pros vs. cons to pass a fair judgment	I've always been held back by these biased tests!	Tests have always enabled me to show how much I know!

thinking is comparable to what we do as we revise our own work, so clearly we are reading another's text from the writer's perspective.

We might also "revise" another's writing when someone asks us about a book or article we've read: "What is Adrian Nicole LeBlanc's *Random Family* about?" In summarizing that contemporary work of creative nonfiction, we would use our own words to shorten a three-hundred-page work to one or two paragraphs. In fact, while you are reading such a text, you are summarizing it to yourself—during the actual reading or during breaks between readings. Thus, to understand a text means, in a sense, to rewrite the author's ideas so that we blend them with our own ideas. Such rewriting is built into the very nature of reading. We cannot truly comprehend a text without doing so.

Active Versus Passive Reading

In the sense that to read means processing written language in order to understand it, all reading is "active." But some forms of reading represent a greater challenge to the comprehension process than others. A letter from a loved one may be processed relatively swiftly and efficiently, almost as a photograph would, whereas a demanding legal or technical document of the same length may need to be processed in a much more methodical manner.

When we read primarily for pleasure—whether a novel, a work of nonfiction, or a friend's email—we are concerned primarily about content: What is going to happen to the characters in the novel? What is the author's premise in the work of nonfiction? What fun activities did the friend experience in London over the summer?

But when we read for a purpose besides (or in addition to) pleasure, we need to think more consciously of our reading process so that we can make necessary modifications. Such reading is task-oriented: to find out certain information, to summarize the work, to analyze the structure of the work, to assess the merits of the argument, to determine how the information coincides with our position on the issue.

You can adopt certain strategies to become a more active reader. It may seem strange to think of a "strategy" of reading. The only strategy that leaps to mind is moving our eyes across the page from left to right and top to bottom (for readers of most Western languages). But from a psychological and linguistic perspective, we are pulling off complex feats of cognition. At the simplest level we are doing any or all of the following, more or less simultaneously:

- *Linking* one part of a sentence with another, for example, linking a subordinate clause to a main clause or nouns and verbs to their respective adjectival or adverbial modifiers, or linking the data in a visual aid such as a graph or diagram to the discussion of those data in the body of the argument. Visuals themselves possess components that need to be linked together when they are read. Imagine a pie chart that breaks down someone's college-related expenses for a given month. The reader links each slice of the chart with the others, reflecting on proportions. If 40 percent of the pie is given over to the cost of meals, for example, the reader may agree or disagree with your claim that food costs on this campus are disproportionate relative to food costs on other college campuses.

- *Tracking* the constantly shifting parameters of meaning from word to word, phrase to phrase, sentence to sentence, paragraph to paragraph

- *Relating* any given sentence or paragraph to a premise or theme, whether implied or explicitly stated

Those are just some of the *basic* strategies. As students of writing, you read not just for understanding but for insight into the way in which an author organizes and develops an argument. This type of active reader needs to do the following:

- Determine the *framework* of the author's argument. What is the claim, data, and warrant?

- Evaluate the *data* (evidence) presented. Is it accurate? Sufficient? Appropriate? Relevant?

- Evaluate the author's *organizational strategy*. Why does the author bring in X before Y and after W? Is the sequence beyond dispute, or is there no clear rhetorical purpose behind the sequence? Should the author have arranged things differently?

- Speculate on the *significance* of what is being argued. What are the short- and long-term consequences of the author's views? If the author argues that student athletes are treated unfairly in the classroom, for example, and uses compelling evidence to back up that claim, then the significance of the argument is that it could persuade classroom teachers to be more flexible, say, in permitting student athletes to miss class in order to participate in out-of-town athletic competitions.

- Analyze the *logic* of the argument. Has the writer inadvertently committed any of the logical fallacies covered later on in Chapter 6?

Each of these cognitive acts works together to comprise active reading. Passive reading, by contrast, means reading without reflecting or "talking back" to the text—that is, without forming questions that can and should be asked of an author who is trying to communicate with us.

 Exercise 2.1

1. Assess your reading process. What kinds of material do you read actively? Passively? What about the material encourages one mode of reading rather than another?

2. Select a short piece such as a magazine feature or editorial on a social or political issue and discuss it in terms of the four concerns of an active reader (framework, data, organizational strategy, and significance).

3. Read a short piece for coherence alone. Explain how the author "glues" sentences and paragraphs together to make them interrelate clearly and meaningfully.

Reading as a Writer of Arguments

Chapter 1 describes the role that supporting data and expert opinion play in building your argument. As you read to find sources of support for your argument, use the following strategies: previewing, in-depth reading, and postreading.

Previewing

Imagine Bob, a first-year student, trying to study for a political science quiz the next day. He's having trouble reading the textbook chapter being tested. It seems like more pages than he has time or inclination to absorb. So he finds his classmate Julie in the library and tells her he's having trouble motivating himself to do all that reading. Julie, who's already read the chapter, encourages him by saying, "Oh Bob, the chapter essentially covers only four points about the economic conditions on the Greek islands comprising Santorini." Relieved that the chapter highlights only four main points, Bob returns to his room motivated to read but also with a sense of how to read the chapter productively. Julie has given him a *preview* of what to expect. Previewing is typically a two-stage process: (1) prereading, and (2) skimming.

Anything worth reading typically requires several readings, so you approach this previewing stage knowing that you will read the assignment more thoroughly later on.

To read as critical thinkers and writers, you must read to ensure that you

- understand the content and progression of the story or argument,
- can determine the rhetorical strategy (for example, the validity and significance of the claim, the data, and the warrant), and
- are able to incorporate the author's views into your own.

Prereading You preread the text to determine its central purpose and approach. You may do this at the beginning of the term, when, standing in line to purchase your textbook, you peruse the table of contents and the introductions to each of the chapters. You also preread when you read the topic sentences of the paragraphs in the introduction. (The topic sentence usually appears in the first, second, or last sentence.)

To preread an article or chapter from a work of nonfiction, you can rely on the structure that writers in the Western tradition have used for centuries and handed down to the modern college composition course:

- Introduction

- Thesis statement

- Topic sentences

- Transitional paragraphs

- Conclusion

Remember that the purpose of prereading is not to understand the whole piece but to identify the key points of the piece so that when you do read it in its entirety, you already have a clear sense of its framework.

After reading the introduction in full, read the topic sentences of the body paragraphs. These tend to be in one of three spots: first, last, or second. Topic sentences most frequently appear as the first sentences of the paragraphs, just where you have been taught to put them. But they also may occur as the last sentence in the paragraph when the writer has organized the content of the paragraph by presenting his or her evidence before the claim. And the topic sentence sometimes is the second sentence of the paragraph (the third most frequent position) when the first sentence is transitional, linking the paragraph before to the one that follows. In these cases, you will read both the transitional sentences and the topic sentences. You may need to read a bit of the article or essay to gain a sense of the writer's style—that is, where he or she tends to position the topic sentence.

Here is an example of a paragraph in which the topic sentence appears at the very end, a technique that this particular author, Carl Sagan, uses quite commonly in his writing. This selection is from Sagan's *The Demon-Haunted World: Science as a Candle in the Dark* (1995):

> What do we actually see when we look up at the Moon with the naked eye? We make out a configuration of irregular bright and dark markings—not a close representation of any familiar object. But, almost irresistibly, our eyes connect the markings, emphasizing some, ignoring others. We seek a pattern, and we find one. In world myth and folklore, many images are seen: a woman weaving, stands of laurel trees, an elephant jumping off a cliff, a girl with a basket on her back, a rabbit, . . . a woman pounding tapa cloth, a four-eyed jaguar. People of one culture have trouble understanding how such bizarre things could be seen by the people of another.

The pattern Sagan uses in this paragraph is this: He opens with a question, gives a string of examples to illustrate the basis of the question, and then answers the question, that is, posits the topic sentence. Such rhetorical patterning provides a coherence that enables readers to follow the strands of a complex discussion.

The final step in prereading is paying close attention to concluding paragraph or paragraphs of the argument. Writers often summarize their main points here. They may also point out implications of the ideas or perhaps let readers know what steps they should take. To return to the chapter from *The Demon-Haunted World* that focuses on the difficulty of observing nature objectively, we arrive at Sagan's conclusion:

> By and large, scientists' minds are open when exploring new worlds. If we [scientists] knew beforehand what we'd find, it would be unnecessary to go [there]. In future missions to Mars or to the other fascinating worlds in our neck of the cosmic woods, surprises—even some of mythic proportions—are possible, maybe even likely. But we humans have a talent for deceiving ourselves. Skepticism must be a component of the explorer's toolkit, or we will lose our way. There are wonders enough out there without our inventing any.

Sagan not only stresses his central idea about the need to maintain objectivity in the search for truth, but also assures us that the search for truth will reward us with discoveries every bit as wondrous as anything we could concoct.

By following a pattern of prereading, you may not yet fully understand the text, but at this stage you are just trying to provide yourself with an overview. You are also giving yourself a sense of how much energy you will need to invest before reading the piece fully.

Skim-Reading   At this stage, read the article in full, including the parts you have preread. But read swiftly, keeping alert for the key words in each sentence. To skim well, take advantage of your peripheral vision: You do not have to look directly at a word to see it; your eyes notice it just by looking in its general vicinity. Also, you already have an idea of the general parts of the article, and you are fleshing out those generalizations via the specifics that the writer provides. This enables you to grasp more readily the writer's logical progression of ideas and use of evidence. By the time you reach the conclusion, you should feel more comfortable with whatever the author is summarizing or exhorting readers to do.

If the piece you are reading is printed in columns, you probably will make your eyes stop once every line, approximately following a pattern indicated by the *x*'s in the passage that follows:

x
As you read these two columns,
    x
you'll notice that there are x's above
    x
the typed lines, one to the left on the
        x
first line and then one to the right on
    x
the second line. The x's continue to
            x
alternate down the columns. Fixing

x
your eyes on those x's, you can see
            x
the words written below them—not
        x
just the words directly below the x's
            x
but the words before and after those
        x
as well. If you were looking just for
                x
a particular date, such as June 20,

x
2000, then you would be looking just
x
for that particular configuration of
x
numbers. Looking somewhat above
x
the lines rather than directly at
x
the words on the lines helps you
x
not to read the words but more
x
to focus on the particular pattern of
x
words or numbers that you are

x
looking for. (The date of June 20,
x
2000, was chosen because that's the
x
wedding date of two British friends,
x
Dave and Jenny.) You see how you
x
could systematically skim for just
x
the two occasions of a date-like
x
configuration. Essentially, that's
x
skimming.

When skimming a page with visuals, return to the visual after skimming the text. First look for connections between the text and the visual; then, look for points of comparison and contrasts within the visual itself—for example, in a multiple bar graph that shows changes in use of coal versus oil for heating in three different decades in the United States (represented by three different-colored bars), you want to notice the degree of difference between coal and oil, and whether such a difference is significant in arguing, say, that the United States has been doing a good job in becoming less oil-dependent from one decade to the next.

In-Depth Reading

The previewing strategies detail methods that you can follow if you wish to locate specific, brief information or to quickly scope out the gist of a piece. As a writer of arguments, you read for other reasons as well:

- *Summarizing* to demonstrate an ability and willingness to present another's ideas in a fair, unbiased way (see "Writing a Summary," pages 60–61)

- *Analyzing* the structure of the piece to understand precisely the logic the writer uses, to determine whether the writer omits some important causal or temporal element, or whether the writer fairly and accurately represents all major viewpoints regarding the issue

- *Assessing* the strengths and weaknesses of the argument and determining the extent to which the writer's position influences your own

- *Annotating* in the margins to maintain an ongoing critical-response dialogue with the author as you are reading (see "Reading with a Pencil," page 62)

Postreading

You follow the full reading with a postreading. Essentially, you read the same parts of the piece as you had for the preread. The purpose for a postread is to reinforce the framework of the whole in your mind and to distinguish between details and main points of a piece. In a postread, you cement in your mind the structure and logic of the piece by going back over it and reviewing its contents. During the postread, follow these steps:

1. Ask yourself, What is the most important thing I learned from this piece, and where is it most clearly expressed? At this stage, not any earlier, you begin to mark the text. Highlight this passage with a marker and make a marginal note briefly summarizing the passage in your own words. Summarizing helps you reinforce what you have read.

2. Now ask, What evidence does the author use that supports the claim most convincingly? Highlight and annotate this passage as well.

3. Ask finally, What concluding insight does the author leave me with? Again, highlight and then annotate this segment of text in your own words.

Once you get into the habit of previewing, in-depth reading, and postreading articles and essays, you will find it an efficient and satisfying process.

 Exercise 2.2

1. Choose an article from your campus newspaper. First, preview the article and jot down what you remember immediately afterward. Next, read the article in depth and jot down new things you had not obtained during the preread. Finally, postread the article, and answer the questions posed in the three steps above.

2. Preview an article in one of your favorite magazines or from the Clusters in Part II. Write down all the information you obtain from this preview reading. Next, read the article as you normally would and write down any information you had not obtained from the prereading. Write a brief assessment of the value of prereading based on this experience.

Writing a Summary

One of the most effective ways of reinforcing your comprehension of a piece is to write a formal *summary* of it shortly after you read it. As you already know, a summary is a concise but accurate rephrasing, primarily in your own words, of the premise of a work. Writing summaries of works you read is a valuable exercise for three reasons:

1. To summarize is to demonstrate (to yourself and to others) the degree to which you understand the piece as the author means it to be understood— realizing, of course, that there is no way of knowing whether one's

understanding of an argument corresponds *exactly* to what the author has in mind. Unfortunately, readers sometimes praise or criticize a work based on a misreading or a misunderstanding of what the author is trying to convey. Writing a concise summary of the thesis statement and the principal support statements can help you avoid that problem.

2. Writing a summary helps you better integrate into your knowledge base what you have learned from the piece.

3. Summaries of related articles and books serve as an important resource for a research paper. You may be reading many different sources on a given topic. Summarizing each one immediately after reading the work helps you to internalize the material better and keep various sources straight in your mind. Sometimes you will use these summaries when preparing an annotated bibliography. (See Chapter 8 for how to format an annotated bibliography.)

Typically, a summary is about one-fourth the length of the original, but a special type of summary is referred to as an *abstract*. Abstracts of books are generally a single page long, and those of articles, a single paragraph. Volumes of abstracts, such as *Resources in Education* (which summarizes thousands of articles on education collected in a vast *database* known as ERIC) and *Chemical Abstracts* (which maintains a similar service for articles on chemistry), are located in your school library and often online.

Writing a summary returns you to the skeletal outline of your essay, where you are better able to isolate the key points. The procedure of summarizing is relatively simple in principle, but in practice it can be tricky. Some pieces are more difficult to summarize than others, depending on whether the key ideas are presented explicitly or implicitly. Here are the steps you should take:

1. Determine the thesis of the essay, rephrase it in your own words, and make that the opening sentence of your summary.

2. Locate the supporting statements. Sometimes these are the topic sentences of each paragraph, but some writers are inventive with paragraph structure. Rephrase the supporting statements in your own words.

3. Write a concluding sentence, paraphrasing the author's own conclusion if possible.

◎⁄◎ Exercise 2.3

1. Do an in-depth reading of the article you preread for the second item in Exercise 2.2. How does the prereading help you to absorb the discussion as you encountered it in the in-depth reading?

2. Write a summary of Martin Luther King, Jr.'s, essay, "Letter from Birmingham Jail," found on pages 143–156.

3. After everyone in class has written a summary of the King essay, compare the summaries in small groups. How do they differ? How are they alike? How do you know? What accounts for the similarities among the summaries? What accounts for the dissimilarities? Are the differences and similarities significant? In what way?

4. Consider the differences and similarities found in question 3 above to see whether they account for greater accuracy of some summaries.

5. Explain the relationship between summary writing and reading comprehension.

Reading with a Pencil

To help you pay special attention to key ideas during a postreading, write marginal comments, underline text, or use visual icons such as asterisks, checkmarks, or arrows. Such annotations, or marginalia, enhance your involvement with the reading material and reinforce understanding. (*Note:* Of course, if you are reading library books or books belonging to someone else, do not put a mark of any kind in them. Instead, jot your notes down in a journal.) If you are not in the habit of writing in the margins or in journals, it is a valuable habit to cultivate. Here are some types of marginalia to try:

- **Glosses:** One-sentence summaries of what each paragraph is about.

- **Comparisons:** Notes to yourself reinforcing correspondences you notice. Say you want to compare a passage with something you have read earlier in the piece or in a different piece. The abbreviation *cf.* (Latin for "compare") is most often used; it means compare and/or contrast this passage with such-and-such a passage on such-and-such a page.

- **Questions or reactions:** Spur-of-the-moment concerns you have about an assertion, the validity of the data or other kinds of evidence, or something the author overlooks or overstates.

- **Icons:** These are your own personal symbols—asterisks, wavy lines, checkmarks, bullets, smiley faces, and so on—that instantly convey to you on rereading whether the passage marked is problematic or especially noteworthy.

Let us take a look at one possible way of annotating a piece. Study the example that follows.

Say No to Trash | Samuel Lipman

Why is the NEA "Congressionally embattled"?

Or—maybe they were saying no to work that offended the most viewers.

In canceling the Robert Mapplethorpe exhibition last week, Washington's Corcoran Gallery did more than refuse to show a few raunchy photographs of what the press, unable to print them, primly called "explicit homoerotic and violent images." Because the exhibition was supported in part by public funds from the Congressionally embattled National Endowment for the Arts, the Corcoran doubtless considered financial self-interest in arriving at its decision. One hopes those responsible are aware that in saying no to Mapplethorpe, they were exercising the right to say no to an entire theory of art.

Graffiti also outrages many. Should graffiti be considered art too?

This theory assumes, to quote an official of the neighboring Hirshhorn Museum, that art "often deals with extremities of the human condition. It is not to be expected that, when it does that, everyone is going to be pleased or happy with it." The criterion of art thus becomes its ability to outrage, to (in the Hirshhorn official's words) "really touch raw nerves."

Despite its occasional usefulness, this theory ignores the vast corpus of great art that elevates, enlightens, consoles and encourages our lives. The shock appeal of art is questionable when it encompasses only such fripperies as displaying inane texts on electronic signboards in the fashion of Jenny Holzer; it becomes vastly more deleterious when it advances, as Mapplethorpe does, gross images of sexual profligacy, sadomasochism and the bestial treatment of human beings.

I don't know what "immediately injurious" means.

In a free society, it is neither possible nor desirable to go very far in prohibiting the private activities that inspire this outré art. People have always had their private pleasures, and as long as these pleasures remain private, confined to consenting adults, and not immediately injurious, the public weal remains undisturbed. But now we are told that what has been private must be made public. We are told that it is the true function of art to accommodate us to feelings and action that we—and societies and nations before us—have found objectionable and even appalling.

Source: Samuel Lipman, "Say No to Trash." Originally published in *The New York Times,* 23 June 1989. Copyright © 1989. Reprinted by permission of Jeaneane Dowis Lipman.

In evaluating art, the viewer's role is thus only to 5
approve. We are told that whatever the content of art, its
very status as art entitles it to immunity from restraint.
There are certainly those who will claim that the
Mapplethorpe photographs are art, and therefore to be criticized, if at all, solely on aesthetic, never on moral, grounds.
Are we to believe that the moral neutrality with which we
are urged to view this art is shared by its proponents? Can
it, rather, be possible that it is the very content so many find
objectionable that recommends the art to its highly vocal
backers?

Further, there are those who would have us believe that

Can any work of art ever be morally neutral?

because we are not compelled to witness what we as individuals find morally unacceptable, we cannot refuse to make it
available for others. Taking this position not only ignores our

A key concern: exposure of erotic art to children.

responsibility for others; it ignores the dreadful changes
made in our own lives, and the lives of our children, by the
availability of this decadence everywhere, from high art to
popular culture.

It is undeniable that there is a large market for the hitherto forbidden. Upscale magazines trumpet the most shocking manifestations of what passes for new art. A rampant
media culture profits hugely from the pleasing, and the lowering, of every taste.

Just as it is neither possible nor desirable to do much
about regulating private sexual behavior, little can be done
legally about the moral outrages of culture, either high or
popular. But we can say no, and not only to our own participation as individuals in this trash. We can decline to make it
available to the public through the use of our private facilities and funds; this, the Corcoran, acting as a private institution, has now done.

There is still more to be done. Acting on our behalf as citizens, our Government agencies—in particular the National
Endowment for the Arts—can redirect their energies away
from being the validators of the latest fancies to hit the art mar-

Much "great art of the past" was shocking in its day.

ket. Instead, public art support might more fully concentrate
on what it does so well: the championing of the great art of the
past, its regeneration in the present and its transmission to the
future. This would mean saying yes to civilization. It is a policy change that deserves our prompt attention. One hopes that
the Corcoran, by saying no to Robert Mapplethorpe, has begun
the process.

Exercise 2.4

1. Your instructor will distribute a short article for everyone in class to annotate. Then, share your manner of annotating. What useful methods of annotation do you learn from other classmates?

2. Clip a relatively short newspaper story, paste or photocopy it on a sheet of paper, leaving very wide margins, and then annotate the article fully.

Reading Visuals in Argument

You might be thinking, who needs to be shown how to read a visual? All you need to do is look at it! Well, that might be true for the consumer—in fact, advertisers *hope* that consumers will simply look at their images so that the hidden persuasive appeals can work their alchemy. As writers of argument, however, you need to read visuals critically, just as you would read any book or article critically. But how does one read an image critically? Graphs and charts are virtually self-explanatory; their captions in effect tell you how to read them, so let's set this type of visual aside for the moment and focus instead on photographs and drawings.

As simple and unified as a photograph or drawing might be, it generates several different kinds of relationships: external, internal (that is, the interplay of particular visual elements within the whole image), and rhetorical (that is, what the different elements in the visual communicate or seem to communicate to the audience).

External Relationships

- The relationship of the visual to the text surrounding it and/or to the text referring to it

- The relationship of the visual to other visuals in the article, if any

Internal Relationships

- The interplay of figure and ground

The terms "figure" and "ground" refer to the object of focus (the figure), which dominates the photograph or drawing, and what is in the background. In a visual everything in an image establishes a relationship of some sort with everything else, simply by its presence.

Before deciding on including a particular visual for your article, ask yourself these two questions:

1. Do the figure and ground elements interconnect in ways that enhance the purpose of the image? Study David Plowden's photograph "The Hand of Man on America."

Notice how the foreground objects interact with the background object, the Statue of Liberty. One of the many ironies of this image is that the Statue of Liberty not only dominates the image even though it's in the background (the telephoto lens used to take the photograph makes it appear larger than it would otherwise), but it also embodies the implicit conflict between the precious liberties it symbolizes and the ways in which those liberties are sometimes abused by environmentally damaging technology and industry.

2. Do all the objects in the foreground or background serve a unifying purpose? Are there extraneous elements in the ground that could prove to be distracting? Test the criterion of unity on Plowden's photograph. Can anything be deleted from the image without diminishing its impact? The cranes in the background? No, they, along with the telephone poles and the piles of refuse, contribute to the ironic contrast between the dark images of abuse and the bright image of liberty.

◎/◎ Exercise 2.5

Write an analysis of the compositional technique of one of your favorite photographs or paintings. Pay attention to the interplay of foreground objects with background objects, and the way each object in the image contributes to a central idea.

Exercise 2.6

Consider the advertisements in Chapter 1. In each case, decide whether the appeal is basically visual or basically verbal—that is, whether the photographs or the words are most important to the impact of the ad. Why do you think as you do?

Becoming a Highly Motivated Reader

People read for many reasons: to be entertained; to be informed of global, local, and job-related events; to enhance their general knowledge of fields such as history, science and technology, commerce, politics, social developments, and the arts; to improve their personal lives and health.

You, however, have an additional reason to read: to become a better writer. To realize this goal, you must become not only an alert, active reader but a highly motivated one as well.

To acquire a sense of the rich possibilities of argumentative writing, begin to read (if you don't already) any or all of the following material:

- Newspaper editorials and op-ed pieces (familiarize yourself not only with the editorial section of your local newspaper but with those of the *New York Times* and the *Washington Post* as well)

- Essays that appear in magazines and journals noted for high-quality commentary on important issues, journals such as *Newsweek, Time, Harper's Magazine,* the *Atlantic Monthly,* and the *New York Review of Books*

- Books that take strong stands on current, intensely debated issues, books such as John Mueller's *Overblown: How Politicians and the Terrorism Industry Inflate National Security Threats, and Why We Believe Them* (Free Press, 2006) or Victoria de Grazia's analysis of the influence of the United States on Europe after World War II, *Irresistible Empire: American's Advance through Twentieth-Century Europe* (Belknap Press/Harvard University Press, 2006)

You likely are already a motivated reader, or else you could not have made it into college. Your goal now is to capitalize on your already strong reading skills by reading even more widely and avidly. Here are a few suggestions to consider:

1. Begin by thinking of each reading experience—each opportunity to scrutinize an argument—as a chance to recruit more brain cells. It is said that we use only 10 percent of our brain capacity, so there's no danger in running out of cells!

2. Think of each reading experience as yet another opportunity to study a talented writer's craft, an important step toward helping you develop your own craft.

3. Select books for reading that you have intended to read but "never got around to." Do not be overly ambitious; you do not want to disappoint yourself. It is not necessary to give yourself page quotas (for example, a hundred pages a night); that has a way of backfiring when you have an already busy schedule. The key is to read *regularly,* every day, at the same time, just as you might with exercising, so that reading becomes a habit. And be patient with yourself: It sometimes takes a while for a habit to take hold. After about three or four weeks of "forcing" yourself to read, say, one hour of noncourse-required reading every morning, the ritual will become so engrained that it will feel as natural (and as enjoyable) as eating.

4. Finally, take the time to keep a reading journal. This does not have to be elaborate. After each reading session, take about fifteen minutes to jot down your reflections on or reactions to the reading you have just finished. In addition to reinforcing your comprehension of the material and your insights into it, the journal will serve as a logbook of your reading experiences.

Once again, it is impossible to overemphasize the importance of reading to learning, to the life of the mind, to what it means to be educated in this complex, information-driven, competitive world. Reading is truly your ticket to the treasures of knowledge and understanding.

 Exercise 2.7

1. Write a reading autobiography in which you describe your childhood and early adolescent reading experiences and tastes. Note how your tastes in and habits of reading have changed over the years.

2. Keep a record of your reading activities over the next four weeks. Record the time you spend reading each day. List everything you read, but only after you finish reading it (individual chapters can count as separate pieces). Divide the material into "required" and "nonrequired" reading. Do an "active reader" critique of each work (refer back to the list on page 55). At the end of the fourth week, evaluate your reading. Did your motivation to read improve? When? Did your reading become more efficient? Be as honest with yourself as you can.

3. If you consider yourself a slow or inefficient reader, make a special effort to improve. If it takes you longer than an hour to read fifty pages of a book, you are probably subvocalizing (sounding out one word at a time in your head, as if you were reading aloud). Practice reading *clusters* of words and be sure your pacing is swift and smooth, not jerky. Check to see whether your campus offers classes in speed reading or efficient reading.

4. Keep a reading improvement log. Each day for the next four weeks, record the number of pages you read in a given time (say, half an hour). Do not

sacrifice your comprehension as you work on improving your efficiency. The more efficient your reading process, the more your comprehension should improve.

Reading Responsibly

To read arguments responsibly is to engage in a three-step procedure:

1. Read to learn the author's position on the issue.

2. Reread to understand fully that position.

3. Reread to compare and contrast the author's views with the views of others.

Every time we read or listen to someone's views about an issue, we may feel prematurely inclined to agree or disagree. Remaining neutral is sometimes difficult, especially if the writer or speaker presents his or her ideas with passion, eloquence, and wit. As a responsible reader, you do not need to maintain neutrality permanently, only to delay judgment. Before judging an issue, regard any argument as but one perspective, and assume that many perspectives must be considered before a fair judgment can be made.

Reading well is like listening well. Good readers give writers the benefit of the doubt, at least momentarily, and respect the author's point of view, believing it worthy of serious attention (unless the author demonstrates negligence, such as distorting another author's views). But disagreement should never be confused with contentiousness, even if the author comes across as adversarial. You will comprehend and subsequently respond more successfully if you read the argument attentively, if you assume that the writer has considered the argument's assertions with great care, and if you are willing to give the writer the benefit of any doubts, at least for the time being. Once you have read the argument and reflected on it, go over it again, making sure you have understood everything. Then, before you do a third reading, place the writer's point of view in the context of others' views. The third reading is the critical one in which you ask questions of every assertion, questions that reflect the larger conversation produced by other essays.

◎/◎   Exercise 2.8

1. Make a list of ten to fifteen books you plan to read during the quarter or semester. After each title, briefly state your reason for wanting to read the book.

2. Keep a reader's log for each book you read. Each entry might include the following information:

   • Author, title, publication data, and number of pages in the book

   • Dates you began and finished the book

- Your reason for wanting to read the book
- The most important things you learned from the book
- Any criticisms or questions you have of the book

3. Use active reading strategies to read the following editorial on the need to combat global warming. *Preread* the editorial to get a sense of its premise and key points. *Skim* it straight through without critical questioning, allowing the author to present his case without interruption, so to speak. Then *read* the essay in depth, paying close attention to the way in which the writer develops the argument. Finally, *postread* it to reinforce full comprehension, making notes in the margins as recommended above.

High Noon

Global warming is here. It is moving as fast as scientists had feared. If it is not checked, children born today may live to see massive shifting and destruction of the ecosystems we know now. They may witness the proliferation of violent storms, floods, and droughts that cause terrible losses of human life.

The good news is that we are not helpless. We can still curb the greenhouse trend. Our next, best chance will come November 13–24 in the Netherlands, when the nations of the world negotiate again over the terms of the global warming treaty called the Kyoto Protocol. If we lose this chance, we may lose momentum for the entire protocol, and with it five or more years of precious time. But if we win a strong treaty in the Netherlands, it will start real movement on the long road to change.

Evidence and Damage

Like trackers on the trail of a grizzly, scientists read the presence of global warming in certain large-scale, planet-wide events. Over the last century, the surface of the planet heated up by about one degree Fahrenheit. More rain and snow began falling worldwide, an increase of 1 percent over all the continents. The oceans rose 6–8 inches. If these numbers applied to local weather, they would be trivial. As planetary averages, they are momentous. The past decade was the warmest in at least a thousand years. A graph of average global temperatures since the year 1000 shows a precipitous rise that starts at about the time of the Industrial Revolution and shoots upward to our own time.

The results may be profound and unpredictable. In altering the climate of the planet, we are playing with a vastly complicated system we barely understand. As Columbia University scientist Wallace Broecker has said, climate is an angry beast, and we are poking it with sticks.

We may already be feeling its anger. Of course, weather happens in   5
spurts, with or without global warming. It is impossible to know whether
this storm or that drought was an ordinary event, say the effect of a little
extra moisture carried over the West Coast by El Nino, or whether it was a
flick of the tail of the global warming beast.

What is certain is that the kinds of catastrophes global warming will
cause are already happening all over the world. Hundreds of people died in
exceptionally high monsoon floods in India and Bangladesh this fall. Three
dozen died last month in mud slides in the Alps; the floodwaters rushing
out of the mountains were said to have raised one lake to its highest point
in 160 years. A heat wave last year across much of this country claimed
271 lives. Penguins in the Antarctic are finding it harder and harder to find
food for their chicks, as the shrimplike krill they eat grow scarcer in warmer
waters. Disease-bearing mosquitoes have moved to altitudes and longitudes
they usually never reach: malaria has come to the Kenyan highlands; the
West Nile virus thrives in New York City.

If global warming continues unchecked, the next hundred years will be
a century of dislocations. Ecosystems cannot simply pick up and move
north. Many will break apart as temperatures shift too far and too fast for
all their plants and animals to follow. Others, such as alpine tundra, will
die out in many places because they have nowhere to go.

According to some climate models, by the year 2100 the southern tip of
Florida may be under water and much of the Everglades may be drowned.
Vermont may be too warm for sugar maples; wide swaths of the forests of
the Southeast may become savannah; droughts may be frequent on the
Great Plains. Meanwhile, according to the UN's Intergovernmental Panel
on Climate Change, heat-related human deaths will double in many large
cities around the world and tropical diseases will spread. Deaths from
malaria alone may rise by more than a million a year.

Problem and Solution

There is no scientific question about the cause of global warming. Carbon
dioxide and other "greenhouse gases" in the atmosphere trap heat. For
millennia, the planet's temperature has moved in lockstep with the concentration of carbon dioxide in the atmosphere. Humans have now increased
that concentration by 30 percent since the pre-industrial era, principally by
burning oil, coal, and other fossil fuels. Today we have the highest atmos-
pheric carbon concentration since the evolution of Homo sapiens.

The United States is the world's biggest greenhouse gas polluter. We   10
have only 5 percent of the world's population, but we produce more than
20 percent of its greenhouse gases. In the face of climate chaos, we continue
to increase our pollution. Power plants are the fastest-growing source of
U.S. carbon dioxide emissions, primarily because we are increasing the
output from old, inefficient coal plants, many of which don't meet current
standards. Cars are another major and growing source.

To stop piling up carbon dioxide, we need to shift to cutting-edge technologies for energy efficiency and for renewable energy from the sun, wind, and geothermal sources. Prosperity doesn't require fossil fuels. According to the American Council for an Energy-Efficient Economy, U.S. carbon intensity (carbon emissions per unit of gross domestic product) has been cut almost in half since 1970. Even during 1997–1999—at the height of an economic boom and with the subsidies and policies that reinforce fossil fuel use still deeply entrenched—the United States achieved a steep decline in carbon intensity, partly through the use of advanced efficiency technologies. Just tightening up national fuel economy standards would eliminate 450 million tons of carbon dioxide per year by 2010.

As the biggest polluter, the United States should take the lead in dealing with global warming. Instead, for most of the past decade, we have obstructed progress. One reason is obvious: the enormously powerful and wealthy fossil fuel lobby, whose campaign contributions subvert the relationship between Congress and the public.

As a result, the Kyoto Protocol is far weaker than it should be. Though many other industrialized countries had pushed for deep cuts in greenhouse gas pollution, U.S. intransigence kept the final agreement conservative. The protocol requires the industrialized nations to reduce their greenhouse gas emissions only 5 percent below 1990 levels by 2012. But for the moment, the protocol is our best hope for nationwide and global progress.

What happens in the Netherlands will be critical in making the Kyoto Protocol work, because the rules on exactly how countries can meet their targets have yet to be written. Three issues stand out:

- The protocol allows a country to meet part of its target by buying greenhouse gas "credits" from nations that emit less than their quota. The negotiators at the Netherlands must make sure that any credits traded represent real pollution cuts, not just paper-pushing.
- The protocol needs strong rules on enforcement. Countries that fail to act and countries with slipshod accounting cannot be permitted to undermine the effort.
- Growing trees absorb carbon, and the protocol allows a nation to meet some of its target by planting trees. The negotiators must make sure that the rules do not permit countries either to raze ancient forests and replant (which releases more carbon than it takes up) or to start counting all the plantings they would have undertaken anyway as new, climate-friendly tactics.

The United States must push to eliminate all of these carbon loopholes. If we get a good treaty, it could be the impetus we need to start modernizing our power plants, vehicles, factories, and buildings. Study after study has shown that these steps will create thousands of new jobs and reduce consumers' energy bills. And, for the sake of future generations, it is our responsibility to change our ways.

We have an enormous job to do. It's time to roll up our sleeves and get to work.   15

To support a strong U.S. position in the Netherlands, contact Undersecretary Frank Loy, State Department Building, 2201 C Street, N.W., Washington, D.C. 20520; phone 202-647-6240; fax 202-647-0753. For more information as the negotiations proceed, see the global warming homepage. ◎/◎

1. Write a one-paragraph summary of the article to ensure that you accurately understand the author's premise and line of reasoning. What is the most important insight you gain from this editorial? What do you most agree with? Least agree with?

2. How does the editorial compare with other commentary on global warming, such as Al Gore's book and film, *An Inconvenient Truth* (2006)? Do a subject or keyword search using your library's online catalog or your Internet search engine, or consult one of the periodical indexes in your library's reference room, such as the *Environmental Index* or the *Reader's Guide to Periodical Literature*. Keep in mind the simple but easily overlooked fact that a single argument is but one voice in a multitudinous conversation. As John Stuart Mill wisely states, "He who knows only his own side of a case knows little." Before you can fully understand the complexities of an issue, let alone take a stance on it, you must become thoroughly familiar with the ongoing conversation, not just with one or two isolated voices.

3. If you had the opportunity to address this topic in an essay of your own, what would be your thesis? How would you defend it? Is there anything missing from the editorialist's argument that should be included? Why do you suppose he omitted it? Out of ignorance? His wish to hide a persuasive contrary view? His assumption that it is irrelevant? Do you find anything in the writer's treatment of the topic that seems especially illuminating or, on the contrary, misleading or confusing?

4. Rewrite the opening paragraph of the editorial. What expectations does your paragraph set up for your readers? How do they differ, if at all, from the expectation the editorialist sets up with his original opening?

5. Consider the author's style, identifying as many stylistic elements as you can. Examples include use of metaphor, manner of incorporating or alluding to outside sources, manner of emphasizing a point, devices used to connect one idea with another, orchestration of sentence patterns, choices of words and phrases, manner of integrating outside sources, overall readability, and concision. What about his style most delights you? Annoys you? What would you do differently and why?

6. Describe the author's concluding paragraphs. Suggest an alternative conclusion for the editorial.

7. Locate up-to-date information about the Kyoto Protocol. How justifiable is the editorialist's faith in this treaty? How would you rewrite the editorial, if at all, in light of your findings?

Active Reading as Shared Reading

Most of the reading you do is in solitude. However, a significant chunk of learning takes place in social contexts such as classrooms or college learning assistance centers, book discussion groups, or student-coordinated study groups. Whenever possible, arrange to have an in-depth discussion of an assigned essay with another classmate or friend, ideally with two or three other classmates or friends. Here is how to make your reading discussion group most productive:

- After the group reads the piece once, have each person go through it again, following the annotating suggestions given in "Reading with a Pencil," page 62.
- Discuss each writer's strategies identified by the group.
- Discuss the strengths and weaknesses of the argument, keeping tabs on any common ground that is mentioned (see the discussion of Rogerian argument in Chapter 5).
- Also keep tabs on any outside sources mentioned by group members. If at all possible, everyone in the group should consult these sources before trying to reach a consensus (see next point below).
- Attempt to reach consensus, despite differences of opinion. What unified position statement can your group produce that fairly represents the view (by now quite likely modified) of each individual member?

◎/◎ Exercise 2.9

1. Reflect on your private reading experience in relation to your public one. What does each reading context contribute toward your understanding and enjoyment of the text? Draw from actual reading experiences that included both a private and a public phase.

2. Does reading with others increase or decrease your comprehension of the text? What do you think accounts for this difference?

Using the Modes of Argument as a Schema for Analysis

To analyze the logic and merits of an argument, first determine which of the predominant general patterns of argument introduced in Chapter 1 and discussed in detail in Chapters 3 through 5—Classical, Toulmin, Rogerian—the argument fits into.

- If the piece follows the Classical (Aristotelian) model, you might ask: Is the intended audience uninformed or well informed on the issue?

- If the piece follows the Toulmin model, you might ask: Are the warrants on solid or shaky ground? Do they need to be made more explicit?

- If the piece follows the Rogerian model, you might ask: Is the tone sufficiently conciliatory to reduce the possibility of reader hostility?

The Importance of Open-Mindedness When Reading

One of the most important attributes that an education affords, along with self-discipline and attentiveness, is open-mindedness—the willingness to suspend judgment until one considers as many differing viewpoints as possible.

Learning to be truly open-minded takes effort. Everyone has deeply rooted beliefs, some of which even border on superstition. When these beliefs are challenged for whatever reasons, no matter how logical the reasons offered are, we resist—sometimes against our own better judgment. Beliefs often operate outside the realm of intellectual control and are entwined with our values and emotions. If, for example, someone in your family earns his or her livelihood in the Pacific Northwest logging industry, you may find it difficult to sympathize with environmentalists who advocate putting an end to logging in that region, even though a part of you wishes to preserve any species threatened with extinction due to continued deforestation.

Being predisposed toward a certain viewpoint is to be expected. Rare is the individual who goes through life with a neutral attitude toward all controversial issues. But one can be predisposed toward a certain view or value system and still be open-minded. For example, you might be highly skeptical of the existence of extraterrestrial creatures yet be willing to suspend that skepticism to give a writer a fair chance at trying to change your mind. Your willingness to be open-minded may increase, of course, if the author is a scientist or if the body of evidence presented has been shared with the entire scientific community for independent evaluations.

Sometimes we feel defensive when a long-held conviction is suddenly challenged. We may wish to guard the sanctity of that conviction so jealously that we may delude ourselves into thinking that we're being open-minded when we're not. When Galileo made his astronomical discoveries of the lunar craters and the moons of Jupiter known in 1610, he was promptly accused of heresy. We may think, from our enlightened perspective at the dawn of the twenty-first century, that the church was narrow-minded and intolerant, neglecting to realize that at the dawn of the seventeenth century modern science had not yet come into being. Most people's conception of "the heavens" was literally that: The night sky was a window to Heaven. And celestial (that is, heavenly) objects like planets, stars, and the moon all occupied divine niches in that Heaven; they were called the crystal spheres. Galileo's modest telescopic observations revolutionized our conception of the universe, but it did not happen overnight, particularly because Galileo recanted his "heresy"—or, rather, was persuaded to recant by the threat of execution. We know that Galileo never wavered in his convictions because even while under house arrest he continued to write about his discoveries.

The moral of Galileo's story, and the stories of many other daring thinkers throughout history, is that open-mindedness is precious, despite its difficulties. Take a few steps to ensure that you will not judge an argument prematurely or unfairly:

1. Identify and perhaps write down in your notebook the specific nature of the resistance you experience toward the author's point of view. Is it that you're a Republican reading a Democrat's evaluation of a Republican presidential administration? A strict vegetarian or vegan and animal-rights activist reading an article about the importance of preserving the cattle industry? An evolutionist reading an article by a creationist questioning the validity of the hominid fossil record? Consciously identifying your predisposition helps you approach neutrality and open-mindedness.

2. Allow yourself to accept the author's premise at least temporarily. What are the consequences of doing so? Are there any reasonable facets to the argument? Can you establish some kind of common ground with the author? Does the author perhaps expose weaknesses in the viewpoint that you would advocate?

   Exercise 2.10

Read the excerpt from Galileo's "Letter to the Grand Duchess Christina," which illustrates a famous example of reading (in this case the Bible) with an open mind.

Letter to the Grand Duchess Christina | Galileo Galilei

... The reason produced for condemning the opinion that the earth moves and the sun stands still is that in many places in the Bible one may read that the sun moves and the earth stands still. Since the Bible cannot err, it follows as a necessary consequence that anyone takes an erroneous and heretical position who maintains that the sun is inherently motionless and the earth movable.

With regard to this argument, I think in the first place that it is very pious to say and prudent to affirm that the holy Bible can never speak untruth— whenever its true meaning is understood. But I believe nobody

Source: Galileo Galilei, "Letter to the Grand Duchess Christina," from *Discoveries and Opinions of Galileo* by Galileo Galilei, translated by Stillman Drake, copyright © 1957 by Stillman Drake. Used by permission of Doubleday, a division of Random House, Inc.

*Galileo (1564–1642) is here lectur-
ing on the Copernican or heliocentric (sun-
centered) theory of the solar system. He
helped to confirm this theory, with
detailed telescopic observations of the
movements of Venus, the moons of Jupiter,
and sunspots.*

will deny that it is often very abstruse, and may say things which are quite
different from what its bare words signify. Hence in expounding the Bible
if one were always to confine oneself to the unadorned grammatical meaning, one might fall into error. Not only contradictions and propositions far
from true might thus be made to appear in the Bible, but even grave here-
sies and follies. Thus it would be necessary to assign to God feet, hands,
and eyes, as well as corporeal and human affections, such as anger, repen-
tance, hatred, and sometimes even the forgetting of things past and ignorance of those to come. These propositions uttered by the Holy Ghost were
set down in that manner by the sacred scribes in order to accommodate
them to the capacities of the common people, who are rude and unlearned.
For the sake of those who deserve to be separated from the herd, it is necessary that wise expositors should produce the true senses of such passages, together with the special reasons for which they were set down in
these words. This doctrine is so widespread and so definite with all theologians that it would be superfluous to adduce evidence for it.

Hence I think that I may reasonably conclude that whenever the Bible
has occasion to speak of any physical conclusion (especially those which are
very abstruse and hard to understand), the rule has been observed of avoiding confusion in the minds of the common people which would render them
contumacious toward the higher mysteries. Now the Bible, merely to conde-
scend to popular capacity, has not hesitated to obscure some very important
pronouncements, attributing to God himself some qualities extremely remote
from (and even contrary to) His essence. Who, then, would positively
declare that this principle has been set aside, and the Bible has confined itself
rigorously to the bare and restricted sense of its words, when speaking but

casually of the earth, of water, of the sun, or of any other created thing? Especially in view of the fact that these things in no way concern the primary purpose of the sacred writings, which is the service of God and the salvation of souls— matters infinitely beyond the comprehension of the common people.

This being granted, I think that in discussions of physical problems we ought to begin not from the authority of scriptural passages, but from sense-experiences and necessary demonstrations; for the holy Bible and the phenomena of nature proceed alike from the divine Word, the former as the dictate of the Holy Ghost and the latter as the observant executrix of God's commands. It is necessary for the Bible, in order to be accommodated to the understanding of every man, to speak many things which appear to differ from the absolute truth so far as the bare meaning of the words is concerned. But Nature, on the other hand, is inexorable and immutable; she never transgresses the laws imposed upon her, or cares a whit whether her abstruse reasons and methods of operation are understandable to men. For that reason it appears that nothing physical which sense-experience sets before our eyes, or which necessary demonstrations prove to us, ought to be called in question (much less condemned) upon the testimony of biblical passages which may have some different meaning beneath their words. For the Bible is not chained in every expression to conditions as strict as those which govern all physical effects; nor is God any less excellently revealed in Nature's actions than in the sacred statements of the Bible. Perhaps this is what Tertullian meant by these words:

"We conclude that God is known first through Nature, and then again, 5 more particularly, by doctrine; by Nature in His works, and by doctrine in His revealed word."[1]

From this I do not mean to infer that we need not have an extraordinary esteem for the passages of holy Scripture. On the contrary, having arrived at any certainties in physics, we ought to utilize these as the most appropriate aids in the true exposition of the Bible and in the investigation of those meanings which are necessarily contained therein, for these must be concordant with demonstrated truths. I should judge that the authority of the Bible was designed to persuade men of those articles and propositions which, surpassing all human reasoning, could not be made credible by science, or by any other means than through the very mouth of the Holy Spirit.

Yet even in those propositions which are not matters of faith, this authority ought to be preferred over that of all human writings which are supported only by bare assertions or probable arguments, and not set forth in a demonstrative way. This I hold to be necessary and proper to the same extent that divine wisdom surpasses all human judgment and conjecture.

But I do not feel obliged to believe that that same God who has endowed us with senses, reason, and intellect has intended to forgo their use and by some other means to give us knowledge which we can attain by them. He would not require us to deny sense and reason in physical matters which are set before our eyes and minds by direct experience or necessary demonstrations.

This must be especially true in those sciences of which but the faintest trace (and that consisting of conclusions) is to be found in the Bible. Of astronomy, for instance, so little is found that none of the planets except Venus are so much as mentioned, and this only once or twice under the name of "Lucifer." If the sacred scribes had had any intention of teaching people certain arrangements and motions of the heavenly bodies, or had they wished us to derive such knowledge from the Bible, then in my opinion they would not have spoken of these matters so sparingly in comparison with the infinite number of admirable conclusions which are demonstrated in that science. Far from pretending to teach us the constitution and motions of the heavens and the stars, with their shapes, magnitudes, and distances, the authors of the Bible intentionally forbore to speak of these things, though all were quite well known to them. Such is the opinion of the holiest and most learned Fathers, and in St. Augustine we find the following words:

"It is likewise commonly asked what we may believe about the form and shape of the heavens according to the Scriptures, for many contend much about these matters. But with superior prudence our authors have forborne to speak of this, as in no way furthering the student with respect to a blessed life—and, more important still, as taking up much of that time which should be spent in holy exercises. What is it to me whether heaven, like a sphere, surrounds the earth on all sides as a mass balanced in the center of the universe, or whether like a dish it merely covers and overcasts the earth? Belief in Scripture is urged rather for the reason we have often mentioned; that is, in order that no one, through ignorance of divine passages, finding anything in our Bibles or hearing anything cited from them of such a nature as may seem to oppose manifest conclusions, should be induced to suspect their truth when they teach, relate, and deliver more profitable matters. Hence let it be said briefly, touching the form of heaven, that our authors knew the truth but the Holy Spirit did not desire that men should learn things that are useful to no one for salvation."[2]

The same disregard of these sacred authors toward beliefs about the phenomena of the celestial bodies is repeated to us by St. Augustine in his next chapter. On the question whether we are to believe that the heaven moves or stands still, he writes thus:

"Some of the brethren raise a question concerning the motion of heaven, whether it is fixed or moved. If it is moved, they say, how is it a firmament? If it stands still, how do these stars which are held fixed in it go round from east to west, the more northerly performing shorter circuits near the pole, so that heaven (if there is another pole unknown to us) may seem to revolve upon some axis, or (if there is no other pole) may be thought to move as a discus? To these men I reply that it would require many subtle and profound reasonings to find out which of these things is actually so; but to undertake this and discuss it is consistent neither with my leisure nor with the duty of those whom I desire to instruct in essential matters more directly conducing to their salvation and to the benefit of the holy Church."[3]

10

From these things it follows as a necessary consequence that, since the Holy Ghost did not intend to teach us whether heaven moves or stands still, whether its shape is spherical or like a discus or extended in a plane, nor whether the earth is located at its center or off to one side, then so much the less was it intended to settle for us any other conclusion of the same kind. And the motion or rest of the earth and the sun is so closely linked with the things just named, that without a determination of the one, neither side can be taken in the other matters. Now if the Holy Spirit has purposely neglected to teach us propositions of this sort as irrelevant to the highest goal (that is, to our salvation), how can anyone affirm that it is obligatory to take sides on them, and that one belief is required by faith, while the other side is erroneous? Can an opinion be heretical and yet have no concern with the salvation of souls? Can the Holy Ghost be asserted not to have intended teaching us something that does concern our salvation? I would say here something that was heard from an ecclesiastic of the most eminent degree: "That the intention of the Holy Ghost is to teach us how one goes to heaven, not how heaven goes."[4]

But let us again consider the degree to which necessary demonstrations and sense experiences ought to be respected in physical conclusions, and the authority they have enjoyed at the hands of holy and learned theologians. From among a hundred attestations I have selected the following:

"We must also take heed, in handling the doctrine of Moses, that we altogether avoid saying positively and confidently anything which contradicts manifest experiences and the reasoning of philosophy or the other sciences. For since every truth is in agreement with all other truth, the truth of Holy Writ cannot be contrary to the solid reasons and experiences of human knowledge."[5]

And in St. Augustine we read: "If anyone shall set the authority of Holy Writ against clear and manifest reason, he who does this knows not what he has undertaken; for he opposes to the truth not the meaning of the Bible, which is beyond his comprehension, but rather his own interpretation; not what is in the Bible, but what he has found in himself and imagines to be there."[6]

This granted, and it being true that two truths cannot contradict one another, it is the function of wise expositors to seek out the true senses of scriptural texts. These will unquestionably accord with the physical conclusions which manifest sense and necessary demonstrations have previously made certain to us. Now the Bible, as has been remarked, admits in many places expositions that are remote from the signification of the words for reasons we have already given. Moreover, we are unable to affirm that all interpreters of the Bible speak by divine inspiration, for if that were so there would exist no differences between them about the sense of a given passage. Hence I should think it would be the part of prudence not to permit anyone to usurp scriptural texts and force them in some way to maintain any physical conclusion to be true, when at some future time the senses and demonstrative or necessary reasons may show the contrary. Who indeed will set bounds to human ingenuity? Who will assert that everything in the universe capable of being perceived is already discovered and known? Let us rather confess quite truly that "Those truths which we know are very few in comparison with those which we do not know." . . . ◎/◎

Notes

1. *Adversus Marcionem,* ii, 18.
2. *De Genesi ad literam,* ii, 9. Galileo has noted also: "The same is to be read in Peter the Lombard, master of opinions."
3. *Ibid.,* ii, 10.
4. A marginal note by Galileo assigns this epigram to Cardinal Baronius (1538–1607). Baronius visited Padua with Cardinal Bellarmine in 1598, and Galileo probably met him at that time.
5. Pererius on Genesis, near the beginning.
6. In the seventh letter to Marcellinus.

1. How convincing is Galileo's effort to reconcile Scripture with his findings?

2. Describe Galileo's attitude toward his audience. To what degree does his manner of supporting his assertions reflect this attitude?

3. How does Galileo connect his different points together? What is his central thesis? Do all of his points relate clearly to this thesis?

4. Why do you suppose Galileo chose to present his argument to a noble-woman and in the form of a letter? Does the letter itself provide any clues?

Chapter Summary

Reading and writing are interconnected modes of thinking. We critically read our own writing (for sense of direction, development of ideas, coherence, clarity, persuasive force, and so on) as well as the writing of others. We construct meaning (a kind of internal writing) when we read in depth—that is, we read actively rather than passively whenever we read critically. To read effectively also means to read in stages: previewing (prereading and skim-reading) to grasp the central purpose of the piece; in-depth reading to understand the content, progression, and rhetorical strategies at work in the piece; and postreading to reinforce the framework of the whole argument. To read effectively also means to respond spontaneously with a pencil, writing marginal glosses, comparisons, and questions in the margins. Finally, reading effectively means to read with an open mind, in a highly motivated manner, as if you are interacting with the author on paper, attempting to reconcile your views with the author's.

Checklist

1. Have I read the assigned essays, as well as the drafts of my fellow students, in three stages: first previewing, then reading in depth, and then postreading?

2. When reading in depth, do I determine the framework of the argument? Evaluate the data presented? Evaluate the author's organizational strategy? Speculate on the significance of what is being argued?

3. Do I understand what it means to read responsibly? Open-mindedly?

Writing Projects

1. Write a critical response to one of the following quotations about reading.

   a. "To write down one's impressions of Hamlet as one reads it year after year would be virtually to record one's own autobiography, for as we know more of life, Shakespeare comments on what we know." (Virginia Woolf)

   b. "We read often with as much talent as we write." (Ralph Waldo Emerson)

   c. "The greatest part of a writer's time is spent in reading." (Samuel Johnson, as quoted by James Boswell)

   d. "To read well . . . is a noble exercise. . . . It requires a training such as the athletes underwent, the steady intention almost of the whole life to this object." (Henry David Thoreau)

   e. "A reasoning passion" (how the French novelist Colette described her experience of reading Victor Hugo's *Les Miserables*).

2. Write an essay in which you propose ways of improving one's reading strategies. You may want to discuss these strategies in relation to particular types of reading materials.

3. Find a print, television, or radio advertisement for an Internet dating service. Write an essay evaluating how convincingly the ad argues for the effectiveness of the service in securing a romantic relationship with someone. Add to your argument by visiting the websites of various Internet dating services, including the one featured in the ad. What assurances do they give? How reliable are they? What hard evidence can you bring to bear on your point of view? Finally, incorporate two or three appropriate visual aids (photographs, a graph or a chart summarizing statistical data, etc.) into your argument.

3 Using the Classical Model in Your Arguments

We need the capacity effectively to urge contradictory positions . . . not so that we may adopt either of the two (it is quite wrong to persuade men to evil), but that we should be aware how the case stands and be able, if our adversary deploys his arguments unjustly, to refute them.
—Aristotle

Rhetoric, or the art of using language persuasively, has a long history. The work of ancient rhetoricians such as Plato, Aristotle, Quintilian, and Cicero has influenced Western education and literature for nearly two thousand years, shaping public discourse and public life. Though rooted in the past, rhetoric plays an integral role in today's judicial, political, religious, and educational institutions.

Argument in the Ancient World

In the ancient world, rhetoric was taught as oratory (public speaking) and was basic preparation for students entering law, politics, and teaching. Students learned how to communicate a point of view clearly and convincingly. There were three categories of argumentative oratory in the ancient world, corresponding to three different functions. Two of these functions were professional or quasi-professional, such as presenting lectures and debates emulating professional situations; one function was political (*deliberative*), such as deliberating over military and civic policies; the other was legal (*forensic*), such as courtroom prosecution or defense motions. The third category of oratory—celebratory (*epideictic*)—generally falls outside the scope of argument. This kind of oratory was used in eulogies, commendations, dedications, and so on. Early rhetoricians, itinerant teachers known as *Sophists,* emphasized the pragmatic skills to be developed in winning an argument. Later, the Platonic school gained ascendancy, valuing philosophical reasoning over mere "training." Plato's student, Aristotle, achieved a sort of middle ground between the idealistic truth-seeking of his mentor and the mercenary pragmatism of the Sophists by viewing rhetoric as the art of finding the best available means of persuasion in a given case—that is, by applying the rigors of philosophical reasoning to actual problems.

Another important element of ancient rhetoric was its system of topic development. For ancient orators, topics were preestablished "modes of thought" regionalized in the mind (the word *topic* comes from the Greek *topos*, meaning place) to aid the memory when speaking. The first topic, logically enough, is definition, followed by comparison, temporal/causal connection, circumstance (for example, what is capable or incapable of happening), and testimony (use of authority, laws, or concrete examples to establish authenticity).

In addition to the ancients' everyday uses of argument in law, politics, religion, athletics, and the military, oratorical competitions were held. Individuals or teams would argue an issue, and an impartial judge would determine the winner based on each argument's strengths (much like what happens in debate tournaments today). Debating, we might say, is the "sport" side of argument—a show of argumentative skill for its own sake and valuable for the development of such skill.

The Classical Model of Argument

The Classical model for structuring an argument is both simple and versatile. First, here is a look at it in outline form:

I. Introduction

  A. Lead-in

  B. Overview of the situation

  C. Background

II. Position statement (thesis)

III. Appeals (ethos, pathos, logos) and evidence

  A. Appeals: to ethics, character, authority (ethos); to emotions (pathos); to reason (logos)

  B. Evidence: citing of statistics, results, findings, examples, laws, relevant passages from authoritative texts

IV. Refutation (often presented simultaneously with the evidence)

V. Conclusion (peroration)

  A. Highlights of key points presented (if appropriate)

  B. Recommendations (if appropriate)

  C. Illuminating restatement of thesis

Argument structure was given its fullest examination by the Roman rhetorician Quintilian, who not only described the five parts of a discourse—the introduction, the statement of facts relating to the issue, the evidence, the refutation of

Aristotle (384–322 B.C.E.) wrote Rhetoric. *It was the first systematic study of argument and reasoning for practical purposes—political, judicial, and ceremonial.*

challenging views, and the conclusion—but stressed the importance of exercising judgment in using them. Rhetorical arrangement, after all, is an art, not a rote computer program. Hence, not all introductions are alike in scope or tone; in fact, sometimes the orator may dispense with an introduction altogether—as when someone wants to hear only "the bottom line." Similarly, the orator may want to refute opposing views before presenting the evidence. The orator may also decide whether the evidence should be strictly factual—that is, appeal exclusively to reason—or should include ethical and emotional appeals as well.

Organizing Your Argument Using the Classical Model

The Classical argument introduces the problem and states the thesis; it next presents background information in the form of a narrative. It then presents the evidence in support of the thesis, including refutation of opposing views. Finally it reaches a conclusion.

Consider the case of student Justine Hearn, who is writing a paper on the folly of developing a tourist resort in Trinidad and Tobago, an environmentally sensitive twin-island nation in the West Indies. Justine has a good idea of what points she wants to make in her argument but is not sure what sequence to use in laying it out. She understands the Classical structure but is not quite sure how specifically she can make her essay adhere to it. Using the Classical model serves as a heuristic device—a set of hints that may be recast as questions:

1. What is my reason for writing the paper?

2. What is the best way to introduce the problem, given my evidence and audience?

3. What definitions of concepts or explanations do my readers require?

4. What exactly is my position on the matter?

5. How will my readers most likely react? Indifferently? Skeptically? Enthusiastically? How can I deal with it in advance? (For example, if the audience is likely to be skeptical, can I say things that would remove some of their skepticism?)

Exercise 3.1

Read Justine's first draft of her argument on how land development damages the ecology of Trinidad and Tobago. Then answer the questions that follow.

Justine Hearn

Ecology vs. Land Development in Trinidad and Tobago

Lead-in

Overview

        The island republic of Trinidad and Tobago in the West Indies is facing unprecedented land development. It does have some land preserved, but even this protected land is in danger of being lost to farming and illegal practices. Thousands of acres of pristine rain forest are without governmental protection and are thus left to be destroyed without oversight or penalty.

Background

        Although the smaller island of Tobago is home to the world's oldest legally protected forest, the Crown Point Reserve (1776), this legacy is not being continued. Instead, it appears that the government has made its decisions in favor of unchecked development benefiting the tourism and petrochemical industries. There exists a number of narrowly-based laws, some of which overlap, that offer environmental protection. However, these laws are not broad enough or modern enough to carry much weight. Activists have been petitioning the government to establish a more comprehensive set of laws, but this has yet to be taken seriously by politicians.

Statistics

        One of the obstacles to environmental reform is the high unemployment rate: 24 percent of the general public, and twice that for young adults. According to Julian Kenney and Christine Toppin-Allahan in a videotaped lecture on August 4,

Introduction

Thesis

1995, this has created a rift in interests that is cleaved along social status lines. Environmental concerns are expressed mostly by those in the upper classes, while the lower classes are often perceived to be the cause for certain environmental problems.

Another obstacle is that of the squatter farmers who illegally occupy government land squatters account

Statistics

for one-fifth of Trinidad and Tobago's population, according to Kenny and Toppin-Allahan. The Nariva Swamp and its inhabitants demonstrate the historical struggle between the people's attempt to establish an adequate

Appeal (emotion)

livelihood and the government's effort to uphold established legislation. This state-owned swamp, the only existing freshwater marsh of its kind in the Caribbean, has become a squatting site of rice farmers. In the

Historical facts

1960s, people began to move into the area to burn and clear Nariva's forest and marshland in order to plant rice. Although this was and still is an illegal practice, farmers continued to move in to take advantage of the open land, encouraged especially by the government's subsidies on locally grown rice. With no budget and little

training, Forestry and Wildlife officers had little success in removing the squatters from the land. In fact, the government considered allowing the squatters to purchase the lands they were using, a practice that often takes place on other state-owned lands throughout the islands. In the late 1980s, commercial farmers moved in with heavy equipment to begin large-scale farming, digging canals to regulate water levels, using chemicals, and bulldozing the swamp's forests.

The human health and general pollution laws are the weakest of the environmental legislation. The Public Health Acts, which were established in the 1920s, discuss mosquito control and human waste disposal and regulate pollution in the form of "noxious substances" and "black smoke"— qualities of waste materials that were relevant at the time of the bill's creation but have since lost their

bearing. Chemical spills and toxic fumes are not a part of this
legislation and are thus not under state jurisdiction.

How might Trinidad and Tobago best solve these serious threats to
their environment? It seems that international influences might be one
of the best vectors of change, just as the World Bank and Greenpeace
influenced the government of Trinidad and Tobago during the early
years of the Environmental Management Authority (EMA). However, it is
important to the success of the new legislation and ongoing preservation efforts that a sense of imperialism does not develop as a result
of the intervention of outside forces. Furthermore, public support is
necessary for government legitimacy, but a society will invest in an
issue only if its people have at least an elementary sense of security. For many citizens, this would require an improvement in their
quality of life, which necessitates the creation of jobs. Yet this
leads to the question of sustainability, because a rise in industry
usually results in some form of environmental degradation. If
Trinidad and Tobago's economy were based in the country's biodiversity, a sustainable framework for jobs could be created that would also
encourage conservation interests. Ecotourism, bio-prospecting, and controlled sustainable agriculture would be possible answers in this scenario.

1. How convincingly does Justine support her thesis?

2. How relevant to her argument are the statistics that she cites? Are they sufficiently recent? Are they reliable? Are her sources credible? Why or why not?

3. How effectively does Justine refute challenging views? How might she
   develop her refutation?

4. Does the solution Justine proposes appear to solve the problem? What
   alternative solutions does she discuss?

5. Suggest ways in which Justine could further develop or otherwise
   strengthen her essay.

Elements of a Classical Argument in Action

Now let us examine each element in detail and see how it operates in a particular
argument. Keep in mind that outlines serve to remind writers of
the basic strategy for developing a sound argument; they should not be followed
slavishly as if they were some unalterable blueprint for constructing a house.

Introduction   A good introduction accomplishes three things:

1. It presents the topic of inquiry or the problem requiring attention and perhaps briefly states the thesis.

2. It establishes a clear context for the problem.

3. It engages the reader's attention and desire to get "the whole picture."

Consider the following introduction to an argument against the use of school vouchers, a system whereby the state promises to pay parents a percentage of tuition for attending a quality school of the parents' choice:

> Most Americans believe that improving our system of education should be a top priority for government at the local, state, and Federal levels. Legislators, school boards, education professionals, parent groups and community organizations are attempting to implement innovative ideas to rescue children from failing school systems, particularly in inner-city neighborhoods. Many such groups champion voucher programs. The standard program proposed in dozens of states across the country would distribute monetary vouchers (typically valued between $2,500–$5,000) to parents of school-age children, usually in troubled inner-city school districts. Parents could then use the vouchers towards the cost of tuition at private schools—including those dedicated to religious indoctrination.
>
> Superficially, school vouchers might seem a relatively benign way to increase the options poor parents have for educating their children. In fact, vouchers pose a serious threat to values that are vital to the health of American democracy. These programs subvert the constitutional principle of separation of church and state and threaten to undermine our system of public education.

How well do these two paragraphs meet the criteria for a strong introduction to an argument? First, the author (an anonymous writer for the Anti-Defamation League) introduces the problem: the need to improve our educational system and the fact that vouchers are considered to be a promising solution of that problem. The second paragraph presents the thesis: Vouchers are a bad idea. Finally, the author engages the reader's attention by using strong, dramatic language to convey a sense of urgency to the matter: Vouchers "pose a serious threat to values that are vital to the health of American democracy" and "subvert the constitutional principle of separation of church and state." Such language not only piques interest but heightens anticipation: How is this writer going to convince me that such an assertion makes sense?

Appeals and Evidence   At the heart of any Classical argument is the evidence, reinforced by the persuasive appeals (see pages 4–6) that will ideally demonstrate, beyond doubt, the validity and reasonableness of the thesis. To be persuasive—that is, to change the minds of readers who otherwise would reject your thesis—facts and appeals must be conveyed in a way that allows readers to see the path by which they lead directly to the thesis.

Let us consider the way in which the three appeals are applied to the argument on school vouchers.

1. *Ethos* (the appeal to ethics, character, valid authority). When the school vouchers author argues that a voucher program would undermine the ideals on which this country was founded, he or she is evoking the appeal of ethos: It would be unethical, or a sign of bad character, to undermine what are considered the fundamental ideals of American democracy and liberty. It should be taken for granted, the author implies, that the authority of the U.S. Constitution must always be upheld.

2. *Pathos* (the appeal to emotion, compassion, sympathy). By alluding to "a serious threat" that vouchers pose to American values, the author is evoking the appeal of pathos—specifically, the fear of what might happen if states violated the U.S. Constitution.

3. *Logos* (the appeal to logic, to sound, reason-based decision making). Note how the author sets up a logical connection between separation of church and state and the American system of public education: If the former is violated, the integrity of the latter is threatened. This is an example of the appeal to logic and reason: There is a logical connection to be made between A and B.

Appeals go a long way toward persuading readers, but strong evidence is also needed. Two kinds of evidence are appropriate to Classical argumentative writing—direct and indirect. *Direct evidence* consists of data from surveys, scientific experiments, and cases-in-point—phenomena that clearly point to a causal agency ("where there's smoke, there's fire"). Facts represent evidence that anyone can check first-hand at any time. *Indirect evidence* consists of formal analytical and mathematical reasoning. Here, the author takes the reader through a step-by-step analysis of, say, causes that lead to inevitable effects.

Reinforcing Aristotelian Appeals with Visuals

Good argumentative writing makes its claims convincing by appealing to readers' emotions, values, and reason (as Aristotelian appeals demand), as well as by providing "hard" evidence through data—and even hard data should be "warranted" on a platform of values as the Toulmin method of argument demands (see Chapter 4).

Using Visuals to Reinforce Ethical Appeals

Many of the public service ads published by humanist and religious organizations to help raise public consciousness demonstrate how visuals can

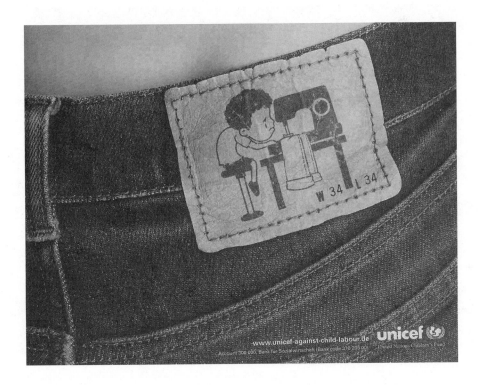

appeal to one's sense of ethics. The UNICEF ad above, for example, dramatically illustrates the unethical practice of child-labor exploitation in sweatshops.

Using Visuals to Reinforce Emotional Appeals

Sometimes raising reader consciousness needs to be reinforced with an emotional jolt appealing to our deepest psychological needs: safety, love, youth, tradition (for example family, custom), longevity, strength or power, or compassion. Here are some examples:

- **Security, freedom from fear**. Say you wanted to incorporate visuals for an essay on the seriousness of domestic violence. You might consider using the following photograph of a run-down city block with the words "It's safer here" [superimposed on the street] "than here" [superimposed beneath an upstairs window].

THAN HERE.

IT'S SAFER HERE

For many women and children, there is no more dangerous place to be than home.
Call **1.877.868.4JOE** or go to **www.joetorre.org** to help make home safe again.

JOE TORRE
Safe At Home
FOUNDATION

- **Strength, Power**. If you plan to write an essay on the ways in which the armed forces help develop leadership skills, you may want to consider matching expectations (as reflected in the U.S. Army ad on page 93) against actualities.

- **Appeal to youth**. For an essay arguing that keeping in shape will keep you youthful, you might incorporate an image similar to this photograph of two runners.

- **Appeal to compassion.** World events that affect large numbers of people may generate strong feelings of compassion. These emotions can be stirred up for years to come by using evocative imagery. This memorial of American flags, shown on page 94, marked the first anniversary of 9/11. The layout of the flags, resembling a graveyard, presents a powerful and moving visual reminder of those who lost their lives on that day in 2001.

Using Visuals to Reinforce Appeals

Frequently in argumentative writing it is necessary to provide hard data such as statistics or findings from surveys or experiments to support a claim. Using charts, graphs, and tables to capture in images what you analyze in the body of your argument aids in comprehension and in turn makes your claim more convincing.

If you happen to be writing about population growth, for example, and wanted not only to support your claim that the world population has grown exponentially in recent history but also to convey the fact as dramatically as possible, you might choose to use this graph:

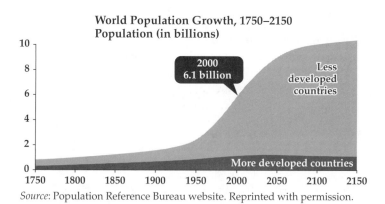

Source: Population Reference Bureau website. Reprinted with permission.

Note how the data is laid out in a way that emphasizes the relationship between the variables on each axis—in this case the quantity variable on the horizontal (x) axis and the temporal variable on the vertical (y) axis. What would take readers thirty seconds or more to read in a paragraph-long explanation can be perceived—and understood with greater clarity—in just two or three seconds via the graph. By the way, there's no reason why you need to restrict yourself to just a line graph. You can, for example, combine drawings and graphs into what are known as pictographs, as in the following example:

*Pictorial varia-
tion of a simple
bar graph.*

The 10 most frequently performed surgeries

Arteriography and angiocardiography: 2.1 million

Cardiac catheterizations: 1.3 million

Endoscopy of small intestine: 1.1 million

Computerized axial tomography (CAT scans): 828,000

Diagnostic ultrasound: 813,000

Balloon angioplasty of coronary artery: 664,000

Reduction of fracture: 667,000

Hysterectomy: 617,000

Insertion of coronary artery stents: 615,000

Endoscopy of large intestine: 596,000

During 2004, 45 million procedures were performed on hospital inpatients in the United States. Here are the 2004 figures for the ten most frequently performed procedures in non-Federal short-stay hospitals.

Combining the Appeals

Most arguments combine all three appeals. Here is a case in point: Imagine that your instructor has assigned the class to investigate the issue of the arts funding in public-school education. As state educational budgets are cut back, school boards tend to target arts programs—music, dance, theater, applied arts and crafts classes in painting or illustration, and so on—for elimination. Your task is to write an argument defending or challenging a decision to eliminate an arts program. What kinds of appeals might you use to persuade readers to accept your point of view? What kind of visual will you select or design that would reinforce those appeals?

To get the research ball rolling, your instructor shows you the ad on page 97, by an organization called Americans for the Arts.

First, take a few moments to contemplate the ad, noticing how the visual elements interact with the text in order to enhance the persuasive force of the message. For example, you notice how the image of the box of graham crackers is labeled, absurdly "Martha Grahams"; directly on the other side of the first column of text is a larger image of Martha Graham herself in a classic dance pose—one of her skills being that of using dance to tell a story. The caption wittily recontextualizes the original aim of that photograph: "Ms. Graham told stories using movement. Here, she tells us how sad it is that kids aren't getting enough art." The third image, positioned within the second column of text and below the Martha Graham photo is the schematic of the human brain. Perhaps you will incorporate the ad into your argument.

The next step, you decide, is to access the Americans for the Arts website, *http://www.AmericansForTheArts.org.*

Here you discover a wealth of links to information resources, field services, events, and ways to become involved with their cause. Here you will find the support data you need to make your claim convincing. You will also find testimonials from parents and teachers describing the impact of an arts education on children's success in and out of school.

Visuals can be effective in argumentative writing because they seem to demonstrate something irrefutable about the nature of what is being represented. As Susan Sontag says in her book-length essay *On Photography* (Delta, 1977), "Photographed images do not seem to be statements about the world so much as pieces of it" (4). That is why they so effectively convey evidence, despite the fact that photographs can be faked or misrepresented.

No matter what type of evidence is used, it must be tested for its relevance, accuracy, thoroughness, and timeliness.

- **Relevance.** The evidence must relate directly to the claims being made. If an argument claims that high school teachers tend subtly to discourage young women from pursuing careers in science or engineering, but then cites instances of that problem only from colleges or private schools, critics would argue that the evidence is not relevant to the claim.

THERE'S NOT ENOUGH ART IN OUR SCHOOLS.

NO WONDER PEOPLE THINK

MARTHA GRAHAM

IS A SNACK CRACKER.

Hardly a fitting legacy for the woman who, despite getting a late start at the positively elderly age of 17, became

the mother of American interpretive dance.

With verve and nearly single-handedly, Martha Graham brought her dance style into the 20th century.

A misconception. Not to mention an overlooked marketing opportunity.

She did nothing less than create an entirely new genre of dance, while

Ms. Graham told stories using movement. Here, she tells us how sad it is that kids aren't getting enough art.

shattering the expectations of audiences and critics alike with her percussive, angular movement style. She was one of the first dancers to collaborate with contemporary composers instead of using the 18th- and 19th-century compositions her predecessors favored. Her dances have been called "motion pictures for the sophisticated"; her theories on movement and kinesthetics are still vital today; and there is scarcely a dancer alive who doesn't

can you do to reverse this trend?

Speak up now. Demand your child's fair share of the arts. To find out how to help, or for more information about the benefits of arts education, please visit us at AmericansForTheArts.org. Otherwise, even a legacy as rich as Martha Graham's can crumble to nothing.

owe a huge debt to her sharp creative mind and fierce perfectionism.

And to think she could have made it her entire life without experiencing the arts. Just like so many kids today.

Each day, more and more of the arts are being completely drained from our children's schools. Yet studies show parents believe dance and music and art and drama make their kids better students and better people. So what

READIN'

ART

'RITING

'RITHMETIC

Let art borrow some brain. It'll return it in better condition.

ART. ASK FOR MORE.

 For more information about the importance of arts education, contact www.AmericansForTheArts.org.

©Barbara Morgan, from "Martha Graham: Sixteen Dances in Photographs" by Barbara Morgan.

AMERICANS for the ARTS

DD
DORIS DUKE
CHARITABLE FOUNDATION

- **Accuracy.** Inaccurate evidence is worse than useless: It can deceive—and even harm. Facts and figures must always be double-checked. Experts or passages from texts must be quoted or paraphrased accurately. Accuracy also requires a degree of precision relevant to what is being argued. It may be acceptable to say "water was brought to a boil" in reference to a recipe, but when describing a chemical experiment involving a water temperature to a precise fraction of a degree, such a statement would be problematic.

- **Thoroughness.** The evidence must cover every facet or implication of the claim. If a writer claims that teenagers in the United States have fewer traffic accidents today than they did ten years ago but then cites accident statistics from only three states, readers rightly would argue that the evidence could be made more thorough by including statistics from all fifty states.

- **Timeliness.** The evidence must be appropriately recent. If a writer argues that teenagers are safer drivers "today" but presents statistics from 1995, then one rightly could argue that the evidence needs to be updated.

Refutation   Closely associated with evidence is refutation, the reference to opposing views and rebutting them. Refuting viewpoints that challenge our own is seldom easy; quite often it is the most difficult stage in writing an effective argument. To refute effectively, we must assume that the challengers are equally convinced of their views. We may be tempted to trivialize or misrepresent an adversarial point by leaving out certain information or giving a faulty interpretation. Disagreements tend to be rooted in deeply personal values and beliefs, so we instinctively try to protect these beliefs. They have worked for us, have stabilized our sense of the world, have helped us cope. Any challenges are avoided. Yet, unless we have the courage to permit these beliefs to be challenged, perhaps modified, maybe even abandoned, learning and personal growth cannot take place.

Knowledge consists not of disembodied facts but of negotiated ideas. What we know we have assimilated from innumerable points of view. The health of our own ideas depends on a steady influx of fresh viewpoints, just as a body of water must be continuously replenished to avoid becoming stagnant. Such receptivity to new ideas requires courage, of course. It is never easy to say of those who argue against us, "Maybe there is some validity to these challenging views; maybe I should adopt some of them."

If after a careful and critical analysis of opponents' arguments we still hold to our overall stance and, in fact, have found flaws in theirs, we are ready to refute them. The aim of refutation is to demonstrate the limitations or errors of challenging views. It is not necessary to establish a distinct boundary between evidence and refutation since evidence may be brought in as part of the refutation process. Notice that in the body of the article on school vouchers (reprinted on pages 100–103), the author refutes the pro-voucher argument by first stating the opposition's rationale and then showing why that rationale is in error:

> Proponents of vouchers argue that these programs would allow poor students to attend good schools previously only available to the middle class. The facts tell a different story. A $2,500 voucher supplement may make the difference for some families. . . . But voucher programs offer nothing of value to families who cannot come up with the rest of the money to cover tuition costs.

The refutation is clearly articulated, but is it convincing? Skeptics probably would demand that the anti-vouchers author supply more in the way of evidence to substantiate the claim that vouchers undermine the integrity of American public schools.

How thorough is the evidence in support of the Anti-Defamation League's thesis that vouchers are harmful? The author brings in important facts that appear to demonstrate the unconstitutionality of vouchers, such as the Supreme Court's quoting of the Establishment Clause or its striking down "education programs that allow parents of parochial school students to recover a portion of their educational expenses from the state." However, much of the argument relies on speculation. There is no way of knowing for sure that the Supreme Court would judge vouchers to be unconstitutional, nor is there any way of knowing for sure that voucher programs "would force citizens—Christians, Jews, Muslims and atheists—to pay for the religious indoctrination of schoolchildren."

Effective argument depends on not only the kinds of evidence used but the degree to which that evidence resolves the stated problem.

Conclusion   The minimal task of a conclusion is to provide a final wisdom about the thesis just argued. Some conclusions summarize the key points of the argument, a strategy that can be much appreciated in a long and complicated argument but may be unnecessary otherwise. Quite often, such summary statements are followed by recommendations for what actions to take. Other conclusions are more speculative: Instead of recommending what should be done, they focus on what *might* be done. And still other conclusions are more open-ended, offering not summative statements but questions for the readers to consider.

The Anti-Defamation League writer on school vouchers does not present as full-fledged a conclusion as he or she does an introduction. Is the conclusion sufficient?

School voucher programs undermine two great American traditions: universal public education and the separation of church and state. Instead of embracing vouchers, communities across the country should dedicate themselves to finding solutions that will be available to every American schoolchild and that take into account the important legacy of the First Amendment.

The author succinctly restates the problem and leaves the reader with the provocative suggestion found in the concluding sentence. But what sort of solution will solve that complex problem? The author brings the readers no closer to a real solution.

  Exercise 3.2

Read the complete text of "School Vouchers: The Wrong Choice for Public Education." Then answer the questions that follow.

School Vouchers
The Wrong Choice for Public Education | Anti-Defamation League

Most Americans believe that improving our system of education should be a top priority for government at the local, state and Federal levels. Legislators, school boards, education professionals, parent groups and community organizations are attempting to implement innovative ideas to rescue children from failing school systems, particularly in inner-city neighborhoods. Many such groups champion voucher programs. The standard program proposed in dozens of states across the country would distribute monetary vouchers (typically valued between $2,500–$5,000) to parents of school-age children, usually in troubled inner-city school districts. Parents could then use the vouchers towards the cost of tuition at private schools—including those dedicated to religious indoctrination.

Superficially, school vouchers might seem a relatively benign way to increase the options poor parents have for educating their children. In fact, vouchers pose a serious threat to values that are vital to the health of American democracy. These programs subvert the constitutional principle of separation of church and state and threaten to undermine our system of public education.

Vouchers Are Constitutionally Suspect

Proponents of vouchers are asking Americans to do something contrary to the very ideals upon which this country was founded. Thomas Jefferson, one of the architects of religious freedom in America, said, "To compel a man to furnish contributions of money for the propagation of opinions which he disbelieves . . . is sinful and tyrannical." Yet voucher programs would do just that; they would force citizens—Christians, Jews, Muslims and atheists—to pay for the religious indoctrination of schoolchildren at schools with narrow parochial agendas. In many areas, 80 percent of vouchers would be used in schools whose central mission is religious training. In most such schools, religion permeates the classroom, the lunchroom, even the football practice field. Channeling public money to these institutions flies in the face of the constitutional mandate of separation of church and state.

While the Supreme Court has upheld school vouchers in the *Zelman v. Simmons-Harris* case, vouchers have not been given a green light by the Court beyond the narrow facts of this case. Indeed, Cleveland's voucher program was upheld in a close (5–4) ruling that required a voucher program to (among other things):

- be a part of a much wider program of multiple educational options, such as magnet schools and after-school tutorial assistance,

- offer parents a real choice between religious and non-religious education (perhaps even providing incentives for non-religious education),

- not only address private schools, but to ensure that benefits go to schools regardless of whether they are public or private, religious or not.

This decision also does not disturb the bedrock constitutional idea that no government program may be designed to advance religious institutions over non-religious institutions. Finally, and of critical importance, many state constitutions provide for a higher wall of separation between church and state—and thus voucher programs will likely have a hard time surviving litigation in state courts.

Thus, other states will likely have a very hard time reproducing the very narrow set of circumstances found in the Cleveland program.   5

Vouchers Undermine Public Schools

Implementation of voucher programs sends a clear message that we are giving up on public education. Undoubtedly, vouchers would help some students. But the glory of the American system of public education is that it is for *all* children, regardless of their religion, their academic talents or their ability to pay a fee. This policy of inclusiveness has made public schools the backbone of American democracy.

Private schools are allowed to discriminate on a variety of grounds. These institutions regularly reject applicants because of low achievement, discipline problems, and sometimes for no reason at all. Further, some private schools promote agendas antithetical to the American ideal. Under a system of vouchers, it may be difficult to prevent schools run by extremist groups like the Nation of Islam or the Ku Klux Klan from receiving public funds to subsidize their racist and anti-Semitic agendas. Indeed, the proud legacy of *Brown v. Board of Education* may be tossed away as tax dollars are siphoned off to deliberately segregated schools.

Proponents of vouchers argue that these programs would allow poor students to attend good schools previously only available to the middle class. The facts tell a different story. A $2,500 voucher supplement may make the difference for some families, giving them just enough to cover the tuition at a private school (with some schools charging over $10,000 per year, they would still have to pay several thousand dollars). But voucher programs offer nothing of value to families who cannot come up with the rest of the money to cover tuition costs.

In many cases, voucher programs will offer students the choice between attending their current public school or attending a school run by the local church. Not all students benefit from a religious school atmosphere—even when the religion being taught is their own. For these students, voucher programs offer only one option: to remain in a public school that is likely to deteriorate even further.

As our country becomes increasingly diverse, the public school system stands out as an institution that unifies Americans. Under voucher programs, our educational system—and our country—would become even more Balkanized than it already is. With the help of taxpayers' dollars, private schools would be filled with well-to-do and middle-class students and a handful of the best, most motivated students from inner cities. Some public schools would be left with fewer dollars to teach the poorest of the poor and other students who, for one reason or another, were not private school material. Such a scenario can hardly benefit public education.

Finally, as an empirical matter, reports on the effectiveness of voucher programs have been mixed. Initial reports on Cleveland's voucher program, published by the American Federation of Teachers, suggest that it has been less effective than proponents argue. Milwaukee's program has resulted in a huge budget shortfall, leaving the public schools scrambling for funds. While some studies suggest that vouchers are good for public schools, there is, as yet, little evidence that they ultimately improve the quality of public education for those who need it most.

Vouchers Are Not Universally Popular

When offered the opportunity to vote on voucher-like programs, the public has consistently rejected them; voters in 19 states have rejected such proposals in referendum ballots. In the November 1998 election, for example,

Colorado voters rejected a proposed constitutional amendment that would have allowed parochial schools to receive public funds through a complicated tuition tax-credit scheme. Indeed, voters have rejected all but one of the tuition voucher proposals put to the ballot since the first such vote over 30 years ago.

Voucher proposals have also made little progress in legislatures across the country. While 20 states have introduced voucher bills, only two have been put into law. Congress has considered several voucher plans for the District of Columbia, but none has been enacted.

A recent poll conducted by the Joint Center for Political and Economic Studies demonstrates that support for vouchers has declined over the last year. Published in October 1998, the Poll revealed that support for school vouchers declined from 57.3 percent to 48.1 percent among Blacks, and from 47 to 41.3 percent among whites. Overall, 50.2 percent of Americans now oppose voucher programs; only 42 percent support them.

Conclusion

School voucher programs undermine two great American traditions: universal public education and the separation of church and state. Instead of embracing vouchers, communities across the country should dedicate themselves to finding solutions that will be available to every American schoolchild and that take into account the important legacy of the First Amendment. ◎/◎

15

1. Suggest one or more alternative ways in which the Anti-Defamation League author might have structured the essay, keeping within the general framework of Classical organizational strategy. What may gain or lose emphasis as a result of the reordering?

2. Evaluate the author's use of facts and appeals. What additional facts and appeals, if any, might have been appropriate?

3. How convincing is the author's argument that school vouchers are constitutionally suspect?

◎/◎   **Exercise 3.3**

Read "Why School Vouchers Can Help Inner-City Children," an argument by Kurt L. Schmoke, Mayor of Baltimore, in support of school vouchers. Then answer the questions that follow.

Why School Vouchers Can Help Inner-City Children | The Honorable Kurt L. Schmoke

I have been a strong supporter of public education during my tenure as mayor. In 1987 I said that it was my goal as mayor to one day have Baltimore be known as "The City That Reads." In doing that I underscored my commitment to improving all levels of education and getting people in our city focused on lifelong learning.

The state of Baltimore's economy was one of a variety of reasons for this commitment. Thirty years before I came into office, the largest private employer in Baltimore was the Bethlehem Steel Corporation's Sparrow's Point Plant. When I entered into office, however, the largest private employer in Baltimore was the Johns Hopkins University and Medical Center.

This transition meant that though there were jobs available, they would require a level of education that was higher than that which our children's parents and grandparents had to attain. It was clear to me that a commitment to improving literacy and understanding that education is a lifelong process was vitally important to our city.

With this knowledge in mind, I worked to improve our library system and our community college. Additionally, we created a Literacy Corporation to combat illiteracy in our city. In fact, President Bush present- ed Baltimore with the National Literacy Award in 1992.

In addition to my public responsibility for the Baltimore educational system, I also have a strong private interest in our city's schools. I have two children who are graduates of city public high schools. In fact, both of my children have at some point while growing up attended both public and private schools, so I have been able to observe my own children in differ- ent educational environments.

What I've found as a result of my experiences in pursuing a better-edu- cated Baltimore, and a better-educated family, is a major void in current school reform efforts. I believe that the issues of competition and accounta- bility are all too often ignored in efforts to improve public education.

My years of experience in education have led me to be in favor of school choice: quite simply, I believe in giving parents more choice about where to educate their children. My support of school choice is founded in the com- mon sense premise that no parent should be forced to send a child to a poorly performing school.

Unfortunately, however, countless parents, especially in the inner cities, are now forced to do just that. Parents in middle- and upper-class communi- ties have long practiced school choice. They made sure that their children

5

Source: Kurt L. Schmoke, "Why School Vouchers Can Help Inner-City Children," *Civic Bulletin* No. 20 Aug. 1999. Reprinted by permission of The Manhattan Institute.

attended schools where they would get the best possible education. There is no reason why this option should be closed to low-income parents.

The consequences of this unfairness are not at all difficult to grasp. As one perceptive observer of urban education has written "Education used to be the poor child's ticket out of the slums. Now it's part of the system that traps people in the underclass."

This was part of the thinking behind what people in Baltimore call my conversion to school choice. It did not happen overnight. It evolved slowly. My belief in school choice grew out of my experiences and, yes, my *frustrations* in trying to improve Baltimore's public schools over the last twelve years.   10

Under my watch as mayor we have tried all sorts of programs to reform the schools. Looking back, some of these programs showed promise, and some of our schools did demonstrate that they were doing a good job of educating our children.

Our successes, however, were still the exceptions, not the norm. I feared that, unless we took drastic action, this pattern would only continue. I considered school choice to be an innovation strong enough to change the course of what was widely recognized as an ailing system.

Why school choice? Two reasons: excellence and accountability. Parents want academic *excellence* for their children. They also want to know that there is someone in their child's school who is *accountable* for achieving those high academic standards.

In most cities in this nation, however, if your child is zoned into a school that is not performing well academically, and where teachers and administrators don't see themselves as being responsible for academic performance, parents have no recourse. Parents can only send their child to that school and hope for the best.

Under a school choice plan, a parent would have options. There would be consequences for a school's poor performance. Parents could pull their children out of poorly performing schools and enroll them someplace else. If exercising this option leads to a mass exodus from certain underachieving schools, schools will learn this painful lesson: schools will either improve, or close due to declining enrollments.   15

Any corporation that tolerated mediocre performance among its employees, unresponsiveness to the complaints of its customers, and the promotion of a large number of failed products, would not survive in the marketplace very long. What is true of corporations should also be true of poorly performing and poorly run schools.

These are some of the ideas that I expressed when I first came out in support of school choice in a speech at Johns Hopkins University in March of 1996, not as a panacea, but as another way to improve public education. Though I thought my remarks were relatively benign, the speech sparked a great deal of controversy.

One of my own aides even joked that he wanted to see my voter registration card to see if I was still a Democrat. Well, I am still a Democrat and I have no plans to change my political affiliation. I, nonetheless, believe that the Democratic Party should reevaluate its position on school choice issues.

In actuality, choice should not be included in partisan rhetoric. School choice should be about giving our nation's children the best possible educational foundation.

The same week as my speech at Johns Hopkins, I appointed a task force [20] to explore the idea of school choice. I asked the task force to consider the pros and cons of school choice programs in all their variations, including programs such as the system implemented in Los Angeles where parents and students have the freedom to choose any school in the public system. I also asked that they investigate private school voucher plans such as the program in Milwaukee, as well as charter and magnet schools.

The task force released a report in that year which recommended that the Baltimore school system expand magnet schools and initiate a system-wide open enrollment program as a way to provide more educational options for parents and their children.

In my view, the task force unfortunately stopped short of endorsing publicly funded vouchers as a way to achieve the goal of school choice. The group, however, did leave open the door for reconsideration of the voucher issue later on. Meanwhile, the Baltimore city public school system has now implemented a variation of the school choice idea through what is called the New Schools Initiative.

These "New Schools" are very similar to charter schools. They are publicly funded schools that are planned and operated by parents or institutions or other non-traditional sponsors.

I recently spoke at Coppin State University for commencement. Coppin State is an historically black college in Baltimore that started out as a teacher training school. Today, under one of the New School Initiatives, Coppin is managing an elementary school in its home neighborhood drawing on its teaching and research to improve that school.

Now, three years after that Hopkins speech, I continue to believe that [25] choice holds the greatest hope for instilling excellence and accountability in the nation's public schools.

At that time, as a Democrat and an African-American mayor, I was considered a maverick, or worse, for expressing that idea. No longer. A ground-swell of support for choice is rising all over the nation, including from some unlikely quarters. Certainly, there's no greater proof of this than the tremendous response to the Children's Scholarship Fund funded by Wal-Mart heir John Walton and financier Ted Forstmann.

Under this program, the parents of some 1.25 million low-income children across the country applied for partial scholarships to help their children attend private and parochial schools. Civil rights pioneer and former mayor of Atlanta Andrew Young wrote these words in a nationally syndicated newspaper column shortly after the results of the scholarship drive were announced: "1.25 million cries for help, voiced by poor, largely minority families, seeking something most Americans take for granted. A decent education for their children."

In that column, Young described the collective cry for help as "a moment of moral awakening" that promises to be just as pivotal in America's civil rights struggle as Rosa Park's refusal to give up her bus seat in Montgomery, Alabama more than 40 years ago.

Such moments of moral awakening, Young observed, force us to reevaluate our beliefs and finally to take action. In Baltimore, that particular scholarship program attracted twenty thousand applicants. This represents an astonishing 44 percent of city children who were eligible.

The conclusions that can be drawn from these figures are unmistakable. The *Baltimore Sun* education editor wrote, "We know now that there's a pent- up demand for school choice in the city. And we know that poor parents do care about the education of their children."

In fact, some low-income African-American parents in our city have shown they care so much that they will even go so far as to look *halfway around the world* in order to find a good school for their children. The school which I refer to is called Baraka, which means blessings in Swahili. It's located in rural Kenya, 10,000 miles and eight time zones from inner-city Baltimore. And it's funded by a Baltimore-based foundation, The Abell Foundation. The Foundation recruits and selects at-risk seventh- and eighth-grade boys from the Baltimore city public schools to participate in this bold education experiment.

The kids chosen for this program are generally headed for serious trouble. It is safe to assume that many of the boys in the Baraka program would have ended up incarcerated, or worse, had they not been selected.

Baraka School is going to begin its fourth year of operation in the fall. With 30 graduates to date, the school is having remarkable success in boosting the academic achievement of these at-risk youngsters and truly turning around their lives.

Because of the persistent resistance to school choice by some Maryland politicians, however, the State Education Department has refused to fund the Baraka School project. I do not speak of any extra funding here. I am only talking about taking the state's cost of educating each Baraka student, which would normally have gone to the school that they had been assigned to had they remained in the public system, and allowing it to be used to educate the students in this alternative environment.

The state has absolutely refused. Were it not for the support of the Foundation, the Baraka School, which has done such an excellent job for these young men, would have closed.

So, despite greater acceptance of school choice it's certainly premature to declare victory in the public opinion contest. Indeed, criticisms of school choice are as strident as ever and I am sure you have heard the more familiar ones.

Some say that school choice, especially vouchers, will weaken public education. My response is that choice can only strengthen public education by introducing competition and accountability into the mix. Others claim that school choice is undemocratic. My response to them is that choice is in keeping with the aspirations for freedom that formed the core of American democracy. As former Delaware Governor Pete Du Pont once wrote, "It's about the liberty to choose what's best for your children." All of us should have that choice.

Some say that school choice is elitist, or even racist. The truth is that black low-income children are among the prime victims of the nation's failing public schools. African-American parents know this all too well. This is why they have been so open to the idea of school choice.

A recent national poll released by the Joint Center for Political and Economic Studies found a trend toward growing support of tuition vouchers among African-American parents.

Another common criticism of school choice, and especially vouchers, is   40 that it violates the principle of separation of church and state.

A properly structured voucher program is no more a violation of the principle of separation of church and state than is the GI Bill. This program allowed military veterans to use government dollars to attend any university of their choice, public or private, religious or secular.

I am convinced that with time, and through open dialogue, critics of school choice will come to see this movement for what it is: part of an emerging new civil rights battle for the millennium, the battle for education equity. We need to give poor children the same right that children from more affluent households have long enjoyed. The right to an education that will prepare them to make a meaningful contribution to society. It is that simple.

In speaking of battles, and in closing, I remind you of those few words of wisdom from Victor Hugo: "Greater than the tread of Mighty Armies, is an Idea whose Time has Come . . ." As we look to the future, evidence is increasingly compelling, that school choice is such an idea. ◎/◎

1. Compare Schmoke's method of arguing his thesis with the Anti-Defamation League's method. Is one method more effective than the other? Why or why not?

2. Critique the essay in terms of (a) the effectiveness of its introduction; (b) the strength of its evidence and appeals; (c) the strength of its refutations; (d) its conclusion.

3. Prepare an outline of your own essay on school vouchers. What will be your thesis? What kind of evidence will you present? How will you refute challenging views?

FIGURE 3.1

Classical Model Flowchart

What *issue* am I going to investigate? [Example: The issue of visual arts education in U.S. public schools.]

What is my *thesis*? [Example: Acquiring basic skills in painting, illustrating, and sculpting is as important as acquiring basic math and reading skills.]

What *evidence* can I use to support my thesis convincingly? [Example: Timely published reports by properly credentialed experts (such as educational psychologists) that explain why acquiring visual arts related skills are as important as math and reading skills.]

What are the opposing views that I must acknowledge and *refute*? [Example: The argument that math and reading skills must take priority over visual arts skills in today's world overlooks the fact that creative thinking is just as important as analytical thinking.]

In light of my evidence and refutation of opposing views, what are my *recommendations* for resolving the problem? [Example: We must find ways to integrate math and reading with painting and illustrating.]

What are my *concluding reflections*?

Using the above information, what can I say in my opening paragraph that would best *introduce* my argument and engage my reader's attention?

Chapter Summary

The Classical model of argument dates back to ancient Greece and Rome, and it is still used. In effect, the Classical model presents a template, a preestablished structure for framing an argument. It includes these elements:

- An introduction, which presents the claim to be argued and gives necessary background information

- A body of collected data or evidence and appeals, which together attempt to persuade the audience that the claim is convincing, and acknowledgment and refutation of challenging views

- A conclusion, which may summarize key points, reflect on implications and consequences, or make recommendations (if appropriate)

- In addition, the content of an argument was generated by modes of thought or topics, which included definition, comparison, temporal/causal connection, circumstance, and testimony.

Argument in the ancient world was conducted mainly through oratory, the art of speechmaking. Training for a profession in which argument was part of the job included being trained in the rhetorical strategies needed for giving speeches in that profession. Hence, aspiring politicians were trained in deliberative oratory, aspiring lawyers in forensic oratory. Everyone involved in public life was probably trained in celebratory oratory, which was used for honoring individuals and events.

Checklist

1. Does my paper include the elements of Classical argument structure in proper sequence?

2. Does my introduction clearly present my thesis and necessary background information?

3. Have I acknowledged and accurately presented challenging views? Have I refuted them thoroughly?

4. Does my conclusion summarize the key points of my argument, present insightful interpretations, or make appropriate predictions or recommendations?

Writing Projects

1. Using the Classical model of argument structure, write a three-page position paper on one of the following topics:

   a. Students should (should not) be required to take fewer core courses and allowed to take more electives.

   b. First-year composition courses should (should not) be an elective instead of a requirement.

   c. The college bookstore's buyback policy should (should not) be reformed.

2. Using the Classical model of argument, write an essay defending or challenging the value or usefulness of an existing law, policy, or program, such as the electoral college, the National Endowment for the Arts, the banning of prayer from public schools, or the minimum drinking age.

4 Using the Toulmin Model in Your Arguments

> Rationality has to be understood in terms of formal argumentation.
> —Stephen Toulmin

Stephen Toulmin (b. 1922), an English philosopher of science and the history of ideas, developed a system of argument that has proven useful and influential in the modern world of complex rhetorical situations. Toulmin's model of argument is systematic in its reasoning; at the same time, it demands that this reasoning be scrutinized for its ethical underpinnings. It is not enough to present a claim and try to "prove" it with evidence. The arguer must also examine the evidence itself, to scrutinize the assumptions we make about the evidence, and even to ensure that *those* assumptions are similarly scrutinized for their ethical underpinnings. Toulmin argument, then, insists that logic alone cannot resolve complex human issues. Ethics and values play as important a role in argumentation as logical reasoning.

Let's take a closer look at the elements that comprise Toulmin argument.

The Toulmin Model of Argument

The terms we encounter in the Toulmin model immediately call attention to the complexity of the social interaction required for responsible argumentation:

- An argument begins with a *claim* to be made, which must be articulated as clearly and as accurately as possible. The claim is the thesis or premise of your argument that you want your audience to accept.

- To accomplish this goal, you must produce compelling *data*, the grounds or evidence. It is important to keep in mind that "evidence" means different things in different disciplines. In the sciences, for example, the data probably consist of results obtained from experiments, close observations, or mathematical analyses. In other contexts, the data probably consist of rules, laws, policies, highly valued social customs, or *quotations* from works of literature.

- Next, you need to ask of any argument whether the data used to support the claim truly are valid and are based on a sound sense of values. In other

Stephen Toulmin (b. 1922) is a philosopher of science with a special interest in the role that rhetoric plays in conveying ideas about ethics and morality. His context-based theory of argument provides an influential alternative to rigid, logic-driven theories.

words, you must determine one or more underlying warrants, assurances that the data are based on some sensible and ethical foundation. Anyone can conjure up all sorts of data and manipulate it to give the appearance of validating a claim. As Shakespeare in *The Merchant of Venice* reminds us through the mouth of the merchant Antonio, "The Devil can cite Scripture for his purpose." For example, sometimes it is not enough to cite a law; it may be necessary to decide if the law is just or unjust.

- Just as the validity of the data is reinforced and sanctioned by one or more underlying warrants, so too must the validity of the warrants be reinforced. As Stephen Toulmin himself explains in *An Introduction to Reasoning* (1979), "Warrants are not-self-validating . . . [and] normally draw their strength and solidity from further substantial supporting considerations" (58). These further supporting considerations Toulmin calls the *backing*. To return to the example of unjust laws, the arguer would need to ask: What *assurance* can I give that the law is unjust?

- Finally, you must be prepared to bring in one or more *qualifiers* to your claim—that is, be prepared to call attention to any exceptions to the claim under certain circumstances. Consider: "The right of free speech must be protected in all situations except when it can endanger life or safety, such as yelling 'Fire!' in a crowded theater." The qualifier—the exception to the rule—prevents the claim from losing touch with complex social situations.

The ability to anticipate qualifiers to one's claim is the mark of a responsible arguer. Toulmin refers to this phase of argument as the *rebuttal*. Of course, no arguer can anticipate every possible exception, and that is why audience feedback is so important in argumentation.

Now let us examine each of these elements in more detail.

The Claim

You know this feature as the thesis, premise, or central assumption. Toulmin chooses to call it the *claim* because that term suggests a thesis or assertion that is particularly *open to challenge*. The term comes from the Latin word *clamare*, to cry out, reminding us of the spontaneity with which claims are often made and hence how easily they can reach human ears and eyes without sufficient evidence to support them. The Latin root also reminds us to pay attention to how open to public scrutiny the claim is likely to be once it is presented as a speech or as a printed document in a periodical or book, on the Internet, in a court of law, or in a college paper.

For an argument to succeed, the writer first must ensure that the claim offered is worthy of deliberation. Some claims are not arguable. For example, it would be foolish to argue seriously that in general red is a superior color to blue. The claim is too dependent on subjective taste to be arguable. As the Latin maxim goes, *De gustibus non est disputandum*—of taste there is no disputing. But let's say you are an interior decorator and you have studied the effects of color on mood. You might argue that particular colors work best in particular types of rooms within a house. Here the claim is based not on personal taste but on statistical fact: Researchers have shown that pale blue helps relax people; therefore pale blue would be an appropriate color for bedroom walls.

There are two basic types of claims, objective and subjective. *Objective claims* assert that something *actually* exists and present evidence that is demonstrably factual—not only in the sense of scientifically factual but legally factual, as in the case of laws, regulations, and policies. Here are some examples of objective claims:

- Video games heighten a child's hand-eye coordination and visual perception, but they impede the development of language processing skills.

- It is a myth that science is based only on logical reasoning and that art is based only on imagination. Logical reasoning and imagination are equally important to science and to art.

- Those who wish to speak out against the U.S. Constitution have just as much constitutional right to communicate their views in public as those who support the Constitution.

The above claims present themselves as objective truths. But they are not *self-evident* truths; they must be supported with the appropriate evidence before readers can accept them as factual. Thus, before the first claim can be accepted as factual, the arguer must show, for example, that psychologists have compared the learning behaviors of children who play video games with those children who do not and have found enough evidence to establish a causal link between video-game playing and abstract reasoning.

Before the second claim can be accepted as factual, the arguer must provide convincing examples of the way imagination works in science and the way logical reasoning works in art. For example, the arguer might refer to autobiographical statements of scientists such as Albert Einstein or mathematicians such as Jules Henri Poincaré, who at various times obtained scientific understanding through dreams or imaginary "thought experiments."

Before the third claim can be accepted as factual, the arguer must demonstrate how the Constitution, paradoxical as it may seem, actually protects the rights of those who wish to speak out against it. This proof would entail careful analysis and interpretation of selected passages from the Constitution.

Subjective claims, on the other hand, assert that something *should* exist and present evidence derived from ethical, moral, or aesthetic convictions. Someone who argues, for example, that all college students should be required to take at least one course in literature to graduate or that animals should be treated with dignity is making a subjective claim. Although each claim is based on personal values, one cannot dismiss them as a kind of anything-goes relativism. The arguer, for example, might demonstrate that the benefits derived from studying literature improve one's ability to understand human nature, a valuable asset when one interacts with people.

The Data or Grounds

The Toulmin model demands that writers take pains to ensure that the supporting evidence fully validates the claim. The word *data* suggests "hard facts"—results from experiments, statistics from surveys, as well as historical, legal, and biographical facts. For more indirect kinds of evidence, such as testimonials or interpretations, the term *grounds* is more appropriate.

Thus, we can identify five different kinds of data to authenticate a claim: (1) *legal data* (such as laws, policies, regulations, and codes); (2) *scientific data*, such as findings obtained from mathematical calculations and laboratory experiments (keep in mind that experiments such as DNA testing and ballistics analyses, used to help solve crimes, are an inherent part of legal data and are often referred to as *forensic* data); (3) *testimonial* or *experiential* data, which is based on firsthand experience (for example, eyewitness testimony and oral histories as gathered by anthropologists); (4) *scholarly* or *documentary* data (that is, data obtained from secondary sources published in book or electronic form); and (5) *statistical data*, which may be obtained firsthand (in which case it would be akin to but not identical with scientific data unless the statistics were derived from laboratory experiments instead of, say, opinion polls).

Like claims, data or grounds must be presented as accurately and as unambiguously as possible. Someone who argues, for example, that essay exams test student comprehension of literature better than multiple-choice exams do, and who in so arguing relies on the testimonials of students, would want to make sure that those testimonials contain clear *demonstrations* of better comprehension for students taking essay exams. Of course, the criteria for "better comprehension" would need to be clarified before they could be used as valid grounds for a claim. The criteria might include richly detailed (as opposed to generalized) recollection of the content of literary works; they might also include insightful critical assessment or comparison of the thematic material of the works (as opposed to, say, superficial explanation of its strengths and weaknesses).

The Warrant and Its Backing

A warrant is the assurance that the evidence brought in to support the claim is completely reliable and that it rests on sound principles or values. Thus, just as the data legitimate the claim, a warrant, often implicit in the argument, legitimates the data. As Stephen Toulmin writes in *The Uses of Argument,* warrants "indicate the bearing of [the] conclusion of the data already produced" (98). By "bearing" Toulmin is referring to the need for readers to recognize and accept an appropriate direction in which the argument takes shape from claim to data to warrant. Warrants remind us of the humanizing dimension of argument: An argument, no matter how "heated," must always be principled rather than stem from vague or questionable motives.

Let us see how warrants operate in a given argument. Consider an essay in which a student, Melissa, argues for the abolition of letter grades in formal education. Melissa's claim is as follows:

```
Letter grades should be abolished because they result in unhealthy
competition, distract students from truly learning the subject matter,
and constitute an inadequate gauge of student performance.
```

Melissa chooses to support her claim with data that compares the performance of students in a letter-graded class with the performance of students in a Pass/No Pass class. Melissa's warrant might go something like this: "Learning for its own sake is more satisfying to students than learning to achieve predetermined standards of proficiency." As backing for this warrant, Melissa might conclude something like the following: "The more satisfying the learning experience, the more students are likely to learn." Melissa may not need to state these sentences explicitly, but the evidence she uses to support her claim should make the warrant and backing apparent.

We might diagram the relationship between Melissa's claim, data, warrant, and backing as in Figure 4.1.

FIGURE 4.1

Relationship Between the
Claim, Data, Warrant, and
Backing

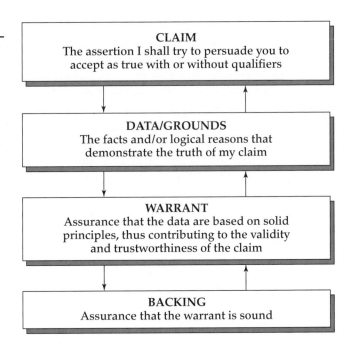

CLAIM
The assertion I shall try to persuade you to
accept as true with or without qualifiers

DATA/GROUNDS
The facts and/or logical reasons that
demonstrate the truth of my claim

WARRANT
Assurance that the data are based on solid
principles, thus contributing to the validity
and trustworthiness of the claim

BACKING
Assurance that the warrant is sound

Compelling warrants are just as vital to the force of an argument as are compelling data because they reinforce the trustworthiness of the data. Unsuccessful warrants often seem disconnected from, or even contradictory to, the evidence. Consider the following claim:

Students should not be required to attend class.

If the evidence presented is the college's pledge to inculcate self-reliance in students, then the warrant—the conviction that self-reliance is compromised when professors require students to attend class—would seem contradictory to many readers because it is often assumed that such requirements are designed to *promote* self-reliance. Similarly, backing can be faulty. For example, in an argument claiming that every sixteen-year-old who drops out of school should be denied a driver's license, a warrant might involve the conviction that there is never any legitimate justification for dropping out of school; however, it would be difficult to find backing for this warrant that would apply in every circumstance.

There are three kinds of warrants, which roughly correspond to the three kinds of appeals in Classical argument: logical or scientific warrants, ethical or forensic-based warrants, and emotional or artistic-based warrants.

1. *Logical or scientific warrants.* These warrants reinforce the trustworthiness of logical progression of scientific reasoning. If a meteorologist predicts a smog alert on the basis of 90-degree temperatures, little or no winds, and heavy traffic, her warrant would be that such a formula for smog predication is reliable.

2. *Ethical or forensic-based warrants.* A warrant is ethical when it relates to values or codes of conduct such as honor, integrity, altruism, honesty, and

compassion. If one argues that underrepresented minorities should be allowed the opportunity to attend college even if their admissions test scores are not quite as high as those of the majority of admissions candidates, and uses as evidence the success rate of those given such opportunity, then the warrant is that society is ethically obligated to compensate minorities for past injustices by giving them such opportunities. Where affirmative action measures have become law we could say that the warrant justifies enactment of that law.

3. *Emotional or artistic-based warrants.* If someone argues that profanity in films weakens instead of strengthens his enjoyment of those films and uses personal testimony as evidence, then the arguer's warrant is that such negative reactions to profanity in movies is a reliable criterion for evaluating the strength or weakness of a film.

Backing may also be logical, ethical, and emotional.

Keep in mind when analyzing the arguments of others (and even your own arguments) that, as stated earlier, warrants—and, consequently, backing—often remain unstated. They may be certain fundamental principles or beliefs that the writer simply assumes his or her reader shares. In fact, such principles or beliefs may well be open to challenge, thus undermining the claim of the argument. But to make such a challenge, you first have to identify the unstated warrant. In making arguments of your own, consider the possibility that a good number of your readers may not share your warrant. If that is the case, it is best to state the warrant and backing directly and perhaps even offer some defense for one or both.

The Qualifier

Claims are rarely absolute; that is, a claim may be valid in many circumstances, but not necessarily in all. If that is the case, an arguer would want to *qualify* the claim so that her readers would understand how she is limiting its range. For example, someone who claims that dress codes should be eliminated in the workplace might qualify that claim by excluding workplaces where uniforms are required for reasons of security (as is the case with police or military uniforms) or where certain articles of clothing are prohibited for reasons of personal safety (for example, someone cannot wear a necktie when operating heavy machinery). Someone writing about the negative influence of television on learning might qualify the claim by noting that watching television for the specific purpose of studying its negative effects could have a positive benefit on learning.

A radical form of qualification is known as the *rebuttal*. This is similar to refutation in Classical argument (see pages 98–99), except that in the Toulmin scheme, rebuttal aims not to invalidate the claim but to show that the claim may not be valid in certain situations. Let's use the example of dress codes mentioned earlier. Instead of merely qualifying the claim that dress codes should be eliminated *except for* police uniforms, the arguer might rebut the claim entirely by agreeing that dress codes should be maintained without exception whenever there is consensus among employers and employees alike that it is necessary or desirable.

A Sample Analysis Using the Toulmin Model

Read the following argument by Virginia Woolf, noting the claim, data, warrant, and backing, as indicated by the marginal annotations.

Professions for Women | Virginia Woolf

Woolf begins by providing necessary background information for her argument.

When your secretary invited me to come here, she told me that your Society is concerned with the employment of women and she suggested that I might tell you something about my own professional experiences. It is true I am a woman; it is true I am employed; but what professional experiences have I had? It is difficult to say. My profession is literature; and in that profession there are fewer experiences for women than in any other, with the exception of the stage—fewer, I mean, that are peculiar to women. For the road was cut many years ago—by Fanny Burney, by Aphra Behn, by Harriet Martineau, by Jane Austen, by George Eliot—many famous women, and many more unknown and forgotten, have been before me, making the path smooth, and regulating my steps. Thus, when I came to write, there were very few material obstacles in my way. Writing was a reputable and harmless occupation. The family peace was not broken by the scratching of a pen. No demand was made upon the family purse. For ten and sixpence one can buy paper enough to write all the plays of Shakespeare—if one has a mind that way. Pianos and models, Paris, Vienna, and Berlin, masters and mistresses, are not needed by a writer. The cheapness of writing paper is, of course, the reason why women have succeeded as writers before they have succeeded in the other professions.

But to tell you my story—it is a simple one. You have only got to figure to yourselves a girl in a bedroom with a pen in her hand. She had only to move that pen from left to right—from ten o'clock to one. Then it occurred to her to do what is simple and cheap enough after all—to slip a few of those pages into an envelope, fix a penny stamp in the corner, and drop the envelope into the red box at the corner. It was thus that I became a journalist; and my effort was rewarded on the first day of the following month—a very glorious day it was for me—by a letter from an editor containing a cheque for one pound ten shillings and sixpence. But to show you how little I deserve to be called a professional woman, how little I know of the struggles and difficulties of such lives, I have to admit that instead of spending that sum upon bread and butter, rent, shoes and stockings, or butcher's bills, I went out and bought a cat—a beautiful cat, a Persian cat, which very soon involved me in bitter disputes with my neighbors.

What could be easier than to write articles and to buy Persian cats with the profits? But wait a moment. Articles have to be about something. Mine, I seem to remember, was about a novel by a famous man. And while I was writing this review, I discovered that if I were going to review books I should need to do battle with a certain phantom. And the phantom was a woman, and when I came to know her better I called her after the heroine of a famous poem. The Angel in the House. It was she who used to come between me and my paper when I was writing reviews. It was she who bothered me and wasted my time and so tormented me that at last I killed her. You who come of a younger and happier generation may not have heard of her—you may not know what I mean by The Angel in the House. I will describe her as shortly as I can. She was intensely sympathetic. She was immensely charming. She was utterly unselfish. She excelled in the difficult arts of family life. She sacrificed herself daily. If there was chicken, she took the leg; if there was a draught she sat in it—in short she was so constituted that she never had a mind or a wish of her own, but preferred to sympathize always with the minds and wishes of others. Above all—I need not say it—she was pure. Her purity was supposed to be her chief beauty—her blushes, her great grace. In those days—the last of Queen Victoria—every house had its Angel. And when I came to write I encountered her with the very first words. The shadow of her wings fell on my page; I heard the rustling of her skirts in the room. Directly, that is to say, I took my pen in my hand to review that novel by a famous man, she slipped behind me and whispered: "My

Woolf's claim emerges here through implication: Women who aspire to write must do all they can to "kill" the Angel in the House.

dear, you are a young woman. You are writing about a book that has been written by a man. Be sympathetic; be tender; flatter; deceive; use all the arts and wiles of our sex. Never let anybody guess that you have a mind of your own. Above all, be pure." And she made as if to guide my pen. I now record the one act for which I take some credit to myself, though the credit rightly belongs to some excellent ancestors of mine who left me a certain sum of money—shall we say five hundred pounds a year?—so that it was not necessary for me to depend solely on charm for my living. I turned upon her and caught her by the throat. I did my best to kill her. My excuse if I were to be had up at a court of law, would be that I acted in self-defence. Had I not killed her she would have killed me. She would have plucked the heart out of my writing. For as I found directly, as I put pen to paper, you cannot review even a novel without having a mind of your own, without expressing what you think to be the truth about human relations, morality, sex. And all these questions, according to the Angel of the House cannot be dealt with freely and openly by women; they must charm, they must conciliate, they must—to put it bluntly—tell lies if they are to succeed. Thus, whenever I felt the shadow of her wing or the radiance of her halo upon my page, I took up the inkpot and flung it at her. She died hard. Her fictitious nature was of great assistance to her. It is far harder to kill a phantom than a reality. She was always creeping back when I thought I had dispatched her. Though I flatter myself that I killed her in the end, the struggle was severe; it took much time that had better have been spent upon learning Greek grammar; or in roaming the world in search of adventures. But it was a real experience; it was an experience that was bound to befall all women writers at that time. Killing the Angel in the House was part of the occupation of a woman writer.

But to continue my story. The Angel was dead; what then remained? You may say that what remained was a simple and common object—a young woman in a bedroom with an inkpot. In other words, now that she had rid herself of falsehood, that young woman had only to be herself. Ah, but what is "herself"? I mean, what is a woman? I assure you, I do not know. I do not believe that you know. I do not believe that anybody can know until she has expressed herself in all the arts and professions open to human skill. That indeed is one of the reasons why I have come here—out of respect for you, who are in process of showing us by your experiments

Woolf is more explicit about her claim here: The "Angel," if not killed, will pluck the heart out of a woman's writing.

The data (grounds) Woolf uses to support her claim: Women writers are forced to conciliate, tell lies.

Woolf's warrant, implied here, is that women writers must be free to be themselves, whatever that might be.

what a woman is, who are in process of providing us, by your failures and successes, with that extremely important piece of information.

But to continue the story of my professional experi- 5 ences. I made one pound ten and six by my first review; and I bought a Persian cat with the proceeds. Then I grew ambitious. A Persian cat is all very well, I said; but a Persian cat is not enough. I must have a motor-car. And it was thus that I became a novelist—for it is a very strange thing that people will give you a motor-car if you will tell them a story. It is a still stranger thing that there is nothing so delightful in the world as telling stories. It is far pleasanter than writing reviews of famous novels. And yet, if I am to obey your secretary and tell you my professional experiences as a novelist, I must tell you about a very strange experience that befell me as a novelist. And to understand it you must try first to imagine a novelist's state of mind. I hope I am not giving away professional secrets if I say that a novelist's chief desire is to be as unconscious as possible. He has to induce in himself a state of perpetual lethargy. He wants life to proceed with the utmost quiet and regularity. He wants to see the same faces, to read the same books, to do the same things day after day, month after month, while he is writing, so that nothing may break the illusion in which he is living—so that nothing may disturb or disquiet the mysterious nosings about, feelings round, darts, dashes, and sudden discoveries of that very shy and illusive spirit, the imagination. I suspect that this state is the same both for men and women. Be that as it may, I want you to imagine me writing a novel in a state of trance. I want you to figure to yourselves a girl sitting with a pen in her hand, which for minutes, and indeed for hours, she never dips into the inkpot. The image that comes to my mind when I think of this girl is the image of a fisherman lying sunk in dreams on the verge of a deep lake with a rod held out over the water. She was letting her imagination sweep unchecked round every rock and cranny of the world that lies submerged in the depths of our unconscious being. Now came the experience that I believe to be far commoner with women writers than with men. The line raced through the girl's fingers. Her imagination had rushed away. It had sought the pools, the depths, the dark places where the largest fish slumber. And then there was a smash. There

To provide *backing* to her warrant, Woolf describes her own experience as a writer to demonstrate how uncompromising one must be in communicating his or her true convictions.

was an explosion. There was foam and confusion. The imagination had dashed itself against something hard. The girl was roused from her dream. She was indeed in a state of the most acute and difficult distress. To speak without figure, she had thought of something, something about the body, about the passion, which it was unfitting for her as a woman to say. Men, her reason told her, would be shocked. The consciousness of what men will say of a woman who speaks the truth about her passions had roused her from her artist's state of unconsciousness. She could write no more. The trance was over. Her imagination could work no longer. This I believe to be a very common experience with women writers—they are impeded by the extreme conventionality of the other sex. For though men sensibly allow themselves great freedom in these respects, I doubt that they realize or can control the extreme severity with which they condemn such freedom in women.

These then were two very genuine experiences of my own. These were two of the adventures of my professional life. The first—killing the Angel in the House—I think I solved. She died. But the second, telling the truth about my own experiences as a body, I do not think I solved. I doubt that any woman has solved it yet. The obstacles against her are still immensely powerful—and yet they are very difficult to define. Outwardly, what is simpler than to write books? Outwardly, what obstacles are there for a woman rather than for a man? Inwardly, I think, the case is very different; she has still many ghosts to fight, many prejudices to overcome. Indeed it will be a long time still, I think, before a woman can sit down to write a book without finding a phantom to be slain, a rock to be dashed against. And if this is so in literature, the freest of all professions for women, how is it in the new professions which you are now for the first time entering?

Those are the questions that I should like, had I time, to ask you. And indeed, if I have laid stress upon these professional experiences of mine, it is because I believe that they are, though in different forms, yours also. Even when the path is nominally open—when there is nothing to prevent a woman from being a doctor, a lawyer, a civil servant—there are many phantoms and obstacles, as I believe, looming in her way. To discuss and define them is I think of great value and importance; for thus only can the labour be shared, the difficulties be solved. But besides this, it is necessary also to discuss the ends and the aims

Woolf *qualifies* her claim by emphasizing the fact that the obstacles facing women have not yet been overcome.

for which we are fighting, for which we are doing battle with these formidable obstacles. Those aims cannot be taken for granted; they must be perpetually questioned and examined. The whole position, as I see it—here in this hall surrounded by women practising for the first time in history I know not how many different professions—is one of extraordinary interest and importance. You have won rooms of your own in the house hitherto exclusively owned by men. You are able, though not without great labour and effort, to pay the rent. You are earning your five hundred pounds a year. But this freedom is only a beginning; the room is your own, but it is still bare. It has to be furnished; it has to be decorated; it has to be shared. How are you going to furnish it, how are you going to decorate it? With whom are you going to share it, and upon what terms? These, I think are questions of the utmost importance and interest. For the first time in history you are able to ask them; for the first time you are able to decide for yourselves what the answers should be. Willingly would I stay and discuss those questions and answers—but not tonight. My time is up; and I must cease. ◎/◎

◎/◎ Exercise 4.1

Should the tobacco industry be held responsible for individuals who smoke and become ill because of it? Or should individuals be responsible for their own decisions? Student Daniel Neal decides to take the latter position and shapes his argument according to the Toulmin model. Read Daniel's paper; then respond to the questions that follow.

Daniel Neal

Tobacco: Ignorance Is No Longer an Excuse

Any individual who chooses to use tobacco today is making an informed decision. The negative effects of tobacco are known, admitted, and even advertised by tobacco companies. Simply put, ignorance is no longer an excuse for smoking. And since the government has settled with the tobacco companies, ignorance is no longer an excuse for legal action. Because of the tobacco settlement, individuals must now be responsible for the consequences of choosing to use tobacco.

Part of this settlement requires the tobacco companies begin "spending hundreds of millions of dollars on efforts to discourage and deglamorize tobacco use" (Klein 463). Because it will highlight the dangers of tobacco, some argue that this will in fact encourage youth tobacco use. Richard Klein holds that "emphasizing that tobacco is dangerous and disapproved will enhance the glamour, prestige, and attractiveness of cigarettes, particularly among the young" (463). Klein's point is valid: Teenagers are attracted to what is dangerous and disapproved. No one debates that youth tobacco use is undesirable and should be prevented. It is wrong, however, to blame tobacco companies for youth tobacco use for the simple reason that they are not the ones directly selling it to minors. The tobacco companies cannot be held accountable for the actions of independent retailers who choose to sell tobacco to children. Instead of arguing that the settlement will increase youth tobacco use, those who are concerned should attack the way teens get tobacco: dishonest retailers willing to sell tobacco products illegally to minors. The tobacco settlement has not changed the illegality of underage tobacco use—that minors may choose to smoke illegally is irrelevant. It is unquestionably positive, however, that the tobacco settlement will fund education efforts so that these minors, when adults, can make informed and responsible decisions about tobacco use.

Other critics of the settlement feel that the tobacco industry will receive unfair protection from further lawsuits. In her essay". . . Or a Payoff to Purveyors of Poison?" Elizabeth M. Whelan writes:

> Whatever the parties' motivation, the deal that resulted gave the tobacco industry a major boost by providing limited immunity against future litigation. While technically allowing smokers (or their survivors) to continue to sue cigarette companies for damages caused by smoking, the settlement would put a yearly cap of $5 billion on damages, an amount that is a trivial cost of doing business for the industry. This cap will serve as a disincentive

to future plaintiff's attorneys, who will incur
enormous costs in any challenges they choose to
mount against the wealthy tobacco companies (467).

If the dangers of tobacco were still concealed by the
tobacco companies, Whelan's argument would be quite valid.
However, that tobacco use is harmful to one's health is plain
knowledge today. Since anyone considering tobacco use today has
been fully informed of the dangers by many sources (including
the tobacco industry), how can anyone but that individual be
responsible for damages resulting from smoking? While Whelan
holds that limited immunity for tobacco companies is a negative
thing, it is in fact quite positive: By setting limits on the
liability of tobacco companies, the government is forcing
individuals to take responsibility for their actions. Later in
her essay, Whelan continues: "This is analogous to a scenario
in which a corporation admits to polluting the water supply,
pays some damages, then returns immediately to dumping toxins
down the well—and gets away with it" (467). In this analogy
Whelan neglects to include a key participant: the individual
choosing to use tobacco. Borrowing her terms, while the well
may be toxic, not only is it clearly labeled so, but none is
forced to drink from it. The tobacco settlement is quite fair
because it places the responsibility for tobacco use into the
hands of the informed consumers who use it.

Instead of continuing to demonize the tobacco industry,
we should demand that the individuals who choose to use tobacco
take personal responsibility for the damages caused by it.
Consider alcohol, a substance harmful both when used as
intended (killing brain cells) and when abused (driving while
intoxicated, alcohol poisoning, alcoholism, etc.). We have, as
a society, accepted the idea of individual responsibility for
the consequences of alcohol use. It is time we do the same for
tobacco. An individual choosing to smoke today must realize
that he or she has been amply warned. By providing the tobacco
industry protection against future litigation, the tobacco
settlement has justly moved the onus of responsibility from the
corporation to the informed consumer.

Works Cited

Klein, Richard. "The Tobacco Deal: Prohibition II . . ." <u>Wall</u>
    <u>Street</u> <u>Journal</u> 26 June 1997: A-18.
Whelan, Elizabeth M. ". . . Or a Payoff to Purveyors of Poison?"
    <u>Wall Street Journal</u> 26 June 1997: A-18.

1. Identify Daniel's claim, data, warrant, and backing (keeping in mind that the final two may be implied).

2. How effectively does Daniel use the Toulmin method? What might he do differently?

3. Critique Daniel's method of organizing the argument. Which parts of the essay, if any, could he organize more effectively? Why?

Organizing Your Argument Using the Toulmin Model

Preparing to write an argument using the Toulmin model puts you into an intense questioning mode about the nature of your claim, the reliability of your data, and the ethical strength of your warrant and backing.

To begin, write down your claim, data, warrant, and backing. Then jot down questions about each of them. One student, organizing an argument on the hazards of secondhand cigarette smoke, prepares the following list:

My Claim

Secondhand cigarette smoke is hazardous enough to justify prohibiting smoking in all public places.

Questions About My Claim

1. Is it valid? What makes it valid?

2. Is it practical? Can it actually be acted on?

3. Are there qualifications I must make to my claim?

4. What will be some of the possible challenges to my claim?

5. Who could benefit most from accepting my claim? Benefit least or be harmed?

My Data

1. Statistical information from the American Cancer Society, the American Lung Association, and the American Medical Association

2. The most recent Surgeon General's report on secondhand smoke

3. Personal testimonials of those who became seriously ill as a result of long-term exposure to secondhand smoke

Questions About My Data

1. Do I have sufficient data to support my claim?

2. Are there other important sources of information that I have overlooked?

3. Are my data reliable (not biased or manipulated)? Timely? Accurate?

4. How can I test the data for reliability, timeliness, and accuracy?

5. Which data are the most compelling? Least compelling?

My Warrant

It is more important for people to have the freedom to breathe clean air than for smokers to have the freedom to befoul the air.

Questions About My Warrant

1. Do I really believe that "freedom" in the context of smoking has to be qualified to include freedom from encroaching on one's right to breathe smoke-free air?

2. What other warrants might underlie the one I have identified? Am I too intolerant of smokers? Am I exaggerating the seriousness of the problem?

3. Am I prepared to stand behind my warrant, regardless of how others might challenge it?

My Backing

Freedom *from* things that cause distress in others is more important than freedom *to do* things that cause distress in others.

Questions About My Backing

1. Does my backing apply in all cases? For example, does ambient smoke <u>always</u> cause distress in others?

2. What makes me so sure that "freedom from" things that might cause distress is <u>more</u> important than "freedom to do" things that might cause distress?

The student then prepares the following tentative outline based on this list:

Thesis

Because secondhand smoke is so hazardous, smoking should be banned from all public facilities.

```
  I. Introduction: The problem of secondhand smoke

     A. First example: Woman breathes in secondhand smoke in a
        restaurant and has an asthma attack

     B. Second example: Child in a shopping mall, allergic to
        secondhand smoke, becomes seriously ill when a group of
        smoking teens pass by him

     C. Claim, with allusions to underlying warrants, that
        secondhand smoke is hazardous enough to justify banning
        smoking from all public places

 II. Data in support of the claim

     A. Scientific data from ACS, ALA, and AMA + discussion of data

     B. Testimonial data from physicians + discussion

III. Deeper considerations (warrants and backing) behind the
     claim
```

[*Note:* This discussion would approximate refutation in the classical model but would give more emphasis to a shared value system with the audience.]

```
 IV. Concluding remarks
```

◎/◉ Exercise 4.2

1. For each of the following claims, suggest at least one qualifier, two kinds of evidence, and one warrant for which you may also discover backing. Also suggest a counterclaim with counterdata and a counter-warrant for each.

   a. Our mayor should be removed from office because we just learned that he was once arrested for possession of marijuana.

   b. Any novel that includes the use of racial slurs should be banned from public school classrooms.

   c. Beef in restaurants should be prepared well done regardless of customer preference because of the danger of *E. coli* infection.

2. Work up two versions of an outline for an essay on improving conditions where you live. Use the Classical model to structure the first outline and the Toulmin model to structure the second. Which of the two outlines would you use as the basis for the paper, and why?

3. Rewrite each of the following claims by using more specific terms or references. *Example:* UFO sightings are a bunch of nonsense. *Rewrite:* UFO sightings are difficult to document because trick photography is easy to accomplish.

   a. Books are an environmental problem.

   b. Cats make better pets than dogs.

   c. Students should be admitted to college on the basis of merit only.

4. Suggest one or two possible warrants for each of the following claims:

   a. All college students should be required to take at least one course in economics.

   b. More college courses should be conducted over the Internet.

   c. High school sex education courses are inadequate.

5. Suggest at least one backing for the warrants you proposed in number 4.

 Exercise 4.3

Read Thomas Jefferson's Declaration of Independence and identify its claim, data, warrant, and backing.

Declaration of Independence | Thomas Jefferson

When in the Course of human events, it becomes necessary for one people to dissolve the political bands which have connected them with another, and to assume among the Powers of the earth, the separate and equal station to which the Laws of Nature and of Nature's God entitle them, a decent respect to the opinions of mankind requires that they should declare the causes which impel them to the separation.—We hold these truths to be self-evident, that all men are created equal, that they are endowed by their Creator with certain unalienable Rights, that among these are Life, Liberty and the pursuit of Happiness.—That to secure these rights, Governments are instituted among Men, deriving their just powers from the consent of the governed.—That whenever any Form of Government becomes destructive of these ends, it is the Right of the People to alter or to abolish it, and to institute new Government, laying its foundation on such principles and organizing its powers in such form, as to them shall seem most likely to effect their Safety and Happiness. Prudence, indeed, will dictate that Governments long established should not be changed for light and transient causes; and accordingly all experience hath shewn, that mankind are more disposed to suffer, while evils are sufferable, than to right themselves by abolishing the forms to which they are accustomed. But when a long train of abuses and usurpations, pursing invariably the same Object evinces a design to reduce them under absolute Despotism, it is their right, it is their duty, to throw off such Government, and to provide new Guards for their future security.—Such has been the patient sufferance of these Colonies; and such is now the necessity which constrains them to alter their former Systems of Government. The history of the present King of Great Britain is a history of repeated injuries and usurpations, all having in direct object the establishment of an absolute Tyranny over these States. To prove this, let Facts be submitted to a candid world.—He has refused his Assent to Laws, the most wholesome and necessary for the public good.—He has forbidden his Governors to pass Laws of immediate and pressing importance, unless suspended in their operation till his Assent should be obtained; and when so suspended, he has utterly neglected to attend to them.—He has refused to pass other Laws for the accommodation of large districts of people, unless those people would relinquish the right of Representation in the Legislature, a right inestimable to them and formidable to tyrants only.—He has called together legislative bodies at places unusual, uncomfortable, and distant from the depository of their public Records, for the sole purpose of fatiguing them into compliance with his measures.—He has dissolved Representative Houses repeatedly, for opposing with manly firmness his invasions of the rights of the people.—He has refused for a long time, after such dissolutions, to cause others to be elected; whereby the Legislative powers, incapable of Annihilation, have returned to the People at large for their exercise; the State remaining in the mean time exposed to all the dangers of invasion from without, and convulsions within.—He has endeavoured to prevent the population of these States; for that purpose obstructing the Laws of Naturalization of Foreigners; refusing to pass others to encourage their migrations hither, and raising the conditions of new Appropriations of Lands.—He has obstructed the Administration of Justice, by refusing his Assent to Laws for establishing Judiciary powers.— He has made Judges dependent on his Will alone, for the tenure of their offices, and the amount and payment of their salaries.—He has erected a multitude of New Offices, and sent hither swarms of Officers to harrass our people, and eat out their substance.—He has kept among us, in times of peace, Standing Armies without the Consent of our legislatures.—He has affected to render the Military independent of and superior to the Civil power.—He has combined with others to subject us to a jurisdiction foreign to our constitution, and unacknowledged by our laws; giving his Assent to their Acts of pretended Legislation:—For quartering large bodies of armed troops among us:—For protecting them, by a mock Trial, from punishment for any Murders which they should commit on the Inhabitants of these States:—For cutting off our Trade with all parts of the world:—For imposing Taxes on us without our Consent:—For depriving us in many cases, of the benefits of Trial by Jury:—For transporting us beyond Seas to be tried for pretended offences:—For abolishing the free System of English Laws in a neighbouring Province, establishing therein an Arbitrary government, and enlarging its Boundaries so as to render it at once an example and fit instrument for introducing the same absolute rule into these Colonies:—For taking away our Charters, abolishing our most valuable Laws, and altering fundamentally the Forms of our Governments:—For suspending our own Legislatures, and declaring themselves invested with power to legislate for us in all cases whatsoever.—He has abdicated Government here, by declaring us out of his Protection and waging War against us.—He has plundered our seas, ravaged our Coasts, burnt our towns, and destroyed the Lives of our people.—He is at this time transporting large Armies of foreign Mercenaries to complete the works of death, desolation and tyranny, already begun with circumstances of Cruelty and perfidy scarcely paralleled in the most barbarous ages, and totally unworthy the Head of a civilized nation.— He has constrained our fellow Citizens taken Captive on the high Seas to bear Arms against their Country, to become the executioners of their friends and Brethren, or to fall themselves by their Hands.—He has excited domestic insurrections amongst us, and has endeavoured to bring on the inhabitants of our frontiers, the merciless Indian Savages, whose known rule of warfare, is an undistinguished destruction of all ages, sexes, and conditions. In every stage of these Oppressions We have Petitioned for Redress in the most humble terms: Our repeated Petitions have been answered only by repeated injury. A Prince, whose character is thus marked by every act which may define a Tyrant, is unfit to be the ruler of a free people. Nor have We been wanting in attentions to our British brethren. We have warned them from time to time of attempts by their legislature to extend an unwarrantable jurisdiction over us. We have reminded them of the circumstances of our emigration and settlement here. We have appealed to their native justice and magnanimity, and we have conjured them by the ties of our common kindred to disavow these usurpations, which, would inevitably interrupt our connections and correspondence. They too have been deaf to the voice of justice and of consanguinity. We must, therefore, acquiesce in the necessity, which denounces our Separation, and hold them, as we hold the rest of mankind, Enemies in War, in Peace Friends.—

We, therefore, the Representatives of the *United States of America,* in General Congress, Assembled, appealing to the Supreme Judge of the world for the rectitude of our intentions, do, in the Name, and by Authority of the good People of these Colonies, solemnly publish and declare, That these United Colonies are, and of Right ought to be *Free and Independent States;* that they are Absolved from all Allegiance to the British Crown, and that all political connection between them and the State of Great Britain, is and ought to be totally dissolved; and that as Free and Independent States, they have full Power to levy War, conclude Peace, contract Alliances, establish Commerce, and to do all other Acts and Things which Independent States may of right do.—And for the support of this Declaration, with a firm reliance on the protection of divine Providence, we mutually pledge to each other our Lives, our Fortunes and our sacred Honor. ◎/◎

FIGURE 4.2
_____

Toulmin Model
Flowchart

What *issue* am I going to investigate? [Example: The issue of visual-arts education in U.S. public schools.]

↓

What is my *claim*? [Example: Acquiring basic skills in painting, illustrating, and sculpting is as important as acquiring basic skills in math and reading.]

↓

What *grounds* (data) can I produce that would authenticate my claim? [Example: Testimonials from educational psychologists, from adults whose public-school education consisted of visual-arts training vs. adults whose education did not.]

↓

What underlying *warrant* (ethical validity) underlies my grounds? [Example: Personal testimonials are more reliable than abstract theorizing; give greater emphasis to firsthand experience.]

↓

What *backing* can I give to my warrant? [Example: Firsthand experience provides more compelling grounding because it can demonstrate better than abstract theory the impact of early learning on adult behavior.

↓

In light of challenging views, how will I need to *qualify* my claim, if at all? [Example: We should allow for individual difference in students (some are more analytically minded than others).]

↓

What *concluding reflections* can I give to my argument?

↓

Using the above information, what can I say in my opening paragraph that would best *introduce* my argument and engage my reader's attention?

Chapter Summary

The Toulmin model of argument goes beyond Classical argument in its efforts to bring values to bear on reasoning. Toulmin argument recognizes that logical reasoning, while necessary, is not enough to resolve complex social issues. For that reason, it is especially suitable in courts of law. The Toulmin argumentation method consists of presenting a carefully articulated claim (thesis to be argued). It recognizes that a claim, whether objective (based on scientific or logical issues) or subjective (based on aesthetic, ethical, or moral issues), must be grounded by data—hard facts, statistics, experimental results, valid testimony, and/or logical analysis, depending upon the nature of the claim. The claim must also be tested for possible qualifiers, exceptions to the rule; this is the rebuttal phase of an argument. Perhaps the most distinctive feature of the Toulmin method of argument is that it does not assume the data to be automatically self-justifying. Instead, the data must rest on one or more warrants, trustworthy foundations that give validity to the data. There must also be assurance—through backing—that the warrants themselves are sound.

Checklist

1. Have I stated my claim clearly and accurately enough for public scrutiny, making sure that it is arguable?

2. Have I added one or more qualifiers to my claim, that is, anticipated possible exceptions to it?

3. Have I included the right kinds of data (evidence) appropriate to my claim in order to support it convincingly?

4. Have I ensured that my data are reliable, timely, accurate, and sufficient for demonstrating the validity and truthfulness of my claim?

5. Have I included one or more warrants to validate the trustworthiness of my data?

6. Have I ensured that my warrants, in turn, are valid? In other words, do my warrants have sufficient backing?

Writing Projects

1. Prepare an argumentative essay on a topic of your own or your instructor's choosing that follows the Toulmin model. Include a preliminary synopsis of your argument, divided into five sections: (1) your claim; (2) a qualifier to your claim; (3) your data, subdivided into hard facts and reason-based evidence, both objective and subjective; (4) your warrant, which renders your data trustworthy; (5) your backing, which reinforces and legitimizes the warrant.

2. Write a Toulmin-based argument in which you defend or challenge the view that anyone elected to public office (mayor, governor, secretary of state, president of the United States, and so on) is obliged to live a morally exemplary life. Be sure to define "morally exemplary."

5 | Using the Rogerian Model in Your Arguments

> The relationship which I have found helpful is characterized
> by . . . an acceptance of [the] other person as a separate
> person with value in his own right, and by a deep empathic
> understanding which enables me to see his private world
> through his eyes.
> —Carl Rogers

In the last two chapters we have examined the art of effective argumentation as it has been practiced in Western culture since ancient times. Classical argument continues to function as a versatile basis for presenting and defending a point of view. Toulmin argument has enhanced the dynamics of Classical argument to meet the complexities of contemporary situations, adding, as you'll recall from Chapter 4, an ethical emphasis (by way of warrants and their backing) to the presentation of evidence, an emphasis that is not explicitly included in Classical argument. Toulmin argument also embraces the complexity of a claim: It must often be qualified, even refuted in certain contexts, by the arguer. This last feature might be regarded as a precursor to the method of modern argument we consider in this chapter, Rogerian argument.

Carl Rogers (1902–1987) was a psychologist of the "humanist" school, seeing cooperative interpersonal relationships as the key to a healthy society. As a therapist, Rogers urged self-realization and believed that to function fully as a person in society, one must be open to new experiences. Rigidity of thought and defensiveness breed intolerance. One way such openness is cultivated is through cooperative methods of communication.

The Rogerian Model of Argument

From Rogers's view, the Classical model of argument and even the more flexible Toulmin model tend to divide people into two camps: proponents and opponents, "good guys" versus "bad guys." The traditional language of argument, for example, is filled with militaristic metaphors: We *win* or *lose* arguments rather than resolve them. We *attack* someone's thesis rather than work to build consensus for resolving points of disagreement. We *marshal* evidence as if gathering troops. Even the seemingly neutral term *debate* is of military origin (from *battre*, to do battle). For Rogers, this combative approach to argument does more harm than good; it generates ill will and antagonism between discussants rather than cooperation.

Finding Common Ground

But, you ask, how can people cooperate or interact harmoniously if they hold diametrically opposed views about an issue? Rogers's answer is that you find a common ground and start from there. Returning to the rhetorical rhombus (see Figure 1.2), we see the emphasis here on *audience*. A paper in the Rogerian mode assumes that readers firmly hold differing views and therefore will resist hearing others' positions. Yet no matter how debatable or controversial a view is, one can locate views on the issue that both can agree on. It might take a while to find them, but they are there. Consider the controversy for and against capital punishment, for example:

- Both sides consider human life to be sacred and precious.
- Both sides feel that capital crimes must be deterred as effectively as possible.
- Both sides agree that someone convicted of a capital crime is a threat to society.

The virtue of finding common ground is that one can isolate and resolve the points of opposition more effectively after identifying the points of agreement because one can reduce any hostility the audience has by demonstrating a true understanding of the audience's perspective.

The Rogerian model modifies the Classical model by emphasizing common ground (points of agreement) *before* calling attention to points of disagreement. The writer's goal is not to win or to prove wrong; it is to work together cooperatively to arrive at an agreed-on truth. From its opening sentence, a Rogerian argument communicates a desire for harmonious interaction rather than combative opposition.

I. Introduction: What is our shared problem? Let's see if we can work together to resolve it.

II. What we agree on.

III. Where we differ: misunderstandings, such as drawbacks or limited application to others' solutions, and the possible reasons behind these drawbacks or limitations.

IV. Possible drawbacks or limitations to writers' solutions, followed by greater benefits of writers' solutions.

V. How we can resolve our differences; or, an exhortation to resolving differences together.

Carl Rogers (1902–1987) was known for his "humanist" client-centered approach to therapy. He advocated nonthreatening methods of interpersonal communication.

Developing Multiple Perspectives

Rogerian persuasion requires writers to work hard at developing multiple perspectives toward issues. You must be tolerant and respectful enough of differing viewpoints to take the time to fathom the value systems that underlie them. The first step toward achieving this goal, according to Rogers, is deceptively simple: It is *to listen with understanding.*

Listening with understanding is a skill that takes time to develop. You may think you are listening with understanding when you permit challengers to speak their minds, but you may be only allowing them their say rather than genuinely paying close attention to what they are telling you.

Here are some suggestions for listening with understanding, in Rogers's sense of the phrase, that also can be applied to reading with understanding:

- Be as attentive as possible. Assume that the speaker's remarks have value.

- Suspend your own judgments while listening, keeping an open mind so as not to run the risk of prematurely judging the speaker's views before you have the chance to consider them carefully.

- If anything is unclear to you or you find yourself disagreeing with anything, ask questions—but only after the person has finished speaking.

- Try to see the speaker's claims in terms of his or her warrants (underlying values or ideology on which the claims are based). One better understands and appreciates a speaker's position if one is aware of these warrants.

- Think of ways in which the speaker's point of view and your own can somehow work together, despite seeming contradictory. Even if you oppose capital punishment and the speaker supports it, both of you could approach a common ground by thinking of extreme situations on either side that would discourage an inflexible stance.

Using Rogerian argument in conversation is one thing; using it in writing is another. When writing, you do not have your audience in front of you to give you immediate feedback. Instead you have to anticipate questions and counter-responses that challengers would have for you (in other words, automatically consider the needs of your audience). By considering the audience's needs and values and the merits of their beliefs, you will be more inclined to take a cooperative stance rather than a defensive or combative one.

Arguing cooperatively also means including in your Rogerian essay specific instances in which the differing views are logically sound. That way, you show yourself to have listened well to those perspectives. This in turn prepares your audience for listening more carefully and sympathetically to *your* side of things. You also demonstrate your awareness of the limitations to your proposal—no position is perfect, after all—even while you show how your position works in more varied or complex or more frequent occurrences of the common problem. You and your audience both become receptive to "give and take."

Organizing Your Argument Using the Rogerian Model

To write an argument based on the Rogerian ideals of cooperation, find common ground with your audience regardless of their views about your claim. You need to become especially sensitive to attitudes and values other than your own. You should focus on the *issue* and the best way to resolve it, not on "winning" the argument over your "opposition."

As with the Classical and Toulmin models, begin thinking about your essay with questions about your audience, the similarities between your views and your audience's (insofar as you are aware of them), and the points at which you differ most, along with possible strategies for resolving those differences.

Consider these questions:

1. Can I be objective enough to represent views and evaluate evidence fairly?

2. How much sense do the points of difference make? Do they make more sense than some of my views? If so, do I have the courage to adopt them, or at least modify them to accommodate my views?

3. Am I genuinely interested in establishing a common ground with my audience? What else can I include that could better facilitate this goal?

When constructing an outline for a Rogerian argument, think in terms of thesis, support of thesis, and concluding judgments based on that support—just as you do when using the Classical and Toulmin models. But with the Rogerian model, you are more concerned with establishing common ground with readers who otherwise would reject the thesis. Here is how an argument using the Rogerian approach might take shape:

I. Introduction to the problem

   A. First scenario: A vignette that illustrates the problem, for example

   B. Second scenario: Another vignette that illustrates the problem, but one with greater complexity that some solutions wouldn't handle well

   C. Thesis

II. Alternative views worth sharing with the target audience, and why these views are worth considering

III. Points of difference, along with reflection on how to resolve them

IV. Conclusion: The implications of finding a solution in light of the evidence presented, that would benefit everyone, plus discussion of the great benefits derived from the solution that all audience members would most likely find to their liking

◎/◎   Exercise 5.1

Read the following essay in which the author uses the Rogerian method to tackle the difficult issue of sexual harassment in the early teen years. Then answer the questions that follow.

Let's Talk About Sexual Harassment in Middle School | Kimberly Shearer Palmer

Like every new employee at the *Washington Post*, I was given a "Codes of Conduct" packet—the company's policies on everything from smoking to taking medical leave.[1] It was the section on sexual harassment that startled me most. Perhaps it shouldn't have. But the prohibition against vulgar jokes and "brushing up against another's body" brought home to me the stark contrast between the informal codes of conduct my friends and I had learned to live by in middle school and what's permissible in the working world today.

Source: Kimberly Shearer Palmer, "Let's Talk About Sexual Harassment in Middle School," *Social Education*, May–June 2003, p. M2. © National Council for the Social Studies. Reprinted by permission.

The situations are very different, of course: There aren't the same sort of power relationships in school that make harassment such a complex problem in the working world. But, looking back, I'm still left wondering why so many teenagers I knew put up with unwelcome sexual behavior. And why adults consistently turned a blind eye. Twelve years ago, when I was in middle school, overt sexual advances were everyday events and usually overlooked by teachers. Boys grabbed girls' breasts in the stairwells and cafeteria as casually as they would say "hello," and our daily routines were punctuated by unwelcome slaps on the behind.

The shared sex-harassment problems children in grades 8–11 have faced

As it turns out, my experience wasn't unusual. According to the American Association of University Women, 65 percent of girls in public school, grades eight to eleven, say they experience "touching, grabbing, and/or pinching in a sexual way."[2] My friends and I used to let boys touch, grab, and pinch us, and I don't think things have gotten all that much better. Sure, there's greater awareness: today, the districts have a sexual harassment policy that schools rely on and teachers can refer to. But the issue doesn't always reach administrators, much less the students. My recent conversations with today's teenagers suggest that it wasn't just my grade; it wasn't just my school; and it wasn't just back then. Many kids think—as my friends and I did—that the unwanted touching is just flirtation.

I have since learned to fight back when men harass me. In Paris a few years ago, when a guy grabbed my breasts, I shoved him away from me and yelled at him. After that, he left me alone. Now, when I think back to all the times in middle school when I didn't make guys leave me alone, I feel angry. So I decided to go back and find boys from my class and ask them why. I got out my old phone directory and called the same boys who would have been too cool for me to call in middle school. Most had moved, and the listed numbers were no longer valid. The ones I found shared my memories of unwanted touching in the hallways. They are, as far as I can tell, good boyfriend material. They are by all accounts sensitive and perceptive; my younger sister knows one well, and my close friend at college dated another. I found out they were just as confused as we girls were in those adolescent years.

What we both agreed on: the touching and grabbing behavior

One old classmate remembers the casual touching. "Even good guys did that," he said. "It wasn't sexual. . . . I don't know what it was. I can't think it's a good thing." He also recalled walking girls to class because they felt threatened. We didn't speak in terms of apologies, but wonderment. It seemed so very strange

that touching someone's breasts or bottom in the hallways was   5
considered friendly behavior. Another one of my classmates told
me that he remembered the same sorts of things. "Not until tenth
grade would guys . . . realize it was not the best way to get a girl
to like you," he said. Grabbing girls was normal behavior, we
both agreed. It happened in public, in front of teachers. No one
told us it was wrong. No one even seemed worried about the
possibility of lawsuits, despite the 1992 Supreme Court decision
that warned schools they could be held responsible for harassment.[3] Maybe the teachers looked at our sometimes giggly and
embarrassed reactions and thought there wouldn't be a problem.

Basis for the
misunderstandings   One male graduate told me that boys bothered girls back
then because they didn't know what else to do. "No one
knows how to act [at that age]. . . . You're self-conscious, no
one has self-esteem." Boys, I realized, were just as insecure
as I remember feeling. We were blindly following what we
assumed was routine social conduct—grabbing, pinching,
being pinched. Who knew there was another way to flirt?
Boys, he told me, were just trying to bridge the gap between
girls and guys. "It wasn't meant to hurt," he said.

Looking back now, he knows that what some boys did probably bothered some girls. But the girls didn't show it. "They
probably didn't want to seem snobby or stuck up," he remembered. As I spoke to these men, I realized how different they
were from the guy who bothered me in Paris. The rules were so
blurry to both girls and boys in middle school that neither gender really knew when lines were crossed. For example, when my
crotch was grabbed on a school bus one afternoon, it wasn't okay
with me, but I didn't even tell my parents because at some level
it seemed so similar to what happened every day in school. I still
feel mad, but I could hardly blame my former classmates when
they were just acting out of friendship or flirtation—however
misguided that was. And the more I talked with my female
friends, the more I realized how often we gave the wrong signals.
Some girls remembered enjoying the attention, sometimes laughing along. One recalled two boys dragging her into the boys'
bathroom, as she tried to kick her way free. But she didn't
remember being angry. "It was the only way to express ourselves," she now says. But something else gave her further pause.
She said she thought that "teachers let it slide" like the other
dumb behavior that happens among adolescents.

Fault lay with the
teachers who avoided
dealing with the
problem.   They shouldn't have. I remember only one teacher who
stood in the front of her class and yelled at the boys for grabbing girls. Finally a teacher noticed, I remember thinking.

Why was she the only one? And if the teacher noticed, why didn't she inform the principal, and start a school-wide discussion? My annoyance with my former classmates redirected itself as I realized that adults who could have explained and enforced the differences between right and wrong behavior—our teachers—often did not. The fact is, no one taught us the right way to act. But as Peggy Orenstein, author of *Schoolgirls: Young Women, Self-Esteem, and the Confidence Gap,* says, "It still must stop."[4] For me, it stopped as soon as I emerged from the achingly self-conscious early teenage years. Assertiveness came from the natural confidence that comes with getting rid of braces and glasses.

And yet, would early lessons have done much good?

Shouldn't we have been helped to learn those lessons earlier? An insecure seventh-grade girl shouldn't have to deal with aggressive boys grabbing her. But I keep asking myself: What would I have wanted my parents to tell me? What could they have possibly told me? "Don't let boys touch you"? "Tell me if anyone's bothering you"? I'm sure they told me those things. I'm sure I dismissed them, way too embarrassed to talk to them about anything dealing with boy-girl relationships. How can you help a shy seventh-grade girl who doesn't even know whether to feel grateful for the attention or angry at the violation?

Admission that solutions are difficult

There are no easy solutions. Zero-tolerance policies make no 10 sense, considering the level of confusion surrounding social behavior. Parents can try to teach their daughters to be tough; teachers can integrate into class discussions of what distinguishes flirtation from harassment. There's plenty of inspiration, in anything from the writings of Shakespeare to Maya Angelou, as Wellesley College sexual harassment scholar Nan Stein suggests in *Flirting or Hurting? A Teacher's Guide on Student-to-Student Sexual Harassment in Schools.*[5] And adults can talk to boys about limits.

Yet one thing remains clear

The fact is, my former classmates did not turn into bad men. They don't bother women at work or college. And the women I knew in school have also learned where to draw the line. But we should all have learned the rules earlier, well before it comes time to sign those company policies. ◎/◎

Notes

1. This essay first appeared in the *Washington Post* on August 20, 2000. Reprinted by permission.

2. American Association of University Women, *Hostile Hallways: Bullying, Teasing, and Sexual Harassment in School* (Washington: AAUW, 2001).

3. Office of Civil Rights, "Revised Sexual Harassment Guidance" (Washington: U.S. Department of Education, 2001), http://www.ed.gov/offices//OCR/shguide/index.html.

4. Peggy Orenstein, *Schoolgirls: Young Women, Self-Esteem, and the Confidence Gap* (Landover Hills: Anchor, 1995).

5. Nan Stein, *Flirting or Hurting? A Teacher's Guide on Student-to-Student Sexual Harassment in Schools* (Washington: National Education Association, 1994).

1. What rhetorical devices—phrases, words, tone, details—suggest that Palmer is using the Rogerian method of argument?

2. What is most Rogerian about Palmer's approach to her topic? Least Rogerian?

3. Briefly, what is Palmer's position on the matter of sexual harassment in middle school?

4. Critics sometimes say that Rogerian argument is "wishy-washy." Is Palmer being wishy-washy about her middle school experiences with sexual harassment? Why or why not?

5. What, if anything, would you suggest to Palmer to strengthen her argument?

◎/◎   **Exercise 5.2**

In April 1963, Martin Luther King, Jr. was sentenced to a week in jail because of his antisegregationist campaign in Birmingham, Alabama. While in jail, Dr. King wrote the following letter defending his activities to eight members of the Birmingham clergy. As you read this masterpiece of persuasive writing, notice how King makes a concerted effort to seek common ground with his audience and to avoid the "good guys" versus "bad guys" combative stance. Look for specific points of emphasis and specific explanations that make his stance Rogerian. After reading, answer the questions that follow.

Letter from Birmingham Jail | Martin Luther King, Jr.

APRIL 16, 1963

My Dear Fellow Clergymen:
    While confined here in the Birmingham city jail, I came across your recent statement calling my present activities "unwise and untimely."[1] Seldom do I pause to answer criticism of my work and ideas. If I sought to answer all the criticisms that cross my desk, my secretaries would have little time for anything other than such correspondence in the course of the day, and I would have no time for constructive work. But since I feel that you are men of genuine good will and that your criticisms are sincerely set forth, I want to try to answer your statement in what I hope will be patient and reasonable terms.

    I think I should indicate why I am here in Birmingham, since you have been influenced by the view which argues against "outsiders coming in." I have the honor of serving as president of the Southern Christian Leadership Conference, an organization operating in every southern state, with headquarters in Atlanta, Georgia. We have some eighty-five affiliated organizations across the South, and one of them is the Alabama Christian Movement for Human Rights. Frequently we share staff, educational, and financial resources with our affiliates. Several months ago the affiliate here in Birmingham asked us to be on call to engage in a nonviolent direct-action program if such were deemed necessary. We readily consented, and when the hour came we lived up to our promise. So I, along with several members of my staff, am here because I was invited here. I am here because I have organizational ties here.

    But more basically, I am in Birmingham because injustice is here. Just as the prophets of the eighth century B.C. left their villages and carried their "thus saith the Lord" far beyond the boundaries of their home towns, and just as the Apostle Paul left his village of Tarsus and carried the gospel of Jesus Christ to the far corners of the Greco-Roman world, so am I compelled to carry the gospel of freedom beyond my own home town. Like Paul, I must constantly respond to the Macedonian call for aid.

    Moreover, I am cognizant of the interrelatedness of all communities and states. I cannot sit idly by in Atlanta and not be concerned about what happens in Birmingham. Injustice anywhere is a threat to justice everywhere. We are caught in an inescapable network of mutuality; tied in a single garment of detiny. Whatever affects one directly, affects all indirectly. Never again can we afford to live with the narrow, provincial "outside agitator"

Source: Martin Luther King Jr., "Letter from Birmingham Jail," April 16, 1963. Reprinted by arrangement with the Estate of Martin Luther King Jr., c/o Writers House as agent for the proprietor, New York, NY. Copyright 1963 Martin Luther King Jr., copyright renewed 1991 Coretta Scott King.

idea. Anyone who lives inside the United States can never be considered an outsider anywhere within its bounds.

You deplore the demonstrations taking place in Birmingham. But your statement, I am sorry to say, fails to express a similar concern for the conditions that brought about the demonstrations. I am sure that none of you would want to rest content with the superficial kind of social analysis that deals merely with effects and does not grapple with underlying causes. It is unfortunate that demonstrations are taking place in Birmingham, but it is even more unfortunate that the city's white power structure left the Negro community with no alternative.

In any nonviolent campaign there are four basic steps: collection of the facts to determine whether injustices exist; negotiation; self-purification; and direct action. We have gone through all these steps in Birmingham. There can be no gainsaying the fact that racial injustice engulfs this community. Birmingham is probably the most thoroughly segregated city in the United States. Its ugly record of brutality is widely known. Negroes have experienced grossly unjust treatment in the courts. There have been more unsolved bombings of Negro homes and churches in Birmingham than in any other city in the nation. These are the hard, brutal facts of the case. On the basis of these conditions, Negro leaders sought to negotiate with the city fathers. But the latter consistently refused to engage in good-faith negotiation.

Then, last September, came the opportunity to talk with leaders of Birmingham's economic community. In the course of the negotiations, certain promises were made by the merchants—for example, to remove the stores' humiliating racial signs. On the basis of these promises, the Reverend Fred Shuttlesworth and the leaders of the Alabama Christian Movement for Human Rights agreed to a moratorium on all demonstrations. As the weeks and months went by, we realized that we were the victims of a broken promise. A few signs, briefly removed, returned; the others remained.

As in so many past experiences, our hopes had been blasted, and the shadow of deep disappointment settled upon us. We had no alternative except to prepare for direct action, whereby we would present our very bodies as a means of laying our case before the conscience of the local and the national community. Mindful of the difficulties involved, we decided to undertake a process of self-purification. We began a series of workshops on nonviolence, and we repeatedly asked ourselves: "Are you able to accept blows without retaliating?" "Are you able to endure the ordeal of jail?" We decided to schedule our direct-action program for the Easter season, realizing that except for Christmas, this is the main shopping period of the year. Knowing that a strong economic-withdrawal program would be the by-product of direct action, we felt that this would be the best time to bring pressure to bear on the merchants for the needed change.

Then it occurred to us that Birmingham's mayoralty election was coming up in March, and we speedily decided to postpone action until after election day. When we discovered that the Commissioner of Public Safety, Eugene "Bull" Conner, had piled up enough votes to be in the run-off, we decided again to postpone action until the day after the run-off so that the demonstrations could not be used to cloud the issues. Like many others, we waited to see Mr. Conner defeated, and to this end we endured postponement after postponement. Having aided in this community need, we felt that our direct-action program could be delayed no longer.

You may well ask: "Why direct action? Why sit-ins, marches, and so forth? Isn't negotiation a better path?" You are quite right in calling for negotiation. Indeed, this is the very purpose of direct action. Nonviolent direct action seeks to create such a crisis and foster such a tension that a community which has constantly refused to negotiate is forced to confront the issue. It seeks so to dramatize the issue that it can no longer be ignored. My citing the creation of tension as part of the work of the nonviolent-resister may sound rather shocking. But I must confess that I am not afraid of the word "tension." I have earnestly opposed violent tension, but there is a type of constructive, nonviolent tension which is necessary for growth. Just as Socrates felt that it was necessary to create a tension in the mind so that individuals could rise from the bondage of myths and half-truths to the unfettered realm of creative analysis and objective appraisal, so must we see the need for nonviolent gadflies to create the kind of tension in society that will help men rise from the dark depths of prejudice and racism to the majestic heights of understanding and brotherhood.

The purpose of our direct-action program is to create a situation so crisis-packed that it will inevitably open the door to negotiation. I therefore concur with you in your call for negotiation. Too long has our beloved Southland been bogged down in a tragic effort to live in monologue rather than dialogue.

One of the basic points in your statement is that the action that I and my associates have taken in Birmingham is untimely. Some have asked: "Why didn't you give the new city administration time to act?" The only answer that I can give to this query is that the new Birmingham administration must be prodded about as much as the outgoing one, before it will act. We are sadly mistaken if we feel that the election of Albert Boutwell as mayor will bring the millennium to Birmingham. While Mr. Boutwell is a much more gentle person than Mr. Connor, they are both segregationists, dedicated to maintenance of the status quo. I have hope that Mr. Boutwell will be reasonable enough to see the futility of massive resistance to desegregation. But he will not see this without pressure from devotees of civil rights. My friends, I must say to you that we have not made a single gain in civil rights without determined legal and nonviolent pressure. Lamentably, it is an historical fact that privileged groups seldom give up their privileges voluntarily. Individuals may see the moral light and voluntarily give up their unjust posture; but as Reinhold Niebuhr[2] has reminded us, groups tend to be more immoral than individuals.

We know through painful experience that freedom is never voluntarily given by the oppressor; it must be demanded by the oppressed. Frankly, I have yet to engage in a direct-action campaign that was "well timed" in the view of those who have not suffered unduly from the disease of segregation. For years now I have heard the word "Wait!" It rings in the ear of every Negro with piercing familiarity. This "Wait" has almost always meant "Never." We must come to see, with one of our distinguished jurists, that "justice too long delayed is justice denied."[3]

We have waited for more than 340 years for our constitutional and God-given rights. The nations of Asia and Africa are moving with jetlike speed toward gaining political independence, but we still creep at horse-and-buggy pace toward gaining a cup of coffee at a lunch counter. Perhaps it is easy for those who have never felt the stinging darts of segregation to say, "Wait." But when you have seen vicious mobs lynch your mothers and fathers at will and drown your sisters and brothers at whim; when you have seen hate-filled policemen curse, kick, and even kill your black brothers and sisters; when you see the vast majority of your twenty million Negro brothers smothering in an airtight cage of poverty in the midst of an affluent society; when you suddenly find your tongue twisted and your speech stammering as you seek to explain to your six-year-old daughter why she can't go to the public amusement park that has just been advertised on television, and see tears welling up in her eyes when she is told that Funtown is closed to colored children, and see ominous clouds of inferiority beginning to form in her little mental sky, and see her beginning to distort her personality by developing an unconscious bitterness toward white people; when you have to concoct an answer for a five-year-old son who is asking: "Daddy, why do white people treat colored people so mean?"; when you take a cross-country drive and find it necessary to sleep night after night in the uncomfortable corners of your automobile because no motel will accept you; when you are humiliated day in and day out by nagging signs reading "white" and "colored"; when your first name becomes "nigger," your middle name becomes "boy" (however old you are) and your last name becomes "John," and your wife and mother are never given the respected title "Mrs."; when you are harried by day and haunted by night by the fact that you are a Negro, living constantly at tiptoe stance, never quite knowing what to expect next, and are plagued with inner fears and outer resentments; when you are forever fighting a degenerating sense of "nobodiness"—then you will understand why we find it difficult to wait. There comes a time when the cup of endurance runs over, and men are no longer willing to be plunged into the abyss of despair. I hope, sirs, you can understand our legitimate and unavoidable impatience.

You express a great deal of anxiety over our willingness to break laws.   15
This is certainly a legitimate concern. Since we so diligently urge people to obey the Supreme Court's decision of 1954 outlawing segregation in the public schools, at first glance it may seem rather paradoxical for us

consciously to break laws. One may well ask: "How can you advocate breaking some laws and obeying others?" The answer lies in the fact that there are two types of laws: just and unjust. I would be the first to advocate to obey just laws. One has not only a legal but a moral responsibility to obey just laws. Conversely, one has a moral responsibility to disobey unjust laws. I would agree with St. Augustine that "an unjust law is no law at all."

Now, what is the difference between the two? How does one determine whether a law is just or unjust? A just law is a man-made code that squares with the moral law or the law of God. An unjust law is a code that is out of harmony with the moral law. To put it in the terms of St. Thomas Aquinas: An unjust law is a human law that is not rooted in eternal law and natural law. Any law that uplifts human personality is just. Any law that degrades human personality is unjust. All segregation statutes are unjust because segregation distorts the soul and damages the personality. It give the segregator a false sense of superiority and the segregated a false sense of inferiority. Segregation, to use the terminology of the Jewish philosopher Martin Buber, substitutes an "I-it" relationship for an "I-thou" relationship and ends up relegating persons to the status of things. Hence segregation is not only politically, economically, and sociologically unsound, it is morally wrong and sinful. Paul Tillich[4] has said that sin is separation. Is not segregation an existential expression of man's tragic separation, his awful estrangement, his terrible sinfulness? Thus it is that I can urge men to obey the 1954 decision of the Supreme Court, for it is morally right; and I can urge them to disobey segregation ordinances, for they are morally wrong.

Let us consider a more concrete example of just and unjust laws. An unjust law is a code that a numerical or power majority group compels a minority group to obey but does not make binding on itself. This is *difference* made legal. By the same token, a just law is a code that a majority compels a minority to follow and that it is willing to follow itself. This is *sameness* made legal.

Let me give another explanation. A law is unjust if it is inflicted on a minority that, as a result of being denied the right to vote, had no part in enacting or devising the law. Who can say that the legislature of Alabama which set up that state's segregation laws was democratically elected? Throughout Alabama all sorts of devious methods are used to prevent Negroes from becoming registered voters, and there are some counties in which, even though Negroes constitute a majority of the population, not a single Negro is registered. Can any law enacted under such circumstances be considered democratically structured?

Sometimes a law is just on its face and unjust in its application. For instance, I have been arrested on a charge of parading without a permit. Now, there is nothing wrong in having an ordinance which requires a permit for a parade. But such an ordinance becomes unjust when it is used to maintain segregation and to deny citizens the First Amendment privilege of peaceful assembly and protest.

I hope you are able to see the distinction I am trying to point out. In no   20
sense do I advocate evading or defying the law, as would the rabid segre-
gationist. That would lead to anarchy. One who breaks an unjust law must
do so openly, lovingly, and with a willingness to accept the penalty. I submit that an individual who breaks a law that conscience tells him is unjust,
and who willingly accepts the penalty of imprisonment in order to arouse
the conscience of the community over its injustice, is in reality expressing
the highest respect for law.

Of course, there is nothing new about this kind of civil disobedience. It was
evidenced sublimely in the refusal of Shadrach, Meshach, and Abednego to
obey the laws of Nebuchadnezzar, on the ground that a higher moral law was
at stake. It was practiced superbly by the early Christians, who were willing to
face hungry lions and the excruciating pain of chopping blocks rather than submit to certain unjust laws of the Roman Empire. To a degree, academic freedom
is a reality today because Socrates practiced civil disobedience. In our own
nation, the Boston Tea Party represented a massive act of civil disobedience.

We should never forget that everything Adolf Hitler did in Germany
was "legal" and everything the Hungarian freedom fighters did in Hungary
was "illegal." It was "illegal" to aid and comfort a Jew in Hitler's Germany.
Even so, I am sure that, had I lived in Germany at the time, I would have
aided and comforted my Jewish brothers. If today I lived in a Communist
country where certain principles dear to the Christian faith are suppressed, I
would openly advocate disobeying that country's anti-religious laws.

I must make two honest confessions to you, my Christian and Jewish
brothers. First, I must confess that over the past few years I have been gravely
disappointed with the white moderate. I have almost reached the regrettable
conclusion that the Negro's great stumbling block in his stride toward
freedom is not the White Citizen's Counciler or the Ku Klux Klanner, but the
white moderate, who is more devoted to "order" than to justice; who prefers
a negative peace which is the absence of tension to a positive peace which is
the presence of justice; who constantly says: "I agree with you in the goal you
seek, but I cannot agree with your methods or direct action"; who paternalis-
tically believes he can set the timetable for another man's freedom; who lives
by a mythical concept of time and who constantly advises the Negro to wait
for a "more convenient season." Shallow understanding from people of good
will is more frustrating than absolute misunderstanding from people of ill
will. Lukewarm acceptance is much more bewildering than outright rejection.

I had hoped that the white moderate would understand that law and
order exist for the purpose of establishing justice and that when they fail in
this purpose they become the dangerously structured dams that block the
flow of social progress. I had hoped that the white moderate would understand that the present tension in the South is a necessary phase of the transition from an obnoxious negative peace, in which the Negro passively
accepted his unjust plight, to a substantive and positive peace, in which all
men will respect the dignity and worth of human personality. Actually, we

who engage in nonviolent direct action are not the creators of tension. We merely bring to the surface the hidden tension that is already alive. We bring it out in the open, where it can be seen and dealt with. Like a boil that can never be cured so long as it is covered up but must be opened with all its ugliness to the natural medicines of air and light, injustice must be exposed, with all the tension its exposure creates, to the light of human conscience and the air of national opinion before it can be cured.

In your statement you assert that our actions, even though peaceful, must be condemned because they precipitate violence. But is this a logical assertion? Isn't this like condemning a robbed man because his possession of money precipitated the evil act of robbery? Isn't this like condemning Socrates because his unswerving commitment to truth and his philosophical inquiries precipitated the act by the misguided populace in which they made him drink hemlock? Isn't this like condemning Jesus because his unique God-consciousness and never-ceasing devotion to God's will precipitated the evil act of crucifixion? We must come to see that, as the federal courts have consistently affirmed, it is wrong to urge an individual to cease his efforts to gain his basic constitutional rights because the quest may precipitate violence. Society must protect the robbed and punish the robber.

I had also hoped that the white moderate would reject the myth concerning time in relation to the struggle for freedom. I have just received a letter from a white brother in Texas. He writes: "All Christians know that the colored people will receive equal rights eventually, but it is possible that you are in too great a religious hurry. It has taken Christianity almost two thousand years to accomplish what it has. The teachings of Christ take time to come to earth." Such an attitude stems from a tragic misconception of time, from the strangely irrational notion that there is something in the very flow of time that will inevitably cure all ills. Actually, time itself is neutral; it can be used either destructively or constructively. More and more I feel that the people of ill will have used time much more effectively than have the people of good will. We will have to repent in this generation not merely for the hateful words and actions of the bad people but for the appalling silence of the good people. Human progress never rolls in on wheels of inevitability; it comes through the tireless efforts of men willing to be co-workers with God, and without this hard work, time itself becomes an ally of the forces of social stagnation. We must use time creatively, in the knowledge that the time is always ripe to do right. Now is the time to make real the promise of democracy and transform our pending national elegy into a creative psalm of brotherhood. Now is the time to lift our national policy from the quicksand of racial injustice to the solid rock of human dignity.

You speak of our activity in Birmingham as extreme. At first I was rather disappointed that fellow clergymen would see my nonviolent efforts as those of an extremist. I began thinking about the fact that I stand in the middle of two opposing forces in the Negro community. One is a force of complacency, made up in part of Negroes who, as a result of long years of oppression, are so drained of self-respect and a sense of "somebodiness" that they have adjusted to segregation; and in part of a few middle-class Negroes who, because of a degree of academic and economic security and because in some ways they profit by segregation, have become insensitive to the problems of the masses. The other force is one of bitterness and hatred, and it comes perilously close to advocating violence. It is expressed in the various black nationalist groups that are springing up across the nation, the largest and best-known being Elijah Muhammad's Muslim movement. Nourished by the Negro's frustration over the continued existence of racial discrimination, this movement is made up of people who have lost faith in America, who have absolutely repudiated Christianity, and who have concluded that the white man is an incorrigible "devil."

I have tried to stand between these two forces, saying that we need emulate neither the "do-nothingism" of the complacent nor the hatred and despair of the black nationalist. For there is the more excellent way of love and nonviolent protest. I am grateful to God that, through the influence of the Negro church, the way of nonviolence became an integral part of our struggle.

If this philosophy had not emerged, by now many streets of the South should, I am convinced, be flowing with blood. And I am further convinced that if our white brothers dismiss as "rabble-rousers" and "outside agitators" those of us who employ nonviolent direct action, and if they refuse to support our nonviolent efforts, millions of Negroes will, out of frustration and despair, seek solace and security in black-nationalist ideologies—a development that would inevitably lead to a frightening racial nightmare.

Oppressed people cannot remain oppressed forever. The yearning for   30
freedom eventually manifests itself, and that is what has happened to the American Negro. Something within has reminded him of his birthright of freedom, and something without has reminded him that it can be gained. Consciously or unconsciously, he has been caught up by the *Zeitgeist*,[5] and with his black brothers of Africa and his brown and yellow brothers of Asia, South America, and the Caribbean, the United States Negro is moving with a sense of great urgency toward the promised land of racial justice. If one recognizes this vital urge that has engulfed the Negro community, one should readily understand why public demonstrations are taking place. The Negro has many pent-up resentments and latent frustrations, and he must release them. So let him march; let him make prayer pilgrimages to the city hall; let him go on freedom rides—and try to understand why he must do so. If his repressed emotions are not released in nonviolent ways, they will seek expression through violence; this is not a threat but a fact of history. So I have not said to my people: "Get rid of your discontent." Rather, I have tried to say that this

normal and healthy discontent can be channeled into the creative outlet of nonviolent direct action. And now this approach is being termed extremist.

But though I was initially disappointed at being categorized as an extremist, as I continued to think about the matter I gradually gained a measure of satisfaction from the label. Was not Jesus an extremist for love: "Love your enemies, bless them that curse you, do good to them that hate you, and pray for them which despitefully use you, and persecute you." Was not Amos an extremist for justice: "Let justice roll down like waters and righteousness like an ever-flowing stream." Was not Paul an extremist for the Christian gospel: "I bear in my body the marks of the Lord Jesus." Was not Martin Luther an extremist: "Here I stand; I cannot do otherwise, so help me God." And John Bunyan: "I will stay in jail to the end of my days before I make a butchery of my conscience." And Abraham Lincoln: "This nation cannot survive half slave and half free." And Thomas Jefferson: "We hold these truths to be self-evident, that all men are created equal. . . ." So the question is not whether we will be extremists, but what kind of extremists we will be. Will we be extremists for hate or for love? Will we be extremists for the preservation of injustice or for the extension of justice? In that dramatic scene on Calvary's hill three men were crucified. We must never forget that all three were crucified for the same crime—the crime of extremism. Two were extremists for immorality, and thus fell below their environment. The other, Jesus Christ, was an extremist for love, truth, and goodness, and thereby rose above his environment. Perhaps the South, the nation, and the world are in dire need of creative extremists.

I had hoped that the white moderate would see this need. Perhaps I was too optimistic; perhaps I expected too much. I suppose I should have realized that few members of the oppressor race can understand the deep groans and passionate yearnings of the oppressed race, and still fewer have the vision to see that injustice must be rooted out by strong, persistent, and determined action. I am thankful, however, that some of our white brothers in the South have grasped the meaning of this social revolution and committed themselves to it. They are still all too few in quantity, but they are big in quality. Some—such as Ralph McGill, Lillian Smith, Harry Golden, James McBride Dabbs, Ann Braden, and Sarah Patton Boyle—have written about our struggle in eloquent and prophetic terms. Others have marched with us down nameless streets of the South. They have languished in filthy, roach-infested jails, suffering the abuse and brutality of policemen who view them as "dirty nigger-lovers." Unlike so many of their moderate brothers and sisters, they have recognized the urgency of the moment and sensed the need for powerful "action" antidotes to combat the disease of segregation.

Let me take note of my other major disappointment. I have been so greatly disappointed with the white church and its leadership. Of course, there are some notable exceptions. I am not unmindful of the fact that each of you has taken some significant stands on this issue. I commend you, Reverend

Stallings, for your Christian stand on this past Sunday, in welcoming Negroes to your worship service on a nonsegregated basis. I commend the Catholic leaders of this state for integrating Spring Hill College several years ago.

But despite these notable exceptions, I must honestly reiterate that I have been disappointed with the church. I do not say this as one of those negative critics who can always find something wrong with the church. I say this as a minister of the gospel, who loves the church; who was nurtured in its bosom; who has been sustained by its spiritual blessings and who will remain true to it as long as the cord of life shall lengthen.

When I was suddenly catapulted into the leadership of the bus protest in   35
Montgomery, Alabama, a few years ago, I felt we would be supported by the white church. I felt that the white ministers, priests, and rabbis of the South would be among our strongest allies. Instead, some have been outright opponents, refusing to understand the freedom movement and misrepresenting its leaders; all too many others have been more cautious than courageous and have remained silent behind the anesthetizing security of stained-glass windows.

In spite of my shattered dreams, I came to Birmingham with the hope that the white religious leadership of this community would see the justice of our cause and, with deep moral concern, would serve as the channel through which our just grievances could reach the power structure. I had hoped that each of you would understand. But again I have been disappointed.

I have heard numerous southern religious leaders admonish their worshipers to comply with a desegregation decision because it is the law, but I have longed to hear white ministers declare: "Follow this decree because integration is morally right and because the Negro is your brother." In the midst of blatant injustices inflicted upon the Negro, I have watched white churchmen stand on the sideline and mouth pious irrelevancies and sanctimonious trivialities. In the midst of a mighty struggle to rid our nation of racial and economic injustice, I have heard many ministers say: "Those are social issues, with which the gospel has no real concern." And I have watched many churches commit themselves to a completely otherworldly religion which makes a strange, unbiblical distinction between body and soul, between the sacred and the secular.

I have traveled the length and breadth of Alabama, Mississippi, and all the other southern states. On sweltering summer days and crisp autumn mornings I have looked at the South's beautiful churches with their lofty spires pointing heavenward. I have beheld the impressive outlines of her massive religious-education buildings. Over and over I have found myself saying: "What kind of people worship here? Who is their God? Where were their voices when the lips of Governor Barnett dripped with words of interposition and nullification? Where were they when Governor Wallace gave a clarion call for defiance and hatred? Where were their voices of support when bruised and weary Negro men and women decided to rise from the dark dungeons of complacency to the bright hills of creative protest?"

Yes, these questions are still in my mind. In deep disappointment I have wept over the laxity of the church. But be assured that my tears have been tears of love. There can be no deep disappointment where there is not deep love. Yes, I love the church. How could I do otherwise? I am in the rather unique position of being the son, the grandson, and the great-grandson of preachers. Yes, I see the church as the body of Christ. But, Oh! How we have blemished and scarred that body through social neglect and through fear of being nonconformists.

There was a time when the church was very powerful—in the time when the early Christians rejoiced at being deemed worthy to suffer for what they believed. In those days the church was not merely a thermometer that recorded the ideas and principles of popular opinion; it was a thermostat that transformed the mores of society. Whenever the early Christians entered a town, the people in power became disturbed and immediately sought to convict the Christians for being "disturbers of the peace" and "outside agitators." But the Christians pressed on, in the conviction that they were "a colony of heaven," called to obey God rather than man. Small in number, they were big in commitment. They were too God-intoxicated to be "astronomically intimidated." By their effort and example they brought an end to such ancient evils as infanticide and gladiatorial contests.

Things are different now. So often the contemporary church is a weak, ineffectual voice with an uncertain sound. So often it is an archdefender of the status quo. Far from being disturbed by the presence of the church, the power structure of the average community is consoled by the church's silent—and often even vocal—sanction of things as they are.

But the judgment of God is upon the church as never before. If today's church does not recapture the sacrificial spirit of the early church, it will lose its authenticity, forfeit the loyalty of millions, and be dismissed as an irrelevant social club with no meaning for the twentieth century. Every day I meet young people whose disappointment with the church has turned into outright disgust.

Perhaps I have once again been too optimistic. Is organized religion too inextricably bound to the status quo to save our nation and the world? Perhaps I must turn my faith to the inner spiritual church, the church within the church, as the true *ekklesia* and the hope of the world. But again I am thankful to God that some noble souls from the ranks of organized religion have broken loose from the paralyzing chains of conformity and joined us as active partners in the struggle for freedom. They have left their secure congregations and walked the streets of Albany, Georgia, with us. They have gone down the highways of the South on tortuous rides for freedom. Yes, they have gone to jail with us. Some have been dismissed from their churches, have lost the support of their bishops and fellow ministers. But they have acted in the faith that right defeated is stronger than evil triumphant. Their witness has been the spiritual salt that has preserved the true meaning of

40

the gospel in these troubled times. They have carved a tunnel of hope through the dark mountain of disappointment.

I hope the church as a whole will meet the challenge of this decisive hour. But even if the church does not come to the aid of justice, I have no despair about the future. I have no fear about the outcome of our struggle in Birmingham, even if our motives are at present misunderstood. We will reach the goal of freedom in Birmingham and all over the nation, because the goal of America is freedom. Abused and scorned though we may be, our destiny is tied up with America's destiny. Before the pilgrims landed at Plymouth, we were here. Before the pen of Jefferson etched the majestic words of the Declaration of Independence across the pages of history, we were here. For more than two centuries our forebears labored in this country without wages; they made cotton king; they built the homes of their masters while suffering gross injustice and shameful humiliation—and yet out of a bottomless vitality they continue to thrive and develop. If the inexpressible cruelties of slavery could not stop us, the opposition we now face will surely fail. We will win our freedom because the sacred heritage of our nation and the eternal will of God are embodied in our echoing demands.

Before closing I feel impelled to mention one other point in your statement that has troubled me profoundly. You warmly commended the Birmingham police force for keeping "order" and "preventing violence." I doubt that you would have so warmly commended the police force if you had seen its dogs sinking their teeth into unarmed, nonviolent Negroes. I doubt that you would so quickly commend the policemen if you were to observe their ugly and inhumane treatment of Negroes here in the city jail; if you were to watch them push and curse old Negro women and young Negro girls; if you were to see them slap and kick old Negro men and young boys; if you were to observe them, as they did on two occasions, refuse to give us food because we wanted to sing our grace together. I cannot join you in your praise of the Birmingham police department.

It is true that the police have exercised a degree of discipline in handling the demonstrators. In this sense they have conducted themselves rather "nonviolently" in public. But for what purpose? To preserve the evil system of segregation. Over the past few years I have consistently preached that nonviolence demands that the means we use must be as pure as the ends we seek. I have tried to make clear that it is wrong to use immoral means to attain moral ends. But now I must affirm that it is just as wrong, or perhaps even more so, to use moral means to preserve immoral ends. Perhaps Mr. Connor and his policemen have been rather nonviolent in public, as was Chief Pritchett in Albany, Georgia, but they used the moral means of nonviolence to maintain the immoral end of racial injustice. As T. S. Eliot has said: "The last temptation is the greatest treason: To do the right deed for the wrong reason."

I wish you had commended the Negro sit-inners and demonstrators of Birmingham for their sublime courage, their willingness to suffer, and their

45

amazing discipline in the midst of great provocation. One day the South will recognize its real heroes. They will be the James Merediths, with the noble sense of purpose that enables them to face jeering and hostile mobs, and with the agonizing loneliness that characterizes the life of the pioneer. They will be old, oppressed, battered Negro women, symbolized in a seventy-two-year-old woman in Montgomery, Alabama, who rose up with a sense of dignity and with her people decided not to ride segregated buses, and who responded with ungrammatical profundity to one who inquired about her weariness: "My feets is tired, but my soul is at rest." They will be the young high school and college students, the young ministers of the gospel and a host of their elders, courageously and nonviolently sitting in at lunch counters and willingly going to jail for conscience' sake. One day the South will know that when these disinherited children of God sat down at lunch counters, they were in reality standing up for what is best in the American dream and for the most sacred values in our Judaeo-Christian heritage, thereby bringing our nation back to those great wells of democracy which were dug deep by the founding fathers in their formulation of the Constitution and the Declaration of Independence.

Never before have I written so long a letter. I'm afraid it is much too long to take your precious time. I can assure you that it would have been much shorter if I had been writing from a comfortable desk, but what else can one do when he is alone in a narrow jail cell, other than write long letters, think long thoughts, and pray long prayers?

If I have said anything in this letter that overstates the truth and indicates an unreasonable impatience, I beg you to forgive me. If I have said anything that understates the truth and indicates my having a patience that allows me to settle for anything less than brotherhood, I beg God to forgive me.

I hope this letter finds you strong in the faith. I also hope that circumstances will soon make it possible for me to meet each of you, not as an integrationist or a civil-rights leader but as a fellow clergyman and a Christian brother. Let us all hope that the dark clouds of racial prejudice will soon pass away and the deep fog of misunderstanding will be lifted from our fear-drenched communities, and in some not too distant tomorrow the radiant stars of love and brotherhood will shine over our great nation with all their scintillating beauty.

—Yours for the cause of Peace and Brotherhood,
Martin Luther King, Jr. ◎/◎

Notes

1. This response to a published statement by eight fellow clergymen from Alabama (Bishop C. C. J. Carpenter, Bishop Joseph A. Durick, Rabbi Milton L. Grafman, Bishop Paul Hardin, Bishop Nolan B. Harmon, the Reverend George M. Murray, the Reverend Edward V. Ramage, and the Reverend Earl Stallings) was composed under somewhat constricting circumstances. Begun on the margins of the newspaper in which the statement appeared while I was in jail, the letter was continued on

scraps of writing paper supplied by a friendly Negro trusty, and concluded on a pad my attorneys were eventually permitted to leave me. Although the text remains in substance unaltered, I have indulged in the author's prerogative of polishing it for publication. [King's note.]

2. **Reinhold Niebuhr** Niebuhr (1892–1971) was a minister, political activist, author, and professor of applied Christianity at Union Theological Seminary. [All notes are the editors' unless otherwise specified.]

3. **justice . . . denied** A quotation attributed to William E. Gladstone (1809–1898), British statesman and prime minister.

4. **Paul Tillich** Tillich (1886–1965), born in Germany, taught theology at several German universities, but in 1933 he was dismissed from his post at the University of Frankfurt because of his opposition to the Nazi regime. At the invitation of Reinhold Niebuhr, he came to the United States and taught at Union Theological Seminary.

5. *Zeitgeist* German for "spirit of the age."

1. King chose to present his views in the form of a letter instead of, say, a manifesto. How might King's choice be explained from a Rogerian perspective?

2. Where do you see King making an effort to establish common ground with his audience? Explain whether you think he succeeded in doing so.

3. Do any moments in King's letter seem un-Rogerian? How so? What positive or negative effect might they have on his intended readers?

4. Does King use any of the three Aristotelian appeals of ethos, pathos, or logos described in Chapter 1? If so, which one(s)? Where do they appear? Why do you suppose King uses them?

5. Where does King most clearly reveal a special effort to reach his audience of fellow clergy?

6. Outline the key points in King's essay. Is there anything Rogerian about the way King sequences and emphasizes some of these points?

7. Should King have taken a more aggressive approach in his "Letter" (i.e., used a classical argument strategy)? Why or why not?

Chapter Summary

A successful argument structured along Rogerian principles, like the Classical and Toulmin models, includes thorough, accurate, and relevant evidence in support of its claim; unlike these models, however, the aim of Rogerian persuasion is not to "win" the argument but to find common ground and to build consensus on an issue troubling both the writer and the audience. Instead of being considered "opponents," those with differing views are encouraged to reach

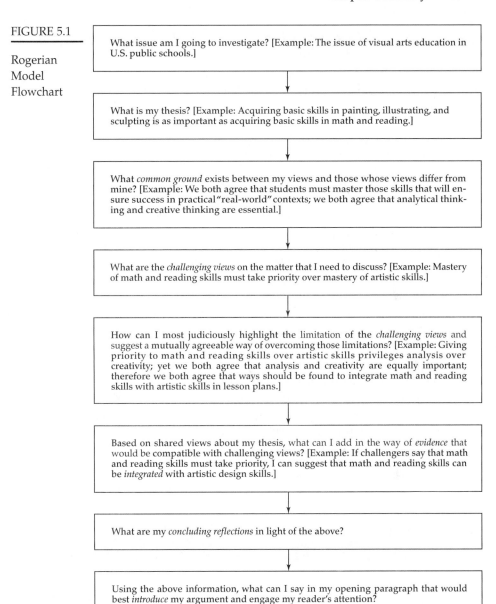

FIGURE 5.1

Rogerian
Model
Flowchart

What issue am I going to investigate? [Example: The issue of visual arts education in U.S. public schools.]

What is my thesis? [Example: Acquiring basic skills in painting, illustrating, and sculpting is as important as acquiring basic skills in math and reading.]

What *common ground* exists between my views and those whose views differ from mine? [Example: We both agree that students must master those skills that will ensure success in practical "real-world" contexts; we both agree that analytical thinking and creative thinking are essential.]

What are the *challenging views* on the matter that I need to discuss? [Example: Mastery of math and reading skills must take priority over mastery of artistic skills.]

How can I most judiciously highlight the limitation of the *challenging views* and suggest a mutually agreeable way of overcoming those limitations? [Example: Giving priority to math and reading skills over artistic skills privileges analysis over creativity; yet we both agree that analysis and creativity are equally important; therefore we both agree that ways should be found to integrate math and reading skills with artistic skills in lesson plans.]

Based on shared views about my thesis, what can I add in the way of *evidence* that would be compatible with challenging views? [Example: If challengers say that math and reading skills must take priority, I can suggest that math and reading skills can be *integrated* with artistic design skills.]

What are my *concluding reflections* in light of the above?

Using the above information, what can I say in my opening paragraph that would best *introduce* my argument and engage my reader's attention?

consensus and to enter into a cooperative dialogue with the writer. For such a cooperative dialogue to succeed, arguers need to listen with care and open-mindedness to divergent points of view. When considering taking a Rogerian approach to your argument, remember to ask yourself three questions: Can I represent challenging views and evaluate the evidence fairly and objectively? Do any of the challenging views make sense to some degree, and, if so, can I find a way to incorporate them into my own views? Am I sincere in my desire to establish common ground with those who take issue with me?

Summary and Comparison of the Classical, Toulmin, and Rogerian Models

Classical Model

- Based on philosophical ideals of sound thinking, incorporating the Aristotelian appeals of ethos (ethical principles, recognized authority, and shared values), pathos (stirring of emotions), and logos (dialectical reasoning)

- Follows a predetermined arrangement of elements: An *introduction* that states the problem and the thesis, presentation of the *evidence, refutation* of challenging views, and a *conclusion*

Toulmin Model

- Based on the pragmatics of the judicial system rather than the ideals of philosophical thinking

- Approaches an argument in terms of its *claims* (which are presented more as hypotheses being opened to challenge than as truths to be proven), its *data,* and its underlying *warrants,* and *backing* justifying those warrants, that make the data trustworthy

- Recognizes the "real-world" complexities of an argument; gives special emphasis to refutation

Rogerian Model

- Based on humanistic values that take into account the importance of social cooperation in argument (that is, finding common ground is valued over "beating the opposition")

- (1) Emphasizes points of agreement over points of disagreement, and (2) treats the issue as a common problem for both the writer and the audience

- Urges arguers to cultivate multiple perspectives toward issues

Checklist

1. Do I find common ground with those whose views differ from my own?

2. Do I carefully consider the weaknesses or limitations of my point of view, as well as those of others'? Do I share these with my readers?

3. Is my tone cooperative rather than confrontational?

4. Do I encourage multiple perspectives rather than a singular one toward the issue?

5. Do I treat views with which I disagree respectfully? Do I give more emphasis to the points of agreement than the points of disagreement?

Writing Projects

1. Write an argumentative essay, following the Rogerian model, in which you defend or challenge one of the following issues:

   a. Books, especially textbooks, should be published online.

   b. Because the Second Amendment to the U.S. Constitution gives citizens the right to bear arms, students over the age of eighteen cannot be prohibited from bringing a firearm onto campus if they feel the need for self-protection.

   c. Libraries should become media centers, using more of their budgets for electronic resources than for print resources.

2. Write an essay in which you use the Rogerian model to argue for one feasible way of improving living conditions with one or more roommates.

3. Write a comparative evaluation of the Classical, Toulmin, and Rogerian models of argument.

4. Read the following essay, "Who Owns Our Children?" by student Daniela Gibson. Then critique it in terms of her use of Rogerian persuasion.

Daniela Gibson

Who Owns Our Children?

Every morning when I go to the bus stop, I pass by a poster with a smiling mother and toddler. On the poster, it says, "You are your child's first teacher." Unfortunately, today, many parents feel that this caring and loving relationship with their children is threatened by a dark force—child violence. The reality of this threat is manifested in tragic events such as the shooting at Columbine where two high school students killed twelve students and a teacher, leaving several wounded. In the face of such tragedies, it is not surprising that parents are desperately seeking a cause. Recently, many have turned to the media and argued that violence on TV is responsible for violence among children. Many parents now feel that only TV censorship by the government can bring child violence to a halt.

These parents, together with several journalists, sociologists, and psychologists, see a parallel between TV violence and child violence. In support of their claim, they cite people like David Walsh, director of the National Institute of Media and the Family, who notes that "it is estimated the average American kid has seen 200,000 acts of violence on television by the time he or she graduates from high school" (Hunt). They further refer to Professor Brandon Centerwall whose studies suggest that "when English-language TV came to South Africa in 1975, having previously been banned by the Afrikaans-speaking government . . . there was a spectacular increase in violent crime, most especially among the young" (Kristol). Another argument against TV is that its violence desensitizes both adults and children from the violence in the real world "to the point where nothing is revolting. Where nothing makes us blush" (Jacoby). Arguments like these have let people conclude that "the government . . . will have to step in to help the parents"—a call, of course, for censorship (Kristol).

These reactions are understandable and reflect the fears and concerns of the parents. I think that everybody will agree that violence is bad, that TV can promote violence among young children, and that this is especially the case when TV replaces a parent or other caretaker. It clearly is in the interest of our children and our society that children do not have unlimited access to television. The question is, however, who should be in charge of regulating TV for our children. The government or the parents? I strongly believe that the latter should be in charge. I believe that child violence can only be reduced if parents stop holding the TV media responsible for the violence and instead acknowledge and act upon their responsibilities as parents.

To blame the media for child violence and call for censorship of television is a mistake, for the causal link between child violence and TV has not been sufficiently established and censorship is not only impractical but also dangerous. First, if we see television as the main cause for child violence, we mistake a correlation for a cause. As one author explains: "epidemiological research . . . consists of observing groups of people and then showing statistical associations between their life-styles or behavior and what happens to them later. Scientists know, as the public often does not, that such [. . .] research tells us nothing about cause and effect" (Glasser). The same author continues, "many people will falsely conclude after reading such statistical associations" that "'[t]elevision is the cause' [of violence]." To illustrate the problems with this epidemiological research, let us look at the argument that TV brought violence to South Africa. This claim is based on a correlation of the introduction of English-language TV and an increase in "violent crime, most especially among the young." To say, however, that TV is the cause of the crime is to exclude all kinds of other factors. For example, we know that in the particular case in South Africa, English-language TV had previously "been banned by the Afrikaans-speaking government." This information suggests tension between the native population and a pro-English movement. Now, I am not saying that I can prove this tension or that it is the real cause for the increase in violence. What I am saying is that we cannot conclude a cause if we only have a simple correlation. To say that English-language TV is the cause for growing violence is to say that "owning more than one television set caused heart disease" just because an "epidemiologic research showed a statistical association between heart disease and the number of television sets a person owned" (in fact, "[c]linical trials demonstrated that cholesterol, but not the number of television sets one owned, was causally related") (Glasser).

Furthermore, not only are the grounds for TV censorship shaky, but such censorship would also be impractical and potentially dangerous. The following quote points at the impracticality of censorship: "claiming we have to reprogram the media watched by 99.99 percent of us to influence the behavior of 0.01 percent is to be rendered helpless by a much smaller problem" (Jenkins). Although I am not sure about the accuracy of these numbers, I do think that the statement demonstrates well the unwillingness of many people to give up their freedom of watching whatever they want on TV in favor of child sensitive censorship. Furthermore, to trust the government with the regulation of TV programs is also dangerous, for it would be unclear by which and whose standards this censorship would be carried out. The difficulty of finding a standard that corresponds to the values of all parents is demonstrated by the claim of an author who argues that most TV shows are in fact portraying the right values. In support of his claim, he refers to the TV show *Friends* and asks, "Is there a more wholesome group of kids than the cute boys and girls on *Friends*. They are all white and hetero" (Hirschorn). Now, I know several parents who would strongly object to "all white and hetero" as the right message. On the other hand, I also know parents who would endorse such a message. Not only does this disagreement show the difficulty of having someone else than the parents, namely the government, define the "right" values for children, but it also points to the danger of children being indoctrinated with values that conflict with those of their parents.

Being aware of the shortcomings of TV censorship, it is important now to look at the benefits of responsible parenting with respect to TV and violence. I believe that parent regulation of TV shows, a dialogue between parent and child about TV shows, and the offering of alternatives to TV can not only reduce child violence but also increase the happiness of child and parent.

First, responsible parents should regulate the TV exposure of their children. This allows parents not only to reduce the violence their children are exposed to while watching TV but also to monitor the time their children spend in front of the TV. For reasons that I will address under point three, I believe that it is important for the mental and physical health of the child that the time spent in front of a TV is limited. The danger with government regulation is that it might give parents a false sense of security. They think because violence has been censored, TV can no longer harm their children. They will feel comfortable about their children watching TV. Suddenly, the TV has become a convenient babysitter.

But responsible parents know not only what and when their children watch TV but also how they respond to what they see. This brings me to my second attribute of responsible parents: Responsible parents also use TV shows as an opportunity for dialogue with their children. In the case where children actually do watch violence, parents could ask, "Can you imagine how much this must hurt?" to give children a sense of the pain that accompanies violence. And of course, parents should also disagree with the violence shown and tell the child, "I really disagree with the way the character treated his friend. I think it would have been much better if he had talked to him instead of beating him." The point is that watching TV together with your child is more than just a means to shield your child from an overdose of TV violence. It can also be a great opportunity to encourage conversations that foster critical thinking skills and verbal skills and allow parents to understand their children better.

And third, responsible parents should also offer their children alternatives to TV. If a child spends most of his or her time in front of a TV, even if the violence is minimal, the child's physical and mental well-being is threatened. The hour-long sitting prohibits the child from getting enough exercise. Furthermore, the lonely hours in front of the TV would cause the child to become alienated from others and to be less and less able to distinguish reality from the world on TV. On the other hand, spending time with the child on other activities can be very rewarding both for the child and the parent. An example is the weekend my husband and I spent with our five-year-old nephew, Mason. He arrived with a video that he was determined to watch. However, when we suggested going to the park, the video was soon forgotten. Moreover, walking all over the park and visiting the planetarium, aquarium, and playground was time well spent: Mason felt proud that he could keep up with us grownups without being carried on my husband's shoulders; he got plenty of exercise, not only from the walking but also from the playground; he became completely fascinated with the planetarium; he got the sense that he was important and loved; and he just had a real fun time. At the same time, because this day was full of interaction and talking with Mason, my husband and I learned so much more about our nephew than we would have ever done if we had watched TV. (Also all these activities caused Mason to fall asleep after dinner, so that my husband and I had a calm and restful evening—something that TV would have never accomplished.)

Censorship might shield children from TV violence. But responsible parenting can do the same. And while TV censorship is problematic its causal grounds are shaky, its practicality and standards are doubtful—responsible parenting is so much more rewarding. When parents not only monitor the shows their children watch and the hours their children spend in front of a TV, but also encourage dialogue about the shows and offer alternative activities to TV, the children will learn to think critically, feel loved, have ample opportunities to release extra energies, and be much happier. And having happier children appears to be the best prevention of violence. In the end, I still believe in the truth of the poster, that "you are your child's first teacher."

Works Cited

Glasser, Ira. "TV Causes Violence? Try Again." <u>New York Times</u>
     15 June 1994: A19.
Hirschorn, Michael. "The Myth of Television Depravity."
     <u>New York Times</u> 4 Sept. 1995: A21.
Hunt, Albert R. "Teen Violence Spawned by Guns and Cultural
     Rot." <u>Wall Street Journal</u> 11 June 1998: 12.
Jacoby, Jeff. "A Desensitized Society Drenched in Sleaze."
     <u>Boston Globe</u> 8 June 1995: 16.
Jenkins, Holman W., Jr. "Violence Never Solved Anything but
     It's Entertaining." <u>Wall Street Journal</u> 28 Oct.
     1998: 14.
Kristol, Irving. "Sex, Violence, and Videotape." <u>Wall Street
     Journal</u> 31 May 1998: 28.

6 Reasoning: Methods and Fallacies

Come now, and let us reason together.
—Isaiah 1:18

As we have seen in the preceding chapters, argumentative writing involves the use of many skills: making rhetorical choices regarding audience, purpose, expectations, and the nature of the subject matter; outlining and drafting arguments; deciding to use Classical, Toulmin, or Rogerian methods of argument. This chapter looks closely at another fundamental skill for writers of arguments—reasoning. By taking care to improve your ability to think critically and logically, you will be less likely to slip into errors of reasoning when supporting a claim.

Argumentative Reasoning

All arguments are imperfect to some degree. Unlike the tight logic of mathematics, in which a problem is solved methodically and objectively and turns out either correct or incorrect, most genuine arguments are based on complex human situations—complex because they have unpredictable elements. It is one thing to prove that force is equal to the product of mass times acceleration ($F = ma$) or that Socrates is mortal (given the fact that all humans are mortal); it is quite another matter to prove that reading to children, say, dramatically increases their chances of college success. To argue that claim convincingly, you would first need to be aware of variables such as the availability of controlled studies on this topic, the characteristics of the students used in the studies, the types of readings the children had been exposed to, the frequency of being read to, and so on. Because of such complex variables, no argument can be 100 percent beyond dispute.

Thus, opportunities to make an argument stronger than it is always exist. Good arguers, however, strive to create not the perfect argument but the most efficient one—the one that will ethically and logically persuade the readers. An argument, then, is most successful when its weaknesses are minimized as much as possible. As a writer of arguments, you should familiarize yourself with the most common argumentative errors, which are known as *fallacies*. Learning to recognize fallacies does not guarantee that you will always avoid them, but it does increase the likelihood that you'll recognize them. You can use the information about fallacies to read others' arguments, resources, and your own drafts so that eventually your ability to recognize fallacies will improve your ability to construct sound and convincing arguments.

The Nature of Fallacies

Arguers rarely use fallacies deliberately. Inadvertent lapses in judgment, fallacies usually arise from lack of experience with the subject matter, lack of familiarity with other points of view, and undeveloped methods of argumentative reasoning. Let us examine each of these problems.

- **Lack of experience with the subject matter.** The more informed you are, the more material you have to defend your views. Most arguments fail to convince because they do not draw sufficiently from experience (personal experience as well as experience acquired from intensive research). You may feel passionately about the need to save the rain forests, but unless you thoroughly understand the nature of rain forests, the reasons they are so precious, and the ways in which they are so threatened, your argument will lack substance. You would have no choice but to rely on broad generalities, such as "Rain forests are filled with important species." Unless you can name and describe such species and describe their importance, readers are unlikely to be convinced that the assertion was valid.

- **Lack of familiarity with other points of view.** In addition to acquiring a knowledge base about the topic, you also need to be familiar with the range of representative views on that topic. Before you can defend your views on an issue, you need to understand challenging arguments, find reasons why those arguments are not as effective as yours, and be open to the possibility of adjusting your position if another is actually more reasonable.

- **Underdeveloped methods of argumentative reasoning.** You not only need to be knowledgeable about issues and familiar with the spectrum of views on those issues, but you also need to know how arguments progress logically from one point to the next. In addition to the methods of presenting an argument (the Classical, Toulmin, and Rogerian methods discussed in Chapters 3–5), there are particular *reasoning strategies* or patterns of thinking that enable you to frame an assertion logically.

Strategies of Reasoning

The reasoning strategies most relevant to argumentative writing are as follows:

- **Deduction:** Drawing conclusions from assertions that you know to be true (insofar as you can determine); reasoning from the general to the specific

- **Induction:** Arriving at a conclusion that is based on what you judge to be sufficient (not necessarily conclusive) available evidence; reasoning from the specific to the general

- **Categorization:** Placing an idea or issue in a larger context using the strategies of definition, classification, and division

- **Analogy:** Attempting to enhance the validity of a claim by finding a similar situation in a different context

- **Authorization:** Establishing the validity of a claim by invoking authority, either in the form of personal testimonial from an expert or of preestablished policy or law

- **Plea:** Using emotionally charged expressions of feeling to aid in defending an assertion

The sections that follow look more closely at the ways in which each of these reasoning strategies operates.

Deduction

When you reason deductively, you break down an assertion into formal statements that are logically connected. A *syllogism* is one formula used in deductive reasoning, consisting of a *major premise,* a *minor premise,* and a *conclusion.*

Major premise: All cats meow.

Minor premise: Cordelia is a cat.

Conclusion: Therefore, Cordelia meows.

As this simple example reveals, to reason deductively means to accept the major premise without question. To call the major premise into question ("Is it true that all cats meow?") is to move from deduction to induction, whereby one looks at the evidence leading up to the hypothesis to determine its truthfulness.

In commonplace arguments, an assumption often goes unstated because it is taken for granted that the audience already shares it. From the perspective of formal logic, this is considered an incomplete syllogism; but from the perspective of argumentative discourse, it is considered sufficient and is referred to as an *enthymeme.* Thus, the statement "Cordelia meows because she is a cat" is an enthymeme because the writer takes for granted that the audience accepts the unstated assumption that all cats meow.

Deductive reasoning can be especially powerful when one is refuting a claim. (If you need to refresh your memory about the process of refutation, review the discussion of Classical argument in Chapter 3.) For example, if a friend claims that to accept a government-run program is to reject a free-market economy, you could refute the claim by asserting that a government program and a free-market economy are not as mutually exclusive as the friend's claim implies. Such dichotomous ("either-or") thinking is a commonly occurring example of flawed deductive reasoning. By calling attention to the many-sided complexity of a problem, you raise the consciousness of your audience; you in effect *teach* your readers to recognize the "gray areas" that aren't as conspicuous as the "black and white ones" but that usually bring the truth much closer.

To refute a claim, you may need to do a deductive analysis of the author's reasoning strategies. Here is a five-step method for such analysis:

1. Identify contradictions.

2. Identify inconsistencies.

3. Identify omissions or oversights.

4. Reduce an unsound claim to its logical absurdity (*reductio ad absurdum*) so as to expose the flawed reasoning more conspicuously.

5. Identify oversimplifications.

Identify Contradictions   Someone asserts that making handgun sales illegal would increase crime because more guns would be obtained illegally. You could reveal a contradiction by showing (using statistics from a reputable survey) how that claim contradicts reality: that crime actually has decreased by a certain percentage in one or more places where such a law had been enacted. Similarly, if a writer asserts that playing video games excessively damages one's ability to think effectively and then proceeds to describe her own experiences with video games in an effective manner, you could point out the contradiction between the authors writing effectively and the alleged damage to her thinking skills from years of playing video games.

Identify Inconsistencies   If you claim that people should give up eating meat but then proceed to eat a bowl of chicken soup, reasoning that such a small quantity of chicken is negligible or that even vegetarians need a "meat break" now and then, you are being logically inconsistent. Or consider this somewhat more complex example: Arlene is against abortion because she equates abortion with murder. However, Arlene agrees that in cases of rape, incest, or grave danger to the mother's life, abortion is permissible. Arlene is being logically inconsistent because her exceptions seem irrelevant to her own definition of abortion as fetal murder.

Identify Omissions or Oversights   A friend advises you not to take a course from Professor Krupp because Krupp gives difficult exams, grades rigorously, and assigns a heavy reading load. At first, you think that these are pretty good reasons for not enrolling in Professor Krupp's course. But then you wonder whether any positive things about this professor might balance out the bad, so you ask: "Did you learn a lot in her course?" Your friend replies, "Oh yes—more than in any other course I've taken." You have just identified a deliberate omission or an accidental oversight in your friend's assessment of Professor Krupp.

Reduce an Unsound Claim to Its Logical Absurdity Someone argues against a company's policy that employees wear shirts and ties or dresses and skirts by claiming that employees can think well even when dressed casually in jeans and T-shirts. You could refute that claim by taking it to the logical extreme. Why wouldn't the first person show up in pajamas or a swimsuit for work then? The point of the dress code is not to affect one's ability to think but to present a certain image of the company.

Identify Oversimplifications Recall the earlier example of the friend who argues that a government-run program is never compatible with a free-market economy. This kind of dichotomous thinking oversimplifies the reality of a free-market society such as that of the United States, where government programs such as Social Security and NASA are quite compatible with a market economy. Oversimplification results from an insufficiently investigated or thought-out premise on which the argument rests.

Exercise 6.1

1. Examine the following four arguments and describe the method or methods of deductive reasoning that each author is using or representing.

   a. Watching the Republican Party try to come to terms with several million gay voters reminds me a little of my uncle. He's the only family member I'm estranged from, because he regards my sexual orientation as a deliberate rebuke to God. When he heard I had contracted HIV, he told me in a letter, in so many words, that I deserved it and that only the Holy Spirit could cure me. He's also, I might add, a good person: kind, loving, and decent, if not the brightest bulb on the Christmas tree.

   The human question is: How do I get along with him? My human answer: I don't. After his letter about my illness, in which he couldn't even bring himself to ask how I was, I cut him off. In most families with gay members there's something of this sort going on. So I completely understand the impulse to ostracize someone who has decided that a religious fiat, which by definition cannot be challenged, requires him to reject and hurt a loved one.

   In a family, we can get away with such anger and hurt. But in politics such emotionally satisfying options come at a price: impasse, conflict, and little progress. That's why the knee-jerk attempt to turn George W. Bush into a homophobe is, in my view, misguided. It's misguided, first of all, because it's clear he isn't one. And it's misguided also because it will create an atmosphere that, while making a few gays feel better, makes many more worse off. We need to change a paradigm in which one side sees only bigots and the other side sees only perverts. This election presents us with a chance.

How? The first step is to resist at every opportunity the notion that homosexuals are defined by victimhood. If you look at the agenda of, say, the leading gay lobby, the Human Rights Campaign, you'll see what I mean. Its priorities are laws that protect gays from hate crimes and employment discrimination. Both proposals rely for their effectiveness on the notion that gay men and women be seen as the objects of physical violence and routine oppression in the workplace. But the number of hate crimes perpetrated against gay people is relatively puny, and such crimes are already covered under existing criminal law. And it's ludicrous to look at the gay population and see millions of people who have a hard time finding or keeping a job. In those states where anti-discrimination laws for gays are in effect, the number of lawsuits filed is negligible. But the real harm of these campaigns isn't just that they add new, largely pointless laws; it's that they portray homosexuals as downtrodden and weak.

To put it bluntly, we're not. We have survived a health crisis that would have destroyed—and is destroying—other populations, due in no small part to our tenacity, compassion, and organization. We are represented in almost every major cultural, political, and social organization, often leading them. Gay strength can be seen everywhere—from courageous high school kids organizing support groups to a young lesbian serving as an indispensable aide to Dick Cheney's vice presidential campaign. The media is saturated with gay talent, images, and skill. An honest gay agenda should capitalize on this truth, not flee from it.—Andrew Sullivan

b. If the Darwinian [evolutionary] process really took place, remains of plants and animals [that is, the fossil record] should show a gradual and continual change from one type of animal or plant into another. One of the things that worried Darwin in his day, as well as [what worries] modern evolutionists, was that the fossil record did not supply these intermediate life forms. —Donald E. Chittick

c. Until the census is focused on individuals, not households, the situation of women and children may continue to be distorted—just as it might be if there were only one vote per household. There is such a wide range of constituencies with an interest in Census Bureau policies that journalists have coined the phrase "census politics." But social justice movements haven't yet focused on the fact that census categories also determine what is counted as work, and who is defined as a worker. . . . —Gloria Steinem

d. Aristotle felt that the mortal horse of Appearance which ate grass and took people places and gave birth to little horses deserved far more attention than Plato was giving it. He said that the horse is not mere Appearance. The Appearances cling to something which is independent of them and which, like Ideas, is unchanging. The "something" that Appearances cling to he named "substance." And at that moment . . . our modern scientific understanding of reality was born. —Robert Pirsig

2. Bring in a short article such as a newspaper editorial and discuss it in terms of its use of deductive reasoning. Point out any flaws you see in the deductive reasoning.

Induction

You engage in inductive reasoning when you strive to make sense of things you experience. Unlike deductive reasoning, you do not begin with a premise assumed to be true and then determine a logical foundation for supporting it. Instead, you build a hypothesis out of your observations of phenomena. To return to our simple example of whether all cats meow, the inductive writer would examine the evidence—Cat A, Cat B, Cat C, and so on—until observing enough cats to warrant the conclusion, "Yes, all cats meow," or to reject it ("No, not all cats meow; Siberian tigers are cats, and they growl"), or to qualify it ("Yes, all cats meow, provided they're members of the subgenus *Felix domesticus*").

Because in inductive reasoning the strength of the conclusion rests entirely on the sufficiency of the evidence observed, you must use an adequate number of reliable samples.

Number of Samples   How many samples must be observed before it is reasonable to make the "inductive leap"? Technically, of course, no conclusion arrived at inductively is absolutely indisputable. For that to be the case in our cat argument, for example, you would have to observe every domestic cat on earth! At some point, every inductive reasoner must say, "I have observed enough to draw a reliable conclusion." This decision can be tricky and, indeed, is a major point of disputation in science—which relies preeminently on the inductive method (better known as the scientific method) for testing the validity of hypotheses.

Reliability of Samples   If the purpose of your paper is to argue whether a clear correlation exists between alcohol consumption and health problems, you may decide first to conduct a campus survey to see whether health problems are more frequent among drinking students than among nondrinking ones. In addition to interviewing an adequate number of students from each group (a 20 to 25 percent response rate to your survey from the total student population would be considered substantial), you will want the sample to be reliable in other ways. For example, it should be representative of different groups within the student body. Having only women, only men, only athletes, or only Mormons included would make your sample survey on college drinking unreliable.

 **Exercise 6.2**

Describe the sequence of likely steps in inductive reasoning one might take for each of the following tasks:

1. Buying a new or a used car

2. Choosing a birthday gift for a friend or parent

3. Determining the chemical composition of an unknown gas

Categorization

Without systems of classification and division, we would be unable to make much sense out of reality. Perhaps the best illustration of this is the Linnean system of taxonomy. With its binomial schema (genus name + species name, as in *Felix domesticus* or *Homo sapiens*), all life on earth has been classified. Think for a moment about how valuable such a schema is for understanding the relationship of life forms to each other.

People categorize foods into groups such as savory or sweet, or main course or dessert, to determine what they'll serve for dinner—a useful strategy for knowing what to buy for a dinner party. People break the large category of sports into basketball, baseball, and so on, and then divide those subgroups further into professional and amateur leagues. College football teams would fall into amateur leagues, which then play on their NCAA division level—IA, IAA, IIA, whatever. Imagine the injuries without such classification—an NFL football team playing a IIIA college team! Categorization in sports helps ensure a level playing field.

Categorization is just as important outside of science; for example, we can plan our day better by grouping our activities into "chores," "business transactions," "recreation," etc. However, problems often arise. When people try to categorize human beings neatly according to ethnicity or cultural differences, the danger of stereotyping arises. Superficial differences such as skin color or manner of dress or speech are given more significance than they deserve. Racism, homophobia, and gender-based discrimination are often the ugly results. Categorizing works best when it serves as an initial gauge for differentiating A from B or A and B from C, and so forth. For example, if you were examining the study habits of college students, you might group your sample students by gender or age or major, just in case a correlation between the category selected and the kind of study habits would show up.

Another facet of categorization is definition, which is necessary for "fine-tuning" the distinctions between one thing and another within the same category. The very word *define* means "to determine or fix the boundaries or extent of" (*Random House Webster's College Dictionary*). Formal definitions use categorizing techniques themselves. In the definition of the word *chaplet*, for example—"a wreath or garland for the head" (*Random House Webster's College Dictionary*)—the first half of the definition ("a wreath or garland") establishes the broad category, or genus, and the second half ("for the head") pinpoints its distinguishing (specific) characteristics.

Exercise 6.3

1. Study the definitions of the following words in two unabridged dictionaries (for Example, *The Oxford English Dictionary* and *Webster's Unabridged Dictionary*). Report the differences in the way each dictionary presents the broad category (genus) and the distinguishing (specific) characteristics:

   a. volcano

   b. emphysema

   c. magician

   d. cathedral

2. Write a brief explanation of the way knowledge is categorized in your major field of study (or in a subject you are currently studying).

Analogy

To make an analogy is to draw a correspondence between two things that are superficially different but not essentially different. Analogies are used to enhance comprehension. If you are trying to help readers understand the nature of a radio wave, for example, you might use the more familiar analogy of a water wave. A river and an artery are not superficially alike, but they behave in similar enough ways for one to say that water flows in a river the way blood flows in an artery. A more readily perceived phenomenon like a flowing river is easier to understand than the flow of blood through an artery. The author's goal is to enable ease of understanding over precision of explanation.

However, to say that people are like ants because they swarm in large numbers to sporting events is to generate a distorted (and demeaning) image of fans' behavior. Using analogy in argumentative writing is a give-and-take situation: You give your readers greater comprehension of the idea, but you take away precision. The rule of thumb, then, is to use analogies carefully.

Exercise 6.4

Create an analogy to help explain each of the following concepts:

1. Doppler effect

2. Cardiac function

3. Eye function

4. Heaven

Authorization

Writers sometimes need to support an assertion by including the testimony of an expert in the field in question. If you are arguing about the dangers of ultraviolet radiation and urging people to consider sunbathing a risky activity due to the alleged link between ultraviolet radiation and skin cancer, you are likely to present empirical evidence from, say, several medical studies. You could also add drama to your claim by quoting a startling statement made by a leading skin cancer expert. In such a situation you are resorting to the ethos, the reliable character, of the expert.

Sometimes finding the appropriate authority to obtain testimony in support of a claim can be tricky, depending on the claim. If you wish to argue that using genetic material from human embryos is unethical, should you include testimony from geneticists or religious leaders, or other kinds of experts? It might be easy to find experts who will agree with you—but are they the right experts?

◎⁄◎   Exercise 6.5

Suggest appropriate credentials for one or more authority figures brought in to offer testimony for each of the following topics:

1. Depletion of South American rain forests

2. The need for greater tsunami preparedness in certain regions of the world

3. A new dieting program

4. Cultivating the habit of reading in children

Plea

Emotional response is often highly persuasive. In formal argument, therefore, you may try to persuade your audience to accept your views by way of sympathy or compassion as well as by way of logical reasoning. Thus, if your goal is fundraising for the homeless, you might tell stories about the way homeless people suffer when they have to go without eating for two or three days or shiver during cold winter nights on a park bench. If you wish to emphasize the importance of reading aloud to children, you might create a little scenario in which you dramatize the way that listening to stories delights and heightens the intellectual curiosity of young children who are absorbed in what their parents are reading to them.

The plea strategy uses the Aristotelian appeals to emotion or to ethics. Appealing to the audience's compassion, ethical responsibility, need for security, comfort, and so on reinforces rather than counteracts the logical and analytical; for that reason such appeals are an important rhetorical tool in the art of persuasion.

 **Exercise 6.6**

Suggest possible uses of the plea strategy for each of the following topics:

1. An article on improving airport security
2. An article on preserving the individual's right to privacy
3. An article on teaching children to swim before age five
4. An article on reducing the risk of drowning accidents among children

Errors in Reasoning: A Taxonomy

Now that we have examined the methods of reasoning, it is time to look closely at the pitfalls that can occur. To some degree errors in reasoning are almost unavoidable because reasoning is a complex mental act that requires a concerted effort to perfect. Nonetheless, the more alert you become to the way in which a given line of reasoning violates a principle of logic, of ethics, or of emotional integrity, the less likely it is that your arguments will be criticized for their fallacies.

Let us begin by becoming familiar with the common fallacies; we then examine each of them in more detail and look at the ways they subtly creep into an argument. We also examine these fallacies to identify faulty logic in the sources we may consult for our topics. Seeing faulty logic in supposedly informed sources helps us to decide not to use such sources ourselves and to know what we can rebut in arguments that challenge our own.

Errors of Deduction

In this group of fallacies, the line of reasoning that stems from statements assumed to be true are flawed or the statements themselves may be flawed. Many errors in deductive reasoning occur because the author fails to connect premises to conclusions logically. Some common types of deductive fallacies follow.

Fourth Term   Careless arguers sometimes substitute one term for another, assuming the terms mean or suggest the same things, when in fact the terms have different meanings. The way to demonstrate the illogic of such a substitution is to think about the terms in a formal syllogism (the pattern of formal deductive reasoning discussed on page 167–169): major, minor, and middle, as follows:

	[Maj]	[Mid]
Major premise:	All **dogs** are **mammals.**	

	[Min]	[Maj]
Minor premise:	**Rascal** is a **dog.**	

	[Min]	[Mid]
Conclusion:	Therefore, **Rascal** is a **mammal.**	

In any valid syllogism, the major term is the subject that must be equated with both a generic classification (middle term) and an individual one (minor term). In the above example, the major term *dog* is equated with the middle term *mammal* (dog = mammal) and the minor term Rascal (dog = Rascal).

Now consider this syllogism:

All prerequisites for the major in chemistry are difficult.

Chem. 50 is highly recommended for the major in chemistry.

Therefore, Chem. 50 is difficult.

Instead of seeing the major term *prerequisites* appear in the minor premise, a substitute fourth term—*highly recommended*—appears, thus rendering the syllogism invalid (even though in actuality it may be true).

Non Sequitur   In a non sequitur ("It does not follow"), an assertion cannot be tied logically to the premise it attempts to demonstrate. Consider the premise, "Nellie is obsessed with basketball." The reason presented is "because she attends a basketball game every week." The fact that one attends a basketball game every week—or every day—does not in itself demonstrate an obsession. Nellie could be an employee at the arena, or her brother could be one of the players, or she could be a sportswriter, or she could be conducting research on the game of basketball, or she could simply love the game in a positive sense. *Obsession* implies that something in one's behavior is beyond control; if that is the case, then your statements should reflect it: "Nellie is obsessed with basketball because, despite being threatened with losing her job if she doesn't go to work rather than the basketball games, she attends them anyway."

Ad Hominem   An ad hominem ("against the individual person") is a form of non sequitur in which the arguer argues against an individual's qualifications by attacking his or her personal life or trying to create a negative link between life and work. "Sherwood would not make a good mayor because he spends too much of his free time reading murder mysteries." The reverse situation—*pro hominem*—is equally fallacious, even though it would seldom be reported: "Sherwood would make a terrific mayor because he spends a lot of his time reading the Bible."

Denying the Antecedent/Affirming the Consequent   This fallacy occurs in hypothetical ("if-then") assertions. The first part of the assertion (the "if" clause) is called the *antecedent*; the second part (the "then" clause) is called the *consequent*. In a valid hypothetical assertion, the antecedent may be affirmed or the consequent denied—but not vice versa. Thus, in the hypothetical assertion,

If it snows today, then classes will be canceled.

the antecedent may correctly be affirmed (*It is snowing today;* therefore classes are canceled), or the consequent correctly denied (*Classes were not canceled today;* therefore it must not be snowing). But asserting the opposite in each case would be fallacious, as follows:

> Antecedent denied: *"It is not snowing today;* therefore classes are not canceled." (Classes could still be canceled even if it weren't snowing—for example, teachers may have gone on strike.)

> Consequent affirmed: *"Classes have been canceled today;* therefore it is snowing." (Again, classes could have been canceled for reasons other than snowfall.)

Errors of Induction

In this group of fallacies, the process of drawing conclusions or arriving at reliable generalizations based on observed particulars is faulty.

Unsupported Generalization   Generalizing is an important tool for critical thinkers, but a good generalization is derived from evidence. When the evidence is lacking, we say that the generalization is unsupported. *Evidence* in this context refers not only to statistics such as trends, tallies, or percentages but also to cases in point. For example, if you read somewhere that more physicians are being sued for malpractice in the current year than in the year preceding, you would be making an unsupported generalization if you neglected to provide statistical support for your assertion. It would also be a good idea to refer to individual cases that *demonstrated* incompetence. Why? Perhaps the increase in malpractice suits was based on other factors, such as more aggressive efforts to sue for malpractice; or perhaps the criteria defining *malpractice* had changed from one year to the next. As a critical thinker, you always need to be aware of alternative possibilities and explanations.

Another example of an unsupported generalization might be termed an assumption of hidden motive (or hidden agenda), or simply the *motive fallacy*, as the British philosopher Jamie Whyte terms it in his witty and incisive exposé of muddled thinking, *Crimes against Logic* (2004). If you're a manager and one of your employees praises you for landing an important contract, you will fall prey to the motive fallacy if you assume that the employee's motive for praise was, say, to reinforce his or her job security rather than simply wanting to praise you for your achievement. Whyte uses a courtroom example of the motive fallacy. A juror might secretly assume that a defense attorney is "motivated" to defend her client's innocence only because she is being paid to do so; but that juror obviously must consider only the evidence, not any hidden motives. "If we followed the method of the motive fallacy in civil trials," Whyte quips, "they would be rather simple. Decide against the side of the lawyer who was paid more. She has the greater corrupting motive" (12).

Hasty Generalization   A hasty generalization occurs when one leaps to a *premature conclusion*—not because the arguer provided faulty evidence or no evidence at all but because the evidence provided was insufficient to convincingly support the claim being made. Writers of argument can fall prey to hasty generalization when they do not check out enough cases before reaching their conclusion. If you claim, for example, that burglary has increased in your neighborhood and use as your only evidence the fact that two houses on your block have been burglarized, you would be guilty of a hasty generalization—*unless* you could also demonstrate that this number is greater for the same time frame of a year ago. Always make sure your evidence is thorough.

Red Herring   In British fox hunting, red herrings (very odorous) are sometimes dragged across a trail to throw the dogs off scent. This practice serves as a metaphor for raising an issue that has little or nothing to do with what is being argued in order to force the argument in a new direction. For example, say that after listening to a voter's concern that the community's high school needs to receive major funds to upgrade its facilities, a candidate responds, "I understand your concern and have asked the school board to review its policies." The candidate has thrown the voter a red herring by changing the subject from inadequate facilities to the school board's educational policies.

Poisoning the Well   Like the red herring, this fallacy aims to interfere with normal argumentative progression. But whereas the red herring aims to derail an argument in progress, poisoning the well aims to corrupt the argument before it even begins—usually by passing judgment on the quality of the argument before listeners have a chance to evaluate it. If you ask your friends to listen to a debate on whether the public library should be funded for building a videotape collection but then say that one of the debaters will be presenting an argument that has already been successfully repudiated, you would be guilty of poisoning the well with your own evaluation before giving your friends the opportunity to judge for themselves.

Post Hoc Ergo Propter Hoc   The phrase (sometimes simply post hoc) means "after the fact, therefore because of the fact." An effect (say, tripping and falling) is attributed to a cause (say, the sudden appearance of a black cat) only because of proximity, not because of any logical connection. The post hoc fallacy forms the basis for superstitious thinking and preempts any effort to determine a logical cause (for example, the ground was slippery or the person who fell was not paying any attention to the ground).

Begging the Question   This is an error of both deductive and inductive reasoning. As a deductive fallacy, question begging takes the form of circular reasoning in which a conclusion is nothing more than a reworded premise, as in this example:

A required course is one that is essential for a well-rounded education.

Composition is essential for a well-rounded education.

Therefore, composition is a required course.

The reasoning looks sound at first glance, but nothing has been "reasoned" at all. "Required course" is just another way of saying "necessary for a well-rounded education" in the context of the above syllogism. The question that remains—that is "begged"—is "What is meant by 'necessary for a well-rounded education' "?

Question begging can also present itself as an error in inductive reasoning. Essentially, it voices a conclusion that requires inductive testing as if the testing had already been conducted, as in the assertion, "Impractical courses like Ancient History will no longer be required for graduation." Instead of applying a test of impracticality (whatever such a test would be like) to the course in question, the speaker assumes by her phrasing that such a test would be unnecessary.

Slippery Slope   This is an example of induction run rampant. Here a person forecasts a series of events (usually disastrous) that will befall one if the first stated step is taken. Thus, the person who asserts the following is committing a slippery slope fallacy:

If medical researchers continue to increase human longevity, then the population will soar out of control, mass famine will occur, the global economy will collapse, and the very survival of the species will be threatened.

Factors capable of compensating for the consequences of population increase have not been considered.

Errors of Categorization

In this group of fallacies, arguers tend to see things in terms of black and white instead of color gradations, so to speak—or they confuse one group of objects or ideas with another.

False Dichotomy (Either/Or)   This error of reasoning assumes there are only two options to resolving a given situation, when in fact there may be many. Assertions such as, "If you're not part of the solution, you're part of the problem," "America: love it or leave it," or "If you love nature, then you cannot possibly support industrial development" are examples of dichotomous thinking. To address the last example mentioned, for instance, factors that complicate the industry/nature dichotomy include the fact that recycling, land reclaiming, and alternative energy use (wind, solar, geothermal, biomass) are industries.

Apples and Oranges   We often hear people comparing two things that are not comparable (because they are not part of the same category). A statement like

"The physics lecture was not as good as the dinner we had at Antoine's last night" does not convey much meaning. Likewise, it is illogical to claim that Placido Domingo is a better singer than Johnny Cash because opera and country-western are two different kinds of music, with fundamentally different criteria for excellence.

Errors of Analogy

Errors in analogies occur when the analogy distorts, misrepresents, or oversimplifies the reality.

False or Invalid Analogy   An analogy is considered false when it distorts what is essentially true about what is being analogized. If a student dislikes an instructor's strict, regimented classroom tactics and says that the classroom is like Hitler's Third Reich, the student is using a false analogy. Yes, it is true that Hitler used strict military tactics; but that fact alone cannot serve to parallel the situation in a classroom—unless the professor hired secret police agents (Gestapo), put dissenters into horrific concentration camps, and instituted mass extermination plans. Parallel activities of students and professionals often breed false analogies: "It isn't fair that I can't write on anything I want, any way I want. Nobody tells Amy Tan or Stephen King how or what to write!"

Faulty Analogy   Sometimes the analogy we use to parallel an idea or object is something of a half-truth instead of a complete falsehood; that is, it might work in one context, but not in others. To compare human courtship rituals to those of peacocks, for example, might amusingly highlight the similarities, but the differences are too major to take the analogy seriously.

Tu Quoque   (pronounced *too qwo-kway,* Latin for "you also") You'd think that the likelihood of commiting this fallacy would have vanished shortly after one's tenth birthday, but for some reason it lingers into adulthood. This is the error of analogy whereby Teddy says to Betty, "Don't you dare accuse *me* of cheating on the exam; I saw you cheating also."

Errors of Authorization

In this group of fallacies, authority figures or their testimonials are used vaguely or erroneously.

Vague Authority   In the sentence, "Science tells us that a catastrophic earthquake will strike Southern California within the next ten years," we would do well to question the term *science.* (In a similar vein, recall the commercial that begins, "Four out of five doctors recommend . . .") We have no idea who or even what authority *science* is referring to since *science* refers to a vast body of disciplines, not any particular authority. To remove the vagueness, the author would have to say something to this effect: "Seismologists at Cal Tech [or better yet, Dr. So-and-So, a seismologist at Cal Tech] predicts that a catastrophic earthquake will strike Southern California within the next ten years."

Suspect Authority   Sometimes it is not easy to tell whether an authority is reliable. Using the above example, if the credentials of the scientist predicting the earthquake are not disclosed—or if her field of expertise is a discipline other than seismology—we have a right to suspect that person's authority.

The suspect authority fallacy is encountered most frequently in advertisements. When a film star tells us that a certain brand of shampoo gives a "deep bodied" luster to hair, we wonder what the basis for authority possibly could be, even assuming that everyone agrees on how a "deep bodied" luster looks.

Keep in mind, of course, that such a commercial is not an example of false advertising. The commercial never states that the film star has the proper credentials to evaluate a product's quality, only that the product is the star's personal choice. The audience is left to make any further inferences, such as, "Gosh, if Wilma Superstar uses that shampoo, then it *must* be terrific."

Errors of Pleading

These fallacies stem from erroneous or improper use of the Aristotelian appeals discussed in Chapter 1.

Appeal to Fear   Anyone who has heard commercials for security alarm systems or auto-theft prevention devices is quite familiar with this appeal. The advertiser typically presents scenarios of coming home to find the place ransacked. "Better to be safe than sorry" is the common phrase brandished here. Keep in mind that this appeal becomes an error in pleading when it is excessive or when the scenarios presented are so extreme as to distort reality. If the advertiser for security alarms paints a lurid picture of you and your family being tortured or murdered by burglars, for example, such an appeal to fear likely would be excessive and thus erroneous.

Appeal to the Bandwagon   Appeal to the bandwagon is the fallacy behind peer pressure. "Hey, everyone else is going to the beach today; don't be a nerd and stay cooped up in the library on such a gorgeous day!" Being able to say no, to maintain your own integrity, and to do what is most responsible and best for you in the long term are hard when you are the only one following that path. If you discover that everyone is suddenly buying or selling shares of stock that you own, the temptation is great to do likewise. It sometimes takes courage to say, "I'm going to think this out on my own and not follow the crowd."

Of course, sometimes an appeal to the bandwagon makes sense, as in the case of sound medical or health-care advice: "Millions of people get their teeth cleaned regularly (because they are far less likely to suffer from gum disease if they do so), so you should get your teeth cleaned too."

Appeal to Ignorance   The basis of the appeal here is that we can decide based on what is *not* known. For example, "We have every reason to believe that Martians exist because we have no way of knowing that they *don't* exist." The problem with this kind of reasoning, of course, is that there is no way to prove or disprove the claim.

One often encounters appeals to ignorance in informal scientific speculation. Have you ever gotten into a conversation about the likelihood of intelligent life on other worlds? You might commonly hear a line of reasoning that goes something like this:

> True, we haven't the slightest blip of evidence that intelligent beings exist beyond earth; but the universe is so vast and our understanding of what the universe could contain is so meager that there must be intelligent life out there somewhere!

Although one might argue that the probability of intelligent life increases in proportion to the size of the field, that probability does not necessarily approach inevitability unless compelling evidence is uncovered (indirect evidence of intelligent habitation, such as industrial pollutants in the atmosphere of a distant planet, for example).

◎/◎ Exercise 6.7

1. What is the connection between a method of reasoning and an error in reasoning?

2. State the principal difference between inductive and deductive reasoning.

3. For each of the following passages,

   - give the method of reasoning it belongs to;

   - indicate whether it is an appropriate or erroneous use of that method; and

   - if the latter, identify the error and suggest a way to resolve it.
     Note: There may be more than one error in a given passage or no errors at all.

   a. Cats are just like people: They're intensely curious, and they get into trouble as a result of their curiosity.

   b. The idiots who gave my car a tune-up forgot to clean the fuel injection system.

c. God is beyond logical understanding; therefore, one should never question the truth of God's existence.

d. All honors students are high achievers. José is a straight-A student. Therefore, José is a high achiever.

e. Jane: What do you think of my new boyfriend?

   Ann: I think he's a jerk.

   Jane: You just say that because you want him for yourself!

f. After interviewing a dozen students about their reading habits, I am convinced that students these days do not like to read poetry.

g. All of my friends who want to attend law school have signed up for the Advanced Argumentation course. Since you plan on going to law school, you should take this course too.

h. It's a good idea to wash fresh fruit before eating it; the last time I forgot to wash the strawberries I ate, I came down with food poisoning.

i. Music appreciation classes seem like a waste of time. I know what I like to listen to, and no music expert is going to change my mind about it.

j. Chicken is much tastier than oatmeal.

k. Libraries are clearly becoming obsolete because the Internet is growing so rapidly.

l. To answer your question about whether taxes should be raised, let me first call your attention to the fact that the unemployment rate in this state is lower than it has ever been.

m. Sound waves, just like light waves, can be low frequency or high frequency.

n. If children love to read, they will do well in school. Erika does well in school. Therefore, Erika loves to read.

o. Why should I vote? You haven't voted in years.

4. For each of the above passages, suggest ways in which the error, if one exists, may be corrected.

 Exercise 6.8

Read "Love Is a Fallacy" by Max Shulman, a mid-twentieth-century humorist. In it he attempts to demonstrate logical fallacies in action. Then answer the questions that follow.

Love Is a Fallacy | Max Shulman

Cool was I and logical. Keen, calculating, perspicacious, acute and astute—I was all of these. My brain was as powerful as a dynamo, as precise Fas a chemist's scales, as penetrating as a scalpel. And—think of it!—I was only eighteen.

It is not often that one so young has such a giant intellect. Take, for example, Petey Burch, my roommate at the University of Minnesota. Same age, same background, but dumb as an ox. A nice enough fellow, you understand, but nothing upstairs. Emotional type, unstable. Impressionable. Worst of all, a faddist. Fads, I submit are the very negation of reason. To be swept up in every new craze that comes along, to surrender yourself to idiocy just because everybody else is doing it—this, to me, is the acme of mindlessness. Not, however, to Petey.

One afternoon I found Petey lying on his bed with an expression of such distress on his face that I immediately diagnosed appendicitis. "Don't move," I said. "Don't take a laxative. I'll get a doctor."

"Raccoon," he mumbled thickly.

"Raccoon?" I said, pausing in my flight.   5

"I want a raccoon coat," he wailed.

I perceived that his trouble was not physical, but mental. "Why do you want a raccoon coat?"

"I should have known it," he cried, pounding his temples. "I should have known they'd come back when the Charleston came back. Like a fool I spent all my money for textbooks, and now I can't get a raccoon coat."

"Can you mean," I said incredulously, "that people are actually wearing raccoon coats again?"

"All the Big Men on Campus are wearing them. Where've you been?"   10

"In the library," I said, naming a place not frequented by Big Men on Campus.

He leaped from the bed and paced the room. "I've got to have a raccoon coat," he said passionately. "I've got to!"

"Petey, why? Look at it rationally. Raccoon coats are unsanitary. They shed. They smell bad. They weigh too much. They're unsightly. They —"

"You don't understand," he interrupted impatiently. "It's the thing to do. Don't you want to be in the swim?"

"No," I said truthfully.   15

"Well, I do," he declared. "I'd give anything for a raccoon coat. Anything!"

My brain, that precision instrument, slipped into high gear. " Anything?" I asked, looking at him narrowly.

"Anything," he affirmed in ringing tones.

Source: Max Shulman, "Love Is a Fallacy" from *The Personal View*, 40–48. Copyright 1951 by Max Shulman, © renewed 1979. Reprinted by permission of Harold Matson Co., Inc.

I stroked my chin thoughtfully. It so happened that I knew where to get my hands on a raccoon coat. My father had had one in his undergraduate days; it lay now in a trunk in the attic back home. It also happened that Petey had something I wanted. He didn't *have* it exactly, but at least he had first rights on it. I refer to his girl, Polly Espy.

I had long coveted Polly Espy. Let me emphasize that my desire for this 20 young woman was not emotional in nature. She was, to be sure, a girl who excited the emotions, but I was not one to let my heart rule my head. I wanted Polly for a shrewdly calculated, entirely cerebral reason.

I was a freshman in law school. In a few years I would be out in practice. I was well aware of the importance of the right kind of wife in furthering a lawyer's career. The successful lawyers I had observed were, almost without exception, married to beautiful, gracious, intelligent women. With one omission, Polly fitted these specifications perfectly.

Beautiful she was. She was not yet of pin-up proportions, but I felt sure that time would supply the lack. She already had the makings.

Gracious she was. By gracious I mean full of graces. She had an erectness of carriage, an ease of bearing, a poise that clearly indicated the best of breeding. At table her manners were exquisite. I had seen her at the Kozy Kampus Korner eating the speciality of the house—a sandwich that contained scraps of pot roast, gravy, chopped nuts, and a dipper of sauerkraut—without even getting her fingers moist.

Intelligent she was not. In fact, she veered in the opposite direction. But I believed that under my guidance she would smarten up. At any rate, it was worth a try. It is, after all, easier to make a beautiful dumb girl smart than to make an ugly smart girl beautiful.

"Petey," I said, "are you in love with Polly Espy?"   25

"I think she's a keen kid," he replied, "but I don't know if you'd call it love. Why?"

"Do you," I asked, "have any kind of formal arrangement with her? I mean are you going steady or anything like that?"

"No. We see each other quite a bit, but we both have other dates. Why?"

"Is there," I asked, "any other man for whom she has a particular fondness?"

"Not that I know of. Why?"   30

I nodded with satisfaction. "In other words, if you were out of the picture, the field would be open. Is that right?"

"I guess so. What are you getting at?"

"Nothing, nothing," I said innocently, and took my suitcase out of the closet.

"Where are you going?" asked Petey.

"Home for the weekend." I threw a few things into the bag.   35

"Listen," he said, clutching my arm eagerly, "while you're home, you couldn't get some money from your old man, could you, and lend it to me so I can buy a raccoon coat?"

"I may do better than that," I said with a mysterious wink and closed my bag and left.

"Look," I said to Petey when I got back Monday morning. I threw open the suitcase and revealed the huge, hairy, gamy object that my father had worn in his Stutz Bearcat in 1925.

"Holy Toledo!" said Petey reverently. He plunged his hands into the raccoon coat and then his face. "Holy Toledo!" he repeated fifteen or twenty times.

"Would you like it?" I asked.   40

"Oh yes!" he cried, clutching the greasy pelt to him. Then a canny look came into his eyes. "What do you want for it?"

"Your girl," I said, mincing no words.

"Polly?" he said in a horrified whisper. "You want Polly?"

"That's right."

He flung the coat from him. "Never," he said stoutly.   45

I shrugged. "Okay. If you don't want to be in the swim. I guess it's your business."

I sat down in a chair and pretended to read a book, but out of the corner of my eye I kept watching Petey. He was a torn man. First he looked at the coat with the expression of a waif at a bakery window. Then he turned away and set his jaw resolutely. Then he looked back at the coat, with even more longing in his face. Then he turned away, but with not so much resolution this time. Back and forth his head swiveled, desire waxing, resolution waning. Finally he didn't turn away at all; he just stood and stared with mad lust at the coat.

"It isn't as though I was in love with Polly," he said thickly. "Or going steady or anything like that."

"That's right," I murmured.

"What's Polly to me, or me to Polly?"   50

"Not a thing," said I.

"It's just been a casual kick—just a few laughs, that's all."

"Try on the coat," said I.

He complied. The coat bunched high over his ears and dropped all the way down to his shoe tops. He looked like a mound of dead raccoons. "Fits fine," he said happily.

I rose from my chair. "Is it a deal?" I asked, extending my hand.   55

He swallowed. "It's a deal," he said and shook my hand.

I had my first date with Polly the following evening. This was in the nature of a survey; I wanted to find out just how much work I had to do to get her mind up to the standard I required. I took her first to dinner. "Gee, that was a delish dinner," she said as we left the restaurant. Then I took her to a movie. "Gee, that was a marvy movie," she said as we left the theater. And then I took her home. "Gee, I had a sensaysh time," she said as she bade me good night.

I went back to my room with a heavy heart. I had gravely underestimated the size of my task. This girl's lack of information was terrifying. Nor would it be enough merely to supply her with information. First she had to be taught to *think*. This loomed as a project of no small dimensions, and at first I was tempted to give her back to Petey. But then I got to thinking about her abundant physical charms and about the way she entered the room and the way she handled a knife and fork, and I decided to make an effort.

I went about it, as in all things, systematically. I gave her a course in logic. It happened that I, as a law student, was taking a course in logic myself, so I had all the facts at my finger tips. "Polly," I said to her when I picked her up on our next date, "tonight we are going over to the Knoll and talk."

"Oo, terrif," she replied. One thing I will say for this girl: you would go   60
far to find another so agreeable.

We went to the Knoll, the campus trysting place, and we sat down under an old oak, and she looked at me expectantly. "What are we going to talk about?" she asked.

"Logic."

She thought this over for a minute and decided she liked it. "Magnif," she said.

"Logic," I said, clearing my throat, "is the science of thinking. Before we can think correctly, we must first learn to recognize the common fallacies of logic. These we will take up tonight."

"Wow-dow!" she cried, clapping her hands delightedly.

I winced, but went bravely on. "First let us examine the fallacy called   65
Dicto Simpliciter."

"By all means," she urged, batting her lashes eagerly.

"Dicto Simpliciter means an argument based on an unqualified generalization. For example: Exercise is good. Therefore everybody should exercise."

"I agree," said Polly earnestly. "I mean exercise is wonderful. I mean it builds the body and everything."

"Polly," I said gently, "the argument is a fallacy. *Exercise is good* is an unqualified generalization. For instance, if you have heart disease, exercise   70
is bad, not good. Many people are ordered by their doctors *not* to exercise. You must *qualify* the generalization. You must say exercise is *usually* good, or exercise is good *for most people*. Otherwise you have committed a Dicto Simpliciter. Do you see?"

"No," she confessed. "But this is marvy. Do more! Do more!"

"It will be better if you stop tugging at my sleeve," I told her, and when she desisted, I continued. "Next we take up a fallacy called Hasty Generalization. Listen carefully: You can't speak French. I can't speak French. Petey Burch can't speak French. I must therefore conclude that nobody at the University of Minnesota can speak French."

"Really?" said Polly, amazed. "*Nobody?*"

I hid my exasperation. "Polly, it's a fallacy. The generalization is reached too hastily. There are too few instances to support such a conclusion."

"Know any more fallacies?" she asked breathlessly. "This is more fun   75
than dancing even."

I fought off a wave of despair. I was getting nowhere with this girl, absolutely nowhere. Still, I am nothing if not persistent. I continued. "Next comes Post Hoc. Listen to this: Let's not take Bill on our picnic. Every time we take him out with us, it rains."

"I know somebody just like that," she exclaimed. "A girl back home— Eula Becker, her name is. It never fails. Every single time we take her on a picnic—"

"Polly," I said sharply, "it's a fallacy. Eula Becker doesn't *cause* the rain. She has no connection with the rain. You are guilty of Post Hoc if you blame Eula Becker."

"I'll never do it again," she promised contritely. "Are you mad at me?"

I sighed deeply. "No, Polly, I'm not mad."   80

"Then tell me some more fallacies."

"All right. Let's try Contradictory Premises."

"Yes, let's," she chirped, blinking her eyes happily.

I frowned, but plunged ahead. "Here's an example of Contradictory Premises: If God can do anything, can He make a stone so heavy that He won't be able to lift it?"

"Of course," she replied promptly.   85

"But if He can do anything, He can lift the stone," I pointed out.

"Yeah," she said thoughtfully. "Well, then I guess He can't make the stone."

"But He can do anything," I reminded her.

She scratched her pretty, empty head. "I'm all confused," she admitted.

"Of course you are. Because when the premises of an argument contra-   90
dict each other, there can be no argument. If there is an irresistible force, there can be no immovable object. If there is an immovable object, there can be no irresistible force. Get it?"

"Tell me some more of this keen stuff," she said eagerly.

I consulted my watch. "I think we'd better call it a night. I'll take you home now, and you go over all the things you've learned. We'll have another session tomorrow night."

I deposited her at the girl's dormitory, where she assured me that she had had a perfectly terrif evening, and I went glumly home to my room. Petey lay snoring in his bed, the raccoon coat huddled like a great hairy beast at his feet. For a moment I considered waking him and telling him that he could have his girl back. It seemed clear that my project was doomed to failure. The girl simply had a logic-proof head.

But then I reconsidered, I had wasted one evening; I might as well waste another. Who knew? Maybe somewhere in the extinct crater of her mind, a few embers still smoldered. Maybe somehow I could fan them into flame. Admittedly it was not a prospect fraught with hope, but I decided to give it one more try.

Seated under the oak the next evening I said, "Our first fallacy tonight is   95
called Ad Misericordiam."

She quivered with delight.

"Listen closely," I said. "A man applies for a job. When the boss asks him what his qualifications are, he replies that he has a wife and six children at home, the wife is a helpless cripple, the children have nothing to eat, no clothes to wear, no shoes on their feet, there are no beds in the house, no coal in the cellar, and winter is coming."

A tear rolled down each of Polly's pink cheeks. "Oh, this is awful, awful," she sobbed.

"Yes, it's awful," I agreed, "but it's no argument. The man never answered the boss's question about his qualifications. Instead he appealed to the boss's sympathy. He committed the fallacy of Ad Misericordiam. Do you understand?"

"Have you got a handkerchief?" she blubbered.   100

I handed her a handkerchief and tried to keep from screaming while she wiped her eyes. "Next," I said in a carefully controlled tone, "we will discuss False Analogy. Here is an example: Students should be allowed to look at their textbooks during examinations. After all, surgeons have X-rays to guide them during an operation, lawyers have briefs to guide them during a trial, carpenters have blueprints to guide them when they are building a house. Why, then, shouldn't students be allowed to look at their textbooks during an examination?"

"There now," she said enthusiastically, "is the most marvy idea I've heard in years."

"Polly," I said testily, "the argument is all wrong. Doctors, lawyers, and carpenters aren't taking a test to see how much they have learned, but students are. The situations are altogether different, and you can't make an analogy between them."

"I still think it's a good idea," said Polly.

"Nuts," I muttered. Doggedly I pressed on. "Next we'll try Hypothesis   105
Contrary to Fact."

"Sounds yummy," was Polly's reaction.

"Listen: If Madame Curie had not happened to leave a photographic plate in a drawer with a chunk of pitchblende, the world today would not know about radium."

"True, true," said Polly, nodding her head. "Did you see the movie? Oh, it just knocked me out. That Walter Pidgeon is so dreamy. I mean he fractures me."

"If you can forget Mr. Pidgeon for a moment," I said coldly, "I would like to point out that the statement is a fallacy. Maybe Madame Curie would have discovered radium at some later date. Maybe somebody else would have discovered it. Maybe any number of things would have happened. You can't start with a hypothesis that is not true and then draw any supportable conclusions from it."

"They ought to put Walter Pidgeon in more pictures," said Polly. "I   110
hardly ever see him any more."

One more chance, I decided. But just one more. There is a limit to what flesh and blood can bear. "The next fallacy is called Poisoning the Well."

"How cute!" she gurgled.

"Two men are having a debate. The first one gets up and says, 'My opponent is a notorious liar. You can't believe a word that he is going to say.' Now, Polly, think. Think hard. What's wrong?"

I watched her closely as she knit her creamy brow in concentration. Suddenly a glimmer of intelligence—the first I had seen—came into her eyes. "It's not fair," she said with indignation. "It's not a bit fair. What chance has the second man got if the first man calls him a liar before he even begins talking?"

"Right!" I cried exultantly. "One hundred per cent right. It's not fair.   115
The first man has *poisoned the well* before anybody could drink from it. He has hamstrung his opponent before he could even start. . . . Polly, I'm proud of you."

"Pshaw," she murmured, blushing with pleasure.

"You see, my dear, these things aren't so hard. All you have to do is concentrate. Think—examine—evaluate. Come now, let's review everything we have learned."

"Fire away," she said with an airy wave of her hand.

Heartened by the knowledge that Polly was not altogether a cretin, I began a long, patient review of all I had told her. Over and over and over again I cited instances, pointed out flaws, kept hammering away without let up. It was like digging a tunnel. At first everything was work, sweat, and darkness. I had no idea when I would reach the light, or even *if* I would. But I persisted. I pounded and clawed and scraped, and finally I was rewarded. I saw a chink of light. And then the chink got bigger and the sun came pouring in and all was bright.

Five grueling nights this took, but it was worth it. I had made a logician   120
out of Polly; I had taught her to think. My job was done. She was worthy of me at last. She was a fit wife for me, a proper hostess for my many mansions, a suitable mother for my well-heeled children.

It must not be thought that I was without love for this girl. Quite the contrary. Just as Pygmalion loved the perfect woman he had fashioned, so I loved mine. I determined to acquaint her with my feelings at our very next meeting. The time had come to change our relationship from academic to romantic.

"Polly," I said when next we sat beneath our oak, "tonight we will not discuss fallacies."

"Aw, gee," she said, disappointed.

"My dear," I said, favoring her with a smile, "we have now spent five evenings together. We have gotten along splendidly. It is clear that we are well matched."   125

"Hasty Generalization," said Polly brightly.

"I beg your pardon," said I.

"Hasty Generalization," she repeated. "How can you say that we are well matched on the basis of only five dates?"

I chuckled with amusement. The dear child had learned her lessons well. "My dear," I said, patting her hand in a tolerant manner, "five dates is plenty. After all, you don't have to eat a whole cake to know that it's good."

"False Analogy," said Polly promptly. "I'm not a cake. I'm a girl."

I chuckled with somewhat less amusement. The dear child had learned   130 her lessons perhaps too well. I decided to change tactics. Obviously the best approach was a simple, strong, direct declaration of love. I paused for a moment while my massive brain chose the proper words. Then I began:

"Polly, I love you. You are the whole world to me, and the moon and the stars and the constellations of outer space. Please, my darling, say that you will go steady with me, for if you will not, life will be meaningless. I will languish. I will refuse my meals. I will wander the face of the earth, a shambling, hollow-eyed hulk."

There, I thought, folding my arms, that ought to do it.

"Ad Misericordiam," said Polly.

I ground my teeth. I was not Pygmalion; I was Frankenstein, and my monster had me by the throat. Frantically I fought back the tide of panic surging through me. At all costs I had to keep cool.

"Well, Polly," I said, forcing a smile, "you certainly have learned your   135 fallacies."

"You're darn right," she said with a vigorous nod.

"And who taught them to you, Polly?"

"You did."

"That's right. So you do owe me something, don't you, my dear? If I   140 hadn't come along you never would have learned about fallacies."

"Hypothesis Contrary to Fact," she said instantly.

I dashed perspiration from my brow. "Polly," I croaked, "you mustn't take all these things so literally. I mean this is just classroom stuff. You know that the things you learn in school don't have anything to do with life."

"Dicto Simpliciter," she said, wagging her finger at me playfully.

That did it. I leaped to my feet, bellowing like a bull. "Will you or will you not go steady with me?"

"I will not," she replied.   145

"Why not?" I demanded.

"Because this afternoon I promised Petey Burch that I would go steady with him."

I reeled back, overcome with the infamy of it. After he promised, after he made a deal, after he shook my hand! "The rat!" I shrieked, kicking up great chunks of turf. "You can't go with him, Polly. He's a liar. He's a cheat. He's a rat."

"Poisoning the Well," said Polly, "and stop shouting. I think shouting must be a fallacy too."

With an immense effort of will, I modulated my voice. "All right, I said. "You're a logician. Let's look at this thing logically. How could you choose Petey Burch over me? Look at me—a brilliant student, a tremendous intellectual, a man with an assured future. Look at Petey—a knothead, a jitterbug, a guy who'll never know where his next meal is coming from. Can you give me one logical reason why you should go steady with Petey Burch?"

"I certainly can," declared Polly. "He's got a raccoon coat."   150

1. Shulman ironically relies on fallacies of his own (such as gender stereotyping) as a way of generating humor. Suggest ways in which the piece could be revised without having to rely on such fallacies.

2. How reliable is this piece as a gauge of problematic reasoning among college students? Although its humor is somewhat dated, does it possess enough of an underlying seriousness to warrant further analysis of the reasoning skills of today's college students?

Chapter Summary

Argumentative writing requires careful reasoning, the ability to think critically and logically about the issues you are investigating and to recognize errors in logic. Such errors—known as fallacies (for example, false analogy and ad hominem)—often arise when writers are not sufficiently knowledgeable about their subject or have not thought sufficiently about possible counterarguments to their thesis. The principal strategies that constitute good reasoning in argument are deduction, induction, categorization, analogy, authorization, and plea. Deduction involves identifying contradictions, inconsistencies, omissions, and oversimplifications as well as reducing unsound claims to their logical absurdity. Induction involves determining a sufficient quantity for the sample as well as determining the reliability of that sample. Categorization involves classifying items according to similar characteristics. Analogy is used to help readers understand a concept by comparing it to one that is simpler and more familiar. Authorization refers to the use of testimony by experts as a supplement to empirical evidence to support claims. Plea refers to use of emotional appeals to motivate readers to take action. When learning to recognize errors in reasoning, don't worry excessively about using fallacies inadvertently; the goal is to become sufficiently familiar with them to reduce the likelihood of their occurring.

Checklist

1. Is the line of reasoning used in my argument logical and coherent?

2. Do I cover all facets of my argument?

3. Do I anticipate counterarguments?

4. Do I commit any errors in reasoning?

   a. Fallacies of deduction such as fourth term, non sequitur, and ad hominem?

   b. Fallacies of induction such as unsupported generalization, red herring, poisoning the well, and begging the question?

   c. Fallacies of categorization such as false dichotomy and mixing apples with oranges?

   d. Fallacies of analogy such as false analogy and faulty analogy?

   e. Fallacies of authorization such as vague authority and suspect authority?

   f. Fallacies of pleading such as appeal to fear, appeal to the bandwagon, and appeal to ignorance?

Writing Projects

1. Read several newspaper or magazine editorial or opinion pieces on a given topic; then write a comparative evaluation of each piece based on the presence and frequency of deductive and inductive errors in reasoning you detect in them.

2. Write an essay on the importance of good reasoning in establishing healthy human relationships, such as romantic or business relationships, friendships, parent-sibling relationships, and so on. Focus on specific kinds of errors in reasoning that occur, using actual or representative examples.

3. Initiate an informal argument on one of the Cluster topics in Part 2 of this book with two or more of your classmates in a small group, and while you are arguing, jot down any fallacies you detect. (To be fair to your classmates, ask them to jot down any fallacies they catch *you* falling prey to.) Afterward, write up the argument, supporting the claim you feel most committed to. Do all you can to rid the argument of the detected fallacies.

7 Researching Your Argument

I have always come to life after coming to books.
—Jorge Luis Borges

Much of the writing you do in college—as well as beyond—requires *research*, which refers to three interconnected activities: (1) searching for and retrieving information you need for your writing project, (2) taking notes, and (3) integrating the necessary information into your paper. These activities enable you to acquire in-depth knowledge of the subject and, in turn, to strengthen the premise of your argument.

The Three Faces of Research

Research involves finding information and applying it to your own purposes. One major reason for writing an argument is to present to readers new information and insights into a topic. At the same time, however, readers need to be informed or reminded about the old information to see how the new perspective (yours) adds to the discussion of the issue and merits consideration. You therefore must learn as much as possible about your topic and know how to incorporate only the best and most relevant researched data. Sometimes students try to incorporate so much data into their papers that the papers begin to read like mere summaries of what others have written about the topic. Readers want to see your original argument *reinforced* by the findings of others.

Searching Before You Research: Taking a Mental Inventory

One of the most important steps in gathering information may seem like the least necessary: making clear to yourself how much you already know about the topic. The step is necessary because a lot of what you learn, if it is not used every day, ends up in the equivalent of deep storage in the brain. Some good ways for retrieving it include listing, clustering, and freewriting—predrafting strategies described in Chapter 1. These information-gathering techniques help you generate questions, ideas, and "paths" to pursue in your research.

Consider this case in point: Before Marian, a first-year composition student, sets out to research her chosen topic—possible long-term effects of secondhand cigarette smoke on children—she opens a blank document in her word processing program and begins freewriting (rapidly recording all that she already knows or associates with the topic). Ignoring word choice, sentence correctness, or paragraph structure for the moment, Marian focuses only on content.

```
My parents both smoked and I remembered coughing a lot when I was
around them, and sometimes my eyes burned. I never connected my cough-
ing and burning eyes to their smoking because I assumed that they
would never do anything to undermine my health. Children can't get
away from smoke. In the family, are stuck, have no choice in the mat-
ter. And then I remember that my best friend Julia's parents also
smoked, even more than my parents did, and that she would cough all
the time, and come down with the flu a lot. Not long afterwards (when?
what year?), the Surgeon General issued a warning that ambient smoke
can be just as harmful as firsthand smoke. Question: has government
done studies comparing effects on children vs. adults? I also read
recently that medical researchers have established a link between sec-
ondhand smoke and chronic respiratory illnesses, such as asthma.
Question: I wonder if the recent upturn in asthma rates in children
relates to parents' smoking? I also know that some researchers or
tobacco industry people or maybe just average smokers argue that the
connection is exaggerated, people's fears get overblown—Question—how
to determine how real is the danger?
```

Marian's freewriting inventory on secondhand smoke is not extensive, but she has written down enough for questions to start occurring to her—questions that help direct and focus the research process. Also, the freewriting gets her thinking about possible opposing views as well as helps her establish a link between her personal experience with the topic and her more objective knowledge of it.

◎/◎ **Exercise 7.1**

1. Freewrite on one of the following argumentative topics:
   a. Ways to improve my local fitness center
   b. How to improve the parking situation on campus
   c. Studying to prepare for a career versus studying for the pleasure of learning

2. Write down all that you already know about a topic you enjoy reading about; then generate a list of questions about aspects of the topic you need to know more about to increase your knowledge or expertise.

Focusing Your Research for Argumentative Essays

Once you have a sense of what you need to find out about your topic, you can guide your researching activities with sets of questions to keep your information-gathering activities in focus. Once again, recall the purpose-audience-writer-subject interconnections of the rhetorical rhombus introduced in Chapter 1 (see Figure 7.1).

Generate your questions in the context of each point on the rhombus. If you are arguing against the authenticity of UFO reports, for example, you might generate sets of questions similar to those in the following four sections.

Purpose-Based Questions

Purpose-based questions are interpretive and based on values, for example:

1. What is the thesis (claim) of my essay? Is it sufficiently clear and convincing? (The next section helps you formulate a strong thesis for your papers.)

2. What values (called warrants in the Toulmin model) are implied by the kind of evidence I bring to the claim?

3. What larger implications are conveyed by the thesis?

4. How do I want my intended audience to think or act after reading my paper? To vote to discontinue funding of UFO research? To stop making unsubstantiated claims?

Audience-Based Questions

Audience-based questions enable you to concentrate on your readers' expectations about the subject matter, on the ways they might respond to your assertions,

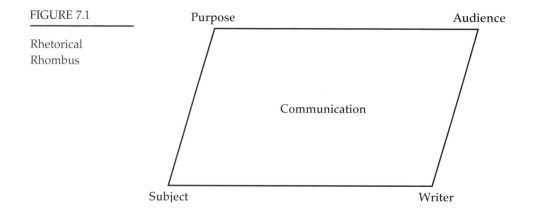

FIGURE 7.1

Rhetorical
Rhombus

and on how you might counterrespond to their reactions. Here are some examples of audience-based questions:

1. Who are the readers I'd like to reach? Those who will support funding of future research on UFOs? Those who are writing the UFO reports to show them their bias?

2. What is my audience's opinion on the authenticity of UFOs? How strongly is that opinion held?

3. What kinds of sources are best suited to my audience? If uninformed, they need background information provided. If hostile, they need to be convinced that I understand their position fully and fairly.

4. What are my audience's main sources of information about UFOs? How reliable are these sources?

5. Exactly how does my audience benefit from reading this essay?

Writer-Based Questions

Writer-based questions enable you to concentrate on your existing knowledge in and understanding of the subject matter and on whether you need to gather more information on it. Here are some examples of writer-based questions:

1. Why is it so important to spend time considering this anti-UFO stance?

2. Do I actually feel strongly one way or another on this issue?

3. How much do I already know about UFO reports?

Subject-Based Questions

Subject-based questions focus on the factual content of your topic. Facts are universally verifiable; that is, they can be tested or verified by anyone. They must be distinguished from interpretations, judgments, or conclusions, which are subjective responses *derived* from your analysis of the facts. Here are some examples of subject-based questions:

1. Do existing UFO reports share common elements? Do these elements reinforce authenticity or fraud?

2. What are the *scientific* data for the claims in the most notable UFO reports? How do I know those scientific data are authentic and reliable?

3. What do I need to research to discuss or refute the claims presented by the UFO reports?

4. Do I carefully consider potential challenges to my views and the best way to interpret their validity?

You can see how the answers to questions in these four areas will affect the text, from its content, to its organization, to its tone.

Formulating a Strong Thesis

You already know what a thesis is: It is the main point you wish to argue, the claim you are making and are trying to persuade your audience to accept, using the strongest evidence you can find. However, you may like to gain more skill in coming up with a strong, compelling thesis for your argumentative essays. Here are three steps you can take to ensure that the thesis you come up with is a good one:

1. Write down an assertion (viewpoint, claim) on a particular topic. For example, if your topic is music censorship, you might write down, "Music censorship is wrong."

2. Ask probing questions about the clarity and specificity of your assertion, making sure that you replace vague or ambiguous language with specific, precise language. If the above statement about music censorship appeared as a thesis statement, readers would have some of the following questions:

   • What is meant by *wrong?* Unethical? Illegal? Misguided?

   • What is meant by *music?* The music itself or the lyrics to songs? If songs, then what kinds of songs? Country-Western? Rap? Rock? Jazz? Rhythm and Blues? Hip Hop? What about the songs do some people find objectionable? Swear words? Obscenity? Political references? Actions seemingly advocated by the lyrics?

   • What is meant by *censorship?* Bleeping certain words or phrases of certain songs? Restricting sales only to those of a certain age? Banning the music altogether?

3. Turn your assertion into a well-focused, specifically worded thesis statement. For example, "Expurgating or banning rap songs because of their alleged profanity or obscenity is against the law because it violates rights guaranteed by the First Amendment."

By taking the time to examine your trial thesis statement from the point of view of its clarity and specificity, you produce effective thesis statements that in turn help you to produce more effective arguments.

◎◎   Exercise 7.2

1. Generate three questions for each of the four elements of the rhetorical rhombus (purpose, audience, writer, subject) for an essay you have recently finished or one you are currently working on.

2. Imagine that you are writing a paper that argues for the best ways of dealing with sexual harassment in the workplace. Generate questions in each of these categories: purpose based, audience based, writer based, subject based.

3. Revise each of the following assertions so that they can serve as strong thesis statements:

   a. Water quality needs to be improved.

   b. Males are the dominant sex because they are stronger.

   c. The university should offer more courses for minorities.

Researching Using the Internet

A late twentieth-century invention, the Internet has become, in little more than a decade, the most revolutionary information resource since the invention of printing about 550 years ago. Its dramatic proliferation brings problems, however, as well as benefits. Some sources on the Net are superficial, irrelevant, or unreliable. Usually, you know right away what is junk and what isn't—but sometimes it is not so easy.

You need to acquire an eye for distinguishing between documents that are substantive and relevant and those that are not. Here are a few questions to ask about Internet documents to help you make that distinction:

1. Are the authors experts in their fields? If no biographical information about the authors is included at the site, check the library or search the Web to see whether these credentials are located elsewhere.

2. Do the authors go beyond mere generalized assertions in order to produce useful new knowledge about the subject? For example, if you find an article that argues either for or against the use of exit tests as a condition for high school graduation, does the author back up those assertions with actual data comparing the performance of students who have prepared for such a test with those who have not?

3. Do the authors provide a scholarly context for their arguments? That is, do they relate their points of view to others who have also conducted scholarly inquiry into the subject?

4. Is the subject matter treated seriously and professionally? Be wary of an amateurish tone. For example, in debates over controversial issues such as whether the state should require creationist doctrine to be given equal standing with evolutionary theory in a high school biology class, one side might easily caricature the other side as "religious fanatics" or "radical atheists." Such pigeonholing or name calling works against the very purpose of argument, which is to examine both sides of an issue critically,

carefully, and responsibly, in order to arrive at a reasonable understanding of what really is or should be. When in doubt, weigh the tone and treatment of a questionable document with documents you know are authentic and significant.

Useful Types of Internet Resources

The most common types of information resources available on the Internet include listservers, newsgroups, databases, and online forums. The sections that follow take a closer look at each of these. *Note:* Regardless which of the below sources you consult, it is always a good idea to double-check information you access, especially when acquiring information from unknown individuals participating in a listserv, newsgroup, or forum.

Listservers

A listserver (more commonly referred to as a *listserv*) is a discussion group subscription service in which commentary and information about a given topic are exchanged with all members of the group who are all connected by email. Listserv members often participate in ongoing conversations or debates over key issues. When a great many experts and enthusiasts from all over the world argue heatedly on a given topic, a wealth of information and viewpoints is generated. For this reason, participation in such discussion groups can be an excellent way of staying informed and developing your argumentative skills at the same time.

Newsgroups

Newsgroups (also usenets or bulletin boards) are topic-based electronic discussion groups that anyone can join. Members with an interest in, say, art history can access useful information that is arranged by subtopic and posted by other members. If you are interested in Italian Renaissance art, for example, you quite likely could find, on a home page menu, a newsgroup devoted to that area. Many of these newsgroups archive their postings, so that they become valuable for research.

Databases

Databases are invaluable compilations of sources in a given subject, such as a compilation of books and articles on health care, biochemistry, ancient Egyptian history, economics, or any other subject. Although many databases are accessed online, some of them, like the *Modern Language Association (MLA) International Bibliography of Language and Literature,* the *Readers Guide to Periodical Literature,* and the *Congressional Record Index* continue to be published in hard copy or put on CD-ROM disks. See the reference librarian at your college library when uncertain about locating a particular database for your research project.

Your college library most likely subscribes to a database company that packages electronic bibliographies. The most popular is InfoTrac, which may include newspaper bibliographies (such as those for the *Wall Street Journal*, the *New York Times*, and newspapers from your local area) as well as general reference articles across the disciplines. Your librarian will be happy to inform you of the databases to which the library subscribes, and may provide you with handouts describing each kind.

The catalogs of most academic and research libraries are available online. The Library of Congress's catalog is also available and contains more than 12 million items. The Library of Congress also has accessible special collections, such as the National Agricultural Library and the National Library of Medicine. Access any of the Library of Congress's catalogs at http://www.loc.gov

Forums

A forum is an ongoing discussion group in real time. Forums exist for just about any subject matter and professional interest imaginable. Such forums can be an excellent way of finding highly knowledgeable people and learning from them, while enjoying interactive conversations with people all across the country or even the world. Be careful, however. The knowledge base of participants varies in these discussions, and some participants may purposefully or inadvertently give out misleading information.

Searching on the Web

Searching for information on the Web is easy—almost too easy. All you do is click on a search engine icon at your Internet service provider's home page or enter a Web address for one of the many existing search engines. Some search engines are more powerful than others, however. Among the most reliable are Google, WebCrawler, Yahoo!, AltaVista, Dogpile, *Ask* and Lycos. Here are their URL (Uniform Resource Locator) addresses:

http://www.google.com

http://www.webcrawler.com

http://www.yahoo.com

http://www.altavista.com

http://www.dogpile.com

http://www.ask.com

http://www.lycos.com

http://en.wikipedia.org/wiki/Main-Page

http://scholar.google.com

http://www.metacrawler.com

http://www.hotbot.com

Every search engine is different. Some, like AltaVista and Dogpile, include brief descriptions of every site called up.

The next step is to type keywords in the narrow blank rectangle provided—and here things can get a little tricky. You need to decide which three or four words come closest to the sort of information you hope to find. Use the most "official" terms you know for your subject. If you are looking for general pro-con arguments on school vouchers, for example, you might enter the keywords *school, voucher,* and *programs.* If you want to find material on vouchers relating to your state, enter the name of your state in the keyword field as well. If you wish to focus on specific concerns within the voucher system, you may need to enter an additional relevant keyword such as *curriculum, class size,* or *teaching excellence.*

Search engines usually retrieve far more sites than you can review in a reasonable time, so you have to be selective. If you're looking for substantive, scholarly commentary, then look for sites from academic institutions. (You can recognize these sites by their URL extension, *.edu.*) Or look for online magazines, or *e-zines* as they are sometimes called.

Google has a time-saving search option, an "I'm feeling lucky" button that, when clicked on, brings up far fewer hits, but those hits are likely the most relevant to the keywords you have entered.

Another problem to be aware of when searching for relevant sites is timeliness. If you require the latest information, be sure to check the dates of the sites you bring up. Some of them may be several years old.

Using Boolean Search Strategies

A Boolean search is one in which you customize your search keywords using what are called operators. The three most common Boolean operators are

and	^
not	+
or	&

Let's say you are searching the Expanded Academic Index (an international general database for source materials in the humanities, social and general sciences) for articles on logging policies or logging practices but not articles having to do with the history of logging. Instead of merely entering the keyword *logging,* you can use the Boolean operators *and* and *not* to restrict your search as follows:

> Logging policies and practices not histories

Another device useful in searches is the asterisk (*) which works as a wildcard: It instructs the search engine to bring up all forms of the word attached to the word segment typed in before the asterisk. Thus, if you're looking for information about cosmology and want to bring up articles with all forms of the word *cosmology* at once instead of searching for each one separately, you would simply type in *cosm**. The search engine would then bring up database articles containing all the words bearing that segment, for example:

cosmic

cosmological

cosmologist

cosmologists

cosmology

cosmos

Of course, you would also get a lot of unwanted entries relating to words that begin with the segment *cosm* but that have nothing to do with the nature of the universe:

cosmetic

cosmetics

cosmetologist

cosmetologists

cosmetology

Useful Websites for Writers of Arguments

The list that follows gives some useful Web addresses for your research. Note, however, that websites often disappear, are updated, or change their addresses. Consider using a current *Internet Yellow Pages* (available in most bookstores and libraries) to locate sources.

For Humanities Resources
http://vos.ucsb.edu/

For Statistics from the U.S. Department of Education
http://nces.ed.gov/pubsearch/

For Resources in Religious Studies
http://www.bu.edu/sth/library/index.html

For Information About World History
http://www.hartford-hwp.com/archives   The website for the World History Archives.

For Health-Related Information from the Centers for Disease Control
http://www.cdc.gov/

For Information About Population from the U.S. Census Bureau
http://www.census.gov/

For Information About Public Policy Issues
http://www.speakout.com/activism/

Media Web Sites

http://www.cnn.com/   The website of the Cable News Network.

http://www.pbs.org/   The website of the Public Broadcasting Service (educational television programming).

http://www.npr.org/   The website of National Public Radio.

http://www.ecola.com/archs.php   A website directory with links to newspapers that allow back-issue searches.

http://www.nytimes.com   The website of *the New York Times*.

http://www.nytimes.com/pages/readersopinions/index.html   This website takes you to *the New York Times* forums, where you can read numerous postings on dozens of subjects by forum members. By subscribing for free, you can post your own views and responses to the postings of others.

Finally, there are websites to help you find information on the Internet as well as to think critically about available resources:

A Tutorial for Finding Information Online
http://www.lib.berkeley.edu/TeachingLib/Guides/Internet/FindInfo.html
This site introduces you to the basics of Web searching.

Guidelines for Evaluating websites

http://www.tucolib.info/   A bibliography of online resources for evaluating websites.

◎/◎   Exercise 7.3

1. Compare the effectiveness of two different search engines, such as Yahoo!, Alta Vista, Dogpile, or Google. Write out a description of their respective strengths and weaknesses.

2. Enter an online forum such as Salon.com on a topic that interests you and then report your experience orally or in an essay. What did you learn about your topic as a result of interacting with other members of the forum?

3. Using the latest *Internet Yellow Pages* in your college library's reference room, locate three or four websites that seem relevant to the topic you are currently writing about. Then go to these sites. Which of them were most useful, and why? Which were least useful, and why?

Researching Using Print Resources

Without doubt, the Internet is a helpful, high-speed information-accessing tool, and its resources are expanding continuously. But hard-copy resources—reference books, trade books, periodicals (specialized and nonspecialized), historical documents, maps, and newspapers—continue to be indispensable. Much if not most academic scholarship continues to be published in traditional print journals, for example. Scholars often find "hard copy" easier to consult.

Locating Articles

To locate important article sources, begin with the Expanded Academic Index in your library's electronic catalog. The listing will tell you whether your library carries the periodical that the article is in. If not, you may be able to have your library obtain a fax of it for a nominal fee or obtain a book through interlibrary loan.

Other important print periodical indexes include:

Applied Sciences Index

Education Index

Environmental Index

General Science Index

Humanities Index

National Newspaper Index

Social Sciences Index

Using Additional Print Reference Works

In addition to periodical indexes, you may already be familiar with the following hard-copy reference works: encyclopedias (general and specialized), dictionaries, abstracts and digests, handbooks and sourcebooks, and atlases.

Encyclopedias   General or subject-specific encyclopedias are often a good place to begin your formal research because they offer a panoramic view of the topic you are working with and provide references for further reading. An encyclopedia article is essentially a detailed summary of the most important facts about a topic, accompanied by a bibliography. You probably have used general encyclopedias that cover the whole spectrum of knowledge. You may not have used specialized ency-clopedias, which are limited to only one subject, such as psychology or religion.

Here is just a small sampling of the kinds of encyclopedias you will find in your library's reference room:

General	Subject-Specific
Collier's Encyclopedia	*Encyclopedia of Environmental Studies*
The Columbia Encyclopedia	*Encyclopedia of Psychoactive Drugs*
Encyclopedia Britannica	*Macmillan Encyclopedia of Computers*
World Book Encyclopedia	*The Wellness Encyclopedia*

Dictionaries   A dictionary provides more than highly concise definitions and explanations; in the case of biographical dictionaries, for example, you will find profiles of notable individuals. Most dictionaries are devoted to words in general, but there are specialized dictionaries as well. Important dictionaries include:

American Biographical Dictionary

A Dictionary of Biology

McGraw-Hill Dictionary of Scientific and Technical Terms

The Merriam-Webster Book of Word Histories

New Dictionary of American Slang

The Oxford English Dictionary

Who's Who

Who's Who Among African Americans

Who's Who Among America's Teachers

Who's Who Among Asian Americans

Who's Who Among Hispanic Americans

Who's Who in American History

Abstracts and Digests   An abstract is a formal summary of a scholarly or scientific paper. Virtually all disciplines publish compilations of abstracts. Digests are summaries of less formal works such as book *reviews*. Here is a sampling of abstracts and digests:

Book Review Digest

Chemical Abstracts

Dissertation Abstracts

Ecology Abstracts

Handbooks and Sourcebooks   These types of reference books provide you with guidelines and references for particular disciplines, such as English literature, philosophy, geology, economics, mathematics, and computer science. Some handbooks and sourcebooks are:

> *A Field Guide to Rocks and Minerals* (similar Field Guides exist for most subjects in the general sciences)
>
> A Handbook to Literature
>
> *Opposing Viewpoints* (collections of pro-con position statements on a wide range of topics)

Atlases   Atlases are collections of maps (of countries, states, cities, the world) and may be historical, topographical (depicting landmasses of different elevations), or geographical (depicting regions in terms of population, natural resources, industries, and the like).

   Exercise 7.4

1. At your library, consult *Opposing Viewpoints* (see listing under "Handbooks and Sourcebooks" above) and write a brief summary of each side of a particular topic that you find interesting. Decide which side is argued most convincingly and why.

2. Look up a single item in three different encyclopedias or dictionaries. Describe how the coverage differs from source to source.

3. Using *Book Review Digest* (see listing under "Abstracts and Digests" above), locate three different reviews of a single book and write a comparative evaluation of the three reviews. Which reviewer provides the most useful information about the book's subject matter? About the author?

Gathering Information from Email, Telephone Conversations, Interviews, and Surveys

As a college student, you are part of a complex community of educators, researchers, and specialists in numerous disciplines. Name your topic and someone on your college faculty, staff, or student body will be an expert in it. But how do you contact these individuals? Very simply: by email or telephone.

Using Email or the Telephone

Obtain a campus phone directory listing faculty and staff and their respective departments or offices; there you will see each person's telephone extension number and email address, along with his or her office location. You can also check your school's website to find what specialties are listed for faculty members or to learn where the various offices and departments are on campus so that you can visit them to find out who is an expert in what. Next, email or phone that person, explain who you are and what you are researching, and ask to set up a time convenient for a telephone interview or a personal interview. If the information you require is relatively complex or the person in question is too busy to be interviewed, request an email exchange.

Conducting an Interview

An interview is a focused, carefully directed conversation on a predetermined topic, usually involving the interviewee's personal involvement in the topic being discussed. Interviews can be formal or informal, depending on the nature of the topic and the relationship between interviewer and interviewee.

Information derived from interviews is valuable for two reasons:

1. It is timely (you may be getting "cutting edge" information before it is published).

2. It provides the opportunity for obtaining personal insights into the subject matter.

Experts can also be extremely helpful in directing you to additional sources and thinking about other aspects of the topic you may not be aware of.

When conducting the interview, keep the following suggestions in mind:

1. Always make an appointment with the person you wish to interview and be clear about what you wish to discuss and why.

2. Prepare questions to ask during the interview, but don't use them rigidly or present them in rote fashion as in an interrogation. Rather, try to work them spontaneously into your discussion. Ask specific, well-focused questions about what you need to know.

3. It is all right to engage in "ice-breaking" small talk, but once the discussion begins, try not to go off on tangents. Remember: You are there to interview the individual, not to have a casual conversation, so listen more than you talk.

4. Be alert for "spinoff" questions—unanticipated questions that occur to you in light of the way the interviewee answers a previous question. Be sure, however, that spinoff questions are relevant to the topic.

5. Avoid leading questions, whereby your manner of wording the questions reveals a bias on your part. For example, a leading question would be "Wouldn't you agree that the dangers from ozone depletion are highly exaggerated?" You want more than a yes or no response anyway.

6. Always ask for clarification of a complex idea or for definition of an unfamiliar term. Also, ask for the correct spelling of names or terms you are uncertain about.

7. If you wish to record the interview on tape, request permission to do so beforehand. But don't expect to transcribe it all. You will use the tape just to capture precise wording of an elegant or particularly apt phrase, just as when you quote a written source directly.

8. Ask the interviewee for permission to contact him or her for follow-up questions after the interview or perhaps suggest a follow-up interview.

9. Write a thank-you note to the interviewee after the interview: Show that you acknowledge that the individual is a busy person who set aside time for you. Such common courtesy is justified and appropriate. It also makes it more likely that the individual will respond if you need any follow-up help.

Conducting a Survey

To obtain information from a large number of individuals, you can conduct a survey. The first step is to prepare a questionnaire—a set of questions with room on the sheet for answers—to distribute to individuals. These questions should be carefully worded so that (1) the respondents can answer them quickly, and (2) the survey will yield valid and useful information for your purposes.

The second step is to conduct the survey. This may be done via email, using a distribution list so it could be sent, for example, to the entire student body at once, or via personal distribution, where you simply question individuals directly or ask them to fill out your questionnaire while you wait. Also, it would be a good idea to check with your school's Human Subjects Board or Computer Center about any policies governing such actions.

Designing a Questionnaire

A good questionnaire is a model of relevance, clarity, and concision. Word questions carefully, making sure that binary (for example, yes or no) questions do not stem from a false dichotomy (that is, where answers other than yes or no are possible). Also, do not word questions that are leading or that conceal a bias. The following is an example of a biased question:

What percentage of old-growth forest should be logged?
_____10%   _____50%   _____75%   _____85%   _____100%

This set of options is biased because (1) there is no 0% (the opposite equivalent of 100%), and (2) there is only one option below 50% but two options above 50%.
The following is an example of a leading question:

Do you agree that the sexist practices of the labor union should be stopped?
_____Yes   _____No   _____Not Sure

Sexist is judgmental and therefore risks leading the respondent to agree with that judgment. The question should describe actual documented actions that may or may not be judged as sexist, such as "Should the labor union continue to deny membership to women?"

It is usually a good idea to avoid questions that readers would not be sure how to answer or that would require long answers. Instead, choose questions that ask respondents to choose among the options you provide:

> Which of the following long-term space exploration policies should NASA adopt? (Check all that apply.)
>
> _____Lunar colonization
> _____Robot probes of outer planets
> _____Human exploration of Mars
> _____Lunar-orbiting telescope

Finally, introduce your questionnaire in a brief, courteous paragraph that includes your name, the purpose of your research, and how much time you estimate it will take to answer the questions. Thank your readers in advance for their time.

Taking Effective Research Notes

The notes you take while reading outside sources for your argument-in-progress will come in handy when you decide which sources you need to integrate into the body of your paper. (See also "Incorporating Outside Sources into Your Argument" on pages 216–218.) The following suggestions will make your note-taking more efficient and productive.

1. Unless you have a laptop computer to take with you into the library, use index cards for taking notes (4" × 6" size is ideal): You can easily shuffle and rearrange them, as well as annotate them. Some students find that it helps to use differently colored cards for different purposes, that is, white for direct quotations, yellow for bibliography, green for the writer's own ideas. Photocopying articles and passages from books is another option, but photocopying can get expensive and can take as much time as writing out notes. Also, photocopied pages are harder to sort through and review.

2. Write out the complete bibliographic citation for every source you use; that way, you will be able to locate the source again easily if you need to and will be able to prepare your Works Cited page more quickly. Guidelines for citing sources appear in Chapter 8, Documenting Your Sources: MLA and APA Styles.

3. Read each source straight through to get an idea of all that it includes. Then return to the beginning and copy passages that seem most useful for your needs. Always double-check to make sure you are copying the

passage accurately. If you need to omit part of a passage, indicate the omission with ellipsis dots (. . .). If you need to add a word or date to make a quoted passage understandable or coherent, place it in brackets:

According to the *Cedarville Gazette,* "Last year [2003], local automobile-related fatalities numbered more than 1,500."

The Role of Serendipity in Research

Writers benefit greatly from methodical research, but not all researching is methodical. Some of it is results from good fortune or a special kind of good fortune call *serendipity.*

Serendipity refers to the capacity for discovering important things in an unexpected manner or in an unexpected place. Serendipity seems most likely to occur when you are immersed in your work. Because your senses are on full alert, you pick up things you might not have otherwise noticed or make connections between two ideas that you would never have made in a less engaged state of mind.

Two students described the following serendipitous discoveries:

Student 1

While I was working on my paper on unfair hiring practices, I happened to notice a news story on the Internet that described how frustrating it is to follow user manuals because their instructions are seldom clear enough. That made a light flash inside my head! Perhaps hiring practices are often unfair because the policies describing them are poorly written!

Student 2

Here I was stumped about how to develop my topic on the way students can study effectively in groups. While I was eating lunch, I overheard two students discussing getting together with their Western Civilization study group to prepare for a midterm. I introduced myself and asked them if they would tell me about how they formed their group, how beneficial they thought it was, and what sorts of pitfalls to avoid.

These examples illustrate the way in which mental alertness and engagement can help you discover new approaches to your topic in unexpected ways.

  Exercise 7.5

1. Over the next four or five days, in addition to using methods of methodical researching, do the following:

   a. Browse for half an hour or so among the library stacks, in subject areas relevant to the topic you are working on.

    b. Listen closely for connections, however seemingly tangential, while talking with classmates or friends.

    c. Find some encyclopedia articles related to the topic you are working on and write down any ideas that might be worth incorporating into your essay.

    d. Review your lecture notes from other classes.

2. Report on any serendipitous discoveries that you were able to use for your paper. Compare your serendipity experiences with those of your classmates. If you hear of one you have not experienced, then try to experience it for yourself.

Evaluating Your Sources

It is tempting to assume that just because information is published it is reliable. Because that is not the case, unfortunately, you need to ensure that the sources you incorporate into your argument are trustworthy. Evaluate every outside source you incorporate into your paper using these five criteria:

1. *Accuracy* of information presented
2. *Relevance* to your thesis
3. *Reliability* of the author and the periodical that originally published the material
4. *Clarity*
5. *Thoroughness*

The sections that follow consider each criterion in turn.

Accuracy

Factual information needs to be checked for accuracy. Data, such as population trends, the latest nutritional information about a dietary supplement, academic program policies and offerings, and so on, sometimes change so frequently that the print source at your fingertips may not be the most recent information. Carefully check dates of publication, check with the campus specialist, or search the Internet for more current information.

Relevance

Does the information you plan to use in your argument truly contribute to your thesis? If you are writing about the importance of animals in medical research but use information drawn from the use of animals in cosmetic research, there may be a problem with relevance unless you can draw a medical connection to cosmetic use (for example, certain dyes in mascara can cause an allergic reaction).

Reliability

When considering the reliability of information, think about the credentials of the author presenting it. For example, if an author is conveying information about the toxins in local ground water, that person should be a recognized authority in environmental chemistry, not just a local politician.

Clarity

Important data are sometimes presented in a way that is difficult to understand. In such cases, you may need to *paraphrase* the source material instead of quoting it directly, or to quote it directly but add your own explanation afterwards. Technical information, while clear to you, might be confusing to nonspecialized readers. In such cases, you may need to provide a somewhat elaborate interpretation of the data.

Thoroughness

It is important to ensure that your data are not perfunctory bits of quotations or statistics that fail to provide sufficient grounding for your claim. The more debatable your claims, the more you need to provide sufficient data to remove any doubts from readers' minds.

Understanding and Avoiding Plagiarism

From the Latin word for kidnapper, *plagiarism* refers to two connected acts:

1. Using someone else's work, *published* or *unpublished,* as if it were your own

2. Incorporating someone else's words or *ideas* into your own writing without explicit acknowledgment of authorship or source

You are most likely aware of the seriousness of plagiarism. Quite simply, it is a crime. People's ideas and ways of expressing them are a form of property—intellectual property—and are as worthy of protection from theft as material property. Thus, when a person plagiarizes, he or she is stealing.

Use the following guidelines to determine what kind of material should be acknowledged and what need not be.

1. Paraphrases of someone else's ideas must be acknowledged (that is, cited). Even though you are putting a passage into your own words, you are

nonetheless using another's ideas. Consider this original passage and the paraphrase that follows.

Original passage: "It is too soon to know with certainty if melting polar ice taking place right now will result in coastal flooding within the next five years" (Climatologist Gail Jones).

Plagiarized paraphrase: Will the melting polar ice currently taking place lead to coastal flooding within five years? It is too early to tell.

The author of the paraphrase gives no indication that the information conveyed was taken from the article by Gail Jones. Yes, it's possible that the author simply forgot to cite the source (sometimes referred to as *accidental plagiarism*)—but it is still full-fledged plagiarism. It is every author's responsibility to remember, and properly acknowledge, all sources. The above paraphrase must be revised accordingly. For example:

Acceptable paraphrase: Could the melting polar ice currently taking place, climatologist Gail Jones wonders, lead to coastal flooding within five years? According to Jones, it is too early to tell.

By the way, you need also to be aware of *faulty paraphrasing*. When you recast someone else's ideas into your own words, you must be careful not to distort that original idea. Consider the following paraphrase of the Gail Jones passage:

Faulty paraphrase: It is impossible to determine whether melting polar ice will result in coastal flooding in the near future.

This is a faulty paraphrase. Jones asserted that it was too soon to know with certainty, not that it was impossible. The paraphrase also fails to capture the fact that Jones referred to melting polar ice *that is currently taking place.*

2. Any information considered common knowledge does not require acknowledgment. Facts such as historical dates that are readily looked up in at least three different sources constitute common knowledge. The key word is *readily.* Some factual information is clearly the product of individual research and, as such, is not readily available.

3. When you need to quote verbatim (using the author's exact words), be mindful of these pointers:

   a. Quote only what is necessary to convey the author's ideas. Too many or too lengthy quotations can make a paper difficult to read.

   b. Do not rely on quoted material to carry your argument forward. This is a common pitfall of beginning writers. You want your paper to represent *your* way of thinking, not that of the experts you are quoting.

c. Besides quoting, *comment* on a quotation of one to two sentences or longer. Do not drop a quotation in if your reason for quoting someone else is not patently clear.

d. Use quotation marks around all material quoted verbatim. If the passage you are quoting runs more than four lines, then place the passage, without quotation marks, in a separate paragraph, indented ten spaces from the main text.

Exercise 7.6

1. Label each of the following statements as common knowledge (not requiring acknowledgment) or not common knowledge (requiring acknowledgment).

   a. Some books should be savored slowly, others devoured ravenously.

   b. Like the 1995 flooding of the Rhine, the inundation of the upper Mississippi and Missouri Rivers in 1993 provided a dramatic and costly lesson on the effects of treating the natural flow of rivers as a pathological condition (Janet Abramovitz, *Imperiled Waters, Impoverished Future* 16.).

   c. The Battle of Hastings took place in 1066 C.E.

   d. Many educators these days tend to regard the Internet as a cure-all for getting students to read.

2. Choose any one of the arguments from Part 2, "Reading Clusters," and evaluate in writing its evidence in terms of the five criteria: accuracy, relevance, reliability, clarity, and thoroughness.

3. Study the following passage and the paraphrases that follow. Determine which of the paraphrases (if any) are acceptable and which are unacceptable. If unacceptable, explain why (that is, faulty, plagiarized).

   The market forces of globalization are invading the Amazon, hastening the demise of the forest and thwarting its most committed stewards. In the past three decades, hundreds of people have died in land wars; countless others endure fear and uncertainty, their lives threatened by those who profit from the theft of timber and land. Scott Wallace, "Last of the Amazon," *National Geographic*, Jan. 2007: 43.

   a. **Paraphrase A:** The forces of globalization are destroying the Amazon forests. In the past thirty years, hundreds of people have died in the land wars there; many others experience fear, their lives threatened by timber profiteers.

   b. **Paraphrase B:** Worldwide market forces, notes Scott Wallace, are contributing to the rapid destruction of the Amazon forests. According to

Wallace, land wars are endangering the lives of hundreds (*National Geographic* 43).

c. **Paraphrase C:** According to Scott Wallace, timber barons have all but destroyed the remaining Amazon forests and are murdering anyone who gets in their way (*National Geographic* 43).

Incorporating Outside Sources into Your Argument

The purpose of bringing outside sources into your argument is to add depth and authority to your own original insights. Make sure, then, when incorporating these sources into your paper, that you do not bury your thread of discussion, that your own voice prevails. You may be tempted to relinquish your voice to those of scholars who are recognized experts in their fields; but keep in mind that experts become so as a result of doing what you are beginning to do seriously as a writer: developing an original thesis so that other scholars will learn from you.

Notice, in the following passage, how the writer's voice becomes obscured by the voice of the authority she quotes:

> Academic integrity is taken seriously at Santa Clara University. "The University is committed to a pursuit of truth and knowledge that requires both personal honesty and intellectual integrity as fundamental to teaching, learning, scholarship, and service. Therefore, all members of the University community are expected to be honest in their academic endeavors, whether they are working independently or collaboratively, especially by distinguishing clearly between their own original work and ideas, and those of others, whether published or not" (*Undergraduate Bulletin*, 2003–05: 2). This should be a clear sign to students that academic integrity is part of the learning experience.

In that last sentence, the writer makes an important, original contribution to the conversation about academic integrity, but it is all but lost in the excessively long quotation that precedes it. It's as if the writer is saying to her audience, "Don't listen to me—I'm just a lowly student; listen to what the university administration says!" But that defeats the very reason for writing, which is to contribute to new knowledge or to new ways of thinking about old knowledge. Seeing her mistake, the student revised the passage as follows:

> Academic integrity at Santa Clara University is taken seriously, mainly because such integrity is part of the learning experience. That explains why the new SCU *Undergraduate Bulletin* for 2003–05 goes into elaborate detail about the issue. Administrators emphasize that the "pursuit of truth" to which the University is committed "*requires* [emphasis mine] both personal

honesty and intellectual integrity" (2). In other words, you cannot truly become an educated person if you are unable or unwilling to make a clear, explicit distinction between what you know and what others know; between what you can contribute to an area of study and what others have contributed.

With this revision, the student asserts herself as a worthy contributor to the conversation on academic integrity. She has earned her stripes as an authority in her own right.

Also, all writing needs to "flow" for the points to unfold logically and smoothly for the reader. An important element in a smoothly developed argument is a clear link between each general point and the specific reference to outside sources. The writer's text should lead into the quoted material not just with a reference to who made the statement but also with the credentials of the source.

When you are incorporating others' ideas into your argument, you will want to lead into the borrowed material with signals that you are about to use a source to support your claim and that your source is a reliable one for your claim.

Finally, check to make sure that you have fully *synthesized* the material from outside sources with the new information that you have contributed. Synthesis occurs when you show that the outside (pre-existing) information together with the new information that you bring to the discussion results in new understanding—A + B = C. Returning to our endangered Amazon forests example in Exercise 7.6, assume that the new information you want to bring into the discussion is your own sense of the global disaster that could arise if Amazon forests are depleted. That insight, combined with the factual information from Scott Wallace, might lead you the following synthesis.

> Preserving the South American forests represent our planet's greatest hope for an environmentally sound future. If, through application of aggressive international policies, we can find a way to stop the destruction in the Amazon, we will have opened a new chapter in twenty-first century forest stewardship that will prevent not one environmental disaster but many.

To quote or paraphrase? Generally, you should quote another's exact words when one of the following three reasons is true:

1. The precise phrasing is so elegant or apt that you wish to reproduce it intact.

2. You are going to focus on the wording itself (or some part of it).

3. You could not rephrase it without significantly changing the meaning or coming close to plagiarizing.

If none of those three reasons applies, you probably should paraphrase the source, remembering still to lead into the paraphrased material as you would a direct quotation and to provide appropriate documentation at the end of the paraphrase. Your readers should be able to tell precisely where another's ideas begin and end and where yours begin anew.

Consider the following passage:

> We may be a lot more creative than we realize. "Although we each have nearly limitless potential to live creatively, most people use only a small percentage of their creative gifts" (John Chaffee, *Critical Thinking, Thoughtful Writing*, 1st ed. 64). Therefore, we should work harder to cultivate these gifts.

Does it seem awkward or clunky to you? Can you tell what causes the awkwardness? Now read the following revision:

> We may be more creative than we realize. As John Chaffee points out in his book, *Critical Thinking, Thoughtful Writing*, "[M]ost people use only a small percentage of their creative gifts" (64). Taking the time to cultivate our creativity thus sounds like a wise investment.

This revised version makes the link between general comment and specific reference smoother and more coherent. Note that the writer trims back some of the original quotation, using only what is essential. The reader is thus able to process the information more efficiently.

Another important principle to keep in mind when you quote from outside sources is not to overquote. Use only that portion of a passage essential to making your point. Remember that you can leave out parts of a passage that seem irrelevant by using an ellipsis (. . .) to let readers know that words, phrases, or sentences are being omitted. Always make certain, however, that in choosing words to delete you do not distort the meaning of the original passage. In cases where you need to convey a lot of information from a source, consider combining direct quotation with paraphrase, or simply rely entirely on paraphrase (making sure your paraphrase remains faithful to the essential point of the source).

◎◎ Exercise 7.7

Examine the following passage to determine how well the writer has incorporated outside sources. Revise the passage where necessary to make it more coherent. In class, compare your revision with those of other students. You will need to consult the book being quoted to make your determination.

> Libraries that receive public money should as a condition of funding be required to publish monthly lists of discards on their websites, "so that the public has some way of determining which of them are acting on behalf of their collections," recommends Nicholson Baker in his book about the way libraries have been destroying or selling off their hard-copy newspaper collections, *Double Fold: Libraries and the Assault on Paper* (New York: Random, 2001) 270. His other recommendations are that "The Library of Congress should lease or build a large building" in which to store any print materials they don't have room for; that several libraries around the country should

work together to save the nation's newspapers in bound form; and that the N.E.H. should ban the current U.S. newspaper program in which newspapers are destroyed after they are microfilmed (270).

Chapter Summary

Argumentative writing often requires research, which is a dynamic multitask process that involves searching for background information and integrating that information effectively into your paper. The research process can include many activities: searching databases to which your college library subscribes; using online search engines to search for material on the Internet; conducting surveys; interviewing specialists, such as the faculty and staff members in your university community; and using the many kinds of print sources (abstracts, atlases, bibliographies, books, government documents, indexes, and so on) available in your library. While most of your research activities should be planned and well organized, allow for serendipitous discovery—stumbling on unexpected sources as a result of being immersed in your planned research. By acquiring a thorough knowledge of their topics supported by careful research, writers argue their claims more authoritatively. Good research begins with taking a mental inventory and generating questions (writer-based, audience-based, subject-based, and purpose-based) about the topic that need answering. Purpose-based questions lead to formulating a strong thesis. A strong thesis, in turn, helps keep writers on track as they conduct research on the Internet, in the library, and with experts through well-prepared interviews.

Checklist

1. Do I take a thorough mental inventory of my topic?

2. Do I ask myself good purpose-, audience-, writer-, and subject-based questions about my topic?

3. Is my thesis strong and well focused?

4. Do I screen my Internet and print sources to make sure they meet the criteria for accuracy, relevance, reliability, clarity, and thoroughness?

5. Do I cite sources where necessary? Use proper documentation format?

6. Do I interview experts on campus or elsewhere about my topic?

7. Do I integrate researched information into my argument smoothly and clearly?

8. Do I check to ensure that I have paraphrased accurately?

9. Do I properly acknowledge the source of paraphrased as well as verbatim-quoted information?

10. Am I certain not to overlook acknowledging a source of outside information?

Writing Projects

1. Keep a detailed log of all your research-based activities for your upcoming writing assignment. Include idea-generating; initial outlining; initial searches through various print and online reference works (list search engines used); more methodical and focused research, interviews, and surveys. Describe your method of preparing the drafts—rough draft, first draft, and subsequent revisions.

2. Write a critical commentary on the usefulness of the Internet as a research tool. Comment on degrees of usefulness of various websites and different search engines, as well as the timeliness, reliability, and thoroughness of the information found in selected sites.

3. Write a comparative evaluation of print resources (as housed in your college library) versus Internet resources. Are both resources equally valuable? One more valuable than the other? Defend your assertions as fully as possible using specific examples.

4. Prepare a set of ten interview questions based on the topic you are currently researching or are planning to research. Next, search through your college's faculty directory or bulletin to locate faculty or staff members who might serve as good interview subjects for your research.

8 Documenting Your Sources: MLA and APA Styles

I quote others only the better to express myself.
—Montaigne

Citation of Source Material: A Rationale

You must acknowledge information and ideas taken from sources not your own (commonly referred to as *outside sources*). There are two main reasons for doing so:

1. **Original ideas are a form of property known as *intellectual property*.** Published material is protected from theft by copyright law. Plagiarism, which means to pass off someone else's ideas or writings as your own, is, quite simply, against the law. Thus, by acknowledging your sources explicitly, you protect yourself from being accused of and prosecuted for copyright violation (see "Understanding and Avoiding Plagiarism" in Chapter 7, pages 213–215).

2. **Acknowledging your sources provides an important service to other scholars.** People who read your essays are often interested in consulting the sources you consult to obtain more detailed information.

Which Documentation Style to Use?

The MLA style is commonly used to document sources in writing done within the humanities disciplines (for example, English and the foreign languages). The APA style is commonly used to document sources in writing done within the social sciences (for example, psychology and sociology). Clarify with your instructor whether you should follow the MLA style (see page 222), APA style (see page 241), or some other system. (For example, *Chicago* style, based on *The Chicago Manual of Style*, 15th edition, is commonly used to document sources in writing done within history and sometimes other humanities disciplines.)

No one expects you to memorize all the details of any particular system of documentation, but you are expected to know how to look up and apply these details each time you write a paper that includes references to other sources. You are expected to know how to follow the instructions and examples given in documentation manuals and to make your citations complete and consistent with the recommendations of an established documentation style. Therefore, get into the habit of checking the proper format either in this chapter or in the other MLA or APA reference manuals listed in this chapter.

A Guide to MLA Documentation Style

The following guide presents the system for documenting sources established by the Modern Language Association (MLA). For more detailed information on how to document a wide variety of both print and electronic sources with the MLA style, see Joseph Gibaldi, *MLA Handbook for Writers of Research Papers,* 6th ed. (New York: MLA, 2003); Joseph Gibaldi, *MLA Style Manual,* 2nd ed. (New York: MLA, 1998); and the MLA Web site at http://www.mla.org.

Remember the following about the MLA documentation system:

1. In the body of your paper, you must (a) inform readers of the last name of the author or authors for each source as you use it in your paper, and (b) give the page number where each source appears originally in a larger work. These elements of the MLA system together form what is called the *author/page in-text citation.* Note that no page numbers are needed if your source is an online one or if it is less than a page long.

2. At the end of your paper, beginning on a new numbered page, you must list in alphabetical order by authors' last names, doubled-spaced, all the sources you refer to within your paper. This list is called *Works Cited.*

Before we look at the details of how to cite various types of sources in your text and the way to list them in your Works Cited, let us look at how to present quoted material and how to paraphrase.

Presenting Quoted Material

When quoting or paraphrasing in MLA style, mention the author's surname and indicate the page number of the passage parenthetically. List the page number (or numbers) without the "p." or "pp." abbreviation. If you are citing more than one page number, indicate them in the following way: 15–16; 140–42; 201–04; 390–401.

Using Quotation Marks and Block-Style Quotation Format

Use double quotation marks around the words quoted if the passage is no more than four lines.

```
According to Charles Lamb, Shakespeare's plays "are grounded deep in
nature, so deep that the depth of them lies out of the reach of most
of us" (7).
```

Lamb's name (last name first) and the title of the essay, "On the Tragedies of Shakespeare," appear in the Works Cited, along with more information about the publisher and date of the essay.

Because you are already using double quotation marks to indicate another author's work, substitute single quotation marks for any double quotations that appear in the original author's material.

```
The distinguished teacher of creative writing, Brenda Ueland, insists
that taking long walks is a good way to generate thoughts: "If I do
not walk one day, I seem to have on the next what Van Gogh calls
'the meagerness'" (42).
```

The end punctuation should be placed as follows: close inner quotation, close outer quotation, insert page number of quotation in parentheses, period.

If the passage is four lines or longer, use block-style quotation. Set the passage off as a separate paragraph and indent each line ten spaces from the margin. If you are quoting two or more paragraphs in the block quotation, indent the first line of each an additional three spaces (that is, thirteen spaces from the left margin). Quotation marks are not used with block-style quotations: Consider indentation to take the place of quotation marks.

```
Commenting on Shakespeare's villains, Charles Lamb notes that while we
are reading any of his great criminal characters—Macbeth, Richard, even
Iago—we think not so much of the crimes which they commit, as of the
ambition, the aspiring spirit, the intellectual activity, which prompts
them to over-leap those moral fences. (12)
```

The period at the end of a block quotation precedes the parenthetical information.

Quoting Verbatim

Do not change punctuation or spelling (for example, changing the British spelling of "colour" to color"). In rare cases in which the author or printer makes a spelling or grammatical error, follow the error with the Latin word *sic* (meaning "thus") in brackets to indicate that the word appears this way in the original source.

Using an Ellipsis

Indicate omission of any *unnecessary* portion of the passage with an ellipsis— three dots separated from each other by a single space.

Original passage: "The timing, as I mentioned earlier, had to be precise."

Quoted passage, using ellipsis: "The timing [. . .] had to be precise."

Be certain that the words you omit from a passage do not alter its essential meaning.

Paraphrasing

A paraphrase is a rewording of an author's idea that presents it more concisely or clearly. By paraphrasing instead of quoting directly, you can more clearly and efficiently integrate the author's thoughts with your own. Of course, you must thoroughly understand the material you wish to paraphrase to avoid distorting it. You must also cite the author's name and a page number as if the paraphrase were a direct quotation. A paraphrase of the Charles Lamb passage quoted previously might be worded like this:

```
Lamb claims that we regard Macbeth, Richard III, and Iago less
as criminals than as high-reaching spirits marked by great
intelligence (12).
```

Make sure your readers will be able to tell which ideas are yours and which are the paraphrased ideas of another author. Do not, for example, merely list a name and page number at the end of a long paragraph. Readers will not be able to tell whether the paraphrase is the last sentence only or the entire paragraph being paraphrased, as in the following example:

```
Revenge takes many forms. Most often it is a hot-tempered reaction
to a perceived injustice. But sometimes it is cool and calculated,
like Iago's revenge against Othello. Either kind, though, can be
thought of as a kind of wild justice which, the more we are
tempted by it, the more urgently we must weed it out (Bacon 72).
```

The writer of the above passage does not make it clear whether the entire paragraph is a paraphrase of Francis Bacon's essay, just the last sentence, or even one portion of the last sentence. A simple revision clarifies the matter:

```
Revenge takes many forms. Sometimes it is cool and calculated,
like Iago's revenge against Othello. Other times it is what Fran-
cis Bacon, Shakespeare's contemporary, once defined as wild jus-
tice. As Bacon put it, the more we are tempted to run to it, the
more urgently we should weed it out (72).
```

Index for Citing Sources: MLA Style

Author/Page In-Text Citations

See the following pages for instruction and examples.

List of Works Cited

See the following pages for instruction and examples.

Citing Print Sources

Citing Nonprint Sources

Using Author/Page In-Text Citations

As you write the body of your paper, you will weave in references to the work of others to support or amplify the points you are making. Make sure that your readers can easily distinguish between your words and ideas, and the words and ideas of others. To create this clear distinction, refer by name to whomever you are quoting or paraphrasing. You can either include the author's name in a lead-in remark:

author's full name mentioned in lead-in remark

```
As Eliot Asinof describes the reaction to the 1919 baseball
scandal, "The American people were at first shocked, then
sickened" (197).
```

or you can include the author's last name in parentheses with the page number after the quotation or paraphrasing:

```
In reacting to the 1919 baseball scandal, "[t]he American
people were at first shocked, then sickened" (Asinof 197).
```

author's last name mentioned in parentheses   no comma   page number

The preferable style is to use the author's name in your lead-in.

Note the following variations on this pattern, depending on the type of source you are citing and whether you are including the author's name in a lead-in remark.

1. Author Named in Lead-In Remarks. As long as you mention the author's last name in your lead-in remarks, the only information needed in parentheses is the page number because the full citation will appear in the Works Cited at the end of your paper.

author

```
According to John Jones, a colony on Mars would rapidly pay
for itself (15).
```

page number   period

author

```
In her biography of Alice James, Jean Strouse writes that the
James children "learned to see and not see, say and not say,
reveal and conceal, all at the same time" (xii).
```

quotation   page number   period

When citing a piece from an anthology or edited volume, cite the name of the author of the piece to which you are referring, not the editor or editors of the anthology.

2. Author Not Named in Lead-In Remarks.   If you do not name the author as you lead into a quotation or paraphrase, place the author's name in parentheses along with the page number of the source.

> No one person in 1919 knew all of the factors that contributed
> to the Black Sox Scandal or could tell the whole story
> (Asinof 11).

author's last name no comma page number

3. Two or More Authors.   If you are citing a work that has two or three authors, mention all their names in your lead-in remarks or in parentheses after the reference.

> Critical reading involves going beyond simple decoding of the
> literal meanings of the written word (Cooley and Powell 3).

authors' last names   no comma   page number

If you are citing a work with four or more authors, state the first author's last name and then write "et al." (a Latin phrase meaning "and others").

4. Multiple Works by the Same Author.   If you are referring to more than one work by the same author, refer to the work's title in your lead-in remarks.

> In *Teaching a Stone to Talk,* Dillard describes the drama of the
> moon blocking the sun during a total eclipse by saying, "It did
> not look like the moon. It was enormous and black. . . . It
> looked like a lens cover, or the lid of a pot. It materialized
> out of thin air—black, and flat, and sliding, outlined in
> flame" (94).

page number

Alternately you can include a short form of the title in parentheses, along with the page number.

> One observer described the mystery of the eclipse by saying,
> "If I had not read that it was the moon, I could have seen the
> sight a hundred times and never thought of the moon once"
> (Dillard, Teaching 94).

author   comma   abbreviated title   page number

5. Works with Anonymous or Corporate Authorship.   Cite works that name no author or editor as follows:

> According to the Consumer Protection Agency, the number of car
> owners who report being cheated by dishonest mechanics has dropped
> by 15 percent in 2000 (7).

6. Internet Sources.   For most electronic sources, it is not possible to pro-vide a page number in the in-text citation. Instead, check to see if an author's name is given and if there are numbered paragraphs or other text divisions. If so, use these pieces of information in place of page numbers in your in-text citation.

```
Some universities have been questioning their use of Aztec
signs and symbols and the use of mascots like "Monty Montezuma"
(Weber, par. 6).
```
author   comma   numbered paragraph

Preparing the MLA List of Works Cited

Definition.   The list of Works Cited is an alphabetical listing of all the sources cited or paraphrased or referred to in a paper. The list of Works Cited does not include additional readings, no matter how relevant; however, your instructor may ask you to prepare a separate list of additional readings.

Purpose.   The main purpose of the list of Works Cited is to assist readers who wish to obtain more information about the topic by consulting the same sources you have. A secondary purpose is to give readers an opportunity to double-check the accuracy and appropriateness of your quotations and paraphrases. It is possible to quote someone accurately but in a way that misrepresents that author's original intentions—of course, not something you intend to do but may accidentally do.

General Procedure

1. Begin the list of Works Cited on a separate page.

2. Title the page Works Cited and center the heading.

3. List everything alphabetically by author's surname. List the author's surname first. If a work has more than one author, alphabetize the entry according to the surname of the author listed first. If no author is listed, enter the title alphabetically. Titles of books and pamphlets are under-scored. Include the city of publication, the abbreviated name of the publisher, and the date of publication.

4. Begin each entry at the left margin. If an entry runs longer than one line, those subsequent lines are indented five spaces.

In the following examples and in the sample student paper beginning on page 233, note the MLA style for citing various types of sources in the list of Works Cited.

Citing Print Sources

1. Single-author Book or Pamphlet

> Jones, John. <u>Colonizing Mars</u>. New York: Far Out, 2002.

2. Book with More than One Author

> Witt, Linda, Karen M. Paget, and Glenna Matthews. <u>Running as a Woman: Gender and Power in American Politics</u>. New York: Free, 1994.

When more than three authors, use the name of the first author and follow it with "et al."

> Johnson, Eric, et al. <u>Smart Shopping</u>. Boston: Lifestyle, 1999.

3. Chapter from a Book

> Blair, John. "The Anglo-Saxon Period." <u>The Oxford History of Britain</u>. Ed. Kenneth O. Morgan. New York: Oxford UP, 1988. 60–119.

4. Government Document

Author Byline Given:

> Elkouri, Frank, and Edna Asper. <u>Resolving Drug Issues</u>. Washington: Bureau of National Affairs, 1993.

No Author Byline Given:

> United States. Dept. of Health and Human Services. <u>Summary Report of the Graduate Medical Educational National Advisory Committee</u>. Washington: GPO, 1980.

5. Article from a Periodical

Magazine:

> Singer, Mark. "God and Football." <u>New Yorker</u> 25 Sept. 2000: 38–42.

Academic Journal:

> Gibson, Ann. "Universality and Difference in Women's Abstract Painting." <u>Yale Journal of Criticism</u> 8 (Spring 1995): 103–32.

Newspaper:

> Revkin, Andrew C. "A West African Monkey Is Extinct, Scientists Say." <u>New York Times</u> 12 Sept. 2000: A20.

Letter to the Editor:

> Kenny, Shirley Strum. "The Useless SAT." Letter. <u>New York Times</u> 19 Mar. 2001: A22.

Unsigned Editorial:

> "Flawed Election in Uganda." Editorial. <u>New York Times</u> 16 Mar. 2001: A20.

6. Book Review

Titled Review of a Work:

> Dowd, Maureen. "The Man in White." Rev. of <u>Hooking Up,</u> by Tom Wolfe. <u>New York Times Book Review</u> 5 Nov. 2000: 6.

Untitled Review of a Work:

> Warren, Charles. Rev. of <u>The Material Ghost: Films and Their Medium,</u> by Gilberto Perez. <u>Georgia Review</u> 54 (Spring 2000): 170–74.

Citing Nonprint Sources

7. Interview

Personal Interview:

> Sanders, Julia. Personal interview. 15 Oct. 2006.

Telephone Interview:

> Ellis, Mark. Telephone interview. 17 Oct. 2006.

8. Correspondence

Paper Letter:

> Beaumont, Clyde. Letter to the author. 10 Jan. 2007.

Email Letter

> Beaumont, Clyde. Email to the author. 10 Jan. 2007.

If a paper letter is not dated, use the date of the postmark. Email messages are dated automatically.

9. Web Page   When your source is a web page—an electronic document from an Internet site—include in your citation (1) the author's name; (2) the title of the document in quotation marks; (3) information about a print version of the same document (if any is given on the website); (4) information about the document's electronic publication; and (5) Web access information such as a URL that will allow your reader to find the material that you are citing. If you cannot locate within your electronic source all of these five categories of information, include as much in your citation as possible, always with the goal of allowing your reader to find your source.

Document from an Internet Newspaper or Journal Site:

author   title

Stein, Charles. "After the Last Whistle: Some Workers, Towns

Have Rebounded Amid the Loss of Factory Jobs. Others Won't

information about print publication   information about electronic publication

Make It." <u>Boston Globe</u> 23 Oct. 2003: D1+1. <u>Boston Globe</u>

<u>Online</u>. 23 Oct. 2003 <http://www.boston.com/business/globe/

date of access

articles/2003/10/23/after_the_last_whistle/>.

URL; if URL goes to a new line, break after a slash

Fredman, Allen. "To the Point: The Adapted Landscape of a
    Former Baltimore Factory Stays True to its Sudsy Past."
    <u>Landscape Architecture</u>. Nov. 2003. American Society of
    Landscape Architects. 29 Oct. 2003 <http://www.asla.org/
    lamag/feature3.html>.

Document from an Article in a Reference Database:

Heitz, Thomas R. "Babe Ruth." <u>Encarta</u>. 2003. <u>MSN Learning and</u>
    <u>Research</u>. 13 Oct. 2003 <http://encarta.msn.com/encnet/
    refpages/SRPage.aspx?search=Babe+Ruth&Submit2=Go>.

Article from an Online Posting:

"NASA Chief Predicts Scientific Tsunami." Online posting.
    20 Oct. 2000. 21 Oct. 2000 <metanews@meta-list.org>.

Rather than citing a posting, the writer should try to locate any article cited therein at its proper Web address, so readers will be able to find it. Thus, for instance, though the article "NASA Chief Predicts Scientific Tsunami" was originally discovered on the Metanews listserv, it should be cited as follows:

"NASA Chief Predicts Scientific Tsunami." Online posting.
    20 Oct. 2000. 21 Oct. 2000 <http://www.space.com/
    business/technology/business/goldin_tsunami_001011.htm>.

10. Television or Radio Program

"Senators Battle Over Judicial Nominee." <u>Newshour</u>. Narr. Jim
    Lehrer. PBS. WGBH, Boston. 23 Oct. 2003.

11. Recording

Audiocassette:

> Churchill, Winston S. <u>The Great Republic</u>. Audiocassette.
>   Random House Audiobooks, 1998.

Videocassette (VCR):

> <u>Witness</u>. Dir. Peter Weir. Perf. Harrison Ford and Kelly
>   McGillis. Videocassette. Paramount, 1985.

Compact Disc (CD):

> Von Bingen, Hildegard. <u>Canticles of Ecstasy</u>. Perf. Sequentia.
>   Deutsche Harmonia Mundi, 1994.

When the recording medium is a compact disc, that fact is not stated in the entry. It is assumed that the sound recording is made on a compact disc unless another medium is indicated.

Digital Video Disc (DVD):

> <u>South Pacific in Concert</u>. Dir. Paul Gemignani. Perf. Reba
>   McEntire, Brian Stokes Mitchell, Alec Baldwin. DVD. Great
>   Performances, 2005.

12. Film

> <u>The Queen</u>. Dir. Stephen Frears. Perf. Helen Mirren,
>   James Cromwell, Alex Jennings. Miramax, 2006.

13. Lecture

> Chaudhuri, Haridas. "The Philosophy of History." Lecture. Cultural
>   Intergration Fellowship, San Francisco. Jan. 7, 2007.

14. Art Work (Painting, Sculpture, or Photograph)

> Munch, Edvard. <u>The Scream</u>. National Gallery, Oslo.

Note: If you are referring to a reproduction of the work in a book, cite the book instead of the location of the work, as follows:

> Munch, Edvard. <u>The Scream</u>. In <u>Edvard Munch</u>. Köln, Germany:
>   Benedict Taschen Verlag, 1988.

15. Figure (published chart, graph, table)

Note: Citation must appear directly underneath the figure (following the caption, and prefaced by the word "Source") as well as in the Works Cited page.

United Nations, World Population Prospects, the 1998 Revision.
Population Referrence Bureau. <http://www.prb.org/Content/
NavigationMenu/PRB/Educators/Human_Population>.

16. Map

Central Asia. Map. Hammond Odyssey Atlas of the World,
1994: 31.

17. Advertisement

Cannon HD Camcorder. Advertisement. *National Geographic* Jan.
2007: 12–13.

Sample Student Paper: MLA Documentation Format

1 inch
margins

½" }

1/2 inch
from top of
page

Gibson 1

Running
head: stu-
dent name
+ number
on every
page

Daniela Gibson

Name,
course,
instructor,
date

Argumentation

Professor Billings

May 16, 2006

Famous case
serves as
attention-
grabbing
opening

Double-
space paper
throughout

Why We Should Punish

The caning of a young American in Singapore in
1994 for minor vandalism has added new fuel to a
centuries-old debate about proper forms of punishment.
Logic demands, however, that prior to the decision of
the proper form of punishment, we must decide on the
proper aim or purpose of punishment. The views on the
proper aim of punishment seem to vary widely. Writers
such as Barbara Wootton and H. L. A. Hart believe that
the proper aim of punishment is the rehabilitation
of the criminal. Others, in contrast, argue for
retribution as the proper aim of punishment. Criminal
Justice professor Graeme Newman, for example, writes,
"Punishment must, above all else, be painful" (40).

Title, cen-
tered, not
underlined

No extra
space
between title
and first line
of text

Paraphrased
sources;
quotation
marks not
used

Gibson 2

Summary of source

A third view of the proper purpose of punishment is deterrence, "removing the criminal from activity and serving as a caution to would-be-criminals" (Rottenberg 41). One recently profiled advocate of punishment as deterrence is Joe Arpaio, sheriff of Maricopa County, Arizona (Phoenix area). According to Arpaio, "Jail should be about punishment and the punishment should be so unpleasant that no one who experienced it would ever want to go through it again" (Graham 61).

Page number reference all that is needed since author mentioned in the discussion

Scope of the question of punishment described

The overall function of punishment is to enforce and protect the moral values of a society, a function that appears to be incompatible with the idea of retribution and only partly compatible with the ideas of deterrence and rehabilitation.

Statement of thesis

The punishment and the moral values of a society are inseparably linked by the laws of that society. Our laws always reflect and are based on our core values. Most societies recognize the right to life as a core value. In the case of our American society, core values are also the ownership of property and the freedom of speech. Consequently, America has laws that protect private property and the freedom of speech. Theft is against the law and so is violation of the freedom of speech. Furthermore, since these laws are based on values, and values always imply a right and wrong, a trespassing of these laws must have consequences that reflect and uphold these moral judgments. Walter Berns addresses this interdependence between morality and punishment when he writes the following about the death penalty:

Punishment linked to society score values

Block-style quotation indented ten spaces from margin; double-spaced; no quotation marks used, except for those that appear in the original source

> [It] serves to remind us of the majesty of the moral order that is embodied in our law and of the terrible consequences of its breach. . . . The criminal law must be made awful, by which I mean awe-inspiring, or commanding "profound respect or reverential fear." It must remind us

Gibson 3

of the moral order by which alone we can live as human beings. (12)

Although I do not necessarily agree with the need for the death penalty and "reverential fear," Berns's observation is significant: Punishment, indeed, must always "remind us of the moral order" by which we live, for if the breaking of the law would have no consequences, our moral values would be void (85). If, for example, the violation of the freedom of speech had no consequences, such a violation could take place again and again. But then, it could hardly be called a value since we would not seem to care about it and would not protect it.

Why one scholar's view of punishment makes sense

Those in favor of retribution as the aim of punishment agree that a criminal act must have legal consequences for the criminal. Despite this very broad similarity between retribution and the protection of moral values, retribution appears impractical and morally wrong in the context of the American value system. Advocates of retribution often refer to Kant, who writes that the principle for legal justice is "[n]one other than the principle of equality . . . any undeserved evil that you inflict on someone else among the people is one that you do to yourself. . . . Only the law of retribution can determine exactly the kind and degree of punishment" (qtd. in Berns 18). Such a view, however, is impracticable, for who would rape a rapist (and how) for retribution of the crime? In addition to these questions, it seems hardly possible that the loss of one individual can truly be retributed by the execution of the murderer.

Author presents challenging view

Reference to a source quoted by another author

Yet retribution is precisely the major motive behind capital punishment. The danger with this extreme form of punishment is irreversible miscarriage of justice, as when an innocent man or woman is sentenced to death (Berlow) or when racist lawyers eliminate Blacks, Hispanics, and other racial minorities

Author refutes challenging view

as potential jurors during jury selection—which was
shown to be the case with Nevada death-row inmate
Thomas Nevius (Amnesty International).

References to
Internet
sources

But more importantly, retribution as the goal of
punishment is immoral, at least in the context of our
value system. Mark Costanzo, chair of the Department
of Social Psychology at Claremont McKenna College,
correctly identifies that "[o]ur efforts to mitigate
punishments arise out of the recognition that we must
not sink to the level of the criminal; raping a rapist
would debase us, weaken our moral solidarity, and
undermine the moral authority of the state" (23). If
we punish via retribution, the danger is that we would
focus too narrowly on one crime and in doing so would
lose sight of the moral code that makes the crime a
crime. In other words, the crime would move to the
foreground and would overshadow the moral authority
that it violates. For example, if someone hits my car,
I could exercise the punishment of retribution by
hitting that person's car in return. However, doing so
fails not only to fix my car but also to ensure me
that there is a moral code and its representative law
that will protect me from similar instances in the
future. Hence, retribution undermines the very same
moral law that punishment is supposed to uphold.

In contrast to retribution, which must be
rejected as the proper aim of punishment on moral and
practical grounds, deterrence appears to be partly
compatible with the upholding of moral values. Ernest
van den Haag, a retired professor of Jurisprudence,
expresses the views of deterrence advocates when he
writes that "[h]arsher penalties are more deterrent
than milder ones" (114). In his explanation, he draws
an analogy to everyday life situations:

Deterrence vs.
retribution as a
basis for
punishment

> All other things equal, we penalize our
> children, our friends, or our business partners
> the more harshly the more we feel we must deter

Gibson 5

them and others in the future from a wrong
they have done. Social life would not be
possible if we did not believe that we
can attract people to actions we desire
by giving them incentives, and deter
them from actions we do not desire by
disincentives. (115)

Van den Haag's analogy works—up to a certain
point. Clearly, if we care about our values, we need
to protect them, and one way of doing so is to punish
offenders as a means of deterrence. And in some
situations, deterrence might be the only way of
communicating what is right and wrong. I remember, for
example, when I was three years old, I took doll
clothing home from preschool. I did so because I
liked to play with it more at home, and I did not
understand that it was not mine. When my parents found
out, they did the right thing: They told me if I ever
did that again, I could no longer play with my dolls.
In that situation deterrence was necessary since I
was too young to understand the concept of private
property and its proper relationship to right and
wrong; I understood, however, that I wanted to play
with my dolls and that I could no longer do so if I
would take doll clothing home again.

There is a danger, however, in viewing deterrence
as the only proper aim of punishment: it could
disconnect that what is feared from what is
morally bad, what is desired from what is morally
good. The Oxford English Dictionary defines
deterrence as "deterring or preventing by fear."
If I, when I was old enough to grasp the meaning
of right and wrong beyond immediate desires,
would have not been taught why it is wrong to take
what is not mine, but instead would have been
continuously motivated by fear, I could have never
developed a deep respect for moral values. Rather, I

Author addresses punishment as rehabilitation

Author qualifies her preceding claim

would have learned to associate fear with my parents' knowledge of my "wrongdoing," but not with the wrongdoing itself. Thus, I would have most likely sought to avoid my parents' knowledge or that of any other authority but not to avoid the deed itself. I believe that this example is generally applicable to deterrence as the main purpose of punishment: Criminals and potential criminals would be taught not that their acts were wrong on moral grounds, but that they should seek to avoid conflicts with authority. But such an attitude would instill in them a distrust for the laws rather than an understanding and respect for the values that they represent.

Another view of punishment is rehabilitation. Rehabilitation in the sense of education seems compatible with and even part of our value system. However, we need to ensure that rehabilitation qua education is not conflicting with other essential values. Costanzo points to the importance that background and circumstances can play in a crime (27). For example, it would seem naēve to expect from a young man proper law-abiding behavior if that man had suffered from "routine beatings from an abusive father" and "grew up in a poverty-ridden, gang-infested neighborhood and received very little in the way of parental guidance or supervision" (31). If that man had committed a crime, rehabilitation that includes a positive alternative to the values or lack thereof of his childhood upbringing seems appropriate. It might not only protect our societal values by preventing further criminal acts by this young man, if the rehabilitation was successful, but it would also reinforce our values, for the effort of rehabilitation shows that we are taking these values seriously and are deeply caring about them.

Yet, as commendable as such rehabilitation efforts are, we cannot allow them to replace other important

Why rehabilitation cannot be the sole basis for punishment

values such as responsibility and justice. By rationalizing a criminal behavior with the criminal's disadvantageous upbringing, we are in danger of denying individual responsibility, a core value of our society. Further, by granting college loans and "grants," books, "compassion and understanding," to criminals, as one former prisoner demands, we would also commit injustice (Stratton 67). For how could we explain this special treatment to all those who have abided by the law, some even despite their background, but do not enjoy grants, loans, etc.? Because these aims are potentially in conflict with each other and because our highest responsibility is to defend the values of our society, rehabilitation can be an integral part of punishment, but it should never replace punishment.

The discourse about the proper aim of punishment is indeed complex. But exactly because of this complexity, we need to approach the question of punishment step by step. It would be fatal to jump to the question of the proper forms of punishment before the question of the proper aim of punishment has been settled. It is absolutely mandatory that the question of the proper aim of punishment is addressed a priori. With respect to its answer, if the upholding of the moral values of a society is any indicator, we should dismiss retribution, and very cautiously consider deterrence and rehabilitation—but by no means should we draw any hasty conclusions.

Concluding
reflections

No extra
space
between
title and
first line
of text

Second and
subsequent
lines
indented

Sources
listed in
alphabetical
order

Gibson 8

Works Cited

Amnesty International. "Serious Allegations of Racism and
   Injustice in Nevada Death Penalty Case." 6 Apr. 2001.
   30 Apr. 2001 <http://www.amnesty.org>.

Berlow, Alan. "The Wrong Man." Atlantic Monthly. Nov. 1999.
   6 Apr.2001 <http://www.theatlantic.com/issues/99nov/
   9911wrongman.htm>.

Berns, Walter. For Capital Punishment. New York: Basic, 1991.

Costanzo, Mark. Just Revenge. New York: St. Martin's, 1997.

"Deterrence." Oxford English Dictionary. 2nd ed. CD. Vers.
   1.13 Oxford: Oxford UP, 1994.

Graham, Barry. "Star of Justice: On the Job with America's
   Toughest Sheriff." Harper's Magazine Apr. 2001: 59–68.

Hart, H. L. A. Law, Liberty, and Morality. Stanford: Stanford
   UP, 1963.

Newman, Graeme R. Just and Painful: A Case for Corporeal
   Punishment of Criminals. London: Macmillan, 1983.

Rottenberg, Annette T., ed. Elements of Argument. 6th ed.
   New York: Bedford, 2000. 569.

Stratton, Richard. "Even Prisoners Must Hope." Newsweek 17
   Oct. 1994: 67.

van den Haag, Ernest. The Death Penalty Pro and Con: A
   Debate. New York: Plenum, 1983.

Wootton, Barbara. Crime and Penal Policy. London: Allen, 1978.

A Guide to APA Documentation Style

The following guide presents the system for documenting sources established by the American Psychological Association (APA). For more detailed information on how to document a wide variety of sources, both print and electronic, see the *Publication Manual of the American Psychological Association*, 5th ed. (Washington, DC: APA, 2001) and the APA *Publication Manual* at http://www.apastyle.org. Remember the following about the APA documentation system:

1. In the body of your paper, you must (a) inform readers of the last name of the author or authors for each source as you use it in your paper, and (b) give the year of publication. These elements of the APA system together form what is called the *author/year in-text citation.*

2. At the end of your paper, beginning on a new numbered page, you must list in alphabetical order by authors' last names, double-spaced, all the sources you refer to within your paper. This list is called *References.*

Before we look at the details of how to cite the various types of sources in your text and how to list them in your References, let us look at how to present quoted material and how to paraphrase.

Presenting Quoted Material

When quoting or paraphrasing in APA style, indicate the surnames of each author, together with the year the source was published.

        According to Freud (1900) . . .

At the end of the quoted or paraphrased passage, indicate only the page number, preceded by the abbreviation for page ("p.") or pages ("pp.") (the abbreviation "pg." is not standard).

Using Quotation Marks and Block-Style Quotation Format

Use double quotation marks around the words quoted if the passage has fewer than forty words.

        Freud (1900) notes that "in the psychic life there exist repressed wishes" (p. 288).

This passage is from *The Interpretation of Dreams,* but it is not necessary to put that information at the end of the quotation because it will appear in the References, along with other relevant publication information.

Because you are already using double quotation marks to indicate another author's work, substitute single quotation marks for double quotations that appear in the original author's material.

```
Henry Petroski (1992) reports that in 1900 "an American patent was
issued to Cornelius Brosnan . . . for a 'paper clip' which has
been regarded in the industry as the 'first successful bent wire
paper clip'" (pp. 62–63).
```

If the passage is forty or more words long, use block-style quotation. Set the passage off as a separate paragraph and indent each line five spaces from the margin. If you are quoting two or more paragraphs in the block quotation, indent the first line of each new paragraph an additional five spaces (that is, ten spaces from the left margin). Quotation marks are not used with block-style quotations.

```
What we recollect of the dream, and what we subject to our
methods of interpretation, is, in the first place, mutilated by
the unfaithfulness of our memory, which seems quite peculiarly
incapable of retaining dreams, and which may have omitted precise-
ly the most significant parts of their content. (p. 470)
```

This passage is also from *The Interpretation of Dreams.*

Quoting Verbatim

Always double-check to ensure that you have quoted the passage accurately. Do not change punctuation or spelling (for example, changing the British spelling of "colour" to "color"). In rare cases in which the author or printer makes a spelling error, follow the word with the Latin word *sic* (meaning "thus") in brackets to indicate that the word appears this way in the original source.

Using an Ellipsis

Indicate omission of any *unnecessary* portion of the passage with an ellipsis—three dots separated from each other by a single space.

Original passage: According to Clifford Geertz (1973), "We are, in sum, incomplete or unfinished animals who complete or finish ourselves through culture" (p. 49).

Quoted passage, using ellipsis: According to Clifford Geertz (1973), "We are . . . incomplete or unfinished animals who complete or finish ourselves through culture" (p. 49).

Always check to make sure that the ellipsis does not distort the original intention of the author.

Paraphrasing

A paraphrase is a rewording of an author's idea that presents it more concisely or clearly. You must cite the author's name and the year of publication as if the paraphrase were a direct quotation. Although APA style does not require that a page number be given with a paraphrase, it suggests that you do so. A paraphrase of the Clifford Geertz passage quoted previously might be worded like this:

```
According to Geertz (1973), humans are incomplete animals who
reach completeness through culture (p. 49).
```

Make sure your readers will be able to tell which ideas are your own and which are the paraphrased ideas of another author. Do not, for example, merely list a name and page number at the end of a long paragraph. Readers will not be able to tell whether the paraphrase is the last sentence only or the entire paragraph.

Index for Citing Sources: APA Style

Author/Page In-Text Citations

See the following pages for instructions and examples.

List of References

See the following pages for instructions and examples.

Citing Print Sources

Using Author/Year In-Text Citations

Introduce outside information smoothly and explicitly so that readers will be able to distinguish between your ideas and the outside source authors' ideas. You provide this clear distinction by referring by name to whomever you are quoting or paraphrasing, as in the following examples.

1. Author Named in Lead-In Remarks

author's full name mentioned in lead-in remark

According to Carolyn Heilbrun (1979), womanhood must be reinvented (p. 29).

So long as you mention the author's last name, the only other necessary information is the page number because the full citation will appear in the References.

2. Author Not Named in Lead-In Remarks

One feminist scholar asserts that womanhood must be invented (Heilbrun, 1979, p. 29).

author's last name   date   page number
comma

3. Two or More Authors

authors listed alphabetically separated by commas date in parens

Colombo, Cullen, and Lisle (2001) emphasize that critical thinking involves cultivating the ability to imagine and the curiosity to question one's own point of view (p. 2).

4. Multiple Works by the Same Author

date followed by letter to indicate the different works

Jones (1998b, p. 130) considers colonization of space a vital step in human evolution. He even argues that our survivability as a species depends on it (1998a, pp. 47–51).

date followed by letter to indicate the different works

The letters *a* and *b* following the date are assigned according to the alphabetized order of the publications' titles. Thus, in the list of references, Jones's 1998a publication appears alphabetically before her 1998b publication, even if the 1998b reference is cited first in the text. Works by the same author published in different years are indicated with one instance of the surname, followed by dates: (Jones, 1999, 2001). When citing two or more different authors sharing the same surname, be sure to include each author's initials: (A. Jones, 1957; C. Jones, 2001).

5. Works with Anonymous or Corporate Authorship

corporate authorship

According to the Consumer Protection Agency (2001), the number of car owners reported being cheated by dishonest mechanics dropped 15% in 2000 (p. 7).

6. Internet Sources

Page from a Website:

According to the Coalition for Affordable and Reliable Energy (2001), coal fuels more than half the country's electricity.

Article from an Online Periodical:

author of online article

Farmer (2001) envisions a memory chip that, when implanted, will give humans the ability to process information one hundred times faster and more efficiently.

Posting from an Online Forum:

Dr. Charles Taylor (2001), a biologist, claims in an online forum that human cloning will pose no dangers to cloned person's senses of selfhood because "the mind and personality can never be cloned."

Note that you do not need to include more than the author's name and the date when citing online sources. Information such as Web addresses will appear in the References.

Preparing the APA List of References

Definition.   The list of References is an alphabetical listing of all the sources cited or paraphrased or referred to in a paper. The list of References does not include additional or recommended readings, no matter how relevant; however, your instructor may ask you to prepare a separate list of supplemental readings.

Purpose.   The main purpose of the list of References is to assist readers who wish to obtain more information about the topic by consulting the same sources you have. A secondary purpose is to give readers an opportunity to double-check the accuracy and appropriateness of your quotations and paraphrases. It is possible to quote someone accurately but in a way that misrepresents that author's original intentions—of course, not something you intend to do but may accidentally do.

General Procedure

1. Begin the list of References on a separate page.

2. Title the page References and center the heading.

3. List everything alphabetically by author surname. List the author's surname first, followed by initials. Authors' or editors' full names are not given in APA format. If the work has more than one author, alphabetize according to the surname of the author listed first. If no author is listed, enter the title alphabetically. List the year of publication in parentheses after the authors' names. Titles of books or names of periodicals are italicized; titles of articles use neither italics nor quotation marks. Capitalize only the first word of book titles and article titles, but not of journal titles. Also, the first word after a colon, be it a book, journal, or article, should be capitalized.

4. Begin the first line of each entry flush with the left margin; turnover lines are indented five spaces.

In the following examples and in the sample student paper beginning on page 250, note the APA style for citing various types of sources in the list of References.

Citing Print Sources

1. Single-author Book or Pamphlet

Boorstin, D. J. (1987). *Hidden history.* New York: Harper & Row.

2. Book with More than One Author

Witt, L., Paget, K., & Matthews, G. (1994). *Running as a woman: Gender and power in American politics.* New York: Free Press.

3. Chapter from a Book

Blair, J. (1988). The Anglo-Saxon period. In K. O. Morgan (Ed.), *The Oxford history of Britain* (pp. 60–119). New York: Oxford University Press.

4. Article from a Periodical

Magazine:

Singer, M. (2000, September 25). God and football. *The New Yorker, 76,* 38–42.

Academic Journal:

Gibson, A. (1995, Spring). Universality and difference in women's abstract painting. *The Yale Journal of Criticism, 8,* 103–132.

Newspaper:

Revkin, A. C. (2000, September 12). A West African monkey is extinct, scientists say. *The New York Times,* p. A20.

Letter to the Editor:

Kenny, S. S. (2001, March 19). The useless SAT [Letter to the editor]. *The New York Times,* p. A22.

Unsigned Editorial:

Flawed election in Uganda. (2001, March 16). Editorial. *The New York Times,* p. A20.

In APA format, if a journal article has more than six authors, after the sixth author's name and initial, use "et al." to indicate the remaining authors of the article.

5. Book Review

Titled Review of Work:

> Dowd, M. (2000, November 5). The man in white [Review of the
>   book *Hooking up*]. *The New York Times Book Review*, p. 6.

Untitled Review of Work:

> Warren, C. (2000, Spring). [Review of the book *The material
>   ghost: Films and their medium*]. *The Georgia Review, 54*,
>   170–174.

6. Government Document

Author Byline Given:

> Elkouri, F., & Asper, E. (1993). *Resolving drug issues.*
>   Washington, DC: Bureau of National Affairs.

No Author Byline Given:

> U.S. Department of Health and Human Services. (1980, April).
>   *Summary report of the Graduate Medical Educational
>   National Advisory Committee.* Washington, DC: U.S.
>   government Printing Office.

Citing Nonprint Sources

7. Web Pages   Treat sources from the Internet just as you do print sources. Cite the author and the title of the work, publication data such as journal names and volume or issue numbers, and the publication date. In addition, however, you need to give the date the site was last updated (if different from the publication date), the date you accessed the site, and the Web address. The reason for the latter information is that websites sometimes disappear or the addresses change.

Periodical Article from Web Page:

> Sharlet, J. (2000, September 15). A philosopher's call to end
>   all paradigms. *The Chronicle of Higher Education.*
>   Retrieved <date>, from http://chronicle.com/cgi2-bin/
>   printable.cgi

Original Web Page Article:

> Williams, A. D. (1994). Jigsaw puzzles: Not just for children
>   anymore. Retrieved <date>, from http://www.ahc.uwater
>   loo.ca/ ~museum/ puzzles/jigsaw/essay.html.

Message Posted to an Electronic Mailing List or Newsgroup:

> NASA chief predicts scientific tsunami. (2000, October 20).
>   Message posted to metanews@meta-list.org.

8. Television Program

> Turner Broadcasting. (2000, November 8). *CNN evening news*
>   [Television broadcast]. Atlanta: Cable News Network.

9. Recording

Audiocassette:

> Churchill, W. S. (Speaker). (1998). *The great republic*
>   (Audiocassette, Random House Audiobooks #RH 850). New
>   York: Random House.

Videocassette:

> Weir, P. (Director). (1985). *Witness* [Videocassette,
>   Paramount #1736]. Los Angeles: Paramount Pictures.

Compact Disc:

> Von Bingen, H. (1994). O choruscans stellarum [Recorded by
>   Sequentia]. On *Canticles of Ecstasy* [CD]. <city>:
>   Deutsche Harmonia Mundi.

10. Film

> Nimoy, L. (Director). (1984). *Star trek IV: The voyage home.*
>   [Motion picture]. United States: Paramount Pictures.

11. Do not include nonprint sources such as interviews or correspondence in references.

Sample Student Paper: APA Documentation Format

1 inch
margins
left and
right

Running head:
short title +
page number

Child Molestation 1

Jarrett Green

Argumentation

Professor Billings

May 16, 2001

Name, course,
instructor,
date; double-
spaced

Abstract

Title, centered

Concisely
states the
problem, the-
sis, and how
the problem
can be solved.

Child molestation has been established as a
disease in both the physiological and psychological
sense of the word. For this reason, prison sentences
fail to cure the molester, as researchers have
demonstrated. Once out of prison, molesters easily
reestablish their concealed identities. Clearly,
alternative measures are needed, such as forcing
released molesters to publicly identify themselves
as such and having the media warn the public of
molesters' reestablished presence in the community.

Child Molestation: Anything but Your Typical Crime

"I've got these urges, and I can't control myself" (Friedman, 1991, p. 2). Although these words come from the mouth of one particular child molester, they easily could have been uttered by thousands of others. Child molesters come in all shapes and sizes, and live in all types of communities—from small farming towns to large metropolitan cities. All child molesters, however, have one very important trait in common: They have an intense sexual fixation with or attraction to children. What makes this trait so dangerous is that it causes immense damage and, at times, destruction to the lives of countless innocent children. Child molestation, unlike any other illegal or stigmatized act, directly attacks our nation's youth—our nation's future. Most states continue to simply imprison child molesters. Some states, on the other hand, have implemented minimal publicity programs that give communities access to information on released child molesters.

The question of how to punish or deal with child molesters is not an easy one. I, however, believe that attaining a proper understanding of the nature of this crime makes its solution crystal clear. Child molestation is unlike any other crime[1] for two reasons: (1) It has been established to be a physiological and psychological disease, and (2) it requires secrecy and identity concealment. This exceptional combination requires that we treat molesters differently than we treat burglars and car-jackers. More specifically, it requires that we *publicize*[2] child molesters, not to *shame* or *embarrass* them, but to *disable* them.

Child molestation is anything but a typical crime. In fact, it has been established as a physiological and psychological disease. Doctor Kieran Sullivan, Ph.D.,

Quotation works as a concrete lead-in to the topic

Give author's name, year, page number if author not mentioned in the sentence

Explanation of uniqueness of the problem

Child Molestation 3

an Associate Professor in the Santa Clara University Psychology Department, explains that pedophilia (or the disorder from which child molesters suffer) "is officially recognized as a diagnostic mental disorder by the *DSM IV,* the psychiatrist's bible" (K. Sullivan, personal interview, March 10, 2001). More importantly, Sullivan explains that child molestation is

Block style quotations (of more than 40 words) are indented 5 spaces from margin and double-spaced

> the only crime that is actually a psychological disorder. Although we consider serial killers to be "insane," their crime is not a direct manifestation of a physiological/psychological disease. Child molesters, on the other hand, have an overwhelming inner compulsion to engage in sexual interaction with children. It is an ever-present disease that drives them and controls them. This is what makes child molesters so unique. (K. Sullivan, personal interview, April 10, 2001)

Sharon Rice is a psychiatric nurse who currently works in the Ohio Veteran's Administration Outpatient Child Clinic. She has counseled hundreds of child molesters throughout her career, both in one-on-one and group settings. Rice claims that child molesters are

Expert description of psychopathology

> inflicted with a horrible disease. Nearly all of the child molesters claim that if they are released, they will be unable to not molest again. Most of them think that pedophilia should be legalized, as they believe that they are just giving children love and care. The others, though, believe their behavior is destructive and harmful toward children—and they feel

Child Molestation 4

incredible guilt and depression for what they have done. When asked whether or not they believe they could overcome their feelings if released, most believed that they could not. They believed their yearning would eventually be too powerful for them to control. Child molestation is really a disease that overpowers the will of the individual. (S. Rice, telephone interview, April 16, 2001)

Child molestation is obviously a unique crime. The child molester suffers from a disease that overpowers any and all restrictions (such as society's ethical standards or the molester's personal guilt). His[3] external acts are dominated by a physiological and psychological disorder.

Because child molestation is a physiological and psychological disease, even the harshest prison time usually fails in deterring the molester from recidivating. The overall rates of recidivism, although very difficult to determine, are extremely high. One examination, which studied 197 convicted male child molesters, found that 42% of the men were reconvicted within the next 31 years (Hanson, Steffy, & Gauthier, 1993, p. 646). The study offers the following important clarification:

Explanation of why current strategies have failed

> Although reconviction rates were used as the recidivism criteria in this study, it is likely that reconviction rates underestimate the rate of reoffending. It is widely recognized that only a fraction of the sexual offenses against children result in the offender being convicted. Consequently, it is possible that all of the men in our study could have reoffended but that only about one half got caught. (p. 650)

Child Molestation 5

    Mary Sue Barone is the Assistant Prosecuting Attorney for the Criminal Division of the Wood County District in the state of Ohio. During her years as a prosecuting attorney she has prosecuted nearly every offense in the book, including numerous child molestation cases. Barone (telephone interview, April 16, 2001) claims that "recidivism rates of child molestation are consistently the highest of any crime, including drug abuse. It is a disease that plagues a child molester for his entire life." When asked whether prison is the proper solution for such a "disease," she replied, "We live in a society of politics. Families and society want to see the child molester locked up. Unfortunately, prison time doesn't seem to do much good the moment the child molester is released." I cannot stress this point enough: Child molestation is a disease—it is a sickness. Locking someone up for six to eight months is not going to suppress the disease. Even if the prison time is harsh, the child molester reenters society with a physiological and psychological urge that remains unimpeded. Thus, the prison's lesson goes in one ear, and the disease throws it out the other. Child molestation is not a typical crime.

    The second reason child molestation is an atypical crime is due to the fact that it is inherently dependent on secrecy and identity concealment. Rarely are child molesters strangers who abuse random children at the playground. In nearly all cases, the child molester is the little league coach, the day-care assistant, the family friend, or the next-door neighbor. Everybody assumes that he is a harmless, good person. The child molester conceals his true self. He hides his destructive fantasies and intentions so that he can earn the trust of the child's parents. Having gained the trust of others, he commits the crime. But his crime is dependent on secrecy and concealment of his true identity.

Our current system of throwing child molesters in prison only makes the process by which they conceal their identities easier. We catch child molesters after they have *secretly* damaged or ruined the lives of countless children. Next we *hide* them in prison cells for the length of their terms and then toss them back *without warning* into the world of children. Although mere prison time is undoubtedly a "feel-good" solution, it is really no authentic solution at all. Child molesters come out of prison and are far too easily able to reestablish their concealed identities. They once again hide their molestating selves and, once again, use this concealment to poison and destroy the lives of innocent children.

Because child molestation is a truly unique crime (since it is a *disease* that undermines prison's function as a deterrent and it is inherently dependent on identity concealment), it screams for alternative state reaction, namely, publicity. Because child molestation is a disease that plagues child molesters, we cannot release them with the expectation that they will never molest again. Consequently, we must do all that we can to decrease the ease by which the disease controls child molesters' lives and damages children's lives. Publicity is this road block. It will make it difficult for child molesters to act on hidden dangerous impulses, since others will be aware of their disease. It will prevent them from succeeding in manipulatively gaining parents' trust and children's friendships so as to satisfy their harmful desires.

Emotional appeal

If we care about the lives of our children, we must make it as difficult as possible for child molesters

Child Molestation 7

to satisfy their harmful impulses through identity
concealment. We must prevent them from deceiving the
world into trusting them. We must rob them of the
tools used to molest children: secrecy and identity
concealment. As I explained before, child molesters do
not just molest random kids while in line for the
movies. We can and must obstruct such development of
Explanation   loyalty and trust by *publicizing* child molesters. Each
of a potential   child molester, on release from prison, should be
solution   publicized by a combination of four "awareness"
tactics. First, newspapers should publish the names
and photographs of child molesters as they reenter
society. Second, local television news programs should
warn communities of the release of child molesters.
News programs frequently display the names and
snapshots of so-called "dangerous" citizens (such as
people who are currently wanted by the police).
Released child molesters are at least as dangerous and
arguably more dangerous than on-the-run convicts or
prison escapees (depending on the crime, of course).
Third, child molesters should be forced under
supervision to go door-to-door throughout their entire
neighborhood (if not further) and inform people of
their danger to children. Fourth, and last, child
molesters should be forced to hold up signs (such as
"I am a child molester and have recently been released
from prison") in popular public locations (such as
inside shopping malls or outside movie theatres) in
their communities.

The combination of these four "awareness" tactics
makes it far more difficult for the child molester
reentering society simultaneously to reenter the lives
of children. Because the child molester so desperately
needs his disease covered up if he is successfully to
form new relationships with children, *publicizing* his

disease will make it far more difficult for him to dupe parents and children into thinking that he is harmless. Thus, publicity does far more than *shame* the child molester (which it may or may not actually succeed in doing); it *disables* him by depriving him of the one tool that he *needs* in order to molest more children: identity concealment.

Disabling child molesters by depriving them of their necessary tool (i.e., identity concealment) is not much different than the ancient punishment of depriving pick-pocketers and thieves of their necessary tool (i.e., their fingers). Pick-pocketers and thieves obviously depended on their fingers in order to commit their crimes. Cutting off their fingers was a simple way of preventing them from repeating their crimes. Similarly, child molesters depend on the concealment of their identities in order to commit their crimes. Depriving them of their concealment via *publicity* is really the only way we can save countless children from being sexually molested. Child molestation is possibly the only crime that fully depends on (which is to say—is impossible without) the concealment of identity. For this reason, crimes such as assault and robbery (which do not depend on the secrecy and deception of identity) should not be countered by publicity. Child molestation is a unique crime. It requires a unique punishment.

My opponents, at this time, would claim that such a punishment is unjustifiably excessive. They would argue that although publicity would disable a molester from molesting, it would also disable him from successfully seeking and holding a job. Additionally, because the child molester has *already* served his time, he now ought to be permitted to reestablish a normal life, which necessarily involves getting a job so that he may feed, clothe and house himself. Some, such as Judith Shepphard

Acknowledge-
ment of
challenging
view

Child Molestation 9

(1997), a journalism professor at Auburn University, argue
that publicizing child molesters is indefensible because
it constitutes double punishment (p. 37).

Refutation of
challenging
view

I respond by arguing that we must use publicity
against child molesters *in place* of full prison terms.
I am advocating a decrease in (but not elimination of)
prison sentences so that publicity becomes a normal
part of "serving one's time." Thus, my opponents'
argument that publicity is unfair because child
molesters have *already served* their time is moot. The
publicity with which they will be forced to deal is
not *in addition* to their time; it *is* their time. A
typical "punishment" for child molestation should be
two-pronged: It should begin with a (shortened,
according to today's norms) prison sentence, and
conclude with a powerful dosage of public exposure.
This public exposure is obviously not going to help
child molesters get jobs (of course, our current system
requires that molesters admit in their job applications
that they were convicted of child molestation, which
doesn't help this cause much either).

Melvin Watt, the Democratic senator from North
Carolina, claims that "our Constitution says to us
that a criminal defendant is presumed innocent until
he or she is proven guilty. . . . The underlying
assumption of this [argument] is that once you have
committed one crime of this kind, you are presumed
guilty for the rest of your life" (Tougher "Megan's
law," 1996). Senator Watt's point demonstrates a
blatant misunderstanding of the nature of child
molestation. As we established earlier in the paper,
child molestation is a physiological and psychological
disease from which child molesters suffer. It is not
as if they were only *suffering* from the disease the
moment they committed the act that led to their

When author-
ship is not
given, state
title; in this
case, no page
number is
given since the
source is from
a website

Child Molestation 10

convictions. In reality, molesters continuously *suffer* from the disease—it is a mental disorder that they cannot escape. Child molesters are not "presumed guilty" for the rest of their lives; they are, however, presumed dangerous for the rest of their lives. This presumption, due to the nature of molestation, seems fair to make.

The final rebuttal that my opponents make is that publicity violates the convicted child molester's right to privacy. Although at an initial glance this argument appears persuasive, a proper understanding of government-enforced punishment defeats it. If a person assaults another, he is put in prison. Every individual in America has an inalienable right to liberty. We believe, however, that an individual can sacrifice this right by behaving in certain ways (such as by assaulting an innocent other). If we so easily accept that the state can violate an individual's right to liberty, why is it so shocking for me to suggest a punishment in which the state violates the individual's right to privacy? We are simply accustomed to the violation of liberty (which, by the way, is a truly sacred right). The fact that the right to privacy is not regularly violated by the government (in response to illegal behavior) does not entail that it is unjustifiable. In the case of the child molester, the violation of this right is perfectly justifiable.

Thus, I do not support the publicity of child molesters so that we might slowly eliminate individual rights or eventually revert back to our days of public shaming. I support publicity because it can *disable* and *handicap* people who leave prison prepared, due to their controlling disease, to molest more children. Although it will not put an end to the molestation of children, it will make it far more difficult for child

Restatement of thesis and concluding remarks

Child Molestation 11

molesters to reenter society and effortlessly start up where they left off.

Footnotes

[1] If a crime exists that I am presently unaware of that satisfies each of the two stated criteria, it would also be subject to *publicity* as a "punishment."

[2] I acknowledge that this use of *publicize* is atypical; however, the need for such a use will become clear later in this paper. Also later in this paper, I will specify the exact manner in which child molesters will be publicized.

[3] Throughout this paper, I intentionally use the male pronoun in referring to child molesters since the great majority of child molesters are male.

Note use of footnotes for informational purposes

Child Molestation 12

References

Friedman, S. (1991). *Outpatient treatment of child molesters.* Sarasota, FL: Professional Resource Exchange.

Hansen, K. R., Steffy, R. A., & Gauthier, R. (1993). Long-term recidivism of child molesters. *Journal of Consulting and Clinical Psychology, 61*(4), 646–652.

Shepphard, J. (1997). Double punishment?: Megan's law on child molesters. *American Journalism Review, 19*(9), 37–41.

Tougher "Megan's law" would require notification. (1996). Retrieved March 3, 2001, from http://www.cgi.cnn.com/ALLPOLITICS. . ./9605/08/sexoffenders/index.shtml.

Title is centered

Indent second and successive lines of each entry 5 spaces

Entries are listed in alphabetical order by author surname (or by title if no author listed)

Ampersand used before name of last author listed

First word in article title and journal title capitalized; journal title and volume number italicized

Part II

Reading Clusters

1 | Athletics and Academics: How Do They Benefit Each Other?

Introduction

For some faculty—and students as well—"athletics" and "academics" are mutually repellant. College, they argue, should be a place for cultivating the mind, not the body. It is certainly not a place for engaging in the kinds of recruitment strategies and profiteering associated with professional sports. Athletics programs, dissenters argue, interfere with the very process of classroom education, as when student athletes skip class to participate in out-of-town competitions.

For others, however, college athletics programs are as essential to education ("education of the whole person") as any academic program; they hold that the mind-body dichotomy is a false one. If athletic programs are going to be scrapped, they argue, then why not scrap theater and dance programs as well? Moreover, athletic scholarships give many students their only opportunity to gain a foothold in academe, and successful athletic programs give many otherwise unknown institutions a chance to have a nationwide reputation. Athletic alumni are often the most generous of alumni in terms of donations to the universities—not just to the athletic programs. Top Division I academic institutions, such as Stanford, show that student athletes can excel at both. (Students from Stanford have won Olympic medals and been part of teams that won have national collegiate titles. Stanford annually supplies both Rhodes and Fullbright scholars). In fact, some would argue that a university cannot be considered great unless it is a leader in both academics and athletics.

The issues associated with the role of sports in college are many, as the range of essays in this cluster indicates. How should we deal with the "dumb jock" stereotyping of student athletes? How do we solve the abuses in athletic programs that do indeed occur? What, exactly, should students "learn" from playing sports? How can an athletic program help the host college financially without resorting to exploitation of the athletes? What would constitute the most ethical recruitment policies?

Are Student Athletes Really Students?

Game Score, Test Scores | Edward Koren

Edward Koren's cartoon depicting a scoreboard for test scores as well as for game scores whimsically calls attention to the concern of everyone—educators, parents, and sports fans, as well as the athletes themselves—that participation in sports not compromise academic achievement. Edward Koren is a prolific cartoonist, having published nearly a thousand cartoons in the New Yorker, Time, Newsweek, Sports Illustrated, *and other periodicals.*

(School basketball game has two score boards. One is for the game score, and one for test scores.)

Reflections and Inquiries

1. What serious point does Koren make with his cartoon?

2. Should GPA (as opposed to other means of determining academic excellence) be the sole criterion for determining eligibility? If so, explain. If not, what other criteria should be used?

3. What might have been Koren's rationale for depicting a basketball game (rather than, say, a football or baseball game) in his cartoon?

Reading to Write

1. Write an essay supporting or challenging the use of minimum test scores as a way of qualifying high school or college students for participation in school-sponsored athletic events. Use the Classical, Toulmin, or Rogerian method in developing your argument.

2. Research what your school requires for its teams' minimum G.P.A. for student athletes to play. Write an essay supporting or challenging that minimum G.P.A.

Brawn & Brains:
Student Athletes Get a Bum Rap | Dave Newhouse

Few would disagree that college should be a place where stereotyping—a major roadblock to learning—is eliminated; yet the collegiate athlete persists in being a victim of stereotyping. At the University of California at Berkeley, however, the image of the college athlete is undergoing a transformation, thanks to the efforts of Herb Simons, a professor in Cal's Graduate School of Education. He has developed a master's program called "Athletics and Academic Achievement." In the following article, Dave Newhouse, a staff writer for the San Mateo County Times *(a newspaper serving the Bay Area peninsula county just south of San Francisco) describes some of the unexpected findings of Simons's program and Cal's Athletic Study Center.*

Athletically, it goes with the turf, it's an unwritten part of every scholarship, and there's no escaping it even if you attend Cal, rated the nation's No. 1 public university.

You're a "dumb jock" regardless.

"I've done a study on this, and athletes at this university are stigmatized," said Herb Simons, a Cal professor who oversees a unique master's program that focuses on the academic side of student-athletes. "They're assumed to be not smart enough or interested enough."

This assumption, Simons said, is held by students and faculty.

"If you're an athlete, it's the opinion that you're not as smart as a regular   5
student," he said. "In my study, some athletes shut up in class or drop the class if the professor says something negative (about them).

"Another thing student-athletes do is try to keep their identity hidden. They don't wear their athletic clothing to class. They do not want to be known as an athlete. They try to keep it a secret."

Cal athletes qualify for NCAA tournaments and play in bowl games, but the same students who cheer them on denigrate them in the classroom.

"They hear things like, 'This test is easy. Even athletes can pass,' " Simons said. "Or, 'You're degrading my degree and my major.' "

The dumb-jock image is nothing new at Cal or at most institutions; it's a stigma that traces back to college athletics' roots in the mid-1800s. The athlete is systematically branded as lacking in intelligence.

Perhaps unfairly.   10

"Athletes *are* successful students," Simons emphasized. "They know how to work hard, how to deal with failure, how to manage their time. Being an athlete takes so much determination and motivation. They're interested in trying anything. They take on the task."

And, despite the negativity that student-athletes encounter from peers and professors, they're very successful in completing the task.

Derek Van Rheenen, director of Cal's Athletic Study Center, offers the following evidence: Half of Cal's 900 student-athletes have 3.0 (B) grade-point averages or higher; five of Cal's 13 men's teams and 10 of its 14 women's teams have cumulative 3.0 GPAs; of the 26 Cal football players who completed their eligibility in 2004, 22 have graduated, or 85 percent.

"Eighty-five percent is comparable to the overall graduation rate at Berkeley," Van Rheenen said. "The *Los Angeles Times* wrote last year that Cal was a model for the rest of the country in terms of the student-athlete, and if there was a Heisman Trophy for that, we would be the recipient."

The Athletic Study Center, founded in 1984, provides tutors for student-   15
athletes with the most critical academic needs. The Student Learning Center is for all Cal students. Van Rheenen reports directly to the vice provost, not the athletic department, thereby reducing pressure from coaches.

Simons, 68—a professor in the Graduate School of Education specializing in language and literacy, society and culture—has been at Cal 35 years, having chosen education over a career in optometry. He believes the general public has no concept of the rigors confronting student-athletes.

"It's the demands on the kids, which are enormous, the amount of time they have to put in," he said.

The NCAA restricts an athlete to 20 hours of participation in his or her sport weekly; however, what the NCAA dictates, it can't always see.

"There are many exceptions," Simons said of that rule. "Weight training doesn't count. Voluntary activity doesn't count; it's more like voluntary/mandatory. The more competitive the university has become playing football, the more the demands increase.

"It's amazing that these athletes do well academically. They get injured,   20
they're exhausted, their sport is year-round. One athlete told me, 'You don't have to work at it all summer, but you'll be third string.' "

Non-athletes don't experience these same demands at Cal. So who's denigrating which classroom, which degree, which major? The student-athlete should serve as a beacon of education rather than as a blight.

One such student-athlete was Keasara "Kiki" Williams. She started on the Cal women's basketball team, earned her master's degree in Simons' program and now is a first-year law student at Hastings in San Francisco.

2005 NCAA graduation chart

Beginning with the 1998-99 academic year, based on a four-year average.

	All students	Student-athletes
PAC-10		
Arizona	55%	58%
Arizona State	52%	57%
Oregon	60%	64%
Oregon State	59%	57%
Cal	84%	69%
Stanford	94%	88%
USC	78%	61%
UCLA	85%	62%
Washington	71%	68%
Washington State	61%	61%
Other Bay Area Division I schools		
St. Mary's	68%	68%
Santa Clara	82%	76%
San Jose State	38%	44%
USF	66%	58%
UOP	68%	70%
Various national Division I schools		
Alabama	61%	55%
Bradley	70%	77%
Connecticut	70%	62%
Duke	93%	90%
Gonzaga	77%	68%
Florida	76%	58%
Florida State	64%	62%
Georgia	71%	55%
Memphis	33%	45%
Miami Florida	67%	60%
Michigan	85%	77%
Nevada	48%	50%
Nevada-Las Vegas	38%	38%
Northwestern	92%	86%
Notre Dame	95%	90%

	All students	Student-athletes
Ohio State	60%	62%
Oklahoma	54%	55%
Penn State	82%	80%
Tennessee	59%	55%
Texas	72%	56%
Vanderbilt	84%	77%
Virginia Tech	74%	70%
Wisconsin	76%	70%

Service academies and Ivy League schools don't offer athletic scholarships per se.
Source: NCAA

"Some teachers at Cal tell students that if they can't be there for finals because of a sporting event, don't take the class," Williams said.

Despite the strict demands placed upon her athletically and academically, Williams graduated with a 3.3 GPA in sociology in four years.

"A lot of student-athletes are doing the same thing," she said of the four-year 25 window. "It's a lot of time management."

Because Williams redshirted as a freshman, she began her master's work during her fifth year at Cal while completing her eligibility in basketball.

"He really cares about the athletes," she said of Simons. "He sees things we haven't thought of before, like study habits and picking whatever issue we wanted for our thesis. I did mine (in partnership) on NCAA violations and how they affect different schools and conferences differently."

Simons' master's candidates must complete 24 units in one academic year, plus write a thesis, to earn their degree from his program, called "Athletes and Academic Achievement." A minimum 3.0 GPA is required to enter any master's or doctoral program at Berkeley, but student-athletes who have entered Simons' program have a combined 3.46 GPA average.

Dumb jock, his eye.

"So often, student-athletes are seen as having low academics," said for- 30 mer Cal football player Tyler Fredrickson. "Most of the time, you hear negative things about guys barely getting into school."

In 2003, Fredrickson kicked game-winning field goals against USC and Virginia Tech in the Insight Bowl. A 3.4 GPA student in film studies, Fredrickson also produced an acclaimed documentary on that '03 Cal team for his master's thesis.

"The thing that's great about Herb is his flexibility," said Fredrickson, who recently signed with the Denver Broncos. "He wants people to pursue their academics at a higher level, and not take a ballroom dancing class like (USC quarterback) Matt Leinart.

"There's so much knowledge that a student-athlete brings to the table that the average student can't bring regarding life experience. There's so much in athletics that prepares you for a post-athletic career that you don't get from just studying in the classroom."

Simons also runs Cal's tutoring program for student-athletes. He hires graduate students as his tutors.

"Though the athletes we work with are the least prepared, some are very 35 successful," he said. "There are differences in ability, never mind skills. Some are really smart kids who don't have the skills. Some are not used to writing papers. A series of drafts are surprising to them. But they should be able to get a degree if they're willing to work at it."

The NCAA's most recent graduation rates, released in 2005, cover both students and student-athletes. These graduation rates begin with the 1998-99 academic year and encompass a four-year period, although some students and student-athletes need more than four years to graduate.

The NCAA reported that 84 percent of Cal students graduated, compared with 67 percent of its student-athletes; however, athletes who transferred or left school early to pursue a professional sport or Olympic competition still counted against Cal's graduation rate, even if they graduated elsewhere. Stanford's comparable graduation rates provided by the NCAA: Students, 94 percent, student-athletes, 88 percent.

"It's no secret that Stanford has higher entrance standards for athletes than Cal," Simons said. "But private schools, traditionally, have higher graduation rates than public schools. If someone is paying $40,000 {for a child's education}, they don't let them slip through the cracks."

Simons said Cal's athletic department is given exceptions by the admissions office in terms of admitting student-athletes with special needs.

"Cal can 'tag' 200 athletes it wants to get in, who vary in SAT scores," he said. 40 "It's true everywhere that there's a certain tagging system, even in the Ivy League."

Some Cal athletes are assigned one tutor; some are assigned two. These athletes meet twice weekly with a tutor, a total of three hours, and once a week with a supervisor for an hour. Plus the tutors meet with Simons weekly.

"My interest is making sure these athletes get the education they were promised when they came here," Simons said. "The (academic) turnaround can happen in a year if they're motivated."

Tutors help the athletes beyond their academic concerns. Simons discovered the athletes, mostly first-year students, will tell tutors things they don't tell anyone else. In other words, a tutorial confessional.

Simons, who has written in numerous educational journals, will retire at the end of the current academic year. He will return to Cal in the fall to work exclusively with his master's students. Van Rheenen will take over his tutoring responsibilities.

"My greatest joy has been working with the kids. I haven't met a student- 45 athlete who was a bad kid," Simons said. "Their getting together as a group (socially), that's a different way (of fraternizing). But every one of them has been nice and personable." ◎/◎

Reflections and Inquiries

1. According to Dave Newhouse, "The student athlete should serve as a beacon of education rather than as a blight." On what grounds does Newhouse rest this claim? How adequate, in your opinion, is Newhouse's evidence?

2. What function does Cal's Athletic Study Center serve? How necessary do you think this facility is?

3. What are some of the negative consequences of experiencing discrimination as a student athlete?

Reading to Write

Study the 2005 NCAA graduation chart (included with this article) in which the graduation rates of student athletes are compared to the graduation rates of all students. Compare these data to those from earlier periods (say 1985 and 1995) as well from a more recent period (say, 2007 or 2008). What generalizations are you prepared to make about the graduation rates of student athletes in relation to types of college from which they graduate? You may need to access the websites of some of the colleges to learn more about their athletic programs. Present your conclusions in a detailed essay.

Is Athletics Meeting Its Purpose? | John R. Gerdy

What, exactly, does a college athletic program contribute to a college education? John R. Gerdy, an education consultant based in New York City, discusses eight concerns most often raised about such programs? (1) Do they build character (and if so, what is meant by that expression)? (2) Is it true that student athletes acquire a narrower world view while in college than that of their nonathlete fellow students? (3) Does participation in sports contribute to "good sportsmanship" in the larger sense of the term? (4) Does participation in sports interfere with the student's intellectual development? (5) What influence, if any, does an athletic program have on racial harmony? (6) Do athletic programs add to or drain the financial resources of the host college? (7) Does an athletic program add to a university's "visibility" in positive ways? Finally, (8) How valuable is the entertainment dimension of sports competitions to the host college?

There is a common belief in the value of sport, which we have chosen to view as a myth not because it is untrue, but because it is generally accepted without question. If this common understanding, this myth about sport, is valid, it ought to withstand scrutiny. If it is not valid, we tax-paying citizens who make decisions about the future of our educational system need to know. . . . If sport does live up to the myth surrounding it, even if only in part, perhaps we should invest more

---

Source: "Is Athletics Meeting Its Purpose?" from *The Successful College Athletic Program: The New Standard* by John R. Gerdy. Oryx Press, 1997: 35–54. Copyright © 1997. Reproduced with permission of Greenwood Publishing Group, Westport, CT.

heavily in sports. For example, we could make room for all students in sport, not just the athletically superior. On the other hand, what if it were demonstrated scientifically that most or all of the myths about school sport have no empirical basis, that there are no data to support them, no evidence of positive effects? As a taxpayer, parent, educator, or concerned citizen, what would your response be? What should it be?

Andrew Miracle and C. Roger Rees

Lessons of the Locker Room

It is perhaps axiomatic that challenges to any system are scorned by those fully vested in the system. On the other hand, organizations that do not continually reevaluate their goals and their effectiveness in meeting those goals will eventually become obsolete. Critical analysis of college athletics is particularly important because a fundamental purpose of higher education is to encourage critical thinking by challenging preexisting assumptions in an effort to seek truth. Therefore, the college athletic community should not fear, resist, or ignore such scrutiny; rather, it should welcome the chance to rethink its purpose. Those who criticize college athletics should not be dismissed as simply destructive, particularly if the criticism is well formulated with suggestions for improvement.

Thus, the debate regarding whether athletics is meeting its stated purposes should not center on whether these questions should be asked, but rather on how athletics' contribution to higher education can be maximized. The credibility of any individual or organization depends upon whether the individual or organization does what it says it will. With both academe and the public questioning the role of athletics in higher education, critical debate regarding the effectiveness with which athletics accomplishes its goals should be encouraged. The following sections are intended to facilitate creative debate.

Does Athletics Build Character?

Sports is a vital character builder. It molds the youth of our country for their roles as custodians of the republic. It teaches them to be strong enough to know they are weak and brave enough to face themselves when they are afraid. It teaches them to be proud and unbending in honest defeat, but humble and gentle in victory. . . . It gives them a predominance of courage over timidity, of appetite for adventure over loss of ease. (General Douglas MacArthur in Chu 1989, 65)

For the past 8 years, we have been studying the effects of competition on personality. Our research began with the counseling of problem athletes, but it soon expanded to include athletes from every sport, at every level, from the high school gym to the professional arena. On the evidence gathered in this study, we can make some broad-range value judgments. We found no empirical support for the tradition that sport builds character. Indeed, there is evidence that athletic competition limits growth in some areas. It seems that the personality of the ideal athlete is not the result of any molding process, but comes out of the ruthless selection process that occurs at all levels of sport. Athletic competition has no more beneficial effects than intense endeavor in any other field. (Oglive and Tutko 1985, 268–269)

The claim that "sports builds character" has long been a widely held assumption 5 in the United States. This largely unquestioned belief made the sponsorship of athletic programs seem logical, not only in colleges and universities but in high schools and junior highs as well. While the lessons learned in classrooms and laboratories in English and science were important, so, it seemed, were the lessons in discipline, teamwork, and perseverance taught on the playing fields. Although thousands of former and current student-athletes will swear by the value of competitive athletics, many others look back on their intercollegiate athletic experience with bitterness and regret.

Just as I was exposed to coaches who had a tremendously positive effect on my life, I was also subject to other coaches who had no interest in my personal or academic development or in that of any of my teammates. So from my experience, while there are lessons that participation in competitive athletics teaches, there were some practices that would be hard to defend from an educational standpoint. And as the money, television exposure, and pressure to win have increased, so too have practices that would be questionable in any educational setting.

Many groups have a vested interest in promoting the principle that participation in sport is a character-building activity. To justify their place in the educational community, coaches and athletic administrators must demonstrate that sports have educational value. The widespread acceptance of the educational value of athletics secures their power and status not only in the educational community but also in the public eye.

The justification that "sports build character" serves those in the athletic establishment in another important way. An unquestioned acceptance of this ideal relieves coaches of having to be accountable for teaching in a responsible manner. A coach can justify punishing an "undisciplined" student-athlete, running a few "bad apples" off the team and out of a scholarship, or verbally abusing a student-athlete by simply stating that he or she is "teaching life lessons." Thus, teaching methods deemed unacceptable for the classroom can be justified on the playing fields in the name of "building character."

Coaches and administrators are not alone in having an interest in promoting the "sports build character" ideal. The media, bowl representatives, television executives, and others who make a living off big-time athletics all have a stake in promulgating this belief. If it were determined that participation in major college athletics had no positive educational benefits, athletics' place on the college campus would be difficult to justify. If universities no longer sponsored athletics, coaches and administrators would no longer have jobs, at least not the same jobs. For this reason, the entire athletic community has a tremendous vested interest in promoting the "sports build character" ideal, regardless of its validity.

Not everyone has accepted without question the claim that participation 10
in sports has significant educational benefits. Skepticism regarding the supposed benefits of athletic participation has almost been as much a part of the
culture of sport as the increased heart rate and the sweat-soaked brow. In fact,
the sentiment of higher education leaders that athletics was a frivolous activity prevented it from being sponsored as a university-sanctioned activity
before the late nineteenth century. When it was formally incorporated into
higher education, debate regarding athletics' value and place on campus
intensified.

While athletics' role was debated on individual campuses for years, the
issue was first raised as a national concern with the release of the Carnegie
Foundation Study of American college athletics in 1929. The report addressed
many concerns, including whether athletic participation had substantial educational value and whether all the attention and expense showered upon college athletic programs were justified. The report stated the following:

> To the development of the individual capacities of young men and women,
> their appreciation of true values, their powers of decision and choice, their
> sense of responsibility, and their ability to sustain it when once it comes to
> them—to the development of these and of all other best habits of mind and
> traits of character, college athletics must contribute far more than they have
> in the past if they are to justify the time and effort that are lavished upon
> them. (Savage 1929, 133-34)

Perhaps the most interesting aspect of the report was its analysis of the coach.
It called into question coaches' propensity to make virtually every decision
related to the game and the program themselves, leaving little opportunity for
the students to develop their decision-making skills.

> The exigencies of the game forbid original thinking. Not many coaches
> understand what it means to let their men work out their own plays and
> conduct their own teams accordingly. It is a commonplace of adverse criti-
> cism of present-day coaching methods that many coaches tend to occupy
> too much of their men's time with fundamentals, too little with playing the
> game under conditions of contest. Yet, if athletics are to be "educational,"
> the player must be taught to do his own thinking. In every branch of ath-
> letics the strategy of the game should not be beyond the capacity of the
> alertly-minded undergraduate. As matters now stand, no branch owes
> even a vestige of its strategy to the undergraduates engaged. Such matters
> are the affair of the coach. (Savage 1929, 176)

While the Carnegie report generated discussion, it did not result in much 15
change. The lack of response, however, did not mean that such concerns
would disappear. Since the publication of the Carnegie report, empirical
data has continued to mount, indicating that the educational value of participation in intercollegiate athletics may have been greatly overemphasized.

Some researchers even charge that participation in highly competitive athletics might actually hinder or arrest the development of various positive character traits.

A Narrower World View

One of the most interesting studies of the effect of athletic participation on student-athletes was conducted by sociologists Peter and Patricia Adler. The Adlers virtually became a part of a Division I basketball program for a five-year period. Their observations are outlined in their 1991 book entitled *Backboards and Blackboards: College Athletes and Role Engulfment.* Their conclusions were based upon extensive interviews and observation, and among those conclusions was the finding that after a four- or five-year intercollegiate athletic experience, student-athletes often had a much narrower "world view" than when they entered the university.

The Adlers found that upon initial enrollment, student-athletes had a broad range of interests and goals in the academic, social, and athletic areas. However, during their time on campus, they were forced to make decisions that pitted their academic and social interests against their athletic interests. Invariably, decisions were made in favor of athletic interests. For example, if a student-athlete wanted to go to a movie with a nonathlete, but the coach had planned a social event with someone who supported the athletic program, the student-athlete felt pressure to attend the team function. Or, if a coach thought a particular academic major was too demanding and would thus affect athletic performance, he would "suggest" that the student-athlete enroll in a less demanding major. Because of the intense and constant pressure to show one's "commitment to the program," student-athletes were continually forced to make decisions that would further their athletic goals, while pushing their academic and social aspirations into the background. Like the muscle that atrophies from inactivity, the result was a dwindling of student-athletes' social and academic interests in favor of athletic interests. Although certain activities, such as travel to new and exciting places, expand the student-athlete's "world view," the Adlers argued that the overall experience in some cases was actually to narrow the student-athlete's perspective.

> Despite its structural fit within the trends current in American society, the engulfment of college athletes raises questions and conflicts that cannot be easily answered. On the one hand, these young men are spending formative years sacrificing themselves to entertain and enrich others, lured by the hope of a future that is elusive at best. For other students, this kind of narrowing and intense focus may lead to a prosperous career in such fields as medicine, law, education, or business. For college athletes, however, their specialization, dedication, and abandonment of alternatives leads to their becoming finally proficient at a role that, for

most, will end immediately following the conclusion of their college eligibility. For those fortunate enough to achieve a professional career, the end comes only slightly later.

It is ironic that these athletes are partly socialized to failure; although some sustained the athletic role temporarily, they were released by the system at the end of four years engulfed in a role destined to become an "ex" (Ebaugh 1988). College athletes entered the university thinking that they would expand their horizons and opportunities in a variety of ways. They ended up narrowing their selves enough that their more grandiose expectations were not met. (Adler and Adler 1991, 230)

One of the purposes of college is to broaden the scope of young people's 20 vision and to provide youth with opportunities to make decisions for themselves and hopefully to learn from even those decisions that turned out to be mistakes. College should expand horizons and teach young people the love of learning. Is it possible that involvement in highly competitive athletics might actually do the opposite? Does participation in intercollegiate athletics actually narrow focus and self-identity of young people, and restrict decision-making opportunities?

The preliminary results of a study led by Hans Steiner, a professor of psychiatry and behavioral science at Stanford University, shed some interesting light on the issue of "focus" in athletics. The study, released in 1996, is based on a survey of more than 2,100 high school and college students. It found that high school student-athletes earned better marks on a variety of psychological tests than did their peers who were not student-athletes. But a different picture emerged of the college student-athlete. The same psychological traits that could contribute to the success of college student-athletes on the playing fields and courts also put them at increased risk of drug or alcohol abuse, or academic and personal problems. According to Steiner, student-athletes are taught to repress the notion of failure, which does not contribute to good psychological health. Steiner plans to test his conclusions further with additional student-athletes and students.

The lengths to which coaches and administrators will go to keep their student-athletes focused on their sport can at times be amusing. During my junior year at Davidson, our basketball coach took a sudden and unexpected leave of absence. We returned from our short Christmas break to find that our coach was no longer going to be with us. Worse, none of the other coaches or administrators knew where he was, or if they did, they were not telling. After practice, an administrator addressed the team as follows: "Men, your coach is gone. Don't know where he is. Thinks he's got a brain infection. Thinks he's gonna die. . . . But I tell ya what we're gonna do. We're gonna buy you a big 'ole steak and we're gonna go out and beat Marshall."

Our coach, for whom we all cared deeply, was missing and apparently very sick. Yet foremost on the mind of this administrator was not helping us deal with, or even understand, what had happened to him. Rather the push was to get us focused on beating Marshall. Of course, feeding us a "big 'ole steak" was supposed to help us forget that our coach was missing and to ignore the fact that no one seemed to know where he was. We lost to Marshall by 30 points.

Teaching Honesty and Sportsmanship

The promise of a fair and honest contest forms the foundation upon which athletic competition is allegedly based. Athletic participation, it is argued, naturally enhances a participant's moral and ethical development through the teaching of good sportsmanship. But research supporting this assertion has, to this point, been largely inconclusive. On the contrary, recent studies seem to suggest that the moral and ethical reasoning skills of intercollegiate athletes might actually be less developed than those of nonathletes.

Over the past few years, Jennifer Beller and Sharon Stoll, both of the 25 University of Idaho's Center for Ethics, have evaluated thousands of high school and college student-athletes and their nonathlete peers on their cognitive moral reasoning development. Beller and Stoll have found that "revenue producing athletes, whether at NAIA, Division III, Division II or Division I are significantly lower in moral development than their peer group, and individual and non-revenue producing athletes." Further, they found that "revenue producing athletes are not morally, developmentally dysfunctional when they come to athletics, rather the competitive process appears to cause a masking of moral reasoning processes" (Stoll 1996).

The classic example of the "masking" of the moral reasoning process is pointed out by Stephen Carter in his 1996 book *Integrity*. During a televised football game, a player who had failed to catch a ball thrown his way hit the ground, rolled over, and then jumped up, celebrating as if he had made the catch. Screened from the play, the referee awarded the catch. A review of the replay revealed that the player had dropped the ball. The broadcaster commented, "What a heads up play!," meaning, in Carter's words, "Wow! What a great liar this kid is. Well done!"

> By jumping up and celebrating, he was trying to convey a false impression. He was trying to convince the officials that he had caught the ball. . . . So, in any understanding of the word, he lied. . . . Now, suppose the player had instead gone to the referee and said, "I'm sorry sir, but I did not make that catch. Your call is wrong." Probably his coach and teammates and most of his team's fans would have been furious: he would not have been a good team player. The good team player lies to the referee, and does so in a manner that is at once blatant (because millions of viewers see it) and virtually impossible for the referee to detect. Having pulled off this trickery, the player is congratulated: he is told that he has made a heads-up play. Thus, the ethic of the game turns out to be an ethic that rewards cheating. (Carter 1996, 5)

David L. Shields and Brenda J. Bredemeir from the University of California, Berkeley, reviewed the body of research available regarding sport and character development in their book *Character Development and Physical Activity*. Consider the following excerpt, which calls into question the blind acceptance of the claim that athletics builds character.

> Let us state our conclusion first. The research does not support either position in the debate over sport building character. If any conclusion is justified, it is that the question that is posed is too simplistic. The term *character* is vague, even if modified with the adjective *good*. More important, sport experience is far from uniform. There is certainly nothing intrinsically character-building about batting a ball, jumping over hurdles, or rolling heavy spheres toward pins. The component physical behaviors of sport are not in themselves moral or immoral. When we talk about building character through sport, we are referring to the potential influence of the social interactions that are fostered by the sport experience. The nature of those interactions varies from sport to sport, from team to team, from one geographical region to another, from one level of competition to another, and so on. . . . The word *character* is often used synonymously with *personality*. Not surprisingly, then, a number of early researchers were interested in whether sport influenced the personality characteristics of participants. Most studies conducted on this question have followed one or more of three strategies (Stevenson 1975): a comparison of athletes with non-participants, a comparison of elite athletes with less-advanced sport participants or the general population, or a comparison of athletes participating in different sports. In all three cases, results are inconclusive. (Shields and Bredemeir 1995, 178)

Bredemeir and Shields went beyond assessing whether sport positively 30 affects the "character" of participants; they reviewed the research that attempts to gauge sports participation on more narrowly defined traits such as aggression, sportsmanship, compassion, fairness, and integrity. Once again, they determined that in virtually all categories, the existing research is inconclusive.

A notable exception, however, is research indicating a negative correlation between sport involvement and delinquency; the reason for the correlation was unclear. Delinquency theory suggests that deviant behavior is learned through contact with other deviants. Thus, this correlation might be inferred by the fact that sport participation deters delinquency by encouraging less frequent, shorter, or less intense interaction with deviant others. Even this apparent positive by-product of sport participation may not result from what is being taught on the playing fields but rather from the fact that the individual simply has less contact with "bad influences." That being the case, athletic participation would be no more likely to result in preventing deviant behavior than participation in other extracurricular activities such as band, theater, or the debate club.

If there is one general conclusion to be made from Bredemeir and Shields' work, it is that "whatever advantages or liabilities are associated with sport involvement, they do not come from sport per se, but from the particular blend of social interactions and physical activities that comprise the totality of the sport experience" (Shields and Bredemeir 1995, 184).

Athletic Injuries to the Mind

Present-day researchers are not the only ones who have questioned the "sports build character" myth. Brutus Hamilton, track and field coach at the University of California, Berkeley, from 1933 to 1965, was one of the all-time best coaches. Hamilton was also U.S. Olympic decathlon coach in 1932 and 1936 and head U.S. track and field coach for the 1952 Olympic games in Helsinki. Hamilton, known as a coach who kept life and athletics in perspective, worried more about character development than about winning. He expressed his concern regarding sports participation and its effect on an individual's character development in a unique way at a Marin Sports Injury Conference in 1962.

Further athletic injuries to the boy's character can result in college. If he has chosen a school where sports are emphasized out of proportion to their importance he will find life easy if he performs well on the team. He will be coddled, made over, given parties by avid alumni, and even handed under-the-table payment, if not in cash then in some kind of presents. He's embarrassed at first, but soon comes to accept these things as a matter of course. The moral fiber gradually weakens and by the time his intercollegiate competition is over he is a victim of the system, a slave to gross and violent tastes, standing at the crossroads of Destiny. He was yesterday's headlines; he will be tomorrow's trivia. Now comes the harsh test as he faces the cruel pace of this competitive world in what he considers routine, humdrum chores of business. He has no headlines now; others who are younger are taking his place. Some former athletes make the adjustment rather quickly, others grope for several years and then make the adjustment, usually with the help of some good woman. Others, all too many, drift into middle age and resort to artificial stimulation to substitute for the intoxicating experiences they enjoyed in sports. Maybe sports were only partly to blame, but I believe no one would criticize a doctor who diagnosed these cases as an athletic injury to character suffered in youth. . . .

The sad cases though are the ones which involve the eager, bright lad 35 who goes to college on some kind of an athletic grant and is eager to become an Engineer, Lawyer, Doctor, Teacher or Architect. He becomes a victim of the intensity of the athletic training program. He misses practice to work on problem sets or to write out a book report. The coach suggests that he may be in the wrong course. Maybe he should transfer to a course which is not so demanding on his time. He certainly can't miss any more practices or his grant may be terminated. The boy has little choice, so he submits to the coach's suggestion and gives up his planned career. He may succeed gloriously in this new field but always he will wonder if he didn't make a mistake. He will always consider that he suffered an athletic injury to his mind in college whether anyone else does or not. When the training for an intercollegiate team becomes so time consuming, so intense and so exhausting that it is no longer possible for the student in the sciences or professions to participate, then something is wrong. Someone, perhaps a great many, are suffering an athletic injury to the mind. (Walton 1992, 118–20)

Los Angeles Lakers forward Elden Campbell made a related point, but much more precisely. When asked if he had earned his degree from Clemson University, he supposedly responded, "No, but they gave me one anyway."

Race and Violence
The college athletic community has also used as an educational justification the fact that a tremendous number of minority, particularly black, youngsters have benefited from the educational opportunity afforded them through athletic scholarships. Coaches often argue that athletics is the most discrimination-free enterprise in our country, insisting that the only criteria relevant in their evaluation of a student-athlete's worth is his or her performance on the field or court. The relatively large percentage of black student-athletes, particularly in the sports of football and basketball, provides some credence to the claim that athletic programs are in fact meeting this justification. According to the 1996 NCAA Division I Graduation Rate Report, 44 percent of football, 60 percent of men's basketball, and 34 percent of women's basketball student-athletes are black (National Collegiate Athletic Association 1996, 622). While these numbers are impressive, trumpeting athletics' tolerance of diversity as a significant justification for its place on campus is suspect at best, particularly given the small percentage of minorities in coaching and administrative positions, and athletics' poor record on issues relating to gender equity. . . .

Finally, there is growing concern regarding the effect of athletic participation on the participant's ability to resolve off-the-field conflicts peacefully, with particular attention being paid to violence against women. Accounts of student-athletes physically abusing women appear in our nation's newspapers far too often. One of the few studies of student-athlete violence against women was published in May 1995 in *The Journal of Sport and Social Issues*. The article reviewed 107 cases of sexual assault reported at 30 NCAA Division I institutions from 1991 to 1993. At 10 schools, male student-athletes were accused in 19 percent of the assaults, although they comprised only 3.3 percent of the male student body (Crosset, Benedict, and McDonald 1995, 126–140). Although broad conclusions should not be drawn from such limited research, the study does raise a question. Could it be that student-athletes, conditioned to resolve on-the-field conflicts with violence, have a more difficult time resolving off-the-field conflicts peacefully?

The Issue is Environment

So what does all this mean for athletics' place within higher education? On one hand, there is the widely accepted notion that sports build character. Participation in college athletics, it is argued, teaches young people important lessons about teamwork, discipline, communication, and loyalty—all skills necessary for success beyond the playing field. For the most part, the public has bought fully into the concept. The supposed character-building benefits of sports have become a part of American folklore. From the mythical Frank Merriwell of Yale to the legendary Bud Wilkinson of Oklahoma, sports and those who play them embody the characteristics that make Americans "number one." Those who coach are sage mentors and molders of our future leaders. Those who play are inspirational heroes and role models.

On the other hand, many argue that college athletics is not about educa- 40 tion, in the sense of character development, at all; sport is about money, power, ego, and doing whatever it takes to win. As Oglive and Tutko (1985) pointed out, sport is not educational simply because it is sport. Rather it is the environment within which sports participation occurs that influences the educational, moral, and ethical development of participants. Sport that is overemphasized in relation to other fields of endeavor, particularly when it is conducted under the banner of an educational institution, is harmful. Sport kept in the proper perspective, where the process of participation (education) is not subjugated by the game's result (winning), can be extremely positive.

Along with the notion of athletics as a character builder goes the belief that coaches are effective teachers and positive educational role models. There are, however, too many examples of coaches who force their student-athletes into less demanding majors or discourage them from fully investing in their educational experience. These coaches are more interested in winning next week's game than preparing their student-athletes for life after athletics. Far too many student-athletes discontinue their participation in college athletics after becoming disillusioned with "the system." These dropouts are dismissed as "not having what it takes to be a winner." The successes are a product of the system; the failures are the result of the individual's shortcomings. Coaches refuse to admit the fact that often the individual succeeds despite the system or that it can be the system, rather than the individual, that fails. Therefore, along with questioning sports as inherently character building, we must also accept the fact that a whistle around the neck does not serve to qualify a coach as an educator.

For close to 100 years, we have claimed that big-time athletics is linked to the educational mission of the university, that participation is educational for the student-athlete, and that coaches and athletic administrators are educators. That assumption, however, can no longer be accepted without question.

The purpose in highlighting the rather inconclusive research regarding sports participation's effect upon personality development is, once again, not to attack athletics or to minimize its potential to influence young people positively, but rather to caution the athletic community regarding its cavalier use of the "sports build character" justification. If education is a primary justification for athletics being on the college campus, then the question we must concern ourselves with is whether the environment in our programs is conducive to the positive educational and personal development of the student-athlete. It is time for the college athletic community to seriously rethink how this component of its mission is approached and realized.

Does Athletics Make Money?

Concern regarding making ends meet financially has been as much a part of the history of American higher education as the classroom lecture. As noted earlier, the never-ending search for new revenue streams was the driving force behind athletics' acceptance into the higher education community.

> With the introduction of athletics to the already economically hard-pressed colleges and universities of late 19th and 20th century America, the doctrine of good works [that revenues generated by intercollegiate athletics are so much greater than the cost of the sport that the entire college benefits financially] offered some hope of relief from further financial hardships. Along with claims concerning the educational value of athletics—that sport participation builds character and that it helps student grades—the financial rationale for sport programs eased the entry onto campus of athleticism, a program previously foreign to the cognitively oriented college and university of the era. (Chu, Segrave, and Becker 1985, 289)

A widely held belief is that major college athletic programs generate a huge 45 surplus of revenue for universities through gate receipts, television revenue, and alumni contributions. Even at universities where programs operate at a deficit, the exposure generated through television and the media is thought to increase the institution's stature and generate public interest in the university. Such visibility, it is said, results in increased applications and curries favor with legislators and the surrounding community. The facts, however, paint a different picture.

When institutional support (salaries, cash, tuition waivers, etc.) is not included on the revenue side of the financial ledger, most Division I college athletic programs lose money. According to an NCAA-sponsored report, only 28 percent of Division I programs generate more revenues than they expend. Further, only 46 percent of the 89 Division I-A schools reporting generated a profit. (The total number of Division I-A programs, those with "big-time" football, is 108; Division I-AA has 119 members and I-AAA has 78.) Without general institutional support, barely more than one in four Division I athletic programs would be solvent. A more detailed accounting of the financial statistics from this report follows (Fulks 1995, 19, 33, and 47):

	Profit	Deficit	Even
Division I-A (n=89)	46%	52%	2%
Division I-AA (n=72)	13%	85%	2%
Division I-AAA (n=45)	18%	82%	0%

And, as institutions begin to appropriate the long-overdue resources necessary to meet the demands of Title IX and gender equity, future financial figures may become more sobering.

There is more to the issue of athletics as a sound institutional business investment. The National Association of College and University Business Officers (NACUBO) conducted an analysis of college athletics' finances in its 1993 report entitled *The Financial Management of Intercollegiate Athletics Programs.* The analysis brought to light additional concerns regarding university accounting procedures as they apply to athletic operations. The report concluded that current costs, as high as they are, may not yet be telling the entire financial story. Specifically, the report questioned the practice of institutions paying many indirect or overhead costs generated by the athletic department.

The report identified six data elements that represent indirect expenditures.

- Amortization of facilities (if owned by the university)

- Student support services (academic and financial assistance) provided by the institution

- Student health services provided by the institution

- Athletic staff salaries and benefits for staff employed in other departments

- Proportion of buildings and grounds maintenance

- Proportion of capital equipment used

The report went on to state that   50

> Interviews with personnel in 18 institutions across all athletics divisions showed that only one of these data elements, amortization of facilities, could be calculated with any degree of accuracy, and even then this could be done only by the four Division I-A institutions in the study. Given this difficulty, it seems likely that many indirect or "overhead" expenses attributable to athletics activities are borne by the university as a whole. In institutions that require other programs or divisions to bear their share of indirect costs, allowing athletics to escape this burden creates a basic inequity. (National Association of College and University Business Officers 1993, 20)

We can easily conclude that were athletics' accounting held to a common business standard where all direct and indirect expenses are charged against revenues, significantly fewer than the 28 percent of all Division I institutions would report an athletic department profit.

Inasmuch as athletics was formally and primarily incorporated into higher education for financial and business reasons, it is ironic that more often than not this "business proposition" is a bad one. A successful business generates more money than it expends. After looking at the numbers, the argument can be made that except for the elite programs, athletics actually drains financial resources from the university.

> A review of the reports published over the past decade indicates that, as a whole, American intercollegiate athletics programs are unable to support themselves and that most programs run a deficit. This finding is not surprising in colleges that designate varsity sports as part of the educational budget and make no claim to seek massive crowds. It does warrant concern, however, when one looks at institutions that have established varsity football and/or basketball as major, self-supporting activities intended to produce revenues, with large arenas and stadia and with television audiences. (Thelin and Wiseman 1989, 15)

Due largely to reports of huge television deals and corporate sponsorship agreements, it is easy to assume that major college athletic programs are rolling in money. But based upon actual figures, the claim that athletic programs make money for the university is largely untrue. Yes, athletic programs generate revenue. And yes, occasionally we read about an athletic department writing a check to the university's library or general scholarship fund. But what is not as readily reported is that major college athletic programs also spend a tremendous amount of money, particularly in the sports of football and basketball.

Further, no conclusive evidence exists to prove that a successful athletic program results in increased alumni giving or applications. Yet, the athletic community continues to use the claim as a primary justification for its own existence. While a successful athletic program can be a factor in alumni giving and student applications, it is unlikely that it is as much of a factor as claimed by those in the athletic community. While an institution may experience an immediate, short-term jump in applications or financial support (more than likely earmarked specifically for the athletic program) after a particularly successful football or basketball season, the fact remains that most institutions will continue to attract quality students who, when they graduate, will donate money to their alma maters, with little regard to the quality or even existence of a big-time athletic program.

Does Athletics Generate Positive Visibility?

Despite the probability that collegiate athletics does not generate monies for the university in general, athletic programs do provide significant regional and national visibility and exposure for the university. Games are broadcast on radio and television to a national audience, and newspaper coverage is often extensive. "By 1900, the relationship between football and public relations had been firmly established and almost everywhere acknowledged as one of sport's major justifications" (Rudolph 1990, 385). Clearly, athletic programs generate significant public exposure for universities. What is not so clear, however, is whether that exposure contributes positively to public relations.

The truth has been well documented: all exposure generated through major college athletic is not positive. A striking example of this dichotomy occurred at Florida State University. In winning a national football championship by defeating the University of Nebraska in the 1994 Orange Bowl, FSU garnered a tremendous amount of positive publicity. A national championship in football was evidence of the university's commitment to excellence. FSU was the best in the nation. There was no reason to expect other programs offered by the university were of lesser quality.

But how quickly things can change. Shortly after the Orange Bowl victory, allegations that student-athletes were provided clothes and cash by agents while coaches "looked the other way" quickly changed the type of exposure the football program was generating. If winning a national football championship meant that Florida State University was a winner, what did allegations that the football program won the national championship while breaking NCAA rules mean?

Questions regarding the supposed positive effect of athletic department visibility on the university go beyond the bad publicity associated with a scandal. . . . [T]he argument can be made that the exposure generated through athletics has little to do with advancing positive educational or institutional messages, but that instead such visibility is used simply to promote the specific goals of the athletic department.

Again, the purpose here is not to criticize unduly or to dismiss the posi- 60 tive impact an athletic program can have on a university, financially or otherwise. A well-run program can contribute to the mission of a university in ways that might not show up in the institutional balance sheet. Visibility and stature within the state legislature may in many cases have a positive impact on institutional efforts to attract state funding. And despite inconclusive evidence, a successful athletic team and the visibility it brings has the potential to attract students to campus on an occasional basis. In fact, . . . such contributions must be given greater consideration when evaluating an institution's return on investment in athletics.

Given the financial statements and the inconclusive research regarding alumni giving and applications, however, coaches and athletic administrators can no longer assert without question that athletics is a positive financial proposition for the institution. That being the case, they must be prepared to address this financial reality as they are challenged to justify athletics' place on campus. Like golfing partners who, when playing for money, make each other putt those short distances that are "gimmes" when playing for fun, college athletics no longer has the benefit of the "financial gimme."

Now That's Entertainment

For millions of people, intercollegiate athletic contests provide enjoyable, exciting entertainment. Whether attending a women's tennis match or watching the Final Four on television, the pageantry and spectacle of college athletics offers an exciting reprieve from the ordinary. If there is one thing about college athletics that almost everyone—critics and proponents, fans and faculty—can agree upon, it is that college sports is good entertainment.

College sports is also Big Entertainment. Simply consider the NCAA's current seven-year, $1.7 billion contract with CBS for the television rights to the NCAA Division I Basketball Tournament as proof that college sports is an entertainment Goliath. If that is not proof enough, stand outside any Southeastern Conference or Big Ten football stadium on a Saturday afternoon in the fall and feel the excitement of 80,000 fans preparing for a big game. Concession stands, T-shirt sales, program sales, tailgating, and ticket scalpers—all turning a buck on college athletics. Merchandising, television ratings, corporate sponsors, shoe contracts, media coverage, crowds cheering . . . now that's entertainment!

Entertaining students, alumni, and the surrounding community is indeed a valuable service that higher education provides the public; it should not be trivialized. Higher education's purpose is to serve the needs of society, and athletics' unqualified success in providing this service should be celebrated.

As university enrollments have increased and diversified, athletic teams have 65 promoted institutional unity and "the old college spirit." The entire university family, from faculty, students, and local fans, to alumni living in faraway places, can usually rally around "Ole State" U's football team. And while the firing of a controversial coach or an NCAA investigation can splinter a campus, athletics usually serves a unifying function for the university community. At what other function does so much of the university community gather to rally around the institution? As Paul "Bear" Bryant, the legendary University of Alabama football coach, allegedly said, "Fifty thousand people don't come to watch English class."

> At games, students and other members of the community come together for a common purpose. They are united, at least for the duration of the contest. Personal differences, politics, even business matters may be put aside. Those gathered view themselves as the community, united against another community. Everyone pulls together, and in so doing, the community generates uncommon energy and commitment. With community members acting in unison with the force of passion, for the very dignity of the community is at stake, the whole is more than the sum of its parts. (Miracle and Rees 1994, 160)

There are, however, risks in relying on athletic teams to unify the campus community. Institutions that use athletics to solve the problems of a fragmented community run the risk of making athletics, and not academic excellence, the primary purpose of the institution. Although a football or basketball program can unite a university community in a way that an English department cannot, the primary purpose of the institution remains educational. In short, a winning football team does not make a quality educational institution.

Further, placing such a heavy emphasis on the unifying function of sports promotes a community mind-set that college athletics is more about the fans and campus community than it is about the participation of student-athletes. A successful team in terms of a won-loss record, although pleasing to fans, alumni, and the media, may cover up fundamental problems within an athletic program, such as low graduation rates, illegal activities, or abusive coaches. While a few wins may unite the campus community in the short term, it may result in long-term disintegration of community trust if the athletic department is not meeting its fundamental educational responsibilities to its student-athletes or if it contradicts broader institutional goals.

Thus, the question remains: Are the entertainment and unifying functions of athletics enough to justify athletics' prominence in the university educational system?

What Does All This Mean?

So where does this analysis of principles, missions, and justifications leave 70 us? After having reviewed athletics' three primary justifications for being a part of the higher education community, the answer is still mixed. Whether athletic departments are meeting their fundamental educational and personal-development responsibilities to student-athletes is questionable. Certainly, many coaches and athletic administrators are committed and effective teachers as well as positive educational role models. And thousands of student-athletes earn a quality, well-balanced academic and athletic experience. But unfortunately, as a result of the "win-at-all-cost" mentality that drives the athletic culture, some lessons learned through athletic participation are not positive. Thus, the assertion that participation in college athletics is a positive educational experience can no longer be accepted without question.

Regarding the claim that athletics generates money and visibility for the university, the data are again mixed. While athletic programs generate revenue, most do not generate more than they expend. And finally, not all the visibility that an athletic program brings to the university is positive. Just ask any president of a school that has been placed on NCAA probation.

Thus, only one of the justifications for athletics being a part of higher education is being fully met—the justification of providing entertainment. And ironically, even when using the current standard of measuring the success of an athletic program—championships won—the vast majority of universities fail miserably. The very nature of sport dictates that for every winner there is a loser. Only one team in every league hangs up the championship banner at season's end.

If our athletic programs are not successful in meeting their primary reasons for existence within higher education, we must reconsider how they can justify their existence. Moreover, because so few of our athletic programs achieve success as it is currently defined, we should reconsider whether the current standards of success—championship banners won and revenue generated—are reasonable and relevant. In short, we must go back to the drawing board and consider in fundamental terms just what our athletic programs should be about, what the people associated with these programs should represent, where these programs fit overall within higher education, and, most important, how their success should be measured. ◎/◎

References

Adler, Patricia A., and Peter Adler. 1991. Backboards and Blackboards: College Athletes and Role Engulfment. *New York: Columbia University Press.*

Carter, Stephen L. 1996. Integrity. *New York: Basic Books.*

Chu, Donald. 1989. The Character of American Higher Education and Intercollegiate Sport. *Albany, NY: State University of New York Press.*

Chu, Donald, Jeffrey Segrave, and Beverly Becker. 1985. Sport and Higher Education. *Champaign, IL: Human Kinetics Publishers.*

Crosset, Todd W., Jeffrey R. Benedict, and Mark A. McDonald. 1995. "Male Student-Athletes Reported for Sexual Assault: A Survey of Campus Police Departments and Judicial Affairs." Journal of Sport and Social Issues 19 (2).

Ebaugh, Helen R. 1988. Becoming an Ex. *Chicago. University of Chicago Press.*

Fulks, Daniel L. 1995. Revenues and Expenses of Intercollegiate Athletic Programs: Financial Trends and Relationships. *Overland Park, KS: NCAA.*

Miracle, Andrew, and C. Roger Rees. 1994. Lessons of the Locker Room: The Myth of School Sports. *Amherst, NY: Prometheus Books.*

National Association of College and University Business Officers. 1993. The Financial Management of Intercollegiate Athletics Program. *Washington, DC: NACUBO.*

National Collegiate Athletic Association. 1996. 1996 NCAA Division I Graduation-Rates Report. *Overland Park, KS: NCAA.*

Oglive, Bruce, and Thomas Tutko. 1985. "Sport: If You Want to Build Character, Try Something Else." In Sport and Higher Education, *edited by Donald Chu, Jeffrey Segrave, and Beverly Becker. Champaign, IL: Human Kinetics Publishers.*

Rudolph, Frederick. 1990. The American College and University: A History. *Athens, GA: University of Georgia Press.*

Savage, Howard J., et al. 1929. American College Athletics. *New York: Carnegie Foundation.*

Shields, David L., and Brenda J. Bredemeir. 1995. Character Development and Physical Activity. *Champaign, IL: Human Kinetics Publishers.*

Steiner, Hans. 1991. Research results reported in The Stanford Daily, *May 7 1996.*

Stevenson, C.L. 1975. Socialization Effects of Participation in Sports; A Critical Review of the Research. Research Quarterly, 46, 287–301.

Stoll, Sharon. Letter to John Gerdy. 19 July 1996.

Thelin, John R., and Lawrence L. Wiseman. 1989. The Old College Try: Balancing Athletics and Academics in Higher Education. *Report No. 4. Washington, DC: The George Washington University.*

Walton, Gary M. 1992. Beyond Winning: The Timeless Wisdom of Great Philosopher Coaches. *Champaign, IL: Leisure Press.*

Reflections and Inquiries

1. Do you agree or disagree with Douglas McArthur's description of sports as a character builder, quoted on page 272? Explain.

2. What contributes to the skepticism that usually greets the formulaic assertion that sports builds character?

3. What did the findings of Jennifer Beller and Sharon Stoll, of the University of Idaho's Center for Ethics, reveal about the influence of sports on the moral development of students?

4. Weigh the validity of the Alders' findings, described on page 275.

Reading to Write

After researching possible ways in which participating in sports can build character, write an essay in which you discuss the character building potential of college athletics (or one of the other seven questions Gerdy addresses). Does your data confirm or disprove Gerdy's assertions?

For True Reform, Athletics Scholarships Must Go | John R. Gerdy

In the world of professional athletics, the essence of the sports relationship, as John Gerdy notes, is "pay for play." But are college athletes professionals? According to Gerdy, they are if they have been awarded scholarships, which are tantamount to payment. But Gerdy argues that college athletes are not professionals; hence athletic scholarships should not be awarded to them. John R. Gerdy is a visiting professor in Sports Administration at Ohio University in Athens, Ohio. He is the author of Air Ball: American Education's Failed Experiment with Elite Athletics *(University Press of Mississippi, 2006).*

The president of the National Collegiate Athletics Association, Myles Brand, created a stir recently when he forcefully defended the NCAA's commercial efforts to raise revenues for its member institutions. "Commercialism per se" is not incompatible with the values of higher education, he contended in his 2006 "State of the Association" address. "It depends entirely on how the commercial activity is conducted."

Despite the outcry his comments generated among critics of college athletics, Brand is absolutely correct. If only he had stopped there.

Responding to those who think that "working too hard to generate revenue somehow taints the purity of college sports," Brand cried, "Nonsense!

Source: John R. Gerdy, "For True Reform, Athletics Scholarships Must Go," *Chronicle of Higher Education* 52, May 12, 2006. Reprinted by permission of the author.

This type of thinking is both a misinterpretation and a misapplication of amateurism. 'Amateur' defines the participants, not the enterprise."

Talk about nonsense!

Division I scholarship athletes are professionals—and to claim otherwise   5
is to ignore reality.

Consider the essence of professional athletics: pay for play. Despite Brand's idealistic rhetoric, the contract between the college athlete and the institution no longer represents the "amateur" ideal of "pay (scholarship) for education" when it is plain to everyone—coaches, fans, faculty members, media, and especially the athletes—that they are on the campus, first and foremost, to play ball. That, by any definition, is "pay for play."

The professional model is also about paying whatever you must for coaches, staff members, facilities, scouting, travel, and anything else that coaches believe might make the difference between winning and losing, regardless of how outrageous or remote the actual impact. Professional sports is also about playing anywhere at anytime to reap television revenues. And professional athletics is about the expectation that athletes train year-round and sacrifice their bodies for "the program." In short, Division I athletics, as currently structured and conducted, operates on the same basic principles as professional sports teams.

Yet educational institutions have no business being in the business of professional sports. It is time to dismantle the professional model of college athletics and rebuild it in the image of an educational institution.

Specifically, the athletics scholarship must be eliminated in favor of institutional need-based aid. The athletics scholarship at its foundation is the biggest barrier to athletes' getting a genuine educational opportunity. When you are paid to play, regardless of the form of "payment," everything takes a back seat to athletic performance.

Calls to eliminate the athletics scholarship in favor of need-based aid are   10
not new. In 1952 the Special Committee on Athletic Reform of the American Council on Education recommended that scholarships be awarded based solely on academic need rather than athletic ability. In 1989 the NCAA President's Commission proposed establishing a need-based system for all sports—with the exceptions of football and men's basketball and two women's sports selected by the institution. More recently, the faculty-led Drake Group suggested changing to a need-based aid system as part of its reform agenda. While some may interpret those failed attempts to adopt a need-based aid model as evidence that it will never pass, an alternative view would be that it is an idea whose time has simply yet to come.

At first glance, it would appear that eliminating athletics scholarships in favor of a need-based formula would not be in the best interest of athletes. However, if judged on what is in their best interest for the next 50 years of their lives, rather than the four or five years they are on a campus, it becomes clear that eliminating the athletics grant will contribute significantly to athletes' chances of obtaining a well-balanced college experience.

An athletics scholarship represents a contractual agreement between the athlete and the coach. That contract allows coaches to view athletes as employees, bought and paid for by the athletics department, and has little to do with education and everything to do with athletic performance and control. If the athlete does not do what the coach wants, or fails to meet expectations on the field or court, he or she can be "fired."

A need-based financial aid agreement, however, is a contractual agreement between the student and the institution. Under such a contract, the student would continue to receive his or her financial aid regardless of what transpires on the athletics field. As a result, the student would be less beholden to the athletics department's competitive and business motives and freer to explore the wide diversity of experiences college offers. There is no more effective way to "empower" the athlete because it would fundamentally change the relationships among the athlete, the coach, and the institution.

Some argue that eliminating athletics scholarships would deny opportunity and limit access for many students, most notably black athletes. The question is, access to what? The fields of competition or an opportunity to earn a meaningful degree? With the six-year graduation rates of black basketball players hovering in the high 30-percent range, and black football players in the high 40-percent range, despite years of "academic reform," earning an athletics scholarship under the current system is little more than a chance to play sports.

A more likely result of the change would be that the black athletes would 15 simply be replaced by other black athletes. While they might be a bit less talented and obsessed with athletics, they would probably be better students— or at least somewhat interested in academic achievement rather than simply using college as a springboard to the pros. What's the better lifelong deal: receiving need-based aid that leads to a meaningful degree, or receiving an athletics scholarship that provides an educational experience that is a sham?

Another potential benefit of this change relates to the athletics culture on campus. How much of an impact does receiving a scholarship, and all the benefits and special treatment that accompany it, have on an athlete's sense of entitlement? How much does it contribute not only to the isolation of the athlete and the team from the general student body, but also to the creation of a team culture that is often at odds with broader academic mores and behavioral expectations? Could it be that much of the deviant athlete behavior that has been revealed in recent scandals at the University of Colorado at Boulder in football and now, apparently, Duke University in lacrosse* is in part the result of athletes' believing their status exempts them from the behavioral standards applied to other students? Dropping the athletics scholarship would help to recast the image of the athlete from the current hired mercenary of the gladiator class to simply a student who happens to be a good athlete.

---

* Charges against the Duke Lacrosse individuals have since been dropped.

Finally, the elimination of athletics scholarships would have a tremendous impact beyond the walls of academe. As a society, we have lost perspective regarding the role that sports should play in our schools, communities, and lives. For proof, one has only to read the daily newspaper to see how high-school and youth programs have become increasingly competitive: coaches scream at 7-year-olds for committing errors; parents and coaches push children to specialize in a sport at earlier and earlier ages; parents sue a coach because their child doesn't get enough playing time; parents attack Little League umpires or even fatally beat each other at a youth-hockey game. Far too many parents and youngsters believe sports, rather than education, is the ticket to future success. While moving to a need-based aid system may not completely change that myth, our educational institutions should have absolutely no part in perpetuating it.

Other aspects of the professional model must also be changed. College freshmen should not be eligible for varsity competition. Spring football and out-of-season practices should be eliminated, as should off-campus recruiting. Basketball and football coaching staffs should be cut in half. Seasons should be shortened, schedules reduced, and travel more restricted.

Such changes would significantly shrink the sizes, budgets, and campus influence of athletics departments. Yet if you operate a business where expenses outpace revenue and where revenue streams are almost tapped out, as is the case with athletics at most colleges and universities—how many more stadium boxes can you build, and how much more stadium signage can you sell?—there is only one way to become solvent: Cut expenses and over-head. Shrink the operation. Many college programs and departments have been downsized or shut down when it has become apparent that they fail to meet their purposes or are drains on institutional resources.

Although college presidents have worked diligently to reform athletics, [20] their efforts have failed to change the fundamental culture and operating principles surrounding Division I programs. Raising academic standards may result in a few more athletes' graduating, but history tells us that, more often, it simply heightens the bar for academic fraud, fosters a greater dependence on athletics-department tutoring services, creates pseudomajors to keep athletes eligible, and incites an arms race in the area of academic-support programs and facilities. Change that is more fundamental must occur.

That is not to say that intercollegiate athletics should be eliminated from higher education. To the contrary, the benefits and positive influence of university-sponsored athletics programs that are operated in a fiscally sound and academically responsible manner can be enormous. Even programs with commercial ties can advance an academic agenda and contribute to the institutional mission in meaningful ways.

Indeed, we must accept the notion that as long as we have athletics, commercialism will be a part of it. We must also recognize that the financing of American higher education is radically different from 20 years ago.

Corporate-sponsored research, naming rights, and the commercialization of myriad other aspects of colleges' operations are increasingly common. And given a future economic outlook of increasing costs and declining revenues and state support, the pressure on institutions to set up partnerships with commercial entities to maintain academic excellence will only increase. Against that backdrop, the commercialism of athletics will look increasingly less radical and out of line with the financing of higher education in general.

In such an environment, athletics' potential to generate resources becomes more important. Thus, what's at issue is not whether athletics can or should be used as a commercial entity to advance institutional mission, but rather how to construct and operate the enterprise to maximize both its commercial and its educational values. The fundamental question regarding that challenge is whether the professional model, with its runaway costs, undermining of academic integrity, and win-at-all-cost culture, is the most effective way to achieve those ends.

Despite the growing evidence that the professional model is not, we continue to buy into the notion advanced by the athletics community that what makes college athletics commercially viable is the "level of play." That has led to a drive to mirror professional sports in training and playing, as well as in behavioral and management styles. It has been the athletics establishment's unyielding adherence to that notion of the "quality of the game," coupled with higher-education leaders' lack of courage to confront such claims, that is most responsible for the misguided professionalization and fiscal excesses of college athletics.

Little evidence, however, suggests that changes such as those that I've recommended would have enough impact on the "quality of the game" to adversely affect the long-term entertainment value of the University of Florida, Pennsylvania State University, or the University of California at Los Angeles in the marketplace. The appeal of college athletics rests not only in how high the players jump, how fast they run, whether they participated in spring practice, or whether they are on an athletics scholarship. Rather, a big part of the commercial draw is that the activity is steeped in university tradition and linked to the higher purpose of education. Alabama-Auburn, Harvard-Yale, Michigan-Ohio State, and Oklahoma-Texas will always draw crowds, be covered by the media, and captivate the public's imagination, regardless of the level of play.

The key to a successful athletic-entertainment business is maintaining public confidence and interest. Public perception of your "brand," or what your business stands for, is critical. Like it or not, the current NCAA brand does not stand for students who are pursuing an education, but rather for pampered, mercenary athletes who have little interest in attending class and are using college as a vehicle to play in the pros. A poll released by the Knight Commission on Intercollegiate Athletics in January found that by a 2-to-1 margin, Americans believe that college sports are more like professional sports than amateur sports.

Most people want college athletics to stand for something other than turning a buck, preparing the next generation of professional stars, and winning at any cost. Deprofessionalizing the operation would actually increase college athletics' public and commercial appeal. Not only would its fan base hold steady and probably even expand, but corporate interest would also increase, as companies prefer to associate their products with positive and wholesome institutions. The public would be more likely to continue to support college sports, or, for those who have become disengaged, to reconnect with them.

Realizing change of this magnitude, however, will be neither quick nor easy. It will require the courage and will of college and university leaders to make athletics look like and represent what they want.

Higher education has been at the reform game, with limited success, for decades. That does not mean that there has not been significant progress in building the foundation and critical mass that can serve as backdrop for significant change. Despite a rash of recent scandals that has led many to suggest that reform is a lost cause, upon closer examination, there are many signs that suggest, for the first time, that the table of reform may finally be set. The writer Malcolm Gladwell describes the one dramatic moment or event in a social movement when everything can change at once as the "tipping point," in his book of that title (Little, Brown, 2000). We may finally be approaching the tipping point for revolutionary change in college sports.

Over the past few years, we have been treated to out-of-control coaches, 30 several cases of academic fraud, and even a murder of a basketball player at Baylor University. Despite such discouraging examples, the third incarnation of the Knight Commission in 2003 represented the continuation of what has been a 24-year process of envisioning, articulating, building, and institutionalizing the structure necessary to support meaningful reform. This movement began in earnest in 1983 when the NCAA adopted a set of academic standards that significantly raised the bar for freshman eligibility.

The significance of the type and duration of the reform effort cannot be overemphasized. Reform of college athletics requires the building and coalescing of a critical mass of people, institutions, and organizations over an extended period of time to drive change. Besides the Knight Commission, other "outside" groups such as the Drake Group, the Coalition on Intercollegiate Athletics, and the Association of Governing Boards of Universities and Colleges have been pressing for it.

Further, the context in which college athletics operates has changed—and, in some ways, rather significantly. For example, not only has public pressure for reform increased, but Congress is beginning to look more critically at the business of college athletics. Title IX continues to exert pressure on athletics departments regarding how best to appropriate resources. Increasingly, research is beginning to paint a more critical picture of athletics' impact on institutional values and outcomes. And where 20 years ago, talk of institutional control and compliance was unheard of, a firmly entrenched and growing compliance community now works to instill a culture of accountability and integrity in intercollegiate athletics.

The situation is far different from the athletics cultures that existed during previous reform efforts. The seeds of reform that were advanced in the 1929 report on athletics of the Carnegie Foundation for the Advancement of Teaching, the "Sanity Code" (or "Principles for the Conduct of Intercollegiate Athletics") of 1946, and the ACE proposals of 1952 were strewn on a barren cultural landscape. Today that landscape is much more fertile for seeds of reform to take root. We may finally be on the verge of the intersection of people, institutions, and ideas, coupled with a series of changing contextual factors, needed to transform the role of sports in our educational institutions. As those forces coalesce, the time for systemic change has never been better. All that is needed is the initiative that begins the avalanche of change.

That initiative is the elimination of the athletics scholarship, which would provide American higher education the much-needed opportunity to recalibrate every aspect of its relationship with athletics. We must get beyond the fear that eliminating the athletics scholarship and the department of professional athletics will cause the entire enterprise to collapse. To the contrary, it will make it more educationally sound, more commercially viable, and thus more effective in contributing to larger university purposes. ◎/◎

Reflections and Inquiries

1. Gerdy claims that when college athletes are paid to play "everything takes a back seat to to athletic performance." Do you agree or disagree, and why?

2. Why would a need-based financial aid agreement be preferable to an athletic scholarship, in Gerdy's opinion?

3. How convincingly does Gerdy refute the counterclaim that eliminating athletic scholarships "would deny opportunity and limit access for many students"?

Reading to Write

Write an essay supporting or opposing the awarding of athletic scholarships. In building your case, consider interviewing student athletes, coaches, and administrators. You may also want to look at information provided by the NCAA (e.g., its academic standards for freshman eligibility) or the Coalition on Intercollegiate Athletics.

Student Essay

Academic Performance of Student Athletes | Scott Klausner

Can a college athletic program become too successful? According to Scott Klausner, a senior at Santa Clara University when he wrote this piece, the answer is yes in the sense that athletic success can lead to "the temptation to sacrifice academics for athletic success." He explains why he thinks this is the case in the following essay.

"There was a time when athletics fit nicely into the framework of the university. Now, we have allowed it, in a lot of ways, to overshadow the purpose of the schools. It is now—at some of our nations most prestigious universities—show biz."
—Charlie Vincent, *Detroit Free Press*

Ever since I can remember, I've spent hours of my Saturdays in the fall sitting in front of a television, captivated by the game in front of me. For me, there's always been something almost magical about college football, something that professional football lacks. As with all college athletics, it has a certain purity, a certain charm: these guys go out every Saturday and play their hearts out—not because they have multimillion dollar contracts, but out of love of the game, out of love for their school. There are no trades, no endorsements, and no free agency; there's simply football.

But slowly, I fear, the charm of college football is beginning to fade, becoming lost in the excessive overproduction and commercialization of college athletics. There is not simply football anymore; there is football: a revenue-producing, celebrity-making, university-defining production. To be fair, this has always been true to an extent. Throughout most of the past century, schools like Michigan, USC, and Nebraska have been largely defined by their football programs. And athletes like George Gipp were lionized even in the 1920s because of their successes on the field. However, there is a critical difference between being the subject of national attention and being the subject of corporate attention. It is the increasing prevalence of the latter that I find disconcerting; for as athletic success becomes increasingly valuable, the temptation to sacrifice academics for athletic success becomes harder to avoid.

College athletics is no longer categorized as a simple, friendly competition between two schools; it has grown into a billion dollar a year industry. Gary Funk, author of *Major Violation: The Unbalanced Priorities in Athletics and Academics,* has even gone so far as to say, "Modern collegiate athletics is, essentially, a monetary endeavor . . ." (65). Disheartened by this commercialization (and the scandals that have accompanied it), John and James Knight founded the Knight Foundation Commission on Intercollegiate

Athletics in 1989. In 1991, the Commission released a groundbreaking report that encapsulates the root of the problem facing college athletics:

> Now, instead of the institution alone having a stake in the given team or sport, the circle of involvement includes the television networks and local stations that sell advertising time, the corporations and local businesses that buy it, the boosters living vicariously through the team's success, [and] the local economies critically dependant on the big game. . . . ("Need for Reform," 5)

This increased interest by parties who are unaffiliated with the universities   5
has catapulted college athletics into the industry that it has become.

This expanded circle of involvement is perhaps most clearly manifested in the bowl games that follow the college football regular season. It used to be that bids to attend a bowl game were reserved for only the best football programs in the nation; it was a reward for an exceptional season. But over the past fifteen years, the NCAA has sanctioned more and more bowls, devaluing these post-season games in the process. According to Jon Solomon, staff writer for the *Birmingham News*, nineteen bowl games were played in the 1990–91 season; in contrast, thirty-one (possibly thirty-two) bowls will be played in the 2006–07 season. These games are no longer a reward for an exceptional season (as now, teams with a mediocre 7–5 record are finding themselves bowl eligible). Rather, they have become simply a tool for the corporatization of college sports.

For the universities, corporate sponsors, and television networks, these games represent an economy unto themselves, producing, in 2000, a whopping cumulative payout of $152,200,000 (Rainey). One can presume this number has grown, as payout from the Bowl Championship Series (or BCS) games alone is a staggering $96,160,000 ("BSC," 7). Clearly, there is a lot more than school pride riding on these games. The University of Notre Dame, for example, received nearly eleven million dollars for its appearance in the 2000 Tostitos Fiesta Bowl (Rainey) and over thirteen million for its 2006 appearance. Now, under the latest BSC contract, the Fighting Irish receive just over a million dollars even if they fail to qualify for a bowl game (Hansen). And the stakes are just as high for the corporate sponsors like Nokia and FedEx who shell out millions of dollars to see their name preface the big bowl games. Likewise, television networks pay huge money to be able to broadcast the games; ABC, for example, agreed to pay fifty-seven million dollars to broadcast the BCS games alone (Rainey). (That figure does not account for the price ABC pays to broadcast the non-BCS games.)

With so much money hanging in the balance, universities, now more than ever, are feeling the pressure to succeed athletically. At big-name schools across the country, athletic departments have grown into businesses. As the Knight Commission notes, "Athletics programs are given a special, often unique status within the university. . . . [They] have taken on all the trappings of a major entertainment enterprise" ("Need for Reform," 6–7). Barry Alvarez, beloved football coach turned athletic director at the University of Wisconsin, reflected this sentiment when he commented to the *Milwaukee Journal Sentinel* about what kind of program he is running: "Let's face it," he says, "We're running a business, a $71.2 million dollar a year business" (Walker).

But businesses tend to be cutthroat. As B. David Ridpath, leader of the Drake Group for academic reform of the NCAA and assistant professor of sports administration at Mississippi State University, has noted, "It is a way of life in the arms race of major Division I athletics to maximize revenue by any means necessary . . ." (Walker). In an effort to maximize revenue, many things are sacrificed or compromised. But perhaps the most troubling thing being sacrificed by many Division I schools is the education of its athletes.

The academic performance of student athletes has been a widely discussed, highly contested issue for decades. There have been many studies conducted that investigate athletes' performance in the classroom. Some say athletes fare better then the general student body, some say they fare as well, and many say they fare worse. On this issue, Gary Funk writes, "Research data on the relationship between athletic participation and academic achievement . . . has been sporadic at best, conflicting at worst, and difficult to compare because of methodological, population sample, and reportorial differences" (14). For Funk, however, it does seem as though student athletes, particularly female athletes, generally are performing satisfactorily in the classroom. Athletes like those on the men's tennis team or the women's field hockey team tend to be doing just fine academically. Yet, athletes playing football or basketball—what Funk calls the revenue sports—tend not to be performing as well. Though he states that this is an insufficient way to summarize the problem, Funk notes that "athlete's academic problems tend to surface in the revenue sports . . ." (29).

Funk's hypothesis is particularly disturbing. Diminished academic performances perhaps may be justifiable if they were occurring equally across all athletics. Athletes, after all, have much more rigorous schedules than the average student; they have to spilt their attention between athletics and school, they miss class time as they travel to games, and exhaust far more energy than the average student. Given this, it may be understandable that athletes perform at a lower level than other students. However, Funk's observations suggest that only those athletes who participate in the revenue sports are struggling academically. There are a variety of reasons why this may occur—perhaps these athletes feel more pressure to succeed athletically than members of other teams and therefore struggle academically. Or perhaps universities, in one way or another, facilitate the poor scholastic performance of these revenue-producing athletes.

Evidence of the latter can be found in the attitude many (though certainly not all) major Division I football and basketball programs take toward recruiting. In this arena, the prospect for athletic success and stardom dwarfs any mention that might be made of academics. The university itself is only a marginal focus; the dominant concern is that of the sports team. Academics, then, is often inconsequential. "The implied message becomes loud and clear,"

Funk writes. "Ball is the priority, and academics are a mere nuisance to be dealt with. This message may not be intentional, but the recruited athlete infers it" (87). Thus, these student athletes assume an apathetic attitude towards academics before they ever step foot in a classroom.

Questionable recruitment policies seem to be among the most benign ways in which universities tend to facilitate poor performances in the classroom. Over the course of the past twenty years, numerous scandals have plagued college athletics. From ignoring poor scholastic performances to administering oral exams to athletes, some universities appear more than willing to see their athletes succeed—whatever the cost may be.

Some may recall the story of Jan Kemp, a teacher at the University of Georgia. Kemp took a job teaching remedial English in the developmental studies program. Soon, she was promoted to coordinator of the program and received "glowing performance evaluations" (Cramer K6). A teacher in the department was forced to fail six football players, which—both as a Bulldogs fan and as a teacher—broke Kemp's heart. "I'm sorry we weren't more successful," she told Georgia's assistant vice president, Leroy Ervin (K6). Ervin, however, had a slightly different reaction. According to Kemp, he ordered her to change the grade. When she refused to do so, Kemp says Ervin "screamed, stomped, and flailed his arms. He shook his finger in my face. [He said,] 'Who do you think is more important to this university, you or a star player?'" (26).

What is most disturbing about this incident is that other people shared 15 Ervin's point of view: eventually, the grades were changed and the star players maintained their eligibility. Despondent, Kemp turned to the NCAA to report the violation. According to Tom Farrey, a senior journalist for ESPN, this, too, proved unsuccessful. He writes, "Kemp recalls an NCAA investigator telling her, 'We don't want to hear anything about grades. All we're interested in are cars, or trips, or things of that sort'" ("Georgia"). A resilient Kemp continued to protest, a decision that cost her a pay-cut and, ultimately, her job. Eventually, the school reinstated Kemp after a federal court required them to do so. The incident at Georgia illustrates the lengths that some institutions will go to in order to protect their financially valuable athletes.

In addition to extensively covering Kemp's case, Tom Farrey written about numerous other incidences in which schools have taken reprehensible steps to insure the eligibility of their star performers. At the University of Minnesota, for example, Jan Gangelhoff, a tutor to the men's basketball team, admitted to writing "some 400 papers, take-home tests and other assignments for 20 Gopher men's basketball players from 1994 to 1998" (Farrey, "Minnesota"). Beloved and successful basketball Clem Haskins had knowledge of this, yet played these students regardless. Farrey also has written of alleged academic misconduct at Ohio State University, where former star football player Maurice Clarett appears to have been given preferential treatment in the classroom. In 2002, Clarett apparently walked out of a mid-term examination, but was then allowed to retake the test orally. He was also allowed to take his final orally, though, for the nonathletes of the class, it was a written exam. Norma McGill, a teacher's assistant in the class, claims this was done because Clarett "couldn't read very well" (Farrey, "Ohio State").

Like the case in Georgia, these incidences at Minnesota and Ohio State represent the disturbing price that some major Division I schools are willing to pay to succeed. As Barry Alverez stated, college athletics is essentially a business—one with the potential to be extremely lucrative. As commercialization renders it evermore the business, the risk of the abhorrent exploitation of student athletes grows greater. There is indeed a place where athletics need not be accompanied by academic rigor; that place is in professional sports, not university athletics. And while collegiate sports may be a steppingstone to the professionals for some students, it is not for the vast majority. Those who do not make it to the professional level will have to rely heavily on the education they received in college—an education that universities should never sacrifice for the sake of a profit. ◎/◎

Works Cited

Bowl Championship Series 2005-2006 Media Guide. *27 June 2006. http://www.bcsfootball.org/ mediaguide.pdf.*

Cramer, Jerome. "Winning or Learning: Athletics and Academics in America." Phi Delta Kappan *67.9; (May 1986): K1–K8.*

Farrey, Tom. "Georgia: Better Late Than Never." Espn.com *7 October 2003. 25 June 2006 http://espn.go.com/ncaa/s/2003/1006/1632219.html.*

———. "Minnesota: No More Reservations." Espn.com *7 October 2003. 25 June 2006. http://espn.go.com/ncaa/s/2003/1006/1632216.html.*

———. "Ohio State: Norma the Mental Freak." Espn.com *7 October 2003. 25 June 2006. http://espn.go.com/ncaa/s/2003/1006/1632215.html.*

Funk, Gary D. Major Violation: The Unbalanced Priorities in Athletics and Academics. *Champaign, IL: Leisure Press, 1991.*

Hansen, Eric. "White Sheds Light on Issues." South Bend Tribune *17 May 2006. 27 June 2006. http://www.southbendtribune.com/apps/pbcs.dll/article?AID55/20060517/NDSports02/ 605170372/-1/SPORTS.*

"The Need for Reform." Keeping Faith with the Student Athlete: A New Model for Intercollegiate Athletics. *Miami: Knight Foundation Commission on Intercollegiate Athletics, 1991.*

Rainey, John. "Bowls Payoff Are Big Business—For Some." Memphis Business Journal *22 Dec. 2000. 28 June 2006. http://memphis.bizjournals.com/memphis/stories/2000/12/25/ editorial3.html.*

Solomon, John. "Bowl Survival." Birmingham News *9 May 2006. Westlaw 25 June 2006. http://www.westlaw.com.*

Walker, Don. "Money Game: Big Business at UW, UW Athletics Now a Booming Business." Milwaukee Journal Sentinel *25 Dec. 2005. Westlaw 25 June 2006. http://www.westlaw.com.*

Reflections and Inquiries

1. Klausner asserts that the increased number of bowl games devalues post-season games. What evidence does he give to support this assertion, and how convincing is it, in your opinion?

2. In what ways can the collegiate athletics business be "cutthroat," according to Klausner?

3. Klausner says, "Questionable recruitment policies seem to be among the most benign ways in which universities tend to facilitate poor performances in the classroom." What recruitment policies would be "questionable" in your opinion? How might they be overcome?

Reading to Write

According to college athletics researcher Gary Funk, to whom Klausner refers, athletes performing in the revenue sports of football and basketball do not perform as well academically as other student athletes. Conduct your own research into the issue, beginning with the revenue sports athletes at your own college. If you find that such is the case, what solution might you propose to deal with this problem? Consider visiting your athletic program director and ask to see the latest NCAA certification documents, especially the section on academic integrity.

Issues for Further Research: The Intrinsic Value of College Athletics

Student Essay

"The Faces of Sports" and "Play for Pride, Not for Pay" | Kelly Ryan

Many students these days are publishing their composition course portfolios on the Internet. An especially fine example is the e-portfolio of Kelly Ryan, a first-year student at Clemson University. Two of the essays from her portfolio, a visual argument on the faces of sports consisting of collages with text, and a discussion of why student athletes should not play for pay, are reproduced below. As you might guess, Kelly Ryan is an avid athlete, having participated in tennis, softball, and swimming in high school. She is currently a member of Clemson's field hockey team.

The Faces of Sports

Sports: some say it is a part of life, some say it is life. However one comes to view it, all sports, teams, and players can embody the same feelings and generate the same expressions. In my collages of the faces of sports, many different games are represented, such as football, baseball, basketball, hockey, and rugby. The athletes all play different sports, but represent the same facial expression. Thus, the individual sport does not determine the expression, but the athletes generate the same emotion.

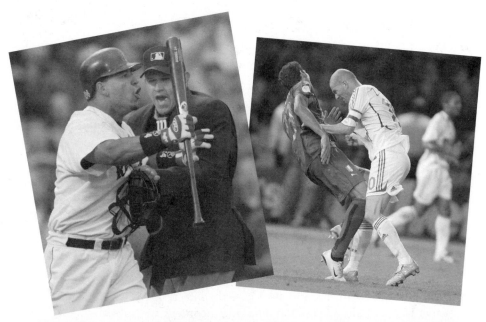

There were three different categories found in most magazine and newspaper cutouts: anger/despair/upset, pride/victory/teamwork, and determination/passion. In discussing my visual with a few dorm mates, they all drew the same conclusion about the label of the three collages before I had marked them with the correct sentiment. Simply, my audience is anyone who can experience or observe emotion; more specifically, people who participate and actively watch sports in general. Pathos (or emotion) is the main focus of my collages. The variety of pathos throughout my collages is easy to determine, but hard to categorize as one theme together. Logos (or logic) is used by the audience to determine what emotion is being portrayed (anger, pride, determination). Finally, ethos (or character) is the athletes themselves who have experienced the sensation, and who therefore show it in their eyes, mouth, and gestures.

Play for Pride, Not for Pay

The debate remains, Should college athletes receive pay? Before you answer, envision this: an alternate universe where college athletes receive compensation to play their sport. You are a five-star football recruit from Greenville, South Carolina. Signing day is quickly approaching. You need to choose between Clemson University, which pays its athletes $50,000 per season, and University of Virginia, which only pays $40,000. They both have comparable programs with excellent academic opportunities as well as a chance to advance and succeed on the field in the National Football League (NFL). Which school will you pick? Clearly, you would choose the school that supplies more money, which is Clemson University. Because it offers more money, it recruits the better athletes than UVA, making Clemson superior to Virginia on the football field. How can this be fair for Virginia? It is not. Now, come back to reality, where student-athletes are not paid for their services in intercollegiate sports. And they should not be.

There are many reasons that college athletes are not rewarded with money for their talents. For one, the amount of special treatment, such as those benefits other than playing time, can be seen as additional pay to the players. Special treatment attracts athletes, which can give an unfair advantage to schools that do not provide this treatment. In addition, the size of the school draws a certain amount of revenue regardless of how amazing or horrible a university may be at a particular sport. More people generate more dollars. Third, the level of compensation to the players for their involvement in the sport is not equal. Are they all worth the same amount? If a player scores a touchdown or makes a game winning three-pointer, is it fair to pay him for his success? Obviously, not everyone on the team has the same amount of talent; and therefore, not everyone is equal. Next, since the football and basketball teams support other intercollegiate team sports, the university can not afford to pay the athletes. Because not all sports are as popular as football and basketball, they do not generate as much income. This would bring about another point: equal pay among all athletes; would football and basketball players receive more pay than a golf or track athlete? Finally, scholarships are important, but it would bring out many finance issues. Where is the line crossed between professionals and amateurs? A professional is someone whose career is solely one's hobby or sport (and in doing so, receives compensation). The point in this definition pertains to jobs. The college athletes' job is not to play his or her sport, but rather to attend classes to get an education.

Sports had not even been introduced into the school system until the late   5
1800s. Donald Chu noted in his book, *Education and Intercollegiate Sport,* that "[sports] did not become an official function of most post-secondary schools until the [1890s]." Thus, academics were the primary focus before sports even existed in universities. The growth of sports in schools has altered the players' mindset into believing they should be paid for playing. However, because the sole focus is not on the sport, but rather on academics, college athletes cannot be classified as professionals. Although some may believe that student-athletes deserve monetary compensation for athletic performance, the reality is that the consequences against supersede any benefit that payment may provide.

In every college and university, additional benefits to student-athletes are prohibited by the National Collegiate Athletic Association (NCAA). The NCAA did not start its organization based on money. In Allen Sack and Ellen Staurowsky's book, *College Athletes for Hire,* they point out that the "men who founded the NCAA . . . had little quarrel with commercialism" (Sack & Staurowsky 79). This suggests that at the time of its foundation in 1905, the goal was not profitable purposes, but rather support and growth of the sport. This special behavior toward the players is currently viewed as payment. Cash payment is forbidden in all schools because it may or may not lure an athlete to a certain school through such benefits.

Since the late 1920s, foundations have disagreed with the expansion of commercialism through college athletics. In the book, *The Political Economy of College Sports,* written by Hart-Nibbrig and Cottingham, the authors bring up the Carnegie Report on American College Athletics. In this report, the issue of concern in intercollegiate sports was that "football was no longer a student's game" (Hart-Nibbrig & Cottingham 23).

This idea recognizes that the sport is not a game, but the issue of money is. Perhaps a player is having a difficult time deciding between schools. One school offers athletes multiple bribes, such as money, a car, and preferred housing, while the other school simply provides them with the opportunity to play on their team. The player will most likely choose the school giving more reimbursement. Enticing potential student-athletes with special treatment lowers entrance standards for the school because it suggests that athletics are more important than academics to the university. People attend college to get an education; if they choose to participate in an intercollegiate sport, that is seen as an extracurricular because it is not all that they do. The mission statement of the NCAA emphasizes that "intercollegiate athletics [are] an integral part of the educational program and the athlete [is] an integral part of the student body" (NCAA Human Resources). Thus, it attests to the point that neither athletics nor the athletes are higher ranked than academics.

Student-athletes feel the need to accept the money, but are still refused access because they attend classes as well as participate in their team sport. The Academic Integrity and College Sports page at the University of Maryland begs to differ:

> Intercollegiate athletics on college campuses plays a constructive role when 10
> it is an amateur pursuit designed to enhance the academic experience. The
> athlete who represents an institution does so as a representative of the student body, engaging in an extracurricular activity designed to enhance his
> or her academic experience. If these activities were not of direct benefit to
> the student participant, there would be no rationale for supporting them.
> (Academic Integrity in Intercollegiate Athletics)

The university believes that academics are just as important as athletics, if not more important. Since the student-athlete is a part of the school and is not a professional, the academic aspect of college life is essential. These teams, people, and behaviors are only sustained through their involvement in their education.

Once a student-athlete attends the school, outsiders known as "boosters" cannot supply the player with any additional benefits that a regular student would not normally receive. For instance, suppose the starting quarterback walks into a restaurant, orders a sandwich, and the manager gives it to the student-athlete free of charge simply because of the great touchdown pass he threw to win the game. This is an example of improper benefits given to student-athletes. The manager would not ordinarily give a person who walks through the door a sandwich for free. So when he presents this athlete with this special accommodation, it is wrong.

Certain universities provide more or fewer amenities depending mainly on the size of the school. Schools with more students produce more money. The smaller Division I schools cannot always afford to attract the number-one high school pick, while the larger Division I schools can. According to Clemson University's web page, the total student enrollment in 2004 was 17,110 (*Clemson University Fact Book*). On the other hand, in 2004 Texas A&M had an enrollment of 44,435 students (*Texas A&M Stats and Facts*). Because of these differences, Texas A&M may make more money through the sale of tickets, water, food, and other items at the stadium. Texas A&M has 27,325 more students than Clemson; therefore, they can give more to their players because they can get more from their audience.

The recruiting system would disappear due to the athletic domination cash payments would create in college sports. In 2002, the NCAA grew suspicious of the University of Michigan. After investigating, officials learned that athletic director Bill Martin had given "loans of more than $600,000 in illegal gambling proceeds to at least four Wolverine players—Chris Webber, Robert Traylor, Maurice Taylor, and Louis Bullock" (Girard). The incentive of payments to players for simply attending the school and participating in the basketball program attracted the best athletes, making their success superior to others. Throughout the 1990s, Michigan men's basketball were NCAA finalists, NIT Champions, and winners of the Big Ten tournament (Girard). In spite of all these major wins, they were worth nothing due to the illegal actions of Bill Martin and the other sixteen members who were involved in the compensation scheme.

If one school provides special treatment, eventually a monopoly would be 15 created, causing the loss of fan base, excitement for playoffs, and certain programs within a school. Special treatment provides dollars to the player, which gives an unfair advantage to certain schools. Because these student-athletes are playing on a Division I team, they are already provided with an abundant amount of other paraphernalia, such as equipment, t-shirts, and television time, which are provided legally. These are authorized special benefits, which all schools may supply to their players.

Through practice, commitment, and games, the student-athletes feel they should be paid for their time. Most of their free time from academics is spent practicing for their sport, and therefore, free time is limited. These athletes feel a need for financial compensation in exchange for their time. In an interview with Sam Perry, the starting forward for Clemson University men's basketball team, he argues that the players should receive compensation because they "generate the money, provide the entertainment, and make the show." Perry argues that without the players, there would be no team; without the team, there would be no money in the first place. While this is all true, Perry continues to state that they are "simply amateurs. Money suggests professional levels . . .," which is not what college athletics spotlight.

Andrew Zimbalist, author of the book *Unpaid Professionals*, outlines where the clear separation is between intercollegiate athletics and professional sports:

> It certainly is not the presence or absence of commercialism and corporate interest. Rather, two differences stand out . . . college athletes don't get paid. . . . [And] the NCAA and its member schools . . . do not pay taxes on their millions from TV deals, sponsorships, licensing, or Final Four tickets. (Zimbalist 5)

Zimbalist says that college athletes are not professionals for these reasons. These athletes generate fame, which brings in the dollars. Zimbalist argues that if the NCAA allowed them to be paid, the NCAA would essentially be paying for the student-athlete's taxes. Furthermore, the college athletes would continuously ask for higher pay (as if they were professionals).

With compensation or not, all athletes are not equally talented. If the players 20 were paid to play, would it be fair to give the starting point guard the same amount as the benchwarmer that never plays? Paying the players may help them reduce their feeling of being "cheated by the university" although they are not obtaining the amount they generated during a game. Jeremy Bloom writes an article in the *New York Times* arguing that all "[he] hear[s] is: 'The NCAA provides a free college education for these kids and that should be enough.'" He addresses that question in two parts. First, "free"? "[The] football players get up at dawn, do an hour of wind sprints, go to classes, spend two hours in the weight room, devote a couple of hours to seven-on-seven drills, study for school, and try to have something of a social life" (Bloom). This all is true, yet Bloom chose to play football; it was not forced upon him. Trying to solve the issue of compensation creates more arguments, which become a continuous cycle.

The powerhouse sports, football and basketball, financially support all the other teams on campus and cannot afford to pay student-athletes. Because other sports, such as swimming, golf, and tennis, lack the immense fan base at events, they also struggle for support. Men's football and basketball repeatedly attract fans that pay for their tickets, food and drinks, and paraphernalia. Because these sports have larger stadiums, they can squeeze many people into sold-out arenas. The revenue made does not simply go solely toward football or basketball; it assists the teams that attract many fewer people to their games.

If all the money accounted from a football game is dispersed to football players, there would be no support for other intercollegiate teams. The less supported teams would quickly diminish and the little profit made during those games would be lost. There are some teams that actually make an ample amount of money, but not nearly enough to keep a program running. For example, in 2003 the Clemson University golf team was ranked the best in the country. Last year, it took home the national championship. However, because it is golf, it got some support, but nothing compared to football. To keep such teams alive, they need the proceeds from the more popular sports.

If the players were paid, will all athletes from each team sport be paid the same amount? Men's football draws more spectators than men's track and field, producing a higher income. Since the two cannot attract an equal number of viewers, each team's fan base will not be represented uniformly. Football is more popular to watch than track. Because there are not as many scholarships for track and field, there are not as many opportunities for these athletes to bring prosperity, publicity, and entertainment to the school.

Athletic scholarships deliberately provide players with unfair financial benefits. They are awarded to obtain the talented players through means of excellent performances. According to Sperber in his book, *College Sports, Inc.,* the NCAA favors the phrase "'grant-in-aid' to 'athletic scholarship' . . . [because 'athletic scholarship' is a] clear indication of college athletes receiving money solely on the basis of their sports abilities" (Sperber 100). These scholarships are used to help those in financial need, not simply to persuade them. The worth of scholarships depends on school location and whether schools are public or not. In-state tuition and out-of-state tuition are the same at private universities. A Clemson University recruit from South Carolina, in actuality, receives less to attend Clemson than an athlete from California. Some may argue that the in-state athlete should receive as much as the out-of-state athlete; nevertheless, they both pay separate amounts for the same product. The difference in tuition remains distinctly unequal whether or not one is a student-athlete. Though there are athletes living a lower socioeconomic lifestyle who desire to receive a good education, athletic scholarships are granted to those who may be wealthy enough to pay for a college education. Academic commitment to the university is promised when the scholarship money is being used. This stresses not only hard work, but also that academics comes before athletics. Some of these athletes feel the pressure to cheat in the classroom to maintain the G.P.A. in order to keep their scholarship. Although this excuse may be true, athletes are not the only people in the school who cheat. Everyone attending a university experiences the need to succeed in the classroom, whether or not they cheat.

Along with athletic scholarships, academic scholarships are awarded; yet 25 both scholarships are utilized the same way. If an intellectual on academic scholarship receives an 'A' on an exam, he should not gain additional benefits, just as if a competitor makes a game-winning interception, he should not acquire special treatment. Because college athletes require an immense amount of training, study time is greatly diminished. Most athletes feel that because they are taken away from studying a lot of the time, they should be repaid with wealth. But the amount received cannot cause a person to study more. Habits are formed by the person who sets the standards, not by the amount of dollars.

A majority of the athletes are on some form of scholarship while attending a Division I school. Because of their status and reputation, athletes and regular students experience a tiny gap in social standings. The more the student-athletes receive, the greater the hole expands. Envy and resentment are evoked toward the players receiving money for their involvement. The sport the athletes participate in is not their profession, so how is it logical to pay for their participation? If someone choses to be on the math team and makes it to state finals, is it fair to pay these scholars for their excellence? The math team (like a sports team) is a supplementary interest, which one choses to be engaged in. These two examples have the same meaning, yet they are generating different outcomes.

Here in the real world, student-athletes are not paid. Still, our generation of college athletes is straying from playing for the love of the sport, and focussing solely on fortune. We live in a capitalist world. You have pictured yourself in an alternate universe. Now imagine yourself in the future. It lies before us, but seems to embody an athletic world where sports are not being played, the money is. The gap is growing as schools are becoming more dependent on football and basketball for revenue. Soon, it will grow to be an everlasting bubble that just may pop. ◎/◎

Works Cited

"Academic Integrity in Intercollegiate Athletics: Principles, Rules, and Best Practices." 4 Oct. 2005 (*www.studenthonorcouncil.umd.edu/intro.html*).

Bloom, Jeremy. "Show Us the Money." New York Times, 1 Aug. 2003: A21.

Chu, Donald. The Character of American Higher Education and Intercollegiate Sport. *Albany: State University of New York Press, 1986.*

Cottingham, Clement, and Nand, Hart-Nibbring. The Political Economy of College Sports. Lexington, MA: Lexington Books, 1986.

Girard, Fred. "U-M Forfeits Basketball Titles and Money in Scandal." Detroit News. 7 Nov. 2002. 30 Sept. 2005 http://www.detnews.com.

James, Nancy. Clemson University Fact Book. 30 Sept. 2005 http://www.clemson.edu.

"NCAA Mission, Values and Goals." NCAA Human Resources. 2 Oct. 2005 http://www1.ncaa.org/eprise/main/Public/hr/mission.html

Perry, Sam. Telephone interview. 27 Sept. 2005.

Sack, Allen, and Ellen Staurowsky. College Athletes for Hire: the Evolution and Legacy of the NCAA's Amateur Myth. Westport, CT: Praeger, 1998.

Sperber, Murray. College Sports Inc: The Athletic Department vs. The University. New York: Henry Holt Facts, 1990.

"Texas A&M Stats and Stats." 28 June 2005. 4 Oct. 2005 www.tamu.edu/home/aboutam/amfacts/index.html

Zimbalist, Andrew. Unpaid Professionals: Commercialism and Conflict in Big-Time College Sports. Princeton, NJ: Princeton, 1999.

Reflections and Inquiries

The Faces of Sports

1. What underlying argument does Ryan's collage-essay convey? What do the collages contribute to the argument?

2. Comment on the way Ryan evokes the Aristotelian appeals in her essay. What more might she have said about each appeal as it relates to sports?

Play for Pride, Not for Pay

3. What are the reasons, according to Ryan, why college athletes are not paid? Do you agree with them? Why or why not?

4. According to Ryan, "Athletic scholarships deliberately provide the players with unfair financial benefits." What does she mean by this?

Reading to Write

1. Support or challenge an existing policy in your school's athletic program. Make sure you are thoroughly familiar with the existing policies beforehand.

2. Create a visual argument in which you celebrate a facet of college sports (or a facet of a particular college sport) that you especially enjoy.

Connections Among the Clusters

1. What influence can college athletic programs have on student diversity and multicultural learning? (See Cluster 4, Multicultural Learning.)

2. What kinds of media regulation or censorship might arise in the context of broadcasting or writing about college sports? How might they be prevented? (See Cluster 3.)

Writing Projects

1. Review your college athletic program's policy on academic standards. What modifications or additions to the existing policy do you recommend and why? Write an essay in which you identify problems and make specific recommendations.

2. Write an essay on the position that participation in a college athletic program benefits or hinders academic performance. You may want to obtain testimonies from several students, as well as from coaches and professors, to support your assertions.

Suggestions for Further Reading

Ashley, Bob. "Can Athletics, Academics at Duke Coexist?" The Durham [NC] *Herald-Sun* 16 June 2006.

Cramer, Jerome. "Winning or Learning: Athletics and Academics in America." *Phi Delta Kappan* 67 (May 1986): K1–8.

Funk, Gary D. *Major Violation: The Unbalanced Priorities in Athletics and Academics.* Champaign, IL: Leisure Press, 1991.

Gerdy, John R. *Sports in School: The Future of an Institution.* New York: Teachers College, 2000.

Schulman, James L., and William G. Bowen. *The Game of Life: College Sports and Educational Values.* Princeton: Princeton UP, 2001.

Zimbalist, Andrew. "A Conversation with Andrew Zimablist." *U.S. Society and Values* December 2003.

Zimbalist, Andrew, and Bob Costas. *May the Best Team Win: Baseball Economics and Public Policy.* Washington, DC: Brookings Institution, 2004.

2 Intellectual Property: How Should IP Rights Be Protected?

Introduction

What is intellectual property? According to the World Intellectual Property Organization (WIPO), IP (as it is commonly called) refers to "creations of the mind: inventions, literary and artistic work and symbols, names, images, and designs used in commerce" (http://www.wipo.int). The WIPO goes on to explain that IP is divided into two categories: (1) industrial property (inventions, patents, trademarks, industrial designs) and (2) copyright (literary and artistic works such as novels, photographs, paintings, sculptures; theatrical and cinematic works; musical works and performances; and architectural designs).

What has made IP law a hotbed of controversy in recent years is the Internet. What regulations should be imposed on Internet distribution of IP? What ethical guidelines should be adopted? These questions are difficult to answer and have been the topic of numerous books and international conferences. One recent example: The theme selected for the sixth annual Ethics and Technology Conference held at Boston College in June 2003 was "Intellectual Property Rights in a Networked World." The topics of the papers presented at this conference reflect the complexity and scope of the issue:

- Ethical distribution of digital music

- The future of copyright law

- Website interconnectivity (how hyperlinks should be used)

- Online privacy problems

- Unauthorized noncommercial copying of computer programs

- Copyright protection vs. sharing of digital information

- Information ethics and globalization

The most controversial topic of all seems to be that of music downloading, as you'll probably agree after reading the first seven selections of this cluster.

How Might the Downloading of Music Files Best Be Regulated?

Troubletown | Lloyd Dangle

Many people feel that whatever appears on the Internet should be downloadable for free. If it's legal to record televised movies without charge, why shouldn't it also be legal to download music without charge? Such was the rationale behind the original Napster music-sharing software application; but in December 1999, the Recording Industry Association of America sued Napster for copyright violation. In the following panel from his syndicated "Troubletown" editorial comic series, Lloyd Dangle takes a satirical approach to Napster's rationale.

Source: Lloyd Dangle Comics and Illustration.

Reflections and Inquiries

1. What assumptions does Dangle seem to hold about the way young people regard intellectual property? Are any or all of these assumptions valid? Why or why not?

2. What negative aspects of IP ownership do Dangle's cartoon characters seem to embody?

3. What point is being made with the car thief and the police officer in the third frame? Is it logically sound or fallacious? Explain.

Reading to Write

Search the Web for additional cartoons and comic strips that convey a point of view about IP use. Then draw your own cartoon panel or compose a satiric essay that reveals your own viewpoint about IP rights.

Jim Rogan Speaks on Intellectual Property Rights
"We Have to Treat Theft as Theft" | U.S. Newswire

Is the downloading of songs from the Internet without payment a form of theft that is no different from other kinds of theft? Three experts addressed this issue during a briefing sponsored by Frontiers of Freedom Institute: Jim Rogan, a former congressman and director of the U.S. Patent and Trademark Office; George Landrith, of Frontiers of Freedom; and Jim DeLong of the Progress & Freedom Foundation.

Downloading songs off the internet for free is "no different than walking into Tower Records and grabbing CDs and sticking them under your coat," said James Rogan, former Congressman and now Under Secretary of Commerce for Intellectual Property and Director of United States Patent and Trademark Office at the U.S. Capitol. The briefing, sponsored by Frontiers of Freedom Institute, explored the state of Intellectual Property rights in America. Rogan, joined by George Landrith of Frontiers of Freedom and Jim DeLong of The Progress & Freedom Foundation, spoke to a large crowd of Congressional staff, local attorneys, and representatives from think-tanks and major associations.

Source: Jim Rogan, "We Have to Treat Theft as Theft," from *U.S. Newswire,* 30 July 2003. Reprinted by permission.

"With the ease of file sharing people with the click of a mouse are now able to download all kinds of free music and they think it's great," began Rogan. "The only problem is it's theft." Rogan explained the popular notion that because something is easy to obtain on the internet, and because people are doing it in the privacy of their own homes, that it's none of the government's business.

"They truly feel that they have this right to take things off the net because it's free and easy," Rogan continued. "Therefore they can subsume someone else's private property rights. It is someone else's private property, it is their creation, they have a right to determine how that creation will be disseminated. And they have a right to be compensated for it."

Rogan also addressed the transformation of America from an agrarian colony to a great economic and technological giant and asserts that the primary reason is the protection of intellectual property. He concluded, "This is why we have to maintain our vigilance in this area, we have to treat theft as theft—irrespective of ease—and if we do that we can look forward to a strong economy and a great technological future."

George Landrith focused his remarks on the importance of all brands of 5 property rights. "Many believe that the First Amendment is the most important right we enjoy in this country. Not so, it is property rights that is the cornerstone of freedom."

"We speak out because we know we cannot have property rights taken from us," Landrith said. "We have no fear of our government taking our home or property when we criticize them. Without the comfort of knowing that property rights always rule the day, we would have no such ability to speak out and exercise those First Amendment rights. Property rights are fundamental."

Jim DeLong, Senior Fellow and Director of the Center for the Study of Digital Property, addressed the role of intellectual property rights in today's markets. "We are all consumers and producers," said DeLong. "Markets bring us together to institutionalize reciprocity."

"For example, if I buy Madonna's latest CD it sends a message that she's done something right," he stated. "It provides incentive to her to continue producing. She produces and we consume. All of us produce our own services and receive compensation. We take that compensation and buy products or services from others."

Concluded DeLong, "Consumers should want to pay, it is how we send a message about what's important to us and what we're willing to pay for. Stealing sends the wrong message to the producers."

Reflections and Inquiries

1. How valid is Rogan's assertion that downloading songs from the Internet is as much an act of stealing as "walking into Tower Records and grabbing CDs and sticking them under your coat"?

2. What does Rogan consider to be the reason so many young people have no qualms about such unauthorized downloading of music? Is this a valid reason, in your opinion? Why or why not?

3. Landrith asserts that "property rights . . . is the cornerstone of freedom." Do you agree or disagree? Why?

4. According to DeLong, paying for a CD sends a message to the artists "about what's important to us." Could downloading the same CD without payment send the same message? Why or why not?

Reading to Write

Conduct a survey in which you gather as many reasons for or against free downloading of music as you can. Next, examine the various reasons, pro and con, for their logical soundness. Prepare an assessment of which reasons are the strongest, which reasons are the weakest, and why.

Protecting Music | Lawrence Lessig

In The Future of Ideas, *from which the following selection is taken, Lawrence Lessig argues that the Internet used to thrive because it created what he calls a "commons"—a place where information, ideas, sounds, and images were made easily available for the public to use as it wished, where creativity could flourish. But now, Lessig argues, corporations and media giants are forcing the rewriting of copyright laws to protect their interests. In "Protecting Music" Lessig, a professor of law at Stanford University, provides a dramatic case in point.*

The Net has created a world where content is free. Napster is the most salient example of this world, but it is not the only one. At any time a user can select the channel of music he or she wants. A song from your childhood? Search on the lyrics and find a recording. Within seconds you can hear any music you want.

This freedom the recording industry calls theft. But they don't call it theft when I hear an old favorite of mine on the radio. They don't call it theft when they are recording takeoffs of prior recorded music. And they don't call it theft when they make a new version of "Jingle Bells." They don't, in other words, call it theft when *they* are using music for free in ways that have been defined by the copyright system as fair and appropriate uses.

The issue we must confront is whether this free distribution should continue to be free. And the solution to that question is to keep an important distinction in mind: As we've seen, there is a distinction between music being "free" and music being available at zero cost. Artists should be paid, but it doesn't follow that selling music like chewing gum is the only possible way.

Here, too, a bit of history helps. . . . [T]here have been many contexts where Congress had to balance the rights of free access against the rights of control. When the courts said piano rolls were not "copies" of sheet music, Congress balanced the rights of composers against the rights to mechanically reproduce what was composed. It balanced these rights through a compulsory license that enabled payment to artists while assuring free access to the work produced. The same is true in the context of cable TV. . . . [T]he Supreme Court twice said that cable TV providers had a right, under existing law, to free TV. Congress finally changed those rights, but again, in a balanced and sensible way. Cable providers got access to television broadcasts, but broadcasters and copyright holders had a right to compensation for that access. This compensation again was set by a compulsory licensing term. Congress protected the author, but not through a *property* right.

The same solution is possible in the context of music on the Net. But here, rather than balance, the rhetoric is about "theft" and "crime." But was it "theft" when cable TV took television broadcasts? 5

Congress should empower file sharing by recognizing a similar system of compulsory licenses. These fees should not be set by an industry intent on killing this new mode of distribution. They should be set, as they have always been set, by a policy maker keen on striking a balance. If only such a policy maker were somewhere to be found. @/@

Reflections and Inquiries

1. One of Lessig's argumentative strategies in this selection is to use analogies. How effective are Lessig's analogies—for example, listening to a song on the radio as analogous to listening to a song on the Internet?

2. What does the example of cable television illustrate? Is it sufficiently analogous to the Internet? Why or why not?

Reading to Write

Argue for or against Lessig's assertion that "Congress should empower file sharing by recognizing a . . . system of compulsory licenses" similar to those used for cable television. Locate sources that support and/or refute Lessig's views.

The Internet Debacle: An Alternate View | Janis Ian

Is it possible that free downloading of music (or other kinds of intellectual property) could actually prove beneficial rather than detrimental to the artists' royalties? Such is the conviction of Janis Ian, a singer who in the 1970s produced several hit records, such as Society's Child. *Ian, as you will tell from the article that follows, fiercely defends free access to entertainment available on the Internet.*

The Internet, and downloading, are here to stay. . . . Anyone who thinks otherwise should prepare themselves to end up on the slagheap of history.

(Janis Ian during a live European radio interview, 9–1–98)

When I research an article, I normally send 30 or so emails to friends and acquaintances asking for opinions and anecdotes. I usually receive 10–20 in reply. But not so on this subject!

I sent 36 emails requesting opinions and facts on free music downloading from the Net. I stated that I planned to adopt the viewpoint of devil's advocate: free Internet downloads are good for the music industry and its artists.

I've received, to date, over 300 replies, every single one from someone legitimately "in the music business."

What's more interesting than the emails are the phone calls. I don't know anyone at NARAS (home of the Grammy Awards), and I know Hilary Rosen (head of the Recording Industry Association of America, or RIAA) only vaguely. Yet within 24 hours of sending my original email, I'd received two messages from Rosen and four from NARAS requesting that I call to "discuss the article."

Huh. Didn't know I was that widely read.   5

Ms. Rosen, to be fair, stressed that she was only interested in presenting RIAA's side of the issue, and was kind enough to send me a fair amount of statistics and documentation, including a number of focus group studies RIAA had run on the matter.

However, the problem with focus groups is the same problem anthropologists have when studying peoples in the field—the moment the anthropologist's presence is known, everything changes. Hundreds of scientific studies have shown that any experimental group *wants to please the examiner.* For focus groups, this is particularly true. Coffee and donuts are the least of the pay-offs.

The NARAS people were a bit more pushy. They told me downloads were "destroying sales," "ruining the music industry," and "costing *you* money."

Costing *me* money? I don't pretend to be an expert on intellectual property law, but I do know one thing. If a music industry executive claims I should agree with their agenda because it will make me more money, I put my hand on my wallet . . . and check it after they leave, just to make sure nothing's missing.

Am I suspicious of all this hysteria? You bet. Do I think the issue has been   10 badly handled? Absolutely. Am I concerned about losing friends, opportunities, my 10th Grammy nomination by publishing this article? Yeah. I am. But sometimes things are just *wrong*, and when they're *that* wrong, they have to be addressed.

The premise of all this ballyhoo is that the industry (and its artists) are being harmed by free downloading.

Nonsense. Let's take it from my personal experience. My site (www.janisian.com) gets an average of 75,000 hits a year. Not bad for someone whose last hit record was in 1975. When Napster was running full-tilt, we received about 100 hits a month from people who'd downloaded *Society's Child* or *At Seventeen* for free, then decided they wanted more information. Of those 100 people (and these are only the ones who let us know how they'd found the site), 15 bought CDs. Not huge sales, right? No record company is interested in 180 extra sales a year. But . . . that translates into $2700, which is a lot of money in my book. And that doesn't include the ones who bought the CDs in stores, or who came to my shows.

Or take author Mercedes Lackey, who occupies entire shelves in stores and libraries. As she said herself: "For the past ten years, my three 'Arrows' books, which were published by DAW about 15 years ago, have been generating a nice, steady royalty check per pay-period each. A reasonable amount, for fifteen-year-old books. However . . . I just got the first half of my DAW royalties. . . . And suddenly, out of nowhere, each Arrows book has paid me three times the normal amount! . . . And because those books have never been out of print, and have always been promoted along with the rest of the back-list, the only significant change during that pay-period was something that happened over at Baen, one of my other publishers. That was when I had my co-author Eric Flint put the first of my Baen books on the Baen Free Library site. Because I have significantly more books with DAW than with Baen, the increases showed up at DAW first. There's an increase in all of the books on that statement, actually, and what it looks like is what I'd expect to happen if a steady line of people who'd never read my stuff encountered it on the Free Library—a certain percentage of them liked it, and started to work through my backlist, beginning with the earliest books published. The really interesting thing is, of course, that these aren't Baen books, they're DAW—another publisher—so it's 'name loyalty' rather than 'brand loyalty.' I'll tell you what, I'm sold. Free works."

I've found that to be true myself; every time we make a few songs available on my website, sales of all the CDs go up. A lot.

And I don't know about you, but as an artist with an in-print record catalogue 15 that dates back to 1965, I'd be *thrilled* to see sales on my old catalogue rise.

Now, RIAA and NARAS, as well as most of the entrenched music industry, are arguing that free downloads hurt sales. (More than hurt—they're saying it's destroying the industry.)

Alas, the music industry needs no outside help to destroy itself. We're doing a very adequate job of that on our own, thank you.

Here are a few statements from the RIAA's website:

1. "Analysts report that just one of the many peer-to-peer systems in operation is responsible for over 1.8 billion unauthorized downloads per month." (Hilary B. Rosen letter to the Honorable Rick Boucher, Congressman, February 28, 2002)

2. "Sales of blank CD-R discs have . . . grown nearly 2 1/2 times in the last two years . . . if just half the blank discs sold in 2001 were used to copy music, the number of burned CDs worldwide is about the same as the number of CDs sold at retail." (Hilary B. Rosen letter to the Honorable Rick Boucher, Congressman, February 28, 2002)

3. "Music sales are already suffering from the impact . . . in the United States, sales decreased by more than 10% in 2001." (Hilary B. Rosen letter to the Honorable Rick Boucher, Congressman, February 28, 2002)

4. "In a recent survey of music consumers, 23% . . . said they are not buying more music because they are downloading or copying their music for free." (Hilary B. Rosen letter to the Honorable Rick Boucher, Congressman, February 28, 2002)

Let's take these points one by one, but before that, let me remind you of something: the music industry had *exactly* the same response to the advent of reel-to-reel home tape recorders, cassettes, DATs, minidiscs, VHS, BETA, music videos ("Why buy the record when you can tape it?"), MTV, and a host of other technological advances designed to make the consumer's life easier and better. I know because I was there.

The only reason they didn't react that way publicly to the advent of CDs 20 was because *they believed CDs were uncopyable.* I was told this personally by a former head of Sony marketing, when they asked me to license *Between the Lines* in CD format at a reduced royalty rate. ("Because it's a brand new technology.")

1. Who's to say that any of those people would have bought the CDs if the songs weren't available for free? I can't find a single study on this, one where a reputable surveyor such as Gallup actually asks people that question. I think no one's run one because everyone is afraid of the truth—most

of the downloads are people who want to try an artist out, or who can't find the music in print.

And if a percentage of that 1.8 billion is because people are downloading a current hit by Britney or In Sync [*sic*], who's to say it really hurt their sales? Soft statistics are easily manipulated. How many of those people went out and bought an album that had been over-played at radio for months, just because they downloaded a portion of it?

2. Sales of blank CDs have grown? You bet. I bought a new Vaio in December (ironically enough, made by Sony), and now back up all my files onto CD. I go through 7–15 CDs a week that way, or about 500 a year. Most new PCs come with XP, which makes backing up to CD painless; how many people are doing what I'm doing? Additionally, when I buy a new CD, I make a copy for my car, a copy for upstairs, and a copy for my partner. That's three blank discs per CD. So I alone account for around 750 blank CDs yearly.

3. I'm sure the sales decrease had nothing to do with the economy's decrease, or a steady downward spiral in the music industry, or the garbage being pushed by record companies. Aren't you? There were *32,000 new titles* released in this country in 2001, and that's not including re-issues, DIY's, or smaller labels that don't report to SoundScan. Our "Unreleased" series, which we haven't bothered SoundScanning, sold 6,000+ copies last year. A conservative estimate would place the number of "newly available" CDs per year at 100,000. That's an awful lot of releases for an industry that's being destroyed. And to make matters worse, we hear music everywhere, whether we want to or not; stores, amusement parks, highway rest stops. The original concept of Muzak (to be played in elevators so quietly that its soothing effect would be subliminal) has run amok. Why buy records when you can learn the entire Top 40 just by going shopping for groceries?

4. Which music consumers? College kids who can't afford to buy 10 new CDs a month, but want to hear their favorite groups? When I bought my nephews a new Backstreet Boys CD, I asked why they hadn't downloaded it instead. They patiently explained to their senile aunt that the download wouldn't give them the cool artwork, and more important, the video they could see only on the CD.

Realistically, why do most people download music? *To hear new music, or records that have been deleted and are no longer available for purchase.* Not to avoid paying $5 at the local used CD store, or taping it off the radio, but to hear music they can't find anywhere else. Face it—most people can't afford to spend $15.99 to experiment. That's why listening booths (which labels fought against, too) are such a success.

You can't hear new music on radio these days; I live in Nashville, "Music City USA," and we have exactly one station willing to play a non-top-40 format. On a clear day, I can even tune it in. The situation's not much better in Los Angeles or New York. College stations are sometimes bolder, but their wattage is so low that most of us can't get them.

One other major point: in the hysteria of the moment, everyone is forgetting the main way an artist becomes successful—*exposure.* Without exposure, no one comes to shows, no one buys CDs, no one enables you to earn a living doing what you love. Again, from personal experience: in 37 years as a recording artist, I've created 25+1 albums for major labels, and I've *never once* received a royalty check that didn't show I owed *them* money. So I make the bulk of my living from live touring, playing for 80–1500 people a night, doing my own show. I spend hours each week doing press, writing articles, making sure my website tour information is up to date. Why? Because all of that gives me exposure to an audience that might not come otherwise. So when someone writes and tells me they came to my show because they'd downloaded a song and gotten curious, I am thrilled!

Who gets hurt by free downloads? Save a handful of super-successes like Celine Dion, none of us. We only get helped.

But not to hear Congress tell it. Senator Fritz Hollings, chairman of the 25 Senate Commerce Committee studying this, said "When Congress sits idly by in the face of these [file-sharing] activities, we essentially sanction the Internet as a haven for thievery," then went on to charge "over 10 million people" with stealing (Steven Levy, *Newsweek* 3/11/02). That's what we think of consumers— they're thieves, out to get something for nothing.

Baloney. Most consumers have no problem paying for entertainment. One has only to look at the success of Fictionwise.com and the few other websites offering books and music at reasonable prices to understand that. If the music industry had a shred of sense, they'd have addressed this problem seven years ago, when people like Michael Camp were trying to obtain legitimate licenses for music online. Instead, the industry-wide attitude was *"It'll go away."* That's the same attitude CBS Records had about rock 'n' roll when Mitch Miller was head of A&R. (And you wondered why they passed on The Beatles and The Rolling Stones.)

I don't blame the RIAA for Holling's attitude. They are, after all, the *Recording Industry* Association of America, formed so the labels would have a lobbying group in Washington. (In other words, they're permitted to make contributions to politicians and their parties.) But given that our industry's success is based on communication, the industry response to the Internet has been abysmal. Statements like the one above do nothing to help the cause.

Of course, communication has always been the artist's job, not the executives. That's why it's so scary when people like current NARAS president Michael Greene begin using shows like the Grammy Awards to drive their point home.

Grammy viewership hit a six-year low in 2002. Personally, I found the program so scintillating that it made me long for Rob Lowe dancing with

Snow White, which at least was so bad that it was entertaining. Moves like the ridiculous Elton John–Eminem duet did little to make people want to watch again the next year. And we're not going to go into the *Los Angeles Times'* Pulitzer Prize-winning series on Greene and NARAS, where they pointed out that MusiCares has spent less than 10% of its revenue on disbursing emergency funds for people in the music industry (its primary purpose), or that Greene recorded his own album, pitched it to record executives while discussing Grammy business, then negotiated a $250,000 contract with Mercury Records for it (later withdrawn after the public flap). Or that NARAs quietly paid out at least $650,000 to settle a sexual harassment suit against him, a portion of which the non-profit Academy paid. Or that he's paid two million dollars a year, along with "perks" like his million-dollar country club membership and Mercedes. (Though it does make one wonder when he last entered a record store and bought something with his own earned money.)

Let's just note that in his speech he told the viewing audience that 30 NARAS and RIAA were, in large part, taking their stance to protect artists. He hired three teenagers to spend a couple of days doing nothing but downloading, and they managed to download "6,000 songs." Come on. For free "front-row seats" at the Grammys and an appearance on national TV, I'd download twice that amount! But . . . who's got time to download that many songs? Does Greene really think people out there are spending twelve hours a day downloading our music? If they are, they must be starving to death, because they're not making a living or going to school. How many of us can afford a T-1 line?

This sort of thing is indicative of the way statistics and information are being tossed around. It's dreadful to think that consumers are being asked to take responsibility for the industry's problems, which have been around far longer than the Internet. It's even worse to think that the consumer is being told they are charged with protecting us, the artists, when our own industry squanders the dollars we earn on waste and personal vendettas.

Greene went on to say that "many of the nominees here tonight, especially the new, less-established artists, are in immediate danger of being marginalized out of our business." Right. Any "new" artist who manages to make the Grammys has millions of dollars in record company money behind them. The "real" new artists aren't people you're going to see on national TV, or hear on most radio. They're people you'll hear because someone gave you a disc, or they opened at a show you attended, or were lucky enough to be featured on NPR or another program still open to playing records that aren't already hits.

As to artists being "marginalized out of our business," the only people being marginalized out are the employees of our Enron-minded record companies, who are being fired in droves because the higher-ups are incompetent.

And it's difficult to convince an educated audience that artists and record labels are about to go down the drain because they, the consumer, are downloading music. Particularly when they're paying $50–$125 apiece for concert tickets, and $15.99 for a new CD they know costs less than a couple of dollars to manufacture and distribute.

I suspect Greene thinks of downloaders as the equivalent of an old-style 35 television drug dealer, lurking next to playgrounds, wearing big coats and whipping them open for wide-eyed children who then purchase black market CD's at generous prices.

What's the new industry byword? *Encryption.* They're going to make sure no one can copy CDs, even for themselves, or download them for free. Brilliant, except that it flouts previous court decisions about blank cassettes, blank videotapes, etc. And it pisses people off.

How many of you know that many car makers are now manufacturing all their CD players to also play DVD's or that part of the encryption record companies are using doesn't allow your store-bought CD to be played on a DVD player, because that's the same technology as your computer? And if you've had trouble playing your own self-recorded copy of *O Brother Where Art Thou* in the car, it's because of this lunacy.

The industry's answer is to put on the label: "This audio CD is protected against unauthorized copying. It is designed to play in standard audio CD players and computers running Windows O/S; however, playback problems may be experienced. If you experience such problems, return this disc for a refund."

Now I ask you. After three or four experiences like that, *shlepping* to the store to buy it, then *shlepping* back to return it (and you still don't have your music), who's going to bother buying CDs?

The industry has been complaining for years about the stranglehold the 40 middle-man has on their dollars, yet they wish to do nothing to offend those middle-men. (BMG has a strict policy for artists buying their own CDs to sell at concerts—$11 per CD. They know very well that most of us lose money if we have to pay that much; the point is to keep the big record stores happy by ensuring sales go to them. What actually happens is no sales to us *or* the stores.) NARAS and RIAA are moaning about the little mom & pop stores being shoved out of business; no one worked harder to shove them out than our own industry, which greeted every new Tower or mega-music store with glee, and offered steep discounts to Target and Wal-Mart et al. for stocking CDs. The Internet has zero to do with store closings and lowered sales.

And for those of us with major label contracts who *want* some of our music available for free downloading . . . well, the record companies own our masters, our outtakes, even our demos, and they won't allow it. Furthermore, they own our *voices* for the duration of the contract, so we can't even post a live track for downloading!

If you think about it, the music industry should be rejoicing at this new technological advance! Here's a fool-proof way to deliver music to millions who might otherwise never purchase a CD in a store. The cross-marketing opportunities are unbelievable. It's instantaneous, costs are minimal, shipping non-existent . . . a staggering vehicle for higher earnings and lower costs. Instead, they're running around like chickens with their heads cut off, bleeding on everyone and making no sense. . . .

Greene and the RIAA are correct in one thing—these are times of great change in our industry. But at a time when there are arguably only four record labels left in America (Sony, AOL/Time/Warner, Universal, BMG—and where is the RICO act when we need it?) . . . when entire *genres* are glorifying the gangster mentality and losing their biggest voices to violence . . . when executives change positions as often as Zsa Zsa Gabor changed clothes, and "A&R" has become a euphemism for "Absent & Redundant" . . . well, we have other things to worry about.

It's absurd for us, as artists, to sanction—or countenance—the shutting down of something like this. It's sheer stupidity to rejoice at the Napster decision. Short-sighted, and ignorant.

Free exposure is practically a thing of the past for entertainers. Getting 45 your record played at radio costs more money than most of us dream of ever earning. Free downloading gives a chance to every do-it-yourselfer out there. Every act that can't get signed to a major, for whatever reason, can reach literally millions of new listeners, enticing them to buy the CD and come to the concerts. Where else can a new act, or one that doesn't have a label deal, get that kind of exposure?

Please note that I am *not* advocating indiscriminate downloading without the artist's permission. I am *not* saying copyrights are meaningless. I am objecting to the RIAA spin that they are doing this to protect "the artists," and make us more money. I am annoyed that so many records I once owned are out of print, and the only place I could find them was Napster. Most of all, I'd like to see an end to the hysteria that causes a group like RIAA to spend over 45 million dollars in 2001 lobbying "on our behalf," when every record company out there is complaining that they have no money.

We'll turn into Microsoft if we're not careful, folks, insisting that any household wanting an extra copy for the car, the kids, or the portable CD player, has to go out and "license" multiple copies.

As artists, we have the ear of the masses. We have the trust of the masses. By speaking out in our concerts and in the press, we can do a great deal to damp this hysteria, and put the blame for the state of our industry right back where it belongs—in the laps of record companies, radio programmers, and our own apparent inability to organize ourselves in order to better our own lives—and those of our fans. If we don't take the reins, no one will. ◎/◎

Reflections and Inquiries

1. How convincingly does Ian support her assertions? How reliable is her evidence?

2. Ian claims that most people download music, not to avoid paying for CDs, but simply *"to hear new music, or records that have been deleted and are no longer available for purchase."* Do you agree or disagree with Ian's claim? On what grounds?

3. According to Ian, recording companies are actually losing money by prohibiting free downloading. How is this possible?

Reading to Write

Prepare a defense of or rebuttal to Ian's thesis, drawing from your own interpretation of policies dealing with music downloading, other selections in this cluster, or any updating of regulations.

Thread My Music's Yours | Bill Thompson

Bill Thompson, like Janis Ian, is a writer with plenty of attitude. In the following short piece from Internet Magazine, the publication he works for as a staff writer, Thompson explains that he originally preferred physical CDs because he liked having sleeve notes and printed lyrics. He changed his mind because the RIAA (Recording Industry Association of America) "has driven [him] over the edge." Thompson, who has published books about the Internet for children, also teaches online journalism at City University, London.

If you like David Bowie, Bob Dylan, the Rolling Stones or the Beatles then I've got some good news for you.

I'm in the process of ripping my entire CD collection, and putting the MP3s onto my hard drive where they can be shared with anyone using the popular Kazaa peer-to-peer file-sharing network.

Over the decades these artists have made millions from their music, and I'm sure that everyone who thinks that it's worth shelling out 15 quid for a copy of a thirty-year-old album has already bought it. So I can't see that I'm doing them any real harm.

Sadly, of course, the artists themselves may not see it that way, greedy as they often are to squeeze another few dollars from their fans. And the record companies who own the copyright in the recordings that I'm so shamelessly copying will certainly disagree with my actions.

Source: Bill Thompson, "Thread My Music's Yours," *Internet Magazine*, August 2003, p. 14. Reprinted by permission of the author.

Up to now, I've made very little use of the file-sharing networks, partly   5
because I like to have sleeve notes, lyrics and the other things that come with
a physical CD, and partly because I don't really have the time to wade
through lists of MP3s and download several until I find a decent quality
recording of the song I want.

But the recent behaviour of the record companies, and especially their US
trade body, the Recording Industry Association of America (RIAA), has driven
me over the edge.

In the last few months the RIAA has used the US courts to get Verizon, an
ISP, to reveal the identity of one of its subscribers in a clear breach of the
principles of natural justice. It has persuaded colleges to deny Net access to
students who they claim are sharing files over college networks. It has damaged the careers of students at a naval academy by accusing them of downloading music files. And it has taken students to court and had them fined
thousands of dollars for trading files.

In addition, it has persuaded several US states to pass laws making it a
criminal offence to add a wireless LAN to your cable modem without written
permission from your ISP. It has filled the file sharing networks with empty
files, and has spammed millions of P2P users.

And it has done all this because it wants to make even more money out of
the Internet than the record companies it represents have made from selling
CDs over the past 20 years.

These companies don't care about music. They don't care about the fans.   10
They only care about their corporate profits, and in an attempt to make even
more money they have declared war on anyone who dares to challenge them.

Well, I've joined the army—on the other side. I'm not going to buy any more
CDs until there's a decent online music service that lets me get the music I want.

I'm happy to pay. I'm just not happy to be ripped off. In the meantime, if
anyone wants my MP3s, just come and get them. ◎/◎

Reflections and Inquiries

1. Why, according to Thompson, has the RIAA persuaded colleges to deny
   Internet access to their students?

2. Thompson asserts that the record companies represented by the RIAA
   "don't care about music." What does he mean by this? Do you agree or
   disagree? Why?

3. How is Thompson being "ripped off," as he asserts in the last paragraph?

Reading to Write

Find out all you can about the RIAA and its policies, and then prepare a
defense of or rebuttal to Thompson's thesis.

Penalties Frighten Music Traders

Survey Reports Copyright Laws Are Not Daunting | Benny Evangelista

In the following article, Benny Evangelista, a staff writer for the San Francisco Chronicle, *reports on the results of surveys conducted to see who in the general population downloads music, who among them expresses concern over whether the music they download is copyright-protected, and what might be the effect of the threat of lawsuits from the RIAA.*

About two-thirds of the people who use online file-sharing programs say they don't care whether the songs are protected by copyrights, according to a new study by a nonprofit Washington group.

Yet in a survey by a technology industry research firm, an equal number would stop downloading if the penalty was a big fine or jail time.

Those two findings seem to bolster the Recording Industry Association of America's latest attempt to quash online file sharing by suing thousands of consumers.

But while the RIAA's copyright crackdown could help slow the deluge of free songs now shared on the Internet, analysts said record companies also must give music fans more ways to buy their songs online.

"If you scare them and they stop downloading, there's no guarantee   5 they're going to go out and buy more CDs,"said Josh Bernoff, an entertainment industry analyst for Forrester Research Inc. "If you want to win them back, you're going to have to make it really easy to pay (for online music)."

The RIAA, the Washington trade group that represents the U.S. recording industry, is pressing forward with plans to file civil lawsuits against individuals who use programs like Kazaa.

TABLE 1   **Who Downloads Music**

The figures reflect the percentage of each group of Internet users who downloaded music from March to May 2003.

Men	32%	Blacks	37%
Women	26	Hispanics	35
Whites	28	All adults	29

Source: Pew Internet & American Life Project Surveys, March–May 2003.

Note: More demographic information from the surveys can be found in [the next table on page 328].

Source: Benny Evangelista, "Penalties Frighten Music Traders," *Survey Reports Copyright Laws Are Not Daunting. San Francisco Chronicle,* 4 Aug. 2003: E1, E5. Copyright 2003 by *San Francisco Chronicle.*

TABLE 2   **Who Downloads Music**

The figures reflect the percent of each group of Internet users who downloaded music.

By age group		Education	
18–29	52%	Less than high school	39%
39–49	27	High school graduate	31
50+	12	Some college	33
		College degree or more	23
Household income		**Internet user experience**	
Under $30,000	38	Less than 6 months	26*
$30,000–$50,000	30	6 mos. to 1 yr	26*
$50,000–$75,000	28	2–3 yrs	29
$75,000 and up	26	3 or more yrs	59

Source: Pew Internet & American Life Project Surveys.

Note: * represents music downloaders who have been online less than one year.

In its lawsuits, the RIAA is going after users who offer to share songs on their computers for others to download. The industry is relying on laws that provide for anywhere from $750 to $150,000 in damages per violation.

Whether the lawsuits prove to be an effective deterrent remains to be seen, but the RIAA's tactic should raise the awareness of the issues to a public that is generally indifferent to copyright laws, said Lee Rainie, director of the Pew Internet & American Life Project, the nonprofit group which did the study.

"On the other side of the coin, so many people are so indifferent to this that it's not really clear what will get their attention," Rainie said. "This is one of the core economic issues of the digital age."

The Pew group released a study last week that showed 67 percent of peo- 10 ple who downloaded music from the Internet did not care whether the songs they downloaded or shared were protected by copyrights.

And 82 percent of people aged 18 to 29 said they did not care about copyright protection. The percentage was similar for file sharers with an annual household income of less than $30,000. In the higher income bracket of $75,000 or more, 61 percent said they weren't worried about the status of songs on their hard drives.

The results were from a survey of 2,515 adults during one week in March and the last week in April, before the RIAA announced its plans to file lawsuits.

That show of indifference stems from the public's general unfamiliarity with the details of copyright laws and "the considerable shades of gray in the law for what constitutes fair use," Rainie said.

For example, copying songs on a tape for a friend "seems to be OK, but if I'm trying to make money off it, that's not OK," he said.

Many file sharers don't consider the activity theft; they look at it as a way 15 to sample music or otherwise supplement the way they buy music, he said.

Both Rainie and Bernoff also noted an underlying feeling among the respondents that file sharing is a backlash from people feeling that the record industry has "gotten away" with overcharging for music for years.

A common complaint is "why should I pay $18 for a CD when it only costs $1 to make," Bernoff said.

"Lawsuits against individual consumers may not be as big a public relations risk for the music industry," he added.

"If that's your image, it's not going to get any worse if you sue people," Bernoff said. "They already hate the music industry."

In a separate Forrester survey of 1,170 people aged 12 to 22, 68 percent of 20 the downloaders surveyed said they would stop if there was a risk of going to jail or being fined for downloading music. That study was conducted in June, just after the RIAA announced it was setting up digital dragnets.

Thirty percent said they would stop if downloading music took twice as long as it did.

Those results show the record industry must use both a carrot and a stick, Bernoff said.

"You can't destroy piracy, but at the same time, you can create a culture where paying for downloading music is easy, moral and fun," he said.

A variety of legal, for-profit online music services may be coming to the rescue of the music industry, which in turn is becoming more comfortable with services like Apple Computer Inc.'s iTunes Music Store.

Started in April, the iTunes Music Store sells downloadable songs for 25 99 cents each and albums for $9.99 each. Apple has sold more than 6.5 million songs, even though the service is only available to users of Macintosh computers.

The early but limited success of iTunes has spurred plans for a dozen more competitors that may be operating by next spring, Bernoff said. BuyMusic.com has already started, while technology companies like Microsoft and Amazon have shown interest in selling downloadable tunes.

Meanwhile, Apple's marketing of its iTunes has raised the overall awareness of legal online music.

A report released last week by the research firm NPD Group of Port Washington, N.Y., said that 20 percent of all consumers 13 years or older knew of iTunes, compared to 14 percent for older music industry sanctioned services like Listen.com's Rhapsody.

While sales of CDs "may decline forever," online music sales should grow to about $2 billion a year by 2007, Bernoff said. ◎/◎

Reflections and Inquiries

1. What assumptions, if any, are you willing to make about the "Who Downloads Music" survey results? For example, are you willing to say that more men download music than women because men are less willing to

pay for music than women? Whatever assumptions you make, prepare to reinforce them with additional evidence from other sources.

2. How legitimate is the rationale that music downloading is permissible because CDs are unreasonably expensive?

3. Evangelista reports that "two-thirds of the people who use online file-sharing programs say they don't care whether the songs are protected by copyrights." What, in your opinion, accounts for this indifference?

Reading to Write

Conduct your own survey of who downloads music on your college campus. Use the same categories as the polls whose survey results Evangelista reports (for example, by gender, race, age group, Internet-user experience), or come up with your own categories. Prepare a detailed analysis of your survey results.

Student Essay

Why I've Stopped Sharing Music

On April 3, the Recording Industry Association of America Filed Suit Against My College Hall Mate | Powell Fraser

In the following piece, Powell Fraser, an undergraduate at Princeton University and an intern at CNN, tells the story of a Princeton computer whiz who ran a search engine that located and downloaded both songs and movies and who subsequently was sued by the music industry. It was enough to make the author change his ways.

Daniel Peng, 17, a computer wiz who skipped two grades before coming to Princeton University, ran a campus-wide search engine that could be used to locate and download songs and movies.

The music industry slapped him with a lawsuit seeking potentially billions of dollars in damages for distributing copyrighted works. His site was shut down and his life thrown into chaos.

Dan, a junior, lived right down the hall from me last semester, and his plight made me rethink the whole issue of sharing music online.

Students Wipe Hard Drives

News of Dan's situation exploded on the New Jersey campus. Some students sprinted back to their dorm rooms to wipe their hard disks clean of any record of unauthorized downloads.

Those who ran similar sites pulled the plug on their machines and waited, 5 fearfully, to see if they would be targeted. Others simply shrugged, opened up Kazaa and went on swapping music.

With Dan's site gone, these bolder souls simply sought another. But Dan's experience revolutionized the way I download music: I started paying for it.

Having researched various subscription services for a term paper, I made a quick transition to Roxio's Pressplay client and began to pay a monthly fee for unlimited downloads through their service.

After a while, my collection of MP3s had grown so large I could no longer tell which ones were legally mine.

Seeking Donations to Pay Fine

After the industry settled out of court with Dan, who agreed to pay $15,000, he replaced his Wake search engine with a page seeking contributions to help pay his settlement.

I used my credit card to send him $20 and students nationwide banded 10 together to help Dan, who told me he has raised almost $4,000. A few of us helped him out of sympathy, perhaps inspired by a guilty conscience.

Until Dan's case showed us how far the music industry would go to stop Internet downloads, a lot of students thought this was an infraction similar to speeding on the highway. The case against Dan persuaded many to slow down.

Still, when I hear a timeless Beatles classic on the radio and then go home to look for it on Pressplay or ITunes and it isn't there, I tend to longingly eye the Kazaa icon that still sits on my desktop, beckoning me to return to piracy.

Only fear and Dan Peng's ordeal keep me in line. ◎/◎

Reflections and Inquiries

1. How would you characterize Fraser's decision to start paying for music he downloaded? Cowardly? Smart? Somewhere in-between?

2. How would you characterize Fraser's sense of ethics on the basis of his quick reference to researching subscription services for term papers?

3. In light of Fraser's change of attitude, how do you explain his concluding paragraph?

Reading to Write

Write an essay arguing whether you consider it fair for the recording industry to fine students for downloading music. Choose the Classical, Toulmin, or Rogerian method of argument in your approach to the topic.

Student Essay

A Language All Their Own | Nathan Salha

One of the most curious of current trends in intellectual property regulation is that of trademarking commonly used slogans. Is this an example of capitalism out of control? In the following paper, Nathan Salha, a senior pre-law student at Santa Clara University, tackles this perplexing trend, using the Paris Hilton's request to trademark "That's hot!" and Donald Trump's request to trademark "You're fired!"— the key slogan of his television series, The Apprentice—*as cases in point.*

"You're fired." What do you think of when you hear this phrase? Is there a definite connotation that comes to mind? Do you think of Donald Trump and his thriving reality series, *The Apprentice?* Does it remind you of a witty supplier of bulletproof vests? Sallyjo Levine claims the phrase is inextricably linked to her ceramics company, You're Fired Inc. (Kramer). Or do you, like most people, think of unemployment and the loss of salary when you hear such a direct, unpolished phrase? Such a question actually came before the U.S. Patent and Trademark Office in early 2004. The Donald and a few others were officially squabbling over the rights to this common, well-known phrase. Should one person be granted the rights to common utterances? What about "Just do it"? "Get more"? Of course one shouldn't. But at the same time, some protection is necessary for the sake of healthy competition. Ideally, trademarks, like patents and copyrights, should be distributed only to protect intellectual invention and the reputations of associated companies.

To understand such limitations, we must start at the extreme. Why should trademarks be dispensed at all? Many believe they shouldn't. This nation is built on certain inherent freedoms—one of these is the freedom of speech. Except in extreme cases harmful or slanderous to others, American citizens may legally say what they please. In saying what they please, citizens are also granted freedom of expression (in words, phrases, etc.). Such highly valued national liberties take precedence as the First Amendment in our founding Bill of Rights. Privileging some with the exclusive rights to universally used phrases (or any phrase at all for that matter) would limit the verbal freedom of others. We have established, however, that such limitation is unconstitutional and unethical. Nonetheless, trademarks do not limit one's freedom of speech. Were Nike granted a trademark on "Just do it," your mother could still bark it out in response to your complaints. And had Mr. Trump secured the rights to "You're fired," the phrase would nonetheless remain in your employer's repertoire. Trademarks do not limit the private use of catch phrases and slogans; they regulate the use of such slogans throughout the business environment.

Having secured our liberties, we may now proceed to the true purpose of a trademark. Are trademarks necessary at all? Again, many believe they aren't. Now, defendants of trademarks and patents may ask their more liberal critics to analyze the Constitution once more. Article I, Section 8, Clause 8 rationalizes such protection "to promote the progress of science and useful arts." Our founding fathers provided for such protection hoping to facilitate science. Logically, businesses, as the developers of science, should qualify for such protection. More specifically, "a trademark is a word, phrase, symbol or design, or a combination [thereof] that identifies and distinguishes the source of the goods of one party from those of others" ("Trademark"). By protecting corporate slogans, the U.S. Patent and Trademark Office also protects corporations.

Here, once again, the trademarking process meets opposition. Some consider the protection of corporations an unnecessary facilitation of greedy corporate capitalism. Protected phrases amount to higher corporate profits. This accusation is true; profits generally do increase. Trademarks do not exist to improve further the financial status of these companies, however. The clever ways in which corporations employ the existing legal framework account for their gains and losses. Trademarks, on the other hand, exist as necessary protection to prevent market deterioration. Firms invest much of their capital in the fickle business of advertising. If hard work and creative invention produce a slogan which appeals to the masses, more product is likely to sell. People will rush out to buy "the breakfast of champions." If the rights to such a phrase are not secured, however, Post Cereals and the Kellogg Company may plaster "breakfast of champions" on whichever products they please and thereby capitalize on the work and money inputted by General Mills. Slogan stealing is not only ethically unsound but also economically detrimental. If just anyone could take up established slogans, General Mills would effectively lose its advantage and any incentive to be creative and competitive. Advertising would become uncreative and mundane. Competition would deteriorate, and quality would soon follow. Hence, trademark phrases, like patented inventions, preserve creativity and promote self-improvement.

But the preservation of slogans does more than aid corporations—it benefits consumers as well. The allocation of specific phrases to specific companies establishes a system of identification. One can become accustomed to buying the soup that is "M'mm, M'mm, Good." If this largely original phrase is not trademarked, however, any generic can of soup may make identical claims. Consumers may be dissatisfied with generic soups that tote the same slogan. Consumers may also mistakenly attribute this dissatisfaction to the Campbell Soup Company. Corporations commit significant resources in an attempt to associate their products with symbols and slogans. We, as consumers, rely on these slogans as indications of quality. If corporate phrases are not protected, however, consumers may be intentionally duped into buying inferior products. By granting companies exclusive rights to the use of certain creative phrases, the government increases the indicators available to consumers to distinguish between market goods.

Clearly, there is a time and a place for trademarks as a protective market measure. The most frequent problems do not require the abolition of the trademark in general; they simply call for its consistent, logical application. Paris

Hilton's modern request to trademark "That's hot" (an exemplar for most modern controversial proposals) is ludicrous. We have enumerated the purposes of a trademark. Like patents and copyrights, trademarks are designed to protect creative invention. Slogans like "You're fired" and "That's hot" are completely void of creativity—they are common vernacular. The simple form of these phrases does not lend itself to trademark either. Any combination of two or three small words is hardly unique and will undoubtedly raise objections. One would be more likely to grant the phrase, "Do you smell what the Rock is cookin'?" As primitive as it may be, it at least exhibits sufficient length and creativity.

Even if we set aside the incompatibility of such basic slogans, the phrases chosen by these celebrities are also unjustifiable. Neither Trump nor Hilton could prove any overwhelming association with such widely used phrases. The phrases are hardly an indicator of their respective empires. And, seeing as these utterances long predate their sponsors, any mild association is the result of poor strategic decisions. If Trump wished to establish his own unique catch phrase, he should have thought of something unique. And if Paris hopes to capitalize on her own limited vocabulary, she should focus on something distinct. While a few businesses may be able to take advantage of the mild associations now established to these phrases, the slogans simply do not lend themselves to protection.

Clearly, intellectual property is an increasingly controversial subject. Should Verizon Wireless have exclusive rights to a phrase as generic as "Get more"? They undoubtedly should not. The only way to protect individual creative contributions is to limit their exploitation. While slogans are admittedly less inventive than most musical scores, software, and other intangible creations, they are nonetheless dependent on their creativity. The unique characteristics of a competitive market only further the cause for creative distinction and brand loyalty. As we have seen, the rights of the individual are not limited through the use of corporate trademark; they are fostered. And the preservation of strategic slogans is clearly justifiable from a market standpoint. We need only to protect this practice from preposterous proposals arising from vanity, greed, and publicity stunts. Creative invention of any kind is equally defendable. Our forefathers were warranted in their protective actions. As long as we distribute such rights with discretion, there is no reason corporations cannot continue to promise, to tempt, and to entertain with a language all their own. ◎/◎

Works Cited

Kramer, Irwin R. "The Donald's New Game of Trademark Monopoly: Can Trump Register the Rights to the Words 'You're Fired'?" Legal Commentary 29 March, 2004. Kramer & Connolly 23 April, 2004 http://www.kramerslaw.com/ trademark_law.htm.

United States Patent and Trademark Office. "Trademark, Copyright or Patent?" Basic Facts 8 November, 2004. 23 April, 2004 http://www.uspto.gov/web/offices/tac/doc/basic/ trade_defin.htm.

Reflections and Inquiries

1. Salha begins his argument by asking why trademarks of any kind should be dispensed. How does his response to this question prepare for his stance on Trump's and Hilton's rationale for their respective slogans?

2. According to Salha, the preservation of slogans benefits consumers and aids the corporations that trademark them. Do you agree? If so, would you also agree that the benefit would extend to the slogans Hilton and Trump were trying to trademark? Why or why not?

3. How, exactly, should we draw the line between a trademark that makes a "creative contribution" to commerce and one that does not?

Reading to Write

The next time you're in a supermarket, take note of as many trademarks as you can. Later, analyze them for their originality or distinctiveness. Which ones seem more original or distinctive (hence more deserving of trademark protection) Which ones seem less deserving? What criteria have you established to validate your assessment?

Issues for Further Research: Copyright Term Limits

Mouse Trap: Disney's Copyright Conquest | Jeffrey Rosen

Most people agree that while copyright protection is a good thing, it must be limited. As Jeffrey Rosen explains in the following essay, the framers of the Constitution understood how copyright monopolies could hinder the very creativity they were trying to protect. Nevertheless, Congress recently extended copyright protection from life of the author plus fifty years to life of the author plus seventy years. Such an extension benefits private-interest groups and their heirs by allowing them to continue to control materials, such as Walt Disney icons, that otherwise would be ready to enter the public domain. Jeffrey Rosen, the public affairs writer for the New Republic and a professor of law at George Washington University, weighs the consequences of such an extension.

Imagine this: While interviewing students for a documentary about inner-city schools, a filmmaker accidentally captures a television playing in the background, in which you can just make out three seconds of an episode of

---

Source: Jeffrey Rosen, "Mouse Trap: Disney's Copyright Conquest," *The New Republic,* 28 Oct. 2002: 12–14. Reprinted by permission.

"The Little Rascals." He can't include the interview in his film unless he gets permission from the copyright holder to use the three seconds of TV footage. After dozens of phone calls to The Hal Roach Studio, he is passed along to a company lawyer who tells him that he can include the fleeting glimpse of Alfalfa in his nonprofit film, but only if he's willing to pay $25,000. He can't, and so he cuts the entire scene.

Today every American who wants to use copyrighted material on his or her personal website—even in passing—is in the same position as the documentary filmmaker. And if the Supreme Court upholds the Copyright Term Extension Act of 1998, or the CTEA, these restrictions on free speech on the Internet will continue for decades to come. The act extended the copyright term for original works by 20 years—from the life of the author plus 50 years to the life of the author plus 70 years. This makes a vast number of films, photographs, and books from the 1920s and 1930s unavailable to the public for another generation. And this dramatic constriction of the public domain comes at a time when the Internet is making possible an explosion of creativity, as digital archives put film clips, MP3 files, and text on the Web. The Internet converts every reader into a potential publisher, enabling scholars, historians, or interested amateurs to put together innovative presentations about, for example, the politics and culture of the New Deal using clips of FDR and Woody Guthrie. If the CTEA remains in place, however, none of these clips can be posted unless their copyrights are cleared—an impossibility for the average Internet publisher, given the prohibitive expenses of tracking down each of the original copyright holders. The CTEA also prevents scholars from quoting works from the '20s and '30s on the Web because of the difficulty in obtaining permission. "If we lose, the burden on creating and restructuring content on the Internet will be extremely high for another generation," Stanford Law School's Lawrence Lessig told me after arguing the copyright case before the Supreme Court last week.

During oral arguments the Supreme Court seemed to understand that the CTEA was a naked giveaway to the heirs of Walt Disney, who persuaded Congress to extend copyright terms for their own private benefit. In 1998, after heavy lobbying by the Walt Disney Company—which feared the imminent return of Mickey Mouse and other copyrighted Disney icons to the public domain and with it the loss of lucrative licensing fees—Congress extended the copyright term for an additional 20 years. That's bad enough on its face. But before the Supreme Court, Lessig argued that upholding the CTEA would grant Congress the power to pass future retroactive copyright extensions to benefit wealthy special interests—making it possible for Disney's copyrights to be extended and re-extended perpetually. This, he argued, violates the plain language of the copyright clause of the Constitution, which grants Congress the power "to promote the Progress of Science" by securing authors the exclusive rights to their writings "for limited Times."

But although they recognized it as a bad law, Chief Justice William Rehnquist and his colleagues expressed skepticism about the constitutional basis for striking down this flamboyant piece of special interest legislation. "We've said there was a general grant" of power to Congress "and that Congress was free to run with it in many respects," Rehnquist told Lessig in an uncharacteristic burst of deference to Congress. In fact, the constitutional arguments against the CTEA are the same ones Rehnquist has made the centerpiece of his judicial legacy: that the Constitution grants Congress limited powers, which may only be exercised for carefully enumerated purposes. Seen in this light, the case for striking down the CTEA is actually stronger than the case for striking down the Violence Against Women Act, the Brady Bill, the Gun-Free School Zones Act, and other federal laws that Rehnquist and his conservative colleagues have held exceed Congress's enumerated powers. If the Court upholds the CTEA while continuing to strike down far less objectionable statutes in the name of limited federal government, Rehnquist's crusade to limit Congress's power will be clearly revealed to be based not on devotion to constitutional text and history but on the political and economic interests that a given law serves.

Lessig (who is my friend and has written for this magazine) argues that the   5
copyright clause, as originally understood, authorized Congress to grant an exclusive monopoly to authors and writers for a specific purpose: to promote creativity. The terms must be limited, the framers insisted, because they recognized that perpetual monopolies over creative works could inhibit creativity by preventing works from entering the public domain. (In contrast to today's life-plus-70-years copyright term, the original term in 1790 granted copyrights for only 14 years with the possibility of one optional 14-year extension.) At the Supreme Court argument, the justices seemed to agree that the CTEA will almost certainly inhibit far more creative speech than it promotes. By definition, as Justice Sandra Day O'Connor recognized, a retrospective copyright extension such as the CTEA *can't* encourage the creation of new works since it applies to works already in existence. And a prospective copyright extension that adds 20 years—long after the death of the author— adds only the most remote additional incentive for him to create during his lifetime: As Justice Stephen Breyer noted, for an 80-year-old composer like Verdi, the prospective of a few more pennies in royalties "an extra twenty years way down the pike" won't make a noticeable difference in spurring him on to finish *Otello*.

In Congress, defenders of the CTEA came up with only one argument for how the act might promote creativity. They testified that the act could encourage major studios to digitize hit films from the '20s and '30s by extending their economic value. But this argument is not convincing. As the head of The Hal Roach Studio—the leading restorer of *Laurel and Hardy* and other films from the '20s and '30s—argued in a principled brief that clashed with his financial interests, the CTEA extends the copyright for 19,000 films made between 1923 and 1942. Of these, only 5,000 continue to earn royalties, which means that the remaining 14,000 have little economic value but are of great historical interest. Many of these are "orphan" films whose copyright holders are very difficult to track down today. The CTEA makes restorations of such films economically prohibitive by requiring nonprofit restorers to hire private detectives to track down the lost copyright holders for the music, the credits, and so forth. As a result, the orphan films will continue to rot unwatched in the Library of Congress. And even if the CTEA actually did increase the incentive to restore these films, as Congress unconvincingly concluded, the preservation of 14,000 films hardly justifies the removal of more than 400,000 other creative works—books, poems, songs, and photographs—from the public domain.

In the hope of appealing to the conservative justices, Lessig argued that the text and original understanding of the copyright clause suggest that the CTEA is exactly the kind of special interest monopoly the framers of the Constitution meant to prohibit. The framers wanted to forbid the practice of sixteenth- and seventeenth-century English monarchs, who granted indefinite publishing monopolies to court favorites not to publish new works but to print existing classics—such as Shakespeare and Milton—that had long been enjoyed by the public. Like the Disney act, this raw political patronage suppressed speech that should be in the public domain. Parliament broke up these monopolies in 1710 by imposing term limits on copyrights; when the Constitution was drafted, the framers looked to the English example in specifying that copyrights could only be granted "for limited Times."

But far from being persuaded by Lessig's argument, Chief Justice Rehnquist suggested it was unprecedented. "Every morning," Lessig recalls, "I wake up with an image of the Chief Justice in my head saying, 'Well, counsel, maybe the fact that nobody raised this question for one hundred fifty years indicates that there is no issue here.'" But there are, Lessig notes, several reasons that no one has challenged retrospective copyright extensions in the past. In the eighteenth century "exclusive rights" in intellectual property meant only the right to print and publish. Today, by contrast, thanks to a vast expansion of copyright protections in 1976, a single copyright includes the right to control derivative works, public performances, and display rights. When copyright only regulated commercial publishers, there was no reason to object to a retrospective copyright extension because publishers, on balance, benefited from the extension more than they were harmed by it. By contrast, in the Internet age, every citizen is a potential publisher, and every publication on the Internet runs the risk of clashing with the tangle of rights that copyright law now protects. Today, a retrospective copyright extension benefits a handful of commercial publishers who hold the most valuable copyrights—such as Disney and AOL—but it harms the millions of citizens, scholars, librarians, and students who want to use historical material in ways that aren't commercially viable.

Another reason that nobody "raised this question" until now is Rehnquist's own judicial legacy. From the New Deal until 1995, the Supreme Court almost never struck down an act of Congress as exceeding Congress's constitutional powers. But beginning in 1995, thanks to Rehnquist's vision of limited federal government, the Supreme Court has dramatically switched course, striking down as many as 26 laws for exceeding Congress's enumerated powers. Many of these opinions were written by Rehnquist, such as the case in 1995 where he said that Congress had no power to pass the Gun-Free School Zones Act because it didn't "substantially affect" interstate commerce. In this and other opinions, Rehriquist was openly contemptuous of the very claim that the government is now pressing in the CTEA case: that Congress should have broad discretion to decide the limits of its own power.

Taking Rehnquist at his word, Lessig argues that the case against the CTEA 10 is far more powerful than the case for invalidating the Gun-Free School Zones Act or the Violence Against Women Act. The reason the Supreme Court got out of the business of striking down acts of Congress in the mid-twentieth century was that it presumed that economic interests could ordinarily fend for themselves in the political process. And there is no claim that champions of gun rights or opponents of federalizing state criminal law can't defend their own interests in Congress. But there is an undeniable case that the public interest isn't adequately represented in the political process when rich donors like Disney lobby Congress to milk their own copyrights for as long as possible. The CTEA is precisely the kind of special interest monopoly that judges throughout American history have invalidated as favoring private interests over the public interest.

By the same token, liberal justices such as Breyer and David Souter, who are ordinarily (and properly) skeptical of imposing limits on Congress's power, could vote to strike down the CTEA while continuing to object to the Court's decision to strike down federal laws under the commerce clause. The commerce clause of the Constitution has no explicit limits at all—it gives Congress the power to "regulate Commerce . . . among the several States"— while the copyright clause has explicit limitations: It gives Congress the power to grant exclusive rights "for limited Times" for the purpose of promoting creativity. Breyer and Souter could write an opinion saying that the Court should only enforce limits on Congress's power when the Constitution is explicit about those limits, as in this case.

Decades from now Rehnquist and his conservative colleagues will be remembered above all for their decisions restricting Congress's power. These decisions have been legitimately criticized for being based more on an abstract devotion to states' rights than on the text and history of the Constitution. Now the Court has before it a law that is constitutionally offensive on every level: It clashes with the explicit limits on Congress's power set out in the text and original understanding of the copyright clause, it represents a naked transfer of wealth to a handful of greedy heirs of pop-culture icons from the '20s, and it threatens to constrict public domain on the Internet for generations to come. If the Court sets limits on Congress's power in the context of commerce but not in the context of copyright, the only difference would be one of political perspective. If there ever were a case in which it makes sense to hope that the conservatives are true to their purported strict constructionist principles, this is it. ◉⃝◎

Reflections and Inquiries

1. What purpose does Rosen's opening anecdote serve?

2. What problems, according to Rosen, can arise if the CTEA is upheld?

3. According to Rosen, only one argument for how the CTEA could promote creativity was given. What is it, and why does Rosen reject it?

4. Rosen provides considerable background into the history of copyright legislation. What purpose does this historical information serve?

Reading to Write

Defend or challenge the value of the CTEA. Draw from Rosen's essay as well as from other articles you might come across having to do with copyright legislation.

Needed: Sane IP Laws │ Jason Brooks

What sorts of regulations are most appropriate for protecting intellectual property? Part of the problem is determining what kinds of IP should be protected and what kinds should not. In the following piece, Jason Brooks, a member of the eWeek editorial board, assesses the problem and offers a possible solution.

Intellectual property regulation in the United States is out of control. The thicket of legislation, policy and precedent through which we grant private monopolies on ideas has become, in many places, disconnected from its Constitutional mandate of promoting the progress of science and useful arts.

We've taken the U.S. patent system to task in this space previously, but equally suspect in our view is the DMCA (Digital Millennium Copyright Act). We take particular note of the provisions of the act that outlaw efforts to

---

circumvent the digital locks that content distributors place on their copy-righted works—even though no copyrights are infringed in the process.

The DMCA's anti-circumvention provisions have failed to reduce the unauthorized trafficking of copyrighted works on the Internet. Peer-to-peer networks are pumping as many bits as ever, and virtually all users who obtain unauthorized copies of content or software obtain those copies precracked. Worse than the DMCA's failures are its perverse successes. The law has been used as an anti-competitive bludgeon with which entrenched businesses have beaten back potential rivals with threats of lawsuits, which small businesses, developers and researchers cannot afford to combat.

For instance, Lexmark used the DMCA's anti-circumvention provisions to keep the printer cartridge refilling services of third-party rival Static Control Components off the market for 19 months before the much smaller company eventually prevailed in court. In addition, Adobe Systems used the DMCA to throw Russian programmer Dimitry Sklyarov in jail for daring to develop software that enabled blind people to access encrypted e-books with their screen readers. And, recently, fear of DMCA-driven retribution forestalled the outing of Sony's harmful CD rootkit DRM (digital rights management) scheme.

As if things weren't bad enough, there's talk of a new law, the Intellectual Property Protection Act of 2006, that would bolster the anti-circumvention provisions of the DMCA, expand government wiretapping and seizure pow-ers for investigating IP crime, and lengthen jail terms for noncommercial copyright infringement.

It's time to stop the multiplication of regulations designed to defend vested interests and return to the concept of individual rights. We call on enterprises and the IT vendors that serve them not only to stand against the Intellectual Property Protection Act of 2006 but also to work to repeal the DMCA's misguided anti-circumvention provisions. A good start would be to demand the resurrection of the Digital Media Consumers' Rights Act, which decriminalizes DRM circumvention for legal, noninfringing purposes. Technology freedoms are as important as other civil rights. The restrictions that the DMCA puts on these freedoms ought not to stand. ◎/◎

Reflections and Inquiries

1. Brooks begins his piece with the startling assertion that "intellectual property regulation in the United States is out of control." What evidence does he use to justify that claim?

2. What problems does Brooks have with the DMCA's anticircumvention provisions? How legitimate are these problems in your estimation?

3. Why does Brooks advocate resurrecting the Digital Media Consumers' Rights Act? Do you favor this move?

Reading to Write

Do some background reading on the Digital Millennium Copyright Act, the Intellectual Property Protection Act, and the Digital Media Consumers' Rights Act. Write an essay in which you determine which of these organizations takes the best approach to intellectual property regulation. Keep in mind that your goal is to encourage the other organizations to improve their approaches.

Issues for Further Research: Copyright Complexities

Changing Copyright | Negativland

Can there be a middle ground between rigid copyright laws prohibiting any kind of use of copyrighted material and the opposite extreme of doing away with such protection altogether? Negativland, a music and art collective, argues that there is. Whenever artists reuse copyrighted material in such a way as to create new works— what it calls "collage"—then that use should not constitute an infringement of copyright.

In an attempt to suggest a culturally sane solution to the continuing legal confrontations between owners of copyrighted cultural material and others who collage such material into new creations, we advocate a broadening of the copyright concept of Fair Use. We want the Fair Use statutes within copyright law to allow for a much broader variety of free, creative reuses of existing work whenever they are used in the creation of new work. The worldwide corporate assumption of private cultural ownership is now fencing off such timely artistic directions by using copyright law to assert that virtually any form of reuse without payment or permission is theft. From their economic point of view, cultural owners now use copyright law as a convenient shield from "direct reference" criticism, and a legal justification for total spin control and informational monopolization in the marketplace.

However, from an artistic point of view, it is ponderously delusional to try to paint all these new forms of fragmentary sampling as economically motivated "theft," "piracy," or "bootlegging." We reserve these terms for the unauthorized

---

Source: Negativland is an audio/video/radio/performance/activist group who have been making appropriation-based art since 1980 and have been sued twice because of their work. For more information about their current projects, please visit their website at www.negativland.com.

taking of whole works and reselling them for one's own profit. Artists who routinely appropriate, on the other hand, are not attempting to profit from the marketability of their subjects at all. They are using elements, fragments, or pieces of someone else's created artifact in the creation of a new one for artistic reasons. These elements may remain identifiable, or they may be transformed to varying degrees as they are incorporated into the new creation, where there may be many other fragments all in a new context, forming a new "whole." This becomes a new "original," neither reminiscent of nor competitive with any of the many "originals" it may draw from. This is also a brief description of collage techniques which have developed throughout this century, and which are universally celebrated as artistically valid, socially aware, and conceptually stimulating to all, it seems, except perhaps those who are "borrowed" from.

No one much cared about the centuries old tradition of appropriation in classical music as long as it could only be heard when it was played live in front of your ears. But now all music exists as a mass produced, saleable object, electronically frozen for all time, and seen by its owners to be in continuous, simultaneous economic competition with all other music. The previously interesting idea that someone's music might freely include some appropriated music of another has now been made into a criminal activity. This example is typical of how copyright laws now actually serve to inhibit or prevent the creative process, itself, from proceeding in certain interesting ways, both traditional and new.

This has become a pressing problem for creativity now because the creative technique of appropriation has jumped from the mediums in which it first appeared (principally in the visual fine arts of painting, printmaking, and sculpture) to popular, electronic mass distributed mediums such as photography, recorded music, and multimedia. The appearance of appropriation techniques in these more recent mass mediums have occasioned a huge increase in owner litigations of such appropriation based works because the commercial entrepreneurs who now own and operate mass culture are apparently intent on obliterating all distinctions between the needs of art and the needs of commerce. These owners of mass produced cultural material claim that similarly mass produced works of appropriation are a new and devastating threat to their total control over the exclusive profits which their properties might produce in the same mass marketplace. They claim that, art or not, an unauthorized appropriation of any kind cannot be allowed to directly compete in the appropriated material's avenue of commerce, as if they were equal in content, and equal in intent. The degree to which the unique nature and needs of art practice do not play any part in this thinking is more than slightly insane.

Consider the starkly stupid proposition that collage has now become 5 illegal in music unless the artist can afford to pay for each and every fragment he or she might want to use, as well as gain permission from each and every owner. Consider how this puts a stop to all independent, non-corporate forms of collage in music, and how those corporately funded collage works which can afford the tolls had better be flattering to the owner in their usage. Where does such a routine thwarting of common free expression lead to? Society does not thrive on commerce alone, and an enlightened one would have long ago established the legal primacy of artistic intent and authority to be at least equal to that of private commercial activities when these two social forces come to blows within our free market system. One feeds the mouth, but the other feeds the spirit, and either one without the other can only be seen as a form of societal decline. And if you don't think the overwhelming colonization and monopolization of creative formats by economic interests has had a debilitating effect on the very practice of creativity, you have already succumbed to that homogenized haze of inconsequence which commercial media surrounds us with day in and day out.

Because art is not defined as a business, yet must compete for economic survival in the business marketplace, we think certain legal priorities in the idea of copyright should be turned upside down. Specifically, a revision of the Fair Use statutes should throw the benefit of the doubt to artistic reuse and place the burden of proof on the owner/litigator. When a copyright owner wished to contend an unauthorized reuse of their property, they would have to show essentially that the usage does not result in anything new beyond the original work appropriated. However, if the new work is judged to significantly fragment, transform, rearrange, or recompose the appropriated material, and particularly does not use the entire work appropriated from, then it should be seen as a valid fair use—an original attempt at new art whether or not the result is successful and pleasing to the original artist, the owners of his or her work, or the court.

This would fully protect the owner's undisputed right not to be bootlegged, and it's *not* difficult to determine! Think of any past or present examples of unauthorized bootlegging, and any past or present examples of artistic appropriation, and you will find it is always perfectly obvious which is which. The difference between any kind of fragmentary transformation of existing work, and the unmanipulated presentation of whole works by others, which is required for successful bootlegging, would be as clear to courts and juries as it is to us. But this is precisely the crucial distinction in methodology which present law seems unwilling to acknowledge, thus throwing all kinds of valuable creative techniques and motivations into the same criminal hopper with economically motivated ripoffs. Both our courts and our corporations are now in the untenable position of assuming that once a work becomes a saleable object, that becomes its only significant role in society, and that role is the only one the law should be concerned with.

We acknowledge there are some complex difficulties in delineating exactly how fragmentary appropriation and esthetic motivation might be defined and allowed within revised Fair Use statutes. But awkward as that process may seem, we think that effort is possible. We presently see neither wisdom nor integrity in a set of laws that, except for very narrowly interpreted "fair use" allowances, simply ignores the validity, even the very existence of various established and valued art practices based on "direct referencing" (Surrealism for example) which have evolved through art formats of all kinds since the turn of this Century, yet do not necessarily fit within the Fair Use guidelines. Now it is implied that artists should actually strive to fit within the narrowly specified "Fair Use" government guidelines whenever attempting to use appropriated elements in new work. But when you become aware of the tiny sliver of specific artistic activity which Fair Use now allows, it doesn't take an artist to see that there is much more to be done with all the media influences which surround us. These ideas range far, wide, and weird, not always following the strictly defined "rules" of parody or carefully controlled commentary which the tiny tunnel of Fair Use statutes now provide for.

Please consider the ungenerous and uncreative logic we are overlaying our culture with. Artists will always be interested in sampling from existing cultural icons and artifacts precisely because of how they express and symbolize something potently recognizable about the culture from which both they and this new work spring. The owners of such artifacts and icons are seldom happy to see their properties in unauthorized contexts which may be antithetical to the way they are spinning them. Their kneejerk use of copyright restrictions to crush this kind of work now amounts to corporate censorship of unwanted independent work. Unlike the basic thrust of all the rest of U.S. law, copyright law actually assumes that all unauthorized uses are illegal until proven innocent, and any contested "fair use" always requires a legal defense, which remains beyond the financial grasp of most accused "infringers." This financial intimidation results in the vast majority of art appropriators caving in and settling out of court, their work being consigned to oblivion, and the "owners" having it all their way, including their expenses paid under the guise of "damages."

The question we want you to consider is this: Should those who might be 10 borrowed from have an absolute right to prevent any such future reuses of their properties, even when the reuse is obviously part of a new and unique work? Do we want to actually put all forms of free reuse under the heading of "theft" and criminalize a valuable art form such as collage—a form which may involve controversial social/cultural references and cannot operate true to its vision when permission is required? Present copyright prohibitions appear unable to appreciate the flow of the art forest because they are forever fixated on the money trees. One might say that Soviet Communism finally fell because it insisted on ignoring the human nature of its own citizens. Here in the land of the free, as well as everywhere else, it is basic to human nature to copy for our own creative purposes—in fact, it's how we got to this level of civilization. This ageless aspect of human creativity is nothing but desirable and need not be criminalized when the motive is to create new work.

The law must acknowledge the logical and inalienable right of artists, not publishers and manufacturers, to determine what new art will consist of. The current corporate control over our technologically based culture has an ominous feel to it because these private owners of our common cultural life have succeeded in removing the concept of culture from a pluralistic dispersement of esthetic ideas, born and realized by individual creative impulses, and given it over to fewer and fewer corporate committees of molders and marketers who are driven only by an overriding need to maintain an ever rising bottom line for their shareholders in the culture market. Is the admittedly pivotal role which society places on commerce really so unassailably useful when it begins to inhibit and channel the very direction of an "independent" art form, "allowing" it to evolve this way, but not that way? Is the role of Federal Law to serve the demands of private income, or to promote the public good through free cultural expression? Both?

Then the crux of the debate we hope to raise is how are we going to maintain reasonable forms of fair compensation for artists and their whole parasitic entourage of associated agents without inhibiting, stifling, or criminalizing perfectly healthy and valuable forms of independent music/art practice which arise out of new, enabling technology? We believe the promotion of artistic freedom should, for the first time, find a balanced representation with the purely commercial guidelines which now dominate copyright law.

Finally, this shift in the mental paradigm which now deifies all-encompassing private ownership must be forged and supported in all the little areas which now attend it. For instance, contract clauses between music labels and their artists which assert the label's exclusive right to market the artists' work could conceivably be renegotiated by fair use supporters to include the possibility of a subsequent fair use of the artist's work by anyone else. The clear and crucial distinction between bootlegging and fair uses, and the change in attitude towards the artistic legitimacy of Fair Use, should be reflected in the very legal documents of private enterprise which occasion all these lawsuits in the first place. Contracted artists who support Fair Use could begin demanding such clause adjustments in their contracts now, and in fact, this would be an interesting means for the traditionally "helpless" artist to actually begin affecting this artistically desirable change in our present legal system, as they are apparently the only people involved who are capable of putting art before profit, and no one else involved appears willing to push this convention challenging juggernaut into reality. ◎/◎

Reflections and Inquiries

1. According to Negativland, "cultural owners now use copyright law as a . . . legal justification for total spin control and informational monopolization in the marketplace." What do you suppose they mean by "spin control" and "informational monopolization of the marketplace"? Explain why you think such an accusation is valid or invalid.

2. What seems to be Negativland's major reason for wanting music collage freed of the restrictions of existing copyright laws?

3. What is "direct referencing"—for example, as used by Surrealist artists? How might this serve as an example of legitimate free use of copyrighted material?

Reading to Write

Examine examples of "collage" art (works of art that incorporate aspects of other works—for example, Andy Warhol's reuse of a Marilyn Monroe photograph for his own artistic purposes). Argue whether such appropriation of copyrighted art should fall under copyright protection.

Issues for Further Research: Plagiarism

The Rules of Attribution | Deborah R. Gerhardt

Ignorance of the law—including intellectual property law—is no excuse, as the cliché goes. For anyone who takes pen to paper (or fingers to keyboard)—students and professional authors alike—it pays to learn about the way intellectual property is protected. Using the case of Harvard undergraduate Kaavya Viswanathan, whose novel How Opal Mehta Got Kissed, Got Wild, and Got a Life *(published by Little, Brown in 2006) was shown to contain unattributed passages from two novels by Megan McCafferty, Deborah R. Gerhardt argues that existing copyright laws are counterintuitive and that teachers need to do more to clarify these laws if they want to prevent plagiarism. Part of the problem, it seems—and this is one of the points Gerhardt raises—has to do with the complexity of copyright law. Deborah Gerhardt is the director of copyright and scholarly communications at the University of North Carolina, Chapel Hill.*

Why do smart students commit plagiarism? Why would a top high-school writer—so accomplished that she would eventually attend Harvard—commit professional suicide by publishing text copied from another author's popular novel? In reading the gotcha press coverage on Kaavya Viswanathan's novel *How Opal Mehta Got Kissed, Got Wild, and Got a Life,* I can't help wondering how much Ms. Viswanathan knew about copyright infringement and plagiarism while she was writing. We don't send our high-school basketball stars onto the court without teaching them the rules of the game, but I fear that too often we send our high-school writing stars to college and graduate school without teaching them the academic and legal rules that govern their creative work.

Source: Deborah R. Gerhardt, "The Rules of Attribution," *Chronicle of Higher Education* 52, May 26 2006. Reprinted by permission of Deborah R. Gerhardt.

Ms. Viswanathan's book was inspired by two novels that resonated with her own experience: Megan McCafferty's *Sloppy Firsts* and *Second Helpings.* She readily admits to having read the novels three or four times. Many passages are so similar that last month the young novelist was accused of plagiarism and copyright infringement, and her public comments about those charges reflect genuine contrition and confusion. She told *The New York Times:* "All I really want to do is apologize to Ms. McCafferty. I don't want her to think I intended to cause her distress, because I admire her so much." This month she was accused of using content from another author's work as well.

In college basketball, the rules are not taught once during a brief orientation and then forgotten. They are repeatedly discussed as the season progresses. As we push young writers into the creative arena, the rules of the writing game should get the same attention. Plagiarism rules are not there just to deter literary thieves. They are codes of honor designed to nurture academic integrity by teaching students to honor the voices of others on the way to finding their own.

Copyright law cannot be understood without thoughtful reflection, because it contains many contradictions. Copyright protection is not supposed to extend to facts, ideas, or general plot lines, yet the copyright laws tell us that the right to create derivative works—for example, a movie from a novel—belongs exclusively to the author. Copyright laws provide broad protection for authors and publishers by assuring that their work will not be copied without compensation, yet they still permit fair use, such as copying excerpts for criticism, comment, or parody. Trying to define the scope of fair use can be a maddening endeavor, but we would serve our students well by at least alerting them to the known ends of the spectrum, to give them some compass to guide them in determining when and how they may use another's content.

We should not expect our students to absorb these complex rules on their own. If we stop to look at our cultural environment through the eyes of Ms. Viswanathan and her peers, we will see that the concepts of plagiarism and copyright are counterintuitive. Copying is essential to learning. When a toddler repeats a word, it is great cause for celebration. That same child will learn to write by copying letters seen in print. In high school and college, students memorize their lecture notes and redeliver this content back to professors on exams, often without the expectation of attribution. The ability to repeat back what they learned (generally without attribution) is richly rewarded.

We encourage our students to recycle objects and ideas they get from others. Discarding paper and plastic in appropriate receptacles has become a routine responsibility in our schools. Students create collages and sculptures from discarded items such as milk jugs and magazines. We assign them to groups to share ideas. We teach them that great writers recycled ideas they found in other great works. A high-school student will learn that Shakespeare brilliantly recast the plot of Tristan and Isolde to create Romeo and Juliet. She may also learn that Thomas Jefferson could not have drafted the Declaration of Independence without recasting the thoughts of other great philosophers such as John Locke. We would serve our students better if we enriched these lessons with discussions about plagiarism and copyright laws so our students would understand the principles that govern their work in different contexts. They need to learn that they can still work within those principles to create new works inspired by their creative heroes.

When the school day ends, students are inundated with an infinite quantity of recycled content in popular culture. They listen to music that uses famous riffs from other songs. They read books that are turned into movies, and then the characters from those movies appear on an endless array of products, such as breakfast cereals, clothing, toys, and video games. Most students do not know that it takes hours of negotiation and boxes of trademark and copyright licenses to make all this borrowing appear so seamless. The recording industry's lawsuits against students who pirate digital music may have taught our students that copying an entire work can get them in trouble. We must alert our students to the reality that sometimes copyright laws also prohibit copying smaller portions of a work.

It is quite possible—and I believe likely—that Ms Viswanathan's editors and advisers pushed her to write and publish without first taking the time to explain to her the basic principles of plagiarism and copyright. Much of the alleged copying in her work is not verbatim lifting but the creative recycling of ideas. The rules of what can be borrowed and when attribution must be given are complex and require vigilant attention. She confessed to *The New York Times:* "I feel as confused as anyone about it, because it happened so many times." It is so unfortunate to see a promising young writer taken out of the game because she did not understand the rules. My hope is that this incident will motivate parents and educators to remember that creative work has its rules, and if they want to stay in the game, our students should know them. ◎/◎

Reflections and Inquiries

1. According to Gerhardt, what can teachers learn from basketball coaches in teaching students about plagiarism?

2. What makes copyright law so difficult to understand? What strategy might teachers use to get around this problem?

3. If "copying is essential to learning," as Gerhardt points out, why do you suppose plagiarism is such a serious offense?

Reading to Write

Locate three or four additional articles on plagiarism, then write an essay in which you distinguish between fair use of existing ideas (e.g., taking a well-known plot such as that of *The Wizard of Oz*, either in L. Frank Baum's book (1900), or the 1925 or 1939 Hollywood film adaptations, and using it as the basis for an "original" work, such as Gregory Maguire's novel, *Wicked: The Life and Times of the Wicked Witch of the West* (HarperCollins, 1995).

Rule No. 1: Don't Copy | Lisa Takeuchi Cullen

We always hear about plagiarism among students, but these days we also commonly hear about plagiarism committed by published authors and corporate executives, such as the CEO of the defense contractor Raytheon. In the following news story, Lisa Takeuchi Cullen explains how the cribbing was uncovered. The question remains, however, What would motivate the leader of a multibillion dollar corporation—one so concerned with ethical conduct that it published a rulebook for its employees—to violate such a rule himself? Lisa Takeuchi Cullen, a staff writer for Time *and its Tokyo correspondent, has reported on a wide range of contemporary issues such as resumé padding, plastic surgery among Asians, and the way that corporations have been overcoming gender biases to make fuller use of the talents of their female employees. She is the author of* Remember Me: A Lively Tour of the New American Way of Death *(HarperCollins, 2006).*

The CEO of Raytheon became a management guru with his book of maxims. How he missed a key one.

At first, William Swanson tried to shrug off the discovery that 16 of the rules in his handy and much acclaimed booklet Swanson's Unwritten Rules of Management had been ripped off from an obscure engineering work published more than 60 years ago. Then, when it turned out that other rules had been lifted from the precepts of Defense Secretary Donald Rumsfeld and humorist Dave Barry, the episode became a full-blown public relations disaster for the CEO of Raytheon, a defense contractor based in Waltham, Mass., that has 80,000 employees and more than $22 billion in annual sales. By last week a chastened Swanson apologized at the annual shareholders' meeting, and Raytheon's board docked him the equivalent of $1 million out of a pay package that amounted to $7 million in 2005—a rare move in the chummy world of corporate governance.

How did that happen to Swanson and his collection of folksy phrasings and spot-on aphorisms, which was first published in 2004 and given out free to Raytheon employees before it found a wide and enthusiastic audience that included Warren Buffett and Jack Welch? Credit goes to Carl Durrenberger, a San Diego engineer, who was packing up his cubicle at Hewlett-Packard to move to another division when he came across a copy of a 1944 chestnut given him by a former boss: *The Unwritten Laws of Engineering* by W.J. King.

He flipped through it, smiling at the dated language. Days later, he read a *USA Today* article online about Swanson and his rules. A memory flashed. He swiveled his chair to a box he had yet to unpack and fished out the King manual. Looking at the article and the manual side by side, Durrenberger, 29, was "flabbergasted" to note that 16 of Swanson's 33 rules were in fact King's—rusty lingo and all. "Bill Swanson of Raytheon is a plagiarist!" Durrenberger blasted on his blog.

Add Swanson's tale to this year's ledger of fakery and its fallout. RadioShack CEO David Edmondson resigned over a tarted-up résumé. Harvard sophomore Kaavya Viswanathan has been roasted for her cribbed chick-lit novel. But Raytheon is a major government contractor that sells missiles, not stereos, and Swanson is a big boss, not a teenage undergrad. Still, he insists it all began with an innocent mix-up. Swanson asked staff members to compile a presentation from materials he kept in a file. It was such a hit that he and his staff collected 33 "rules"—one for each of his years at Raytheon—and began disseminating them in a 76-page booklet. "It's clear to me now that this file contained Professor King's book as well as other published material," Swanson says.

A little fumble like that may seem inconsequential in a field known for heavier-weight scandals. But because the defense industry—and corporations in general—is under greater public scrutiny these days, CEOs tend to pay for their blunders. Last year Boeing fired its CEO for having an affair with a subordinate—certainly a lesser infraction than the military procurement scandal that claimed his predecessor, Phil Condit, who, although not personally implicated, left because it happened on his watch. Swanson succeeds a CEO who agreed in March to settle with the Securities and Exchange Commission over accounting irregularities. But there's nothing phony about Raytheon's record under Swanson. Sales grew 8% last year; the stock price and profits have soared. Whatever rules he follows there are working.

Nonetheless, the ethical transgression of a top executive can have powerful repercussions. "If I were a board member or a shareholder, it would raise questions in my mind about how honest, transparent and responsible a CEO is being in other dealings," says Andy Wicks, co-director of the University of Virginia's Olsson Center for Applied Ethics. Jeffrey Sonnenfeld of the Yale School of Management points to the tarnish Swanson leaves on Raytheon, which the CEO had "no problem using as a bully pulpit from which to trumpet his empty clichés."

Lost in all this are the plagiarized. King died two decades ago, but his book remains a best seller for the American Society of Mechanical Engineers, its publisher. Rumsfeld had no comment. As for Barry, whose observation about being nice to waiters was lifted, the whole episode leaves him feeling weirdly connected to the Secretary of Defense—and a bit nervous. "I hope when they build their missiles, they're a little more careful about where they get their information," he says. "Because if they're getting any of that from me—well, if we ever launch anything, it'll land in Vancouver."

Reflections and Inquiries

1. What rationale did Swanson give for having allegedly plagiarized from other sources for his rule book? How valid is such a rationale?

2. Why, according to Takeuchi Cullen, was Swanson's plagiarism so much more serious than that of Kaavya Viswanathan? Do you agree or disagree, and why?

3. Was the fine imposed on Swanson by Rayethon's board of directors appropriate or sufficient, in your opinion? Why or why not?

Reading to Write

Investigate other examples of corporate plagiarism (you might start with the "tarted-up" resume of RadioShack CEO David Edmondson that Takeuchi Cullen mentions), and write an essay in which you argue the seriousness or the probable root causes of this problem.

Connections Among the Clusters

1. Suggest ways in which restrictions on music downloading could have an impact on other kinds of Internet media such as articles and books or material from web pages. See Cluster 3, Media Regulation.

2. How might intellectual property laws help or hinder minorities or economically disadvantaged peoples globally? (See Cluster 4, Multicultural Learning.) For example, should students in third-world countries be permitted to download materials that would otherwise require payment? Why or why not?

3. What potential national security issues, if any, might arise if certain kinds of information, such as information about explosives, were freely available on the Web? What measures should or should not be taken in light of this potential security problem? See Cluster 5, National Security.

Writing Projects

1. Write an essay on the role that ethics should play, if any, in determining intellectual property policy.

2. Are U.S. copyright laws fair or unfair? Write an essay in which you take a stance, but in which you also give careful consideration to views that challenge your own.

3. Take a stance on Internet music downloading in light of your views regarding intellectual property. That is, to what degree should recording artists and composers retain copyright protection for their creative works in light of the public's right to free access to music?

Suggestions for Further Reading

Brinson, J. Dianne, and Mark F. Radcliffe. "An Intellectual Property Law Primer for Multimedia and Web Developers." http://www.eff.org/CAF/law/ip-primer.

Grantz, John, and Jack B. Rochester. *Pirates of the Digital Millennium: How the Intellectual Property Wars Damage Our Personal Freedom, Our Jobs, and the World Economy.* Upper Saddle River, NJ: Financial Times/Prentice-Hall, 2004.

Harris, Lesley. *Digital Property: Currency of the Twenty-First Century.* New York: McGraw-Hill, 1998.

Karoun, Dimirjian. "What Is the Price of Plagiarism? *Christian Science Monitor* 52; 11, May 2006.

Klein, Julia. "Plagiarism and Other Unoriginal Sins." *Chronicle of Higher Education* 52; 11, Nov. 2005.

Lessig, Lawrence. *The Future of Ideas: The Fate of the Commons in a Connected World.* New York: Vintage, 2001.

Litman, Jessica. *Digital Copyright.* New York: Prometheus, 2001.

Lohr, Steve. "Fighting the Idea That All the Internet Is Free." *New York Times* 9 Sept. 2003: C1.

Merges, Robert P. *Intellectual Property in the New Technological Age,* 3rd ed. New York: Aspen Publishers, 2003.

National Research Council Staff. *The Digital Dilemma: The Future of Intellectual Property in the Information Infrastructure.* Washington: National Academy P, 2000.

Shulman, Seth. *Owning the Future.* Boston: Houghton Mifflin, 1999.

"Suing the Music Downloaders." Editorial. *New York Times* 12 Sept. 2003: A26.

Media Regulation: What Are the Issues?

Introduction

Issues of censorship are interwoven with issues of individual freedom, as well as of freedom of speech and the press, which are protected by the First Amendment to the Constitution. But is there ever such a thing as too much free speech? Few would agree that yelling "Fire!" in a crowded theater without there being a fire is merely the exercise of one's First Amendment rights. In certain cases, such as this one, "speech" as it is normally defined is not being exercised at all, but is rather a false alarm that can cause panic and physical injury. The question then arises, Where does one draw the line? Should inflammatory ("hate") speech or works such as *Mein Kampf* or *The Turner Diaries*, both of which advocate white supremacy at all costs, including genocidal war, be banned? After all, the latter book was in the possession of Timothy McVeigh, the convicted Oklahoma City terrorist bomber, although it was never determined that its ideas significantly influenced his decision to blow up the Murrah Federal Building, killing 168 men, women, and children. Again, where does one draw the line between "speaking one's mind" about, say, a public official's allegedly poor performance and defaming that person (a legitimate basis for a lawsuit)? Should students or faculty be permitted to communicate ideas and opinions that most people would consider offensive? The selections in this cluster consider how the First Amendment's guarantee of freedom of speech should be applied, whether violence in the media should be regulated, and the rationale behind banning or "sanitizing" certain books.

How Should the First Amendment's Freedom of Speech Guarantee Be Applied?

Internet and Censorship (editorial cartoon) | Patrick Chappatte

Internet censorship works in two ways: Certain materials can be filtered beforehand, or given the fact that government agencies can spy on what Internet users' access, users

Source: © Chappatte in *International Herald Tribune*, www.globecartoons.com.

censor themselves. Some would argue that both kinds of censorship violate First Amendment rights, although certain kinds of Internet censorship are good things. For example, public libraries add filters to protect children from accessing potentially harmful websites, and government agencies should keep track of anyone using the Internet to, say, organize a terrorist attack. But the old question always surfaces: Where do we draw the line between warranted protection and abuse of individual liberties? Chappatte's cartoon suggests that the latter is becoming more common than the former. Patrick Chappatte's editorial cartoons appear in Le Temps, Neue Zürcher Zeitung, *and the* International Herald Tribune.

Reflections and Inquiries

1. Comment on the expressions on the characters' faces. How do they tie in with the theme of the cartoon?

2. How does the cartoon influence, if at all, your stance on Internet surveillance in the name of combating terrorism?

Reading to Write

1. Study the following cartoon by Chappatte in which an association between terrorism and the Internet is made. Write an essay in which you reflect on the seriousness of Internet terrorism and whether the National Security Association should spy on citizens for possible terrorist uses on the Internet.

   Patrick Chappatte, "Terrorists and the Internet," 21 Dec. 2005 http://www.globecartoon.com. (Search "Internet" and then look for date.)

2. Read the following interview with Patrick Chappatte, "Letting you draw your own conclusions":

International Herald Tribune 9 Feb. 2006 (http://
www.globecartoon.com/caricat.iht060209.html).

Write an essay in which you agree or disagree with Chappatte's views against
censorship of religiously or ethnically sensitive material, such as the
Mohammad cartoons in a Danish newspaper.

Speech Overview | Rodney Smolla

*Whenever free speech seems threatened, people quickly invoke the First Amendment,
which guarantees that no law shall infringe on each citizen's right to free speech.
In the following article, Rodney Smolla, dean of the University of Richmond's School
of Law, provides a detailed explanation of the implications of the First Amendment
and of why it protects speech (including images) considered to be hateful, anti-
American, or even criminal.*

The First Amendment to the Constitution of the United States declares that
"Congress shall make no law . . . abridging the freedom of speech." What
does and should this mean? Justice Oliver Wendell Holmes, in his famous
Abrams v. United States (1919) dissenting opinion, began what may be the sin-
gle most poetic paragraph ever written by a Supreme Court justice on the
meaning of freedom of speech. Here is that improbable opening line:
"Persecution for the expression of opinions seems to me perfectly logical."
What could Holmes have been thinking?

Perhaps Holmes was expressing the view that all of us, individually and collectively, have within us a kind of censorship-impulse. Governments are especially prone to censor. As Holmes went on to put it: "If you have no doubt of your
premises or your power and want a certain result with all your heart you naturally express your wishes in law and sweep away all opposition." Censorship is
thus a kind of social instinct. As caring and responsible citizens of society, *especially* good and decent citizens of a good and decent society, we are likely to want
many results with all our hearts. We want security, we want freedom from fear, we
want order, civility, racial and religious tolerance, we want the well-being of our
children. We want these things with all our hearts, and when others express opinions that seem to threaten these aspirations, who can blame us for being tempted
to express our wishes in law and sweep away the opposition? It is perfectly logical. And that is what, at bottom, freedom of speech is all about.

Over the course of roughly the last 50 years the U.S. Supreme Court has
set our nation on a remarkable experiment, often construing the First
Amendment in a manner that strenuously defies the natural and logical

---

Source: "Speech Overview" by Rodney Smolla, Dean, University of Richmond School of
Law, August 2003. Reprinted by permission of the author.

impulse to censor. In scores of decisions, the Supreme Court has interpreted the First Amendment in a manner that to most of the world seems positively radical. Those decisions are numerous and cover a vast and various terrain, but consider some highlights. Americans have the right to:

- Desecrate the national flag as a symbol of protest.
- Burn the cross as an expression of racial bigotry and hatred.
- Espouse the violent overthrow of the government as long as it is mere abstract advocacy and not an immediate incitement to violence.
- Traffic in sexually explicit erotica as long as it does not meet a rigorous definition of "hard core" obscenity.
- Defame public officials and public figures with falsehoods provided they are not published with knowledge of their falsity or reckless disregard for the truth.
- Disseminate information invading personal privacy if the revelation is deemed "newsworthy."
- Engage in countless other forms of expression that would be outlawed in many nations but are regarded as constitutionally protected here.

Such First Amendment decisions reject the impulse to censor; they are therefore striking as legal doctrines. Perhaps more striking, however, is that these decisions have gained widespread currency within American culture as a whole. The Supreme Court is not alone in its commitment to the free-speech project. While undoubtedly any one decision will often be controversial with the public, which may be deeply divided on topics such as flag-burning or sex on the Internet, on balance what is extraordinary about the evolution of freedom of speech in America over the last 50 years is that it has taken such a strong hold on the American consciousness, a hold that seems to cut across party labels such as "Democrat" or "Republican" or ideological labels such as "liberal" or "conservative." On the Supreme Court itself, for example, justices with hardy conservative credentials such as Antonin Scalia or Clarence Thomas have often been as committed to expansive protection for freedom of speech as justices famous for their liberal views, such as William Brennan or Thurgood Marshall. Appointees of Republican presidents, such as Anthony Kennedy or David Souter, have been as stalwart as appointees of Democratic presidents, such as Stephen Breyer or Ruth Bader Ginsburg, in their articulation of strong free-speech doctrines. So too, in the political arena, views on free-speech issues often do not track along traditional party lines or classic ideological divisions.

This is not to say that in some simplistic sense everybody in America 5 believes in freedom of speech, and certainly it is not to say that everybody in America believes that freedom of speech means the same thing. But it is to say that in a sense both deep and wide, "freedom of speech" is a value that has become powerfully internalized by the American polity. Freedom of speech is a core American belief, almost a kind of secular religious tenet, an article of constitutional faith.

How do we account for the modern American reverence for freedom of speech? Why is this value so solidly entrenched in our constitutional law, and why is it so widely embraced by the general public? Over the years many philosophers, historians, legal scholars and judges have offered theoretical justifications for strong protection of freedom of speech, and in these justifications we may also find explanatory clues.

An obvious starting point is the direct link between freedom of speech and vibrant democracy. Free speech is an indispensable tool of self-governance in a democratic society. Concurring in *Whitney v. California* (1927), Justice Louis Brandeis wrote that "freedom to think as you will and to speak as you think are means indispensable to the discovery and spread of political truth."

On a communal level, free speech facilitates majority rule. It is through talking that we encourage consensus, that we form a collective will. Whether the answers we reach are wise or foolish, free speech helps us ensure that the answers usually conform to what most people think. Americans who are optimists (and optimism is a quintessentially American characteristic) additionally believe that, over the long run, free speech actually *improves* our political decision-making. Just as Americans generally believe in free markets in economic matters, they generally believe in free markets when it comes to ideas, and this includes politics. In the long run the best test of intelligent political policy is its power to gain acceptance at the ballot box.

On an individual level, speech is a means of participation, the vehicle through which individuals debate the issues of the day, cast their votes, and actively join in the process of decision-making that shape the polity. Free speech serves the individual's right to join the political fray, to stand up and be counted, to be an active player in the democracy, not a passive spectator.

Freedom of speech is also an essential contributor to the American belief   10 in government confined by a system of checks and balances, operating as a restraint on tyranny, corruption and ineptitude. For much of the world's history, governments, following the impulse described by Justice Holmes, have presumed to play the role of benevolent but firm censor, on the theory that the wise governance of men proceeds from the wise governance of their opinions. But the United States was founded on the more cantankerous revolutionary principles of John Locke, who taught that under the social compact sovereignty always rests with the people, who never surrender their natural right to protest, or even revolt, when the state exceeds the limits of legitimate authority. Speech is thus a means of "people-power," through which the people may ferret out corruption and discourage tyrannical excesses.

Counter-intuitively, influential American voices have also often argued that robust protection of freedom of speech, *including speech advocating crime and revolution*, actually works to make the country more stable, increasing rather than decreasing our ability to maintain law and order. Again the words of Justice Brandeis in *Whitney v. California* are especially resonant, with his admonition that the framers of the Constitution "knew that order cannot be secured merely through fear of punishment for its infraction; that it is hazardous to discourage thought, hope and imagination; that fear breeds repression; that repression breeds hate; that hate menaces stable government; that the path of safety lies in the opportunity to discuss freely supposed grievances and proposed remedies; and that the fitting remedy for evil counsels is good ones." If a society as wide-open and pluralistic as America is not to explode from festering tensions and conflicts, there must be valves through which citizens with discontent may blow off steam. In America we have come to accept the wisdom that openness fosters resiliency, that peaceful protest displaces more violence than it triggers, and that free debate dissipates more hate than it stirs.

The link between speech and democracy certainly provides some explanation for the American veneration of free speech, but not an entirely satisfying or complete one. For there are many flourishing democracies in the world, but few of them have adopted either the constitutional law or the cultural traditions that support free speech as expansively as America does. Moreover, much of the vast protection we provide to expression in America seems to bear no obvious connection to politics or the democratic process at all. Additional explanation is required.

Probably the most celebrated attempt at explanation is the "marketplace of ideas" metaphor, a notion that is most famously associated with Holmes' great dissent in *Abrams*, in which he argued that "the best test of truth is the power of the thought to get itself accepted in the competition of the market." The marketplace of ideas metaphor does not posit that truth *will* emerge from the free trade in ideas, at least not instantly. That would be asking too much. It merely posits that free trade in ideas is the best *test* of truth, in much the same way that those who believe in laissez-faire economic theory argue that over the long haul free economic markets are superior to command-and-control economies. The American love of the marketplace of ideas metaphor stems in no small part from our irrepressible national optimism, the American "constitutional faith" that, given long enough, good will conquer evil. As long as this optimism is not blind naiveté, but is rather a motive force that encourages us to keep the faith in the long view of history, it can be a self-fulfilling prophecy. Just as we often have nothing to fear but fear, hope is often our best hope. Humanity may be fallible, and truth illusive, but the hope of humanity lies in its faith in progress. The marketplace metaphor reminds us to take the long view. Americans like to believe, and largely *do* believe, that truth has a stubborn and incorrigible persistence. Cut down again and again, truth will still not be extinguished. Truth will out, it will be rediscovered and rejuvenated. It will prevail.

The connection of freedom of speech to self-governance and the appeal of the marketplace of ideas metaphor still, however, do not tell it all. Freedom of speech is linked not merely to such grandiose ends as the service of the democracy or the search for truth. Freedom of speech has value on a more personal and individual level. Freedom of speech is part of the human personality itself, a value intimately intertwined with human autonomy and dignity. In the words of Justice Thurgood Marshall in the 1974 case *Procunier v. Martinez*, "The First Amendment serves not only the needs of the polity but also those of the human spirit—a spirit that demands self-expression."

Many Americans embrace freedom of speech for the same reasons they 15 embrace other aspects of individualism. Freedom of speech is the right to defiantly, robustly and irreverently speak one's mind just because it is one's mind. Freedom of speech is thus bonded in special and unique ways to the human capacity to think, imagine and create. Conscience and consciousness are the sacred precincts of mind and soul. Freedom of speech is intimately linked to freedom of thought, to that central capacity to reason and wonder, hope and believe, that largely defines our humanity.

If these various elements of our culture do in combination provide some insight into why freedom of speech exerts such a dominating presence on the American legal and cultural landscape, they do not by any means come close to explaining the intense and seemingly never-ending legal and cultural debates over the *limits* on freedom of speech.

There *are* limits. The major labor of modern First Amendment law is to articulate the points at which those limits are reached. This ongoing process is often contentious and difficult, and no one simple legal formula or philosophical principle has yet been discovered that is up to the trick of making the job easy. Americans thus continue to debate in political forums and litigate in legal forums such issues as the power of society to censor offensive speech to protect children, the power to arrest speakers spreading violent or hateful propaganda for fear that it will foment crime or terrorism, the permissibility of banning speech that defeats protection of intellectual property, the propriety of curbing speech to shelter personal reputation and privacy, the right to restrict potitical contributions and expenditures to reduce the influence of money on the political process, and countless other free-speech conflicts.

Yet while the country continues to struggle mightily to define the limits and continues to debate vigorously the details, there is surprisingly little struggle and debate over the core of the faith. Americans truly *do* embrace the central belief that freedom of thought, conscience and expression are numinous values, linked to our defining characteristics as human beings. While limits must exist, American culture and law approach such limits with abiding caution and skepticism, embracing freedom of speech as a value of transcendent constitutional importance. ◎/◎

Reflections and Inquiries

1. How does Smolla, by way of Oliver Wendell Holmes, explain the impulse to censor?

2. Smolla calls attention to First Amendment Supreme Court decisions within the last fifty years that "strenuously def[y]" the natural impulse to censor. By what line of reasoning have such activities as hate speech, disseminating information invading personal privacy, or flag burning become worthy of First Amendment protection? Do you challenge any of these rulings, and if so, why?

3. Explain the rationale behind the analogies Smolla makes between freedom of speech and democracy and between freedom of speech and a market economy.

4. The framers of the Constitution, Justice Brandeis wrote in *Whitney v. California*, understood "that it is hazardous to discourage thought." Explain.

Reading to Write

Should there be constraints of some kind on the exercise of free speech? In other words, is there a legitimate basis for censoring certain kinds of speech in special cases? Why or why not? Present your argument in an essay, making sure that you illustrate with cases in point and that you fairly represent and challenge dissenting views.

Campus Speech Issues | Martin P. Golding

Perhaps the trickiest part of settling freedom-of-speech issues is deciding what exactly constitutes "speech." Should the freedom to yell "Fire!" in a crowded theater be protected by the First Amendment when there is no fire? Is it unconstitutional for airport security to prohibit joking about firearms when passing through the metal detectors? Well, then, some would argue, why should Ku Klux Klan members or sympathizers retain their right to speak? Isn't it true that racist speech is tantamount to a physical assault on some people?

Some argue that college communities should adopt speech codes that would ensure a comfortable learning environment for all students. Others counter that students be able to speak their minds and learn to deal with audience reactions, for that is how learning takes place. In the opening chapter of his book, Free Speech on Campus, *Martin P. Golding, a professor of philosophy and of law at Duke University, examines the rationale behind college speech codes.*

Source: Martin P. Golding, "Campus Speech Issues," Ch. 1: *Free Speech on Campus.* Rowman & Littlefield, 2000: 1–13. Reprinted by permission.

From time to time, the Congress of the United States has considered an amendment to the Constitution that would allow Congress and the states to prohibit the physical desecration of the American flag. Were the amendment to be approved (it would need the vote of two-thirds of each House and three-fourths of the states), it would have the effect of reversing the decision of the Supreme Court in the case of *Texas v. Johnson* (491 U.S. 397 [1989]), which held that a statute designed to protect the flag violated the free speech provision of the First Amendment: "Congress shall make no law . . . abridging the freedom of speech or of the press. . . ." Gregory Johnson had burned a flag in protest at the 1984 Republican National Convention. Yet as Justice William J. Brennan wrote:

> If there is a bedrock principle underlying the First Amendment, it is that the Government may not prohibit the expression of an idea simply because society finds the idea itself offensive or disagreeable.

The Court's decision was met with a great deal of outrage, for as the Court itself recognized, the flag is the "unique" symbol of national unity. Hence the move by Congress to reverse the decision.

This so far unsuccessful move has been met by opposition, much of it coming from people who revere the flag and deplore its desecration. They see the proposal as contrary to the "bedrock principle," perhaps just the thin edge of the wedge toward eroding an essential American freedom. It is somewhat ironic, though, that a number of these same people have no hesitation in supporting campus speech codes. While there may be a difference between a government's restriction of the expression of an idea and a college's or university's imposition of a speech code (a difference that evaporates in the case of a public institution), there clearly is some dissonance here. A double standard seems to be at work. But there are complications. Many people may be more resentful of the government's attempts to restrict free speech than a university's.

A university is more of a special-purpose institution, and restrictions on expression, it is sometimes argued, fit in with its aims: restrictions on speech are necessary to promote a "comfortable learning environment." The airing of certain ideas is therefore acceptable, while airing others that are offensive to one or another group is not. Some proponents of speech codes insist that it is not the ideas in the abstract that are of concern so much as "verbal behavior" that may cause hurt. The simplistic old adage, "Sticks and stones may break my bones, but names will never harm me," is rejected. The proscription of certain offensive and disagreeable ideas, or the mode of their expression, is therefore appropriate. Or so it is maintained.

While speech codes have varied in details, these interrelated arguments or sentiments seem to be basic considerations. Another related claim is that punishing "hate speech" teaches people that racism or other prejudice is unacceptable and can bring about tolerance and sensitivity.[1] A school's failure to institute a speech code, it is sometimes said, is tantamount to an endorsement of bigotry and racism. It has also been claimed that the Fourteenth Amendment ("nor shall any State . . . deny to any person within its jurisdiction the equal protection of the laws") mandates that students be protected from demeaning and denigrating speech if they are to be—and feel—equal on campus.[2] At perhaps a lesser level, it has been argued that some Supreme Court opinions legitimize prohibition of certain forms of offensive speech.[3] Whether arguments for speech codes can be sustained is something we examine later.

In line with the above considerations and claims, three basic models of codes have been noted: the fighting words approach, the emotional distress theory, and the nondiscrimination/harassment option.[4] (1) "Fighting words" were forbidden as student misconduct by a University of California code. These are defined as personally abusive epithets inherently likely to provoke a violent reaction whether or not they actually do so, and they constitute harassment when they create a hostile and intimidating educational environment. (2) A University of Texas at Austin code made it a university offense to engage in racial harassment, defined as "extreme or outrageous acts or communications that are intended to harass, intimidate or humiliate a student or students on account of race, color or national origin and that reasonably cause them to suffer severe emotional stress." (3) A third type of code emphasizes "discriminatory harassment." Thus, a proposed code at the University of Massachusetts would have made it a violation for any member of the university community to engage in verbal or physical conduct that the targeted individual or group "would find discriminatorily alters the conditions" for participation in the activities of the university, on the basis of race, color, and national or ethnic origin. The third approach seems the most commonly used, but they all overlap in extent.

Of course, a public college or university, as an agency of government, is required to conform to the provisions of the First Amendment. It is to such an institution that Justice Brennan's bedrock principle applies. In a number of important instances campus speech codes have been struck down by the courts.[5] Private institutions are in a different situation, however. They have more leeway in enacting speech codes.[6] Furthermore, one can easily imagine a church-connected college imposing a speech and conduct code that prohibits on-campus expressions that do not conform to its official beliefs and practices (e.g., opposition to abortion). The courts probably could not disallow such a code, for that may interfere with another First Amendment right, the school's right of "free exercise" of religion.

The similarities and differences that obtain among public, private, and church-connected colleges and universities suggest a broad topic for analysis: the aims of institutions of higher learning. For it is in the context of these aims that arguments for and against campus speech codes take place. Obviously, the topic is too large for full treatment here, but it cannot be avoided entirely. For we are concerned, as it were, with the "constitution" of institutions of higher learning and the extent to which it does contain, or ought to contain, something like Justice Brennan's bedrock principle. . . .

Also, although the bedrock principle of the First Amendment applies head-on only to public institutions, there is much to be gleaned from some of the debate over how far it reaches. The fact is that not all kinds of speech are constitutionally protected, for instance, obscene speech and terrorist threats. Analogies to free speech jurisprudence are frequently found in the speech code literature, even in the case of nonpublic colleges and universities, many of which proclaim their commitment to principles of freedom of expression and inquiry. That they are found is hardly surprising. While George Washington did not receive the Ten Amendments on Mount Vernon, they nevertheless are as close to being our civil religion as anything. So although the First Amendment applies only to governments and their agencies, we often encounter the complaint of people who have been suspended from a private institution, because of an opinion they have expressed, that their right of free speech has been violated.

The issue of free speech on campus is broader than that of speech codes alone. Speech codes are typically directed at students. Academic freedom, on the other hand, is a concept that applies, first of all, to the corporate, institutional autonomy of a university or college, its freedom to determine who shall teach, who shall be admitted, and what shall be taught. Most importantly, however, it refers to the freedom of the individual faculty member to express his or her views (however unpopular with the trustees or college administration) on extramural matters, e.g., on questions of general or local politics, and freedom from reprisal for positions taken.[7] In this respect, the term refers to free speech "off campus," as it were, though such expression might occur on the campus. The status of tenure is regarded as vital to protect this aspect of academic freedom. In fact, many faculty members do not have tenure, and their protection derives from the respect for academic freedom maintained by the intellectual culture of the university.[8]

In another sense of the term, "academic freedom" is associated with the 10 university as a marketplace of ideas and the free speech provision of the university's constitution. . . . In this sense the term refers to political positions and ideological assertions "on campus," positions and assertions expressed in the course of teaching and class discussion or debate. An instructor in economics might be a proponent of the free market or of Marxism and teach from one or the other perspective, and a student might take a contrary position. With regard to an instructor, the term also covers the freedom (jus docens, the right to teach) of a qualified faculty member to control the contents of his or her courses and research, subject to the limits of professional ethics. Academic freedom in this sense may come into conflict with the institutional autonomy of the university, its freedom to determine what shall be taught. Although trustees and administration should not interfere with academic freedom, that doesn't mean "anything goes." Trustees and administration have the responsibility of seeing that standards of scholarship are not eroded; "academic freedom" shouldn't become a mindless device for avoiding this responsibility.[9]

All these aspects of academic freedom border on the battle being fought over the curriculum and "multicultural education." Although some of the arguments voiced in this encounter are germane to the issue of free speech on campus, they will only be glanced at here.[10] In trying to understand the scope of the university as a marketplace of ideas, we shall, however, consider whether there are grounds for *excluding* a subject or field from the university.

Because of the campus disturbances that were common in the 1960s and '70s, "academic freedom" was extended to include the right of students to attend classes and invited lectures free from disruption by students who disapprove of the ideas being expressed therein. Instances of such disruption have occurred in recent years, as well as in the 1980s. On many campuses, conduct codes forbid disruption of classes and lectures, but these provisions seem to be selectively enforced.

The freedom of qualified faculty members to control the content of their courses can raise a free speech issue in another way, as is illustrated by an item in the *New York Times* (May 11, 1994). Under the headline "A Sexual Harassment Case to Test Academic Freedom," there is a report on events that allegedly took place in a class at the Chicago Theological Seminary. The professor, Gordon Snyder, told a story, from the Babylonian Talmud, regarding a man who falls off a roof and accidentally "penetrates" a woman. The point of the story, presumably, was that in the opinion of the Talmud the man is free from sin because his act was unintentional. (Examination of the source will show that the story has nothing at all to do with sin but rather with whether the man is civilly liable for degradation.) A female student believed that the story justified brutality toward women, and she charged the professor with "creating an intimidating, hostile or offensive environment"—he had engaged "in verbal conduct of a sexual nature." The upshot of the incident was that the professor was severely censured by the seminary and had his course placed under strict supervision.

While it is impossible to comment on this incident without having more information, it is easy to see that the outcome could have a "chilling effect" on the conduct of this course and other courses taught at the school. The ethics of teaching does place limits on professors, and the control that they may have over their courses should not be the same thing as professorial whim. Still, it is plain that sexual harassment regulations can raise campus free speech concerns. And they can raise them for students, too. In fact, there appears to be a trend to use anti-harassment regulations as a way of restricting speech, analogous with prohibitions in Employment Law.[11]

By the beginning of 1995 more than 350 American colleges adopted or 15 tried to adopt a speech code. Although, as noted, the speech-restrictive provisions of codes at several public institutions have been invalidated by the courts, many of them remain on the books unchanged, perhaps for public relations or "feel good" reasons. While some codes appear to be merely aspi-rational, others designate punishments for violations, anything from censure to expulsion. Offenders (faculty or student) may sometimes also be required to undergo a process of sensitivity training. Sensitivity and diversity training is one of the growth industries on American campuses, bringing with it a corps of (often high-priced) so-called sensitivity and diversity consultants and facilitators. On many campuses such training is a mandatory part of freshman orientation. Some of the practices that have been reported strike me as bizarre; for instance, requiring students to sit quietly while all sorts of slurs are thrown at them. Certain techniques strike me as ethically questionable, to say the least, such as embarrassing or shaming students to the point of tears. If speech codes forbid anything, it should be these sorts of practices.

As objectionable as sensitivity training may be, it raises an important gen-eral question: Is moral education part of the university's function, and if so, what shape should it take? More specifically for our purposes, do speech codes have a role to play in the process? The former question raises the large issue of curriculum, which is beyond the scope of this book. The latter ques-tion is dealt with indirectly in other chapters. We should keep in mind, of course, that the issue of speech codes is only part of the subject of free speech on campus.

At this point it will be useful to list a number of examples of incidents that are used to raise campus free speech issues. Except for one, all are given here more or less as they are reported in the literature. Almost all of them have occurred in the past ten years. It is sometimes said that the campus speech debate has largely consisted of a rehashing of the same few alleged horror stories whose existence is attested to by anecdotal evidence at best. While a lot of rehashing has occurred, it is my distinct sense that the "alleged horror stories," i.e., incidents of successful or attempted suppression or regulation of speech, are many and not few. But, in an important respect, whether they are many or few really doesn't matter. The incidents raise ques-tions of principle and underlying rationale, which merit discussion in their own right. These questions are the subject matter of this book. Although I shall be looking at real-world incidents, it is not intended as a work of reportage.

1. A group of students hangs a banner reading "Homophobia Sucks" across the entrance to a building.

2. A male student wears a sweatshirt with the words "Fuck Women."

3. One student calls a student who is of Asian descent a "Gook" and says that there are too many of his kind at the university.

4. In a class on race relations in the United States the lecturer refers to a group as Indians rather than Native Americans. As a result the class is disrupted.

5. In order to prevent its circulation, a black student takes copies of an independent campus newspaper; a previous issue contained an article about blacks that he found offensive and "full of lies."

6. A university adopts a rule that prescribes punishment for "derogatory names, inappropriately directed laughter, inconsiderate jokes, and conspicuous exclusion from conversation."

7. In the campus newspaper, an advertisement is published that denies the occurrence of the Holocaust.

8. A black student association withdraws its invitation to a speaker who reportedly gave an anti-Semitic speech on another college campus.

9. A new course proposed by a professor is turned down by the college curriculum committee on the grounds that it is ethnocentric and its syllabus is not sufficiently multicultural. When the instructor objected to such "thought control," her dean declared the objection a threat to academic freedom.

10. In a legal studies class on the Thirteenth Amendment the instructor refers to the black students as ex-slaves. He is required to make a public apology and attend a "sensitivity and racial awareness" session.

11. A mathematics professor writes a letter to the student newspaper about date rape; he states that female students who accept invitations to male students' dormitory rooms must bear some responsibility for such alleged rapes. The professor is temporarily suspended.

12. A professor of biology writes a letter to the student newspaper condoning premarital intercourse between consenting students. The professor is dismissed from his position.

13. A student newspaper runs a cartoon making fun of affirmative action, for which one of the editors is suspended. A student editor at another school writes an article that criticizes the suspension; he, too, is suspended.

14. In a project for a course on contemporary issues in feminist art, some women students distribute posters around the university with the names of fifty men chosen at random from the directory, under the heading "Notice: These Men Are Potential Rapists."

15. A fraternity stages an "Ugly Woman" contest in which one member dresses as a black woman: he wears stringy black hair in curlers, uses pillows to pad his chest and buttocks, and speaks in slang that parodies blacks. As a result, various sanctions are imposed by the university on the fraternity.

Except for one case, the second, these incidents, or incidents like them, are reported to have occurred on North American college or university campuses in the past few years.[12] I used the second case as an example in an undergraduate course. We were discussing John Stuart Mill's defense of free speech in his famous essay *On Liberty*, and I brought up the 1971 Supreme Court case of *Cohen v. California* (403 U.S. 15). Cohen had been convicted in a California court of violating a disturbing-the-peace statute by "offensive conduct." He had worn a jacket bearing the words "Fuck the Draft" in a Los Angeles courthouse corridor. He testified that he did so as a means of informing the public of the depth of his feeling against the Vietnam War and the draft. A majority of the U.S. Supreme Court decided that Cohen's right to freedom of expression had been violated and reversed his conviction.[13]

My class (thirty or so students, mostly seniors, about ten of them women) readily agreed with the result in *Cohen*. Well, I asked, suppose a student wore a sweatshirt emblazoned "Fuck NAFTA" around the Duke campus (the North American Free Trade Agreement was being debated in Congress at the time). Again, my students had no difficulty in saying it should be allowed—a clear case of "political" speech, they said. Well, then, what about a sweatshirt with "Fuck Women"? A brief moment of disquiet could be sensed. Well, what about it? Somewhat to my surprise, given the line being broadcast in many quarters of the campus regarding male-female relations, there was general agreement that this sort of speech or conduct should not be punishable. Even the ten women who were present agreed with that view; at least none of them openly dissented. Unfortunately, I did not pursue the issue. I could at least have inquired whether they thought their view was widely shared by Duke undergraduates. (I think that the general reaction would be quite vocal and negative.) But I was too diffident to press the example. I rarely use the mentioned four-letter word in my own speech, even less in a class, and in more than thirty years of teaching I don't think that I ever uttered it as many times as that day. I did suggest that a generation used to cable television and R-rated movies may have become inured to such language, but that universities and colleges, students and faculty both, perhaps should be held to higher standards of speech and conduct than the rest of society. Because of my diffidence, however, I moved on to other, less discomforting examples. (The concern with single words may seem rather old-fashioned, the sort of thing for which kids would get their mouth washed out with soap. In fact, many speech codes focus on single words, so-called derogatory names.)

Because of my diffidence I also failed to take up a related topic, the possi- 20 ble "chilling" effect on freedom of expression—was my diffidence due in part to that chilling effect? was I committing a verbal sexual assault? will I use this example again in a class? I would not venture to predict whether the students' reaction would be the same, next time.

In order to elicit some of the issues inherent to our subject, it will be useful to look at a few of our opening examples. It will not be necessary to expound each of them with the same degree of detail. Some of them overlap, anyway.

Example (1) is reported as an actual incident at a college in the northeast. A father visiting his son there asked the president of the college whether it would be all right if a group of students hung a banner with the slogan "Homosexuality Sucks" on a college building. "That could never be tolerated," he answered.[14] (As stated, it is not important whether any of this occurred exactly as reported.) Why it couldn't be tolerated isn't clear to me. Perhaps the president merely wanted to avoid dealing with the ruckus that would be aroused. But *shouldn't* it be tolerated? If one banner is the expression of an idea, isn't the other (its opposite) also the expression of an idea? And if it is permissible to express one idea, shouldn't it be permissible to express the other? Various observers of campus goings-on have said that a "double standard" often operates in cases of this kind.[15] Suppose, in example (7) for instance, there is a move to forbid, punish, or (as has been done) severely censure the publication of Holocaust-denying advertisements. Should it matter that they contain blatant falsehoods, as long as they are an expression of ideas? How should such cases be handled?

More fundamentally, though, we need to consider whether there is a principled basis for distinguishing acceptable from unacceptable speech. This is no easy matter, and in the end we may not be able to formulate such a principle, which could be a point of great consequence. Is "Sucks" acceptable on a campus banner, no matter what it is that is supposed to "suck"? The fact is that there may well be levels of unacceptable speech, ranging, as it were, from felonies to misdemeanors. A form of speech may be unacceptable yet not something that should be punishable, as some members of my class seemed to believe in example (2). Is "inappropriately directed laughter," example (6), the sort of thing that should be punished? On one campus a student was suspended after laughing when someone called another student a "faggot" in his presence.

Moreover, much may depend on the context. In the late 1960s and early '70s, expletives and vulgarities were uttered in classrooms in order to cause a disruption; they now are frequently used in student newspapers, and even by some faculty in classes, as a matter of course. But what about "derogatory names"? In example (3), it will be noticed, a derogatory name was directed against a specific person, while in example (10), as described above, the name was used in reference to a group. Should that make a difference to whether a name is acceptable? Of course, regarding these two examples, it could be argued that there isn't much if any difference between them, for in (10), calling the black students "ex-slaves," the name was used in reference to a *present* group. But suppose someone announces more generally that there are too many "Gooks" at the university? Should that be regarded as the expression of an "idea" and hence tolerable, however unacceptable the mode of expression? Suppose the student had merely said that there were too many Asians at the university? The poster with the fifty names, example (14), seems to be the expression of an idea, but does that make it tolerable? If it had said "Notice: All men are potential rapists," would that make it more tolerable?

What makes a name a "derogatory name" anyway? Various kinds of 25
speech (e.g., false accusations) plainly have the capacity to cause harm in a
given context. But if, as the old adage has it, "names will never harm me,"
perhaps what makes a name derogatory and unacceptable is that the recipient
of the name finds it *offensive*—it hurts in a way, even if it doesn't harm.
Sometimes, however, the recipient may find a name to be offensive while the
deliverer does not. Apparently this was the case in example (10); the instructor did not think it offensive to call the black students "ex-slaves," and he did
not *intend* to give offense. (In the actual incident, he initially spoke the word
to a particular black student who couldn't recite the Thirteenth Amendment
to the U.S. Constitution; as an ex-slave, the instructor said, he and all the other
blacks should know the amendment's contents. As a Jew, the instructor later
explained, he didn't mind being called an ex-slave, for as the annual Passover
service states: "We were slaves in Egypt. . . .") If certain words or forms of
expression are to be deemed unacceptable and possibly punishable—but only
if uttered with an intention to offend—it has seemed crucial to many com-
mentators that there be some standard of offensiveness that is not dependent
exclusively on the feelings of those people to whom the remark is directed.
For example, some students at a major state university, which had a speech
code, complained that they were offended when they were called "rednecks."
Some administrators decided that the word itself is not offensive, but were
they the right judges?

Examples (10) and (4) should be compared. A number of students in the
classroom were upset because the lecturer used the word "Indian" instead of
"Native American," and they made it difficult for him to finish out the course.
Assuming that there were no Native Americans in the audience who might
have taken offense (in fact, I've met Native Americans who prefer to be called
Indians), and assuming that no offense was intended, there would seem to
have been no wrong committed.

On the other hand, certain words in our language are recognized as intrinsically derogatory names or deprecatory words, e.g., "stupid." Should we say,
instead, "cognitively challenged"? These words have negative connotations
and express "con" rather than "pro" or neutral attitudes. It is easy to compile
a list of them. But the status of many words is far from clear. Perhaps "Indian"
falls into the unclear or neutral category, though there are some people who
strongly prefer to be called Native Americans, just as there are some people
who prefer to be called African Americans rather than blacks. Whether a name
has an intrinsically derogatory status will often be controversial, and it might
be argued that the recipient, in such a case, just has to tolerate any offense he
or she feels. Some words are generally recognized as derogatory and yet do
not always cause offense. It is imaginable that someone might not be offended
by being called a "nerd." "Zero tolerance" of *anything* that *any*body finds
offensive, which is a principle found in a few campus speech-regulation
policies, clearly creates havoc with free speech.

Aside from the problems raised by offensive words and derogatory names, there are perhaps more important free speech issues raised by "ideas" that offend or are unacceptable at least in some sense. For the notion that certain ideas are unacceptable has as its complement the notion that only certain ideas are acceptable. In effect, this duality was noted regarding the banner in example (1), assuming that the expression of an idea was involved. But it is also present in other examples: taking copies of a newspaper (5), the Holocaust-denying advertisement (7), withdrawing an invitation to speak (8), the letters about date rape and premarital sex (11), (12), and the cartoon (13). Though each of these cases probably raises a particular free speech issue, there is in each one an implicit reference to a complementary pair of acceptable and unacceptable ideas.

Consider, for instance, example (13). A student editor was suspended after writing an article criticizing the suspension of a student editor at another school who ran a cartoon making fun of affirmative action. Of course, one can easily imagine that the cartoon was in bad taste, a not infrequent characteristic of the "humor" that pervades college publications. But how significant should that be? It is hard to believe that the second student editor would have been suspended had he written an article *supporting* the suspension. Apparently, advocacy of affirmative action is acceptable but expressing one's opposition to it is not.[16]

This example and the others just cited raise an important and difficult 30 issue about universities. To what extent should they remain neutral as between conflicting ideas and values? Can they in fact be neutral? Isn't the promotion of certain ideas and values implicit in the very concept of a university? Does it matter if a certain idea is regarded as a blatant falsehood? and by whom? Example (7), the Holocaust-denying advertisement, is a case in point. What, in any event, is the distinction between the expression of an idea and the expression of an attitude (the use of derogatory names), and of what relevance is it? Whether there is a workable distinction is, I believe, a crucial question in the campus speech debate. Attitudes generally reflect the beliefs and opinions one holds, which is one reason why outlawing even deliberate attempts at humiliation could be problematic.

Example (15), which occurred at a public university, raises the interesting issue of the speech–conduct distinction. It generally is agreed that conduct (behavior) is more subject to government regulation and restriction than speech is. But it turns out that conduct will sometimes be regarded as a kind of speech and therefore qualify for First Amendment protection—namely, so-called "expressive conduct," conduct that expresses an idea or attitude. Johnson's burning of the flag and Cohen's wearing of the "Fuck the Draft" slogan were held by the Supreme Court to fall into this category. And so did the incident of example (15), according to the federal court that heard the case: "[The] Fraternity's skit, even as low-level entertainment, was inherently expressive and thus entitled to First Amendment protection."[17] Some proponents of speech codes, however, argue in the other direction. They maintain that speech itself can at times be regarded as a form of conduct and therefore become subject to regulation in the way that other conduct is. Should we accept this argument?

We have not discussed all of the examples given in the detail they deserve. The number listed easily could have been multiplied, especially if we include instances of hoax "hate crimes." But enough has been said to indicate the problems, some of which will turn up in our examination of arguments for speech codes in chapters 4 and 5.[18]

What we need to do now is to consider some fundamentals of the "constitution" of institutions of higher learning (colleges and universities, though "university" is the term we shall generally use) and, particularly, why a free speech provision—something like Justice Brennan's bedrock principle—is a vital element of it. Having such a provision, however, does not by itself resolve all the speech issues that might come up, any more than the words of the First Amendment of the U.S. Constitution do. In order to resolve campus speech issues, recourse must be had to the provision's underlying rationale or justification, and even then problems could remain. (It should be kept in mind that speech codes are only one aspect of the topic, free speech on campus.) That rationale is rendered by the notion of the university as a marketplace of ideas. ◎/◎

Notes

1. See Richard Delgado, "Words That Wound: A Tort Action for Racial Insults, Epithets, and Name-Calling," 17 *Harvard Civil Rights-Civil Liberties Law Rev.* (1982), 148–49. With slight editorial changes and the elimination of some footnotes, this article is reprinted in M. J. Matsuda, C. R. Lawrence III, R. Delgado, and K. W. Crenshaw, *Words That Wound. Critical Race Theory, Assaultive Speech and the First Amendment* (Boulder, Colo.: Westview Press, 1993), 89–110. Three articles from this book are discussed below, in chapters 4 and 5. There is no agreed-on definition of "hate speech," and it is sometimes used interchangeably with "offensive speech." Judging from the literature, though, we can take it to mean: any form of expression (or communication), verbal or nonverbal (e.g., posters, parades, insignia, picket lines) regarded as offensive to racial, ethnic, or religious groups or other discrete minorities (e.g., homosexuals), or to women.
2. See Mari J. Matsuda, "Public Response to Racist Speech: Considering the Victim's Story," 87 *Michigan Law Rev.* (1989), 2320–81. With slight editorial changes and the elimination of some footnotes, this article is reprinted in *Words That Wound*, 17–52.
3. *Chaplinsky v. New Hampshire*, 315 U.S. 568 (1942) ("fighting words," words that "by their very nature inflict injury" and words that "tend to incite an immediate breach of the peace," are not protected by the First Amendment); *Beauharnais v. Illinois*, 343 U.S. 250 (1952) (upholding the constitutionality of a 1917 Illinois group libel law). For a discussion of the erosion of these decisions, see Samuel Walker, *Hate Speech: The History of an American Controversy* (Lincoln: University of Nebraska Press, 1994).
4. See Robert M. O'Neil, *Free Speech in the College Community* (Bloomington: Indiana University Press, 1997), 7–11, for a discussion of the differences. O'Neil's clearly written book covers more topics than we do here, and focuses on public colleges and universities and issues of constitutional law.

5. For an excellent study of the cases, see Timothy C. Shiell, *Campus Hate Speech on Trial* (Lawrence: University of Kansas Press, 1998). . . .

6. In February 1995, a judge of the Santa Clara County (California) Superior Court struck down the Stanford University speech code on the basis of California's 1992 Leonard Law: Private educational institutions may not discipline a student "solely on the basis of . . . speech or other communication that when engaged in outside the campus is protected from government restriction by the First Amendment." The Stanford code, enacted in 1990, prohibited "personal vilification of students on the basis of their sex, race, color, handicap, religion, sexual orientation or national and ethnic origin." There is no Leonard Law in other states, but some individual state constitutions contain speech protections that may apply to private colleges and universities.

7. As put in the 1940 American Association of University Professors *Statement of Principles on Academic Freedom and Tenure:* "When they [teachers] speak or write as citizens, they should be free from institutional censorship or discipline. . . ."

8. Academic freedom is a large subject, on which much has been written. See Richard Hofstadter and Walter P. Metzger, *The Development of Academic Freedom in the United States* (New York: Columbia University Press, 1955). A bibliography from 1940 and articles of historical, legal, and philosophical interest may be found in 53 *Law and Contemporary Problems* (Summer 1990), Freedom and Tenure in the Academy: The Fiftieth Anniversary of the 1940 [American Association of University Professors] Statement of Principles.

9. Academic fields and faculties are generally self-governing and they have the initial responsibility of showing that the "emperor has no clothes." But faculties are notoriously weak (and weak-kneed). The slogan of "academic freedom" too easily becomes a way of avoiding judgments of academic merit. But the issue can have complex dimensions. . . .

10. I have never met a faculty member who is opposed to the teaching of non-Western cultures, languages, and literatures. What is opposed by many faculty is the ideology and policy of multiculturalism, an expression of which is contained in Stanford University's *Affirmative Action Plan* (October 16, 1991): "The Office for Multicultural Development is predicated upon the knowledge that our society is composed of independent, multi-racial/multi-ethnic peoples and that our future requires new thinking and new structures which incorporate diversity as a means to harmony, unity, and equity. Moreover, diversity is fundamental to the pursuit of excellence and knowledge. In understanding and accepting this reality, Stanford University begins a transformation to ensure that multiculturalism is infused into (not appended to) all aspects of teaching, research, planning, policies, practices, achievement, and institutional life. It is the mission of the Office for Multicultural Development to develop the multicultural model of the future and guide Stanford University through the transformation."

    Cited in David O. Sacks and Peter A. Thiel, *The Diversity Myth* (Oakland, Calif.: The Independent Institute, 1995), 24. The authors demonstrate the dependence of Stanford's multiculturalism on an animus against Western culture and ideals. ("Hey hey, ho ho, Western Culture's got to go!") Statements similar to the one cited are found at other universities.

11. See Shiell, n. 5. . . .

12. Example (12) goes back to 1960. It is very doubtful that such a letter would result in dismissal today, whether from a public university or from most private institutions. More than likely, it would not be written, and if written, not attract attention. In the 1950s a number of faculty members were dismissed or not renewed because of

political positions they had taken, because of failure to sign loyalty oaths, because of political affiliations, or because of refusal to testify before government committees (e.g., the House Un-American Activities Committee) about their political affiliations. I have chosen to focus on more recent examples. Example (12) is mentioned because it reminds us of how much historical context counts, when compared with example (13).

13. At some point in First Amendment jurisprudence, the term "freedom of expression" began to be often substituted for the term "free speech." (Even striptease in bars has been claimed to be constitutionally protected expression.) And once we move to "self-expression," political or nonpolitical, it seems that Mr. Cohen has a pretty good case. As Justice John M. Harlan II said in *Cohen:* "We cannot sanction the view that the Constitution, while solicitous of the cognitive content of individual speech, has little or no regard for that emotive function, which, practically speaking, may often be the more important element of the overall message sought to be communicated."

14. College and university administrations do have a large degree of control over the placement of banners, announcements, posters, etc., on campus property, though that control may be subject to First Amendment free speech guarantees in public institutions. Compare the removal of a Malcolm X mural, with anti-Semitic symbols, from a wall at San Francisco State University. In this instance, the university had paid for the mural, and therefore had the right to remove it. *Herald-Sun*, Durham, N.C., May 29, 1994, G8.

15. Employment of a double standard is a kind of hypocrisy, which occurs when a purportedly general standard is applied in one way to one individual or group and differently (or not at all) to another. Such hypocrisy is not infrequent on college campuses, e.g., when administrations condemn newspaper thefts by some groups but not by others, or when they condemn expression of one controversial idea ("Homosexuality Sucks") but not the expression of another ("Homophobia Sucks").

16. Since a public university is subject to the First Amendment, any allowable restriction (e.g., reasonable time, place, and manner restrictions) on speech must be "view-point neutral."

17. *Iota Xi Chapter of Sigma Chi Fraternity v. George Mason University*, 993 F.2d 386 (4th Cir. 1993). At a nearby university some male students sponsored a contest to find the "Biggest JAP on Campus." "JAP" is a derogatory term referring to a stereotypical Jewish American Princess. I do not know whether the school disciplined these students. JAP baiting incidents have been reported on a number of campuses. Slogans such as ZAP-A-JAP and SLAP-A-JAP have been worn on students' T-shirts, for instance. Compare example (2).

18. Example (8) wasn't discussed at all. When the invitation was withdrawn, some people said that the speaker's First Amendment rights had been violated. This claim rests on a misunderstanding. Just as a private association has no duty to provide a speaker with a forum, so may it withdraw an invitation, if there are good grounds for doing so. . . .

Reflections and Inquiries

1. How does Golding distinguish between "free speech" and "speech codes"?

2. Is it useful to draw a distinction between "expression of ideas" and "verbal behavior"? Why?

3. In light of the fact that obscene language is not protected by the First Amendment, defend or challenge Golding's examples of students' use of obscene slogans on articles of clothing as a form of protest. What about Golding's own use of such examples in his classroom?

4. Examine the fifteen examples of freedom-of-speech incidents that Golding lists. Which of these examples, if any, deserve First Amendment protection? Which do not? Explain your reasons.

Reading to Write

1. Find out whether your college or university has a speech code already as one of its policies. If so, examine it to see whether you support the wording as it stands and write a short essay that shows why it is necessary or that shows what you believe needs to be changed. If your college or university has no speech code, write an essay in which you support or argue against the adoption of one.

2. After rereading Golding's commentary on derogatory names, write a position paper in which you defend or challenge the motion that "derogatory" in this context is too subjective to prohibit in a speech code.

The Web Police | Matthew Quirk

Not surprisingly in repressive regimes like those of China and Iran, Internet censorship is a well-developed operation. But as Matthew Quirk, a staff writer for the Atlantic Monthly, *reports, China is but one of several countries that censor Internet use by its citizens. Even so, ingenious Internet users can find ways to slip through undetected. In this article, Quirk reports on the extent of Internet censorship globally, using data gathered by Reporters Without Borders, an organization committed to maintaining freedom of the press worldwide.*

Internet censorship is prevalent not just in China but throughout the world. Can the Web be tamed?

China has become notorious for the extent and sophistication of its Internet censorship. The government constantly adjusts its roster of banned Web sites. Search engines filter content, leaving only pro-government information on sensitive topics. Companies that provide space to bloggers censor hundreds of key words, such as "democracy," "Falun Gong," and "freedom." Chat rooms are monitored by tens of thousands of government workers, who remove offending posts. E-mail is subject to censorship, although less likely to be blocked than public communications. Even text messages are now perused by the authorities.

Source: "The Web Police" by Matthew Quirk. *The Atlantic Monthly,* May 2006. Reprinted with permission of the author.

But China is hardly alone in its vigilance. The [side bar], based on research by Reporters Without Borders, a free-press watchdog group, shows the state of Internet freedom in fifty-five countries worldwide, based on how much of the Web is blocked and how vulnerable citizens are to government intimidation for unsanctioned use.

For the most part, the countries that police the Web most thoroughly are the ones you'd expect: Iran, China, and Vietnam are among the most aggressive, blocking a wide range of political, religious, human-rights, and vice-related sites while tracking Internet users carefully. In Burma and Cuba, only a tiny fraction of users can connect to the Internet at all; the rest can access only their country's intranet, composed mostly of business and government propaganda sites. Several states filter only minimally but make examples of those who speak up on the Web: there are currently fifty-five dissidents imprisoned for online activities worldwide—forty-eight in China, two in Vietnam, two in Iran, and one each in the Maldives, Tunisia, and Syria.

But liberal democracies also filter the Web. Google first censored its search engine on a state's behalf not in January to assist China but nearly four years ago to comply with hate-speech codes in Germany, France, and Switzerland. In America, Pennsylvania's then-attorney general enforced a law requiring Internet service providers to block sites hosting child porn, though the courts have since deemed that law unconstitutional.

Worldwide, the number one target of government filters is not political speech but pornography. In Islamic states, sites featuring lingerie, alcohol, drugs, gay or lesbian images, evangelism, sex education, and criticism of Islam are often blocked. This emphasis on moral matters may reflect the hierarchy of concerns of many governments, but sites catering to vice are also the easiest to block: many government censors rely on off-the-shelf filtering software—originally built to keep employees from engaging in dubious workplace activities—which features ready-made blacklists of offensive sites by category. (This sort of filtering can be clumsy, and inevitably leads to inadvertent blocking. For instance, smut filters have blocked the tourism site of the English county of Essex and temporarily stopped the residents of Scunthorpe from logging on to AOL.) 5

While China has proved that the mass of casual surfers can be effectively blinkered by a committed regime, experienced users can find ways through the firewall. Only the most dedicated governments can keep blacklists up to date on the ever-changing Web, and very often simply trying an alternate address or dropping the prefix "www" will allow access to a banned site. Bloggers can also slip obvious misspellings of banned words past the censors. In Cuba, a black market in Internet access has sprung up.

New software and Web services increasingly allow Internet users to bypass filters. Dissident exiles and groups like the OpenNet Initiative and Electronic Frontier Foundation actively update and distribute such software in a race to stay ahead of the censors, although the censors are fighting back by blocking access to those resources, and even allegedly attacking those writing the codes

INTERNET FREEDOM

The following information is based on the work of Reporters Without Borders, a free-press advocacy group that ranked fifty-five countries in a 2004 survey based on levels of Web censorship, intimidation, and the existence of independent online media.

Russia: Free (For Now)
Vladimir Putin's media crackdown in Russia has largely missed the Web, which is teeming with opposition (although the state has hired hackers, and at least one anti-Putin site has been hacked and replaced with government propaganda). Whether or not to block dissent on the internet remains a contentious debate in the Kremlin.

USA: Collaborators
U.S. companies provide most of the technology for foreign censors. Secure Computing's SmartFilter has been used by Saudi Arabia, Tunisia, and Iran. To comply with China's laws, Google has created a censored search engine, Microsoft has taken down offending blogs, and Yahoo has shared information that landed a Chinese journalist in jail.

SE Asia: Mission Creep
Once begun, filtering sometimes expands beyond its original purposes. In Thailand, for instance, filtering systems established legally to stop certain vice-related online activities were then used secretly to block muckraking and political opposition sites.

Middle East: Popular Policing
Saudi Arabia blocks most drug, sex, and gambling sites—but gay and lesbian, political, news, and alcohol sites are largely accessible, and the Saudi government is open about its filtering activities. In a 1999 survey, while 45 percent of Saudis thought too many sites were blocked, 41 percent thought the level was reasonable and 14 percent wanted more censorship.

China: The Great Firewall
China has built the world's most advanced filtering regime. It can block not just whole domains (like www.amnesty.org) but individual pages within a site (yale.edu is available, but its pages on the Falun Gong are blocked), making its censorship seem less oppressive. Sophisticated technology allows China to automatically search and instantly block new Web content containing politically sensitive key words—the maintenance of "blacklists" is not required.

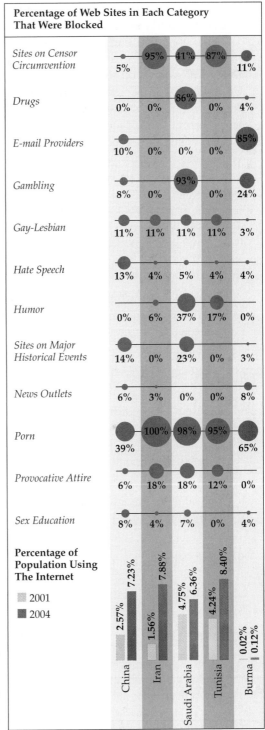

(a Falun Gong specialist in circumventing Chinese filters was rolled in a carpet and beaten, and the computers taken from his Atlanta home, in February).

Like so much early hype surrounding the Internet, talk of the Web's potential as a democratizing force has far exceeded the reality. To date, relatively well-wired countries such as the United Arab Emirates, Singapore, and China have reaped many of the economic benefits of the Web while still stifling the flow of free information. Censorship techniques in these places have become more precise and supple over time.

But it's still too soon to know whether censors will be able to keep the Web under heel. Most governments are not sophisticated in their attempts at censorship—they rely on simple filtering technologies that can be defeated by a determined political opposition. Even in China, information is seeping through. The regime is having trouble staying on top of the 111 million residents now online—less than 10 percent of the country's population. It's hard to imagine how it will keep up as that number swells. ◎／◎

Reflections and Inquiries

1. Notice (in the bar graph) the increase in Internet use from 2001 to 2004 in countries where Internet censorship is heavy. What accounts for this increase, in your opinion?

2. China operates the world's most sophisticated Internet censorship system. What contributes to its effectiveness?

3. What does the graph, "Percentage of Web Sites in Each Category That Were Blocked," suggest about the general attitude censoring regimes have toward certain materials? What surprises or inconsistencies do you see in the table?

Reading to Write

Write an essay in which you speculate on the future failure or success of Internet censorship and on the Internet as a democratizing force, given the information Quirk provides in the last two paragraphs of his article.

Student Essay

Speech Codes: An Insult to Education and a Threat to Our Future | Quentin Clark

How useful are speech codes in society, especially on college campuses where they can influence the educational experience of students? Some argue that they constitute a form of education—of appropriate language etiquette—implying that certain words, like certain physical actions, can be injurious. Others, like Quentin Clark, a student from the University of Melbourne spending his senior year in the United States, argue that speech codes interfere with free speech and prevent learning.

Triumph, failure, outrage, delight, fear, freedom, conviction, fervor, passion, and in an instance, silence. The speed with which censorship transforms the magnificence of enlightenment into the tragedy of ignorance is frightening, and few places necessitate protection from this silence more than the halls of higher education. Universities face an impasse: either foster learning through open debate or control education through censorship and speech codes. One is not compatible with the other, and a university that chooses poorly risks its identity as a place of higher learning.

Thus far, universities across the country have taken this risk by adopting speech codes to combat the expression of views that may be distasteful or offensive. Proposed solutions have invariably become swamped in a subjective sea of double standards and semantic contradictions, leaving students bewildered as to what they can and can't say, and dictating what they may and may not be offended by. In their ambiguous pontification, all these universities manage to achieve is confusion and suppression. They gag that which is the very lifeblood of their institution: knowledge. No answer can be found in limiting dialogue; instead, it must be liberated. An idea, however repugnant it may appear, must be set free. It must be laid bare for all to see, consider, criticize, or commend. Only then can it be truly judged on its merits, or lack there of.

Proponents of speech codes in universities insist that in order to create a "comfortable learning environment," restricting the expression of some ideas and dialogue is necessary (as quoted in Golding). A "comfortable learning environment" is one in which students are not subject to verbal abuse or behavior that intimidates, discriminates, or incites hatred and violence. Martin P. Golding, a professor of philosophy and of law at Duke University (444), notes three basic models of speech codes banning and punishing certain actions used by a number of U.S. universities:

1. "Fighting words," defined as personally abusive epithets inherently likely to provoke a violent reaction whether or not they actually do so; they constitute harassment when they create a hostile and intimidating educational environment.
2. "Racial harassment," defined as extreme or outrageous acts or communications that are intended to harass, intimidate, or humiliate a student or students on account of race, color, or national origin and that reasonably cause them to suffer severe emotional distress.
3. "Discriminatory harassment," defined as verbal or physical conduct that the targeted individual or group would find discriminatorily, alters the conditions for participation in the activities of the university on the basis of race, color, and national or ethnic origin. (445–446).

The problem with such definitions lies in their broadness and subjectivity; depending on context, almost anything may fall under them. For example, would it be unacceptable to screen the movie *Revenge of the Nerds* on campus? "Nerd" was originally used as a derogatory term to discriminate against someone of a socially awkward disposition but proficient in intellectual or technical pursuits (Wikipedia). *Revenge of the Nerds* stereotypes and ridicules this group, as well as another group common to universities, "jocks." It is a clearly offensive film depicting the persecution of one group by another and demonstrating an unfortunate reality on many campuses. However, countless "jocks" and "nerds" do not take offense to the film, and even enjoy it, whether its creators intended them to or not. The term "nerd" has even evolved into a source of pride used to describe a certain level of intellectual acumen or technical skill. Is *Revenge of the Nerds* a deliberate attempt to offend and mock particular groups, is it an important social commentary on university life and the broader community, or is it both? Is it possible for a university board to make a decisive decision on the acceptability or unacceptability of language, themes, and ideas such as those expressed in *Revenge of the Nerds?*

The *Revenge of the Nerds* example highlights important questions   5 surrounding the intention of, and degree of, offensiveness contained in certain language. Language may be used with the intention to offend. Often it achieves its purpose, but many times it does not. If no hostility or intimidation is experienced by the recipient, does an environment of intimidation and hostility exist? And what of the deliverer of allegedly offensive language who never intended to offend? Should this person be as severely sanctioned as the former, their language and any discussion of it indignantly and self-righteously banned? If I were to find an idea or language offensive, I should like the right to voice my offense and challenge the offender. And if someone were to find offense in an idea or language of my own, I should like the opportunity to defend my views, anticipating fair and knowledgeable reply.

During a race relations class, a lecturer referred to a group as "Indians" rather than "Native Americans"; the class was disrupted even though the lecturer did not intend to offend anyone (Golding 449, 453). Has the term "Indian" then taken on an inherent offensiveness whether Native Americans hear it or not, or are even offended if they do? Meaning can easily change depending on perception, circumstance, and historical context. Is it fair for the professor's class to be disrupted if he meant no offense, and the degree of offense felt by students is questionable? Would it not be more beneficial for students to explore and to understand their feelings? Advocates of speech codes would object. They would have the class not only disrupted, but cancelled until a new professor is found and the content has been revised.

Golding provides further examples of universities suppressing contentious debate through sanctions including suspension: a mathematics professor after he stated in a letter to the student newspaper that female students who accept invitations to male students' dormitory rooms must bear some responsibility for the occurrence of alleged rapes (449, 453); the suspension of a student editor for running a cartoon making fun of affirmative action (450, 453); the subsequent suspension of a student editor from another school after the editor wrote an article criticizing the prior suspension (450, 453). In each of these cases, a university chose to handle controversial issues with subjugation. These universities appear to be saying: Advocate the status quo and you will be given voice without challenge; dispute it and you will be punished and censored. Is this a suitable message to send students and professors alike? Is this acceptable practice for a university in a free society? Apart from breeching the right to freedom of speech, as outlined in the First Amendment, what sort of education shelters students from dissenting opinion and prevents them from speaking their own for fear of sanction? An individual unable to speak for self, defend self, or challenge others is no kind of individual, least of all an educated one.

In 2003 a lawsuit was filed against Shippensburg University on behalf of two students who claimed that the school's catalog and student handbook contained "unconstitutionally vague or overly broad language" as well as reprimands pertaining to "unconscious attitudes toward individuals which surface through the use of discriminatory semantics" and the banning of "presumptive statements" and behavior or "attitude" that "annoys" another person or group (As quoted in Calvert & Richards). Such vague policy provides for action against any teacher or student deemed to have caused or intended to cause annoyance to anyone. It is almost impossible for a student to go through university without annoying someone or another, and I doubt there is a university professor alive who could claim never to have annoyed a student or fellow faculty member. With entire university populations susceptible to sanctions, disciplinary boards are now given power they can leverage according to politics, beliefs, orthodoxy, and even personal agendas.

In response to the lawsuit, the University released the following statement:

> As an institution of higher education we encourage and promote free speech among and between individuals and organizations. The university is also committed to the principle that this discussion be conducted appropriately. We do have expectations that our students will conduct themselves in a civil manner that allows them to express their opinions without interfering with the rights of others. (as quoted in Calvert & Richards)

To live life with the right not to be annoyed by anybody, not to have anybody 10 presume anything of us, not to have anybody unconsciously discriminate against us, and not to think for ourselves is to live as an ill-educated drone at best, or a lobotomized hermit at worst. Either that or enroll at Shippensburg University. But don't join a free society.

Shippensburg, after initially declaring that nobody would dictate its policies and procedures, eventually settled the suit, agreeing to costs and to change the unconstitutional elements of its code. Now the university only enforces harassment laws as outlined under state law.

The Shippensburg case was an historic and important win for free speech advocates. However, Shippensburg is a public university and is thus bound by the First Amendment. Private institutions are not compelled by the same obligations. Consequently, it is important to hold private universities accountable to their own standards. The Foundation for Individual Rights in Education (FIRE) contends that if a private college wishes to place a particular set of moral, philosophical, or religious teachings above a commitment to free expression, then it has every right to do so. FIRE goes on to say that students wishing to attend an institution that clearly states it is devoted to a given orthodoxy give their consent for the imposition of such regulations as the university sees fit for the protection and perpetuation of said orthodoxy. Further, the university is in fact contractually obligated to do so (FIRE). Therefore, any private university that promotes itself as a defender of free thought and expression must be held as accountable as a public institution is in protecting that philosophy. They owe it to their students. Not just as a legal obligation, but a moral one.

Shippensburg may have been acting with good intentions, but in the end, it not only limited speech and behavior, but thought as well. When a university outlines such definitions in its policies and regulations, students believe they have an unconditional right to be free from offense, embarrassment, discomfort, or in the case of Shippensburg, annoyance. As a result, censorship becomes self-replicating. Students form attitudes at school that stay with them for life. They learn that jokes, remarks, and visual displays that "offend" someone may justly be forbidden, and will not see cause for alarm when government itself seeks to censor and demand conformity in its citizens. On its website, FIRE warns: A nation that does not educate in freedom will not survive in freedom, and will not even know when it has lost it (FIRE).

Enforcing campus speech codes that restrict freedoms not only damages the learning environment for students but also denies it. Higher education is the culmination of centuries of learning, of ideas fighting to become accepted and of views withstanding challenge upon challenge. During his trial in 399 BC, facing death, Socrates proclaimed to the jury, "If you offered to let me off this time on condition I am not any longer to speak my mind. . . I should say to you, 'Men of Athens, I shall obey the Gods rather than you'" (as quoted in Smith and Torres). Freedom begets knowledge, and knowledge begets freedom. John Milton put it famously when, in defiance of the very licensing laws he was arguing against, he published *Areopagitica* in 1644:

> Give me the liberty to know, to utter, and to argue freely according to conscience, above all liberties. . . . Where there is much desire to learn there of necessity will be much arguing, much writing, many opinions; for opinion in good men is but knowledge in the making. (Milton)

Ideas must be explored and contested; that is the history of humankind encap- 15
sulated by our universities.

Higher education cannot foster institutions of hypocrisy that breed ignorance and undermine their own foundations. Instances of intolerance, harassment, discrimination, and intimidation occurring through free exercise of speech and expression *should* be condemned by a university and its students; but such condemnation must be expressed in discussion and argument, not intimidation and silence. The best way to create a positive learning atmosphere free from "fighting words," "racial harassment," and "discriminatory harassment" is for professors and students to voice their objections and encourage challenges to well thought out and sturdy defenses. The worst possible path lies in limitation and suppression. Confusing and vaguely defined speech codes enforced with sanctimonious hostility only serve to stifle debate, subdue classrooms, and threaten the future of enlightened education. ◎/◎

Works Cited

Calvert, Clay, and Robert, Richards. "Lighting a FIRE on College Campuses: An Inside Perspective on Free Speech, Public Policy and Higher Education." Georgetown Journal of Law and Public Policy *Winter 2005. 20 March 2006.*

Foundation for Individual Rights in Education. "A Great Victory for Free Speech at Shippensburg: University Agrees to Eliminate its Unconstitutional Speech Code." 24 February 2004. *19 March 2006 http://www.thefire.org.*

Golding, Martin P. "Campus Speech Issues." The Well-Crafted Argument. *Ed. White, Fred D., and Simone J. Billings. (Boston: Houghton Mifflin, 2008) 361–374.*

Milton, John. "Areopagitica." Complete Poems and Major Prose, *ed. Merritt Hughes. Indianapolis: Hackett Publishing Co., 2003: 716–49.*

Smith, David, and Luc. Torres, "Timeline: a history of free speech." The Observer 5 *February 2006 http://www.guardian.co.uk.*

Wikipedia: The Free Encyclopedia. *"Nerd." 18 March 2006 http://www.wikipedia.org.*

Reflections and Inquiries

1. According to Clark, before a word is considered offensive, the context in which the remark is uttered needs to be considered; words shouldn't be considered inherently offensive. Suggest situations from your own experience that would support or refute Clark's claim.

2. What was flawed about the charges filed against Shippensburg University in 2003?

3. Clark asserts that "To live life with the right not to be annoyed by anybody, not to have anybody presume anything of us, not to have anybody unconsciously discriminate against us . . . is to live as an ill-educated drone," implying that speech-code restrictions interfere with a college education. Do you agree or disagree, and why?

Reading to Write

Examine your college's speech codes and critique them in an essay. If your college does not have such codes, argue whether or not it should provide them, and what those codes should contain.

Issues for Further Research: Book Banning

A Letter to the Chairman of the Drake School Board | Kurt Vonnegut Jr.

One of America's best-loved novelists, Kurt Vonnegut, is famous for novels that satirize the human condition from unusual perspectives. His most famous novel, Slaughterhouse-Five, *which focuses on the brutality of World War II, has been banned from numerous schools and libraries primarily because of its use of offensive language. In 1973, after the school board in Drake, North Dakota, literally burned the book, Vonnegut wrote the following letter to the chairman of the Drake school board.*

My novel *Slaughterhouse-Five* was actually burned in a furnace by a school janitor in Drake, North Dakota, on instructions from the school committee there, and the school board made public statements about the unwholesomeness of the book. Even by the standards of Queen Victoria, the only offensive line in the entire novel is this: "Get out of the road, you dumb motherfucker." This is spoken by an American antitank gunner to an unarmed American chaplain's assistant during the Battle of the Bulge in Europe in December 1944, the largest single defeat of American arms (the Confederacy excluded) in history. The chaplain's assistant had attracted enemy fire.

So on November 16, 1973, I wrote as follows to Charles McCarthy of Drake, North Dakota:

Dear Mr. McCarthy:

I am writing to you in your capacity as chairman of the Drake School Board. I am among those American writers whose books have been destroyed in the now famous furnace of your school.

Kurt Vonnegut (1922–2007) is well-known for his novels, which satirize war, avarice, and all-around human stupidity.

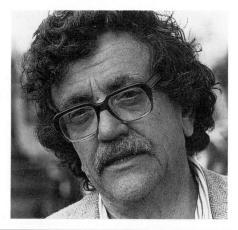

Certain members of your community have suggested that my work is evil. This is extraordinarily insulting to me. The news from Drake indicates to me that books and writers are very unreal to you people. I am writing this letter to let you know how real I am.

I want you to know, too, that my publisher and I have done absolutely nothing to exploit the disgusting news from Drake. We are not clapping each other on the back, crowing about all the books we will sell because of the news. We have declined to go on television, have written no fiery letters to editorial pages, have granted no lengthy interviews. We are angered and sickened and saddened. And no copies of this letter have been sent to anybody else. You now hold the only copy in your hands. It is a strictly private letter from me to the people of Drake, who have done so much to damage my reputation in the eyes of their children and then in the eyes of the world. Do you have the courage and ordinary decency to show this letter to the people, or will it, too, be consigned to the fires of your furnace?

I gather from what I read in the papers and hear on television that you imagine me, and some other writers, too, as being sort of ratlike people who enjoy making money from poisoning the minds of young people. I am in fact a large, strong person, fifty-one years old, who did a lot of farm work as a boy, who is good with tools. I have raised six children, three my own and three adopted. They have all turned out well. Two of them are farmers. I am a combat infantry veteran from World War II, and hold a Purple Heart. I have earned whatever I own by hard work. I have never been arrested or sued for anything. I am so much trusted with young people and by young people that I have served on the faculties of the University of Iowa, Harvard, and the City College of New York. Every year I receive at least a dozen invitations to be commencement speaker at colleges and high schools. My books are probably more widely used in schools than those of any other living American fiction writer.

If you were to bother to read my books, to behave as educated persons would, you would learn that they are not sexy, and do not argue in favor of wildness of any kind. They beg that people be kinder and more responsible than they often are. It is true that some of the characters speak coarsely. That is because people speak coarsely in real life. Especially soldiers and hardworking men speak coarsely, and even our most sheltered children know that. And we all know, too, that those words really don't damage children much. They didn't damage us when we were young. It was evil deeds and lying that hurt us.

After I have said all this, I am sure you are still ready to respond, in effect, "Yes, yes—but it still remains our right and our responsibility to decide what books our children are going to be made to read in our community." This is surely so. But it is also true that if you exercise that right and fulfill that responsibility in an ignorant, harsh, un-American manner, then people are entitled to call you bad citizens and fools. Even your own children are entitled to call you that.

I read in the newspaper that your community is mystified by the outcry from all over the country about what you have done. Well, you have discovered that Drake is a part of American civilization, and your fellow Americans can't stand it that you have behaved in such an uncivilized way. Perhaps you will learn from this that books are sacred to free men for very good reasons, and that wars have been fought against nations which hate books and burn them. If you are an American, you must allow all ideas to circulate freely in your community, not merely your own.

If you and your board are now determined to show that you in fact have   10 wisdom and maturity when you exercise your powers over the education of your young, then you should acknowledge that it was a rotten lesson you taught young people in a free society when you denounced and then burned books—books you hadn't even read. You should also resolve to expose your children to all sorts of opinions and information, in order that they will be better equipped to make decisions and to survive.

Again: you have insulted me, and I am a good citizen, and I am very real. ©/©

Reflections and Inquiries

1. How would you describe the tone of Vonnegut's letter to Charles McCarthy? Is it angry? Upset? Respectable? Sarcastic? A little of each? Something else? What is noteworthy about the tone of the letter?

2. What do you consider to be the most important point that Vonnegut makes in his letter? How convincingly does it come across?

3. Imagine that you are a member of a junior high school book-selection committee. Would you vote to ban Vonnegut's book on the basis of the sentence that he quotes from it? Why or why not?

4. To what extent does Vonnegut consider the views of the Drake school board? Should he have been more sympathetic to them? Explain. You may wish to review Rogerian argumentative strategies in Chapter 5.

5. What seem to be the major factors underlying a public school board's decision to ban books? Which of these factors, if any, seem valid to you?

Reading to Write

Write a letter to Vonnegut in which you support or take issue with his response to the Drake school board.

Student Essays

Point-Counterpoint: Two Student Essays on Book Censorship
Kiley Strong and Gaby Caceres

Is book censorship bad or good? Bad in some cases but good in others? What criteria should be used in judging one way or another? The matter is complicated by the fact that there are many motives for censorship and many situations in which it isn't even clear if works have been censored or not. In the case of the traditional Western canon, is the relative absence of works by women or persons of color the result of censorship? What about censoring certain kinds of books for children of a certain age? The very term "censorship" becomes problematic. In their respective essays, Santa Clara University seniors Kiley Srong and Gaby Caceres take very different views on censorship in schools: Strong on the myth of book censorship and Caceres on when censorship is and is not necessary.

The Myth of Book Censoring Within the American Education System

The traditional literary canon has come under fire in recent years for the exclusion of works by females and cultures outside the western hemisphere. However, some school boards in the United States have aimed the ammunition at some of the literature's content rather than the homogony of the works' authors. For example, students in Savannah, Georgia, in 1999 had to obtain a signed permission slip from parents to read *Hamlet*, *Macbeth*, or *King Lear*. Since when does Shakespeare meet the qualifications of literature which needs to be censored from students? Conservative parents, teachers, and educators should be aware that carrying censorship too far will only result in cheating students of a well-rounded education. The banning of books should not be permitted in the secondary level of public education because the lack of specific criteria makes the process too subjective and limits the ideologies and opinions to which students are exposed.

What exactly does book banning consist of? The Modern Library Association cites two statuses books can be in, based on complaints and recommendations of readers. The first is books which are challenged by educators for their content and are considered books which should be taken off of reading lists in schools and out of public libraries. While these books supposedly contain questionable material, they still remain readily available to the public. If a book is successfully challenged, it becomes a "banned" book, meaning it is removed from public libraries and is not allowed to be sold in bookstores due to its content. The history of book censorship in the United States is interesting and provides a foundation for the arguments against censorship at secondary level in schools. Books have been banned from the public sphere since before the United States existed for reasons ranging from obscenity to racism to curse words to antidemocratic sentiments. Some past banned books include *Hamlet, The Communist Manifesto, Lady Chatterley's Lover,* and *Moll Flanders.* To a contemporary this censorship of classic literature is laughable.

Many Americans willingly accept freedom of speech and recognize the option they have to view the book or not to view it, much like pornography. However, the issue gains heat when considering how students of varying perspectives, backgrounds, and maturity levels will react to literature that contains mature content. In modern American society the media expose children to sex, cursing, violence, and a wide range of political ideologies on a daily basis. Educators and parents naively believe that students' first exposure to this content is through reading books which contain this material. Conservative parent and educator groups who insist on sheltering important ideas and viewpoints from a generation which has already long been exposed to the "real world"—some probably even by watching *The Real World*.

Book censorship remains a mysterious process which does not have any real criteria and remains a local rather than a national level issue. These two facts detract from the credibility of such decisions. Who decides which books should be banned? Mostly it is parents and school board members who are outraged that teachers try to introduce such topics in a classroom setting. School boards then vote to remove books from the libraries only for the reason that parents or faculty believe they are too obscene, too racy, too racist, or too anti-America for children to handle. And if books are to be banned, why is this only done at a local level? If a book is considered inappropriate for 16-year-olds in one county, why not for 16-year-olds across the board? The answer to this question is obviously that there are regional differences in beliefs. But really whose beliefs are these? They are mostly the beliefs of the parents and educators, not the students. Given the chance, most students would rather read a controversial book than, say, *Moby Dick.* If definitive criteria existed by which a book could be judged, then I think the process would seem fairer to everyone and more practical. But how can a book be judged inappropriate in one place, and taught in another?

While the lack of criteria makes banning wrong on a logical level, the real   5
issue at hand is that students could possibly miss out on important and eye-opening experiences. When a teacher chooses a book to teach in an English class, it is usually because the book is an example of fine literature and style and also contains universal themes. Reading provides students with the opportunity to understand other people's perspectives and walk in another person's shoes. For example, *Black Boy* by Richard Wright, a book banned a few decades ago, gives students a chance to experience what it is like to grow up in the South as a black

man. By banning this book from schools, it cheated students of the chance for an eye-opening reality check of what life in the South was actually like. And even if the reality presented is harsh, its better for students as American citizens to be aware of the reality, as opposed to having an idyllic view of Southern society in the past. Another reason books that discuss sex, racism, and other hot topics should be taught to students is that the classroom provides a much better setting to learn about and discuss these topics than anywhere else. Within a structured classroom environment students can hear honest viewpoints provided by teachers and classmates and partake in discussions about what they are reading. This option is preferable to students just hearing about sex and racism from their peers or the media, which most likely would provide exaggerated, untrue, or stereotyped information.

So before teachers and parents start urging the removal of books from school libraries and classrooms, they should take a second look at what ideologies they are exactly removing. By preventing the free consumption of ideas, parents and educators are acting in the same manner as the Chinese government. According to a recent issue of *Time* magazine, when Tiananmen Square is googled in China, the only images which pop up are tourist photos or one of a congressman posing in the square. This kind of censorship is outrageous to Americans and parents should not think that solely exposing children to ideas and hot issues through literature is going to incite children to act in a certain manner or develop certain ideas; rather books give students ideas to think and mull over in their own heads and form their own ideas and not eat the ideals parents forcefeed them.

Richard Wright (1908–1960) is an African American novelist and social critic whose books dramatize racial injustice.

Censorship of Books for Public High Schools: When Necessary, When Not

> "It's not just the books under fire now that worry me. It is the books that will never be written. The books that will never be read. And all due to the fear of censorship. As always, young readers will be the real losers."
> Judy Blume

Censorship is a heated issue affecting all aspects of speech and media. Particularly among school boards, censorship is a longstanding debate with no easy or obvious resolution that will please all board members, teachers, students, parents, and anyone else with connections to these schools. School boards must make many decisions about what is allowed to be taught in classrooms and what is not allowed in the curriculum. Especially among public high school textbooks, censoring of books is a topic of extensive discussion and argument. Obviously not all works are appropriate *required* reading for public high school students—for example, pornographic literature or books advocating devil worship. But because the censorship of schoolbooks has become so prevalent, removing the censorship of schoolbooks in public high schools could not only lead to a broader knowledge for these teenagers but also help these young adults feel more accepted within their family and society.

Many feel that censorship is a thing of the past, but a close look into the complexities and controversies that arise from censorship or attempted censorship reveal that it is a longstanding problem still present in many high school systems, leading to problems for not only high school students but also for their families and teachers. Prominent publishers of public high school textbooks such as Scott, Foresman; McGraw-Hill; and many others delete or reword material that certain groups or authors would most certainly object to. The censorship of high school written material has even developed such strict guidelines and regulations that in some states rejection or significant changes have been made in one-half to two-thirds of the material proposed for use. Publishers use censorship as a way to protect themselves and the readers of their books from reading material that others could claim to be damaging to the readers: reference to possible negative exposure of material that shows sex and drug use; literature showing children challenging parents and authorities; discussion of evolution and/or creationism; racist and/or sexist views. But these issues are not the only reason for censorship. Right-wing conservatives also pressure publishers, as do left-wing liberals, each supporting their views of what should and should not be included in schoolbooks. These influences are supposed to help young adolescents become well educated, but what is really happening is the development of problems that will negatively affect high school students.

One of the main reasons the removal or censoring of school books published for public high schools is seen as necessary is that such books run the risk of misleading and of misrepresenting material. Many publishing companies are scared of the negative publicity from lawsuits that arise from publishing sensitive or offensive material. Publishers are responding to this fear by eliminating or changing large amounts of written material submitted for use in their textbooks. Although publishers must protect themselves from lawsuits, they are now deleting or rewording so much written material that it is jeopardizing the textual integrity of their schoolbooks. For example, one publisher of a high school anthology deleted over three hundred lines of Shakespeare's *Romeo and Juliet*. This is a large quantity of material to eliminate from a play consisting of less than three thousand lines, and it is hard to believe that the substance and meanings behind the play are fully preserved under these conditions. Many critics agree that changing such a large part of this play leads to the corruption and distortion of a famous literary classic. Anne Ravitch, author of *The Language Police*, states "The history texts are reluctant to criticize any dictator unless they are long dead. And even then, there are exceptions like Mao who is praised in one text for modernizing China but his totalitarian rule is not mentioned." Ravitch has also shown her disproval of certain textbooks which display photos of Saudi women working as doctors and nurses, because of the implication that they have gender equality, which everyone knows is not the case.

The publishers' problem is not only the fact that they alter the information 10 published in their textbooks but also that they usually do not note these changes, or simply mention them on the bottom of the acknowledgements page. Many times, even acknowledged alteration of written material is not specific on what or where the changes are.

Another reason to prohibit censorship of school books is that the reading material that publishers consider to be unfit for a public high school curriculum could actually help students better understand themselves, their families, and their societies. Censorship is such a highly subjective issue that publishers are afraid to publish anything. If one group advocates a certain issue in a text, another group denounces that issue and demands its removal, forcing publishers to "dumb down" the books they distribute to avoid any conflict.

Some of the many topics that are constantly challenged and removed from schoolbooks are the ones that deal with issues relevant to today's teenagers and young adults. Any references to sex, drugs, alcohol, violence, or children challenging their parents almost never make their way into literature provided for public high school students. In this day and age, adolescents are going through many changes and are beginning to experience many pressures and desires that will help form their characters in the years to come. Thus, high school students could definitely gain from exposure to some literature discussing these controversial issues. All teenagers question themselves and their place in society; at some point all teenagers wonder whether or not they are normal or whether or not they are living a normal lifestyle. Reading literature that deals with these issues could certainly help young adults relate to issues that are so pertinent to their age group. Adolescents could use this exposure to not only help themselves feel that they are acceptable within their families and society, but also to educate themselves about the dangers and consequences of sex, drugs, alcohol, and violence. Also, this kind of literature can help reduce tensions felt by so many teenagers and can reassure them that it is normal to feel certain pressures and desires at their age. With opportunities to realize that they are normal, to have books to turn to, and to help them relate to certain issues, students can relieve themselves of their anxieties and focus more attention on academics.

The censorship of schoolbooks also has a negative impact on the preparation of future college students and current high school teachers. Since censorship does not substantially affect the textbooks or literary works taught at college level, many high school student, teachers, and college faculty are faced with problems over the preparation of prospective college students. Joan DelFattore, professor of English Education at the University of Delaware, understands the negative effects of censorship and says, "When twelfth-grade textbooks present the following year's college freshman with versions of *The Right Stuff* without expletives, Chaucer without bawdiness, *Hamlet* without overt sexual relations between Gertrude and Claudius, and 'The Train from Rhodesia' without 'piccanins,' these textbooks are giving the students neither an accurate factual background in literature nor adequate preparation to discuss the complexities and controversial elements of the unadulterated literature taught in college."

High school students should be fully prepared for their future schooling at the university level, and the censorship of high school texts unquestionably deters students from achieving that necessary level of preparation. Of course, not all high school graduates attend college, but even when a student will not continue his or her schooling at a higher level, censorship can still leave a negative influence. A student that is taught misrepresented or misleading information will never know that what he or she learned in high school was not accurate information.

Since oftentimes acknowledgements of censored material are not men-   15 tioned in high school books or are inconspicuously printed, teachers are left uninformed on the subjects to be taught. Thus, they can not adequately teach their students, much less properly plan their discussions.

Many argue that censorship of material for high school students is absolutely necessary to have a diverse multicultural education and to avoid the corruption of teenagers. A closer look at these arguments reveals that these claims are false. Liberals argue that censorship is the only way minority authors have the chance to place their works in high school texts; however, since right wing conservatives more commonly lead the pressures that influence publishers, works that represent women and minority writers such as Frederick Douglass and Harriet Beecher Stowe are often replaced by more traditional ones like those written by dead white european males such as Nathaniel Hawthorne and Henry David Thoreau to please the greater pressures of the conservatives. School boards and publishers also challenge or ban books proposed for distribution for a high school curriculum for fear that certain material corrupts teenagers. Even books such as J. K. Rowling's Harry Potter series have been challenged and banned from some school districts because of the claim that they promote witchcraft and deal with dark subjects such as death and evil too often.

Although censorship is a good way to protect students from offensive material, the censorship of one book leads to the censorship of another and another, creating a slippery slope in which students become deprived of the privilege to read books that ultimately encourage the use of their imagination and critical thinking skills. Often schools and publishers also bring too much negative publicity to challenged books, resulting in a motivating factor for students to seek out these books and read them, not the result the censors intended.

Perhaps developing a compromise between those who are against censorship and those who deem it necessary will resolve the longstanding problems that are affecting students across the nation. First and foremost, publishers must be more specific as to what contents they have altered or deleted. Acknowledgements of these alterations should be explicit on each literary work affected so students and teachers can be aware of these changes. Also, allowing students to read certain material that has been considered objectionable should be allowed as long as teachers and parents abide by strict guidelines that might help their students. Teachers and parents should be able to carefully examine the material they propose for students to read and help the students to distinguish between literal and literary ideas. Teachers should also allow themselves to be open to discussion about the uncensored material so that students can discuss their readings and feelings on the taboo issues that affect teenagers each day. If teachers and parents can openly discuss the material that their students read at school, censorship of high school texts would not be such a controversial issue because schools would not have as much to fear for their students.

As a controversy, censorship will not be resolved anytime in the near future. It will, in fact, be a more frequent issue every day. It has a profound impact on students across the United States. Over time, censorship has not only become a personal issue but has led to federal disputes. Authors around the world are deterred from writing about certain things for fear of the detrimental effects others may claim are being imposed on students and the possible lawsuits that could arise against them. If publishers would stop worrying about making the greatest possible profit, high school texts might be more sensitive in teaching tolerance, honor, and courage, all necessary for shaping the future leaders of our nation. High schools need to realize the negative affects of distributing censored material and need to act in order to help high school students learn to their full potential. ◎/◎

Reflections and Inquiries

"The Myth of Book Censoring . . ."

1. How convincingly does Kiley Strong support her claim that banning books from secondary public schools should not be permitted?
2. What problem does Strong see in the differing regional criteria used to determine whether a book should be banned?

"Censorship of Books for Public High Schools . . ."

3. According to Caceres, when can censorship of certain books in public high schools be beneficial? When can it be a problem?
4. Caceres states that a "compromise" between those who advocate censorship and those who are against it could "resolve the longstanding problems that are affecting students across the nation." What kind of compromise? What longstanding problems does Caceres have in mind?
5. Do you find one essay easier to read than the other? Is one essay's ideas clearer than the other? What contributes to these differences?

Reading to Write

Examine the arguments both for and against the censoring of *one* particular book in public high schools, and take a stance on the issue—either for censorship of the work or against it.

Issues for Further Research: Effects of Media Violece

Statement Linking Media Violence to Violence in Kids Draws Criticism | Cheryl Arvidson

In 2000, four major health organizations, including the American Medical Association and the American Academy of Child & Adolescent Psychiatry, issued a statement attesting to overwhelming evidence of a connection between media violence and violent behavior in children. But a number of experts, including one psychiatrist, are not convinced that a significant connection exists. Journalist Cheryl Arvidson summarizes both sides of the issue in the following report.

The decision by four major health organizations to issue a statement linking violent television shows, movies, music lyrics and video games to violence in children was a political one, not one based on conclusive scientific evidence, according to censorship foes and academics who have studied the existing research on violence and the media.

"It's absolutely predictable in the current political climate," said Henry Jenkins, a professor of comparative media studies at the Massachusetts Institute of Technology, about the statement released last week in Washington at a Capitol Hill news conference convened by Sen. Sam Brownback, R-Kan.

"The mixture of the post-Columbine moral climate coupled with an election year is designed to feed the 'culture war' rhetoric," Jenkins said, referring to last year's massacre of 12 students and a teacher by two teen gunmen in a Denver suburb. "It feeds into the hands of various political groups that would like to set themselves up against popular culture for political gain."

"The question I have is, Where's the news here?" said Robert Corn-Revere, a First Amendment specialist with the Washington law firm of Hogan & Hartson. "This isn't based on some new research or new finding. It's not a medical or scientific statement. It's a political statement."

The four organizations issuing the statement—the American Medical 5 Association, the American Academy of Pediatrics, the American Psychological Association, and the American Academy of Child & Adolescent Psychiatry said that more than 1,000 studies "point overwhelmingly to a causal connection between media violence and aggressive behavior in some children."

"The conclusion of the public health community, based on over 30 years of research, is that viewing entertainment violence can lead to increases in aggressive attitudes, values and behavior, particularly in children," the statement said.

"I know the research is not as definitive as people suggest it is and claim it is," said Joan Bertin, executive director of the National Coalition Against Censorship. "Why there is this movement in the medical community I don't know . . . but obviously, somebody has been doing some organizing."

Dr. Edward J. Hill, a spokesman for the American Medical Association, flatly disputed suggestions that the health groups were making a political statement. But he did acknowledge that the statement was issued at the behest of Brownback and some of his congressional colleagues who "wanted to raise the level of public awareness of the epidemic of violence and the youth of America."

Source: Cheryl Arvidson, "Statement Linking Media Violence to Violence in Kids Draws Criticism." *The Freedom Forum Online,* July 31, 2000. Reprinted with permission of The Freedom Forum.

"What's the political advantage of the American Medical Association to go out and talk about a link between media violence and violence?" Hill asked. "I don't see any political advantage to that. I think we have a professional and moral responsibility to point out that there is that link, and parents have to be extremely aware of this link. I think that is extremely responsible."

But Jonathan Freedman, a professor in the University of Toronto 10 Department of Psychology who has studied the research on media violence and violent behavior, said he found the statement of the AMA and other health groups to be "irresponsible."

"It's incredible," he said. "The scientific evidence does not support what they are saying. In fact they claim that it does, and that is simply incorrect in my opinion."

Freedman said that although some studies suggest a causal link between entertainment violence and violent acts in children, "the majority of them do not. Normally, in science, you expect to get consistent results. It's irresponsible for any scientist to say that given the distribution of (these) results, this is proven."

Freedman, a psychologist, said he wouldn't be so upset if the medical groups had issued a statement saying they believed there was a link "based on our intuitions and experience. But putting it in terms of what scientific evidence shows is irresponsible and absolutely wrong. I would challenge the AMA to bring forth any member of their board who has read it (the research).

"First, you have to be trained to read it," he continued. "I imagine the doctors would have a great deal of difficulty reading this kind of research. Even if they were trained to do it, they would have to take the time to do it. It would take a year to read the research carefully. I don't blame them for not reading it; I just blame them for making a statement that suggests they have read it."

Hill, the AMA spokesman, conceded that neither he nor anyone on the 15 board had read the research, "but we have a science department that gives us the information that we utilize. We have to depend upon that science department. I suspect that our science department has thoroughly read that material."

Hill said suggestions that the scientific evidence is not definitive reminded him of the earlier debate over evidence linking tobacco to cancer.

"Forty years ago they said exactly the same thing about tobacco," he said. "Obviously, it has been quite proven that we were not irresponsible. This is another example of that type of rhetoric. They're condemning the quality of science behind this link that we think is a causal link between media violence and real violence in some people."

But Freedman said it was "really insulting" to compare the studies on television, movie, music or video game violence to the smoking and cancer studies. "There the evidence is extremely powerful and consistent and convincing. That is not the case with this kind of (violence) research," he said.

Bertin said that for several years, social scientists have sought to cast the media violence/youth violence debate as the same type of discussion identified cigarettes and guns as public health threats.

"The cause and effect between cigarettes and health and guns and health 20 are clear," she said. "But here, the link between viewing violence in some entertainment format and engaging in a criminal act is not at all clear."

Jenkins, who said he approached the question from the viewpoint of a "humanist" who studies issues of culture, said he was troubled when lawmakers trumpet "fairly simple-minded political solutions to complex problems."

"We're not dealing with this (youth violence) as a complex, cultural concern that requires multiple types of research to be brought together," he said. "That is not to say the media has no effect, it's just that it is much more complicated than the causal claim" cited by the health organizations.

Both Jenkins and Bertin said that when a group as prestigious as the AMA flatly endorses a link between media violence and violence in children, it raises the stakes in the debate and makes it more difficult to get to the heart of the problem.

"It's very, very hard to argue against the AMA because of the aura of authority that we ascribe to medicine and science in our current culture, which means to me the AMA should be more careful" in the positions it takes, Jenkins said. "I'm simply skeptical that my doctor has more to say than I do about the cultural causes of these problems. It's making judgments about things [the doctor] isn't qualified to evaluate."

Although most people "know instinctively that this (media violence) is 25 not what causes people to become violent and it's much more complicated than that . . . it is going to concern people," Berlin said. "It must be countered. I think to the casual observer, it certainly is going to have an influence."

"I wish these organizations had exerted better judgment than to start releasing statements about causal effects," agreed Corn-Revere, the First Amendment lawyer. "With some very limited exceptions, not even the social scientists who conduct the studies make such claims."

Bertin said one way to counter the argument of the health groups is to "go at it the other way and get the people who actually engage in crime and try to work backwards to determine what are the causative actions that actually precipitated this crime. They hardly ever talk about the media. That might be one way to bring a little more clarity to the discussion.

"I don't want to be an apologist for crummy television and movies," she continued. "That's not the point. The point is these claims of causation are not well founded, and they terribly . . . oversimplify a very complex problem."

Bertin said she was not suggesting that "there isn't an occasional person for whom this stimulus is important, but most people think . . . that the person for whom that kind of stimulus is the operative event is like an accident waiting to happen. If it weren't the TV show, it could be a comic book. That person is looking for an excuse, and finds it in the media he chooses to view."

Jenkins said the problem with current research on media violence and behavior is that cultural studies cannot be conducted in a sterile laboratory environment in the same way other medical research is done. For example, he said, "very few of us consume violent media in a sterile laboratory" and cultural factors have a major impact on how an individual reacts. Also, he said, just studying a "neurological response" does not factor in "how people interpret, translate, make sense of the type of violence they are consuming."

The studies also fail to make distinctions between the impact of different types of media violence on different age groups, he said, adding that the studies also measure only the immediate response to violence, but the effect may be quite different after some time has passed.

"There is no direct process we can follow between consuming media violence and committing violent crime," he said. "I think the really good work . . . is very cautious and very qualified." ◎/◎

Reflections and Inquiries

1. On what grounds does Arvidson assert that the health organizations' statement linking media violence to violence in children is a political one? How did the health experts making the statement counterargue? Whose views seem most convincing, and why?

2. One health expert, psychology professor Jonathan Freedman, finds the statement to be irresponsible. On what grounds does he make this assertion?

3. What is problematic about "claims of causation," according to some critics of the statement?

4. What makes research into the media violence effects on children so difficult, according to media expert Henry Jenkins?

Reading to Write

Given the complexity of establishing a causal link between media violence and violence in children, write a paper in which you argue for the best way to proceed. Should we do nothing to curb the kinds or frequency of violence in video games, TV shows, or movies? Why? Or should we take the opposite track and censor excessively violent shows (assuming we can reach consensus on what "excessively violent" means)? Should we design new kinds of experiments? What kinds?

TV Isn't Violent Enough | Mike Oppenheim

Perhaps experiencing violence vicariously through books, movies, and games is good for us. Aristotle used the word catharsis *to describe the purging effect that witnessing something horrific (such as Oedipus's blinding himself after realizing his tragic misdeeds) has on our emotions. Such emotional release might prevent us from being violent ourselves. Freelance writer and physician Mike Oppenheim works with this idea in the following essay. Could it be true that if the media depicted violence more accurately and graphically—as in real life—we would find it completely unappealing?*

Caught in an ambush, there's no way our hero (Matt Dillon, Eliot Ness, Kojak, Hoss Cartwright . . .) can survive. Yet, visibly weakening, he blazes away, and we suspect he'll pull through. Sure enough, he's around for the final clinch wearing the traditional badge of the honorable but harmless wound: a sling.

As a teenager with a budding interest in medicine, I knew this was nonsense and loved to annoy my friends with the facts.

"Aw, the poor guy! He's crippled for life!"

"What do you mean? He's just shot in the shoulder."

"That's the worst place! Vital structures everywhere. There's the blood 5 supply for the arm: axillary artery and vein. One nick and you can bleed to death on the spot."

"So he was lucky."

"OK. If it missed the vessels it hit the brachial plexus: the nerve supply. Paralyzes his arm for life. He's gotta turn in his badge and apply for disability."

"So he's *really* lucky."

"OK. Missed the artery. Missed the vein. Missed the nerves. Just went through the shoulder joint. But joint cartilage doesn't heal so well. A little crease in the bone leaves him with traumatic arthritis. He's in pain the rest of his life—stuffing himself with codeine, spending his money on acupuncture and chiropractors, losing all his friends because he complains all the time. . . . Don't ever get shot in the shoulder. It's the end. . . ."

Today, as a physician, I still sneer at TV violence, though not because of 10 any moral objection. I enjoy a well-done scene of gore and slaughter as well as the next viewer, but "well-done" is something I rarely see on a typical evening in spite of the plethora of shootings, stabbings, muggings, and brawls. Who can believe the stuff they show? Anyone who remembers high-school biology knows the human body can't possibly respond to violent trauma as it's usually portrayed.

On a recent episode, Matt Houston is at a fancy resort, on the trail of a vicious killer who specializes in knifing beautiful women in their hotel rooms in broad daylight. The only actual murder sequence was in the best of taste: all the action off screen, the flash of a knife, moans on the sound track.

In two scenes, Matt arrives only minutes too late. The hotel is alerted, but the killer's identity remains a mystery, Absurd! It's impossible to kill someone instantly with a knife thrust—or even render him unconscious. Several minutes of strenuous work are required to cut enough blood vessels so the victim bleeds to death. Tony Perkins in *Psycho* gave an accurate, though abbreviated, demonstration. Furthermore, anyone who has watched an inexperienced farmhand slaughter a pig knows that the resulting mess must be seen to be believed.

If consulted by Matt Houston, I'd have suggested a clue: "Keep your eyes peeled for someone panting with exhaustion and covered with blood. That might be your man."

Many Americans were puzzled at the films of the assassination attempt on President Reagan. Shot in the chest, he did not behave as TV had taught us to expect ("clutch chest, stagger backward, collapse"). Only after he complained of a vague chest pain and was taken to the hospital did he discover his wound. Many viewers assumed Mr. Reagan is some sort of superman. In fact, there was nothing extraordinary about his behavior. A pistol is certainly a deadly weapon, but not predictably so. Unlike a knife wound, one bullet can kill instantly—provided it strikes a small area at the base of the brain. Otherwise, it's no different: a matter of ripping and tearing enough tissue to cause death by bleeding. Professional gangland killers understand the problem. They prefer a shotgun at close range.

The trail of quiet corpses left by TV's good guys, bad guys, and assorted ill- 15 tempered gun owners is ridiculously unreal. Firearms reliably produce pain, bleeding, and permanent, crippling injury (witness Mr. Reagan's press secretary, James Brady: shot directly in the brain but very much alive). For a quick, clean death, they are no match for Luke Skywalker's light saber.

No less unreal is what happens when T. J. Hooker, Magnum, or a Simon brother meets a bad guy in manly combat. Pow! Our hero's fist crashes into the villain's head. Villain reels backward, tipping over chairs and lamps, finally falling to the floor, unconscious. Handshakes all around. . . . Sheer fantasy! After hitting the villain, our hero would shake no one's hand. He'd be too busy waving his own about wildly, screaming with the pain of a shattered fifth metacarpal (the bone behind the fifth knuckle), an injury so predictable it's called the "boxer's fracture." The human fist is far more delicate than the human skull. In any contest between the two, the fist will lose.

The human skull is tougher than TV writers give it credit. Clunked with a blunt object, such as the traditional pistol butt, most victims would not fall conveniently unconscious for a few minutes. More likely, they'd suffer a nasty scalp laceration, be stunned for a second or two, then be extremely upset. I've sewn up many. A real-life, no-nonsense criminal with a blackjack (a piece of iron weighing several pounds) has a much better success rate. The result is a large number of deaths and permanent damage from brain hemorrhage.

Critics of TV violence claim it teaches children sadism and cruelty. I honestly don't know whether or not TV violence is harmful, but if so the critics have it backward. Children can't learn to enjoy cruelty from the neat, sanitized mayhem on the average series. There isn't any! What they learn is far more malignant: that guns or fists are clean, efficient, exciting ways to deal with a difficult situation. Bang!—you're dead! Bop!—you're unconscious (temporarily)!

"Truth-in-advertising" laws eliminated many absurd commercial claims. I often daydream about what would happen if we had "truth in violence"— if every show had to pass scrutiny by a board of doctors who had no power to censor but could insist that any action scene have at least a vague resemblance to medical reality ("Stop the projector! . . . You have your hero waylaid by three Mafia thugs who beat him brutally before he struggles free. The next day he shows up with this cute little Band-aid over his eyebrow. We can't pass that. You'll have to add one eye swollen shut, three missing front teeth, at least twenty stitches over the lips and eyes, and a wired jaw. Got that? Roll 'em . . .").

Seriously, real-life violence is dirty, painful, bloody, disgusting. It causes 20 mutilation and misery, and it doesn't solve problems. It makes them worse. If we're genuinely interested in protecting our children, we should stop campaigning to "clean up" TV violence. It's already too antiseptic. Ironically, the problem with TV violence is: It's not violent enough.

Reflections and Inquiries

1. Oppenheim published his essay in 1984 and therefore alluded to TV shows of that time. Does his premise still hold true with regard to current TV shows? Give examples one way or another.

2. Why are depictions of gun murders on TV often "ridiculously unreal"?

3. What specifically makes the typically unrealistic depictions of TV murders much more dangerous than realistic ones?

4. Is Oppenheim being entirely serious when he says that TV isn't violent enough? Why or why not?

Reading to Write

How convincing is Oppenheim's support of his thesis? Write an essay in which you defend or challenge his views, referring to his reasons as well as those from one or two other sources.

Issues for Further Research: Textbook Sanitizing

Language Police Bar "Old," "Blind" | CNN Student News

The following news story discusses The Language Police *(2003), by Diane Ravitch, a professor of education at New York University. In this book, Ravitch presents five hundred words that have been banned from textbooks published in the United States on grounds that such words are offensive or discriminatory to one group of people or another.*

Oh heck: Hell hath no place in American primary and high school textbooks.

But then again you can't find anyone riding on a yacht or playing polo in the pages of an American textbook either. The texts also can't say someone has a boyish figure, or is a busboy, or is blind, or suffers a birth defect, or is a biddy, or the best man for the job, a babe, a bookworm, or even a barbarian.

All these words are banned from U.S. textbooks on the grounds that they [are] either elitist (polo, yacht), sexist (babe, boyish figure), offensive (blind, bookworm), ageist (biddy), or just too strong (hell which is replaced with darn or heck). God is also a banned word in the textbooks because he or she is too religious.

To get the full 500-word list of what is banned and why, consult *The Language Police*, a new book by New York University professor of education Dianne Ravitch, a former education official in President George H. W. Bush's administration and a consultant to the Clinton administration.

She says she stumbled on her discovery of what's allowed and not   5 allowed by accident because publishers insist that they do not impose censorship on their history and English textbook authors but merely apply rules of

---

Source: "Language Police Bar 'Old,' 'Blind,'" from Reuters News Service, August 2003. Reprinted by permission of Foster Reprints.

sensitivity—which have expanded mightily since first introduced in the 1970s to weed out gender and racial bias.

Ravitch's book is taking people by surprise the same way that Rachel Carson's *Silent Spring* did in the 1960s in exposing the effects of pesticides.

"The Older Person and the Water"

She says a lot of people are having fun finding new titles for Ernest Hemingway's *The Old Man and the Sea* which presents problems with every word except "and" and "the." Ravitch said old is ageist, man is sexist and sea can't be used in case a student lives inland and doesn't grasp the concept of a large body of water.

But some people say the phenomenon of sanitizing words and thought is not isolated to textbook publishers seeking not to offend anyone so that sales can be as wide as possible.

The New York Times recently reported that National Institute of Health researchers on AIDS are not only avoiding using words like gay and homosexuals in e-mails so as not to offend conservatives in the Bush administration, they are also inventing code words.

Times journalist Erica Goode reported that one researcher was told to 10 "cleanse" the abstract of his grant proposal of words like gay, homosexual and transgender even though his research was on HIV in gay men.

Nor is the government the only source of constraint or censorship in the watch-what-you-say business. Wal-Mart, the nation's largest retailer, recently banned racy men's magazines from its shelves although it continues to sell sexy underwear.

According to Ravitch both the right wing and the left wing get what they want in American textbooks, for example an emphasis on family values and equality among ethnic groups.

"Everyone gets their pet causes incorporated in textbooks. The history texts are reluctant to criticize any dictator unless they are long dead. And even then, there are exceptions, like Mao is praised in one text for modernizing China but his totalitarian rule is not mentioned," she said.

She was also unhappy to see photos in one text of Saudi women working as doctors and nurses because that implied that they had gender equality.

"You also can't say Mother Russia or Fatherland or brotherhood in texts 15 and that's both silly, trivial and breathtaking. It is like George Orwell's 'Newspeak' come to life," she said in an interview, referring to the manipulation of language in *1984*.

Ravitch said that textbook publishing is controlled by four main publishers and they aim to sell texts state by state, thus forcing them to dumb down the books and make the language as inoffensive as possible. "They don't want controversy and they don't want people screaming," she said. ◎/◎

Reflections and Inquiries

1. "They don't want controversy and they don't want people screaming," Diane Ravitch is quoted as explaining some textbook publishers' "bias guidelines" that include lists of words deemed offensive. What "people" do the publishers have in mind, do you suppose?

2. The *CNN.com* article cites not only textbook publishers but also other organizations, such as large retail businesses like Wal-Mart, and governmental organizations like the National Institute of Health, which feel pressure to sanitize words like *gay* and *homosexual*, even in the context of AIDS research. Do you feel such measures actually help eliminate discrimination? Why or why not?

Reading to Write

1. In an interview, Ravitch associated such manipulation of language with the world of George Orwell's *1984*. Write an essay that explores the implications of this connection. You may wish to allude to Orwell's novel.

2. Examine the list of so-called biased words in Ravitch's book or examine an excerpt from the book published in the *Atlantic Monthly* (Mar. 2003): 82–83. Then write an essay in which you discuss why it is either foolish or sensible to censor such expressions.

Connections Among the Clusters

1. How might freedom of speech issues relate to issues of multicultural learning? (See Cluster 4.)

2. Discuss censorship of ideas in terms of the effort of some teachers, administrators, or legislators to ban the teaching of evolution or the teaching of creationist doctrines. (See Cluster 6, Science and Religion.)

3. What connections can you make between library surveillance by government agencies and national security issues? (See Cluster 5.)

Writing Projects

1. Write an essay on hate speech. Should the existing definitions be modified, and if so, why? Does hate speech deserve First Amendment protection? Why or why not? How should it be dealt with? In your study, refer to cases in point (perhaps including incidents you have witnessed).

2. Recently the FCC has been cracking down on talk-show hosts, charging them with indecent language and fining and firing them. Investigate some of these incidents and decide whether the FCC is stepping out of bounds in terms of restricting freedom of speech.

3. Write a position paper in which you defend or refute the following claim: "Violence depicted in comedy routines or cartoons is harmless to children." Support your assertions with specific examples and testimony from appropriate experts.

Suggestions for Further Reading

Alterman, Eric. *What Liberal Media? The Truth About Bias and the News.* New York: Basic, 2003.

Buckingham, David. "Electronic Child Abuse? Rethinking the Media's Effects on Children." *Ill Effects: The Media/Violence Debate.* Ed. Martin Barker and Julian Petley. London: Routledge, 1997. 32–47.

Cox, Archibald. *Freedom of Expression.* Cambridge: Harvard UP, 1981.

Fiss, Owen M. *The Irony of Free Speech.* Cambridge: Harvard UP, 1996.

Foerstel, Herbert N. *Banned in the U.S.A.: A Reference Guide to Book Censorship in Schools and Public Libraries.* Westport, CT: Greenwood Press, 2002.

Harvey, Phillip D. *The Government vs. Erotica: The Siege of Adam and Eve.* Amherst, MA: Prometheus, 2001.

Kamalipour, Yahya R., and Kuldip R. Rampal, eds. *Media, Sex, Violence, and Drugs in the Global Village.* Lanham, MD: Rowan & Littlefield, 2001.

Murdock, Graham. "Visualizing Violence: Television and the Discourse of Disorder." *Rethinking Communication.* Vol. 2. London: Sage, 1989. 226–49.

Robins, Natalie. *Alien Link: The FBI's War on Freedom of Expression.* New York: Morrow, 1992.

Siano, Brian. "Frankenstein Must Be Destroyed: Chasing the Monster of TV Violence." *Humanist* 54 (1994): 20–25.

Spitzer, Matthew. *Seven Dirty Words and Six Other Stories: Controlling the Content of Print and Broadcast.* New Haven: Yale UP, 1986.

Sternheimer, Karen. *It's Not the Media: The Truth about Pop Culture's Influence on Children.* Boulder, CO: Westview Press, 2003.

Strossen, Nadine. *Defending Pornography: Free Speech, Sex, and the Fight for Women's Rights.* New York: Scribner, 1995.

Thoman, Elizabeth. "What Parents Can Do about Media Violence." *Center for Media Literacy.* 13 May 2003 http://www.medialit.org/focus/par_home.html.

4 Multicultural Learning: What Are the Priorities?

Introduction

Ideas about education, like ideas about religion and politics, tend to be categorized as "conservative" or "liberal." Thus stereotyped, they tend to become oversimplified as well. While it is true that to be conservative generally means to find value in traditional practices and that to be liberal generally means to be willing to change existing practices in light of changing values and circumstances, it does not necessarily follow that one view must exclude the other.

Multiculturalism—the study of the way that different cultures and groups interact in a particular context (educational, economic, political)—has shed important light on the possibilities of human progress and cooperation. In education, it has called attention to possible correlations between cultural heritage, sexual orientation, socioeconomic background, and learning; between proficiency in a primary or secondary language and learning; between culturally bound teaching methods and learning.

The following selections address some of the key issues regarding multicultural education: Who, if anyone, benefits from instruction that incorporates multicultural perspectives on language, literature, social studies, and history? What is the relationship between multiculturalism and globalization? What can be done to engage students who have been disenfranchised as a result of cultural, linguistic, or ethnic barriers? Can standardized testing be improved to better meet the needs of minority students?

Who, If Anyone, Benefits from Multicultural Education?

Politically Correct | Jim Huber

Editorial cartoons are popular because of the way they can call attention to the short-comings of a policy or trend in current events. At the same time, there is always the danger of misinterpretation or misrepresentation. Obviously, a cartoon must rely on an immediate visual impact to be effective; the cartoonist doesn't have room to provide explanations and qualifications. That said, what does the following cartoon by the syndicated conservative political cartoonist Jim Huber assume about the nature of majoring in ethnic studies? About multicultural learning in general?

Source: Jim Huber www.conservativecartoons.com.

Reflections and Inquiries

1. What assumptions underlie Huber's notion of majoring in ethnic studies? Are these assumptions valid or invalid? Why?

2. Huber's cartoon raises the concern many students (and their parents) have about the relationship between an undergraduate major and career preparation. What are your views on this relationship?

3. Does taking courses in ethnic studies raise the same concerns as majoring in ethnic studies? Why or why not?

Reading to Write

Study the ethnic or multicultural studies courses and programs at your school. If a major is offered in this area, what is its declared purpose? What are the expected learning outcomes of some of the courses? You may want to interview professors teaching these courses—as well as students taking them or majoring in the field—to acquire a fuller understanding of them. Write a report on your findings or write an essay in which you assess the value of such a program.

Perspectives: Improving Race Relations One Journalism Class at a Time | Breea C. Willingham

Eliminating racial discrimination often seems like an overwhelming challenge, even after more than half a century of civil rights reforms. But according to Breea C. Willingham, a former newspaper reporter and now a journalism professor at St. Bonaventure University in Allegany, New York, one must not overlook the small steps. One of the most important of these small steps is simply to talk about race—but as Willingham explains in the following article, that is not as simple as it sounds.

I was standing in line in the Dollar Tree store recently when a blonde-haired little girl who looked to be about 5 years old flashed a toothless smile at me. "Hello," she said. "You have a black face. How did you get that black face?"

I'm usually quick with a comeback, but the girl caught me off guard. After pausing for a few minutes I simply replied, "I was born with it just like you were born with your white face."

"Oh," the little girl said, and went about her business.

Source: Breea C. Willingham, "Perspectives: Improving Race Relations One Journalism Class at a Time," *Diverse Online,* September 28, 2006. Reprinted by permission.

Imagine that little girl in my classroom 13 years from now. I recognize that little girl in a few of my students.

I'm an African-American faculty member on a predominantly White campus in a town where less than 5 percent of the population is minority. [5]

Many of my students are from White suburban communities or small towns, where diversity is not an issue because there is none. For many of them, their first experiences with minorities and discussions about race happen in my classroom.

Getting my students to talk about race is challenging, at best, on most days.

And on the days when my students write papers where they call Black people "coloreds" or say the majority of crimes in the United States are committed by Black men, that goal seems more frustrating than attainable.

The biggest challenge for me is figuring out how to use those frustrations as learning tools and examples of precisely why diversity is needed across the curriculum. Just as newsrooms across the nation celebrate Time Out for Diversity and Accuracy once a year, journalism educators need to be reminded why they have to bring these issues to the classroom.

I've always been passionate about issues dealing with race, ethnicity and [10] diversity, and how they relate to the media. I covered these matters as a reporter for the *Times Union* in Albany, and I work hard to incorporate them into my courses.

For instance, during an exercise in my "Women, Minorities and the Media" class I drew four columns on the blackboard and labeled each one African-American, Asian American, American Indian or Hispanic. I then asked the students to call out stereotypes for each group.

The students had no problem calling out stereotypes such as "lazy," "like to eat fried chicken" and "can't speak English well." But when I drew a fifth column for White people and asked for the stereotypes, the students were hard pressed to find any. I repeated the exercise asking for positive attributes for each group; the lists for the minorities were considerably shorter.

At the end I asked my students why it was so easy for them to point out the negatives and not the positives. They all blamed the media for portraying negative images of minorities.

I try to teach my students that before they can even begin to report on and write about race-related issues, they have to be willing to talk about them first and confront their prejudices.

Teaching that lesson isn't always easy, and I even became discouraged [15] when I read course evaluations from last fall semester where some students criticized me for talking about diversity too much in class.

But then I read one student's paper in the spring semester. "Because of this class I feel better prepared to deal with many social issues and situations, especially race, on a day-to-day basis," the student wrote. I felt an overwhelming sense of satisfaction knowing I at least reached one.

My efforts so far have taught me that adding diversity to the curriculum is more than just adding a new course to the roster, and simply having a "Women, Minorities and the Media" course is not enough.

I'm learning it's more about changing the way students think about and look at diversity issues, and challenging their biases. Professors also need to learn before they can deal with these issues as an educator; they need to acknowledge and challenge their own biases.

Although I have my moments when I feel like I want to give up trying to teach diversity to the next generation of journalists, my passion for the issue won't let me.

And on the days when I feel my efforts are in vain, I remember the advice 20 a colleague recently gave me: "You're the only education some of these students will ever get on race issues. I don't know if that's more frustrating than consoling, but I see it as a legitimate chance for you to make a difference in some of their lives and in the world around you. Yeah, it seems small-scale, but if the world's gonna change, it's going to be one person at a time. At least you're doing some good things to try to initiate that change. Keep at it."

And so I do. ◎/◎

Reflections and Inquiries

1. What point does Willingham attempt to convey with her opening anecdote, and how effectively does she convey it? If you had encountered a young child who asked the same question about your skin color, how would you have responded, and why?

2. Reflect on the role that language plays in race relations.

3. What do you suppose contributes to so much misinformation about race?

4. Comment on the teaching methods Willingham uses in her classes. What other methods can you think of that might also work to raise student consciousness about race relations?

5. Discuss this article from the standpoint of the three Aristotelian appeals of ethos, pathos, and logos. You might want to review "Using Appeals in Argument" in Chapter 1.

Reading to Write

After obtaining testimonials from teachers on how they help their students acquire understanding and appreciation of racial diversity, write an essay on what you consider to be the most effective teaching methods, and why.

Language and Literature from a Pueblo Indian Perspective | Leslie Marmon Silko

Leslie Marmon Silko is a Native American novelist and essayist whose first novel, Ceremony (1977), the story of a half-breed and veteran of World War II who tries to restore his war-damaged psyche by turning to ancient rituals, has been called one of the greatest twentieth-century novels about modern Indian life. Silko, of Laguna Pueblo, Mexican, and white ancestry, attended reservation schools as a child and graduated from the University of New Mexico in 1969. In the following essay, she discusses the fundamental differences between Anglo and Native American experience with language and stresses the need for Anglo educators responsible for teaching Native American youth to recognize these differences.

Where I come from, the words that are most highly valued are those which are spoken from the heart, unpremeditated and unrehearsed. Among the Pueblo people, a written speech or statement is highly suspect because the true feelings of the speaker remain hidden as he reads words that are detached from the occasion and the audience. I have intentionally not written a formal paper to read to this session because of this and because I want you to hear and to experience English in a nontraditional structure, a structure that follows patterns from the oral tradition. For those of you accustomed to a structure that moves from point A to point B to point C, this presentation may be somewhat difficult to follow because the structure of Pueblo expression resembles something like a spider's web—with many little threads radiating from a center, crisscrossing each other. As with the web, the structure will emerge as it is made and you must simply listen and trust, as the Pueblo people do, that meaning will be made.

I suppose the task that I have today is a formidable one because basically I come here to ask you, at least for a while, to set aside a number of basic approaches that you have been using and probably will continue to use in approaching the study of English or the study of language; first of all, I come to ask you to see language from the Pueblo perspective, which is a perspective that is very much concerned with including the whole of creation and the whole of history and time. And so we very seldom talk about breaking language down into words. As I will continue to relate to you, even the use of a specific language is less important than the one thing—which is the "telling," or the storytelling. And so, as Simon Ortiz has written, if you approach a Pueblo person and want to talk words or, worse than that, to break down an individual word into its components, ofttimes you will just get a blank stare, because we don't think of words as being isolated from the speaker, which, of course, is one element of the oral tradition. Moreover, we don't think of words as being alone: Words are always with other words, and the other words are almost always in a story of some sort.

Today I have brought a number of examples of stories in English because I would like to get around to the question that has been raised, or the topic that has come along here, which is what changes we Pueblo writers might make with English as a language for literature. But at the same time I would like to explain the importance of storytelling and how it relates to a Pueblo theory of language.

So first I would like to go back to the Pueblo Creation story. The reason I go back to that story is because it is an all-inclusive story of creation and how life began. Tséitsínako, Thought Woman, by thinking of her sisters, and together with her sisters, thought of everything which is, and this world was created. And the belief was that everything in this world was a part of the original creation, and that the people at home realized that far away there were others—other human beings. There is even a section of the story which is a prophesy—which describes the origin of the European race, the African, and also remembers the Asian origins.   5

Starting out with this story, with this attitude which includes all things, I would like to point out that the reason the people are more concerned with story and communication and less with a particular language is in part an out-growth of the area [pointing to a map] where we find ourselves. Among the twenty Pueblos there are at least six distinct languages, and possibly seven. Some of the linguists argue—and I don't set myself up to be a linguist at all—about the number of distinct languages. But certainly Zuni is all alone, and Hopi is all alone, and from mesa to mesa there are subtle differences in language— very great differences. I think that this might be the reason that what particular language was being used wasn't as important as what a speaker was trying to say. And this, I think, is reflected and stems or grows out of a particular view of the story—that is, that language *is* story. At Laguna many words have stories which make them. So when one is telling a story, and one is using words to tell the story, each word that one is speaking has a story of its own too. Often the speakers or tellers go into the stories of the words they are using to tell one story so that you get stories within stories, so to speak. This structure becomes very apparent in the storytelling, and what I would like to show you later on by read-ing some pieces that I brought is that this structure also informs the writing and the stories which are currently coming from Pueblo people. I think what is essen-tial is this sense of story, and story within story, and the idea that one story is only the beginning of many stories, and the sense that stories never truly end. I would like to propose that these views of structure and the dynamics of storytelling are some of the contributions which Native American cultures bring to the English language or at least to literature in the English language.

First of all, a lot of people think of storytelling as something that is done at bedtime—that it is something that is done for small children. When I use the term "storytelling," I include a far wider range of telling activity. I also do not limit storytelling to simply old stories, but to again go back to the original view of creation, which sees that it is all part of a whole; we do not differentiate or fragment stories and experiences. In the beginning, Tséitsínako, Thought Woman, thought of all these things, and all of these things are held together as one holds many things together in a single thought.

So in the telling (and today you will hear a few of the dimensions of this telling) first of all, as was pointed out earlier, the storytelling always includes the audience and the listeners, and, in fact, a great deal of the story is believed to be inside the listener, and the storyteller's role is to draw the story out of the listeners. This kind of shared experience grows out of a strong community base. The storytelling goes on and continues from generation to generation.

The Origin story functions basically as a maker of our identity—with the story we know who we are. We are the Lagunas. This is where we came from. We came this way. We came by this place. And so from the time you are very young, you hear these stories, so that when you go out into the wider world, when one asks who you are, or where are you from, you immediately know: We are the people who came down from the north. We are the people of these stories. It continues down into clans so that you are not just talking about Laguna Pueblo people, you are talking about your own clan. Within the clans there are stories which identify the clan.

In the Creation story, Antelope says that he will help knock a hole in the earth so that the people can come up, out into the next world. Antelope tries and tries, and he uses his hooves and is unable to break through; and it is then that Badger says, "Let me help you." And Badger very patiently uses his claws and digs a way through, bringing the people into the world. When the Badger clan people think of themselves, or when the Antelope people think of themselves, it is as people who are of *this* story, and this is *our* place, and we fit into the very beginning when the people first came, before we began our journey south. 10

So you can move, then, from the idea of one's identity as a tribal person into clan identity. Then we begin to get to the extended family, and this is where we begin to get a kind of story coming into play which some people might see as a different kind of story, though Pueblo people do not. Anthropologists and ethnologists have, for a long time, differentiated the types of oral language they find in the Pueblos. They tended to rule out all but the old and sacred and traditional stories and were not interested in family stories and the family's account of itself. But these family stories are just as important as the other stories—the older stories. These family stories are given equal recognition. There is no definite, pre-set pattern for the way one will hear the stories of one's own family, but it is a very critical part of one's childhood, and it continues on throughout one's life. You will hear stories of importance to the family—sometimes wonderful stories—stories about the time a maternal uncle got the biggest deer that was ever seen and brought back from the mountains. And so one's sense of who the family is, and who you are, will then extend from that—"I am from the family of my uncle who brought in this wonderful deer, and it was a wonderful hunt"—so you have this sort of building or sense of identity.

There are also other stories, stories about the time when another uncle, perhaps, did something that wasn't really acceptable. In other words, this process of keeping track, of telling, is an all-inclusive process which begins to create a total picture. So it is very important that you know all of the stories—both positive and not so positive—about one's own family. The reason that it is very important to keep track of all the stories in one's own family is because you are liable to hear a story from somebody else who is perhaps an enemy of the family, and you are liable to hear a version which has been changed, a version which makes your family sound disreputable—something that will taint the honor of the family. But if you have already heard the story, you know your family's version of what *really* happened that night, so when somebody else is mentioning it, you will have a version of the story to counterbalance it. Even when there is no way around it—old Uncle Pete did a terrible thing—by knowing the stories that come out of other families, by keeping very close watch, listening constantly to learn the stories about other families, one is in a sense able to deal with terrible sorts of things that might happen within one's own family. When a member of one's own family does something that cannot be excused, one always knows stories about similar things which happened in other families. And it is not done maliciously. I think it is very important to realize this. Keeping track of all the stories within the community gives a certain distance, a useful perspective which brings incidents down to a level we can deal with. If others have done it before, it cannot be so terrible. If others have endured, so can we.

The stories are always bringing us together, keeping this whole together, keeping this family together, keeping this clan together. "Don't go away, don't isolate yourself, but come here, because we have all had these kinds of experiences"—this is what the people are saying to you when they tell you these other stories. And so there is this constant pulling together to resist what seems to me to be a basic part of human nature: When some violent emotional experience takes place, people get the urge to run off and hide or separate themselves from others. And of course, if we do that, we are not only talking about endangering the group, we are also talking about the individual or the individual family never being able to recover or to survive. Inherent in this belief is the feeling that one does not recover or get well by one's self, but it is together that we look after each other and take care of each other.

In the storytelling, then, we see this process of bringing people together, and it works not only on the family level, but also on the level of the individual. Of course, the whole Pueblo concept of the individual is a little bit different from the usual Western concept of the individual. But one of the beauties of the storytelling is that when something happens to an individual, many people will come to you and take you aside, or maybe a couple of people will come and talk to you. These are occasions of storytelling. These occasions of storytelling are continuous; they are a way of life.

Storytelling lies at the heart of the Pueblo people, and so when someone comes in and says, "When did they tell the stories, or what time of day does the storytelling take place?" that is a ridiculous question. The storytelling goes on constantly—as some old grandmother puts on the shoes of a little child and tells the child the story of a little girl who didn't wear her shoes. At the same time somebody comes into the house for coffee to talk with an adolescent boy who has just been into a lot of trouble, to reassure him that *he* got into that kind of trouble, or somebody else's son got into that kind of trouble too. You have this constant ongoing process, working on many differ- 15 ent levels.

One of the stories I like to bring up about helping the individual in crisis is a recent story, and I want to remind you that we make no distinctions between the stories—whether they are history, whether they are fact, whether they are gossip—these distinctions are not useful when we are talking about this particular experience with language. Anyway, there was a young man who, when he came back from the war in Vietnam, had saved up his Army pay and bought a beautiful red Volkswagen Beetle. He was very proud of it, and one night drove up to a place right across the reservation line. It is a very notorious place for many reasons, but one of the more notorious things about the place is a deep arroyo behind the place. This is the King's Bar. So he ran in to pick up a cold six-pack to take home, but he didn't put on his emergency brake. And his little red Volkswagen rolled back into the arroyo and was all smashed up. He felt very bad about it, but within a few days everybody had come to him and told him stories about other people who had lost cars to that arroyo. And probably the story that made him feel the best was about the time that George Day's station wagon, with his mother-in-law and kids in the back, rolled into that arroyo. So everybody was saying, "Well, at least your mother-in-law and kids weren't in the car when it rolled in," and you can't argue with that kind of story. He felt better then because he wasn't alone anymore. He and his smashed-up Volkswagen were now joined with all the other stories of cars that fell into that arroyo.

There are a great many parallels between Pueblo experiences and the remarks that have been made about South Africa and the Caribbean countries—similarities in experiences so far as language is concerned. More specifically, with the experience of English being imposed upon the people. The Pueblo people, of course, have seen intruders come and intruders go. The first they watched come were the Spaniards; while the Spaniards were there, things had to be conducted in Spanish. But as the old stories say, if you wait long enough, they'll go. And sure enough, they went. Then another bunch came in.

And old stories say, well, if you wait around long enough, not so much that they'll go, but at least their ways will go. One wonders now, when you see what's happening to technocratic-industrial culture, now that we've used up most of the sources of energy, you think perhaps the old people are right.

But anyhow, our experience with English has been different because the Bureau of Indian Affairs schools were so terrible that we never heard of Shakespeare. There was Dick and Jane, and I can remember reading that the robins were heading south for winter, but I knew that all winter the robins were around Laguna. It took me a long time to figure out what was going on. I worried for quite a while about the robins because they didn't leave in the winter, not realizing that the textbooks were written in Boston. The big textbook companies are up here in Boston and *their* robins do go south in the winter. But this freed us and encouraged us to stay with our narratives. Whatever literature we received at school (which was damn little), at home the storytelling, the special regard for telling and bringing together through the telling, was going on constantly. It has continued, and so we have a great body of classical oral literature, both in the narratives and in the chants and songs.

As the old people say, "If you can remember the stories, you will be all right. Just remember the stories." And, of course, usually when they say that to you, when you are young, you wonder what in the world they mean. But when I returned—I had been away from Laguna Pueblo for a couple of years, well more than a couple of years after college and so forth—I returned to Laguna and I went to Laguna-Acoma high school to visit an English class, and I was wondering how the telling was continuing, because Laguna Pueblo, as the anthropologists have said, is one of the more acculturated pueblos. So I walked into this high school English class and there they were sitting, these very beautiful Laguna and Acoma kids. But I knew that out in their lockers they had cassette tape recorders, and I knew that at home they had stereos, and they were listening to Kiss and Led Zeppelin and all those other things. I was almost afraid, but I had to ask—I had with me a book of short fiction (it's called *The Man to Send Rain Clouds* [New York: Viking Press, 1974]), and among the stories of other Native American writers, it has stories that I have written and Simon Ortiz has written. And there is one particular story in the book about the killing of a state policeman in New Mexico by three Acoma Pueblo men. It was an act that was committed in the early fifties. I was afraid to ask, but I had to. I looked at the class and I said, "How many of you heard this story before you read it in the book?" And I was prepared to hear this crushing truth that indeed the anthropologists were right about the old traditions dying out. But it was amazing, you know, almost all but one or two students raised their hands. They had heard that story, just as Simon and I had heard it, when we were young. That was my first indication that storytelling continues on. About half of them had heard it in English, about half of them had heard it in Laguna. I think again, getting back to one of the original statements, that if you begin to look at the core of the importance of the language and how it fits in with the culture, it is the *story* and the feeling of the story which matters more than what language it's told in. ◎/◎

Reflections and Inquiries

1. Silko compares the structure of Pueblo discourse to a spider web. Does the comparison work, in your opinion? Explain how it does or does not.

2. Storytelling, according to Silko, lies at the root of Pueblo expression. Why is storytelling so important?

3. In Pueblo culture, what is the relationship of the speaker to the story being told? What is significant, in terms of communication goals, about this relationship?

4. How, according to Pueblo belief, can the story "be inside the listener"? What are the implications of such an assertion?

Reading to Write

Write an essay in which you speculate on ways the Pueblo and Anglo approaches to language might work together to help underprepared students.

Issues for Further Research: The Canon Debate

Equality and the Classics | Dinesh D'Souza

In the following excerpt from his controversial critique of multicultural educational practices in U.S. universities, Dinesh D'Souza argues against the displacement of Western classics by non-Western ones. This premise feeds into his larger view, developed in his book Illiberal Education, *that multiculturalism is merely a façade for a new kind of racist policy in academe—racist in that it mandates multicultural study and manipulates admissions policies based on race, ethnicity, and gender. D'Souza, a native of India, studied at Dartmouth and Princeton Universities, where he edited conservative newspapers. He was a domestic policy analyst under President Reagan and a research fellow at the American Enterprise Institute.*

. . . Universities can address their curricular problems by devising a required course or sequence for entering freshmen which exposes them to the basic issues of equality and human difference, through a carefully chosen set of classic texts that deal powerfully with those issues. Needless to say, non-Western classics belong in this list when they address questions relevant to the subject matter. Such a solution would retain what Matthew Arnold termed "the best that has been thought and said," but at the same time engage the contemporary questions of ethnocentrism and prejudice in bold and provocative fashion.

It seems that currently both the teaching of Western classics as well as the desire to study other cultures have encountered serious difficulties in the curriculum. As the case of Stanford illustrates, an uncritical examination of non-Western cultures, in order to favorably contrast them with the West, ends up as a new form of cultural imperialism, in which Western intellectuals project their own domestic prejudices into faraway countries, distorting them beyond recognition to serve political ends. Even where universities make a serious effort to avoid this trap, it remains questionable whether they have the academic expertise in the general undergraduate program to teach students about the history, religion, and literature of Asia, Africa, and the Arab world.

The study of other cultures can never compensate for a lack of thorough familiarity with the founding principles of one's own culture. Just as it would be embarrassing to encounter an educated Chinese who had never heard of Confucius, however well versed he may be in Jefferson, so also it would be a failure of liberal education to teach Americans about the Far East without immersing them in their own philosophical and literary tradition "from Homer to the present." Universal in scope, these works prepare Westerners to experience both their own, as well as other, ideas and civilizations.

The problem is that many of the younger generation of faculty in the universities express lack of interest, if not contempt, for the Western classics. Either they regard the books as flawed for their failure to endorse the full emancipation of approved minorities, or they reject their metaphysical questions as outdated and irrelevant. Naturally, young people will not investigate these texts, which are often complex and sometimes written in archaic language, if they do not believe their efforts will be repaid. Unfortunately, many undergraduates today seem disinclined to read the classics, but not because they oppose or detest them. Their alienation is more radical: they are indifferent to them. For them the classics have retreated into what Lovejoy called "the pathos of time."

Yet a survey of these books immediately suggests that many of them are 5 fully aware of, and treat with great subtlety, the problems of prejudice, ethnocentrism, and human difference. Long before Willie Horton raised, in American minds, the specter of a dark-skinned man sexually assaulting a white woman, Iago raised this possibility with Brabantio. Will he allow his "fair daughter" to fall into "the gross clasps of a lascivious Moor"? If he does not intervene, Iago warned, "You'll have your daughter covered with a Barbary horse." *Othello* and the *Merchant of Venice*, Shakespeare's Venetian plays, are both subtle examinations of nativism and ethnocentrism. Both engage issues of ethnic and sexual difference. They reflect a cosmopolitan society's struggle to accommodate the alien, while maintaining its cultural identity. Othello is the tragedy of a foreign warrior who depended on Desdemona's love to legitimate his full citizenship in his new country—when Iago casts that love into doubt, not just his marriage but his identity was fundamentally threatened. By contrast with Othello, Shylock is the outsider who refused to integrate, and pressed his principles into uncompromising conflict with those of Christian civilization. These timeless examples of the tension between community and difference are precisely what young people today should confront, and respond to in terms of their own experience.

The relevance of the classical tradition to questions of beauty and equality and freedom has not gone unrecognized by perceptive black thinkers and writers. Traveling in Vienna, W. E. B. Du Bois wrote, "Here Marcus Aurelius, the Roman Caesar died; here Charlemagne placed the bounds of his empire that ruled the world five centuries. . . . Around Vienna the intrigues and victories of Napoleon centered. . . . And here, after the downfall of the great Tyrant, sat the famous congress which parcelled out the world and declared the African slave a stench in the nostrils of humanity." Du Bois saw the grandeur and degradation in a single unifying thought—slavery was the West's tragic flaw; yet it was tragic precisely because of the greatness of the civilization that encompassed it.

Paul Robeson recalled that his father took him "page by page through Virgil and Homer and other classics." As a result, Robeson says, "a love of learning, a ceaseless quest for truth in all its fulness—this my father taught." Robeson believed that the Latin and Greek classics were just as much the treasure of the American black as of the American white. When Robeson played Othello on Broadway, he created a national sensation. Audiences found *Othello*, in Robeson's words, "painfully immediate in its unfolding of evil, innocence, passion, dignity and nobility, and contemporary in its overtones of a clash of cultures, and of the partial acceptance and consequent effect upon one of a minority group." Othello's jealousy thus "becomes more credible, the blow to his pride more understandable, the final collapse of his individual world more inevitable." In 1943–44 Robeson's *Othello* set a record for a Shakespearean play on Broadway, running for almost three hundred consecutive performances.

For a variety of reasons, university presidents and deans will not implement even the most obvious and sensible reform proposals. First, being for the most part bureaucrats rather than intellectual leaders, they lack the vision and imagination to devise new and innovative policies, preferring to continue familiar programs and echo their accompanying bromides. Second, university officials feel physically and morally intimidated by minority activists; as a result, the activists set the agenda and timorous administrators usually go along. Third, and perhaps most serious, many no longer believe in the emancipation brought about by liberal education, and are quite willing to sacrifice liberal principles to achieve expedient ends.

The liberal university is a distinctive and fragile institution. It is not an all-purpose instrument for social change. Its function is indeed to serve the larger society which supports and sustains it, yet it does not best do this when it makes itself indistinguishable from the helter-skelter of pressure politics, what Professor Susan Shell of Boston College terms "the academic equivalent of Tammany Hall." Nothing in this book should be taken to deny the legitimate claim of minorities who have suffered unfairly, nor should reasonable aid and sympathy be withheld from them. But the current revolution of minority victims threatens to destroy the highest ideals of liberal education, and with them that enlightenment and understanding which hold out the only prospects for racial harmony, social justice, and minority advancement. . . . ◎∕◎

Reflections and Inquiries

1. Why does D'Souza think that Western intellectuals' efforts to include an examination of non-Western cultures in the curriculum constitutes "a new form of cultural imperialism"? Do you agree or disagree with this charge, and why?

2. According to D'Souza, young faculty members lack interest in, or even show contempt for, traditional Western classics. Why? Have you found this to be the case in your experience?

3. Compare D'Souza's use of evidence to support his views with Lawrence W. Levine's in the selection that follows. Which of the two authors provides the most convincing support for his thesis? What errors in reasoning, if any, do you detect in one or both of these authors?

4. D'Souza places much of the blame for curriculum design problems on university presidents and deans. Is this a valid charge? Bring up the matter with the dean or president at your school and weigh his or her responses against those of D'Souza's.

Reading to Write

What grounding in Western classics (for example, Homer's *Iliad* or *Odyssey*, Dante's *Divine Comedy*, any of Shakespeare's plays) have you had? Do you agree with D'Souza that they can offer as much insight into multicultural issues as non-Western classics? Write an essay agreeing or disagreeing with D'Souza's premise.

A Historian in Wonderland | Lawrence W. Levine

In diametric opposition to Dinesh D'Souza, who argues that the inclusion of non-Western works into the Western school curriculum is unnecessary because the Western classics are universal in theme and scope, Lawrence W. Levine argues that the shift to multicultural books and ideas reflects the changing values of U.S. culture. Once suspected as irrelevant, so-called non-Western works are much more reflective of contemporary U.S. society and hence just as essential as the traditional classics. Levine is the Margaret Byrne Professor of History, emeritus, at the University of California, Berkeley, a recipient of the MacArthur Prize Fellowship, and a member of the American Academy of Arts and Letters.

The "traditional" curriculum that prevailed so widely in the decades between the World Wars, and whose decline is lamented with such fervor by the conservative critics, ignored most of the groups that compose the American population whether they were from Africa, Europe, Asia, Central and South America, or from indigenous North American peoples. The primary and often exclusive focus was upon a narrow stratum of those who came from a few Northern and Western European countries whose cultures and mores supposedly became the archetype for those of all Americans in spite of the fact that in reality American culture was forged out of a much larger and more diverse complex of peoples and societies. In addition, this curriculum did not merely teach Western ideas and culture, it taught the *superiority* of Western ideas and culture; it equated Western ways and thought with "Civilization" itself. This tendency is still being championed by contemporary critics of the university. "Is it Eurocentric to believe the life of liberty is superior to the life of the beehive?" Charles Krauthammer inquired in his justification of the European conquest of the Americas. Without pretending to have studied the cultures of Asia or Africa in any depth, Secretary of Education William Bennett did not hesitate to inform the faculty and students of Stanford University that "the West is a source of *incomparable* intellectual complexity and diversity and depth."

To say that a curriculum that questions these parochial assumptions is somehow anti-Western or anti-intellectual is to misunderstand the aims of education. If in fact the traditions of Western science and humanities mean what they say, modern universities are performing precisely the functions institutions of higher learning should perform: to stretch the boundaries of our understanding; to teach the young to value our intellectual heritage not by rote but through comprehension and examination; to continually and perpetually subject the "wisdom" of our society to thorough and thoughtful scrutiny while making

Source: "Through the Looking Glass" from *The Opening of the American Mind* © 1996 by Lawrence W. Levine. Reprinted by permission of Beacon Press, Boston.

the "wisdom" of other societies and other cultures accessible and subject to comparable scrutiny; to refuse to simplify our culture beyond recognition by limiting our focus to only one segment of American society and instead to open up the *entire* society to thoughtful examination.

To require more careful study and more convincing documentation for the charges against the university is not to be pedantic or picayune; it is to hold the critics of the university to the same scholarly standards and the same humanistic values they claim the university itself has abandoned. The irony is that the critics of the contemporary university too often have become parodies of the very thing they're criticizing: ideologues whose research is shallow and whose findings are widely and deeply flawed by exaggerated claims, vituperative attacks, defective evidence, and inadequate knowledge of the history of the university in the United States and of the process by which canons and curricula have been formed and reformed since the beginning of American higher education.

While performing the high task of protecting knowledge and scholarly standards against "barbarians," it is obviously not always possible to observe the purest scholarly standards oneself. Dinesh D'Souza's "research" technique, for example, is summed up by the following incident. While visiting the Berkeley campus of the University of California, he wanted to speak with "Asian American students" as part of his investigation. Students of Asian ancestry then constituted roughly one-third of the undergraduates at Berkeley, but D'Souza had trouble locating interviewees: "It is not easy to find an Asian student willing to talk at Berkeley. I passed up two or three who would talk only on condition of anonymity. I approached one student waiting for the library to open, but he was too eager not to miss a minute of reading time. Eventually I found Thuy Nguyen, a cheerful woman who turned out to be a student at UC-Davis. She knew all about Berkeley, though; she was visiting her friend Cynthia Dong, an undergraduate there." Thus his *entire* direct testimony from "Berkeley" students of Asian descent—a designation covering a wide variety of peoples and cultures—comes from a student enrolled not at Berkeley but at the University of California at Davis, a campus sixty miles away. Ironically, D'Souza's approach is all too typical of those whose concern about the declining standards and ideals of the academic world has led them to level blistering attacks against it.

After a tour of universities Charles Sykes reported back that "tens of thou- 5 sands of books and hundreds of thousands of journal articles . . . bloat libraries with masses of unread, unreadable, and worthless pablum." Alas, we never learn whether Mr. Sykes knows this because he himself has performed the heroic task of carefully examining the tens of thousands of books and hundreds of thousands of articles, or if he is synthesizing the Herculean labors of other investigators who remain anonymous, or if he is merely *assuming* that so many books and articles that sit so inertly on library shelves simply *must* be "worthless pablum." Robert Hughes too can't resist the trap of pretending to be able to sum up the scholarly world without having done more than dip the edge of a toenail into it. "With certain outstanding exceptions like Edward Said, Simon Schama or Robert Darnton," he declared, "relatively few of the people who are actually writing first-rate history, biography or cultural criticism in America have professorial tenure." Since in his entire volume Hughes cites only six works of history directly in his notes, it is impossible to discern how he arrived at this ludicrous judgment of the discipline of history which is in one of its most exciting and original periods and has in the past several decades produced large numbers of significant works that have advanced our thinking about the past considerably.

Without taking the trouble to conduct an actual investigation, Martin Anderson, a Fellow at the Hoover Institution, decided: "The work of scholars that is relevant to the critical issues facing Americans is almost nonexistent." This self-generated observation led him to the conclusion that "taken as a whole, academic research and writing is the greatest intellectual fraud of the twentieth century." Based upon precisely the same sort of self-referential "analysis," the historian Page Smith concluded that "the vast majority of the so-called research turned out in the modern university is essentially worthless," though obviously he could have had no actual familiarity with "the vast majority" of university research, most of which is in fields he knew nothing about. Similarly, Allan Bloom presented no evidence whatever to document his assertions that students today appreciate classical music less than they did thirty years ago, or that sexual liberation has robbed them of their ability to relate to the novels of the past, or that students no longer think about or want to visit the countries of western Europe. Bloom's "research," apart from his own limited personal experience, was primarily internal, conducted largely in the archives of his own mind and the precincts of the sensibilities of the ancient writers as he envisioned them.

In his influential polemic *Tenured Radicals,* Roger Kimball spoke about the "decanonization" of dead, White, European men in recent years but presented no evidence that writers like Shakespeare are actually studied less now than they were before the 1960s. In fact, the most exhaustive surveys of college and university literature courses conducted in 1984–85 and again in 1990 provide no documentation for this accusation made so frequently by conservative critics. The earlier survey concluded that "courses are added to expand the curriculum, not to replace traditional offerings, which remain in place as core requirements for the English major." Of the courses that 80 percent of the English departments insisted their majors take, the three most frequently required were survey courses in British literature, American literature, and Shakespearian drama. The 1990 survey of over nine hundred English teachers indicated that courses in nineteenth-century American literature featured such authors as Nathaniel Hawthorne, Henry David Thoreau, Herman Melville, and Ralph Waldo Emerson, while previously neglected writers like Frederick Douglass and Harriet Beecher Stowe made their way into the curriculum very gradually. "The major works and authors remain preeminent in the courses surveyed," the report concluded. The ways in which curricular change and tradition can and do coexist and constitute the substance of the contemporary university are simply ignored in the impassioned culture of hyperbole which pictures Alice Walker and Toni Morrison displacing Shakespeare.

Like Allan Bloom, Kimball and many of his fellow critics jump from rhetoric to assumption, from assumption to assertion, from assertion to fact. Author after author, critic after critic have recited the catechism concerning how the New Left has captured the academic world. One searches in vain for evidence, for citations, for documentation. Some truths, it seems, are too obvious to require the needless paraphernalia of scholarship. But not too obvious to need constant reiteration so that once again the unproven assertion becomes "documented" through the sheer force of repetition. In 1992, the historian John Diggins asserted that "in the field of American history . . . a liberal Ph.D. who subscribed to consensus instead of class conflict, or a white male conservative who admired Madison more than Marx, had about as much chance of getting hired on some faculty as Woody Allen of starting as point guard for the Knicks." Though Diggins's claim was unaccompanied by any evidence whatever, Lynn Cheney in her 1992 report as chairman of the National Endowment for the Humanities cited it as a "fact" to document her own allegation that a political agenda now often dominated universities and their faculties. Similarly, Professor Jerry Z. Muller has written that political correctness "is a consequence of the institutionalization within the academy of a cohort of New Leftists who came of age politically in the 1960s, who lecture on egalitarianism while practicing elitism, and who exert disproportionate influence through their organizational zeal and commitment to academic politics," and cited Diggins's own totally unsupported assertion that the New Left dominates as his sole "proof." This kind of uninformed and under-researched generalizing is done ostensibly in *defense* of the university by those who seem to understand, or at least to care, little about its purposes, standards, and approaches.

Charges of political advocacy against the university are made also through the process of transforming norms into extremes. Hostility to the writings of "Dead White European Males" is attributed to any scholar who would supplement the canon with the work of those who have been traditionally excluded from it. Afrocentrism and multiculturalism are made synonymous by simply ignoring the large and sophisticated body of recent scholarship on ethnicity which has nothing to do with Afrocentrism *or* Eurocentrism. Practices and processes that have long exemplified the academe are made to appear to be the contemporary fruits of advocacy. Thus vigorously debating the orthodoxies of prior days, or supplementing and replacing canonical texts and subjects, or altering and experimenting with curricula, or using abstruse theories and complex language, or constructing courses to accommodate the changing nature of the student body, or responding to the major social, cultural, and political forces of the day are treated as evidence of the university's current degradation when in fact they have been endemic in the American academic world. Peter Shaw has complained of "resistance to authority of all kinds" in the modern university: "Literary critics rejected traditional interpretations, scholars found the formal limitations of their disciplines stifling, and humanists objected to the established canon of great works." This condition, of course, is hardly peculiar to our own time but has been an evolving characteristic of American universities throughout the nineteenth and twentieth centuries. Universities are about teaching the methods and dispositions necessary to criticize, question, and test authority.

Similarly, when Gertrude Himmelfarb criticizes many of her fellow histo- 10 rians for daring to "impose upon the past their own determinacy," for acting as if "the past has to be deconstructed and constructed anew," she is, in fact, describing the well-established process of historiography. Historians have always reconstructed the past on the basis of new information, new research, new theories, new approaches, new understandings; on the basis of what the historian Jack Hexter once called the "tracking devices" of their own time. The current emphasis on social and cultural history which so troubles contemporary critics is no more permanent than were past emphases on political, intellectual, economic, or diplomatic history. Neither is it any more—or less— politically motivated. It reflects, as earlier historiographies have reflected, the questions, problems, issues that touch our time and help us make sense of the world. It also reflects the fact that history today is written, as it has always been written, by human beings who are part of their own societies and cultures.

Perhaps the most common of the charges that the contemporary university is guilty of behavior that differentiates it qualitatively from its predecessors and makes it an exception in the history of American higher education are those revolving around what has been called "political correctness" (PC) which has allegedly cast a pall on freedom of expression and action on the American campus. Lynn Cheney has argued that today's students "can disagree with professors. But to do so is to take a risk." In fact, when was it *not* risky for a socialist student to confront her economics professor who was teaching about the wonders of the free market, for an atheist student to confront his professor of religion who was teaching about the wonders of monotheism, or for African American students to confront their professor of history who was teaching about the wonders of the Founding Fathers, many of whom were slaveholders? This has always been the case in the university. Those professors who would welcome vigorous debate and disagreement on fundamentals often fail to get it either because students don't think this is their place, or because of those of their colleagues who don't welcome it and have taught students to repress their dissident urges. Students have always had to learn to accommodate to the whims and prejudices of professors, to the attitudes and sensitivities of fellow students, and to the values and beliefs of the larger society; to, that is, the complex of considerations that today is referred to much too simply as "political correctness."

The trouble with critics like Cheney is that they have made this long-standing condition in the academe a partisan one (unique to the Left) and an exceptional one (unique to our time). From reading Cheney and most of her fellow critics, you would never dream that there existed a conservative Republican professor or a centrist Democratic professor who stifled freedom of thought and inquiry in the classroom, who intimidated students into silence, who felt it was a student's function to listen and a professor's to dominate the discourse, who was confident of having the True Word to impart to a captive student audience. The problem Cheney is describing—of students fearing to risk debate—is neither new nor confined to one part of the political spectrum, nor is it unique to our time, nor is it particularly virulent in our time, nor does it really characterize the contemporary university which is a more varied, more open, more dynamic place to be in and near than ever before. This problem is inherent in the university which is a dual institution: on the one hand a center of free inquiry and discourse, on the other hand a center of intellectual authority—two characteristics that don't mesh easily and often lead to contradictory or inconsistent behavior. Ironically, it is most often Cheney's fellow conservative critics who have invoked authority in their vision of the classroom. Thus Gertrude Himmelfarb has argued that "it is reasonable and proper to ask students, even scholars, . . . to accept, at least provisionally, until disproved by powerful evidence, the judgment of posterity about great writers and great books. This calls for an initial suspension of private judgment in favor of authoritative opinion, the collective opinion of generations."

It surely was much simpler when the university community was a homogeneous one, not because there was more freedom but because homogeneity ensured that there was more unanimity about what constituted acceptable ideas and behavior; because, that is, there was *more*, not less, of what today is called political correctness. When Allan Bloom blamed the radical students of the 1960s for opening the university to the "vulgarities present in society at large," he conveniently ignored the truth that long before the student movements universities had hardly transcended the larger society's "vulgarities" but had in fact mirrored its often prejudiced, repressive, and "politically correct" attitudes toward gender, race, and ethnicity in their admissions policies, their hiring practices, and their curricula.

But the American university no longer is and never again will be homogeneous, and much of what we have seen recently in terms of speech codes and the like are a stumbling attempt to adapt to this new heterogeneity. The major consequence of the new heterogeneity on campuses, however, has not been repression but the very opposite—a flowering of ideas and scholarly innovation unmatched in our history. Charles Sykes quotes the educator Robert Maynard Hutchins's dictum that the liberal arts should free the student "from the prison-house of his class, race, time, place, background, family, and even his nation," and goes on to argue that universities today have reversed Hutchins's definition by focusing on race, class, gender, and sexual orientation. On the contrary, today's universities with their diverse student bodies, faculties, and curricula have done more to free us from the confines of self-absorption than Hutchins could have imagined. The problem with Hutchins's vision is that like Bloom's, it was coupled to a homogeneous university community of faculty and students largely from the same class and background who were allowed to assume that *they* were the model and everyone else the deviants, that *they* possessed culture which everyone else lacked. What so troubles many conservatives is the modern university's presumption in believing that it can actually educate a wide array of people and help free them from the prison house of stereotypes and assumptions—those they hold of others and those others hold of them.

The British historian Sir Lewis Namier observed that "the crowning 15 attainment of historical study is a historical sense—an intuitive understanding of how things do *not* happen." It is exactly this understanding of how things do not happen that the leading critics of the contemporary university lack. Thus they freely spin their facile theories of how the survivors of the New Left lost the political wars but won their ultimate triumph by capturing the university and transforming it from an institution of culture and learning to a high-handed and inflexible purveyor of Political Correctness. The problem with such notions—aside from the fact that they are promulgated, to borrow Carl Becker's memorable phrase, without fear and without research—is that they are telling examples of how things do not happen. Universities in the United States are not transformed by small cabals of political and social radicals who somehow (the process is never revealed) capture venerable private and public institutions of higher learning, convert them to their own agendas, overwhelm and silence the vast majority of their colleagues while boards of regents and trustees benignly look on, and mislead generations of gullible and passive college youth who are robbed of their true heritage and thus compelled to stumble forth into the larger world as undereducated and uncultured dupes mouthing the platitudes taught them by the band of radical mesmerists posing as college professors. "I have never fully understood the notion that faculty could brainwash me into believing whatever they wanted me to," a Stanford undergraduate testified. "Reading Hitler did not make me a fascist; reading Sartre did not make me an existentialist. Both simply enabled me to think about those philosophies in ways I hadn't previously." It should not take a great deal of reflection to realize that neither college students nor college faculties nor college administrations operate in the manner posited by the apocalyptic and conspiratorial views of the contemporary university. This is not how things happen in the American university and to comprehend why some people are convinced that they do we might ponder Richard Hofstadter's notions of the "paranoid style" in American politics.

In no sense did Hofstadter equate what he called the paranoid style with psychological pathology. He argued that while clinical paranoia describes an individual who is convinced of the existence of a hostile and conspiratorial world "directed specifically *against him*," the paranoid style involves belief in a conspiracy "directed against a nation, a culture, a way of life." Hofstadter found this style recurring throughout American history in the anti-Masonic and anti-Catholic crusades, and in such manifestations of anti-Communism as McCarthyism and the John Birch Society. But there is nothing particularly retrograde about the style; one can find it in aspects of abolitionism, of Populism, and of antiwar movements as well. It is less tied to particular political goals than to a way of seeing the world, a way of understanding how things work by invoking the process of conspiracy. "The paranoid spokesman," according to Hofstadter, "sees the fate of this conspiracy in apocalyptic terms. . . . He is always manning the barricades of civilization. He constantly lives at a turning point: it is now or never in organizing resistance to conspiracy. Time is forever just running out. . . . The apocalypticism of the paranoid style runs dangerously near to hopeless pessimism, but usually stops just short of it."

I would argue that this manner of envisioning reality has frequently characterized those who resisted the changes taking place in American higher education, and never more so than during the past several decades. Perhaps the most unfortunate aspect of this mode of analysis is not merely that it's incorrect but that it's so simple and pat and that we learn little, if anything, from it. "We are all sufferers from history," Hofstadter concluded, "but the paranoid is a double sufferer, since he is afflicted not only by the real world, with the rest of us, but by his fantasies as well."

What is wrong with the dominant critiques is not that they are mistaken in every instance, nor that there aren't things to criticize in contemporary universities. Of course there are. We need to integrate learning more fully and to have more sequential courses that build on one another. We need to minimize the use of inaccessible jargon wherever possible, particularly in those fields where jargon has become a way of life. We need to make a greater effort to communicate with colleagues in other disciplines, with students, and with the general public. We need to ensure that teaching ability is considered seriously in all faculty personnel decisions. We need to learn how to respond to the considerable challenge of teaching the most wide-ranging and heterogeneous body of students in the history of American higher education. The problem is that the charges against the university are so hyperbolic, so angry, so conspiracy-minded, and so one-sided they can find almost nothing positive to say. They see little if any good coming out of the new research and teaching on race and gender, the multifaceted study of American culture, the attempts to more completely understand the world and its peoples and cultures, the exciting development of a student body and faculty that are increasingly becoming more representative of the nation's population.

There *is* fragmentation in the United States; there *is* distrust; there *is* deep anger—and much of this is reflected in and acted out in universities, but none of it is *caused* by universities or by professors or by young people. Nevertheless, all three are easy scapegoats for the problems of the larger society.

The many changes taking place in the nation's universities have created awkward moments pregnant with the possibilities of progress but also containing an abundance of room for egregious mistakes, and universities have had their share of both. But to collect dozens of anecdotes illustrating the stumbling of many universities in the face of new pressures and challenges—while ignoring all of their many successful adjustments and innovations—and to parade these stories forth as indicative of the great problem we face is mistaken. Those who do so disregard the fact that the real fragmentation confronting this society has nothing to do with the university, which is one of the more successfully integrated and heterogeneous institutions in the United States, and everything to do with the reality that forms of fragmentation—social, ethnic, racial, religious, regional, economic—have been endemic in the United States from the outset. In our own time this historic fragmentation has been exacerbated because a significant part of our population has been removed from the economy and turned into a permanent underclass with no ladders leading out of its predicament and consequently little hope.

Americans' complicated and ambivalent attitudes toward the university 20 have created the myth that universities are not part of the "real" world, and many professors, pleased at the notion that they were apart from and therefore more "objective" about the surrounding society, have been willing to go along with this illusion and to varying extents have even come to believe it. In truth, as this study will illustrate again and again, universities are never far removed from the larger society. To have a literature of crisis built upon the university and the young as *the* enemy, as *the* creators of fragmentation, discontent, and social turmoil, is so bizarre as to almost, but not quite, defy understanding. Rather than face the complex of reasons for our present state of unease, it is easier and certainly much more comforting to locate the source of our dilemma in an institution—the university—that has always been deeply suspect in the United States, in a group—professors—who have always been something of an anomaly in a theoretically egalitarian land, and in a generation—college youth—who have always made us nervous because they never *seem* to be our exact replicas.

The trouble with the widespread apocalyptic view of the sudden takeover of the university by forces essentially alien to its basic spirit is that this vision removes the American university from the context of its own extended history and transforms long-term processes of change and development into short-term accidents. When the Mock Turtle asked Alice to explain where she came from, the Gryphon exclaimed impatiently, "No, no! The adventures first, explanations take such a dreadful time." Contemporary critics of the university have shown a similar impatience. Explanations *do* take time, but they remain essential. To understand where the university is we have to understand where it has been and how its present state was constructed. There is no quicker or easier way to proceed; to fathom today requires some awareness of yesterday. In the process we will learn not only about higher education, we will discover truths about our culture and, hopefully, about ourselves as well. ◎/◎

Reflections and Inquiries

1. What problems does Levine see with the research methods of certain conservative defenders of the Western curriculum, such as Dinesh D'Souza, Charles Sykes, and Roger Kimball? How convincingly does Levine support his claim that these research methods are defective?

2. According to Levine, "Students have always had to learn to accommodate to the whims and prejudices of professors." Drawing from your own experience, do you agree or disagree that it is more difficult to accommodate to the whims of "politically correct" professors?

3. Why does Levine invoke Richard Hofstadter's notion of "the paranoid style" of politics in describing the attitudes of the critics of multicultural education?

4. What does Levine advocate in the way of better dialogue between the critics and the defenders of multicultural education?

Reading to Write

What long-standing myths about the university help prevent deeper understanding of the relationship between higher education and society, according to Levine? In a short essay, suggest what can be done to dispel these myths.

Student Essay

The Importance of Multicultural Education in Global Society | Chris Garber

In a multicultural society, educators have come to realize, one's social identity cannot be ignored. One's race, cultural heritage, gender, and socioeconomic milieu are fundamental ingredients in acquiring a sense of self. Without finding ways of connecting this sense of self to what one is being taught in the classroom, learning may be impeded. In the following essay, Chris Garber, a first-year business major at Santa Clara University, critiques the arguments against multicultural education and calls attention to its benefits.

People speak as if race is something blacks have, sexual orientation is something gays and lesbians have, gender is something women have, ethnicity is something so called "ethnics" have. . . . Thus, if persons do not fit "neatly" into the aforementioned categories, they are not acknowledged as sharing group membership in any particular group. Moreover, if they do not openly identify with the above categories, people assume that they do not have any worries about the various identities.

—Henry Louis Gates (Ferguson and Howard-Hamilton 284)

By 2030, educators estimate language-minority students will make up 40 percent of children in school (Thomas and Collier 26). This statistic represents not only the increasing diversity of the population in the United States, but also a pressing need within the educational community to reevaluate its focus. Currently, an entire portion of the school age population does not benefit from the system of education in our country. Since this group grows larger every year, curriculum needs to be adapted to meet the needs of a more diverse group of students.

Although a concrete, universal definition remains elusive, most educators understand that multicultural education is a method of teaching that exposes students to a wide variety of cultures, traditions, and social groups in an attempt to help them better understand how they fit into society. This also includes bilingual education, which seeks to increase students' proficiency in English while at the same time maintaining their connection with their first language. Multicultural education has grown in popularity throughout the past 15 years as student populations have grown increasingly diverse. The need stems from the fact that "traditional student affairs and psychological research historically has excluded or minimized the importance of the individual's social identities (i.e., ethnicity, gender, sexual orientation) and their relationship within individuals' psychological, interpersonal, leadership, and social development" (Ferguson and Howard-Hamilton 293). It is detrimental to assume that a child who does not know English would benefit from the same type of education as a student who has been speaking English his or her entire life. Multicultural education seeks to allow all students to benefit equally from education.

The debate on this issue remains complex, and as a result it is easier to avoid rather than discuss or address. Activists bring up the fearful image of the "melting pot" in argument against multicultural education. In this social model, programs use education to mold the various cultures of America into one homogeneous group deemed socially acceptable by dominant society. This results in the loss of the history and traditions of the many ethnic groups who inhabit our nation. Supporters believe in order to "make it" in society, minority students are forced to abandon their heritage, thus giving up their personal and cultural identities (Nieto 10). They fear that multicultural education will serve only to destroy the cultural differences making each of us unique. Another accusation against multicultural education is it completely undermines the integrity of the history of Western thought and achievement. Critics shrug off multiculturalism as an identity crisis of the minority population which threatens to destroy Western culture (Giroux 505).

In his book, *The Disuniting of America*, Arthur M. Schlessinger states a contrasting argument as he explores the effects of multiculturalization on society. He comes to the conclusion that while cultural diversity promotes human interaction, the overemphasis of these differences leads to conflict. First, it creates a group Schlessinger refers to as the "militants of ethnicity"—people caught up in upholding cultural differences who become alienated from society and instill social unrest. Second, cultural separation results in "balkinization": a disuniting of society that eventually leads to social breakdown on the premise that no one will be able to relate to any cultural group but their own. Schlessinger argues that the only way to achieve social diversity without the fragmentation of society is to create an education system that lifts up cultural differences and teaches tolerance and understanding. Only through a system of multicultural education can people gain the cross-cultural experience necessary to interact in today's international world.

Multicultural education benefits and improves our society. In "Two   5 Languages Are Better than One," Wayne P. Thomas and Virginia P. Collier argue for multicultural education because, "in the remedial program, English learners receive less access to the standard grade-level curriculum. The achievement and equity gap increases as native English speakers forge ahead while English learners make less progress" (23). The current system of education proves culturally inadequate since it widens the gap in student achievement rather than closes it. Our current programs for bilingual education involve either separating English learners from the school population or minimizing their exposure to core material. Both options alienate them from their peers and deny them the education they need and deserve.

In his book *Hunger of Memory*, Richard Rodriguez writes about the changes in his life as a result of bilingual education. He explains that the biggest barrier in the English learner's quest for acceptance in society remains the sense of separation between his or her culture and the American life he or she is pursuing. Rodriguez insists, "full individuality is achieved, paradoxically, by those who are able to consider themselves members of the crowd. Thus it happened for me: Only when I was able to think of myself as an American, no longer an alien in *gringo* society, could I seek the rights and opportunities necessary for full public individuality" (27). An educational program making all members feel like they belong builds a stronger and less fragmented community. Once a sense of public identity is achieved, the individual understands his or her societal role and can better interact with other people. In this way, education represents the pathway to becoming a member of society.

The argument against multicultural education has taken a number of different forms. Henry A. Giroux's essay, "Democracy and the Discourse of Cultural Difference: Towards a Politics of Border Pedagogy," emphasizes one of the more powerful movements by conservative intellectuals who claim multiculturalism works against the entire institution of Western thought. They argue multicultural proponents hold distorted attitudes that emphasize bigotry and prejudice in Western culture rather than its great achievements. Furthermore, they label multiculturalism as a crisis within the value system of American culture that destroys the "common culture" that has resulted from hundreds of years of shared international discovery. Giroux quotes Roger Kimball, who states:

> Implicit in the politicizing mandate of multiculturalism is an attack on the idea of common culture, the idea that, despite our many differences, we hold in common an intellectual, artistic, and moral legacy, descending largely from the Greeks and the Bible, supplemented and modified over centuries by innumerable contributions from diverse lands and peoples. It is this legacy that has given us our science, our political institutions, and the monuments of artistic and cultural achievement that define us as a civilization. Indeed, it is this legacy, insofar as we live up to it, that preserves us from chaos and barbarism. And it is precisely this legacy that the multiculturalist wishes to dispense with. (519)

Kimball points out that discoveries of people from all nations founded the modern world. Thus, he explains, modern civilization is by definition diverse and emphasizing these differences is unnecessary. Kimball sees multiculturalism replacing the shared identity developed through humankind's achievements. Furthermore, he concludes, the emphasis of cultural differences does not provide common ground, and therefore it dismantles the foundation of modern civilization.

Gloria Anzaldúa, in her book *Borderlands/La Frontera: The New Mestiza,* 10 argues a different point with ramifications similar to Kimball's. She explains that American education forces other cultures to give up their identities for the sake of fitting into popular society. While her ideas place importance on customs and heritage, she does not support multicultural education. She sees it as a method of assimilation diluting the full importance of cultural independence. She explains, "Chicanos and other people of color suffer economically for not acculturating. This voluntary (yet forced) alienation makes for psychological conflict, a kind of dual identity—we don't identify with the Anglo-American cultural values and we don't totally identify with the Mexican cultural values" (43). Anzaldúa claims that forcing outside rules on minority cultures does not draw them in as expected, but rather pushes them away through the destruction of their social identity. As a result, they cannot relate to other social groups and move to the fringes of society. In addition, by losing their cultural identity, they have difficulty if they want to go back to their original beliefs.

Both Anzaldúa's and Kimball's ideas assume multicultural education cannot provide the benefits found in either the institution of Western thought or the cultural history of minority populations. Kimball's statement ignores the argument that accepted Western thought ignores the ideas of minorities while claiming to represent the entire population. The argument is not what would happen if multicultural education is widely implemented, but rather what will happen if it is not. Giroux states, "what is at stake is not the defense or repudiation of a common culture, but the creation of a democratic society in which differences are affirmed and interrogated rather than dismissed as essentialist or disruptive" (509). Without a broader education base, our society will not gain the cultural acceptance necessary for the coming age of diversity, and Schlessinger's fear of "balkanization" could become a reality.

Anzaldúa's pessimistic view of multicultural education can be counter-argued by Rodriguez, who wrote, "Those middle-class ethnics who scorn assimilation seem to me filled with decadent self-pity, obsessed by the burden of public life. Dangerously, they romanticize public separateness and they trivialize the dilemma of the socially disadvantaged" (27). He explains sepa-ratists have become convinced that minorities cannot emerge as members of mainstream society. By citing personal examples, his story argues that one gains personal identity through cultural acceptance and understanding. Further, he states while his family life at home changed as a result of his learn-ing English, "there are two ways a person is individualized" (26). While an individual's private sense and his or her dependence on cultural heritage diminishes with multicultural education, this loss makes the gain of a greater understanding of the self in relation to the rest of the world possible. In the end, the gain results in the forming of a public identity—a sense of belonging within mass society, which Rodriguez claims is essential to being an active member of a community.

For students in the multicultural age of America, English cannot be a sec-ond language. It needs to be a tool that, when combined with a student's first language, not only makes the student a part of American society but allows him or her to achieve at a higher level than possible without it. In light of this, there are a number of ways multicultural education could be implemented to best improve each student's experience.

For example, in "Strength Through Cultural Diversity," multicultural expert Ronald Takaki proposes that courses encouraging diversity should be offered at universities to fulfill social science or humanities requirements as core classes. In this way, students would receive diversity education without having to take extra classes or commit more time to study (Heuberger, Gerber, and Anderson 109). Angela D. Ferguson and Mary F. Howard-Hamilton call for a similar solution in their discussion of college diversity but assert that faculty need to reaffirm their commitment to supporting a diverse student population. They also seek the implementation of courses and programs that not only support diversity but also "emphasize the idea of diversity as includ-ing multiple identities [and] sensitize students to becoming aware that people do not exist under one identity" (291). This argument seeks not only a broad-er curriculum base but also seeks programs supporting ethnic students as well as those of different sexual orientations. It reminds us that a classroom experience can cover only so much information and that the variables includ-ed in a person's identity are infinite, necessitating personalized support and interaction. Furthermore, Leslie Marmon Silko writes from a Pueblo Indian perspective, a culture based in storytelling. She states, "if you begin to look at the core of the importance of the language and how it fits in with the culture, it is the *story* and the feeling of the story which matters more than what language it's told in" (58). Multicultural education should not emphasize the evident differences in language and customs but rather accentuate the common themes that can be better explored by bringing in diverse works. Commenting on a broad scale, Thomas and Collier see that bilingual education would be beneficial to the entire school age population, not just communities including English learners. "The research evidence is overwhelmingly clear that *proficient* bilinguals outperform monolinguals on school tests" (26). With this in mind, multicultural education represents an improvement on the modern education system not only for minority students but for all. A wide-scale implementation of multicultural and bilingual programs can serve only to enhance the experience of English-speaking students while at the same time rectifying the crime being committed by a system serving only the majority.

It is essential that the American education system keep up with the chang- 15 ing needs of our students. As globalization spreads throughout the modern world, contact and interaction with other cultures will become part of daily life. Students need to be given the tools to allow intercultural relations to take place. This can be accomplished by changing curriculum and implementing programs that broaden the scope of topics covered, as well as enacting bilingual programs to make education more effective for the entire school age population. The result is a student who is not only better educated but ready to critically assess, with an open mind and an open heart, situations involving people from all walks of life. ◎/◎

Works Cited

Anzaldúa, Gloria. "How to Tame a Wild Tongue." Ways of Reading: An Anthology for
    Writers. *Eds. David Bartholomae and Anthony Petrosky. 5th ed. Boston: Bedford, 1999. 36–45.*
*Ferguson, Angela D., and Mary F. Howard-Hamilton. "Addressing Issues of Multiple Identities
    for Women of Color on College Campuses."* Toward Acceptance: Sexual Orientation Issues
    on Campus. *Ed. Vernon A. Wall and Nancy J. Evans. Lanham: UP of America, 2000. 283–97.*
*Giroux, Henry A. "Democracy and the Discourse of Cultural Difference: Towards a Politics of
    Border Pedagogy."* British Journal of Sociology of Education *12 (1991): 501–20.*
Heuberger, Barbara, Diane Gerber, and Reed Anderson. "Strength Through Cultural Diversity."
    College Teaching *47 (1999): 107–14.*
Nieto, Sonia. "Affirming Diversity." National Education Association Today *18 (2000): 10.*
Rodriguez, Richard. Hunger of Memory. *Boston: Godine, 1982.*
Schlesinger, Arthur M. The Disuniting of America: Reflection on a Multicultural Society.
    New York: Norton, 1991.
Silko, Leslie Marmon. "Language and Literature from a Pueblo Indian Perspective." English
    Literature: Opening Up the Canon. *Ed. Leslie A. Fiedler and Houston A. Baker Jr.
    Baltimore: Johns Hopkins UP, 1981. 52–58.*
Thomas, Wayne P., and Virginia P. Collier. "Two Languages Are Better than One." Educational
    Leadership *55 (Dec. 1997–Jan. 1998): 23–26.*

Reflections and Inquiries

1. What are Garber's principal arguments against multicultural education? How convincingly does he refute them?

2. Garber argues that English cannot be a second language for students in the United States. Why not? Do you agree or disagree?

3. According to Garber, "A wide-scale implementation of multicultural and bilingual programs can serve only to enhance the experience of English-speaking students." Defend or challenge this assertion.

Reading to Write

After reading about multicultural education programs, curricular and extracurricular, investigate your school's programs. Examine any brochures and catalogs associated with these programs. What do you see as their strengths and shortcomings? Write an essay evaluating one or more of these programs, suggesting improvements if you feel they are warranted.

Issues for Further Research: Bilingual Education

English: The National Language | John Darkow

Many people think that English is the official language of the United States but the United States does not have an official language—nor should it, some will argue, because it is a nation of immigrants, a pluralist society in which many languages are spoken, as John Darkow's cartoon makes dramatically clear. John Darkow is an editorial cartoonist for the Columbia (MO) Daily Tribune.

Source: © John Darkow/Cagle Cartoons.

Reflections and Inquiries

1. What is ironic about Darkow's cartoon?

2. How might the cartoon be altered to reflect support the English as a national language movement?

3. Compare Darkow's approach to the issue to Monte Wolverton's in the cartoon below:

What aspects of the issue does Wolverton's cartoon allude to that Darkow's does not, and vice versa?

Reading to Write

What are the advantages and the disadvantages to making English the official language of the United States? Before arguing your premise, research both sides of the debate.

Bilingual or Immersion? | Kendra Hamilton

To some educators, the question posed by the title of this article is the wrong question to ask about teaching English to nonnative speakers. The real concern is the quality of instruction. Kendra Hamilton, a poet, journalist, and regular contributor to Black Issues in Higher Education, *discusses the efficacy of this point of view in the following article.*

Source: © Monte Wolverton/Cagle Cartoons.
Source: Kendra Hamilton, "Bilingual or Immersion?" *Diverse: Issues in Higher Education* 23.5, April 20, 2006: 23–26, including sidebar, "Six Myths About Bilingual Education." Reprinted by permission.

A new group of studies is providing fresh evidence that it's not the language of instruction that counts, but the quality of education

Eight years ago, Proposition 227 virtually eliminated bilingual education in California's K-12 schools. Since then, the English-only approach has made inroads in states like Arizona and Massachusetts, where ballot initiatives have created even more restrictive "English immersion" programs than California's. In Colorado, backers of a failed ballot initiative are trying again, this time with a campaign for a constitutional amendment.

But a group of new studies is providing fresh evidence of what many researchers have been saying all along: English immersion has more political appeal than educational merit.

"We're saying it's not possible given the data available to definitively answer the question 'which is better—bilingual or immersion?'" says Dr. Amy Merickel, co-author of "Effects of the Implementation of Proposition 227 on the Education of English Learners K-12." The five-year, $2.5 million study was conducted for the state of California by the American Institutes for Research and WestEd.

"We don't see conclusive evidence that bilingual education is superior to English immersion, and we don't see conclusive evidence for the reverse," Merickel says. "We think it's the wrong question. It's not the model of instruction that matters—it's the quality."

Dr. Tim Shanahan, professor of curriculum and instruction at the University   5
of Illinois-Chicago and director of its Center for Literacy, agrees.

Shanahan and a team of more than a dozen researchers from institutions across the nation recently completed a synthesis of all the available research on literacy, including second language literacy for the U.S. Department of Education.

"When we looked at all the past attempts to get at this issue and analyzed their data, essentially what we concluded was that, in fact, kids did somewhat better if they received some amount of instruction in their home language," Shanahan says. "How much? It was not clear from the available data. What should it look like? That wasn't entirely clear either. But across the hoard, the impact of some instruction in home language seemed to be beneficial.

"But one of the things that surprised me and that stood out for me was the sheer volume of the research that was not devoted to these issues," he adds. "If you look at the data, most of the research is on [which] language of instruction [is better]. That issue has so sucked up all the oxygen that all those other issues of quality clearly are being neglected."

Such conclusions run sharply counter to the assertions of many defenders of English immersion. In 1997, millionaire Ron Unz began a campaign against bilingual education, forming an advocacy organization with a simple name and message—English for the Children. That organization helped push Proposition 227 to a landslide victory in California, claiming 61 percent of the vote.

Two years later, citing dramatic gains on test scores for immigrant children, the English for the Children movement moved to Arizona, where Proposition 203 notched 63 percent of the vote. In 2002, Massachusetts followed suit with Question 2, which was passed with 70 percent support. But in Colorado, voters rejected the English-immersion philosophy, turning it down 55 percent to 44 percent at the polls.

But the movement began to fizzle after 2002. The offices of English for the 10 Children have closed, and studies have consistently been punching holes in core tenets of the English-only argument.

First to fall were the "dramatic gains" in test scores. Proponents of English-immersion stated emphatically that test scores for immigrant students had shot up 40 percent between 1998 and 2000. But research teams from Stanford University, Arizona State University and others pointed out that scores had risen for all students during that period. They also noted that the rising test scores were due to the fact that California had introduced a new achievement test and not to the effects of Prop 227.

More damning was the failure of Prop 227 to hold up its central promise. English for the Children had repeatedly claimed that results could be achieved with only a one-year transition period for English learners.

"The one-year limit is a fantasy," says Dr. Stephen Krashen, professor emeritus at the University of Southern California's Rossier School of Education. "In California and Arizona, English learners are currently gaining less than one level per year out of five, where level five means 'ready for the mainstream.'

"That means that a child starting with no English will take at least five years before 'transitioning.' In Massachusetts, after three years of study, only half of the English learners are eligible to be considered for regular instruction," he says.

Merickel's AIR/WestEd research team noted several exemplary programs 15 during the course of their study. Some of the programs were bilingual, others were English immersion and some were "dual immersion"—providing instruction in both Spanish and English.

Prop 227 has actually been a useful tool, she says, for forcing the state to focus much-needed attention on the non-English speaking population. Some former foes of the proposition, she says, "have come to see it as a positive thing."

But Shelly Spiegel-Coleman, president of Californians Together, an advocacy coalition formed in 1998, isn't willing to go so far.

"The truth is Prop 227 was a horrible blow for us, but if that was all that happened to us since 1998, we could have galvanized attention, made our points" and worked to ease the law's most restrictive elements, she says.

But Prop 227 was the first of a wave of reform movements, each more restrictive than its predecessor. First came a flurry of one-size-fits-all, skill-based reading programs, crafted to meet the curricular needs specified in Prop. 227.

"They allow no accommodation for non-native speakers, and they're 20
sweeping the country," Spiegel-Coleman says.

And then there are the harsh accountability systems mandated by No
Child Left Behind.

"There are these people who have so much invested in these English-only
reading programs and accountability systems who do not want to admit that
what they're doing is wrong for kids," Spiegel-Coleman says.

Indeed, the stakes in these political battles over education could not be
higher. According to U.S. Census figures, the number of children living in
homes where English is not the primary language more than doubled from
1979 to 1999, from 6 million to 14 million. California was home to more than
1.4 million English learners—or nearly 40 percent of all such public school students in the nation (excluding Puerto Rico).

These "language minority" students face formidable obstacles in school,
according to the National Center for Education Statistics. The dropout rate is
31 percent for language minority children who speak English, compared with
51 percent for language minority kids who do not and only 10 percent for the
general population.

"At some point," says Shanahan, "we better get serious about immigra- 25
tion, about integrating immigrants as productive, tax-paying and social
security-supporting parts of our work force. To do these things, they have
to be able to do the work that we do in the United States—that means
we have to be making quality choices to provide them with a quality
education."

But the discussion about quality has only begun, says Shanahan, noting
that his review found only 17 studies concerned with educational quality,
compared with more than 450 studies examining types of reading programs.

Meanwhile the discussion about the language of instruction—a discussion Shanahan says is deeply political—seems never-ending. ◎/◎

SIX MYTHS ABOUT BILINGUAL EDUCATION

Myth 1: Bilingual programs are mostly concerned with maintaining the
ethnic culture of the family.

Response: While some bilingual programs encourage development of a
student's native language after English has been mastered, the major goal
of bilingual education is the rapid acquisition of English and mastery of
academic subjects.

Myth 2: Bilingual education doesn't work; it prevents children from acquiring
English.

Response: Scientific studies consistently show that children in bilingual programs typically score higher on tests of English than do children in all-English immersion programs. In fact, three major reviews coming to this conclusion were published last year in professional, scientific journals.

Myth 3: Children languish in bilingual programs for many years, never learning enough English to study in mainstream classes.

Response: According to a recent report from New York City for children entering school at kindergarten and grade 1, only 14 percent were still in bilingual education after six years. From data provided by the state of Texas, I have estimated that for those who started at kindergarten, only 7 percent were still in bilingual education after grade 5.

Most students in bilingual programs in upper grades are those who came to the United States at an older age. These late-comers face a daunting task: Many come with inadequate preparation in their country of origin, and need to acquire English as well as assimilate years of subject matter knowledge.

Myth 4: Bilingual programs teach only in the native language.

Response: Some critics have claimed that bilingual education requires that children spend five to seven years mastering their native language before they can learn English. This is not correct. In properly organized bilingual programs, English is introduced immediately. ESL [English as a Second Language instruction] begins from the first day, and subjects are taught in English as soon as they can be made comprehensible. Research confirms that English is not delayed by bilingual education. According to one study of bilingual programs, by the time children are in third grade, 75 percent of their subject matter is in English, and it is 90 percent by grade 5.

Myth 5: Immigrants, especially Spanish-speakers, are refusing to learn English.

Response: They aren't refusing to learn English. According to the most recent census, only 7 percent of those who said another language was spoken at home cannot speak English. These figures include newcomers. Census data also tells us that Spanish speakers are acquiring English at the same rate as other groups.

Spanish speakers born in the United States report that they speak, read and write English better than they do Spanish by the time they finish high

school. One does, of course, occasionally run into immigrants who don't
speak English. These are usually new arrivals, or those who have not been
able to find the time or opportunity to acquire English.

Myth 6: Bilingual education is not done in other countries, only in the
    United States.
Response: Bilingual education is not the most widely used approach
    for children acquiring a second language, but it is widespread. Most
    European countries provide bilingual education for immigrant
    children, and studies done by European scholars show that children
    in these programs acquire the second language of the country as well
    as and usually better than those in "immersion" programs. There
    are also numerous programs for the languages spoken by indigenous
    minority communities. No member of the European Economic
    Community has passed the equivalent of California's
    Proposition 227.

*—Dr. Stephen Krashen, Professor Emeritus, Rossier School of Education, University of
Southern California*

Reflections and Inquiries

1. What was faulty about the "dramatic gains in test scores" initially reported
   by the English for the Children group (immersion advocates)?

2. What caused the failure of California's Prop 227?

3. Despite the fact that researchers are uncertain about the superiority of one
   mode of English instruction over another, the "Six Myths about Bilingual
   Education" Hamilton appended to her essay reveals her stance on the matter. How convincingly do her responses to the "myths" support the idea
   that bilingual education is the best approach?

Reading to Write

After reviewing current research in education scholarly journals such as the
International Journal of Bilingual Education and Bilingualism, and perhaps interviewing students who have taken bilingual and those who have taken immersion
classes, write an essay discussing what would constitute "quality" in the teaching
of English to nonnative speakers.

Two Languages Are Better Than One

Wayne P. Thomas and Virginia P. Collier

Some educators argue that bilingual education fails because teachers cannot proper-ly teach students to be experts in the language of instruction while simultaneously learning the subject of instruction. But Wayne P. Thomas and Virginia P. Collier set out to prove that thesis wrong. According to these educators, students serve as peer tutors for each other and are able to stimulate natural language acquisition because they keep the level of interaction intellectually stimulating. Thomas is Professor of Research and Evaluation Methods at George Mason University. Collier is Professor of Bilingual, Multicultural, and ESL Education at George Mason University. Both authors are researchers with the U.S. Department of Education's Center for Research on Education, Diversity, and Excellence.

Among the underachieving youth in U.S. schools, students with no proficien-cy in English must overcome enormous equity gaps, school achievement tests in English show. Over the past three decades, schools have developed a wide range of programs to serve these English learners. After much experimen-tation, U.S. schools now have clear achievement data that point to the most powerful models of effective schooling for English learners. What is astounding is that these same programs are also dynamic models for school reform for all students.

Imagine how the 21st century will look. Our world will surely be in con-stant change, for we are facing this pattern now. The predictions of the near future also depict an interconnected world, with global travel and instant international communications. Right now, many U.S. businesses seek employ-ees proficient in both English and another language. Students who graduate with monocultural perspectives will not be prepared to contribute to their societies, for cross-cultural contact is at an all-time high in human history as population mobility continues throughout the world (Cummins in Ovando and Collier 1998). Thus, majority and minority language students together must prepare for a constantly changing world.

Tapping the Power of Linguistic Diversity

For more than three decades, as we have struggled to develop effective mod-els for schooling English learners, we have mostly considered the choices avail-able to us from a deficit perspective. That is, we have often viewed English learners as a "problem" for our schools (oh, no—they don't know English), and so we "remediate" by sending them to a specialist to be "fixed." In the

Source: Wayne P. Thomas & Virginia P. Collier (1997/1998), December/January. "Two Languages Are Better Than One." In *Educational Leadership* 55(4), 23–27. Used with permission.

remedial program, English learners receive less access to the standard grade-level curriculum. The achievement and equity gap increases as native English speakers forge ahead while English learners make less progress. Thus, underachieving groups continue to underachieve in the next generation. Unfortunately, the two most common types of U.S. school services provided for English learners—English as a Second Language (ESL) pullout and transitional bilingual education—are remedial in nature. Participating students and teachers suffer often from the social consequences of this perception.

But when the focus of any special school program is on academic enrichment for all students, the school community perceives that program positively, and students become academically successful and deeply engaged in the learning process. Thus, enrichment programs for English learners are extremely effective when they are intellectually challenging and use students' linguistic and cultural experiences as a resource for interdisciplinary, discovery learning (Chiang 1994, Ovando and Collier 1998, Thomas and Collier 1997). Further, educators who use the enrichment models that were initially developed for English learners are beginning to see the power of these models for *all* students.

A History of Bilingual Enrichment

These innovative enrichment models are called by varying names—*dual language, bilingual immersion, two-way bilingual,* and *developmental bilingual education.* We recommend these models as forms of mainstream education through two languages that will benefit all students. Let's examine the history of their development and some basic characteristics of these models.

Initially, the first two 20th-century experiments with bilingual education in the United States and Canada in the early 1960s came about as a result of parental pressure. Both of these experiments were enrichment models. In Canada, English-speaking parents who wanted their children to develop in both French and English initiated what became known as immersion education. Immersion is a commitment to bilingual schooling throughout grades K–12 in which students are instructed 90 percent of the school day during kindergarten and grade 1 in the *minority* language chosen for the program, and 10 percent of the day in the majority language (English). The hands-on nature of academic work in the early grades is a natural vehicle for proficiency development of the minority language.

Immersion programs emphasize the less dominant language more than English in the first years, because the minority language is less supported by the broader society, and academic uses of the language are less easily acquired outside school. Gradually, with each subsequent grade, the program provides more instruction in the majority language until children learn the curriculum equally through both languages by grade 4 or 5. By grade 6, students have generally developed deep academic proficiency in both languages, and they can work on math, science, social studies, and language arts at or above grade level in *either* language. From the 1960s to the 1990s, immersion bilingual schooling has grown immensely popular in Canada and has achieved high rates of success with majority and minority students, students of middle- and low-income families, as well as students with learning disabilities (Cummins and Swain 1986, Genesee 1987).

About the same time that the first immersion program started in Canada, Cubans arriving in Miami, Florida, initiated the first U.S. experiment with two-way bilingual education in 1963. The term *two-way* refers to two language groups acquiring the curriculum through each other's languages; *one-way* bilingual education refers to one language group receiving schooling through two languages (Stern 1963). Intent on overthrowing Fidel Castro and returning to their country, the Cuban arrivals established private bilingual schools to develop their children's English and maintain their Spanish. The public schools, losing significant enrollment, chose to develop bilingual classes to attract students back. As English-speaking parents enrolled their children in the classes, two-way, integrated bilingual schooling emerged as a new program model in the United States. These classes provided a half day of the grade-level curriculum in Spanish and a half day in English, now known as the 50–50 model of two-way.

Over time, these two experiments have expanded to many states in the United States as school communities recognize the benefits for all students. The immersion model, originally developed in Canada for majority language speakers, has become known as the *90–10* two-way model in the United States because during the first two years both language groups receive 90 percent of the instruction through the *minority* language.

Students as Peer Language Models

Key to the success of all two-way programs is the fact that both language 10 groups stay together throughout the school day, serving as peer tutors for each other. Peer models stimulate natural language acquisition for both groups because they keep the level of interaction cognitively complex (Panfil 1995). Research has consistently demonstrated that academic achievement is very high for all groups of participants compared to control groups who receive schooling only through English. This holds true for students of low socioeconomic status, as well as African-American students and language-minority students, with those in the 90–10 model achieving even higher than those in the 50–50 model (Lindholm 1990, Lindholm and Aclan 1991, Thomas and Collier 1997).

The Role of Careful Planning

What are other essential characteristics of this school reform? An important principle is clear curricular separation of the two languages of instruction. To maintain a continuous cognitive challenge, teachers do not repeat or translate lessons in the second language, but reinforce concepts taught in one language across the two languages in a spiraling curriculum. Teachers alternate the language of instruction by theme or subject area, by time of day, by day of the week, or by the week. If two teachers are teaming, each teacher represents one language. When two teachers share and exchange two classes, this is a cost-effective, mainstream model that adds no additional teachers to a school system's budget. In contrast, ESL pullout is the most costly of all program models for English learners because extra ESL resource teachers must be added to the mainstream staff (Crawford 1997).

Successful two-way bilingual education includes

- a minimum of six years of bilingual instruction;

- focus on the core academic curriculum rather than on a watered-down version;

- quality language arts instruction in both languages;

- separation of the two languages for instruction;

- use of the non-English language for at least 50 percent of the instructional time and as much as 90 percent in the early grades;

- an additive bilingual environment that has full support of school administrators;

- a balanced ratio of students who speak each language (for example, 50–50 or 60–40, preferably not to go below 70–30;

- promotion of positive interdependence among peers and between teachers and students;

- high-quality instructional personnel; and

- active parent-school partnerships (Lindholm 1990).

Demographics influence the feasibility of two-way programs, because the students in each language group serve as peer teachers for each other. A natural choice for many U.S. schools is a Spanish-English two-way program, because Spanish speakers are most often the largest language group. In the 204 two-way bilingual schools identified in the United States in a 1997 survey, other languages of instruction in addition to Spanish include, in order of frequency, Korean, French, Cantonese, Navajo, Japanese, Arabic, Portuguese, Russian, and Mandarin Chinese (Montone et al. 1997).

Closing the Equity Gap Through Bilingual Enrichment

What makes these programs work? To answer this question, let's look at the students who are initially the lowest achievers on tests in English. Most school policymakers commonly assume that students need only a couple of years to learn a second language. But while these students make dramatic progress in English development in the first two years, English language learners are competing with a moving target, the native English speaker, when tested in English.

The average native English speaker typically gains 10 months of academ- 15 ic growth in one 10-month school year in English development because first language acquisition is a natural work in progress throughout the school years, not completed until young adulthood. Although some score higher and some lower, on average they also make a year's progress in a year's time in mathematics, science, and social studies. Thus students not yet proficient in English initially score three or more years below grade level on the tests in English because they cannot yet demonstrate in their second language all that they actually know. These students must outgain the native speaker by making one and one-half years progress on the academic tests in their second language for each of six successive school years (a total of nine years progress in six years) to reach the typical performance level of the constantly advancing native English speaker.

When students do academic work in their primary language for more than two to three years (the typical support time in a transitional bilingual program), they are able to demonstrate with each succeeding year that they are making more gains than the native English speaker—and closing the gap in achievement as measured by tests in English across the curriculum. After five to six years of enrichment bilingual schooling, former English learners (now proficient in English) are able to demonstrate their deep knowledge on the academic tests in English across the curriculum, as well as in their native language, achieving on or above grade level (Thomas and Collier 1997).

Bridging the Gap to a Better Tomorrow

Why is such progress for English learners important for our schools? Language-minority students are predicted to account for about 40 percent of the school-age population by the 2030s (Berliner and Biddle 1995). It is in our pragmatic self-interest to ensure their success as young adults, for they will be key to a robust economy to pay retirement and medical benefits for today's working adults. We must close the equity gap by providing enrichment schooling for all. For native English speakers as well as language-minority students, the enrichment bilingual classes appear to provide a constant stimulus and intellectual challenge similar to that of a gifted and talented class. The research evidence is overwhelmingly clear that *proficient* bilinguals outperform monolinguals on school tests (Collier 1995). Crossing cultural, social class, and language boundaries, students in a bilingual class develop multiple ways of solving human problems and approach ecological and social science issues from a cross-national perspective. These learners acquire deep academic proficiency in two languages, which becomes a valuable resource in adult professional life. And they learn to value each other's knowledge and life experiences—leading to meaningful respect and collaboration that lasts a lifetime. ◎/◎

References

Berliner, D. C., and B. J. Biddle. (1995). The Manufactured Crisis: Myths, Fraud, and the Attack on America's Public Schools. *Reading, Mass.: Addison Wesley.*

Chiang, R. A. (1994). "Recognizing Strengths and Needs of All Bilingual Learners: A Bilingual/Multicultural Perspective." NABE News 17 4: 11, 22–23.

Collier, V. P. (1995). Promoting Academic Success for ESL Students: Understanding Second Language Acquisition for School. *Elizabeth: New Jersey Teachers of English to Speakers of Other Languages-Bilingual Educators.*

Crawford, J. (1997). Best Evidence: Research Foundations of the Bilingual Education Act. *Washington, D.C.: National Clearinghouse for Bilingual Education.*

Cummins, J., and M. Swain. (1986). Bilingualism in Education. *New York: Longman.*

Genesee, F. (1987). Learning Through Two Languages: Studies of Immersion and Bilingual Education. *Cambridge, Mass: Newbury House.*

Lindholm, K. J. (1990). "Bilingual Immersion Education: Criteria for Program Development." In Bilingual Education: Issues and Strategies, *edited by A. M. Padilla, H. H. Fairchild, and C. M. Valadez. Newbury Park, Calif.: Sage.*

Lindholm, K. J., and Z. Aclan. (1991). "Bilingual Proficiency as a Bridge to Academic Achievement: Results from Bilingual/Immersion Programs." Journal of Education 173: 99–113.

Montrone, C., D. Christian, and A. Whitcher. (1997). Directory of Two-Way Bilingual Programs in the United States. *Rev. ed. Washington, D.C.: Center for Applied Linguistics.*

Ovando, C. J., and V. P. Collier. (1998). Bilingual and ESL Classrooms: Teaching in Multicultural Contexts. *2nd ed. New York: McGraw-Hill.*

Panfil, K. (1995). "Learning from One Another: A Collaborative Study of a Two-Way Bilingual Program by Insiders with Multiple Perspectives." Dissertation Abstracts International 56-10A. 3859 *(University Microfilms No. AA196-06004).*

Stern, H. H., ed. (1963). Foreign Languages in Primary Education: The Teaching of Foreign or Second Languages to Younger Children. *Hamburg, Germany: International Studies in Education, UNESCO Institute for Education.*

Thomas, W. P., and V. P. Collier. (1997). School Effectiveness for Language Minority Students. *Washington, D.C.: National Clearinghouse for Bilingual Education.*

Reflections and Inquiries

1. What "enormous equity gaps" must students with no English proficiency overcome? What would be the best way to overcome such equity gaps, according to Thomas and Collier?

2. The authors assert that program enrichment rather than the students' learning problems should be the focus of a bilingual education classroom. What is the point of changing emphasis in this manner? How valid is such a change in emphasis, in your opinion?

3. Why do the authors advocate peer-learner models? How do they work best?

4. What does it mean when the level of peer-student interaction is kept "cognitively complex"? Why is this important?

Reading to Write

Review Thomas's and Collier's criteria for "quality instruction" in a successful bilingual education program. Then discuss in a short essay which two or three of these criteria are most important and why.

Speaking a Public Language | Richard Rodriguez

The son of Mexican immigrant workers, Richard Rodriguez in 1981 published his autobiography, Hunger of Memory, *which has stirred considerable controversy for its antibilingual education stance. In his book, Rodriguez describes his move from a socially disadvantaged and alienated Spanish-speaking child thrust into English-only classrooms in Sacramento to a professor of English literature and writer twenty years later. In the following excerpt from the book, Rodriguez presents his reasons for upholding English-only instruction in American schools.*

Supporters of bilingual education today imply that students like me miss a great deal by not being taught in their family's language. What they seem not to recognize is that, as a socially disadvantaged child, I considered Spanish to be a private language. What I needed to learn in school was that I had the right—and the obligation—to speak the public language of *los gringos*. The odd truth is that my first-grade classmates could have become bilingual, in the conventional sense of that word, more easily than I. Had they been taught (as upper-middle-class children are often taught early) a second language like Spanish or French, they could have regarded it simply as that: another public language. In my case such bilingualism could not have been so quickly achieved. What I did not believe was that I could speak a single public language.

Without question, it would have pleased me to hear my teachers address me in Spanish when I entered the classroom. I would have felt much less afraid. I would have trusted them and responded with ease. But I would have delayed—for how long postponed?—having to learn the language of public society. I would have evaded—and for how long could I have afforded to delay?—learning the great lesson of school, that I had a public identity.

Fortunately, my teachers were unsentimental about their responsibility. What they understood was that I needed to speak a public language. So their voices would search me out, asking me questions. Each time I'd hear them, I'd look up in surprise to see a nun's face frowning at me. I'd mumble, not really meaning to answer. The nun would persist, 'Richard, stand up. Don't look at the floor. Speak up. Speak to the entire class, not just to me!' But I couldn't

---

believe that the English language was mine to use. (In part, I did not want to believe it.) I continued to mumble. I resisted the teacher's demands. (Did I somehow suspect that once I learned public language my pleasing family life would be changed?) Silent, waiting for the bell to sound, I remained dazed, diffident, afraid.

Because I wrongly imagined that English was intrinsically a public language and Spanish an intrinsically private one, I easily noted the difference between classroom language and the language of home. At school, words were directed to a general audience of listeners. ('Boys and girls.') Words were meaningfully ordered. And the point was not self-expression alone but to make oneself understood by many others. The teacher quizzed: 'Boys and girls, why do we use that word in this sentence? Could we think of a better word to use there? Would the sentence change its meaning if the words were differently arranged? And wasn't there a better way of saying much the same thing?' (I couldn't say. I wouldn't try to say.)

Three months. Five. Half a year passed. Unsmiling, ever watchful, my   5
teachers noted my silence. They began to connect my behavior with the difficult progress my older sister and brother were making. Until one Saturday morning three nuns arrived at the house to talk to our parents. Stiffly, they sat on the blue living room sofa. From the doorway of another room, spying the visitors, I noted the incongruity—the clash of two worlds, the faces and voices of school intruding upon the familiar setting of home. I overheard one voice gently wondering, 'Do your children speak only Spanish at home, Mrs. Rodriguez?' While another voice added, 'That Richard especially seems so timid and shy.'

That Rich-heard!

With great tact the visitors continued, 'Is it possible for you and your husband to encourage your children to practice their English when they are home?' Of course, my parents complied. What would they not do for their children's well-being? And how could they have questioned the Church's authority which those women represented? In an instant, they agreed to give up the language (the sounds) that had revealed and accentuated our family's closeness. The moment after the visitors left, the change was observed. '*Ahora,* speak to us *en inglés,*' my father and mother united to tell us.

At first, it seemed a kind of game. After dinner each night, the family gathered to practice 'our' English. (It was still then *inglés,* a language foreign to us, so we felt drawn as strangers to it.) Laughing, we would try to define words we could not pronounce. We played with strange English sounds, often overanglicizing our pronunciations. And we filled the smiling gaps of our sentences with familiar Spanish sounds. But that was cheating, somebody shouted. Everyone laughed. In school, meanwhile, like my brother and sister, I was required to attend a daily tutoring session. I needed a full year of special attention. I also needed my teachers to keep my attention from straying in class by calling out, *Rich-heard*—their English voices slowly prying loose my ties to my other name, its three notes, *Ri-car-do.* Most of all I needed to hear my mother and father speak to me in a moment of seriousness in broken— suddenly heartbreaking—English. The scene was inevitable: One Saturday morning I entered the kitchen where my parents were talking in Spanish. I did not realize that they were talking in Spanish however until, at the moment they saw me, I heard their voices change to speak English. Those *gringo* sounds they uttered startled me. Pushed me away. In that moment of trivial misunderstanding and profound insight, I felt my throat twisted by unsound- ed grief. I turned quickly and left the room. But I had no place to escape to with Spanish. (The spell was broken.) My brother and sisters were speaking English in another part of the house.

Again and again in the days following, increasingly angry, I was obliged to hear my mother and father: 'Speak to us *en inglés.' (Speak.)* Only then did I determine to learn classroom English. Weeks after, it happened: One day in school I raised my hand to volunteer an answer. I spoke out in a loud voice. And I did not think it remarkable when the entire class understood. That day, I moved very far from the disadvantaged child I had been only days earlier. The belief, the calming assurance that I belonged in public, had at last taken hold.

Shortly after, I stopped hearing the high and loud sounds of *los gringos.* 10 A more and more confident speaker of English, I didn't trouble to listen to *how* strangers sounded, speaking to me. And there simply were too many English- speaking people in my day for me to hear American accents anymore. Conversations quickened. Listening to persons who sounded eccentrically pitched voices, I usually noted their sounds for an initial few seconds before I concentrated on *what* they were saying. Conversations became content-full. Transparent. Hearing someone's *tone* of voice—angry or questioning or sar- castic or happy or sad—I didn't distinguish it from the words it expressed. Sound and word were thus tightly wedded. At the end of a day, I was often bemused, always relieved, to realize how 'silent,' though crowded with words, my day in public had been. (This public silence measured and quick- ened the change in my life.)

At last, seven years old, I came to believe what had been technically true since my birth: I was an American citizen.

But the special feeling of closeness at home was diminished by then. Gone was the desperate, urgent, intense feeling of being at home; rare was the expe- rience of feeling myself individualized by family intimates. We remained a loving family, but one greatly changed. No longer so close; no longer bound tight by the pleasing and troubling knowledge of our public separateness. Neither my older brother nor sister rushed home after school anymore. Nor did I. When I arrived home there would often be neighborhood kids in the house. Or the house would be empty of sounds.

Following the dramatic Americanization of their children, even my par- ents grew more publicly confident. Especially my mother. She learned the names of all the people on our block. And she decided we needed to have a telephone installed in the house. My father continued to use the word *gringo*. But it was no longer charged with the old bitterness or distrust. (Stripped of any emotional content, the word simply became a name for those Americans not of Hispanic descent.) Hearing him, sometimes, I wasn't sure if he was pronouncing the Spanish word *gringo* or saying gringo in English.

Matching the silence I started hearing in public was a new quiet at home. The family's quiet was partly due to the fact that, as we children learned more and more English, we shared fewer and fewer words with our parents. Sentences needed to be spoken slowly when a child addressed his mother or father. (Often the parent wouldn't understand.) The child would need to repeat himself. (Still the parent misunderstood.) The young voice, frustrated, would end up saying, 'Never mind'—the subject was closed. Dinners would be noisy with the clinking of knives and forks against dishes. My mother would smile softly between her remarks; my father at the other end of the table would chew and chew at his food, while he stared over the heads of his children.

My *mother*! My *father*! After English became my primary language, I no longer knew what words to use in addressing my parents. The old Spanish words (those tender accents of sound) I had used earlier—*mamá* and *papá*—I couldn't use anymore. They would have been too painful reminders of how much had changed in my life. On the other hand, the words I heard neighborhood kids call *their* parents seemed equally unsatisfactory. *Mother* and *Father; Ma, Papa, Pa, Dad, Pop* (how I hated the all-American sound of that last word especially)—all these terms I felt were unsuitable, not really terms of address for *my* parents. As a result, I never used them at home. Whenever I'd speak to my parents, I would try to get their attention with eye contact alone. In public conversations, I'd refer to 'my parents' or 'my mother and father.'

My mother and father, for their part, responded differently, as their children spoke to them less. She grew restless, seemed troubled and anxious at the scarcity of words exchanged in the house. It was she who would question me about my day when I came home from school. She smiled at small talk. She pried at the edges of my sentences to get me to say something more. (What?) She'd join conversations she overheard, but her intrusions often stopped her children's talking. By contrast, my father seemed reconciled to the new quiet. Though his English improved somewhat, he retired into silence. At dinner he spoke very little. One night his children and even his wife helplessly giggled at his garbled English pronunciation of the Catholic Grace before Meals. Thereafter he made his wife recite the prayer at the start of each meal, even on formal occasions, when there were guests in the house. Hers became the public voice of the family. On official business, it was she, not my father, one would usually hear on the phone or in stores, talking to strangers. His children grew so accustomed to his silence that, years later, they would speak routinely of his shyness. (My mother would often try to explain: Both his parents died when

15

he was eight. He was raised by an uncle who treated him like little more than a menial servant. He was never encouraged to speak. He grew up alone. A man of few words.) But my father was not shy, I realized, when I'd watch him speaking Spanish with relatives. Using Spanish, he was quickly effusive. Especially when talking with other men, his voice would spark, flicker, alive with sounds. In Spanish, he expressed ideas and feelings he rarely revealed in English. With firm Spanish sounds, he conveyed confidence and authority English would never allow him.

The silence at home, however, was finally more than a literal silence. Fewer words passed between parent and child, but more profound was the silence that resulted from my inattention to sounds. At about the time I no longer bothered to listen with care to the sounds of English in public, I grew careless about listening to the sounds family members made when they spoke. Most of the time I heard someone speaking at home and didn't distinguish his sounds from the words people uttered in public. I didn't even pay much attention to my parents' accented and ungrammatical speech. At least not at home. Only when I was with them in public would I grow alert to their accents. Though, even then, their sounds caused me less and less concern. For I was increasingly confident of my own public identity.

I would have been happier about my public success had I not sometimes recalled what it had been like earlier, when my family had conveyed its intimacy through a set of conveniently private sounds. Sometimes in public, hearing a stranger, I'd hark back to my past. A Mexican farmworker approached me downtown to ask directions to somewhere. '¿Hijito . . . ?' he said. And his voice summoned deep longing. Another time, standing beside my mother in the visiting room of a Carmelite convent, before the dense screen which rendered the nuns shadowy figures, I heard several Spanish-speaking nuns—their busy, singsong overlapping voices—assure us that yes, yes, we were remembered, all our family was remembered in their prayers. (Their voices echoed faraway family sounds.) Another day, a dark-faced old woman—her hand light on my shoulder—steadied herself against me as she boarded a bus. She murmured something I couldn't quite comprehend. Her Spanish voice came near, like the face of a never-before-seen relative in the instant before I was kissed. Her voice, like so many of the Spanish voices I'd hear in public, recalled the golden age of my youth. Hearing Spanish then, I continued to be a careful, if sad, listener to sounds. Hearing a Spanish-speaking family walking behind me, I turned to look. I smiled for an instant, before my glance found the Hispanic-looking faces of strangers in the crowd going by.

Today I hear bilingual educators say that children lose a degree of 'individuality' by becoming assimilated into public society. (Bilingual schooling was popularized in the seventies, that decade when middle-class ethnics began to resist the process of assimilation—the American melting pot.) But the bilin-gualists simplistically scorn the value and necessity of assimilation. They do not seem to realize that there are *two* ways a person is individualized. So they do not realize that while one suffers a diminished sense of *private* individual-ity by becoming assimilated into public society, such assimilation makes pos-sible the achievement of *public* individuality.

The bilingualists insist that a student should be reminded of his difference 20 from others in mass society, his heritage. But they equate mere separateness with individuality. The fact is that only in private—with intimates—is separate-ness from the crowd a prerequisite for individuality. (An intimate draws me apart, tells me that I am unique, unlike all others.) In public, by contrast, full individuality is achieved, paradoxically, by those who are able to consider themselves members of the crowd. Thus it happened for me: Only when I was able to think of myself as an American, no longer an alien in *gringo* society, could I seek the rights and opportunities necessary for full public individuality. The social and political advantages I enjoy as a man result from the day that I came to believe that my name, indeed, is *Rich-heard Road-ree-guess.* It is true that my public society today is often impersonal. (My public society is usually mass society.) Yet despite the anonymity of the crowd and despite the fact that the individuality I achieve in public is often tenuous—because it depends on my being one in a crowd—I celebrate the day I acquired my new name. Those middle-class ethnics who scorn assimilation seem to me filled with decadent self-pity, obsessed by the burden of public life. Dangerously, they romanticize public separateness and they trivialize the dilemma of the socially disadvantaged.

My awkward childhood does not prove the necessity of bilingual educa-tion. My story discloses instead an essential myth of childhood—inevitable pain. If I rehearse here the changes in my private life after my Americanization, it is finally to emphasize the public gain. The loss implies the gain: The house I returned to each afternoon was quiet. Intimate sounds no longer rushed to the door to greet me. There were other noises inside. The telephone rang. Neighborhood kids ran past the door of the bedroom where I was reading my schoolbooks—covered with shopping-bag paper. Once I learned public lan-guage, it would never again be easy for me to hear intimate family voices. More and more of my day was spent hearing words. But that may only be a way of saying that the day I raised my hand in class and spoke loudly to an entire roomful of faces, my childhood started to end. ◎/◎

Reflections and Inquiries

1. How does Rodriguez distinguish between "public" and "private" language? Do you agree with this distinction? Why or why not?

2. Describe Rodriguez's reaction to his parents' decision to stop speaking Spanish. Is it consistent or inconsistent with his views about bilingual education? Explain.

3. What exactly is Rodriguez referring to when he mentions "the new quiet" he experienced from his family following the nuns' visit?

4. What had to happen before Rodriguez could experience "full public individuality"? Are any factors besides language-based ones relevant to this change, in your opinion?

Reading to Write

Are the losses Rodriguez describes worth the gains? In a short essay, defend or argue against this manner of language acquisition. How might Rodriguez's experience have been different and less distressing?

Student Essays

Point Counterpoint: Education in English English First

Regina Patzelt
Yung Le

Although both Regina Patzelt, a Santa Clara University junior, and Yung Le, a recent graduate, received bilingual education instruction, their views about the effectiveness of this mode of learning English differ dramatically. Patzelt in "Education in English: The Proven Benefits of a Bilingual Academic Program" argues for bilingual education; Le in "English First" supports an emphasis on English. What conclusions, if any, can you draw about the intrinsic effectiveness of bilingual instruction based on the experiences of these students, both of whom have clearly developed an admirable degree of proficiency in English?

Education in English: The Proven Benefits of a Bilingual Academic Program

"[M]ajority and minority language students together must prepare for a constantly changing world."

—Wayne Thomas and Virginia Collier (443)

With the great influx of minorities in the American population in the past fifty years, education for these students as well as majority students has become the foremost concern for upcoming generations. Obviously, the children need to be taught English if they are to achieve any sort of success in this country; however, therein lies the problem of how best to teach English to these nonnative speakers while simultaneously including their cultural heritage in the education of all the students. Although a few methods do this, it has become apparent that bilingual education is the method that is most beneficial only not to the ESL students but to the English-speaking students as well, for the process inherently allows for mastery of language on both sides. In order to teach children English while maintaining their personal culture, schools need to use a program of bilingual education for this is the most successful way to teach English while also achieving an incorporation of minority students' cultures.

Bilingual education is a program that requires various aspects in order for it to be successful. There are two main types of educational programs: 90–10, in which 90 percent of the school day is taught in the minority language and 10 percent in the majority language, usually English, and the 50–50 model wherein the school day is split equally between the two languages. Both programs require certain basic characteristics to work in the academic setting. One of the main ideas is keeping the English and non-English speaking students together in all the classes so they "serve as peer tutors for each other" (Thomas and Collier 445). This way, the students hear the more formal language of the teachers coupled with the informal language of the native speakers, which promotes a greater understanding and learning of the language. Another important part to the program is the planning of where and when to use the languages so that they complement each other and provide "a continuous cognitive challenge" (445) so that they don't repeat lessons and classes in the opposite language but switch between the languages depending on theme and subject matter as well as day to day or week to week (445). Finally, the program only works if implemented early and continued for 6 or more years. The earlier the students start, the easier it is for them to learn a second language, as proven by psychological research. Learning a language before the age of 12 ensures much more efficient learning and better comprehension due to the fact that even one's first language is not full mastered until the age of 12. Adding another language earlier serves to promote quicker and fuller fluency. The aforementioned aspects constitute the only basic necessities for making two-way educational programs work, for there are also several minor necessary parts. These include such things as support of administration and parents, an almost equal ratio of students who speak the two languages, quality instruction, etc. (446). In general, all these aspects must be combined to create an efficient and successful program.

The other, formerly popular, type of ESL educational program, remedial education, does not work nearly as well as bilingual education and consequently has become much less common. Remedial education is inherently flawed in many ways, beginning with the central premise that it is built on. In this program, children who do not speak English as their first language are seen as "problems" that need to be "remedied," which automatically categorizes these students as inferior. This results in their being seen as negative "issues" that need to be dealt with, when in reality they are just children who happen to be disadvantaged by not knowing the language of the majority. Then, these "problems" are segregated by being placed into separate, special classes where they are supposed to be taught English. However, often there are many problems with their curriculum, as Mike Rose points out in his essay *The Politics of Remediation*. Two minor problems with the curriculum he mentions are a lack of continuity with the lessons he taught and a self-enclosed curriculum that automatically excludes the use of the children's own culture in the exercises such as storytelling. But, as Rose points out, the main problem with the program is that there is no space in the program "to explore the real stuff of literacy" (Rose 673). Because there is so much focus on the very precise, dry, categorical parts of grammar, Rose says that there is a lack of emotion, so the children lose the chance to explore fully the language. Thomas and Collier agree with Rose on this point, saying, "In the remedial program, English learners receive less access to the standard grade-level curriculum" (Thomas and Collier 443–448), All of these problems combined result in an ineffective program and a poor choice for teaching English to students. Additionally, remedial education ignores the diverse cultures of the students, preventing them from making connections between the new ideas and themes in English and their own background.

The strictly "white" approach to teaching English in remedial education programs leads to the ignoring of the cultural heritage of the students. Because of the parameters the program places on the subjects covered, students cannot incorporate familiar aspects of their private life into their learning, an inability that limits their ability to comprehend the subject matter. So the students are forced to forget both their first language as well as most of their cultural familiarities. Yet, the incorporation of their cultural knowledge can supplement the learning of the students and improve their ability to grasp the new concepts. In Leslie Marmon Silko's essay *Language and Literature from a Pueblo Indian Perspective*, she explains the difference between the linear, flat, logical style of English writing and the web-like, interconnected style of Pueblo writing. This difference makes it challenging for Pueblo students to learn English because it is so opposite to the language and writing they are used to. However, she points out how incorporating aspects of Pueblo language in English would benefit the language. It would also probably make it easier for Pueblo students to learn English because they could use their cultural knowledge during the challenging process of learning a new language. This idea that the use of one's own culture in the learning of a new language creates greater and quicker comprehension can extend to students of all cultural backgrounds.

Not only are there are numerous benefits to a bilingual educational program, it also solves the problems found in remedial educational programs. First, it addresses the segregation issues associated with remedial education as it places both ESL and non-ESL students in the same classrooms. This placement 5 also solves the problem of excluding other cultures because they are inherently involved in the bilingual curriculum. In this program the students teach each other about both their language and their culture in a two-way exchange. A second benefit to two-way education is that it solves the predicament of the "moving target" (447), where by the ESL student must compete with the ever-advancing native English speaker who starts out ahead and widens the gap with each passing year. This program starts the students out on equal footing as native speakers from both languages continually mentor each other. This prevents anyone from advancing too quickly as they rely on each other throughout the learning experience. The third advantage to this type of program is that it can be used both ways: English speakers can learn a second language through their ESL peers as the ESL students learn English and teach their language. It ends up being a mutually beneficial situation; the parties involved gain knowledge of another language and culture. Testing statistics have proven the effectiveness of this approach, showing "proficient bilinguals outperform monolinguals on school tests" (Thomas and Collier 447). Overall, research has shown time and again that having fluency in two languages promotes higher achievement in all areas of life, especially academically and occupationally. Truly, bilingual education has shown to have numerous benefits and essentially no disadvantages.

There seems to be only one major disadvantage that opponents bring up, that the program can contribute to the loss of cultural heritage, for the students may forget their past if they are not reminded of it. Rodriguez addresses this point when he laments that he "would have been happier about my public success had I not sometimes recalled what it had been like earlier, when my family had conveyed its intimacy through a set of conveniently private sounds [Spanish]" (Rodriguez 453). Yet he goes on to explain that "loss implies gain" (454) and that by learning English he could "seek the rights and opportunities" (454) that are present in America. So even though he lost some of his culture, he gained a sense of individuality and competency in America. Silko also speaks of this issue and what happens with Native Americans attending English schools by offering a powerful anecdote. In the story, she goes into an English class of Laguna and Acoma Pueblos and asks the students if they know of a particular Pueblo story because storytelling is so fundamental to their culture. She is shocked and pleasantly surprised to discover that most of the students knew of the story, proving "that storytelling continues on" (Silko 416) and displaying that despite their English education the students still were well aware of their heritage. These two authors who have had experience with the bilingual education program show that culture loss is not a great issue with the program.

Overall, it has been proven that bilingual education is one of the most effective ways to teach English to ESL students and to introduce and promote fluency in a second language for native English speakers. Through the various essays, an abundance of evidence and examples proves the success of bilingual education. The world is changing and by the 2030s 40 percent of the school-age population will be language minority students (Thomas and Collier 447); it would be foolish now not to implement more bilingual educational programs. Ignoring the facts and the inevitable increase of minorities in America will only harm the country in the end. It is often said the future lies in the school, and if this is true, we should really try to offer only the best education available to all students. It will benefit the entire American population and prove even more clearly that two-way education is a most effective academic program. ◎/◎

Works Cited

Rodriguez, Richard. "Speaking a Public Language." The Well Crafted Argument 3rd Edition. Ed. Fred D. White and Simone J. Billings. 2008.

Rose, Mike. "The Politics of Remediation." The Well Crafted Argument 2nd Edition. Ed. Fred D. White and Simone J. Billings. 2005.

Silko, Leslie Marmon. "Language and Literature from a Pueblo Indian Perspective." The Well Crafted Argument 3rd Edition. Ed. Fred D. White and Simone J. Billings. 2008.

Thomas, Wayne P. and Virginia Collier, "Two Languages Are Better Than One." The Well Crafted Argument 3rd Edition. Ed. Fred D. White and Simone J. Billings. 2008.

English First

Bilingual education prevents one from learning English. English is arguably the hardest language to learn; even native English speakers struggle with it. Like all languages, English involves continually learning new vocabularies and usage: each new subject is a discovery of the English language. The U.S. public school system, especially on the elementary level, should not stunt the development of a student's English by teaching a bilingual curriculum. Students and their respective families who wish to foster their native language should do so outside of the education system or as an elective.

By no means am I implying that all languages besides English are inferior or that I do not see value in learning a native language or any other languages for that matter. I myself am bilingual without the bilingual education. I do not credit elementary bilingual education for learning another language; I credit my family, outside classes, and foreign language classes throughout high school and college. However, I do credit my English-only education system for learning English, for being able to communicate in all its entailments, and for developing and honing my English throughout my education. My English skills would have never been acquired had I been allowed to use my native language as a handicap in learning and communicating in English at the same level as a native English speaker.

English-only instruction stresses the importance of English skills in a socie- 10 ty that is predominately English speaking. The school system, at least at the elementary level, should not compromise developing English skills by teaching curriculum in another language. If another language is taught, a student will not develop either of the languages fully. For instance, if social studies is taught in Spanish instead of English, students will not learn new ideas and words associated with that subject in English—missing pertinent English language development. In essence, a bilingual education system consisting of 50 percent English and 50 percent Spanish (for example) will only be teaching its students 50 percent of the content and ideas in English. Rather than being adept in one language, students are inept in two.

In elementary school we learn to be adept in English so we can develop our public persona and communicate effectively in society. This development happens regardless of the subjects taught: math, science, or history. Students just entering school have yet to develop their rudimentary English skills, or even their native language. It is unfair to compromise the learning of English—one of the purposes of going to school—to try to accomplish another goal that can be done outside or as an elective. Why should the school system attempt to develop multiple personas when it has a hard time developing one effective persona?

In his autobiography, *Hunger of Memory,* Richard Rodriguez, the son of a Mexican immigrant worker, supports English-only instruction in American schools. He asserts that English-only instruction allowed the development of his public identity: "how long could I have afforded to delay [speaking English]?—learning the great lesson of school, that I had a public identity" (449). Sure, teaching in the student's native language would've made the transition easier, but it would've slowed down the English learning process. As Rodriguez says, "it would have pleased me to hear my teacher address me in Spanish. . . . I would have felt much less afraid. . . . But I would have delayed—for how long postponed?—having to learn the language of public society" (449). From English-only instruction Rodriguez understood the importance of learning English, as all elementary students in the United States need to understand and learn. It is not the school system's concern to worry about a private persona, or any other persona, when one persona is yet to be fully developed. The underdevelopment of English is demonstrated by low English literacy in the United States.

Statistics show that students do not understand English at their level. "A stunning 40 percent of America's 4th graders continue to read below the basic level on national reading assessments" (http://www.edu-cyberpg.com). Why is the school system going to confuse students further by mixing in another language? The literacy rate in the United States is astoundingly low: according to the Children's Literacy Foundation, "one in five American children grows up functionally illiterate" and "three out of four American school children do not have the knowledge or skills needed to write stories and reports proficiently" (http://www.clifonline.org). Shouldn't we focus on trying to teach successfully English to our kids before we insist that they learn another language? In the United States high school students are now required to pass an exit exam—consisting of reading and writing—in order to graduate. How is learning a foreign language in conjunction with English a foundation to passing the exit exam?

The elementary foundation is shaken up further as bilingual education confuses not only the students but also the school system. How is the school system supposed to decide on what language to teach in addition to English? Majority vote? The second most popular language based on demographics? What will happen if the population is split between Spanish and Chinese speakers? The United States is a melting pot of different cultures and ethnicity; in one school district we can find a whole array of languages: who's going to decide which language is more important? If a school decides that Spanish will be the second language, is a Chinese native speaker supposed to learn Spanish, English, and the native language that he or she speaks at home? In essence, the student will be immersed in three different languages—none of which the student knows fluently. Now that's confusing. Imagine the difficulties in crossing over pronunciations, sound, and tone. Even I have to remind myself to make the "th" sound in "the" instead of "duh," and I had an English-only elementary education.

In addition, there are so many opportunities to learn another language 15 at any age or level of learning. Implementing a mandatory bilingual education in elementary schools is counterproductive and unnecessary. Students who wish to master language other than English can take extra classes, such as Saturday school (which I did) or as a school elective. Sure, the students may not develop the other language to the same level as English; but can you really develop another language at the same level as English, when we live in an English-speaking society? For those who want to immerse themselves into a foreign language, there are many opportunities. Students can travel in the summer, take required foreign language classes in high school and college, study abroad, or even go on field trips to areas such as Chinatown or Little Italy. There is no reason to sacrifice pivotal English learning, regardless of subject, when students are able to pursue a foreign language on their own time.

So please, if you're thinking of voting for bilingual education in elementary schools, don't. If you're thinking you're doing bilingual students like me a favor, you're not. If you're worried that not learning another language will give your children less of a competitive edge, don't. There are so many opportunities to learn a foreign language outside an English-only curriculum. Statistics show that our future generations aren't learning English proficiently. We don't need to add another language. We need more qualified teachers and English assistance so students can fully learn the language of English and can effectively communicate their beliefs. ◎/◎

Works Cited

Ellis, Karen. "Educational CyberPlayGround." 1996. Database available online. 08 June 2006. http://www.edu-cyberpg.com.

Rodriguez, Richard. "Speaking a Public Language." The Well Crafted Argument 3rd Edition. Ed. Fred D. White and Simone J. Billings. Boston: Houghton Mifflin, 2008. 449–454.

"Statistics on Children's Literacy." 08 June 2006. http://clifonline.org/lit_intro.html.

Reflections and Inquiries

1. Summarize Patzelt's and Le's respective viewpoints regarding bilingual education. Is one student's evidence supporting her view more convincing than the other's? Explain.

2. How useful is the information Le provides about her family background?

3. Comment on each student's use of outside sources in supporting their views.

Reading to Write

Contact several students who have studied English as a second language and see if you can determine the extent to which nonclassroom language experiences have contributed to their mastery of English. Use your findings in an essay to support your views on the influence of nonclassroom language experience on developing English proficiency.

Literacy Development for Students with No Voice: Scheme and Schema | Ann Russell

Literacy—the ability to process language via reading, speaking, and writing—lies at the heart of learning. Basic literacy skills must be developed in the early grades, and yet, students from lower socioeconomic groups sometimes have difficulty acquiring an "academic" voice in addition to their own voice, which may be very different. Is the cause entirely language-based or culture-based? In the following scholarly paper, Ann Russell, a professor of education at Southwestern Oklahoma State University, makes a case for the latter.

The objective of this paper is to provide a review of current literature with emphasis on the issues of student empowerment, early intervention strategies, and cultural issues in education which may stimulate solutions for restructuring literacy education in response to the No Child Left Behind legislation of 2001.

Examples of problems and solutions are given for both elementary and secondary levels. One of the conclusions illustrated in the paper is that reading failure for speakers of nonstandard English dialect is related more to cultural issues than language differences. The literature has moved from an emphasis on linguistic issues such as dialect barriers and language differences toward student empowerment and instructional techniques such as Reading Recovery that make a difference for the beginning reader.

Source: Ann Russell, EdD (2003, September). "Literacy Development for Students with No Voice: Scheme and Schema," *Reading Improvement*, 40: 104–109. Reprinted by permission of the author.

What type of educational intervention will help to curb the startling figures that define our national rate of illiteracy? The U.S. Department of Education (1993) report *Adult Literacy in America,* provided a look at the results of the National Adult Literacy Survey which included 26,000 adults ages 16 and older.

Translating the sample data into population terms, "between 40 and 44 million adults nationwide demonstrated skills in the lowest literacy level defined" (U.S. Department of Education, 1993). Those in the lowest literacy level could read only short pieces of text or were unable to complete even simple reading tasks. Reasons for their low level of reading were reportedly related to the number of years of schooling, lack of facility with the English language, or reported disabilities.

The objective of this paper is to provide a review of current literature with emphasis on the issues of student empowerment, early intervention strategies, and cultural issues in education which may stimulate solutions for restructuring literacy education.

Creating a New Vision

Educators are unsure how to create an alternative vision of reading instruction related to the recent changes in the No Child Left Behind legislation of 2001. Discussion continues over high stakes testing even as President Bush continues to emphasize, "The heart of educational reform is accountability" (*Reading Today,* April/May 2001). The results of the *Fourth-Grade Reading 2000 Report* from the National Assessment of Educational Progress (NAEP) indicated the average reading achievement has stayed about the same since 1992. However, the gap between the highest and lowest students has widened. The 90th and 75th percentiles rose but the 10th percentile dropped from a score of 170 in 1992 to 163 in 2000. The International Reading Association's response was to emphasize the content areas and "ensure that students have rich and wide experiences engaged with new content in science and social studies. Reading to learn and the concepts required to comprehend these texts are very different from the early stories and texts of initial literacy" (*Reading Today,* June/July 2001).

Emergent Literacy Development for Low-SES Learners

One of the reasons for unsuccessful literacy learning for students classified as low socioeconomic given by McIntyre (1992) is that there is cultural incongruity with school tasks and demands. Children who are inexperienced with print when they begin school may find that the demands are beyond their experience since they lack the schemata for school-type tasks. This factor may cause students to learn dysfunctional strategies for getting along in school and to quit trying. One of the successful strategies McIntyre found was to have the teacher provide one-on-one instruction for these at-risk students to supply support with print awareness until some success was achieved by the student with literacy tasks.

In response to the call for one-on-one instruction, many schools have adopted Reading Recovery, an emergent literacy program for at-risk students developed over 20 years ago by New Zealand child psychologist Marie Clay. Reading Recovery is designed to address the needs of first grade students who have fallen behind in reading and writing skills. In an interview with Dame Marie Clay at the University of London, she admitted that there were more challenges in the inner city than in the suburbs when implementing Reading Recovery (Russell, 1991).

Reading Recovery continues to grow in the United States. A record 142,149 students participated during the 1998–99 school year as opposed to 4,772 a decade ago (*Reading Today*, December 2000/January 2001). One of the keys to the program's success is teacher knowledge and skill. Intensive training programs on university campuses help train teacher leaders to insure that Reading Recovery teachers are able to diagnose individual strengths and weaknesses and respond appropriately to the child's needs with structured reading and writing activities. This one-on-one program provides a potential solution to emergent literacy concerns, if the gains shown in the research can be attained with inner city populations and maintained over time. So far, follow-up programs are impressive. According to Ohio State University researchers, results indicate success. "We can be confident that Reading Recovery teaches even low-achieving children to read and spell. For districts with high numbers of at-risk students we recommend the program as the cornerstone of a comprehensive approach to literacy" (Pinnell, 1990). The hope for early intervention programs is to be able to address reading remediation needs during the first grade so that there will be fewer students who fail because of a poor beginning.

The International Reading Association supports Reading First and Early 10 Reading First legislation, a part of the No Child Left Behind legislation, but emphasizes concerns related to bias in the selection of only a few reading programs and overstated claims that the programs are research-based (*Reading Today*, June/July 2002). The key to effective instruction is the teacher, and therefore emphasis is given to providing professional development and helping teachers gain skills to evaluate whether selected reading programs are research-based (*Reading Today*, June/July 2002).

Teaching in Context of Language and Culture

Reyes (1992) challenges the accepted assumptions that guide literacy instruction for linguistically different students, saying that we must "begin with the explicit premise that each learner brings a valid language and culture to the instructional context."

Reyes criticizes process or whole language instruction because it presumes that students will learn essential skills as a result of participating in reading and writing activities without the teacher's direct assistance. She claims that this method does not work equally well for all students, especially linguistically different students who may need more direct assistance and specific feedback in order to learn a concept.

For example, Reyes observed ESL students in her research who wandered aimlessly and were virtually ignored in a whole language classroom where children were told to choose books from the class library for silent sustained reading. The teacher modeled silent reading, and the rest of the class chose books, while the Asian students were given no assistance.

In another classroom Reyes followed students in their journal activities for two years and found them making the same spelling mistakes even though correct spelling was modeled for them. They were failing to benefit from indirect modeling and limited direct instruction which the constructivist approach provided. Reyes points out that in end-of-the-year interviews the students were surprised to learn that they had errors in their grammar and spelling never corrected by the teacher.

Developing Democratic Voices in Literacy Programs

Shannon (1993) cautions that teachers cannot ignore the connection between   15
the classroom and social life if we are to restructure schools successfully. The numbers of students who live below the poverty line is increasing. Shannon asserts that we need to move away from top-down initiatives that require more emphasis on testing, longer school days, and emphasis on math and science curriculums to make us more competitive internationally. Instead, he claims, we need to emphasize reform of literacy education so that we can educate our population to engage in an active public life and thus create a more equitable future for all.

Shannon criticizes constructivist approaches to literacy education such as "whole language" because he claims that they do not address the political nature of voice nor do they develop intellectual tools to allow analysis of historical and social origins of attitudes, values, and opinions. Yet, many teachers have an understanding of social reform which allows them to develop democratic voices in their literacy programs.

Fears of Naming

Fine (1987) discusses the concept of "silencing" as a fear of talk which pervades low-income urban schools where "undesirable" talk is subverted. In low-income schools the process of inquiry into students' experience is assumed to be unsafe territory. Silencing sustains the belief in schools as a mechanism for social mobility and diverts criticisms away from educational institutions which organize class, race, and gender hierarchies. These circumstances, when examined in the light of classroom experiences, make the concerns, communities, and biographies of low-income minority students irrelevant. In the process, the voices of the students that public education claims to nurture shut down.

The teachers, according to Fine, who felt the least empowered were the most likely to conclude that the students at a low-income, "low-skill" school could not be helped. A social studies teacher at a large New York City high school claimed that the students were not teachable and that he would be lucky to reach 20 percent.

To not name bears consequences, but especially for low-income, minority students. To not name causes students to be alienated, cut off from home, from experience, and to be left out and severed from the educational process. Good students managed the two worlds by learning to speak standard English dialect. They trained themselves to speak in two voices, their own voice alternated with an academic voice which denied race or class. They spoke of hard work and success. Another study of successes in a group of South Bronx students found that those students were significantly more depressed, less politically aware, less likely to be assertive, and more conformist. The price of success may have been muting one's own voice (Fine, 1987).

Several students who had dropped out responded the same way to a 20 question regarding their participation in school as a young kid. Each one answered that they were a good kid and made no trouble, indicating the idea that participation signified poor discipline and rude behavior.

From a research field note comes the following example of silencing in the urban school:

> Patrice is a young black female, in eleventh grade. She says nothing all day in school. She sits perfectly mute. No need to coerce her into silence. She often wears her coat in class. Sometimes she lays her head on her desk. She never disrupts. Never disobeys. Never speaks. And is never identified as a problem. Is she the student who couldn't develop two voices and so silenced both? Is she so filled with anger, she fears to speak? Or so filled with depression she knows not what to say (Fine, 1987)?

The process of education is to allow children and adolescents their voices—to read, write, and critique. We cannot justify institutionalizing silence behind a rhetoric of excellence and progress in a school organized around control (Fine, 1987).

Empowering the Learner

Ashcroft also notes that there are two different aspects of power to be considered—personal and social. She emphasizes that if we are only committed to personal power, we may produce egocentric, disrespectful, isolated or alienated individuals. If we overemphasize the interpersonal aspect of power, we may lose the individual in the collective action, disregard personal belief, inquiry, creativity, and unique contribution.

The concept of empowerment as related to learning focuses on the process of inquiry and discovery which lead to knowledge, something that can only be personally acquired and not given. The 1986 Carnegie Report calls for an educational system that will foster critical thinking, integration, synthesis, and the ability to cooperate with others. The term *empowerment* applied to both inner-personal and inter-personal spheres addresses an educational philosophy which will support the future learner and the future world (Ashcroft, 1987).

An example of empowerment is described by Lewis (1993) who partici- 25 pated in a teaching scenario involving a fourth grade boy's attempt at a critical reading of a fable by Arnold Lobel and the teacher-student interaction that followed. The teacher concluded that the student was unable to process the material as the author intended because of cultural factors related to past experiences and social codes. Instead of accepting the student's voice and allowing him to "own" the reading of the text based on his schema, the teacher continued to guide him toward her more conventional interpretation which matched the author's.

Was it the teacher's job to accept the student's interpretation, or help the student move toward a more conventional reading? Lewis concluded from the experience that it was most effective to encourage the student to "listen for other voices while legitimizing his own" (Lewis, 1993).

Lewis concluded that advising students to use their background information and to relate their experiences to what they read will not work equally well for all students. Students quickly learn that their experiences won't help them if these experiences do not fit the shared culture of the classroom.

Rather than reject the student's answer based on middle-class social codes, Lewis suggested an alternative would be to recognize the social and historical voice of the child as a part of developing critical literacy.

Conclusions

Research direction and pedagogical concerns in literacy education have changed somewhat with regard to emphasis. Progressing from the civil rights movement, literacy education in the 1960's and 1970's focused on research studies concerned with linguistic issues such as dialect training and dialect barriers in improving reading instruction (Cummingham, 1976; Goodman & Buck, 1965; Goodman, 1973; Ruddell, 1965; Rystrom, 1970). Authors worked to codify Black English so that teachers would not take a deficit approach in their instruction of children who spoke differently. There were concerns that children not be penalized for these differences in standardized and informal tests. Since the late 1970's, the heightened concerns for understanding culture were reflected in research and practice by our emphasis on multicultural education themes. "It has moved from correction of errors of omission and commission in portrayals of ethnic experiences to the promotion of ethnic pluralism as a social value at all grade levels" (Gay, 1983).

This change in emphasis is reflected by Labov (1970) who claims that the 30 primary reasons for reading failure are related to differences in culture, not dialect. "The principal problem in reading failure for speakers of nonstandard English dialects is not dialect or grammatical differences but rather cultural conflict between the vernacular culture and the schoolroom" (p. 43).

Looking toward the future of multiethnic education, Gay (1983) challenges practitioners to look at translating theory into practice in terms of student performance and fiscal expenditure in order to provide evidence of its efficacy.

It is interesting to see that the trends in literacy education parallel the trends in multicultural education where the movement has turned from a focus on describing language differences, toward an emphasis on early intervention, empowerment, cultural awareness, and demonstrating results. The future of the nation depends on our efforts to produce classrooms where students will eagerly seek the opportunity to learn to read. ◎/◎

References

Ashcroft, L. (1987). Defusing "empowerment": The what and the why. *Language Arts*, 64, 142–156.

Cunningham, P. M. (1976). Teachers' correction responses to black-dialect miscues which are non-meaning-changing. *Reading Research Quarterly*, 12, 637–653.

Despite the protests, drifts toward testing seem likely. (April/May 2001). *Reading Today*, pp. 1, 4.

Fine, M. (1987). Silencing in public schools. *Language Arts*, 64, 157–174.

Gay, G. (1983). Multiethnic education: Historical developments and future prospects. *Phi Delta Kappan*, 65, 560–563.

Goodman, K. S. (1973). Dialect barriers to reading comprehension. *The Reading Teacher*, 27, 6–12.

Goodman, K. S., with Buck, C. (1965). Dialect barriers to reading comprehension revisited. *Elementary English*, 42, 853–860.

Labov, W. (1970). *The study of nonstandard English*. Urbana, Ill.: National Council of Teachers of English.

Latest NAEP sees little change in past eight years. (June/July 2001). *Reading Today*, pp. 1, 3.

Lewis, C. (1993). Give people a chance: Acknowledging social differences in reading. *Language Arts*, 70, 454–461.

Marrow testifies before House Subcommittee. (June/July 2002), Reading Today, pp. 1, 3.

McIntyre, E. (1992). Individual literacy instruction for young low-SES learners in traditional urban classrooms. *Reading Research and Instruction*, 31, 53–63.

Pinnell, G. S. (1990). Success for low achievers through reading recovery. *Educational Leadership*, 48, 17–21.

Reading recovery growing rapidly. (December 2000/January 2001). *Reading Today*, p. 14.

Reyes, M. (1992). Challenging venerable assumptions: Literacy instruction for linguistically different students. *Harvard Educational Reviews*, 62, 427–446.

Ruddell, R. P. (1965). The effect of the similarity of oral and written patterns of language structure on reading comprehension. *Elementaty English*, 42, 403–410.

Russell, A. (1991). Interview with Marie Clay. Unpublished interview conducted at the University of London, May 12.

Rystrom, R. (1970). Dialect training and reading: A further look. *Reading Research Quarterly*, 5, 581–599.

U.S. Department of Education. (1993). *Adult literacy in America*. Washington, D.C.

Reflections and Inquiries

1. What does Russell say "silencing" is in the context of low-income schools? Why does it occur? What reforms may be needed to prevent it from occurring?

2. Russell speaks of "inner-personal" and "inter-personal" aspects of learning. How might one be cultivated without neglecting the other?

3. How can an understanding of students' respective cultures contribute toward improving those students' literacy?

Reading to Write

Russell calls attention to the "cultural incongruity" arising from teaching conventional school tasks to low-socioeconomic-group students. Using some of the bibliographic references Russell provides (for example, K. S. Goodman, "Dialect Barriers to Reading Comprehension," and G. S. Pinnell, "Success for Low Achievers Through Reading Recovery"), together with your own searches (consider interviewing education professors at your school and elementary school teachers in your community, for example), write an essay in which you propose specific ways in which teachers can help low-socioeconomic, high-risk children improve their literacy skills in the classroom.

Eliminating Standardized Tests in College Admissions: The New Affirmative Action? | Rebecca Zwick

How reliable are standardized test scores for predicting student performance? What does a psychometric investigation—an investigation that focuses on the psychological and sociological dynamics of test-taking and the way these dynamics are reflected in the test scores—reveal about the accuracy of standardized tests in predicting academic achievement regardless of ethnicity? What would happen if colleges decided to eliminate Scholastic Aptitude Test (SAT) scores from consideration and placed more emphasis on grade point averages (GPAs) or other indicators of academic performance? Rebecca Zwick, a professor of education at the University of California, Santa Barbara, reports the results of her formal investigation of these key concerns in the standardized testing controversy.

Source: Rebecca Zwick, "Eliminating Standardized Tests in College Admissions: The New Affirmative Action?" © 1999, Rebecca Zwick. This article first appeared in the December 1999 issue of *Phi Delta Kappan*. Reprinted by permission of the author.

College enrollment figures aren't ordinarily big news, but the 1998 fresh-man enrollment numbers for the University of California's most presti-gious campuses were startling enough to warrant headlines. At the University of California, Berkeley, African American enrollment dropped by more than 60% from 1997 levels, and Latino enrollment dropped by nearly 50%. UCLA experienced dramatic decreases as well.[1]

Since the passage in 1996 of California's Proposition 209, which banned consideration of race or ethnicity in admissions decisions at public colleges and universities, University of California educators have feared just such a plunge in minority representation and have been considering ways to coun-teract it. In 1997 the university settled on an apparently simple solution: elim-inate the SAT as a criterion for admissions. "We . . . have evidence that the SAT loses us 2,000 Latino students this year alone," said Eugene Garcia, dean of the School of Education at Berkeley in a 1997 interview.[2]

Although the university's enthusiasm for eliminating the SAT may have faded, admissions testing remains a source of controversy. A new document from the U.S. Department of Education, "Nondiscrimination in High-Stakes Testing" (still in draft form), advises that colleges may be in legal jeopardy if they rely too heavily on standardized test scores in making admissions or financial aid decisions. The president of the University of California, Richard Atkinson, said in a March 1999 interview that he "would be prepared to for-get that SAT" if the newly approved California high school exit examination proves to be a good test.[3] And a bill that would deemphasize the role of stan-dardized testing in admissions decisions (S.B. 145), introduced for the second time in January 1999, awaits action in the California senate. (An earlier ver-sion of the bill, introduced in 1998, passed both houses of the legislature but was vetoed by the outgoing governor, Pete Wilson.)

Meanwhile, Texas has been grappling with the effects of the *Hopwood* decision, which banned the use of race in admissions programs, and the state of Washington has been faced with the consequences of Initiative 200, a Prop 209 clone that was passed in 1998. These political developments have pro-voked a reconsideration of the role of tests in college admissions and have focused serious attention on two questions: Are standardized admissions tests biased against minorities, as is often argued? Would eradicating these tests produce a more ethnically diverse freshman class?

The Question of Bias

Differences between racial and ethnic groups in their performance on standard- 5 ized tests—including the SAT (from the Educational Testing Service) and its competition, the ACT (from ACT, Inc.)—have been analyzed extensively, both in academic journals and in the popular press. Researchers, social theorists, and politicians have offered an array of reasons for these score differences, ranging from socioeconomic, cultural, linguistic, and genetic factors to test bias. A recent inflammatory contribution to this literature was *The Bell Curve*, by Richard

Herrnstein and Charles Murray, which was published in 1994 and encouraged consideration of genetic explanations for group differences in test scores.[4] But the controversy has not been limited to the *reasons* for the differences in performance. Even the matter of determining which groups are advantaged by standardized tests is less straightforward than it first appears.

In the popular press, the existence of bias in admissions tests is typically assumed to be demonstrated by the persistent pattern of differences between racial groups in average test scores. The idea that score differences are sufficient evidence to establish bias is reflected in the original language of the California standardized testing legislation that is currently under consideration. According to the initial version of the bill, "a test discriminates . . . if there is a statistically significant difference in the outcome on test performance when test subjects are compared on the basis of gender, ethnicity, race, or economic status."[5] Another example of the view that score differences are sufficient evidence for test bias can be found at a website maintained by *Time* and the Princeton Review, a test preparation company: "Studies show persistent . . . race bias in both the SAT and the ACT. . . . The SAT favors white males, who tend to score better than all other groups except Asian-American males."[6]

When academic researchers investigate the fairness of the SAT, however, they don't ordinarily focus on the average scores achieved by each ethnic group. Instead, they consider another aspect of the test results: How well does the SAT predict college grades for each group? Researchers have typically found that using the SAT to predict first-year college grade-point averages (GPAs) results in a *more positive* prediction for black and Latino test-takers than is warranted; that is, the predicted grades tend to exceed the actual grades for these groups.

For example, a 1994 College Board study found that "there were, on average, underpredictions [of college GPAs] for Asian American students (and to a lesser extent, white students) and overpredictions for American Indian, black and Hispanic students."[7] In other words, SAT scores tended to predict higher college grades than were actually attained by African American, Latino, and American Indian students and lower grades than were actually attained by Asian American and white students. In discussing the recurrent finding of inflated predictions for African Americans, Robert Linn, an eminent educational researcher, noted in 1983 that this result is "contrary to a commonly held expectation that tests are unfair to certain minority groups in the sense that they give a misleadingly low indication of the likely performance . . . in school. The overprediction finding suggests that, if anything, just the opposite is true."[8] In their widely acclaimed 1998 book, *The Shape of the River*, William Bowen and Derek Bok also include an extensive discussion of this phenomenon.[9]

What's the real story about differences in ethnic group performance on the SAT? Do black and Latino test-takers tend to score lower, or are predictions of their college grades based on their SAT performance inflated?

Paradoxical as it may seem, *both* these patterns have characterized SAT results for many years.

The 1994 College Board study provides a useful context for illustrating [10] these seemingly contradictory results. This research, based on 1985 data from 45 colleges, represents the most detailed and painstaking analysis of the utility of the SAT as a predictor of college grades. A portion of the results—those for African Americans, Asian Americans, Latinos, and whites—are given here. The much smaller American Indian group is not included. (See Table 1.)

The average SAT scores, high school GPAs, and college GPAs show substantial differences across groups. Average SAT scores are higher for Asian American and white students than for African American and Latino students. The difference is more dramatic for the math score than for the verbal score. The average SAT math score for Asian Americans is about 130 points higher than the average SAT math score for African Americans.[10] (The 1998 SAT results reveal similar patterns.) If a difference in average performance were considered sufficient to demonstrate test bias, then these findings would appear to show bias against African American and Latino test-takers. (If this were the sole criterion, we would have to conclude that high school and college grades were biased as well.)

However, in the world of psychometrics, the assessment of test bias is conceptualized differently. Group performance differences can arise for many reasons that are not a function of the test itself—unequal educational opportunity being the most obvious—so the absence of such differences is not considered a criterion for test fairness. Instead, traditional psychometric analysis focuses on another question: Is the test an effective and accurate predictor of college GPAs for all groups? (Here we consider only ethnic groups, but other demographic groups—males, females, native and non-native speakers of English—are ordinarily examined as well.)

The first step in the psychometric investigation is to assess the validity of the test for students as a whole. Does the SAT lead to better prediction of college

TABLE 1   **Average SAT Scores, High School GPAs, and College GPAs, by Ethnic Group**

	African American	Asian American	Latino	White	Overall
SAT (verbal)	436	484	462	513	505
SAT (math)	466	595	516	564	559
High school GPA	3.18	3.58	3.43	3.40	3.41
College GPA	2.14	2.80	2.37	2.66	2.63
Number of test-takers	2,475	3,848	1,599	36,743	44,849

Source: Adapted from Leonard Ramist, Charles Lewis, and Laura McCamley-Jenkins, *Student Group Differences in Predicting College Grades: Sex, Language, and Ethnic Groups.* (New York: College Entrance Examination Board, College Board Report No. 93–1; ETS Research Report No. 94–27, 1994), p. 9.

grades than could be obtained using high school grades alone? Typically, the effectiveness with which SAT verbal scores, SAT math scores, and high school grades can jointly predict college grades is evaluated through linear regression analysis, a standard statistical procedure that is used in a variety of prediction applications. The regression analysis yields an equation for predicting college grades from high school grades, SAT math scores, and SAT verbal scores (each multiplied by a weighting factor and then added up). Predictive effectiveness is measured by the degree of correspondence between the predicted college grades and the actual college grades. The analysis can then be repeated using high school grades alone as a predictor. Comparing the results of the two analyses yields an estimate of the "value added" by using SAT scores.

After these analyses are completed for the entire group of students, the next step is to perform a separate prediction analysis within each ethnic group and to compare the resulting equations across groups. The College Board study evaluated various combinations of the three key predictors of college grades. Consistent with earlier research, the results showed that high school grades and SAT scores are important predictors in all ethnic groups and that including the SAT did lead to better prediction than using high school grades alone.[11] Research conducted at the University of California in 1997 produced the same conclusion.[12] In the College Board study, prediction was somewhat more effective for white and Asian American test-takers than for African American and Latino test-takers, regardless of which combination of predictors was used. In the African American group, unlike the other groups, SAT scores alone provided slightly more effective prediction than high school grades alone.

Although test validity research involves the computation of separate prediction equations for each ethnic group, admissions decisions within a college are ordinarily made by means of a common prediction equation for all ethnic groups. Will the use of a single equation result in systematic over- or underprediction of college grades for certain groups? This can be determined by comparing the actual first-year college grades to the predicted grades (obtained using the equation based on all students). Table 2 shows the average differences between actual college GPA and predicted college GPA for each group. A minus sign indicates overprediction (actual grades lower than predicted grades); a plus sign, underprediction (actual grades higher than predicted grades).

By definition, the equation will, on average, predict perfectly for the over- 15 all group. The white results will necessarily be similar since whites constitute about 82% of the total group in the study. But how do the results stack up for the remaining ethnic groups? Whether SAT score, high school GPA, or a combination is included in the equation, the results for Asian American test-takers are slightly underpredicted, while the results for African American and Latino test-takers are overpredicted. It is worth noting that overprediction is mitigated by the use of the SAT—it's even worse when only high school GPA

TABLE 2   **Average College GPA Minus Average Predicted College GPA**

Predictors in Equation	African American	Asian American	Latino	White	Overall
High school GPA	−.35	+.02	−.24	+.03	0
SAT (verbal and math)	−.23	+.08	−.13	+.01	0
High school GPA plus SAT (verbal and math)	−.16	+.04	−.13	+.01	0

Source: Adapted from Leonard Ramist, Charles Lewis, and Laura McCamley-Jenkins, *Student Group Differences in Predicting College Grades: Sex, Language, and Ethnic Groups* (New York: College Entrance Examination Board, College Board Report No. 93–1; ETS Research Report No. 94–27, 1994), p. 15. The scale of the GPAs is 0–4.

is used. For example, college GPAs for African Americans are overpredicted by an average of 0.35 when only high school GPAs are used as predictors. When SAT scores are included in the prediction equation, the average over-prediction is reduced to 0.16.[13]

What explains the overprediction? A variety of reasons have been advanced, including differences across groups in high school courses taken or in the stringency of high school grading practices, differences across groups in the choice of college curriculum, and a greater incidence in ethnic minority groups of life difficulties that interfere with academic performance in college.

The results of the College Board study mirror the general findings of SAT validity research from the last several decades. First, for all ethnic groups, tests do contribute to the prediction of college performance as measured by college GPA. Second, there's some evidence of ethnic group differences in the effectiveness and accuracy of prediction. Third, it's possible for a group to have lower average test scores than other groups and still receive inflated predictions of later performance. The overriding conclusion is neither new nor earth-shaking: in crafting a college admissions policy, tests serve as useful, but far from perfect, tools.

Would Eliminating the SAT Improve Ethnic Diversity?

If colleges removed the SAT from admissions criteria, what would be the likely result? This is the very question addressed in a December 1997 report issued by the Office of the President, University of California.[14] It was based on supplementary analyses of data from a study conducted by the California Postsecondary Education Commission (CPEC).[15] Transcripts, test scores, and demographic information from a 6% random sample of 1996 graduates of California public high schools were analyzed to determine the effect of applying various admissions criteria. The study issued by the Office of the President considered how eliminating standardized admissions tests would affect the rates of "UC eligibility," which is based on the completion of certain college-preparatory courses, the GPA for those courses, and (if the GPA is below 3.3) scores on the SAT or ACT.

The study's conclusion was surprising to some: eliminating the admis- 20 sions test requirement, when combined with other mandated features of admissions policy at the University of California, would produce very small changes in the eligibility rates for Latinos (from 3.8% to 4.0%), African Americans (from 2.8% to 2.3%), and Asian Americans (from 30% to 29%). The largest change would be an *increase* in the eligibility rate for whites (from 12.7% to 14.8%).[16]

The analysis that produced these projections of eligibility rates incorporated the provisions of the Master Plan for Higher Education in California, which mandates that 12.5% of the state's high school graduates be declared "UC eligible." If the admissions test requirement were dropped, the minimum GPA for the required college-preparatory courses would need to be raised, a change that leads to the predicted effects on eligibility rates. Dropping the SAT, while simultaneously ignoring the "12.5%" requirement, increased eligibility to 18.7% overall, while leaving the pattern of ethnic-group eligibility virtually unchanged. (This analysis, as well as many of the conjectures in this article, is based on the implicit assumption that eliminating the SAT would not have a substantial impact on high school grading practices. Some educators have raised the concern that rampant grade inflation would occur if the SAT requirement were lifted, rendering high school grades useless as an admissions criterion.)

The minimal changes in the predicted eligibility rates for African American and Latino students are less remarkable in light of the finding that "low test scores rarely are the only reason for a student's ineligibility."[17] In fact, the CPEC report on eligibility shows that only 2.5% of California public high school graduates were ineligible solely on the basis of inadequate test scores. Most students—62.6% of graduates overall—were ineligible because they had "major course omissions" or grade deficiencies or because they attended "schools that did not have a college-preparatory curriculum approved by the University." The percentage of students ineligible for these reasons was higher for African Americans (77%) and Latinos (73.6%) and lower for whites (58.7%) and Asian Americans (39%). Another 13.7% of graduates overall were ineligible because they were missing "only a few" (no more than three) of the required college-preparatory courses.[18]

Because the pattern of ethnic group differences in average high school GPA is usually similar to the pattern of average admissions test scores, an admissions policy that excludes tests but continues to include high school grades is unlikely to produce dramatic change. A case in point is the so-called 4% plan, which will go into effect at the University of California in 2001. The plan offers admission to the top 4% of graduates of every California high school who have completed the required college-preparatory courses, regardless of their test scores. Analyses have predicted that the plan will have "little impact on racial proportions at UC, since any increases in numbers of black, urban students [will] be matched by increases in white, rural students."[19]

Keith Widaman, chair of the universitywide committee that developed the plan, told the *San Francisco Chronicle* that implementing the plan will probably have only a minor effect on the percentage of black and Latino applicants admitted.[20]

The indisputable fact is that both high school grades and scores on admissions tests are reflections of the same education system, with all its flaws and inequities. In a recent colloquium on the future of affirmative action, Christopher Edley, a professor of law at Harvard University and a consultant to President Clinton on issues of race, noted, "The SAT simply recapitulates . . . all of the class advantages, all of the access advantages . . . in the K–12 experiences of the student."[21] The same can also be said of high school grades. By using grades rather than SAT scores as an admissions criterion, said sociologist Christopher Jencks in a 1989 essay, "You are simply substituting tests designed by high school teachers for tests designed by the Educational Testing Service."[22] A college admissions system that relies heavily on either tests or high school grades, then, cannot be the path to the eventual elimination of disparities in educational opportunity.

While there is little basis for concluding that standardized admissions 25 tests are biased against ethnic minorities in the psychometric sense—in fact, they tend to overpredict performance for African American and Latino students—it is clear that an overreliance on tests and other traditional measures of achievement in admissions can perpetuate the underrepresentation of certain groups by, as author Ellis Cose has put it, rewarding "those who have already been well schooled."[23] The *Hopwood* decision, Proposition 209, and similar initiatives exacerbate the problem by removing one method of increasing access to higher education for people of color.

A point on which individuals of every political stripe can agree is that, ultimately, we must fix "the pipeline"—that is, improve K–12 education so that college applicants will be better prepared. But this viewpoint has drawn an impatient response from some educators. "Obviously," says Edley, "we all would prefer the great day in which the pipeline is repaired and students of all kinds show up at our doorsteps prepared, ready, eager to take the best of what we have to offer. But that day is not with us. What do we do in the meantime?"[24]

One avenue for change in the admissions process is the consideration of alternative definitions of college success. Although it has long been argued that the first-year college GPA is not the only outcome of interest, no other criterion has gained wide use. Remaining within the realm of grades, GPA in a student's area of specialization and GPA at graduation have been proposed as alternative criteria. The 1994 College Board study found that the grades earned in individual college courses may be more promising outcome measures than GPA. Other possible criteria are successful completion of the first year of college or successful completion of the bachelor's degree. What distinguishes students who attain these milestones from those who do not? Among the student attributes that warrant further investigation are motivation, perseverance, ability to overcome an adverse environment, and "spike talents" in particular areas. We need research to determine how best to measure these characteristics and how to assess their predictive value.

Of course, none of these approaches is guaranteed to improve the ethnic balance on U.S. campuses. As a society we must determine whether we believe that diversity is beneficial per se—a view that is distinct from the argument that diversity be promoted as a way of righting past or present wrongs. If we support President Clinton's contention that "there are independent educational virtues to a diverse student body,"[25] then we should adopt the goal of diversity explicitly by considering an applicant's membership in an underrepresented group to be a "plus" in the admissions process.

Mounting legal barriers to such explicit consideration of ethnicity have given rise to the idea that eliminating the SAT can serve as a form of covert affirmative action. Although it is certainly possible to design a workable admissions policy that does not include standardized tests, as some 15% of four-year colleges have done, it is not sound policy to eliminate admissions tests in the hope of indirectly furthering a social policy goal. In California, the perennial hotbed of the affirmative action debate, we now know that failure to complete required college-preparatory courses—rather than low test scores—is the main barrier to admission to the University of California for members of all ethnic groups. In any case, both test scores and high school grades are reflections of the very same disparities in educational opportunity. Eliminating standardized tests and relying more heavily on high school achievement in admissions decisions simply cannot result in a dramatic change in the ethnic diversity of the student body. In short, dismantling admissions test requirements as a backdoor affirmative action policy cannot work.

Notes

1. Kenneth R. Weiss, "Fewer Black and Latinos Enroll at UC," *Los Angeles Times,* 21 May 1998, pp. A-3, A-24.
2. Richard Lee Colvin, "Q & A: Should UC Do Away with the SAT?," *Los Angeles Times,* 1 October 1997, p. B-2.
3. Kenneth R. Weiss, "Use of Sat Tests May Not Pass with UC Regents," *Los Angeles Times,* 24 March 1999, Sect. B.
4. Richard J. Herrnstein and Charles Murray, *The Bell Curve* (New York: Free Press, 1994).
5. "Legislative Counsel's Digest, S.B. 1807: Standardized Testing," available from the website of the California State Senate, www.sen.ca.gov, 18 February 1998.
6. "The Best College for You," available from the *Time*/Princeton Review website, www.review.com, April 1997.
7. Leonard Ramist, Charles Lewis, and Laura McCamley-Jenkins, *Student Group Differences in Predicting College Grades: Sex, Language, and Ethnic Groups* (New York: College Entrance Examination Board, College Board Report No. 93-1; ETS Research Report No. 94-27, 1994), p. 32.

8. Robert L. Linn, "Predictive Bias as an Artifact of Selection Procedures," in Howard
    Wainer and Samuel Messick, eds., *Principles of Modern Psychological Measurement: A
    Festschrift for Frederic M. Lord* (Hillsdale, N.J.: Erlbaum, 1983), p. 33.
9. William G. Bowen and Derek Bok, *The Shape of the River: Long-Term Consequences of
    Considering Race in College and University Admissions* (Princeton: Princeton University
    Press, 1998).
10. Ramist, Lewis, and McCamley-Jenkins, p. 9.
11. Ibid., p. 31.
12. Judy A. Kowarsky, *University of California Follow-up Analysis of the 1996 CPEC Eligibility
    Study* (Oakland: Office of the President, Student Academic Services, University of
    California, December 1997), p. 25.
13. Ramist, Lewis, and McCamley-Jenkins, p. 15.
14. Kowarsky, op. cit.
15. *Eligibility of California's 1996 High School Graduates for Admission to the State's Public
    Universities: A Report of the California Postsecondary Education Commission* (Sacramento:
    California Postsecondary Education Commission, 1997).
16. Kowarsky, p. 2.
17. Ibid.
18. *Eligibility of California's 1996 High School Graduates*, pp. 50–61.
19. "Senate Looks into Making Top 4% of Students in Each High School UC-Eligible,"
    Notice: A Publication of the Academic Senate, University of California, March 1998,
    pp. 1–3.
20. Pamela Burdman, "UC Regents Dubious About New Admissions Proposal," *San
    Francisco Chronicle*, 15 May 1998, p. A-21.
21. Christopher Edley, quoted in Daren Bakst, ed., *Hopwood, Bakke, and Beyond: Diversity on
    Our Nation's Campuses*. (Washington, D.C.: American Association of Collegiate
    Registrars and Admissions Officers, 1998), p. 81.
22. Christopher Jencks, "If Not Tests, Then What?," in Bernard R. Gifford, ed., *Test Policy
    and Test Performance* (Boston: Kluwer Academic Publishers, 1989), p. 117.
23. Ellis Cose, *Color-Blind: Seeing Beyond Race in a Race-Obsessed World* (New York: Harper-
    Collins, 1997), p. 117.
24. Edley, quoted in Bakst, p. 80.
25. A Dialogue on Race with President Clinton," *Newshour with Jim Lehrer*, 9 July 1998,
    available from the website of the Public Broadcasting Service, www.pbs.org.

Reflections and Inquiries

1. What, besides average scores achieved by different ethnic groups, do
    researchers investigate when trying to determine the fairness of the SAT?
    Why?

2. What does a psychometric investigation of test bias disclose about the dif-
    ferences in average test scores among ethnic groups?

3. What is the "4% plan" that the University of California launched in 2001?
    Why is it unlikely, according to one researcher, that this plan will be able to
    change racial proportions at UC?

4. How does Zwick account for the tendency of test scores to over- or under-
    predict actual achievement?

Reading to Write

1. Using the data reported by the CPEC, defend or challenge a move to eliminate SAT testing as a way of predicting academic achievement for African-American, Latino, and Asian-American students.

2. Defend or challenge Zwick's conclusion that getting rid of admissions test requirements would fail as a "backdoor affirmative action policy."

Should the SAT Account for Race? | Nathan Glazer *Yes*
Abigail Thernstrom *No*

Few would disagree that a college education should be within the grasp of all young people, regardless of their race, ethnicity, gender, or socioeconomic class. Yet, due to a wide range of inheritable disadvantages, such as growing up in an inner-city environment, attending poor schools, and growing up with little or no parental guidance, some students' chances of getting into college are slim.

What, if anything, can educators and legislators do to help? Affirmative action is one possibility: require that a certain percentage of underrepresented minorities be admitted without regard to test scores such as the Scholastic Aptitude Test (SAT), which is unfavorable to certain ethnic groups. But critics of affirmative action consider any kind of racial targeting wrong, even when the purpose is to compensate for past injustices.

The following debate considers another possibility: equalize the testing playing field with a scoring handicap called a "Strivers" score. Students of underrepresented ethnic groups who come from inner-city areas, for example, would have extra points added to their actual test results. In effect, affirmative action ideals would kick into effect at the testing stage.

Nathan Glazer, who supports the use of a Strivers score, is a contributing editor of *The New Republic*; Abigail Thernstrom, who argues against it, has coauthored the book, *America in Black and White: One Nation, Indivisible* (1997).

YES

This month [Sept. 1999], the Educational Testing Service (ETS), creator and marketer of the SAT—the most widely used test of academic ability and the key measure that colleges and universities take into account when making admissions decisions—announced that it is developing a "Strivers" score, an adjustment of the SAT score to take into account a student's socioeconomic background and race, increasing the scores of those whose socioeconomic

---

Source: Nathan Glazer and Abigail Thernstrom, "Should the SAT Account for Race?" "Yes" (Glazer); "No" (Thernstrom). *The New Republic,* September 27, 1999: 26–29. Reprinted by permission of *The New Republic.*

background or race is considered to put them at a disadvantage. Colleges and universities will be able to use the new Strivers score, if they wish, in making their admissions decisions. The ETS will offer institutions both a "race-blind" model, which includes only social, economic, and educational factors, and a model that also takes into account race—that is, whether the applicant is black, Hispanic, or Native American. ETS's chief competitor, the American College Testing Program, which produces a test used by many institutions instead of the SAT, will be developing a similar model.

Clearly, these developments are a response to the crumbling of the legal support that colleges and universities have relied upon to justify the almost universal practice among selective institutions of giving some kind of preference to black and Hispanic students. And, just as surely, critics of racial preference in college admissions will not be mollified by the new Strivers score and other, similar new strategies. If the formula using race is factored into admissions decisions, the new procedure will be just as legally vulnerable as the existing formal or informal preferences for race that have been struck down by a federal appeals court ruling in a University of Texas case and are now being challenged in an important University of Michigan case. Nor, one would think, would the new approach survive in the courts of the states—California and Washington—where popular referenda have forbidden the states and their agencies, including colleges and universities, to take race into account when making admissions decisions.

And, if the Strivers score without the race factor is used, present statistical patterns show that it will be less effective in identifying black students who may qualify for admission than the score that includes race as part of the formula. For race is indeed a factor in reducing test scores, independent of family wealth, education, and the other socioeconomic factors. It has a particularly strong independent effect in reducing scores for blacks, and, for most institutions, increasing the number of black students is a higher priority than increasing the number of Hispanic students.

What is most striking about the development of the Strivers score is the evidence it gives us of the strength of the commitment to maintaining a higher number of black and Hispanic students in selective institutions than would qualify on the basis of academic promise alone. It is not only the testing agencies that show this commitment. They are, after all, responding to their customers, the educational institutions, whose presidents and administrations universally support racial preference in admissions. They may call it "diversity," a softer and more benign term, but what diversity in practice means is more blacks than they would admit under admissions procedures that didn't take race into account. Writing in *National Review*, Stephan Thernstrom, a strong critic of racial preferences, informs us with disapproval that "[William] Bowen and [Derek] Bok argue [in their study of racial preference *The Shape of the River*] that administrators barred from using racial double-standards in admissions will elect to lower standards for all applicants so as to secure enough non-Asian minorities in the student body."

While this is not quite their position—it is, rather, that administrators 5 will do what they can to maintain the number of black students even when legal bans on taking race into account exist—the fact is that it is not administrators alone who will do this in the effort to evade the clear effect of the elimination of race preference. The Texas legislature voted that the state university should consider the top ten percent of the graduating class of every Texas high school eligible for the state university, a far more radical lowering of the standards for eligibility than any university administrator would have proposed.

Even more remarkably, the Regents of the University of California, who had earlier voted that race could not be taken into account in admissions decisions, have voted that the top four percent of the graduates of every California high school should be eligible for admission to the state university system! The Texas and California actions both radically expand the number of black and Hispanic students eligible for the state universities, for in both states there are many high schools almost exclusively Hispanic and black in composition

Standardized testing is a major education industry. How necessary is it?

that would not be capable of producing students eligible for the top branches of the state university without the new policies.

The faculties of colleges and universities have not played much of a role in all this. Faculty members critical of racial preferences berate their colleagues for not speaking up—indeed, faculty members rarely speak up when a controversial issue does not affect them directly. But recent surveys show that the critics of racial preference will not get much support from university faculties. Although a recent survey of 34,000 faculty members conducted by the Higher Education Research Institute of the University of California at Los Angeles does not ask the racial preference question directly, it does ask whether "promoting diversity leads to the admission of too many underprepared students." Only 28 percent of respondents agreed. And 90.5 percent of respondents agreed with the following statement, admittedly not much more controversial than arguing the virtues of motherhood: "A racially/ethnically diverse student body enhances the educational experience of all students."

Thus college and university faculty and administrators, state legislatures, and the ruling political bodies in charge of public universities all seem to have a commitment to maintaining the number of black and Hispanic students receiving higher education, and, bluntly, are willing to take evasive action to do it. They will use substitutes for race—and, if one substitute does not work, they will look for others. If focusing on applicants who live in a poor neighborhood doesn't help—perhaps there are too many Asians in one poor California neighborhood or another—they will try focusing on applicants who live in housing projects. One way or another, the commitment to enrolling more blacks than would qualify based on academic criteria alone will be pursued.

I believe this commitment, however cloaked in subterfuge it may be, is a valid one. True, it has been clear from the beginning of affirmative action that the majority of the American population—and even a very substantial part of the black population—does not like the idea of making an individual's fate dependent on his or her race or ethnic background. We are all, in principle, in favor of a race-blind society, and clearly that is an important principle, one that we all hope to realize in time. But it has turned out that the use of strict race-blind admissions procedures will radically reduce the number of black students, and in lesser measure the number of Hispanic students, in the selective institutions of higher education—key institutions of our society. This can only serve to further divide non-Asian minorities and whites and to further post-pone the day when we can achieve a truly race-blind, fully integrated society. And this is simply too high a price to pay for adhering to the principle of race-blind admissions today.

If, then, one accepts that admitting more non-Asian minorities than would   10
make the cut through academic criteria alone is a legitimate goal, the Strivers score is not such a terrible way to achieve it. The new score, which is simply an

adjustment of the actual SAT score, is based on the common observation that students from wealthier and more educated families, from well-to-do suburbs, from high schools with better students, and the like, will on average do better on the SAT than students from poorer and less-educated families and from worse high schools—the circumstances of a disproportionate number of minorities. It stands to reason that a student from a materially and education-ally impoverished environment who does fairly well on the SAT and better than other students who come from a similar environment is probably stronger than the unadjusted score indicates. In the past, those colleges and universities whose admissions staffs and procedures permitted individual evaluation of applications took such factors into account informally. With the new Strivers score, they will have a statistical tool that includes no fewer than 14 character-istics that are expected to affect SAT scores. It will, of course, be up to individ-ual institutions to decide whether they want to make use of the Strivers adjustment, just as individual institutions now determine how much weight the SAT score should have in the admissions decision. Still, the Strivers score may make what was essentially an intuitive system more rational.

Of course, there's a strong possibility that it may not survive the inevitable legal challenges. It also remains to be seen just how effective the new approach will be at maintaining or increasing the number of black and Hispanic students in our colleges and universities. For instance, it's possible that the main effect may be instead to increase the number of Asians, in which case the effective-ness of the Strivers adjustment would undoubtedly be reviewed.

But even if the Strivers score approach does not succeed, its introduction has highlighted the need for institutions under legal attack to improve the informal and messy procedures that they have been using to raise their enroll-ment of minority students. Perhaps we can bury the overt emphasis on race while trying to reach the same objective; perhaps race can become the dirty little secret we are trying to take account of without directly saying so. Hypocrisy in the matter may be no minor gain. But it is clear that, for some time, if we are to maintain the appearance of being one nation when by many measures we are, in fact, two, a pure race-blind policy will be so strongly resisted that racial preference will by some means prevail.

NO

The Educational Testing Service (ETS) calls them "strivers." They could just as well be called the "but for" kids: kids who would have done better on their SATs *but for* . . . their racial or ethnic identities, their families' income, the quality of their schools, and so forth. Or so ETS believes. These and other circumstances call for college admissions officers to treat these students' scores differently than they otherwise would, the company suggests. Never mind that selective colleges already take such factors into account when weighing student applications. That inevitably subjective process is inadequate, ETS apparently believes. Schools with high admissions standards need further instruction and a tool to help read scores properly. "A combined score of 1000 on the SATs is not always a 1000," Anthony Carnevale, an ETS vice president who heads the Strivers project, has said. "When you look at a striver who gets a 1000, you're looking at someone who really performs at a 1200."

The students ETS has in mind are those who have done better than their demographic profile would predict. Carnevale suggests the low score is, in effect, a false negative, but ETS has evidently decided to leave the actual process of readjusting scores up to the schools themselves. It will provide the unadjusted score and a statistical formula that colleges can use to convert it to the Strivers number, should they so choose.

Or so it seems. In the wake of negative press, the company released an 15 obfuscating memo denying any current "program or service based upon the Strivers research." But it did not rule out offering a "program or service" once its final report is completed—in about two months. "Researchers" have been "studying the effect of considering additional background information" in order to "provide a richer context for candidates' scores," the memo explained. "ETS is committed to continuing a dialogue about fairness and equity in higher education."

That ongoing "dialogue" has largely been prompted, of course, by the end of the use of racial preferences in admissions decisions in public higher education in Texas, California, and Washington states. Although University of Michigan President Lee Bollinger recently declared diversity to be "as vital as teaching Shakespeare or mathematics," the University of Michigan's own race-based admissions processes will soon be on trial in a federal district court. Suits against other elite colleges (all of which sort students on the basis of race and ethnicity) are sure to follow. But ETS may be riding to the schools' partial rescue with a formula that gives a pseudo-scientific imprimatur to setting lower SAT standards for "disadvantaged" students.

ETS broadens the definition of disadvantage beyond race and ethnicity and is said to be working on two formulas. One will factor in race. The other will reportedly focus on only such variables as the employment status of the student's mother and the kinds of electrical appliances and number of books in the student's home, as reported—accurately or inaccurately—by the student. Thus, the University of California and the handful of other schools that are no longer allowed to make race-based admissions decisions will be able to use it. A formal acknowledgment that disadvantage comes in all colors and many forms would certainly be a step forward. But not a very big one. Expanding the universe of preferential admits does not solve the basic problem. ETS is simply adding more variables to a victimology index and reinforcing the already-too-widespread belief that demography is destiny. And once you start factoring in variables that lead to disadvantage, where do you stop? Should you take into account an applicant's birth order? Her relationship with her parents? The psychologists haven't even gotten into the act yet.

◎/◎ ◎/◎ ◎/◎

Of course, literally no one believes that SAT scores alone should determine who gets into which schools. And, in fact, no college entirely ignores the "context" that ETS wants to stress. But does ETS really want high schools telling a black kid in the Bronx that no one expects him to do as well as the Vietnamese immigrant in his class? Should a teacher say to a white student from a low-income family, "I'll count your C in math as an A? You come to the test with a disadvantage; I understand."

Across the nation, states are getting serious about promoting high academic standards in their elementary and secondary schools. But, in Massachusetts and elsewhere, anti-testing voices have argued that it is simply unfair to expect suburban skills in urban schools with high concentrations of non-Asian minority kids. Teachers, critics say, are being asked to achieve the impossible. Moreover, the Office of Civil Rights in the U.S. Department of Education has recently weighed in with an attack on all high-stakes testing as potentially discriminatory.

Without doubt, school is easier for children who grow up in affluent and 20 educated households. And yet, without tough tests and uniformly high expectations, the academic performance of black and Hispanic children—which, on average, is woefully behind that of whites and Asians—is unlikely to improve. ETS is proposing to send the worst possible message to these kids: If you start out in life with less, we expect less of you—today, tomorrow, maybe forever. The die has been cast. The fix is in.

The students who meet high academic expectations in the kindergarten-through-twelfth-grade years are likely to do well on the SATs, and for most students those tests are excellent predictors of how they will fare in college. As a consequence (as Carnevale surely knows), a score of 1000 is simply not the same as 1200; the lower-scoring student is less academically prepared. Even a score of 1200 means a rough academic ride for students at universities such as Princeton and Stanford, where the median SAT score exceeds 1400.

If elite schools want to become nonselective, or if they want to choose their matriculants randomly from the pool of applicants with scores over, say, 1000, who could object on grounds of principle? Needless to say, their fancy professors and devoted alumni might not like the idea. The physics professor who is a Nobel laureate generally wants to teach high-powered students, and the alumni like the prestige that accompanies highly selective admissions. A more random system would let in plenty of strivers, but the schools themselves would change. Students who were less prepared would require less rigorous courses—unless the colleges suddenly became willing to flunk them out.

ETS is obviously trying to suggest otherwise. Strivers (by definition) have tried harder and thus can do as well as the kid with the much higher SAT, the testing service implies. The disadvantaged student with a score of 1000 will do just as well as the privileged one who got 1200.

Well, maybe, in some cases. But the notion rests on a questionable assumption—namely that a score of 1000, when it beats a racial or other group norm, represents extraordinary effort. That may not be the case. Perhaps the student from an impoverished family who seems to have beaten the SAT odds is simply good at taking standardized tests. Or perhaps her parents have intangible qualities that the ETS formula has failed to capture. It is even possible that she didn't try hard enough—that she is underperforming relative to her intellectual gifts. Her score may reflect academic talent, not hard work. In fact, if ETS is serious about finding the kids who really "strive," it might make much more sense to look at grade point averages, adjusted for the difficulty of the courses taken. Arguably, it is the student with a low SAT score but a high GPA who has demonstrated dedication and perseverance—true grit.

In addition, there is no evidence that students who outscore peers with the same demographic characteristics will experience exceptional intellectual growth in college. In general, for unknown reasons, black students, for 25 instance, earn substantially lower grades in college than their SATs would lead us to predict. (This is one of the buried but depressing facts contained in William Bowen and Derek Bok's pro-affirmative-action book, *The Shape of the River.*) Another recent study, which focused on University of San Diego undergraduates, looked not only at blacks and Hispanics but also at the records of students who attended impoverished high schools, came from low-income families, or lived in neighborhoods with few college graduates. These disadvantaged youths also underperformed, by the measure of their SAT scores.

Most important, why should the measure of achievement be a group norm? Asians do better than whites on math SATs; should whites who outperform the white group norm be given special preference? Should a high-scoring Asian be rejected from MIT if she beats the non-Asian competition but scores lower than Asians in general? In fact, both Asians and Jews will suffer under any leveling scheme that penalizes applicants who come from more prosperous and better-educated homes. These two groups are strikingly overrepresented on elite campuses today, precisely because they score so high on the SATs. Asians constitute only four percent of the population, but they represent almost a quarter of all students scoring above 750 on the math SATs, with the result that they make up nearly one-fifth of the student body at Harvard and a quarter or more at MIT and Cal Tech. It appears that the end of racial preferences in California has primarily benefited Asians.

ETS is perfectly right, of course, to say that race, ethnicity, and socioeconomic status correlate with SAT scores. And SAT scores, the company should add, correlate with college performance. Instead of trafficking in group stereotypes, endlessly tinkering with scores, giving extra points for this or that sort of disadvantage, and pretending lower-scoring students are competitive when they are not, why not just educate the kids? Does ETS believe good schools are an impossible dream? Shame on it, if it does. ◎╱◎

Reflections and Inquiries

1. According to Glazer, those who criticize racial preference in college admissions are not expected to support the Strivers score option. Why not?

2. What reasons does Glazer give that make the Strivers score option a valid one?

3. Glazer feels that measure of achievement should not be a group norm. Why not? Do you agree or disagree?

4. Thernstrom considers the Strivers score option subjective and inadequate. Why?

5. In Thernstrom's view, ETS is merely reinforcing the belief that demography is destiny. What does she mean by that? Do you agree or disagree?

6. How would the Strivers score option affect "elite" universities like Princeton, according to Thernstrom? Would you consider this change a good one? Why or why not?

Reading to Write

1. Write a one- to two-page critique of each debater's use of evidence to support his or her respective claims.

2. Drawing from the information both authors provide and supplementing it with additional background reading, write a position paper in which you recommend that colleges use or not use Strivers scores as a criterion for admission.

Connections Among the Clusters

1. What connections can you make between issues in national security (see Cluster 5) and multicultural learning?

2. How might multicultural education influence the making of connections between science and religion? (See Cluster 6.)

3. What issues in media regulation (see Cluster 3) emerge when we consider bilingual education methods?

Writing Projects

1. Visit your campus's multicultural center or a minority-student organization and obtain information about its most pressing problems. Then write an essay in which you examine these problems, their effect on student learning and student life, the efforts to solve the problems, and the work that remains to be done.

2. Examine the course offerings in your major from the perspective of multicultural learning. Write an essay in which you propose changes, such as adding new courses that focus on minorities and their works or revising existing courses so they embrace multicultural matters.

Suggestions for Further Reading

Banks, James A., and Cherry Banks. *Multicultural Education: Issues and Perspectives.* New York: John Wiley, 2004.

Bloom, Allan David. *The Closing of the American Mind: How Higher Education Has Failed Democracy and Impoverished the Souls of Today's Students.* New York: Simon, 1987.

Giroux, Henry A. *Schooling and the Struggle for Public Life: Critical Pedagogy in the Modern Age.* Minneapolis: U of Minnesota P, 1988.

Harper's Symposium. "Who Needs the Great Works?" *Harper's* Sept. 1989: 43–52.

Kates, Gary. "The Classics of Western Civilization Do Not Belong to Conservatives Alone." *Chronicle of Higher Education* 5 July 1989: A46.

Kimball, Roger. *Tenured Radicals: How Politics Has Corrupted Our Higher Education.* New York: Harper, 1990.

Krauthammer, Charles. "Hale Columbus, Dead White Male." *Time* 27 May 1991: 74.

Moya, Paula. *Learning from Experience: Minority Identities, Multicultural Struggle.* Berkeley: U of California P, 2002.

Nieto, Sonia. *Light in Their Eyes: Creating Multicultural Learning Communities.* New York: Teachers College P, 1999.

Potowski, Kim. "Situational Context of Education: A Window into the World of Bilingual Learners." *International Journal of Bilingual Education and Bilingualism* 9.2; 2006: 281–83.

Sykes, Charles J. *The Hollow Men: Politics and Corruption in Higher Education.* Washington: Regnery, 1990.

Walqui, Aida. "Scaffolding Instruction for English Language Learners: A Conceptual Framework." *International Journal of Bilingual Education and Bilingualism* 9.2; 2006: 159–80.

5 National Security: How Can the United States Best Protect Itself?

Introduction

The history of America, like that of many other nations, is filled with the struggle to preserve two precious possessions: freedom (national and individual) and security (national and individual). One depends on the other—that is, freedom is jeopardized when there is no way to protect it; security does not mean much when freedom is absent. Ever since the end of World War II, when President Truman established the National Security Council, the President of the United States has relied on a team of national security advisers in making policy decisions.

In the best of times, the scales of security and freedom are delicately balanced. But ever since 9/11, some argue, that delicate balance has been lost: Security seems to be taking precedence. A new governmental department, the Department of Homeland Security, has been created. The Patriot Act, in particular, has led to an aggressive effort to filter out potential terrorists. As will become apparent in your reading of the first several articles in this cluster, to many, the Patriot Act is a troublesome overstepping of the boundaries of privacy and individual freedom. The American Civil Liberties Union (ACLU), for example, deems the Patriot Act to be "un-American" in its methods of surveillance and the use of detentions without probable cause. How far are we willing to tip the freedom/security scale in a post–9/11 world?

What Effects Could the Patriot Act Have on Individual Liberties?

"So, It's Agreed" | Chris Slane

Security requires, it seems, a certain loss of freedom. For governments to keep air travel safe, belongings must be x-rayed and searched. For countries to keep their roadways safe, speed limits and drunk driving prohibitions must be enforced. But certain types or degrees of security may demand a greater loss of freedom. A child bargains with Santa Claus, trading the freedom to be "bad" with the security of receiving gifts at Christmas. But, as Chris Slane, a widely syndicated editorial cartoonist hints at in the following editorial cartoon, shadier characters may be sitting at the security bargaining table.

Reflections and Inquiries

1. Slane's cartoon is filled with physical emblems that quickly establish the identities and attributes of the individuals sitting around the conference table. How many can you spot? What are the implications of being able to identify individuals on the basis of emblem alone?

2. Everyone's face is visible to the viewer except that of the devil. What is your explanation for that?

Source: Slane Cartoons Ltd.

3. What justification can you give for the physical emblems associated with the CIA agent and the direct marketing representative?

4. Describe the premise of the cartoon in your own words.

Reading to Write

Locate a few other editorial cartoons that deal with national security and write an essay on recurring views or attitudes toward this complex issue. Are these concerns or attitudes justified, or are they just easy targets for cartoonists?

Patriot Act a Vital Tool Against Terrorism | Kevin V. Ryan

In the wake of the 9/11 terrorist attacks on the United States, measures were taken to heighten domestic security. The controversial Patriot Act is one of them. Arguing for its support is Kevin V. Ryan, a former judge for San Francisco's Superior Court, whom President Bush appointed as U.S. attorney for the Northern District of California.

Two years ago today, we all bore witness to the callous viciousness of our terrorist enemies, as well as the devastation they seek to inflict. That day, more than 3,000 Americans lost their lives, and the fight against terrorism became the Justice Department's first and highest priority.

Thus, when I took office as the U.S. attorney for the Northern District of California in July 2002, I immediately mandated that the highest priority of my office would be the protection of this district from a terrorist attack. I have instructed my prosecutors to use every legal weapon at their disposal to fight the war against terrorism—particularly the USA Patriot Act.

Unfortunately, a small but vocal group of protesters have been mounting a campaign against the Patriot Act. Swayed by these protesters, a few local city councils have passed resolutions opposing the Patriot Act—including the San Francisco Board of Supervisors, which approved a measure directing city employees not to cooperate in federal criminal investigations in certain circumstances. Such efforts are largely based on misinformation and threaten to place the community at greater risk.

Both Democrats and Republicans in Congress came together to pass the Patriot Act: The House of Representatives voted 357–66 to approve it, and the Senate approved the legislation by a near-unanimous 98–1 vote. Among

---

Source: Kevin V. Ryan, "Patriot Act a Vital Tool Against Terrorism," *San Francisco Chronicle,* Sept. 11, 2003: A25. Reprinted by permission of the author.

the local lawmakers voting in favor of the Patriot Act were Sens. Barbara Boxer and Dianne Feinstein, and Rep. Nancy Pelosi, all Democrats.

While the Patriot Act is a key tool in the fight against terrorism, it provided 5 for only modest, incremental changes in the law. The Patriot Act simply took existing legal principles and retrofitted them for the challenges posed by a well-financed and highly coordinated global terrorist network:

- First, the Patriot Act ensured that investigators could use the same tools in terrorism cases that have been available for many years in drug, fraud and racketeering cases. As Sen. Joe Biden of Delaware explained during the congressional floor debate prior to passage of the act, "the FBI could get a wiretap to investigate the Mafia, but they could not get one to investigate terrorists. To put it bluntly, that was crazy! What's good for the mob should be good for terrorists."

- Second, the Patriot Act also brought the law up to date with current technology, so we no longer have to fight a digital-age battle with weapons from an era of rotary telephones.

- Third, the Patriot Act allows information-sharing and cooperation among government agencies so that they can better "connect the dots." The act recognizes that every level of law enforcement and first responders need to cooperate, contribute and share information to deal with the threats we face.

- Fourth, the Patriot Act increased the penalties for those who commit terrorist crimes so that we can take terrorists off the street and out of our communities.

Critics of the Patriot Act have created numerous myths about the act that have no basis in either the text of the law or in law-enforcement practice. For example, critics have charged that the FBI is unlawfully visiting local libraries to monitor the reading records of ordinary citizens. The fact is: business records, including library records, have been available to law enforcement for decades through grand jury investigations. (In the investigation of the Zodiac killer, for instance, police suspected that the murderer was inspired by a Scottish occult poet and wanted to learn who had checked the poet's books out of the library.)

The Patriot Act does not allow federal law enforcement free and unchecked access to libraries, bookstores or other businesses. The act only allows a high-ranking FBI official to ask a federal court to grant an order in specific investigations to "protect against international terrorism or clandestine intelligence activities." As a safeguard of our liberties, the act expressly bars the FBI from investigating citizens solely based on the exercise of their First Amendment rights.

Critics have also claimed that the Patriot Act encourages law enforcement to employ racial profiling and targeting. In fact, the act contains a provision explicitly condemning discrimination against Arab and Muslim Americans. Justice Department policy is that terrorism investigations are to be governed by the principle of neutrality. We target criminal conduct, not nationality.

Lastly, some critics have claimed that the Patriot Act deprives Americans of their constitutional rights. To date, however, not a single provision of the act has been declared unconstitutional by any court. The law both before and after the Patriot Act is that a federal judge must approve requests by law enforcement to conduct wiretaps of terrorism suspects or searches and seizures.

As an immigrant to this country, I appreciate the unique constitutional 10 rights that America offers. To this end, I will not tolerate the abuse of anyone's rights by law enforcement, nor will I accept anything less than the highest standard of ethical conduct by the prosecutors in my office. The protection of all our citizens' rights and privacy is the principle that guides us; failure to do so renders our efforts meaningless.

The Patriot Act, however, provides important tools that law enforcement can and should employ to fight the war on terror. I will not shrink from my sworn duty to do everything I can within the law to protect this district from terrorist attacks. Peoples' lives may well be at stake. ◎/◎

Reflections and Inquiries

1. Describe the organizational strategy of Ryan's argument. How effectively is each section of the argument developed?

2. According to Ryan, "The Patriot Act simply took existing legal principles and retrofitted them" to meet the challenges of a post–9/11 world. What "existing legal principles" do you suppose Ryan is referring to? What does he mean by "retrofitting" them?

3. Law enforcement officials "target criminal conduct, not nationality," Ryan claims. How convincingly does he support this assertion?

Reading to Write

Do background reading to find out how effectively or ineffectively the Patriot Act has achieved its objectives. Report any incidents of what you consider to be efforts made to protect a person's civil rights or, conversely, any abuses of civil rights.

Faking Out the Constitution | Kevin Danaher and Scott Lynch

The authors of the following rebuttal to Kevin Ryan's defense of the Patriot Act (see the preceding selection) are both human rights activists. Kevin Danaher is the director of Global Exchange, a San Francisco-based international human rights group that he founded. Scott Lynch is the communications director of Peace Action, a forty-year-old U.S.-based group devoted to promoting peace and disarmament.

"We think it is important to tell the truth," White House spokesman John Bolton said recently on the topic of North Korea. But the Bush administration has a little trouble telling the truth, a small problem that could have devastating consequences for democracy and freedom in this country.

First, there are those 16 little words that President Bush has been forced to eat. Iraq's alleged plot to purchase African yellowcake for a nuclear weapons program is a falsehood based on forged documents. Yet the White House included the allegation in a presidential speech despite fully knowing the weakness of the charge.

Remember the canisters of poison gas and anthrax that were supposed to be lying around the Iraq desert near Tikrit? None to be found.

There was also a short news flurry about Iraq's alleged mobile biowarfare labs. They were actually used to inflate weather balloons, just as the Iraqis claimed when the "labs" were discovered.

How about those remote-controlled aircraft set to bomb surrounding   5
nations, Israel and even the East Coast of the United States? They were held together with duct tape and chicken wire and are about as precision-guided as a kite.

That is just a small selection of the inaccuracies, shaded truths and outright lies about Iraq the Bush administration has foisted on the American public. The administration's "weapons of mass destruction" talk is merely a front for its own "weapons of mass deception."

Such a state of affairs exists because there are still many Americans who believe that Iraq had something to do with Sept. 11. That carefully stage-managed propaganda has enabled President Bush, Vice President Dick Cheney and Attorney General John Ashcroft to push for Patriot Act II and defend Patriot Act I as necessary in protecting Americans.

Step back and think of the future. When the next major attack on U.S. soil occurs, the Bush administration will be asking for yet another Patriot Act enhancement to "protect" the American population. Let's not give them another blank check.

Source: Kevin Danaher and Scott Lynch, "Faking Out the Constitution," *San Francisco Chronicle,* Sept. 11, 2003: A25. Scott Lynch is the Communications Director for Peace Action, and Dr. Kevin Danaher is a cofounder of Global Exchange. Reprinted with permission.

Why? The Patriot Act was supposed to make the United States safer; instead it has sown terror and fear in immigrant communities, making immigrants—particularly those of Middle Eastern origin—less likely to come forward with any information. So far, 154 communities in 28 states have passed resolutions opposing the Patriot Act, and that includes three statewide resolutions in Vermont, Hawaii and Alaska.

Two scathing internal Justice Department reviews have revealed abuses 10 of power, beatings and harassment of those arrested under the Patriot Act's authority. The full extent of the abuse is unclear, for detainees are held unconstitutionally incommunicado without access to lawyers.

The final government report on Sept. 11 concluded that a failure to prevent the attacks had more to do with institutional inertia, turf wars and lack of communication between the CIA and FBI—not a lack of resources. The intelligence services had more than enough tools for the job, but the Bush administration wanted more. Thus, the Patriot Act sprung from nowhere, as if it had been kept hidden in a bottom drawer ready to be dropped on a terrified population given the right opportunity.

Most members of Congress simply did not read this sweeping abrogation of the Constitution the first time round, which explains why they are feeling a little more skeptical with Patriot Act II. The original Patriot Act enables the Bush administration to subpoena library records, search homes without informing residents, monitor telephone and Internet traffic without notification and detain foreigners indefinitely. It even created a new bogeyman, the domestic terrorist: Anyone who carries out an act that "appears to be intended to intimidate or coerce a civilian population [or] to influence the policy of government by intimidation or coercion." The term is so broadly defined that peaceful protest and civil disobedience could be labeled as terrorism.

Patriot Act II would expand domestic intelligence gathering even more, further erode the role of the courts in governmental oversight, allow secret arrests, create a DNA databank of those suspected of associating with "terrorists" and even yank the citizenship away from Americans who support groups the government would rather not deal with. It sounds like something out of Germany, circa 1938.

No wonder democracies in Europe and around the world are looking on in horror. We don't need a new Patriot Act. We need a new foreign policy based on cooperation and respect, not bludgeoning and fear. We do not need a domestic policy that makes a mockery of America's tradition as a democracy. ◎/◎

Reflections and Inquiries

1. According to Danaher and Lynch, the Patriot Act "has sown terror and fear in immigrant communities." What evidence, if any, do the authors provide to support this assertion?

2. What methods of persuasion are the authors employing in this article? How effectively do they employ these methods? (You might first want to review Chapter 3, Using the Classical Model in Your Arguments.)

3. Defend or refute the authors' claim that we need a new foreign policy based on cooperation, rather than a new Patriot Act.

4. Compare Danaher and Lynch's argument against the Patriot Act with Ryan's argument in defense of it. Which side argues its case more convincingly, in your opinion, and why?

Reading to Write

Follow up on the claims made by the authors of the two previous selections. What information does each side overlook, oversimplify, or distort? This analysis should bring you to a clear articulation of your own stance on the Patriot Act.

USA Patriot Act: What's Next? | George H. Pike

In the following article, George H. Pike summarizes the aims of the original Patriot Act, whose provisions expired on December 31, 2005, the changes made to the Patriot Act renewed on March 9, 2006, and the continuing debate over the continued threat to civil liberties generated by the Patriot Act. George H. Pike is Director of the Barco Law Library and Assistant Professor of Law at the University of Pittsburgh School of Law. His expertise is legal research.

On March 9, the USA PATRIOT Act was renewed. After nearly a year of proposals and counterproposals, two extensions, and ongoing behind-the-scenes negotiations, Congress passed two bills renewing the act. President Bush signed the legislation only hours before it was set to expire.

The USA PATRIOT Act was enacted just 6 weeks after 9/11 in response to lapses in intelligence gathering that may have contributed to the attacks. Congress and the Bush administration were especially concerned that existing statutes had not evolved enough to respond to new communication technologies, such as cell phones, electronic finance and banking, and the Internet.

There was also concern that intelligence and criminal investigation agencies were unable (or unwilling) to exchange information. The 9/11 Commission pointed to a number of information-exchange lapses even within the FBI. Three months prior to 9/11, an FBI agent who was investigating the attack on the USS Cole obtained information about a man who later turned out to be

---

one of the 9/11 hijackers. The information, however, was not shared with other agents/officials because of real or perceived "need to know" barriers.

The Threat to Civil Liberties

The USA PATRIOT Act was intended to break down those barriers and respond to new communication technologies in a number of ways. The act broadened the definition of terrorism, permitted extensive sharing of intelligence information, made it easier to get warrants to conduct intelligence investigations, increased the secrecy relating to search warrants, and expanded the scope of information that could be obtained. Partially due to its haste in passing the act, Congress decreed that many—but not all—of the PATRIOT Act's provisions would expire on Dec. 31, 2005.

While acknowledging that various breakdowns contributed to 9/11, the PATRIOT Act also generated opposition. Critics charged that many of its provisions threatened civil liberties and constitutional rights, including the right to free speech and protections against warrantless searches. Among the most criticized were provisions allowing for "sneak and peek" warrants—issued secretly and without notice until after the search is completed—and expansions in the use of National Security Letters (NSLs), which are warrantless demands for certain records.

Of most concern to librarians and others in the information industry was Section 215, which expanded the definition of business records that could be obtained under a secret warrant to include "any tangible things," a broad definition that would include records from libraries and bookstores.

These criticisms were countered by the Bush administration and supporters of the act who believed that it was necessary, that it was working, and that the concerns about civil liberties were misplaced. Congressional testimony noted that investigations under the act had broken up several potential terrorist threats. Justice Department officials also reported very few verified complaints about civil liberties abuses, and they claimed that Section 215 had never been used to access library records. In the words of former Attorney General John Ashcroft, the Justice Department has neither "the time nor inclination to monitor the reading habits of Americans." He added, "No offense to the American Library Association, but we just don't care."

The Renewal Debate

Against this backdrop, Congress worked on renewing the USA PATRIOT Act through the summer and fall of 2005. Although a consensus quickly developed on a number of the more noncontroversial provisions, a joint House and Senate Conference Committee's proposal was unable to overcome a filibuster about civil liberties concerns. After two extensions to maintain the status quo, a second compromise was ultimately hammered out and approved.

So after months of debate and discussion, the act continues as the law of the land. A number of changes, however, make the new version substantially different from the old one. The new laws made all but two of the PATRIOT Act provisions permanent. Section 215 (dealing with business and library records) and Section 206 (dealing with roving wiretaps) were extended to Dec. 31, 2009.

Changes to Section 215

Several changes were made to Section 215 to address concerns about the 10
threat to civil liberties. First, the standard for obtaining a warrant was changed. (The warrant is obtained from a specific federal court empowered to issue warrants in secret and only for intelligence-gathering purposes.) The request must be approved by the FBI director or deputy director, and must show that the material is "relevant to an authorized investigation . . . to protect against international terrorism."

The recipient of a Section 215 request can disclose the request to an attorney and may challenge the request in a special federal court procedure. However, the other secrecy provisions of Section 215 remained intact.

The second compromise added a new provision that would permit the recipient of a Section 215 order to challenge the secrecy provisions after 1 year has passed. The challenge, which is made in the same kind of special federal court proceeding, can be granted only if the court finds no reason to believe that disclosure would threaten national security or interfere with an ongoing investigation. However, the same compromise gave the Justice Department or FBI the right to "certify" that disclosure would be harmful. If the certification is made in good faith, the court must consider it to be conclusive and enforce the secrecy provision.

National Security Letters

NSLs also figured prominently in the PATRIOT Act renewal legislation. The FBI can issue an NSL to specific individuals or businesses to request specific information. NSLs have been used primarily to get information from "electronic communication service" providers about subscribers. According to an October 2005 lawsuit, at least one NSL was issued to a person identified as a "member of the American Library Association."

The NSL provisions were modified somewhat by the renewal legislation. An NSL recipient can petition his/her local federal court for an order to modify or set aside the NSL. The secrecy provisions remain largely intact, including the threat of criminal charges for unauthorized disclosure, but the NSL can be disclosed to an attorney. The NSL recipient does not have to disclose the name of the attorney to the FBI. Other new provisions provide increased internal auditing and external reporting to Congress on the use of NSLs.

The second compromise also contains specific language stating that a 15
library that provides access to the Internet or digital databases is not an "electronic communication service provider" under the NSL statutes. This should prevent most libraries from receiving NSLs to disclose information about patron Internet or database use. However, if a library acts as an Internet

service provider, it would be subject to NSLs. Some library consortiums that provide Internet access to their members could be considered electronic communication service providers.

More Changes Still Needed?

Other changes to the PATRIOT Act included the Justice Department pointing out 30 new provisions to protect privacy and civil liberties. However, critics continue to argue that the changes do not go far enough. Sen. Russ Feingold, D-Wis., and the ALA recommend that Section 215 be strengthened further to establish a tighter connection to specific terrorist threats before records can be obtained. NSLs remain easy to obtain and subject to extensive secrecy. Finally, the provision for getting a court order to permit disclosure of a Section 215 order after 1 year is very weak.

Will passage of the altered PATRIOT Act end the acrimonious debate now that most of it is permanent? Probably not. Any law can be changed at any time and, already, additional legislation to target these issues is being proposed. Finally, the sunset provisions that remain in the act mean that this debate will again take center stage in 3.5 years.

History's Paradox

But history provides an interesting paradox on whether conditions that provoke civil liberties concerns will eventually change. Civil liberties were restricted in times of national security threat during the Civil War, World War I, and World War II, when some constitutional rights were suspended. But in each of these cases, those suspensions ended when the wars ended.

The war on terrorism, however, is different. There is less likelihood of an Armistice Day or V-E Day that establishes a clear end to the war on terrorism. And if there is no clear end to the war, it will be difficult to end the threat to civil liberties. ◎/◎

Reflections and Inquiries

1. Why is the threat to civil liberties generated by the Patriot Act different from other threats to civil liberties in American history?

2. What are National Security Letters, and how were their provisions modified? Do they represent an improvement or not? Why?

Reading to Write

Study the changes made to the Patriot Act and in an essay argue whether or not they are sufficient. If they are, why do you think so? If not, what more needs to be done?

Candorville | Darrin Bell

What price are we willing to pay for security? To what extent are we willing to sacrifice privacy for protection? Is the government going too far when it monitors the way American citizens use the Internet or the public library? If we agree that this kind of snooping into our private business is going too far by violating our First Amendment rights, what is to prevent domestic terrorists from using the Internet to make bombs or to interact with terrorist cells around the world? In the following Candorville *strip, Darrin Bell takes a humorous approach to the way such snooping might get out of hand. Darrin Bell is the co-creator of the comic strip* Rudy Park, *syndicated to 80 newspapers and websites. A graduate in political science from the University of California, Berkeley, Darrin Bell has been a staff cartoonist for the* Daily Californian *and a regular contributor to the* Los Angeles Times, San Francisco Chronicle *and* Oakland Tribune.

Source: Darrin Bell/Bellcartoons.com.

Reflections and Inquiries

1. What would you say is the central argument of Bell's *Candorville* strip? Where does it come through most clearly?

2. All political cartoons and comic strips exaggerate or satirize to convey their premises humorously as well as emphatically. The possibilities for unjustifiable exaggeration exist, of course. Does Bell exaggerate unjustifiably or not? Explain.

3. Reflect on the way in which Bell depicts his characters. What correlation, if any, do you detect between their physical appearance and roles?

Reading to Write

Examine Darrin Bell's other work by accessing his portfolio at http://www.BellCartoons.com or http://www.candorville.com, and then write an essay that explains Bell's social or political views on one specific topic and that argues for the effectiveness (or lack of effectiveness) of the use of visual argument for conveying that particular viewpoint.

The USA PATRIOT Act and Patron Privacy on Library Internet Terminals | Mary Minow

One of the most controversial aspects of the PATRIOT Act—itself controversial—is that it enables the FBI and other law-enforcement authorities to subpoena library records in order to track the Internet sites visited by library patrons. In the following article, Mary Minow, a consultant in library law for the librarylaw.com website, addresses public concerns regarding how libraries should cooperate with these enhanced surveillance measures allegedly intended to counteract terrorism.

Within hours after the September 11 attacks, the FBI began serving search warrants to major Internet Service Providers [ISPs] to get information about suspected electronic communications.[1] Within a week, police and FBI agents received tips that some suspects used libraries in Hollywood Beach and Delray Beach, Florida. FBI agents have since requested computer sign-in lists from other libraries. President Bush signed the USA PATRIOT Act into law on October 26, 2001. This law is expected to greatly increase the number of requests for sign-in lists at libraries.

Source: Mary Minow, "The USA PATRIOT Act and Patron Privacy on Library Internet Terminals," published Feb. 15, 2002 at www.llrx.com/features/usapatriotact.htm. Reprinted by permission of the author.

What is the USA PATRIOT Act?

The USA PATRIOT Act stands for the Uniting and Strengthening America by Providing Appropriate Tools Required to Intercept and Obstruct Terrorism Act of 2001. The legislation is broad and changes immigration laws, tightens controls on money laundering, and greatly expands the legal use of electronic surveillance.

The Act greatly expands the use of "roving wiretaps." This means that a wiretap order targeted to a person is no longer confined to a particular computer or telephone. Instead, it may "rove" wherever the target goes, which may include library computers. The new law allows a court to issue an order that is valid anywhere in the U.S. This greatly increases a library's exposure to court orders. Further, the use of pen/trap orders is now "technology neutral" and applies to the Internet as well as [to] telephones. Whereas incoming and outgoing phone numbers have long been available upon the mere showing that they are relevant to an ongoing investigation, now email headers and URLs visited are available under the same low standard. Civil liberties advocates argued that such information is not analogous to phone numbers, but far more revealing (including, for example, the keywords used in Google searches such as http://www.google.com/search?hl=en&q=mary+minow).

Much of the Act expands the Foreign Intelligence Surveillance Act (FISA), in which the standards for courts to approve surveillance of foreign intelligence gathering are far less demanding than those required for approval of a criminal wiretap, which requires a showing of probable cause.

Librarians can get a good sense of the legal requirements by reading the guidance just issued to federal agents by the Department of Justice.[2]   5

What does the USA PATRIOT Act mean for libraries?

The upshot is that there will be a great many more surveillance orders, everywhere in the country, and in turn there will be more requests for library records, including Internet use records. Think of law enforcement as needing to enter two doors to apprehend a suspect.

Door One leads to the computer server. Law enforcement can find electronic tracks through email or Internet history logs. They may have intercepted messages through surveillance or other means. This leads to a particular computer terminal, date and time.

Door Two leads to the individual. This person could be someone using the Internet in a library, particularly someone who wishes to remain anonymous. The FBI (or others) will want to see a library record of who was using the library's terminal(s) at a particular date and time. If the library keeps sign-up records, law enforcement will want to see those records.

Will the FBI (or other law enforcement) ask to put surveillance technology on library computers?

In many cases, the surveillance technology will be placed elsewhere, and lead law enforcement directly to Door Two. However, it is possible that the FBI will approach the library and ask to place software (such as the controversial DCS1000 [also known as Carnivore]) on library servers.[3] Libraries should be sure to insist on a court order before complying. Note that libraries that share servers with cities or others may not be directly approached.

Should a library cooperate with the FBI (or other law enforcement) in giving library Internet sign-up lists?

Yes, but advisedly with a court order. This is where the library's individual 10 policies and procedures will become increasingly important. Does the library require sign-ups? If there are no sign-up lists, the inquiry essentially halts. Does the library allow first names only, or made-up names? Does it require identification? Library cards with addresses? Does it keep sign-up records, and if so, for how long? Does it use an automated system that ties library card numbers (tied to registration information) to Internet use? Is such information electronically disengaged after use and electronically shredded? Is it backed up on computer tapes? How long are backup tapes kept?

Search warrants are court orders, signed by a magistrate or a judge. Libraries are explicitly barred under Calif. Gov't Code §6267 from disclosing patron registration or circulation records, excepting staff administrative use, written consent by the patron, or an order from the appropriate superior court.[4]

Whether or not the law protects Internet use records from disclosure without a court order (this includes search warrants) is not entirely clear. Many libraries consider these records as an extension of registration/circulation records, in that personally identifying information linking patron names with content is involved. Additionally, another section of the law known as the "personal privacy" exemption, provides that certain types of information may be kept confidential by a public agency where the disclosure would constitute an unwarranted invasion of personal privacy.[5] Finally, library policies that protect such records, if well drafted, might protect Internet use records. For an argument that the state law should be updated to reflect the use of Internet in *California libraries,* see my article in *California Libraries,* April 4, 1999.[6]

Should my library use sign-ups for Internet terminals? If we use sign-up records, are they subject to the California Public Records Act, making us at risk if we destroy them?

Libraries generally decide on whether and how to use sign-up procedures based on the supply and demand of Internet terminals. Sometimes libraries want identification to afford a measure of accountability, i.e., prevent hacking. Libraries should be aware, however, that the sign-up procedure has considerable privacy implications. If records are kept, it is best if precise information can be extracted (e.g., user at Terminal #2 on November 13, 2001 at 1 p.m.) without giving out other patron data.

Under the California Public Records Act, the library is not required to create or maintain Internet use records, any more than numerous other temporary records libraries may keep, such as reference query logs. Once records are created and kept, however, they are subject to court orders, and possibly to open records requests. (Remember that it's possible these records have the same privacy safeguards as circulation and registration records described above.)

Although libraries are not required to create or maintain such records, it 15 is definitely not advisable to destroy the records after a law enforcement or public request for disclosure. In a case in New Hampshire, a father requested a school's computer Internet logs (in this case, the electronic records of sites visited). He was concerned that the school library's acceptable use policy was inadequate. When the school did not turn over the logs, the father sued under the state's Right-To-Know law. The county superior court ordered the school to turn over the logs, with the user names and passwords omitted. In January 2001, however, the Court found that the school had intentionally deleted the logs after the father filed suit. It found the school to be in contempt of court, and ordered it to produce the remaining records and pay the father his costs and attorney's fees.[7]

In addition, local ordinances may apply. Check with the library's attorney.

I read that the USA PATRIOT Act allows federal agents to get court orders for the production of "business records." Does that include library records?

The Act states that the FBI may apply for an order requiring the "production of any tangible things (including books, records, papers, documents, and other items) for an investigation to protect against international terrorism or clandestine intelligence activities, provided that such investigation of a United States person is not conducted solely upon the basis of activities protected by the first amendment. . . ."[8]

This provision is designed to get ISP records of user billing information. Library patrons who are merely accessing information on Internet terminals should have strong First Amendment arguments. Nevertheless, it's not clear whether they would win. Senator Russ Feingold tried to get an amendment to clarify that the Act would not preempt existing federal and state privacy laws, by maintaining existing criteria for records, such as library records. This amendment failed. Also, it should be noted that this "business records" provision is an amendment of the FISA law, which means that court proceedings are not open and are sealed.

I read that a research librarian tipped off the police in Florida. Can I do that, or must I wait for them to come to me?

If you recognize a picture in the newspaper as one of your patrons, that is not divulging a library record. If, on the other hand, you recognize a suspect's name from library records, you should definitely check in with your attorney before deciding whether to call the police.

In Broward County, Florida, the library was issued an order by a federal [20] grand jury to collect library records when a patron fitting the description of Mohamed Atta, an alleged terrorist leader, was seen using computers with Internet access.[9] The order was given with specific instructions not to release information to anyone other than federal authorities.[10]

Recall that the vast majority of library patrons are not terrorists, and libraries should make all efforts to protect patron privacy.

Wasn't there an FBI program years ago that sent FBI agents into libraries asking for reading habits of suspicious looking people?

Yes. The FBI Library Awareness Program was a program that ran for about 25 years, in which FBI agents tried to enlist the assistance of librarians in monitoring the reading habits of "suspicious" individuals. Such individuals were variously defined as people with Eastern European or Russian-sounding names or accents, or coming from countries hostile to the U.S.[11] During the Library Awareness Program, some FBI agents wrongly claimed that they were not subject to statutes protecting library records.[12] The efforts were largely unsuccessful, due to the tremendous outrage and resistance from those in the library profession.

The most important lesson that libraries learned was the importance of training the "friendly front desk clerk" and even volunteers not to hand over the information, but to refer all inquiries, even by badged FBI agents, to the library director.

How is the library community responding to the anti-terrorism legislation?

The American Library Association joined with the Association of Research Libraries and the Association of American Law Libraries in issuing a statement on the proposed anti-terrorism measures. It says that libraries do not monitor information sought or read by library users. To the extent that libraries "capture" usage information of computer logs, libraries comply with court orders for law enforcement.

The statement is also concerned that the legislation, which makes it easier to access business records, may in some cases apply to library circulation records. It recommends that legislators keep high standards for court orders regarding release of library records.[13]

Where should libraries go to get guidance on FBI search warrants?

The Freedom to Read Foundation is making some legal assistance available to librarians. Librarians are advised to call the ALA Office for Intellectual

Freedom and request legal advice from Jenner & Block without disclosing the existence of a warrant. For more details, see the ALA's recently issued Alert: USA PATRIOT Act.[14] ◎/◎

Notes

1. "FBI turns to Internet for terrorism clues," http://www.cnn.com/2001/TECH/internet/09/13/fbi.isps/ (visited November 15, 2001).
2. See United States. Department of Justice. Computer Crime and Intellectual Property Section. Field Guidance on New Authorities that Relate to Computer Crime and Electronic Evidence Enacted in the USA Patriot Act of 2001, http://www.usdoj.gov/criminal/cybercrime/PatriotAct.htm (visited November 13, 2001).
3. For more on current software/hardware surveillance technology, see Jack Karp, "Chewing on Carnivore," *TechTV,* October 16, 2001 (visited November 13, 2001).
4. See Calif. Gov't Code §6254 and §6267 (2001). The library may not disclose these records except to a) staff within the scope of administrative duties, b) with written consent from the patron, or c) by order of the appropriate superior court. Although California law refers to the "appropriate superior court," the USA PATRIOT Act still requires court orders, but allows courts in any jurisdiction to issue orders. Federal law will supercede state law in this case (unless the Act is later found unconstitutional).
5. Calif. Gov't Code, § 6254(c) (2001).
6. See Mary Minow, "Library patron internet records and freedom of information laws," *California Libraries,* April 4, 1999, pp. 8–9, reprinted at http://www.librarylaw.com/publicrecords.html (visited October 3, 2001).
7. James M. Knight v. School Administrative Unit #16, Docket No. 00-E-307, Rockingham, SS. Superior Court, New Hampshire. See "Exeter Internet Ruling, Complete Ruling," *Portsmouth Herald,* January 8, 2001 at http://www.seacoastonline.com/news/1_8special.htm (visited November 15, 2001).
8. USA PATRIOT Act H.R. 3162, Title II Section 215, amending the Foreign Intelligence Surveillance Act (FISA), Title V, Section 501(a)(1) http://leahy.senate.gov/press/200110/USA.pdf (visited November 13, 2001).
9. Florida Statute §257.261. The Florida Statute is very similar to the Calif. Gov't Code §6254 and §6267.
10. John Holland, Paula McMahon, Fred Schulte and Jonathon King, "Library computers targeted in terrorism investigation," *Sun-Sentinel,* September 18, 2001 at http://www.sun-sentinel.com/news/southflorida/sfl-culprits918.story (visited October 3, 2001).
11. See Herbert N. Foerstel, *Surveillance in the Stacks: The FBI's Library Awareness Program* (Greenwood Press 1991); Ulrika Ekman Ault, "Note: The FBI's Library Awareness Program: Is Big Brother Reading Over Your Shoulder?" 65 *N.Y.U.L.* Rev. 1532 (December, 1990).
12. Senator Simon, Academic Libraries Must Oppose Federal Surveillance of Their Users, 100th Cong. 2nd Sess., 134 Cong. Rec. S 4806 (1988) (republishing an article by Gerald R. Shields, *Chronicle of Higher Education*), cited in Mark Paley, The Library Awareness Program: The FBI in the Bookshelves at http://hometown.aol.com/paleymark/library.htm (visited October 1, 2001).

13. Library Community Statement on Proposed Anti-Terrorism Measures and Library Community Letter to Congress on Anti-Terrorism Legislation (pdf file) at http://www.ala.org/washoff/ (visited October 4, 2001).

14. American Library Association. Office for Intellectual Freedom Alert: USA Patriot Act http://www.ala.org/alaorg/oif/usapatriotact.html.

Reflections and Inquiries

1. What are "roving wiretaps" and how might they affect individual Internet users under the PATRIOT Act?

2. Minow advocates library cooperation in providing the FBI with Internet sign-up slips, but "advisedly with a court order." What does Minow mean by "advisedly"? In your opinion, what kinds of information should the library provide, or not provide, the FBI?

3. Libraries in California "are explicitly barred . . . from disclosing patron registration or circulation records, excepting staff administrative use, written consent by the patron, or an order from the appropriate superior court"— yet, according to Minow, it is not entirely clear "whether or not the law protects Internet use records from disclosure without a court order." Why not? What further steps should libraries take, if any, to better protect their patrons' rights?

Reading to Write

1. Find out more about the use of library records as a means of obtaining information on suspected terrorists. You might begin by interviewing the head librarian of your college library. Next, write an essay advocating or challenging the usefulness of this kind of surveillance.

2. Write an essay in which you argue for or against the tracking of library patrons' Internet use. Does it violate an individual's right to privacy under the First Amendment? Why or why not?

Big Brother Is Listening | James Bamford

The NSA has the ability to eavesdrop on your communications—landlines, cell phones, e-mails, BlackBerry messages, Internet searches, and more—with ease. What happens when the technology of espionage outstrips the law's ability to protect ordinary citizens from it?

The conflict between protecting the security of the United States and protecting the privacy rights of U.S. citizens is ongoing. Many agree that in our post–9/11 era, heightened security measures are needed, but how much is too much? James Bamford, who has joined the American Civil Liberties Union in its lawsuit asking the courts to end the National Security Agency's spying without warrants, has published two books on the NSA and another on intelligence agencies generally: The Puzzle Palace: A Report on NSA, America's Most Secret Agency *(Random House, 1982),* Body of Secrets: Anatomy of the Ultra-Secret National Security Agency *(Random House, 2001), and* A Pretext for War: 9/11, Iraq and the Abuse of American Intelligence Agencies *(Random House, 2005).*

On the first Saturday in April of 2002, the temperature in Washington, D.C., had taken a dive. Tourists were bundled up against the cold, and the cherry trees along the Tidal Basin were fast losing their blossoms to the biting winds. But a few miles to the south, in the Dowden Terrace neighborhood of Alexandria, Virginia, the chilly weather was not deterring Royce C. Lamberth, a bald and burly Texan, from mowing his lawn. He stopped only when four cars filled with FBI agents suddenly pulled up in front of his house. The agents were there not to arrest him but to request an emergency court hearing to obtain seven top-secret warrants to eavesdrop on Americans.

As the presiding justice of the Foreign Intelligence Surveillance Court, known as the FISA court, Lamberth had become accustomed to holding the secret hearings in his living room. "My wife, Janis . . . has to go upstairs because she doesn't have a top-secret clearance," he noted in a speech to a group of Texas lawyers. "My beloved cocker spaniel, Taffy, however, remains at my side on the assumption that the surveillance targets cannot make her talk. The FBI knows Taffy well. They frequently play with her while I read some of those voluminous tomes at home." FBI agents will even knock on the judge's door in the middle of the night. "On the night of the bombings of the U.S. embassies in Africa, I started the first emergency hearings in my living room at 3:00 a.m.," recalled Lamberth. "From the outset, the FBI suspected bin Laden, and the surveillances I approved that night and in the ensuing days and weeks all ended up being critical evidence at the trial in New York.

Source: James Bamford, "Big Brother Is Listening," *The Atlantic Monthly,* April 2006. Reprinted by permission of International Creative Management, Inc. Copyright © 2006 by James Bamford.

"The FISA court is probably the least-known court in Washington," added Lamberth, who stepped down from it in 2002, at the end of his seven-year term, "but it has become one of the most important." Conceived in the aftermath of Watergate, the FISA court traces its origins to the mid-1970s, when the Senate's Church Committee investigated the intelligence commu-nity and the Nixon White House. The panel, chaired by Idaho Democrat Frank Church, exposed a long pattern of abuse, and its work led to biparti-san legislation aimed at preventing a president from unilaterally directing the National Security Agency or the FBI to spy on American citizens. This legislation, the 1978 Foreign Intelligence Surveillance Act, established the FISA court—made up of eleven judges handpicked by the chief justice of the United States—as a secret part of the federal judiciary. The court's job is to decide whether to grant warrants requested by the NSA or the FBI to moni-tor communications of American citizens and legal residents. The law allows the government up to three days after it starts eavesdropping to ask for a warrant; every violation of FISA carries a penalty of up to five years in prison. Between May 18, 1979, when the court opened for business, until the end of 2004, it granted 18,742 NSA and FBI applications; it turned down only four outright.

Such facts worry Jonathan Turley, a George Washington University law professor who worked for the NSA as an intern while in law school in the 1980s. The FISA "courtroom," hidden away on the top floor of the Justice Department building (because even its location is supposed to be secret), is actually a heavily protected, windowless, bug-proof installation known as a Sensitive Compartmented Information Facility, or SCIF. "When I first went into the FISA court as a lowly intern at the NSA, frankly, it started a lifetime of opposition for me to that court," Turley recently told a group of House Democrats looking into the NSA's domestic spying. "I was shocked with what I saw. I was convinced that the judge in that SCIF would have signed anything that we put in front of him. And I wasn't entirely sure that he had actually *read* what we put in front of him. But I remember going back to my supervisor at NSA and saying, 'That place scares the daylights out of me.'"

Lamberth bristles at any suggestion that his court routinely did the 5 administration's bidding. "Those who know me know the chief justice did not put me on this court because I would be a rubber stamp for whatever the exec-utive branch was wanting to do," he said in his speech. "I ask questions. I get into the nitty-gritty. I know exactly what is going to be done and why. And my questions are answered, in every case, before I approve an application."

It is true that the court has been getting tougher. From 1979 through 2000, it modified only two out of 13,087 warrant requests. But from the start of the Bush administration, in 2001, the number of modifications increased to 179 out of 5,645 requests. Most of those—173—involved what the court terms "substantive modifications."

This friction—and especially the requirement that the government show "probable cause" that the American whose communications they are seeking to target is connected in some way to a terrorist group—induced the administration to begin circumventing the court. Concerned about preventing future 9/11-style attacks, President Bush secretly decided in the fall of 2001 that the NSA would no longer be bound by FISA. Although Judge Lamberth was informed of the president's decision, he was ordered to tell no one about it—not even his clerks or his fellow FISA-court judges.

Why the NSA Might Be Listening to *You*

Contrary to popular perception, the NSA does not engage in "wiretapping"; it collects signals intelligence, or "sigint." In contrast to the image we have from movies and television of an FBI agent placing a listening device on a target's phone line, the NSA intercepts entire streams of electronic communications containing millions of telephone calls and e-mails. It runs the intercepts through very powerful computers that screen them for particular names, telephone numbers, Internet addresses, and trigger words or phrases. Any communications containing flagged information are forwarded by the computer for further analysis.

The NSA's task is to listen in on the world outside American shores. During the Cold War, the principal targets were the communications lines used by the Soviet government and military—navy captains calling their ports, fighter pilots getting landing instructions, army commanders out on maneuvers, and diplomats relaying messages to the Kremlin. But now the enemy is one that communicates very little and, when it does, uses the same telecommunications network as everyone else: a complex system of wires, radio signals, and light pulses encircling and crisscrossing the globe like yarn. Picking up just the right thread, and tracing it through the maze of strands, is difficult. Sometimes a thread leads back inside the United States. An internal agency report predicted a few years ago that the NSA's worldwide sigint operation would demand a "powerful and permanent presence" on the global telecommunications networks that carry "protected American communications." The prediction has come true, and the NSA now monitors not only purely "foreign" communications but also "international" ones, where one end of the conversation might be in the United States. As a result, the issue at hand since the revelation last December of the NSA's warrantless spying on American citizens is not the agency's access to the country's communications network—it already has access—but whether the NSA must take legal steps in preparing to target the communications of an American citizen.

It used to be that before the NSA could place the name of an American on 10 its watch list, it had to go before a FISA-court judge and show that it had probable cause—that the facts and circumstances were such that a prudent person would think the individual was somehow connected to terrorism—in order to get a warrant. But under the new procedures put into effect by Bush's 2001 order, warrants do not always have to be obtained, and the critical decision about whether to put an American on a watch list is left to the vague and subjective "reasonable belief" of an NSA shift supervisor. In charge of hundreds of people, the supervisor manages a wide range of sigint specialists, including signals-conversion analysts separating HBO television programs from cell-phone calls, traffic analysts sifting through massive telephone data streams looking for suspicious patterns, cryptanalysts attempting to read e-mail obscured by complex encryption algorithms, voice-language analysts translating the gist of a phone call from Dari into English, and cryptolinguists trying to unscramble a call on a secure telephone. Bypassing the FISA court has meant that the number of Americans targeted by the NSA has increased since 2001 from perhaps a dozen per year to as many as 5,000 over the last four years, knowledgeable sources told *The Washington Post* in February. If telephone records indicate that one of the NSA's targets regularly dials a given telephone number, that number and any names associated with it are added to the watch lists and the communications on that line are screened by computer. Names and information on the watch lists are shared with the FBI, the CIA, the Department of Homeland Security, and foreign intelligence services. Once a person's name is in the files, even if nothing incriminating ever turns up, it will likely remain there forever. There is no way to request removal, because there is no way to confirm that a name is on the list.

In December of 1997, in a small factory outside the southern French city of Toulouse, a salesman got caught in the NSA's electronic web. Agents working for the NSA's British partner, the Government Communications Headquarters, learned of a letter of credit, valued at more than $1.1 million, issued by Iran's defense ministry to the French company Microturbo. According to NSA documents, both the NSA and the GCHQ concluded that Iran was attempting to secretly buy from Microturbo an engine for the embargoed C-802 anti-ship missile. Faxes zapping back and forth between Toulouse and Tehran were intercepted by the GCHQ, which sent them on not just to the NSA but also to the Canadian and Australian sigint agencies, as well as to Britain's M16. The NSA then sent the reports on the salesman making the Iranian deal to a number of CIA stations around the world, including those in Paris and Bonn, and to the U.S. Commerce Department and the Customs Service. Probably several hundred people in at least four countries were reading the company's communications. The question, however, remained: Was Microturbo shipping a missile engine to Iran? In the end, at the insistence of the U.S. government, the French conducted a surprise inspection just before the ship carrying the mysterious crate was set to sail for Iran. Inside were legal generators, not illegal missile engines.

Such events are central to the current debate involving the potential harm caused by the NSA's warrantless domestic eavesdropping operation. Even though the salesman did nothing wrong, his name made its way into the computers and onto the watch lists of intelligence, customs, and other secret and law-enforcement organizations around the world. Maybe nothing will come of it. Maybe the next time he tries to enter the United States or Britain he will be denied, without explanation. Maybe he will be arrested. As the domestic eavesdropping program continues to grow, such uncertainties may plague innocent Americans whose names are being run through the supercomputers even though the NSA has not met the established legal standard for a search warrant. It is only when such citizens are turned down while applying for a job with the federal government—or refused when seeking a Small Business Administration loan, or turned back by British customs agents when flying to London on vacation, or even placed on a "no-fly" list—that they will realize that something is very wrong. But they will never learn why.

More than seventy-five years ago, Supreme Court Justice Louis Brandeis envisioned a day when technology would overtake the law. He wrote:

> Subtler and more far-reaching means of invading privacy have become available to the government . . . The progress of science in furnishing the government with means of espionage is not likely to stop with wiretapping. Ways may some day be developed by which the Government, without removing papers from secret drawers, can reproduce them in court, and by which it will be enabled to expose to a jury the most intimate occurrences of the home . . . Can it be that the Constitution affords no protection against such invasions of individual security?

Brandeis went on to answer his own question, quoting from an earlier Supreme Court decision, *Boyd v. U.S.* (1886): "It is not the breaking of his doors, and the rummaging of his drawers that constitutes the essence of the offence; but it is the invasion of his indefeasible right of personal security, personal liberty, and private property."

Eavesdropping in the Digital Age

Today, the NSA's capability to eavesdrop is far beyond anything ever 15 dreamed of by Justice Brandeis. With the digital revolution came an explosion in eavesdropping technology; the NSA today has the ability to scan tens of millions of electronic communications—e-mails, faxes, instant messages; Web searches, and phone calls—every hour. General Michael Hayden, director of the NSA from 1999 to 2005 and now principal deputy director of national intelligence, noted in 2002 that during the 1990s, e-communications "surpassed traditional communications. That is the same decade when mobile cell phones increased from 16 million to 741 million—an increase of nearly 50 times. That is the same decade when Internet users went from about 4 million to 361 million—an increase of over 90 times. Half as many land lines were laid in the last six years of the 1990s as in the whole previous history of the world. In that same decade of the 1990s, international telephone traffic went from 38 billion minutes to over 100 billion. This year, the world's population will spend over 180 billion minutes on the phone in international calls alone."

Intercepting communications carried by satellite is fairly simple for the NSA. The key conduits are the thirty Intelsat satellites that ring the Earth, 22,300 miles above the equator. Many communications from Europe, Africa, and the Middle East to the eastern half of the United States, for example, are first uplinked to an Intelsat satellite and then downlinked to AT&T's ground station in Etam, West Virginia. From there, phone calls, e-mails, and other communications travel on to various parts of the country. To listen in on that rich stream of information, the NSA built a listening post fifty miles away, near Sugar Grove, West Virginia. Consisting of a group of very large parabolic dishes, hidden in a heavily forested valley and surrounded by tall hills, the post can easily intercept the millions of calls and messages flowing every hour into the Etam station. On the West Coast, high on the edge of a bluff overlooking the Okanogan River, near Brewster, Washington, is the major commercial downlink for communications to and from Asia and the Pacific. Consisting of forty parabolic dishes, it is reportedly the largest satellite antenna farm in the Western Hemisphere. A hundred miles to the south, collecting every whisper, is the NSA's western listening post, hidden away on a 324,000-acre Army base in Yakima, Washington. The NSA posts collect the international traffic beamed down from the Intelsat satellites over the Atlantic and Pacific. But each also has a number of dishes that appear to be directed at domestic telecommunications satellites.

Until recently, most international telecommunications flowing into and out of the United States traveled by satellite. But faster, more reliable undersea fiber-optic cables have taken the lead, and the NSA has adapted. The agency taps into the cables that don't reach our shores by using specially designed submarines, such as the USS *Jimmy Carter*, to attach a complex "bug" to the cable itself. This is difficult, however, and undersea taps are short-lived because the batteries last only a limited time. The fiber-optic transmission cables that enter the United States from Europe and Asia can be tapped more easily at the landing stations where they come ashore. With the acquiescence of the telecommunications companies, it is possible for the NSA to attach monitoring equipment inside the landing station and then run a buried encrypted fiber-optic "backhaul" line to NSA headquarters at Fort Meade, Maryland, where the river of data can be analyzed by supercomputers in near real time.

Tapping into the fiber-optic network that carries the nation's Internet communications is even easier, as much of the information transits through just a few "switches" (similar to the satellite downlinks). Among the busiest are MAE East (Metropolitan Area Ethernet), in Vienna, Virginia, and MAE West, in San Jose, California, both owned by Verizon. By accessing the switch, the NSA can see who's e-mailing with whom over the Internet cables and can copy entire messages. Last September, the Federal Communications Commission further opened the door for the agency. The 1994 Communications Assistance for Law Enforcement Act required telephone companies to rewire their networks to provide the government with secret access. The FCC has now extended the act to cover "any type of broadband Internet access service" and the new Internet phone services—and ordered company officials never to discuss any aspect of the program.

The NSA won't divulge how many people it employs, but it is likely that more than 38,000 worldwide now work for the agency. Most of them are at Fort Meade. Nicknamed Crypto City, hidden from public view, and located halfway between Washington and Baltimore, the NSA's own company town comprises more than fifty buildings—offices, warehouses, factories, laboratories, and a few barracks. Tens of thousands of people work there in absolute secrecy, and most never tell their spouses exactly what they do. Crypto City also houses the nation's largest collection of powerful computers, advanced mathematicians, and skilled language experts.

The NSA maintains a very close and very confidential relationship with 20 key executives in the telecommunications industry through their membership on the NSA's advisory board. Created shortly after the agency's formation, the board was intended to pull together a panel of science wizards from universities, corporate research labs, and think tanks to advise the agency. They keep the agency abreast of the industry's plans and give NSA engineers a critical head start in finding ways to penetrate technologies still in the development phase.

One of the NSA's strategies is to hire people away from the companies that make the critical components for telecommunications systems. Although it's sometimes difficult for the agency to keep up with the tech sector's pay scale, for many people the chance to deal with the ultimate in cutting-edge technology and aid national security makes working for the NSA irresistible. With the help of such workers, the agency reverse-engineers communication system components. For example, among the most crucial pieces of the Internet infrastructure are routers made by Cisco. "Virtually all Internet traffic," says one of the company's television ads, "travels across the systems of one company: Cisco Systems." For the NSA, this is an opportunity. In 1999, Terry Thompson, then the NSA deputy director for services, said, "[Y]ou can see down the road two or three or five years and say, 'Well, I only need this person to do reverse-engineering on Cisco routers (that's a good example) for about three or five years, because I see Cisco going away as a key manufacturer for routers and so I don't need that expertise. But I really need somebody today and for the next couple of years who knows Cisco routers inside and out and can help me understand how they're being used in target networks.'"

The Temptations of Secrecy

The National Security Agency was born in absolute secrecy. Unlike the CIA, which was created publicly by a congressional act, the NSA was brought to life by a top-secret memorandum signed by President Truman in 1952, consolidating the country's various military sigint operations into a single agency. Even its name was secret, and only a few members of Congress were informed of its existence—and they received no information about some of its most important activities. Such secrecy has lent itself to abuse.

During the Vietnam War, for instance, the agency was heavily involved in spying on the domestic opposition to the government. Many of the Americans on the watch lists of that era were there solely for having protested against the war. Among the names in the NSA's supercomputers were those of the folk singer Joan Baez, the pediatrician Benjamin Spock, the actress Jane Fonda, the civil-rights leader Martin Luther King Jr., and the newspaper editor David Kahn, whose standard history of cryptology, *The Codebreakers*, contained information the NSA viewed as classified. Even so much as writing about the NSA could land a person a place on a watch list. The NSA, on behalf of the FBI, was also targeting religious groups. "When J. Edgar Hoover gives you a requirement for complete surveillance of all Quakers in the United States," recalled Frank Raven, a former senior NSA official, "and when Richard M. Nixon is a Quaker and he's the president of the United States, it gets pretty funny."

Of course, such abuses are hardly the exclusive province of the NSA; history has repeatedly shown that simply having the ability to eavesdrop brings with it the temptation to use that ability—whatever the legal barriers against that use may be. For instance, during World War I, the government read and censored thousands of telegrams—the e-mail of the day—sent hourly by telegraph companies. Though the end of the war brought with it a reversion to the Radio Act of 1912, which guaranteed the secrecy of communications, the State and War Departments nevertheless joined together in May of 1919 to create America's first civilian eaves-dropping and code-breaking agency, nicknamed the Black Chamber. By arrangement, messengers visited the telegraph companies each morning and took bundles of hard-copy telegrams to the agency's offices across town. These copies were returned before the close of business that day.

A similar tale followed the end of World War II. In August of 1945, 25 President Truman ordered an end to censorship. That left the Signal Security Agency (the military successor to the Black Chamber, which was shut down in 1929) without its raw intelligence—the telegrams provided by the telegraph companies. The director of the SSA sought access to cable traffic through a secret arrangement with the heads of the three major telegraph companies. The companies agreed to turn all telegrams over to the SSA, under a plan code-named Operation Shamrock. It ran until the government's domestic spying programs were publicly revealed, in the mid-1970s.

The discovery of such abuses in the wake of the Watergate scandal led Congress to create select committees to conduct extensive investigations into the government's domestic spying programs: their origin, extent, and effect on the public. The shocking findings turned up by the Church Committee finally led to the formation of permanent Senate and House intelligence committees, whose primary responsibility was to protect the public from future privacy abuses. They were to be the FISA court's partner in providing checks and balances to the ever-expanding U.S. intelligence agencies. But it remains very much an open question whether these checks are up to the task at hand.

Who Watches the Watchmen?

Today, the NSA has access to more information than ever before. People express their most intimate thoughts in e-mails, send their tax returns over the Internet, satisfy their curiosity and desires with Google searchers, let their hair down in chat rooms, discuss every event over cell phones, make appointments with their BlackBerrys, and do business by computer in WiFi hot spots.

NSA personnel, the customs inspectors of the information superhighway, have the ultimate goal of intercepting and reviewing every syllable and murmur zapping into, out of, or through the United States. They are close to achieving it. More than a dozen years ago, an NSA director gave an indication of the agency's capability. "Just one intelligence-collection system," said Admiral William O. Studeman, referring to a listening post such as Sugar Grove, "can generate a million inputs per half hour." Today, with the secret cooperation of much of the telecommunications industry, massive dishes vacuuming the airwaves, and electronic "packet sniffers," software that monitors network traffic, diverting e-mail and other data from fiber-optic cables, the NSA's hourly take is in the tens of millions of communications. One transatlantic fiber-optic cable alone has the capacity to handle close to 10 million simultaneous calls. While most communications flow through the NSA's electronic net unheard and unread, those messages associated with persons on the agency's watch lists—whether guilty or innocent—get kicked out for review.

As history has shown, the availability of such vast amounts of information is a temptation for an intelligence agency. The criteria for compiling watch lists and collecting information may be very strict at the beginning of such a program, but the reality—in a sort of bureaucratic law of expansion— is that it will draw in more and more people whose only offense was knowing the wrong person or protesting the wrong war.

Moreover, as Internet and wireless communications have grown expo- 30 nentially, users have seen a corresponding decrease in the protections provided by the two institutions set up to shield the public from eavesdroppers. The first, the FISA court, has simply been shunted aside by the executive branch. The second, the congressional intelligence committees, have quite surprisingly abdicated any role. Created to be the watchdogs over the intelligence community, the committees have instead become its most enthusiastic cheerleaders. Rather than fighting for the public's privacy rights, they are constantly battling for more money and more freedom for the spy agencies.

Last November, just a month before *The New York Times* broke the story of the NSA's domestic spying, the American Bar Association publicly expressed concern over Congress's oversight of FISA searches. "The ABA is concerned that there is inadequate congressional oversight of government investigations undertaken pursuant to the Foreign Intelligence Surveillance Act," the group stated, "to assure that such investigations do not violate the First, Fourth, and Fifth Amendments to the Constitution." And while the administration did brief members of Congress on the decision to bypass FISA, the briefings were limited to a "Gang of Eight"—the majority and minority leaders of the House and Senate and the chairmen and ranking members of the two intelligence committees. None of the lawmakers insisted that the decision be debated by the joint committees, even though such hearings are closed.

Frank Church, the Idaho Democrat who led the first probe into the National Security Agency, warned in 1975 that the agency's capabilities

> could be turned around on the American people, and no American would have any privacy left, such [is] the capability to monitor everything: telephone conversations, telegrams, it doesn't matter. There would be no place to hide. If this government ever became a tyranny, if a dictator ever took charge in this country, the technological capacity that the intelligence community has given the government could enable it to impose total tyranny, and there would be no way to fight back, because the most careful effort to combine together in resistance to the government, no matter how privately it is done, is within the reach of the government to know. Such is the capacity of this technology.

It was those fears that caused Congress to enact the Foreign Intelligence Surveillance Act three years later. "I don't want to see this country ever go across the bridge," Senator Church said. "I know the capacity that is there to make tyranny total in America, and we must see to it that [the National Security Agency] and all agencies that possess this technology operate within the law and under proper supervision, so that we never cross over that abyss. That is the abyss from which there is no return." ◎/◎

Reflections and Inquiries

1. How does the NSA gather surveillance information? What, if anything, concerns you about this method?

2. Explain the literary reference in Bamford's title. How accurate a reference is it?

3. What did law professor Jonathan Turley find so frightening about the FISA court? Do you share Turley's apprehension? Explain.

4. The NSA often obtains documents without a warrant. Do you agree or disagree that this is a necessary procedure? Support your view as fully as you can, keeping aware of counterarguments.

Reading to Write

> Go to the NSA's website, http://www.nsa.gov, to learn more about the
> organization. For example, you can learn about the history of signals
> intelligence (SIGINT). Next, compare the way the NSA represents itself to
> the way James Bamford represents it in at least one of his books,
> mentioned above. Finally, using Academic Search Elite or your library's
> electronic catalogue, locate a third perspective on the NSA, ideally one
> that has been published within the last five years and that differs from
> Bamford's perspective. Now write an essay in which you assess the
> ethical foundations of the NSA's surveillance practices.

Student Essay

New British Measure Will Harm Civil Liberties

United Kingdom's Law Will Heighten Tensions By Spying on Muslim Students at Universities | Mohammed Surve

Ever since 9/11, and aggravated by the London subway bombings in 2005, Muslims the world over have been targets of discrimination and harassment. In the following article, Mohammed Surve, an exchange student from the University of California at Berkeley, describes his unease at the prospect of returning to Britain in light of what he considers to be that country's anti-Muslim policies.

When I read an article entitled "Universities urged to spy on Muslims," in an October [2006] issue of the United Kingdom publication "The Guardian," I felt deeply betrayed. The article exposes the British government's request to universities in the United Kingdom to reveal personal information on Muslim students of South Asian appearance as a national security measure.

Such racial and religious profiling is abhorrent. It is a grave and counterproductive policy in the British government's fight against extremism.

As an exchange student from Britain now studying at UC Berkeley, I no longer feel at ease returning to such an environment in what I once considered to be my safe and non-threatening homeland. The United Kingdom's Department of Education has gone so far as to draw up an eighteen-page

---

Source: Mohammed Surve, "New British Measure Will Harm Civil Liberties." *Daily Californian*, November 3, 2006. The Daily Californian. Reprinted with permission.

document openly targeting students—members of society that the government has a duty to protect.

Under this document, lecturers are instructed to notify a special branch of the police force of any "suspicious" student activities. Under such a system, all it would take is a single racist lecturer to report a student to a Gestapo-like secret service employee to cause serious trouble for the student. This could effectively destroy the lives of many Muslims on college campuses all over the United Kingdom. This document also calls for the monitoring of activities within Islamic societies, which the government unfoundedly claims have become political hotbeds.

During my stay at here at UC Berkeley, it has been made clear to me 5 that—when it comes to monitoring Islamic activities—encroaching on civil liberties in a post–Sept. 11 world has become a common practice here in the United States. I did not, however, expect the British government to take such extreme measures in light of its previously exemplary record of cultural and religious accommodation.

It is apparent that now, the British government has decided to emulate the U.S. domestic policy in dealing with the threat of terror. Instead of engaging in productive dialogue, the United Kingdom has chosen to alienate and marginalise South-Asian Muslims, as well as invade their civil rights.

These anti-Muslim, McCarthyist-style witch hunts will serve to victimise British Muslims, leaving them nowhere to turn and driving them to express anger at their homeland. Ironically, such an extreme reaction is precisely what the government claims it is hoping to defeat by instituting the new monitoring measures.

What is more worrisome is that the British government has done nothing to counter the increasing threat of the British right wing parties, who advocate their racist and extreme ideologies on United Kingdom campuses. These groups move up and down the country on a daily basis.

Such double standards serve only to further alienate British Muslims and provide fuel for these student "extremists." I believe that the government should be taking positive steps, such as working with Muslim groups like the Federation of Student Islamic Societies—akin to the Muslim Student Association of here in the United States and in Canada. If it is truly committed to stamping out extremism, then reaching out to these groups is the right place to start.

Thankfully, moderate voices remain. The BBC's coverage of the story, for 10 example, emphasised the government's failure to take on board any of the student federation's concerns upon its development of the eighteen-page document in question. Keeping in mind these important points, we must remember that the way forward is through cooperation between the government and Muslim organisations, not through unilateral action on the behalf of the British government. ◎/◎

Reflections and Inquiries

1. Surve considers Britain's racial profiling practices "abhorrent." Do you agree or disagree with him, and why?

2. According to Surve, the United States, Canada, and the Britain should be "reaching out" to Muslims. What do you suppose he means by that?

Reading to Write

Investigate the ways in which British agencies, such as the Department of Education, have been "openly targeting [Muslim] students." Write an essay in which you report your findings and present your recommendations.

Issues for Further Research: Budgeting for Security

The Cost of Securing the Homeland | Michael Scardaville

It is one thing to think ideally about increasing national security to maximum levels, but quite another to pay for the expense. In the following article, Michael Scardaville, a homeland security policy analyst with the Heritage Foundation in Washington, D.C., (http://www.heritage.org) takes a close, hard look at the costs required for securing a post–9/11 United States.

September 11, 2001, ushered in a new era in American strategic planning in which a premium is being placed on domestic security. Progress, however, does not come without a price. Securing the American homeland from the threat posed by radical Islamic terrorism has led to increased spending by federal, state, and local governments as well as the private sector. In addition, many of the new security programs are likely to result in indirect costs, either monetary or cultural in nature.

One of the greatest challenges the United States will face in coming years will be in meeting these costs responsibly. Every effort must be made to ensure that expenditures for security are the most cost-efficient means of achieving the desired result.

Federal Budget

The federal budget for homeland security has more than doubled since September 11. Congress enacted $16.9 billion in domestic security funds for fiscal year 2001 and $42.6 billion this year; for 2004, President Bush has requested $41.3 billion. These funds are spread throughout many federal

---

Source: Michael Scardaville, "The Cost of Securing the Homeland," *The World and I*, Aug. 18, 2003 p. 54. Reprinted by permission of WorldandIJournal.com.

agencies, with the vast majority allocated to just five departments: Homeland Security, Defense, Health and Human Services, Justice, and Energy.

Not surprisingly, the Department of Homeland Security (DHS) receives the most, at $23 billion in 2003 and with nearly $24 billion requested for 2004. Within the president's request for 2004, 18 percent of the DHS budget is allocated to border and transportation security, 6.8 percent to protecting ports and waterways, 0.8 percent to analyzing intelligence data and applying it to infrastructure protection, 0.8 percent to research and development, 6 percent to disaster response, 1.8 percent to salvaging America's immigration policy, and 1.9 percent toward other costs. In addition, approximately 34 percent of the DHS budget is allocated to its non-homeland security missions (such as search and rescue and responding to natural disasters).

The largest single increase in spending was enacted in the 2002 budget, with funding growing from $13.2 billion in 2000 to $29.3 billion. While another substantial increase occurred in 2003, as the country became more familiar with its homeland security needs, the president's request for 2004 has remained relatively static despite the establishment of the DHS.

In many cases, the Bush administration has also excelled at prioritizing its initiatives. For example, reducing a terrorist's ability to smuggle weapons into the United States must be a top priority. Improving the security of domestic U.S. ports may not be the most effective means of accomplishing this goal. Weapons could still be loaded onto foreign ships departing for American ports, inaccurately listed on a manifest, and enter the country without any illegal activity occurring at the port itself. Further, in the case of a nuclear weapon, the ship would not even have to dock in many cities to achieve its deadly effect, making any port-security initiatives irrelevant.

Instead, the Bush administration has emphasized making smuggling more difficult through earlier and more accurate manifest reporting, point-of-origin inspection, better screening of cargo containers, and partnerships with industry to secure entire supply chains. Securing the physical infrastructure of a port remains important, as these largely unprotected facilities may be tempting targets for terrorists. But if the objective is to prevent the entry of terrorist weapons, port security should defer to customs initiatives.

As 2004 draws near, increases in spending on securing the homeland may come to be driven by election politics. Indeed, presidential candidate Sen. Joseph Lieberman (D-Connecticut) has recently called for an additional $16 billion for homeland security. Some of Lieberman's proposals have merit, such as accelerating the Coast Guard's deepwater modernization program. Others, including his additional $7.5 billion for first-responder grants, may be premature because adequate reform of the existing program has not yet occurred, nor has a detailed analysis of the program's impact and needs been conducted. What is clear is that the federal homeland-security budget is likely to be a major issue during the 2004 election season.

State and Local Costs

Unlike modern U.S. defense policy, homeland security is as much a local responsibility as it is a federal one. As the U.S. Conference of Mayors illustrated in a March 2003 report, "When you dial 9-1-1, the phone doesn't ring in the White House. . . . Those calls come in to your city's police, fire, and emergency medical personnel [offices] . . . our domestic troops." Just as the federal government has a responsibility to maintain the military, local authorities have a duty to provide for their first responders and protect local infrastructure.

The Conference of Mayors estimates that America's cities have spent 10 approximately $2.6 billion on general homeland security needs and another $70 million per week while the nation was at a heightened state of alert during the war in Iraq. Similarly, the National Governors Association has estimated that the states would need to spend from $5 to 7 billion (in state and federal funds) to meet their homeland-security needs. Unfortunately, many jurisdictions are now facing severe budget shortfalls.

Since the mid-1990s, the federal government has made grants available to state and local agencies to provide specialized planning, training, and equipment needed for those terrorist incidents with unusual circumstances (particularly disasters involving weapons of mass destruction). So far in 2003, $3.9 billion has been allocated for such grants; the president has requested an additional $3.5 billion for 2004, approximately a tenfold increase from the pre–September 11 spending levels. Before the program can be fully effective, however, it must better prioritize how money is distributed—a change that should occur before new money is appropriated.

Due to budget problems, many states, counties, cities, and first-responder organizations have been calling for additional federal funding for basic equipment (such as fire trucks and police cruisers), new personnel, and overtime costs associated with heightened states of alert. While all these concerns affect a locality's level of readiness, a failure to achieve a reasonable standard of burden sharing now risks making the program unsustainable for the long run.

The Departments of Homeland Security and Justice recently began to offer federal grants to cover overtime expenses. Doing so sets a bad precedent, suggesting that ultimate responsibility for basic local requirements such as police and fire services rests with the federal government. In his letter to the Senate Appropriations Committee on Homeland Security, Lieberman admitted as much, stating, "This problem is still with us because the federal government hasn't made it a priority. We have basically left it up to the states."

Such an attitude, that all solutions can only come from Washington, doesn't take into account the advantages of local control. As Deputy Secretary of Homeland Security Gordon England recently told *Business Week* magazine, "The people there [at the state and local level] understand their vulnerabilities better than we do. Our job is to help them do their job better."

The federal government should continue to provide grants for such 15 specialized equipment, training, and planning but not for overtime and basic needs, which should be paid for by local governments. State and local authorities will have to plan for such times of greater risk despite their tight budgets.

Private Investment

In addition, the private sector bears responsibility for the physical protection of the facilities it owns. On the micro level, this applies to nearly every structure in the country, from offices to apartment buildings and malls. At the macro level, the focus is on points that the White House says provide "the foundation for our national security, governance, economic vitality, and way of life. . . . A successful strike against [any of these] . . . may result in significant loss of life and property in addition to long-term public health and safety consequences."

Private-sector investment is crucial in securing these assets, because, by most estimates, business interests own some 85 percent of the critical nodes in the country. Fortunately, business already has market-based incentives to invest in security, due to consumer and investor confidence as well as insurance rates. A study by the Data Center Institute, a project of the information-technology management organization known as AFCOM, noted that 50 percent of the data centers surveyed increased security investments by between 5 and 15 percent in the last year without any government mandates. Nationally, Bart Hobijn of the Federal Reserve Bank of New York has estimated that the private sector is likely to spend $32.8 billion annually on security, or nearly the same amount as the federal government.

To determine how much to spend, most industries rely on risk-management tools to identify risks, evaluate how serious they are, and suggest appropriate countermeasures based on the potential likelihood and consequences of a disruptive event. Nevertheless, industry is ill equipped to accurately evaluate the threat without federal assistance. The U.S. government has done comparatively little to ensure that the private sector understands the threat, although such a program was detailed in multiple strategy documents released by the White House.

Indirect Costs

Probably the most difficult homeland-security costs to estimate are indirect expenses resulting from new security programs and regulations. Such costs can come from, among other things, losses in productivity due to delays caused by security checks, compliance with new rules and regulations, and increased insurance costs.

On one hand, Hobijn has estimated that delays business travelers are 20 likely to face at airports will result in a loss of 215 million work hours, with a productivity cost of $5.3 billion. Similarly, Richard Larrabee, director of port commerce for the Port Authority of New York and New Jersey, has estimated that even a 3 percent increase in container inspections at that port alone would create a backlog of 4,500 containers per month, costing industry $1.2 million monthly. In the words of Chris Corrado, vice president for customer service at APL Logistics, a major international shipper, "A cargo hold can add up to real money, real fast. . . . It will slow down your supply chain."

In addition, new regulations imposed on a variety of industries are likely to come with a real cost. For example, congressionally mandated port security measures are likely to cost operators approximately $1.4 billion, according to Coast Guard estimates.

When considering indirect costs, it's also important to consider potential indirect gains. As a January 2003 report from PIERS Global Intelligence Solutions on the indirect costs of port security efforts noted, "On balance, however, there is encouraging evidence that today's security-driven investments will yield . . . added benefits."

Civil Liberties

Finally, the most important cost that must be measured is the loss of individual freedom that could result from new security programs. As Chief Justice William Rehnquist has noted in his now famous book, *All the Laws But One*, "In any civilized society, the most important task is achieving a proper balance between freedom and order. In wartime, reason and history both suggest that this balance shifts to some degree in favor of order—in favor of the government's ability to deal with conditions that threaten the national well-being."

While reductions in freedom cannot be numerically cataloged, the consequences could prove more grave than any economic cost. Sacrificing freedom for security should be avoided whenever possible. If it proves absolutely necessary, it must only be done for a limited duration, with close oversight by Congress.

Homeland security will remain a top national priority for the foreseeable 25 future and represents an area of security planning that has long been neglected in the United States. Consequently, new costs are likely to be incurred for some time, as the nation determines the best parameters for an enduring strategy. Nonetheless, the Bush administration and Congress would be well advised to determine the appropriate level of funding incrementally through frequent program evaluations. Dumping new funds into dysfunctional programs is unlikely to provide a substantial increase in security.

On the other hand, many state and local agencies need to accept that securing the homeland is a shared responsibility that will require them to adapt their budgets to the new security reality. Government and industry must also work more closely together to better understand what the private sector can and should do to secure those vital assets it owns. Finally, the nation must enact new programs in a way that does not come at a noticeable cost to the freedoms for which we are fighting. ◎/◎

Reflections and Inquiries

1. What accounts for the more than doubling of the federal budget for national security since September 11, 2001? Are all of these costs unavoidable, in your opinion? Why or why not?

2. According to Scardaville, one of Senator Lieberman's proposals for additional homeland security spending (first-response grants) may be unwarranted. Why? Has the situation changed since Lieberman first made this proposal in 2003?

3. What individual freedoms may be placed at risk from additional security programs, in Scardaville's opinion? Do you agree or disagree? Support your assertions with specific evidence.

4. Scardaville refers to "a reasonable standard of burden" that jeopardizes the sustainability of the first-response program. How do you believe that phrase should be interpreted?

5. What makes homeland security costs so difficult to determine accurately?

Reading to Write

Do background reading in homeland security costs and priorities, and then sketch out a program that would make the cost of securing the homeland a "shared responsibility," in Scardaville's words.

Issues for Further Research: Border Security

6,000 Guardsmen Are Not Enough | Charlie Norwood

How vital are secure borders for protecting the United States against terrorists? In the following editorial, Charlie Norwood, the late United States congressional representative (R-Georgia) explains why he thinks that President Bush's call for 6,000 National Guard troops to patrol the Mexican–United States border will not stop the flow of illegal aliens into the United States, that ten times that number would be required to do the job. Congressman Norwood (1941–2007), a graduate of Georgia Southern University and Georgetown University's School of Dentistry, served as a captain in the U.S. Army Dental Corps (1967–69) and was in private practice as a dentist in Augusta, Georgia, before entering politics.

Source: Charlie Norwood, "6,000 Guardsmen Are Not Enough," *Human Events* 62: May 22, 2006. Reprinted by permission.

President Bush should be commended for at least showing he is listening to House members and the overwhelming majority of the American people by agreeing to send even some National Guard to our lawless border with Mexico.

He has potentially taken at least a first step in the right direction with his proposal to use our National Guard to provide border security. Now the debate is no longer whether to send them, just how many.

The speech was a first for not only Bush, but for any President in recent history—official acknowledgement of our national nightmare problems from illegal immigration. Congress should take that as an extended hand and get to work showing the President how to improve his plan so it will actually work.

Improvement is mandatory. The specific proposal is too weak in terms of manpower and missions and will not secure the border. Deploying only 6,000 troops for a 2,000-mile border is a maximum of one man on duty per mile per eight-hour shift. Couple that with the fact that none of the troops will even be posted on the border, and that any increase in border presence will be a result of Border Patrol administrative personnel being freed up for patrol duty.

The net result is that the President's plan will do nothing to slow the flood   5 of illegal aliens pouring into the country across the Southern border.

The American people are tired of waiting for a secure border. They want it now, because they know this problem is getting worse every day we leave our Southern border open. Increased technology and infrastructure is a great idea—but it takes years to get in place, and the public patience on this issue is 100% used up.

The political tragedy is that had the President called for a 40,000-man deployment, announced that the United States was fed up with having our borders violated and was putting a stop to it, his approval rating would be back in the 50s if not higher. What an extraordinary missed opportunity!

The people in my district are ready to throw anybody and everybody out of office who won't bring this nightmare to a stop. The plan the President proposed is not what the American people want.

The President said we can't have a secure border without a new guest-worker program. In fact, the opposite is true—we can't have a new guest-worker program without a secure border first. There is no way the House will vote for any new guest-worker plan or how to handle the illegal aliens already in the country until the border is shut down to all but legal traffic.

We have a very good idea of the correct number of people necessary to   10 secure the border with our current infrastructure and technology. The same figures keep coming back from past Border Patrol demonstration projects, the

Minutemen project and from senior officials at the Department of Homeland Security. Somewhere between 36,000 and 50,000 troops are necessary to do the job. Some say 60,000.

To send 6,000 is a small first step, and should be taken as just that. The real potential of the President's decision should be to pave the way for a full deployment over the next several months that will secure our Southern border against a Mexican government that refuses to acknowledge it and officially encourages their citizens to violate our laws and our sovereignty as their "right."

The House and Senate should encourage the President's call for troops to the border by committing to provide funding for up to a five-year military deployment of 48,000 troops, estimated at $2.5 billion per year.

We can support the President's initial deployment of 6,000 troops while Congress moves to approve funds for a long-term deployment. It will also give us several weeks to observe the lack of impact of 6,000 troops on halting illegal immigration.

However, even a properly manned long-term troop deployment is just part of a successful comprehensive plan to combat illegal immigration. Such a plan must include total rejection of any hint of amnesty for those who have broken our laws in coming here. Period.

Reflections and Inquiries

1. What evidence does Representative Norwood use to support his claim that 40,000 guardsmen, not 6,000, are needed to secure the Mexican–U.S. border? How convincing is this evidence in your opinion?

2. Do you agree or disagree with Norwood that the United States cannot have a new guest-worker program without first securing the border—the opposite of what President Bush has argued? What are your reasons?

3. Norwood states his opposition to offering amnesty to immigrants who have entered the U.S. illegally, but does not explicitly give his reasons. Infer from the article what his possible reasons might be, and then explain why you agree or disagree with them.

Reading to Write

Locate information on the current situation with Mexico–U.S. border security; then write an essay in which you argue for ways to resolve the situation. Be sure to acknowledge, and then refute, views that challenge your own.

Mexicans See Insult, Danger in Border Plan | Monica Campbell

In the following piece, Monica Campbell reports on the reactions of Mexican citizens to Bush's border security plan announced in May 2006. Monica Campbell, a freelance journalist based in Mexico City, contributes articles regularly to the Christian Science Monitor, San Francisco Chronicle, *and* USA Today.

The border-security plan President Bush announced Monday as part of his immigration agenda has made him few friends here.

Alfredo Martinez, 56, a tomato seller at an open-air market, shook his head when asked about Bush's plan to send 6,000 National Guard troops to help police the 2,000-mile-long U.S.-Mexico border.

His 22-year-old son crossed the border illegally last year and now sends money home every month from his job in a New York City deli. "I don't think he'll be able to come back and visit for a while," Martinez said. "It's a shame. There should be a way to recognize the work we do up north, a way to see us as laborers and not delinquents."

His complaint was echoed by many Tuesday on the streets of Mexico's capital city.

"I don't understand why the United States must take such a repressive 5 attitude toward us," said Agustin Melgar, 45, who works in the same open-air market as Martinez near Chapultepec Park in the city center. "It's insulting. We all know there's a mutual demand: The gringos need our cheap labor, and we want better pay."

Ruben Aguilar, a spokesman for Mexican President Vicente Fox, said Monday that a security-first policy at the border would not solve the problems created by illegal immigration. Fox has said he prefers a plan that would offer some form of legal status for all undocumented Mexicans now in the USA.

Rafael Femandez de Castro, an international relations expert at the Autonomous Technological Institute of Mexico, characterized the Mexican government's response as muted. "The government here does not want to portray this as a big setback for Mexico," he said. "But it clearly is. Mexico has been given the stick, while the U.S. Congress gets the carrot."

The government began to change its message on Tuesday. Foreign Secretary Luis Ernesto Derbez warned that the United States might face lawsuits if the increased troop presence on the border resulted in human rights abuses. "If we see the National Guard starting to directly participate in detaining people . . . we would immediately start filing lawsuits through our consulates," he told Radio Red, a Mexico City radio station.

Source: Monica Campbell, "Mexicans See Insult, Danger in Border Plan," *USA Today,* May 17, 2006: 8A. Reprinted by permission of the author.

Andres Manuel Lopez Obrador, a former Mexico City mayor who is running for president in July elections, said Tuesday that Fox's government is "mostly responsible. . . There are no jobs in Mexico, so people need to emigrate."

Felipe de Jesus Calderon Hinojosa, the presidential candidate of Fox's 10 party, said Monday that he understands the U.S. government's desire to protect its borders, but adding troops there will only "increase the social and human costs for immigrants."

He was referring to the possibility that hardening the border will force migrants to try to cross at more remote and dangerous points, especially the vast deserts of Arizona and New Mexico. In 2005, 463 migrants died crossing the U.S.–Mexico border, according to the Latin America Working Group, a human rights organization based in Washington.

"We realize that the discussion over how to manage the border has now turned into a win-lose game between the Republicans and Democrats," said Humberto Garza, an expert on Mexican foreign relations at the College of Mexico. "But it's an insult to Mexicans. This discussion clearly lacks foresight. It ignores the fact that no matter how tight you make the border, people will still find a way to cross." ◎/◎

Reflections and Inquiries

1. Compare Campbell's method of presenting her views on the border security issue with Senator Norwood's above. What are the major differences?

2. According to Mexico's Foreign Secretary Luis Ernesto Derbez, interviewed by Campbell, increased troop presence could result in lawsuits if any human rights abuses occurred. What sorts of human rights abuses do you suppose Secretary Derbez has in mind? Do you agree or disagree with him, and why?

3. Do you agree or disagree with Mexican foreign relations expert Humberto Garza that border tightening is "an insult to Mexicans"? On what do you base your response?

Reading to Write

After familiarizing yourself with the current U.S.-Mexico border issues, propose a plan that would, in your opinion, provide a satisfactory policy for Mexican immigration into the United States *and* maintain appropriate antiterrorist border security. (Note that you are to write a problem/solution essay, with an argument that first fully describes the problem and then posits a solution.)

Connections Among the Clusters

1. To what extent do issues of national security impact issues relating to multicultural learning? (See Cluster 4.)

2. Can we draw the line between necessary and unwarranted kinds of speech censorship (Cluster 3) for purposes of national security? Explain.

3. In what way does the Mexico-U.S. border security controversy relate to issues involving multicultural learning? (See Cluster 4.)

Writing Projects

1. Write an essay in which you explore the role that ethics should (or should not) play in developing an effective national security policy.

2. After researching how the courts have ruled on elements of the Patriot Act and other government efforts to fight terrorism and deal with suspected terrorists, evaluate the constitionality of government security policy. Do you agree with the courts? Why or why not?

3. Using Classical, Toulmin, or Rogerian methods of argument, propose—and establish a rationale for—a national security policy for a nation known to possess (or suspected of possessing) nuclear materials (e.g., North Korea, Iran, or Pakistan).

Suggestions for Further Reading

Bleckman, Barry M. *The Politics of National Security: Congress and United States Defense Policy.* New York: Oxford UP, 1990.

Cole, David, et al. *Terrorism and the Constitution: Sacrificing Civil Liberties in the Name of National Security.* New York: New Press, 2002.

Halprin, Morton. *Top Secret: National Security and the Right to Know.* New York: Simon, 1977.

Herda, D. J. *New York Times v. United States: National Security and Censorship.* Hillsdale, NJ: Enslow, 1994.

Riebling, Mark. *Wedge: From Pearl Harbor to 9/11: How the Secret War Between the F.B.I. and the C.I.A. Has Endangered National Security.* New York: Simon, 2002.

Risen, James. *State of War: The Secret History of the C.I.A and the Bush Administration.* New York: Free Press, 2006.

Rothkopf, David J. *Running the World: The Inside Story of the National Security Council and the Architects of American Power.* New York: Public Affairs, 2005.

Tal, Israel. *National Security: The Israeli Experience.* Westport: Praeger, 2000.

6 Science and Religion: If Common Ground Exists, Where Does It Lie?

Introduction

In the seventeenth century, when modern science was born, it was feared that new insights into the eternal mysteries of the universe derived from experimentation and telescopic observation would sound the death knell for religious faith. Before modern science brought new truths, what we now call "outer space" was literally considered Heaven. But if outer space was merely an extension of ordinary space, populated by other worlds made of ordinary matter, then where was Heaven? And where was God?

Ever since 1610 when Galileo turned his telescope to the moon and Jupiter and beheld evidence that other worlds were earthlike, not heavenlike, scientists and theologians have debated the relationship between scientific revelations and theological ones. Galileo himself, a devout Catholic, struggled with the issue, asserting that there must be some way to reconcile divine revelation (for example, as manifested in the Old and New Testaments) with what he had seen through the telescope.

Today, despite our increased understanding of the nature of things—or perhaps because of it—scientists and theologians are finding more common ground. Albert Einstein, one of the greatest scientists of all time, insisted that the sensation of the mystical and the beautiful is fundamental to the pursuit of science. Mystery, one could argue, is built into the very fabric of nature, as quantum mechanics would imply.

The following selections tackle such difficult and highly debatable issues as whether scientific discoveries about the nature of the universe shed light on the "ultimate" questions that concern theologians and the faithful. Does anything about the design of reality point toward a master designer? Can reality accommodate miracles? Does evolutionary biology really contradict scriptural accounts of human origins? What exactly constitutes religious perspectives on human origins, and should they be taught alongside scientific perspectives in the public schools?

What Is the Basis of the Conflict Between Science and Religion?

B.C. | Johnny Hart

Johnny Hart (1931–2007), one of the United States' most famous cartoonists, began his career fifty years ago when he published a cartoon in the Saturday Evening Post. *He began his world-famous* B.C. *strip in 1958, and since that time it has appeared in more than twelve hundred newspapers and has reached more than a hundred million readers. In the 1990s, Hart, a devout Christian and a Sunday school teacher, began to stir controversy when he injected religious views into his comic strips, as in the following strip in which Hart's perspective on the creationism versus evolution debate emerges.*

Reflections and Inquiries

1. How are the first two frames relevant to the rest of the comic strip?

2. Comment on the phrasing of Peter's question in the third frame.

3. Comment on the implications of the answer Peter receives to his question.

Source: Creators Syndicate.

Reading to Write

1. Locate other Hart *B.C.* or *Wizard of Id* comic strips (many are collected in book form) that seem to convey a religious—if not a specifically Christian—message. Write an essay on one of the following topics:

   - Hart's *B.C.* comic strips as occasional arguments supporting his Christian vision

   - Cartoons and comic strips as appropriate venues to convey religious views

2. Compare and contrast Charles Schultz (*Peanuts*) and Hart as Christian cartoonists: Examine obvious and subtle references and arguments each makes, and then evaluate which cartoonist you think conveys his point of view more convincingly.

A Designer Universe? | Steven Weinberg

Does the material universe show signs of having been deliberately designed? That is, can we find evidence in nature not only of God's existence but of God's active involvement in the process of creation? Steven Weinberg responds to this centuries-old theological problem from the perspective not only of contemporary physics and cosmology, but of world history. Weinberg is an eminent physicist—he received the Nobel Prize in 1979 and the National Medal of Science in 1991—and is a professor in the Departments of Astronomy and Physics at the University of Texas, Austin.

I have been asked to comment on whether the universe shows signs of having been designed. I don't see how it's possible to talk about this without having at least some vague idea of what a designer would be like. Any possible universe could be explained as the work of some sort of designer. Even a universe that is completely chaotic, without any laws or regularities at all, could be supposed to have been designed by an idiot.

The question that seems to me to be worth answering, and perhaps not impossible to answer, is whether the universe shows signs of having been designed by a deity more or less like those of traditional monotheistic religions—not necessarily a figure from the ceiling of the Sistine Chapel, but at least some sort of personality, some intelligence, who created the universe and has some special concern with life, in particular with human life. I suppose that this is not the idea of a designer held by many people today. They may tell me that

---

Source: Steven Weinberg, "A Designer Universe?" from *The Best American Science Writing 2000*, HarperCollins, 2000: 239–248, originally published in *The New York Review of Books*. Reprinted by permission of the author.

they are thinking of something much more abstract, some cosmic spirit of order and harmony, as Einstein did. They are certainly free to think that way, but then I don't know why they use words like "designer" or "God," except perhaps as a form of protective coloration.

It used to be obvious that the world was designed by some sort of intelligence. What else could account for fire and rain and lightning and earthquakes? Above all, the wonderful abilities of living things seemed to point to a creator who had a special interest in life. Today we understand most of these things in terms of physical forces acting under impersonal laws. We don't yet know the most fundamental laws, and we can't work out all the consequences of the laws we do know. The human mind remains extraordinarily difficult to understand, but so is the weather. We can't predict whether it will rain one month from today, but we do know the rules that govern the rain, even though we can't always calculate their consequences. I see nothing about the human mind any more than about the weather that stands out as beyond the hope of understanding as a consequence of impersonal laws acting over billions of years.

There do not seem to be any exceptions to this natural order, any miracles. I have the impression that these days most theologians are embarrassed by talk of miracles, but the great monotheistic faiths are founded on miracle stories—the burning bush, the empty tomb, an angel dictating the Koran to Mohammed—and some of these faiths teach that miracles continue at the present day. The evidence for all these miracles seems to me to be considerably weaker than the evidence for cold fusion, and I don't believe in cold fusion. Above all, today we understand that even human beings are the result of natural selection acting over millions of years of breeding and eating.

I'd guess that if we were to see the hand of the designer anywhere, it would   5
be in the fundamental principles, the final laws of nature, the book of rules that govern all natural phenomena. We don't know the final laws yet, but as far as we have been able to see, they are utterly impersonal and quite without any special role for life. There is no life force. As Richard Feynman has said, when you look at the universe and understand its laws, "the theory that it is all arranged as a stage for God to watch man's struggle for good and evil seems inadequate."

True, when quantum mechanics was new, some physicists thought that it put humans back into the picture, because the principles of quantum mechanics tell us how to calculate the probabilities of various results that might be found by a human observer. But, starting with the work of Hugh Everett forty years ago, the tendency of physicists who think deeply about these things has been to reformulate quantum mechanics in an entirely objective way, with observers treated just like everything else. I don't know if this program has been completely successful yet, but I think it will be.

I have to admit that, even when physicists will have gone as far as they can go, when we have a final theory, we will not have a completely satisfying picture of the world, because we will still be left with the question "why?" Why this theory, rather than some other theory? For example, why is the world described by quantum mechanics? Quantum mechanics is the one part of our present physics that is likely to survive intact in any future theory, but there is nothing logically inevitable about quantum mechanics; I can imagine a universe governed by Newtonian mechanics instead. So there seems to be an irreducible mystery that science will not eliminate.

But religious theories of design have the same problem. Either you mean something definite by a God, a designer, or you don't. If you don't, then what are we talking about? If you do mean something definite by "God" or "design," if for instance you believe in a God who is jealous, or loving, or intelligent, or whimsical, then you still must confront the question "why?" A religion may assert that the universe is governed by that sort of God, rather than some other sort of God, and it may offer evidence for this belief, but it cannot explain why this should be so.

In this respect, it seems to me that physics is in a better position to give us a partly satisfying explanation of the world than religion can ever be, because although physicists won't be able to explain why the laws of nature are what they are and not something completely different, at least we may be able to explain why they are not *slightly* different. For instance, no one has been able to think of a logically consistent alternative to quantum mechanics that is only slightly different. Once you start trying to make small changes in quantum mechanics, you get into theories with negative probabilities or other logical absurdities. When you combine quantum mechanics with relativity you increase its logical fragility. You find that unless you arrange the theory in just the right way you get nonsense, like effects preceding causes, or infinite probabilities. Religious theories, on the other hand, seem to be infinitely flexible, with nothing to prevent the invention of deities of any conceivable sort.

Now, it doesn't settle the matter for me to say that we cannot see the hand 10 of a designer in what we know about the fundamental principles of science. It might be that, although these principles do not refer explicitly to life, much less human life, they are nevertheless craftily designed to bring it about.

Some physicists have argued that certain constants of nature have values that seem to have been mysteriously fine-tuned to just the values that allow for the possibility of life, in a way that could only be explained by the intervention of a designer with some special concern for life. I am not impressed with these supposed instances of fine-tuning. For instance, one of the most frequently quoted examples of fine-tuning has to do with a property of the nucleus of the carbon atom. The matter left over from the first few minutes of the universe was almost entirely hydrogen and helium, with virtually none of the heavier elements like carbon, nitrogen, and oxygen that seem to be necessary for life. The heavy elements that we find on earth were built up hundreds of millions of years later in a first generation of stars, and then spewed out into the interstellar gas out of which our solar system eventually formed.

The first step in the sequence of nuclear reactions that created the heavy elements in early stars is usually the formation of a carbon nucleus out of three helium nuclei. There is a negligible chance of producing a carbon nucleus in its normal state (the state of lowest energy) in collisions of three helium nuclei, but it would be possible to produce appreciable amounts of carbon in stars if the carbon nucleus could exist in a radioactive state with an energy roughly 7 million electron volts (MeV) above the energy of the normal state, matching the energy of three helium nuclei, but (for reasons I'll come to presently) not more than 7.7 MeV above the normal state.

This radioactive state of a carbon nucleus could be easily formed in stars from three helium nuclei. After that, there would be no problem in producing ordinary carbon; the carbon nucleus in its radioactive state would spontaneously emit light and turn into carbon in its normal nonradioactive state, the state found on earth. The critical point in producing carbon is the existence of a radioactive state that can be produced in collisions of three helium nuclei.

In fact, the carbon nucleus is known experimentally to have just such a radioactive state, with an energy 7.65 MeV above the normal state. At first sight this may seem like a pretty close call; the energy of this radioactive state of carbon misses being too high to allow the formation of carbon (and hence of us) by only 0.05 MeV, which is less than one percent of 7.65 MeV. It may appear that the constants of nature on which the properties of all nuclei depend have been carefully fine-tuned to make life possible.

Looked at more closely, the fine-tuning of the constants of nature here 15 does not seem so fine. We have to consider the reason why the formation of carbon in stars requires the existence of a radioactive state of carbon with an energy not more than 7.7 MeV above the energy of the normal state. The reason is that the carbon nuclei in this state are actually formed in a two-step process: first, two helium nuclei combine to form the unstable nucleus of a beryllium isotope, beryllium 8, which occasionally, before it falls apart, captures another helium nucleus, forming a carbon nucleus in its radioactive state, which then decays into normal carbon. The total energy of the beryllium 8 nucleus and a helium nucleus at rest is 7.4 MeV above the energy of the normal state of the carbon nucleus; so if the energy of the radioactive state of carbon were more than 7.7 MeV it could only be formed in a collision of a helium nucleus and a beryllium 8 nucleus if the energy of motion of these two nuclei were at least 0.3 MeV—an energy which is extremely unlikely at the temperatures found in stars.

Thus the crucial thing that affects the production of carbon in stars is not the 7.65 MeV energy of the radioactive state of carbon above its normal state, but the 0.25 MeV energy of the radioactive state, an unstable composite of a beryllium 8 nucleus and a helium nucleus, above the energy of those nuclei at rest.[1] This energy misses being too high for the production of carbon by a fractional amount of 0.05 MeV/0.25 MeV, or 20 percent, which is not such a close call after all.

This conclusion about the lessons to be learned from carbon synthesis is somewhat controversial. In any case there *is* one constant whose value does seem remarkably well adjusted in our favor. It is the energy density of empty space, also known as the cosmological constant. It could have any value, but from first principles one would guess that this constant should be very large, and could be positive or negative. If large and positive, the cosmological constant would act as a repulsive force that increases with distance, a force that would prevent matter from clumping together in the early universe, the process that was the first step in forming galaxies and stars and planets and people. If large and negative the cosmological constant would act as an attractive force increasing with distance, a force that would almost immediately reverse the expansion of the universe and cause it to recollapse, leaving no time for the evolution of life. In fact, astronomical observations show that the cosmological constant is quite small, very much smaller than would have been guessed from first principles.

It is still too early to tell whether there is some fundamental principle that can explain why the cosmological constant must be this small. But even if there is no such principle, recent developments in cosmology offer the possibility of an explanation of why the measured values of the cosmological constant and other physical constants are favorable for the appearance of intelligent life. According to the "chaotic inflation" theories of André Linde and others, the expanding cloud of billions of galaxies that we call the big bang may be just one fragment of a much larger universe in which big bangs go off all the time, each one with different values for the fundamental constants.

In any such picture, in which the universe contains many parts with different values for what we call the constants of nature, there would be no difficulty in understanding why these constants take values favorable to intelligent life. There would be a vast number of big bangs in which the constants of nature take values unfavorable for life, and many fewer where life is possible. You don't have to invoke a benevolent designer to explain why we are in one of the parts of the universe where life is possible: in all the other parts of the universe there is no one to raise the question.[2] If any theory of this general type turns out to be correct, then to conclude that the constants of nature have been fine-tuned by a benevolent designer would be like saying, "Isn't it wonderful that God put us here on earth, where there's water and air and the surface gravity and temperature are so comfortable, rather than some horrid place, like Mercury or Pluto?" Where else in the solar system other than on earth could we have evolved?

Reasoning like this is called "anthropic." Sometimes it just amounts to an 20 assertion that the laws of nature are what they are so that we can exist, without further explanation. This seems to me to be little more than mystical mumbo jumbo. On the other hand, if there really is a large number of worlds in which some constants take different values, then the anthropic explanation of why in our world they take values favorable for life is just common sense, like explaining why we live on the earth rather than Mercury or Pluto. The actual value of the cosmological constant, recently measured by observations of the motion of distant supernovas, is about what you would expect from this sort of argument: It is just about small enough so that it does not interfere much with the formation of galaxies. But we don't yet know enough about physics to tell whether there are different parts of the universe in which what are usually called the constants of physics really do take different values. This is not a hopeless question; we will be able to answer it when we know more about the quantum theory of gravitation than we do now.

It would be evidence for a benevolent designer if life were better than could be expected on other grounds. To judge this, we should keep in mind that a certain capacity for pleasure would readily have evolved through natural selection, as an incentive to animals who need to eat and breed in order to pass on their genes. It may not be likely that natural selection on any one planet would produce animals who are fortunate enough to have the leisure and the ability to do science and think abstractly, but our sample of what is produced by evolution is very biased, by the fact that it is only in these fortunate cases that there is anyone thinking about cosmic design. Astronomers call this a selection effect.

The universe is very large, and perhaps infinite, so it should be no surprise that, among the enormous number of planets that may support only unintelligent life and the still vaster number that cannot support life at all, there is some tiny fraction on which there are living beings who are capable of thinking about the universe, as we are doing here. A journalist who has been assigned to interview lottery winners may come to feel that some special providence has been at work on their behalf, but he should keep in mind the much larger number of lottery players whom he is not interviewing because they haven't won anything. Thus, to judge whether our lives show evidence for a benevolent designer, we have not only to ask whether life is better than would be expected in any case from what we know about natural selection, but we need also to take into account the bias introduced by the fact that it is we who are thinking about the problem.

This is a question that you all will have to answer for yourselves. Being a physicist is no help with questions like this, so I have to speak from my own experience. My life has been remarkably happy, perhaps in the upper 99.99 percentile of human happiness, but even so, I have seen a mother die painfully of cancer, a father's personality destroyed by Alzheimer's disease, and scores of second and third cousins murdered in the Holocaust. Signs of a benevolent designer are pretty well hidden.

The prevalence of evil and misery has always bothered those who believe in a benevolent and omnipotent God. Sometimes God is excused by pointing to the need for free will. Milton gives God this argument in *Paradise Lost:*

I formed them free, and free they must remain
Till they enthral themselves: I else must change
Their nature, and revoke the high decree
Unchangeable, eternal, which ordained
Their freedom; they themselves ordained their fall.

It seems a bit unfair to my relatives to be murdered in order to provide an   25 opportunity for free will for Germans, but even putting that aside, how does free will account for cancer? Is it an opportunity of free will for tumors?

I don't need to argue here that the evil in the world proves that the universe is not designed, but only that there are no signs of benevolence that might have shown the hand of a designer. But in fact the perception that God cannot be benevolent is very old. Plays by Aeschylus and Euripides make a quite explicit statement that the gods are selfish and cruel, though they expect better behavior from humans. God in the Old Testament tells us to bash the heads of infidels and demands of us that we be willing to sacrifice our children's lives at His orders, and the God of traditional Christianity and Islam damns us for eternity if we do not worship him in the right manner. Is this a nice way to behave? I know, I know, we are not supposed to judge God according to human standards, but you see the problem here: If we are not yet convinced of His existence, and are looking for signs of His benevolence, then what other standards *can* we use?

The issues that I have been asked to address here will seem to many to be terribly old-fashioned. The "argument from design" made by the English theologian William Paley is not on most people's minds these days. The prestige of religion seems today to derive from what people take to be its moral influence, rather than from what they may think has been its success in accounting for what we see in nature. Conversely, I have to admit that, although I really don't believe in a cosmic designer, the reason that I am taking the trouble to argue about it is that I think that on balance the moral influence of religion has been awful.

This is much too big a question to be settled here. On one side, I could point out endless examples of the harm done by religious enthusiasm, through a long history of pogroms, crusades, and jihads. In our own century it was a Muslim zealot who killed Sadat, a Jewish zealot who killed Rabin, and a Hindu zealot who killed Gandhi. No one would say that Hitler was a Christian zealot, but it is hard to imagine Nazism taking the form it did without the foundation provided by centuries of Christian anti-Semitism. On the other side, many admirers of religion would set countless examples of the good done by religion. For instance, in his recent book *Imagined Worlds*, the distinguished physicist Freeman Dyson has emphasized the role of religious belief in the suppression of slavery. I'd like to comment briefly on this point, not to try to prove anything with one example but just to illustrate what I think about the moral influence of religion.

It is certainly true that the campaign against slavery and the slave trade was greatly strengthened by devout Christians, including the Evangelical layman William Wilberforce in England and the Unitarian minister William Ellery Channing in America. But Christianity, like other great world religions, lived comfortably with slavery for many centuries, and slavery was endorsed in the New Testament. So what was different for anti-slavery Christians like Wilberforce and Channing? There had been no discovery of new sacred scriptures, and neither Wilberforce nor Channing claimed to have received any supernatural revelations. Rather, the eighteenth century had seen a widespread increase in rationality and humanitarianism that led others—for instance, Adam Smith, Jeremy Bentham, and Richard Brinsley Sheridan—also to oppose slavery, on grounds having nothing to do with religion. Lord Mansfield, the author of the decision in *Somersett's Case*, which ended slavery in England (though not its colonies), was no more than conventionally religious, and his decision did not mention religious arguments. Although Wilberforce was the instigator of the campaign against the slave trade in the 1790s, this movement had essential support from many in Parliament like Fox and Pitt, who were not known for their piety. As far as I can tell, the moral tone of religion benefited more from the spirit of the times than the spirit of the times benefited from religion.

Where religion did make a difference, it was more in support of slavery 30 than in opposition to it. Arguments from scripture were used in Parliament to defend the slave trade. Frederick Douglass told in his *Narrative* how his condition as a slave became worse when his master underwent a religious conversion that allowed him to justify slavery as the punishment of the children of Ham. Mark Twain described his mother as a genuinely good person, whose soft heart pitied even Satan, but who had no doubt about the legitimacy of slavery, because in years of living in antebellum Missouri she had never heard any sermon opposing slavery, but only countless sermons preaching that slavery was God's will. With or without religion, good people can behave well and bad people can do evil; but for good people to do evil—that takes religion.

In an e-mail message from the American Association for the Advancement of Science I learned that the aim of this conference is to have a constructive dialogue between science and religion. I am all in favor of a dialogue between science and religion, but not a constructive dialogue. One of the great achievements of science has been, if not to make it impossible for intelligent people to be religious, then at least to make it possible for them not to be religious. We should not retreat from this accomplishment. ◎／◎

Notes

1. This was pointed out in a 1989 paper by M. Livio, D. Hollowell, A. Weiss, and J. W. Truran ("The anthropic significance of the existence of an excited state of 12C," *Nature*, Vol. 340, No. 6231, July 27, 1989). They did the calculation quoted here of the 7.7 MeV maximum energy of the radioactive state of carbon, above which little carbon is formed in stars.
2. The same conclusion may be reached in a more subtle way when quantum mechanics is applied to the whole universe. Through a reinterpretation of earlier work by Stephen Hawking, Sidney Coleman has shown how quantum mechanical effects can lead to a split of the history of the universe (more precisely, in what is called the wave function of the universe) into a huge number of separate possibilities, each one corresponding to a different set of fundamental constants. See Sidney Coleman, "Black Holes as Red Herrings: Topological fluctuations and the loss of quantum coherence," *Nuclear Physics*, Vol. B307 (1988), p. 867.

Reflections and Inquiries

1. What does the opening paragraph reveal about Weinberg's attitude about the universe being designed?

2. Weinberg "does not see any exceptions" to the natural order of things—that is, he sees all that is, including the human mind, "as a consequence of impersonal laws acting over billions of years." How does Weinberg support this claim?

3. Why does Weinberg feel that physics is in a better position than religion to give us a more satisfying explanation of the world?

4. What events in human history have made Weinberg doubtful that a benevolent Creator could exist?

5. Do you agree or disagree with Weinberg's assertion that "with or without religion, good people can behave well and bad people can do evil; but for good people to do evil—that takes religion"? Explain.

Reading to Write

1. Write an analysis of Weinberg's use of logical reasoning to defend his thesis. Does his argument contain any logical fallacies? If so, identify them. (See Chapter 6, Reasoning: Methods and Fallacies.)

2. Weinberg alludes to a number of sophisticated scientific concepts such as carbon synthesis, the cosmological constant, and the anthropic principle. Do additional background reading in these concepts, and then write a paper evaluating Weinberg's use of them to defend his thesis.

The New Convergence | Gregg Easterbrook

One biologist, Nobel laureate Jacques Monod, asserts that science has utterly refuted God; but another biologist, Christian de Duve—also a Nobel laureate—asserts that "there is no sense in which atheism is enforced or established by science"; and a third Nobel laureate, the physicist Charles Townes, states that the recent discoveries in physics "seem to reflect intelligence at work in natural law." Are science and religion achieving what Gregg Easterbrook refers to as a "new convergence"? Are these domains, usually thought to be mutually exclusive, becoming more interactive, even mutually illuminating? The point of convergence lies in that area of cosmology concerned with the creation of the universe. Ever since 1926 when astronomer Fred Hoyle propounded the theory that the universe actually did have a beginning, and that beginning could be traced to a point in time known as the Big Bang, scientific and religious sensibilities do indeed appear to be converging, at least for the time being.

Gregg Easterbrook, is a contributing editor at the Atlantic Monthly *and the* New Republic. *He is the author of* Beside Still Waters: Searching for Meaning in an Age of Doubt *(1999) and, most recently,* The Progress Paradox *(2003).*

"The ancient covenant is in pieces: Man knows at last that he is alone in the universe's unfeeling immensity, out of which he emerged only by chance." So pronounced the Nobel Prize-winning French biologist Jacques Monod in his 1970 treatise *Chance and Necessity*, which maintained that God had been utterly refuted by science. The divine is fiction, faith is hokum, existence is a matter of heartless probability—and this wasn't just speculation, Monod maintained, but *proven*. The essay, which had tremendous influence on the intellectual world, seemed to conclude a millennia-old debate. Theology was in retreat, unable to explain away Darwin's observations; intellectual approval was flowing to thinkers such as the Nobel-winning physicist Steven Weinberg, who in 1977 pronounced, "The more the universe seems comprehensible, the more it also seems pointless." In 1981, the National Academy of Sciences declared, "Religion and science are separate and mutually exclusive realms of human thought." Case closed.

And now reopened. In recent years, Allan Sandage, one of the world's leading astronomers, has declared that the big bang can be understood only as a "miracle." Charles Townes, a Nobel-winning physicist and coinventor of the laser, has said that discoveries of physics "seem to reflect intelligence at work in natural law." Biologist Christian de Duve, also a Nobel winner, points out that science argues neither for nor against the existence of a deity: "There is no sense in which atheism is enforced or established by science." And biologist Francis Collins, director of the National Human Genome Research

---

Source: Gregg Easterbrook, "The New Convergence," *Wired 10* (Dec. 2002): 165–69.

Institute, insists that "a lot of scientists really don't know what they are missing by not exploring their spiritual feelings."

Ever so gingerly, science has been backing away from its case-closed attitude toward the transcendent unknown. Conferences that bring together theologians and physicists are hot, recently taking place at Harvard, the Smithsonian, and other big-deal institutions. The American Association for the Advancement of Science now sponsors a "Dialogue on Science, Ethics, and Religion." Science luminaries who in the '70s shrugged at faith as gobbledygook—including E. O. Wilson and the late Stephen Jay Gould and Carl Sagan—have endorsed some form of reconciliation between science and religion.

Why the renewed scientific interest in spiritual thinking? One reason is the cyclical nature of intellectual fashions. In philosophy, metaphysics is making a comeback after decades ruled by positivism and analytical theory of language. These restrained, empirically based ideas have run their course; now the pendulum is swinging toward the grand vision of metaphysics—someday, surely, to swing away again. Similarly in science, the pure materialistic view that reigned through the 20th century, holding that everything has a natural explanation, couldn't keep other viewpoints at bay forever. The age-old notion that there is more to existence than meets the eye suddenly looks like fresh thinking again.

Meanwhile, decades of inconclusive inquiry have left the science-has-all-the-answers script in tatters. As recently as the '70s, intellectuals assumed that hard science was on track to resolve the two Really Big Questions: why life exists and how the universe began. What's more, both Really Big Answers were assumed to involve strictly deterministic forces. But things haven't worked out that way. Instead, the more scientists have learned, the more mysterious the Really Big Questions have become. 5

Perhaps someday researchers will find wholly natural explanations for life and the cosmos. For the moment, though, discoveries about these two subjects are inspiring awe and wonder, and many scientists are reaching out to spiritual thinkers to help them comprehend what they're learning. And as the era of biotechnology dawns, scientists realize they're stepping into territory best navigated with the aid of philosophers and theologians. We are entering the greatest era of science-religion fusion since the Enlightenment last attempted to reconcile the two, three centuries ago.

Look up into the night sky and scan for the edge of the cosmos. You won't find it—nobody has yet. Instruments such as the Hubble Space Telescope's deep-field scanner have detected at least 50 billion galaxies, and every time the equipment is improved, more galaxies farther away come into focus. Space may be infinite—not merely vast, but *infinite*—encompassing an infinite number of galaxies with an infinite number of stars.

All this stuff—enough to form 50 billion galaxies, maybe fantastically more—is thought to have emerged roughly 14 billion years ago in less than a second, from a point with no physical dimensions. Set aside the many competing explanations of the big bang; *something* made an entire cosmos out of nothing. It is this realization—that something transcendent started it all—which has hard-science types such as Sandage using terms like "miracle."

Initially, scientists found the big bang's miraculous implications off-putting. When, in 1927, Catholic abbé and astronomer Georges Lemaître first hypothesized that existence began with the detonation of a "primordial atom" of infinite density, the idea was ridiculed as a transparent ploy to place Genesis on technical grounding. But Lemaître enclosed a testable prediction—that if there had been a bang, the galaxies would be rushing away from one another. This idea, too, was ridiculed, until Edwin Hubble stunned the scientific world by presenting evidence of cosmic expansion. From Hubble's 1929 discovery on, science has taken big bang thinking seriously.

In 1965, another sort of big bang echo—the cosmic background radiation— 10 was discovered. Soon, it was assumed, cosmologists would be able to say, "Here's how everything happened, steps one, two, and three." Today cosmologists do think they know a fair amount about steps two and three—what the incipient cosmos was like in the instant after the genesis, how matter and energy later separated and formed the first galaxies. But as for step one, no dice. Nobody knows beyond foggy conjecture what caused the big bang, what (if anything) was present before that event, or how there could have been a prior condition in which nothing existed.

Explanations of how the mass of an entire universe could pop out of a void are especially unsatisfying. Experiments announced in July this year by the Brookhaven National Laboratory in New York measured properties of subatomic particles known as muons, finding that they behave as though influenced by other particles that seem to have materialized from nothingness. But no object larger than the tiniest subatomic particle has been observed to do this—and these "virtual" particles are volatile entities that exist for less than a second, while the big bang made a universe that is superbly stable, perhaps even permanent.

About 10 years ago, just as scientists were becoming confident in big bang theory, I asked Alan Dressler—one of the world's leading astronomers, and currently a consultant on the design of the space telescope scheduled to replace the Hubble—what caused the bang. He scrunched his face and said, "I can't stand that question!" At the time, cosmologists tended to assert that the cause and prior condition were unknowable. The bizarre physics of the singularity that preceded the explosion, they explained, represented an information wall that blocked (actually, destroyed) all knowledge of the prior condition and its physical laws. We would never know.

The more scientists testily insisted that the big bang was unfathomable, the more they sounded like medieval priests saying, "Don't ask me what made

God." Researchers, prominently Alan Guth of MIT, began to assert that the big bang could be believed only if its mechanics could be explained. Indeed, Guth went on to propose such an explanation. Suffice it to say that, while Guth asserts science will eventually figure out the cause, he still invokes unknown physical laws in the prior condition. And no matter how you slice it, calling on unknown physical laws sounds awfully like appealing to the supernatural.

The existence of 50 billion galaxies isn't the only mystery that's prompting scientists to rethink their attitudes toward the divine. Beyond this is the puzzle of why the universe is hospitable to living creatures.

In recent years, researchers have calculated that if a value called omega— the ratio between the average density of the universe and the density that would halt cosmic expansion—had not been within about one-quadrillionth of 1 percent of its actual value immediately after the big bang, the incipient universe would have collapsed back on itself or experienced runaway-relativity effects that would render the fabric of time-space weirdly distorted. Instead, the firmament is geometrically smooth—rather than distorted—in the argot of cosmology. If gravity were only slightly stronger, research shows, stars would flame so fiercely they would burn out in a single year; the universe would be a kingdom of cinders, devoid of life. If gravity were only slightly weaker, stars couldn't form and the cosmos would be a thin, undifferentiated blur. Had the strong force that binds atomic nuclei been slightly weaker, all atoms would disperse into vapor.

These cosmic coincidences were necessary to create a universe capable of sustaining life. But life itself required an equally unlikely fine-tuning at the atomic level, yielding vast quantities of carbon. Unlike most elements, carbon needs little energy to form exceedingly complicated molecules, a requirement of biology. As it happens, a quirk of carbon chemistry—an equivalence of nuclear energy levels that allows helium nuclei to meld within stars—makes this vital element possible.

To the late astronomer Fred Hoyle, who calculated the conditions necessary to create carbon in 1953, the odds of this match occurring by chance seemed so phenomenally low that he converted from atheism to a belief that the universe reflects a "purposeful intelligence." Hoyle declared, "The probability of life originating at random is so utterly minuscule as to make the random concept absurd." That is to say, Hoyle's faith in chance was shaken by evidence of purpose, a reversal of the standard postmodern experience, and one shared by many of his successors today.

This web of improbable conditions—making not just life but intelligent life practically inevitable—came to be known as the anthropic principle. To physicist Charles Townes, an anthropic universe resolves a tension that has bedeviled physics since the heyday of quantum theory. "When quantum mechanics overthrew determinism, many scientists, including Einstein, wanted the universe to be deterministic," he points out. "They didn't like quantum theory, because it leaves you looking for a spiritual explanation for why things turned out the way they did. Religion and science are going to be drawn together for a long time trying to figure out the philosophical implications of why the universe turned out favorable to us."

Of course, not every scientist is ready to don choir robes. Hard science's attempt to explain our anthropic universe without any reference to the divine has led to the emerging theory of the multiverse, or multiple universes. Andrei Linde, a researcher at Stanford, has argued for a decade that the big bang wasn't unique. Universes bang into existence all the time, by the billions. It just happens in dimensions we can't see.

Linde starts from the assumption that if the big bang was a chance event 20 driven by some natural mechanism, then such events can be expected to happen repeatedly over eons. Ergo, billions of universes. With each bang, Linde supposes, physical laws and constants are determined anew by random forces. Huge numbers of universes end up with excessive gravity and are crushed out of existence; huge numbers end up with weak gravity and no stars; huge numbers lack carbon. Once in a while, an anthropic cosmos comes about.

Several variations on the multiverse theory are popular in academia because they suggest how our universe could have beaten the odds without a guiding hand. But the multiverse idea rests on assumptions that would be laughed out of town if they came from a religious text. Townes has said that speculation about billions of invisible universes "strikes me as much more freewheeling than any of the church's claims." Tenured professors at Stanford now casually discuss entire unobservable universes. Compare that to religion's proposal of a single invisible plane of existence: the spirit.

Linde admits that we can't observe or verify other universes in any way; for that matter we can't even explain how they might occupy alternate dimensions. (As a scientific concept, extra dimensions are ambiguous at best; none beyond the familiar four have ever been observed, and it's far from clear that a higher number is possible.)

Thus, the multiverse theory requires as much suspension of disbelief as any religion. Join the church that believes in the existence of invisible objects 50 billion galaxies wide! To be fair, the dogmas embraced by science tend to be more flexible than those held by theologians. If empirical evidence of God were to appear, science probably would accept it eventually, if grudgingly; while religion, if presented with an empirical disproof of God, might simply refuse to listen. Nevertheless, while cosmology seems more and more to have a miraculous aspect, the scientifically approved alternatives require an article of faith.

Numerous other areas of contemporary science sound like supernaturalism dressed up. Researchers studying the motions of spiral galaxies have found that the stars and gas clouds within them behave as though they're subject to 20 times more force than can be explained by the gravity from observed matter. This has led to the assumption—now close to a scientific consensus—that much of the cosmos is bound up in an undetectable substance provisionally called dark matter. The ratio of dark to regular matter may be as high as 6 to 1.

Other experiments suggest that as much as two-thirds of the content of 25 the universe may crackle with an equally mysterious dark energy. In 1998, astronomers were surprised to discover that, contrary to expectations, cosmic expansion isn't slowing as the momentum of the big bang peters out. Instead, it appears to be speeding up. Something very powerful is causing the galaxies to fly apart faster all the time.

Then there's the Higgs field. In an attempt to explain the ultimate source of mass, some theorists propose that the universe is permeated by an undiscovered field that confers mass on what would otherwise be zero-mass particles. The Superconducting Supercollider project, canceled in 1993, was intended to test this hypothesis.

These and other mystery forces seem to function based on . . . nothing. That notion, now a fact of life among physicists and cosmologists, would have been considered ridiculous just a few generations ago. Yet Judeo-Christian theology has been teaching for millennia that God made the universe ex nihilo—out of nothing. Maybe these forces work in a wholly natural manner that simply hasn't yet been determined. Certainly, there's a better chance of finding observational evidence for theories of physics than theories of theology. But for the moment, many believers find physics trending in their direction, while physicists themselves are left to ponder transcendent effects they can't explain.

Physicists and theologians hold chummy conferences and drink sherry together, but most biologists still want little to do with spiritual thought, and the feeling is mutual on the part of many believers. More than three-quarters of a century after John Scopes stood trial for teaching evolution, Darwin's theory remains a flash point. Only in September, creationists urged Congress to enact legislation supporting the teaching of alternatives to evolution in public schools.

The battle between evolutionary biology and faith isn't inevitable. As genome researcher Collins says, "I am unaware of any irreconcilable conflict between scientific knowledge about evolution and the idea of a creator God. Why couldn't God use the mechanism of evolution to create?" Mainstream Protestant denominations and most branches of Judaism accept Darwin, and in 1996, Pope John Paul II called Darwin's work "more than just a hypothesis."

Even Christian fundamentalism wasn't always anti-Darwin. When the 30 American movement began at the start of the 20th century, its trumpet call was a popular series of pamphlets called *The Fundamentals,* which were to the decade of the 1910s what the *Left Behind* series of evangelical novels is today. According to *The Fundamentals,* evolution illustrated the subtle beauty of God's creative power.

The tide began to turn a decade later, however, when William Jennings Bryan began preaching against Darwinism. He was influenced by a 1923 book, *The New Geology,* which argued that Earth's apparently ancient age was an artifact created by God to test people's faith. Moreover, Bryan had just spent a year in Germany and was horrified by the incipient Nazi movement, which used social Darwinism—now discredited, but then fashionable on the left as well as the right—to assert that it was only natural for the strong to kill the weak. His crusade against evolutionary theory led to the Scopes trial in 1925, which cemented into American culture the notion that Darwin and religion were opposing forces.

Espousing a theory known as intelligent design, molecular biologist Michael Behe and others are attempting to forge a synthesis. Often—though inaccurately—described as creationism lite, intelligent design admits that evolution operates under current conditions but emphasizes that Darwin is silent on how those conditions came to be. Science doesn't have the slightest idea how life began. No generally accepted theory exists, and the steps leading from a barren primordial world to the fragile chemistry of life seem imponderable.

The late biologist Gerald Soffen, who oversaw the life-seeking experiments carried out by NASA's Viking probes to Mars, once outlined the early milestones in the evolution of living processes: development of organic compounds, self-replication of those compounds, appearance of cells isolating the compounds from their environment, photosynthesis enabling cells to use the sun's energy, and the assembly of DNA. "It's hard to imagine how these things could have happened," Soffen told me before his death in 2000. "Once you reach the point of a single-cell organism with genes, evolution takes command. But the early leaps—they're very mysterious."

Intelligent design trades on this insight to propose that only a designer could create life in the first place. The theory is spiritual, but it's not bound by Scripture, as creationism is. A designer is a nondenominational, ecumenical possibility, not a dogmatic formula.

Did a designer set Earth's life processes in motion? Few questions are 35 more interesting or intellectually rich. Because the evolution debate is so rancorous, however, the how-did-life-begin question is usually lost amid shouting matches between orthodox Darwinians and hard-line creationists.

The biotech era may change this. Biologists and fundamentalists may still want to hurl bricks at one another, but there's no dodging the immediate questions of biological engineering, stem-cell research, transgenic animals, and so on. What is life? Do individual cells have rights? Do human beings have the right to alter human DNA? Is it wise to reengineer the biosphere?

The need to grope our collective way through such quandaries may force theologians, church leaders, biologists, and philosophers to engage one another. Perhaps this debate will get hopelessly hung up in doctrine, for instance on the question of whether life begins when sperm meets egg. But there is at least an equal chance that the pressure of solving biotech questions will force science and theology to find the reasonable points of either field. Unlike cosmology, which poses fascinating questions whose answers have no effect on daily life, biotech will affect almost everyone in an immediate way. A science-and-religion reconciliation on this subject may be needed to write research rules, physician ethics, and, ultimately, law.

Oh, and what did Einstein think about this issue? He said, "Science without religion is lame, religion without science is blind." Einstein was neither convinced there is a God nor convinced there is not; he sensed that it's far too early in the human quest for knowledge to do more than speculate on transcendent questions. Science, which once thought the case for higher power was closed, is now trending back toward his view. ◎/◎

Reflections and Inquiries

1. Easterbrook wonders if the "new convergence" might simply be a fad of sorts ("now the pendulum is swinging toward the grand vision of metaphysics— someday, surely [it will] swing away again"). Do you agree? Why or why not?

2. Why should scientists involved with biotechnology realize that, as Easterbrook states, they will be "stepping into territory best navigated with the aid of philosophers and theologians"? In what ways do you suppose philosophers and theologians could be of service to these scientists?

3. Reflect on whether or not the big bang origin of the universe presupposes the existence of a creator; address challenging views as you do so.

4. What is remarkable about the element carbon in the context of a discussion of science-religion convergence?

Reading to Write

In an essay, write a point-by-point comparison between a strictly secular explanation for the creation of the universe and a religious one. Take care to represent each side as objectively and as accurately as you can. Next, commit to one side or the other and provide a detailed rationale for your commitment.

Miracles and Explanations | Chet Raymo

Miracles and scientific explanations: Could any two concepts be more mutually exclusive? Chet Raymo, a professor of physics and astronomy, explains in the following essay—comprising the first chapter of his book, Skeptics and True Believers *(1998)—that they have more in common than meets the eye. His explanation takes us to the roots of the impulse to make sense of the world—an impulse shared by philosophers, theologians, and scientists alike.*

See! I am God. See! I am in everything. See! I never lift my hands off my works, nor will I ever. See! I lead everything toward the purpose for which I ordained it.
—Julian of Norwich

Like most children, I was raised on miracles. Cows that jump over the moon; a jolly fat man that visits every house in the world in a single night; mice and ducks that talk; little engines that huff and puff and say, "I think I can"; geese that lay golden eggs. This lively exercise of credulity on the part of children is good practice for what follows—for believing the miracle stories of traditional religion, yes, but also for the practice of poetry or science.

Science is based upon our ability to imagine what we cannot see: nuclear reactions in the cores of stars, the spinning of galaxies, the dervish dance of DNA. Science, like the imaginative landscapes of childhood, is a world of make-believe. It is, however, a very special kind of make-believe. Science takes as given that a real world exists "out there," and that it can be represented, albeit imperfectly, in the world of ideas. We struggle mightily to make the partition between the imagined world and the real world as transparent as possible. No scientist will dispute that "atom" is a made-up concept; however, the concept "atom" is the *most concise* way—perhaps the only way—to make sense of our detailed, quantitative experience of the material world. Without the concept "atom," chemistry, X-ray crystallography, nuclear energy, thermodynamics, and other broad territories of external experience make no sense at all. Indeed, so transparent is the partition between "atom" and experience that most scientists would say that atoms are "facts," or at least so close to being facts that no quotation marks are called for.

In the Land of Make-Believe
It is because we retain as adults something of the child's facility for make-believe that we can enthuse with the poet Gerard Manley Hopkins:

Look at the stars! Look, look up at the skies!
O look at all the fire-folk sitting in the air![1]

Source: Chet Raymo, "Miracles and Explanations," Ch. 1 of *Skeptics and True Believers: The Exhilarating Connection Between Science and Religion.* New York: Walker & Co., 1998, pp. 10–26. Reprinted by permission.

It is also because we retain something of the child's facility for make-believe that we can imagine that the stars are vast spheres of hydrogen and helium, powered by nuclear energy, light-years away. Poetic metaphor ("fire-folk") and scientific construct (nuclear-powered spheres of gas) serve useful functions in our lives, but we are confident the latter bears a closer affinity to reality—to whatever is "out there"—than the former. The poetic metaphor conveys a human truth; the scientific construct attempts to remove the human subject from the equation of idea and reality.

The biologist Richard Dawkins has suggested that the credulity of children—the willingness to believe whatever one is told by adults, especially parents—has been reinforced by natural selection for its survival value.[2] The child comes into the world knowing nothing, and must quickly learn how to navigate the perils of life. At first, "Don't touch the stove" and "Be good or Santa won't bring toys" are absorbed with equal credulity. The child is asked by an authority figure to behave as if the stove is hot, and to behave as if Santa exists, and so she does. The challenge of growing up is to learn which sorts of make-believe are useful reality constructs and which are poetic metaphors.

Early on in our lives, we abandon Santa Claus and the tooth fairy as real- 5 ity constructs because we recognize contradictions that are difficult to resolve (the relative sizes of Santa's rotund belly and the chimney pipe, for example), but also because word gets around from other presumably reliable authorities, older siblings perhaps, that the stories are untrue. As for the stove, we learn to exercise a certain skepticism concerning whether or not it is hot, testing in doubtful cases by cautiously touching the surface with a fingertip.

We cannot live without some sorts of make-believe in our lives. Without made-up maps of the world, life is a blooming, buzzing confusion. Some elements of our mental maps (Santa Claus, fire-folk) satisfy emotional or aesthetic *inner needs;* other elements of our mental maps (hot stove, nuclear-powered stars) satisfy intellectual curiosity about the world *out there*. We get in trouble when the two kinds of maps are confused, when we objectify elements of make-believe solely on the basis of inner need. No one takes *fire-folk* literally; but many of us accept the astrological influence of the stars on our lives because it satisfies an inner need, even in the face of convincing evidence to the contrary (every objective test of astrology has proved negative).

The True Believer retains in adulthood an absolute faith in some forms of empirically unverifiable make-believe (such as astrology or the existence of immortal souls), whereas the Skeptic keeps a wary eye even on firmly established facts (such as atoms). Both Skeptic and True Believer use made-up maps of the world.

Is one map as good as any other? Since all knowledge is constructed, can the choice between two contradictory maps (fire-folk versus nuclear-powered spheres of gas, for example) be a matter of personal or political expediency? Not unless we are willing to erect partitions between what we believe to be true on the basis of unambiguous, reproducible evidence and what we merely wish to be true. Apparently, many of us are willing to do just that. A 1995 Gallup poll showed that 79 percent of adult Americans believe in miracles (interestingly, 86 percent of women believe in miracles, compared to 71 percent of men). About half of us are open to the reality of astrological influences. Nearly three-quarters of us believe in life after death. When teenagers were asked, "When scientific and religious explanations conflict, which explanation are you more likely to accept?" the majority chose religion by a factor of two to one.

The Unmiraculous Shroud

A linen cloth preserved in the cathedral at Turin, Italy, the Shroud of Turin, bears the likeness of a man and is purported to be the winding sheet of Christ. The cloth has long been an object of veneration among Christians. In the late 1980s, Roman Catholic authorities allowed scientists to take tiny samples of the shroud for radiocarbon dating. This technique uses the precisely known decay rate of radioactive carbon atoms as a kind of clock to determine when organic substance—bone, wood, charcoal, et cetera—were alive.[3] The method has enjoyed wide use among archaeologists, paleontologists, and historians. It has been calibrated against the ring count of ancient trees and tested successfully many times on historical objects of known age.

In the case of the Shroud of Turin, carbon dating shows when the flax 10 plants were alive from which the linen was made. Three independent carbon-dating labs, in Zurich, Oxford, and Tucson, Arizona, participated in the test.[4] Along with a sample from the shroud, each lab was given three control samples of cloth of known age: linen from a 900-year-old Nubian tomb, linen from a second-century mummy of Cleopatra, and threads from an 800-year-old garment of St. Louis d'Anjou. None of the samples was identified for the researchers. None of the labs communicated with the others until the results were in. After making their measurements, all three labs agreed on the ages of all four samples. All three labs correctly dated the control samples. And all three labs concluded that the Shroud of Turin is medieval, dating from the mid-fourteenth century. Significantly, this is the very time the shroud first appears in historical records.

It is to the credit of Church officials in Italy that they authorized the carbon-dating tests and accepted the results. Their actions are in keeping with a declaration by Pope John Paul II on the relationship of science and theology: "Science can purify religion from error and superstition, and religion can purify science from idolatry and false absolutes."[5]

Is the conclusion of the radiocarbon tests absolute? No, of course not. No scientific test can prove anything with absolute certainty. Is the conclusion convincing? Yes, if you are a Skeptic. No, if you are a True Believer. The person with True Belief in the shroud's authenticity will dismiss any evidence to the contrary.

In fact, carbon dating of the Turin shroud seems only to have enhanced its reputation as the winding sheet of Christ. (Web pages on the Internet are devoted to its cult.) Since the test results were announced, many attempts have been made to explain them away. According to one critic, a burst of neutrons from the body of the risen Christ created extra carbon-14 nuclei, making the cloth appear younger than it actually is. (No mention is made of what might have caused this mysterious neutron burst, other than a miracle.) Another critic has suggested that the presence of bacteria on the cloth might have muddied the result by adding modern-day carbon-14, although no evidence is adduced that such bacteria actually exist on the Shroud of Turin. As I write, several Italian professors claim to have seen the image of a first-century Roman coin on the cloth. No test, no matter how carefully contrived, will dissuade a True Believer from his belief. Given a conflict between scientific and religious explanations, most of us are quite willing to go with the religious explanation if it confirms our deep-seated inner need for miracles.

Early in my education, the Shroud of Turin was offered to me as evidence for the risen Christ, and therefore for the truth of Christianity. I was educated in Roman Catholic schools, where miracles were as much a part of the curriculum as Dick and Jane and the multiplication tables. *The Shroud of Turin. The spinning Sun at Fátima. Having our throats blessed with crossed candles on Candlemas Day, thereby making us immune to choking on chicken bones. St. Brendan the Navigator taking refuge on the back of a whale during his sixth-century voyage to America (my teachers were Irish nuns). Et cetera, et cetera.* We lived within a vast and engaging landscape of miracles, as richly improbable (by empirical standards) as the make-believe landscape of fairy tales, and including, of course, those constant miracles we had with us every day: the Real Presence of Christ's body and blood in the Eucharist, the efficacy of intercessory prayer, angels, devils, heaven, limbo, purgatory, hell, and life everlasting. I absorbed these things, mostly uncritically, because it is the nature of children to be credulous. I didn't ask for evidence; the miracles *were* the evidence.

In retrospect, it is easy to see that the entire panoply of miracles, includ- 15 ing the most outrageously improbable—all those little unbaptized babies in limbo, for instance—were there to bolster the possibility that death is not final. St. Paul said (as we were frequently reminded), "If the dead are not raised, Christ has not been raised, and if Christ has not been raised, your faith is in vain." (1 Cor. 15:17) The Shroud of Turin and all the rest were offered as evidence that our ultimate fate is not to be food for worms.

By the time I went off to the University of Notre Dame, many of the more fanciful miracles of my primary education had faded from the story, but the big miracles remained. The text we used for my freshman theology class was Frank Sheed's *Theology and Sanity*, the thrust of which was that any sane person *must* be a Roman Catholic, so persuasive is the evidence for the objective truth of that faith. Meanwhile, I was studying science and discovering a way of constructing mental maps of the world that allowed no place for miracles.

This is not to say that science proves miracles are impossible. One does not prove the invalidity of a miracle by showing that it is inconsistent with the laws of nature. It is the nature of miracles—the strength of their force as evidence—that they violate natural law. Science works by finding consistent patterns in nature; miracles, if they occur, are by definition one-time things. In my university science classes, I did not learn that miracles are impossible, but that there is no reliable evidence that they occur.

Every miracle, examined closely, has a way of slipping through the fingers. En masse the evidence for miracles looks impressive; but take them one at a time and they become frustratingly evasive. As I searched among the miracles of my faith, I found none that was not contaminated with the likelihood of flawed testimony, fraud, or wishful thinking. Always there was the possibility of a natural explanation. The person whose illness abates after a trip to Lourdes might have been cured by the intercession of the Virgin, but the illness also might have receded on its own or have been ameliorated by positive thinking; both circumstances are recognized within the natural order. The Shroud of Turin might be the winding sheet of the risen Christ, but it might also be an ingeniously contrived fraud or work of art, both of which were common in the fourteenth century. Shine the fierce light of skepticism on the Lourdes cure or the Turin shroud and the "miracle" vanishes.

The Miraculous Red Knot

I learned something else in my study of science, something that had an even greater effect upon my religious faith: None of the miracles I had been offered in my religious training were as impressively revealing of God's power as the facts I was learning in science. In one of his sermons, the poet John Donne writes: "There is nothing that God hath established in a constant course of nature, and which therefore is done every day, but would seem a miracle, and exercise our admiration, if it were done but once."[6] Consider, for example, the flight of juvenile red knots from the islands of northern Canada to Tierra del Fuego, at the southern tip of South America.

The red knot is a sandpiper that twice each year visits the eastern shores of the United States. Every year, these tough little travelers wing more than 18,000 miles, from the southern tip of South America to the arctic islands of northern Canada and back again, stopping briefly along the way on the beaches of Delaware Bay and Cape Cod. 20

During our northern winter, red knots feed on the sunny beaches of Tierra del Fuego. The birds take advantage of the austral summer to replace their tattered feathers in a long molt, which ensures their flight equipment is in top condition when, in February, they lift off in flocks of hundreds or thousands for the journey north. Up the coast of Argentina, across the hump of Brazil, stopping occasionally along the way to fatten up. They know exactly where to find food, returning each year to the same stretches of sand or marsh. From the northern coast of South America, they strike out across the Atlantic on a weeklong nonstop flight that brings them in mid-May to their usual feeding grounds on the marshy shore of Delaware Bay, just as horseshoe crabs are laying eggs by the millions.

For a few weeks the red knots gorge themselves; a single bird might consume 135,000 horseshoe crab eggs. Then, fat and fit again, they take to the air for a nonstop flight to islands of the Canadian archipelago north of Hudson Bay. Here, in the boreal summer, they mate and breed, each female red knot laying four speckled eggs, which she and her mate incubate in turns. Baby knots are up and about as soon as they hatch, growing rapidly and replacing natal down with juvenile feathers in preparation for flight. By mid-July, the female adults abandon their new offspring and head south; male adults follow a few weeks later. The juveniles fend for themselves until late August, when they too commence the 9,000-mile journey to Tierra del Fuego.[7]

Now here is the astonishing thing, and the reason I have told the story. The young red knots, by the thousands and *without adult guides or prior experience*, find their way along the ancient migration route. From northern Canada to New England's Atlantic shore, across the Atlantic Ocean to Guyana and Suriname, then down along the eastern coast of South America, arriving precisely at those feeding grounds along the way where they are sure to find food. At last they join their parents and others of their species on the beaches of Tierra del Fuego for the southern summer.

How do they do it? How do the young birds make their way along a route they have never traveled to a destination they have never seen? How do they unerringly navigate the long stretch of their journey over featureless sea? We know exactly *what* the red knots accomplish—where they go, when they arrive; dedicated ornithologists have banded the birds by the hundreds, watched for them at way stations, counted their comings and goings. But *how* the uninstructed young birds accomplish their epic feat of navigation remains mysterious. The Sun, the stars, the Earth's magnetic field, angles of polarized light—all of these have been shown to be part of the navigational skills of one animal or another (birds, fish, or insects), and singly or in combination these clues must keep the red knots on course.

This much is certain: A map for the journey and the instrumental knowledge to follow it are part of the red knot's genetic inheritance. Each bird begins life as a single fertilized cell. Already, that microscopic cell contains the biological equivalent of a set of charts, a compass, a sextant, and maybe even something akin to a satellite navigation system. This must be true, for every bird is born with the instinct to make its journey. 25

How can a map of the globe and the skill to follow it be contained within a cell too small to be seen with the naked eye? Medieval theologians are said to have debated how many angels can dance on the head of a pin; in the flight of the red knot we are engaged with a mystery more immediately present but no less marvelous. We can call it instinct and let it go at that. But human curiosity will not let it go. We ask: How? The need to find answers is deep within us, anchored at the root of our being. Of all species of life on Earth, we are the one that *wants to know*. We want knowledge that is reliable, public, and universal, based upon unambiguous, reproducible experience that is (or can be) common to all of us—in a word, knowledge that is scientific.

In the case of animal navigation, the answer to our question turns out to be quite incredible. The urge to make the red knot's planet-spanning flight, the map of the journey, and the skills to follow it, are written into a DNA molecule in a language of stunning simplicity. The molecule is shaped like a spiral staircase—the famous double helix. The side rails of the staircase are linked sugar and phosphate molecules. The treads are paired molecules called nucleotides. There are four kinds of nucleotides: adenine, guanine, cytosine, and thymine, designated A, G, C, and T. Adenine always pairs with thymine, and guanine always pairs with cytosine, so that there are four kinds of treads along the DNA staircase: A-T, T-A, G-C, and C-G. It is the sequence of these treads that is the genetic code. The red knot's map and navigational manual are written in a chemical language of only four letters!

In each cell of the red knot's body, there are identical strands of DNA, about an arm's length in all, a blueprint for making a small russet bird with an urge to fly and the skills to make a 9,000-mile unpracticed journey. Can it be possible? There are thirty-two volumes in the *Encyclopaedia Britannica*, 1,000 pages per volume, 1,200 words per page, an average of five letters per word, for a total of 200 million letters. There are several billion nucleotide pairs in an arm's length of DNA. A sequence of three nucleotide pairs (sixty-four possible combinations) is enough to provide a code for each letter of the alphabet, upper- and lowercase plus punctuation. Believe it or not, several sets of the *Encyclopaedia Britannica* could be transcribed into the red knot's genes!

This information is not in doubt. Molecular biologists can isolate DNA, replicate it, photograph it, measure it, read the sequence of nucleotides, change the sequence, modify genes. It is possible in principle to provide a complete transcription of the red knot's DNA (this has been done for many organisms), and to determine which parts of the sequence code for eye, feather, beak, claw. Somewhere along the red knot's double helix—somewhere among those many volumes of information—is the code for constructing those parts of the red knot's brain that contain the map of the migration route and the skills to follow it. The red knot's brain is a flexible organ, capable of wiring itself by experience. But part of the red knot's brain comes already wired with a map of the globe and a navigator's skills.

For some years I have been on the Board of Overseers of Boston's Museum ³⁰ of Science. On my visits to the museum, I always make my way to the ten-foot-high model of a segment of DNA. To my mind, it is the most extraordinary exhibit in the museum. Atoms are represented by colored ball—carbon black, oxygen red, nitrogen blue, hydrogen white—linked by rods. The model contains only a few dozen pairs of nucleotides, a tiny fraction of what is contained within the DNA of even the simplest living organism. If the whole of the red knot's complement of DNA were shown at the scale of the model, it wouldn't fit within the entire museum. Nevertheless, I stand in front of this partial strand, gape-jawed at the beauty, at the simplicity—a simplicity out of which emerges the astonishing diversity and awesome complexity of life. What I feel as I stand before the model cannot be adequately put into words. Call it reverence, awe, praise—in short, the full range of religious feeling.

Nothing I learned during my religious training is more wondrous to me than the flight of the juvenile red knot from northern Canada to Tierra del Fuego, a journey whose map is contained in the red knot's DNA. Such real-world mysteries inspire my awe far more than the so-called miracle on display in the cathedral at Turin. In the red knot's story, we catch a glimpse of a God who never lifts his hand from his work, and who leads everything to the purpose for which it was ordained. As the British writer and cartographer Tim Robinson observed: Miracles are explainable; it is the explanations that are miraculous. ◎/◎

Notes

1. Gerard Manley Hopkins, "The Starlight Night," *The Poetical Works of Gerard Manley Hopkins*, ed. by Norman H. MacKensie (Oxford: Clarendon Press, 1990), p. 139.
2. Richard Dawkins, "Putting Away Childish Things," *Skeptical Inquirer*, January–February 1995, p. 139.
3. Living organisms build their bodies by taking carbon from the atmosphere. There are two kinds of carbon atoms, called isotopes. Carbon-12 has six protons and six neutrons in its nucleus; carbon-14 has two extra neutrons. Carbon-12 nuclei are stable; carbon-14 nuclei are unstable, or radioactive, and disintegrate at a precisely known rate called a half-life (the half-life of carbon-14 is 5,568 years). In spite of the decay, the ratio of carbon-14 to carbon-12 in the atmosphere is approximately constant, maintained by the creation of radioactive carbon-14 nuclei by cosmic rays from outer space. When an organism dies, the carbon-14 in its structure decays without being replaced, changing the ratio of isotopes in a clocklike fashion. The number of atoms of both species in a sample can be determined using a mass spectrometer.
4. P. E. Damon, D. J. Donahue, and B. H. Gore, "Radioactive Dating of the Shroud of Turin," *Nature* 337 (February 16, 1989): 311–15.
5. Pope John Paul II, "Science and Faith," address at the University of Pisa, September 24, 1989. Reprinted in *Origins, Catholic News Service Documentary Service* 19 (October 26, 1989): 21.
6. John Donne, Sermon, Easter Day, March 25, 1627, *The Complete Poetry and Selected Prose of John Donne*, ed. by Charles M. Coffin (New York: Modern Library, 1952), p. 536.
7. For the story of the red knot, I am indebted to Brian Harrington, *The Flight of the Red Knot* (New York: W. W. Norton, 1996).

Reflections and Inquiries

1. Early in the essay Raymo asserts that science "is a world of make-believe." How convincingly does he support this assertion? What does it have to do with the intersection of science with religion?

2. What do skeptics have in common with true believers, according to Raymo? What is the most significant difference between them?

3. According to Pope John Paul II in his effort to reconcile science with theology, "Science can purify religion from error and superstition," while "religion can purify science from idolatry and false absolutes." Do you agree or disagree that science and religion can "purify" each other in this manner? How so? (You will need to provide a possible definition of *purify* as it is used in this context.)

4. According to Raymo, none of the miracles he learned about in his religious training was as revealing of God's power as what he learned about in science. What scientific revelations is he referring to? Do you agree or disagree that these scientific phenomena are more revealing of God's power? Why?

5. What are red knots, and why does Raymo spend so much time in his essay discussing them?

Reading to Write

Read the entirety of Raymo's book, *Skeptics and True Believers*, from which this selection is taken. Then write a detailed critique of Raymo's ability to "converge" science with religion.

Fossils | J. T. Barbarese

Poetry sometimes has a way of probing a complex idea in such a concentrated way that its deepest truths are extracted—although it may take several close readings to understand what those extracted truths are saying. In the following poem, J. T. Barbarese, a professor of English at Rutgers as well as a poet, focuses on the conflict between science and religion. Barbarese has published two volumes of poetry: Under the Blue Moon *(1985) and* New Science *(1989).*

When he was young he used to spend the whole summer
in the abandoned slag heaps around the old mines
outside the city of Scranton. It would take him hours
to pick through the shale stacks, the sweat writing lines
in the dust on his face, and the old ball peen hammer   5
slung from his belt pinching his belly button.
Some days there was nothing to read but the signatures
of ice and erosion and tools. Then he'd find one,
a slate unnaturally filigreed with the fright masks
of a trilobite, ferns, the inferior commissures   10
of ancient clams. He would wrap them in moist newspaper
and carry them carefully home. Once his teacher asked
him to talk to the class about fossils.
      Satan plants them to trick us,
he said. *When I get home I smash them to pieces.*

Source: J. T., Barbarese, "Fossils" from *The Atlantic Monthly* (Sept. 2000): 95.
J. T. Barbarese is a poet and translator who teaches at Rutgers University in Camden, New Jersey. Reprinted by permission.

Reflections and Inquiries

1. What is the attitude of the boy toward the fossils he discovers? How does it differ from the attitude of the narrator (or the poet)? How can you tell?

2. Study the definitions of the terms *trilobite, filigreed,* and *commissures* if you don't already know them. What do they contribute to the thematic elements of the poem?   15

3. Provide a rationale for the boy's destruction of the fossils he collects.

4. Suggest a reason why the poet chooses to frame the poem as the recollection of boyhood, rather than to relate the incident directly.

Reading to Write

A poem can be effective because of what it merely hints at or leaves out altogether. Write an expanded prose version of the poem in your own words, making explicit what is implicit or ambiguous in the original.

Great Minds Needn't Think Alike to Be Right: Advocates of Science, Religion Can Co-Exist | Cynthia Bass

Should Darwinian evolution be regarded as a threat to religion? Cynthia Bass, a free-lance writer based in the San Francisco Bay Area, thinks that it is a mistake to think so because the two domains do not really compete against each other. Bass explains her position in the following article, published on the birthday of two famous people who viewed the world in very different ways.

On this day in 1809, two of the most famous men of the nineteenth century were born under very different circumstances—one in a Kentucky log cabin, the other in an English country house complete with stable and servants' quarters. The first is, of course, Abraham Lincoln.

And the second? None other than Charles Darwin.

That two such influential men should be born on the same day of the same year surely is one of history's most amazing coincidences. In fact, had the second man been anyone else in the world except Charles Darwin, the father of the theory of evolution, it might even be cited as an example of . . . intelligent design!

Needless to say, Darwin's birthday is not a day of great celebration in intelligent design circles. On the contrary: Darwin's theory of evolution has been increasingly under attack by intelligent-design proponents—an attack both shrill and nationwide.

It's important to keep in mind that an overwhelming majority of scien-   5
tists, both here and abroad, consider evolution one of the most established theories in all science. Indeed, modern biology, physiology, biochemistry— and even medicine and immunology—accept and build upon Darwin's naturalistic explanation of both the diversity of species and the complexities of biological systems.

Intelligent design adherents agree with Darwin that species are indeed diverse and biological systems unquestionably complex. It's that naturalistic element they so heartily oppose. According to intelligent design—both its nonscientific supporters and the few fully credentialed scientists who also support it—there are times when diversity is just too diverse, complexity just too complex, for the explanation solely to be natural selection.

The examples most often cited include unexpected biological novelty in the fossil record and the existence of so-called "junk" DNA. If life were really informed by natural selection alone, says intelligent design, these examples should never exist. And yet they do. Therefore, there must have been something (or someone) that (or who) stepped in and, for whatever reason, "designed" them.

Regarding the exact nature of this designing force, intelligent design advocates declare complete neutrality: it can be God, Brahma, Gaia, even the Enlightenment's "Great Clockmaker." They claim they are interested only in making sure students are not misled into thinking that Darwin explains everything.

This is disingenuous in the extreme. There would be no interest in including an intelligent "disclaimer" in a biology class (as was proposed in the recent Dover, Pa., court case), were it not specifically to undermine Darwin. After all, while it's true that modern Darwinian thought doesn't explain everything in biology, there are plenty of unexplained mysteries in physics, too. Astronomy and cosmology also have lots of gaps. But nobody's rushing to insist on "disclaimers" prior to teaching say, the Big Bang. Darwin comes in for this special treatment precisely because some zealous conservative religious believers see evolution as a direct threat to all religious belief in America.

There's a sad irony in this for those of us who are ourselves religious, for the   10
surest way to undermine religion is to insist on playing in Darwin's "ballpark." That's because once you accept the standards of science and the scientific method—which intelligent design vehemently claims to—you run the risk that science will ultimately provide naturalistic explanations to its current mysteries. And if the day comes when a future scientist explains "junk" DNA as concisely as James Watson and Francis Crick explained what at the time seemed equally unsolvable—the mystery of DNA itself—where will this leave religious belief?

A more effective way to bolster religious belief than attacking Darwin is to remember that religion addresses questions that are completely beyond the range of science. The meaning of life, the nature of good conduct, the nature of the human soul: Science is not set up to deal with any of these.

This is why religion remains so potent—and, I think, so positive—a force in modern America. It alone provides answers to the hardest questions we all face. In a health crisis, we want help from a doctor who practices medicine in a completely rational and scientific manner. But our prayers that this medicine helps go to a supernatural being, not to the doctor.

Which returns us to today's other birthday boy.

Lincoln could never have accomplished the great tasks before him, nor inspired others to stay the course through so many defeats, disappointment and death, without recourse to ideas imbued with the deepest spirituality. Whether he declared that "this nation, under God, shall have a new birth of freedom" or called on his fellow Northerners to press on to victory "with malice toward none, with charity for all, with firmness in the right as God gives us to see the right," he clearly saw the unique wisdom and power embodied in the great truths of religion—wisdom certainly different from scientific wisdom, but equally certainly, just as valuable.

This, most of us would agree, is religion at its best: providing spiritual 15 comfort, psychological strength, moral direction and righteous inspiration. In this realm, evolution—wonderful job that it does in explaining the natural world—cannot compete with religion. In its own "ballpark," religion, as Lincoln knew, wins every time. It's only when it strays into the other guy's stadium that it sets itself up for inevitable loss and disappointment. ◎/◎

Reflections and Inquiries

1. What is Bass's reason for beginning her article by commenting on the fact that Abraham Lincoln and Charles Darwin were born on the same day?

2. According to Bass, religion alone "addresses questions that are completely beyond the range of science." What questions are those? Explain why you agree or disagree with Bass's assertion.

3 Describe Bass's attitude toward evolution.

Reading to Write

If you are not familiar with biological evolution, especially the concept of natural selection, spend some time familiarizing yourself with its principles; then write an essay in which you suggest ways in which evolution either can or cannot interact harmoniously with a spiritual view of creation.

Student Essay

Can One Compare Science and Religion? | Kareem Raad

Why is it that science and religion are not as easy to reconcile as might first be believed? Kareem Raad, a senior double-majoring in biology and philosophy at Santa Clara University, investigates the problem by examining the reasons "why people accept certain kinds of knowledge."

L et me describe what I will not do. I will not list the overwhelming scientific evidence for evolution, nor will I try to describe the wonder of nature which, when properly experienced, offers compelling evidence for the existence of a divine being. William Wordsworth would hardly be satisfied with this approach, for he writes:

Where lies the truth? has Man, in wisdom's creed,
A pitiable doom; for respite brief
A care more anxious, or a heavier grief?
Is he ungrateful, and doth little heed
God's bounty, soon forgotten. or indeed,
Must Man, with labour born, awake to sorrow
When Flowers rejoice and Larks with rival speed
Spring from their nests to bid the Sun good morrow? [. . .]
But o'er the contrast wherefore heave a sigh?
Like those aspirants let us soar—our aim,
Through life's worst trials, whether shocks or snares,
A happier, brighter, purer Heaven than theirs
    —William Wordsworth, 1846

But note that Wordsworth can be successful in advancing a position on science and religion (hereafter SAR) only if he presupposes that the evidence he brings forth in his poetry appeals to the reader. Wordsworth's success depends on whether religious ideas ultimately define our interpretation of a poem, or whether our understanding of poetry influences our religious belief. Likewise for science. "Of course they influence each other" might be many people's obvious response. But I will argue that this question is not so simple. Understanding why people accept certain kinds of knowledge at the most fundamental level, then, is the question we should consider here. While this will be a more abstract endeavour, I believe it will ultimately be more fruitful. We will have to set poetry aside in the meantime, but will ultimately return to Wordsworth's dilemma.

I am not suggesting that this is the proper forum to consider one's most fundamental religious and scientific assumptions, but it is a good place to emphasize the importance of the question. Unfortunately the reasons for making such a bold claim will not appear clear until much later in this discourse.

In determining whether there will be a point to these writings, I ask only for the same faith or intellectual curiousity that those who debate science and religion bring to the dispute.

Defining the Issue

Galileo's astronomical discoveries in the sixteenth century marked the first well-known conflict between SAR. In the twenty-first century, a quick "Google News" search of the phrase "intelligent design and evolution" reveals thousands of articles (Google.com). Clearly the debate between defenders of evolution and intelligent design rages on. But what is the basis of the conflict, and more importantly, what should the basis be? The disagreement about intelligent design and evolution is often framed as part of a broader cultural clash between science and religion. In the evolution controversy it is often assumed that because we know what SAR are, we know how they ought to be compared. But is this a fair assumption? Should the term *religion* include religious practices, rituals, and anthropological facts relating to religion—or does it include only propositional religious belief? Is it fair to use the word *science* to refer to more than the application of a principle, viz., the scientific method?

At face value it seems that if one understood religion in the full-blown sense, then it would be difficult to compare science and religion. The scientific method (the principle underlying all "science," indeed, it defines a discipline as scientific) is a principle for gathering knowledge of the natural world, while religion can include attitudes, rituals, beliefs, as well as its own complex epistemology.[1] Comparing Christianity, Judaism, and Islam to the scientific method is thus an unfair contrast, for they are two kinds of entities.

How About Looking at the "Anthropology" of Science?

One option to resolve this dilemma is to suggest that, in the same way that Christian religion is more than a set of principles, being a full-blown culture, we might talk about a culture of science arising out of the scientific habit of mind—members of this scientific community might be skeptical of a proposition until it is repeatedly demonstrated, carefully scrutinize the method underlying the acquisition of knowledge, think of objects in the natural world in relation to the system of objects surrounding them, or radically alter their beliefs to accommodate new information. For example, evidence linking the disease of autism to genetic factors has been slowly built up over decades of research (see Muhle et al. 2005). However, despite this central dogma about the cause of autism, researchers quickly accepted that environmental factors can independently cause the disease once a few studies reporting this fact emerged. This

---

[1]Epistemology is the study of what kind of thing knowledge is, what the correct way to get knowledge is, and what the extent of our knowledge can be.

willingness to rapidly accommodate conflicting evidence arises not only in the scientific professional pursuing research as a vocational end in itself, but to anyone who uses the scientific method to understand the natural world. Thus, we can distinguish between the profession of working as a scientist and the application of the scientific method to understanding the natural world. Just as Christian culture arises out of the interpretation and practice of Biblical principles, we can conceive of a scientific culture arising out of the application of the scientific method to empirical questions.

Science in the Workplace Versus Science as a Principle to Live By

Confusion about the distinction between science defined as the scientific method and science as a world view is the basis of many unnecessary debates between proponents and opponents of evolution. That is, distinguishing between individuals who use the scientific method to understand the natural world and professionals who use it as a tool to fulfill a particular vocational task is important. For example, some might take the existence of an antievolution petition signed by 514 scientists and engineers to be a significant blow to the evolutionary hypothesis (Chang). But Kenneth Chang in the *Detroit News* points out that "of the 128 biologists who signed, few conduct research that would directly address the question of what shaped the history of life" and continues by noting that "the other signers include 76 chemists, 75 engineers, 63 physicists and 24 professors of medicine." Chang fails to realize that one need not be a biologists to understand the evidence for evolution—dozens of evolutionary studies are easily accessible to a non-biologist with college-level English skills. What would be relevant is if these scientists used the scientific method not only in their professional lives but also in their personal lives, and still concluded that the evidence for evolution was shaky. Because of a similar oversight the organizers of the petition do little to show that petition signers apply the scientific method to address scientific questions beyond the limited requirements of their profession: the scientific method can be used as a tool to accomplish a specific task in a specific discipline without requiring one to adopt it as a principle to live by. Obviously the signers might reject evolution citing religious reasons, reasons which do not rely on a scientific basis. A failure to understand what evidence would be relevant to the other party in the debate means both Chang and the petition organizers do not establish their arguments, and their debate is unhelpful.

Problems with the "Anthropology" of SAR

Let us reconsider our first two distinctions: (1) the principle of science as the scientific method and the culture that arises out of that principle; (2) propositional religious belief as presented in a religious holy book such as the Bible versus the culture that arises out of such propositions. Looking at the "anthropology" of SAR is an intriguing possibility as an intellectual endeavour in and of itself. But I maintain that the two principles ought not to be compared this way because comparing the cultures of SAR does little to answer the epistemic question of which approach to belief an individual ought to endorse. Before deciding whether an individual will defend the epistemic approach underlying a culture, it would beg the question to look at what that culture looked like. Because the debate about evolution should be a debate about propositional facts, not about the culture that arises out of those facts, this is the real question we should be concerned with. Truth becomes a meaningless concept if it depends on, for example, how happy accepting a proposition makes us. Furthermore, I would argue that most religious people and scientists hold their beliefs because they deem them true beliefs, not because of convenience. This is an important premise, for if the only way to achieve salvation or get a Nobel Prize is to believe in facts because they are convenient, then the notion of truth becomes distorted. If scientists believe in science because it can be applied to create new technology that improves human existence (i.e., makes one happy) but religious people believe in their religion because they genuinely believe it to be true, there can be little debate. Similarly, if religious people hold their beliefs because of a desire for salvation, while scientists hold their beliefs because of a genuine interest in finding truth, there can be little debate. A common notion of truth undistorted by personal gain is a prerequisite to any debate between SAR.

This principle can be illustrated with a few examples. The above argument arises in debates of radical Islam where on party points to the fact that the contents of the Koran are benign—just as the principles underlying science and religion might be—but the way that Islam is sometimes practiced is shameful. The motivations of the September 11 hijackers, if indeed religiously motivated, mark the epitome of this shamefulness. It is believed the hijackers used a passage in the Koran claiming that martyrs of Jihad will be granted salvation to justify their actions. But note that this passage does not say anything about the moral rightness of flying a plane into the World Trade Center; it merely assures the fulfillment of the hijackers' selfish desires for salvation assuming their cause is just. If we set aside the question of justice here, the morality of the hijackers' actions is undermined by passages in the Koran emphasizing the wrongness of killing, the importance of being spiritually pure (or fighting one's internal jihad) before engaging in the external jihad, and the necessity of avoiding harm to innocents in conflict. For these reasons and others, most Muslims claimed the actions of the September 11 hijackers to be indefensible on religious grounds. Thus, this criticism of extreme Muslims indicates scientific and religious epistemic principles can be abused even if the principles themselves are morally neutral.

Steven Weinberg makes a similar attack on religion in the following passage:

> I could point out endless examples of the harm done by religious enthusiasm, through a long history of pogroms, crusades, and jihads. In our own century it was a Muslim zealot who killed Sadat, a Jewish zealot who killed

Rabin, and a Hindu zealot who killed Gandhi. No one would say that Hitler was a Christian zealot, but it is hard to imagine Nazism taking the form it did without the foundation provided by centuries of Christian anti-Semitism. (539)

Weinberg's criticism of religion makes the same mistake that many scientists 10 accuse the religious of: it attacks religious belief because of the consequences of those beliefs, not because the beliefs are false in themselves. Once again we see how this is analogous to an ad hominem fallacy applied to a system instead of an individual.

Delos B. McKown also mistakenly attacks Christianity. Consider the following claims:

First, it can no longer be maintained that the church is founded on the New Testament; rather the church compiled the New Testament, and out of intensely partisan documents written by churchmen with theological axes to grind. . . . Second, much in the gospels concerning Jesus is suspect. Neither history nor biography, they were written that their recipients might believe in him (John 20:31). . . . Third, the church has always represented Christianity as the religion of and from Jesus, but it is not the religion of Jesus. [Christianity] is the religion about Jesus emanating from St. Paul's paranormal experiences, unmitigated gall, and desire to dominate the movement (Gal. 1:11, 2:11-16; 2 Cor. 11-12). (McKown 589)

How do the above claims address the truth of the proposition that Jesus is the son of God who ensures the resurrection of the body and soul to those who believe in his teachings? Clearly, beyond attacking the motivations of the early church leaders, the above claims do little to answer this latter question. In addition to being useless in resolving the debate between science and religion, ad hominem claims distance both parties in the debate, making further progress difficult. These examples happen to be cases of unwarranted attack on religious belief, but this is not to say that scientific principles have not been mistakenly attacked on similar grounds.

In Defense of the "Anthropology" of SAR

However, in defense of the two parties, even though it might be that one can apply the scientific method as a tool in one's professional life without being committed to it in one's personal life, there still ends up being a psychological correlation between the two. Even though one might accept the theoretical argument that science as a principle and religion stripped of its cultural interpretation are what ought to be compared in debates of evolution, there remains an inevitable psychological connection between culture and principle that makes it difficult to separate the two.

Thus, one may reply that although the above criticisms by McKown and Weinberg do not directly undermine a religious world view, they are still fair criticisms insofar as they are motivated by an awareness of the underlying connection between principle and culture in SAR. For example, in the preceding section Weinberg's argument was dismissed because it does not follow that the moral consequences of religious extremists' beliefs undermine the truth of religious propositions. But Weinberg might want his argument to be interpreted in a more subtle way. Above I argued that a debate between religion and science is only possible if both parties value truth as a concept independent of the consequences of that truth on human existence—we ought not to believe in something simply because it is useful. Although I emphasized the importance of this assumption in order for debate to be possible, I did not give an argument as to why a debate *must* be possible. By emphasizing that religious principle and practice are inseparable—each being understood and reunderstood by the other in a constant flux, so that neither takes precedence— Weinberg might be saying that the evils arising out of religious practice point to a flaw with the underlying principles themselves.

To test this proposal one can look at the practices, culture, "rituals," etc. of those who pursue scientific research in order to compare SAR, that is, look at the "anthropology" of science. After doing this laborious study we could begin to compare ethical, epistemic, and metaphysical attitudes across the two disciplines. This is what many sociologists have done, and there is no real consensus about the nature of the relationship between the expanded conceptions of science and religion. Three of the most influential modern sociologists of religion, Rodney Stark, Laurence Iannaccone, and Roger Finke, published a paper called "Rationality and the Religious Mind," in which they respond to a view of religion "as the irrational product of primitive minds and prescientific times" (Stark 1). Their main conclusion, summing up years of sociological research they have devoted to SAR, is that:

> Despite continuing talk about the secularizing effects of education and academia, our analysis of data from the 1972 through 1996 General Social Surveys find that most highly educated Americans, including most professors and scientists, are as religious as other Americans. Moreover, the college faculty most acquainted with "hard" scientific knowledge—physicists, chemists, biologists, and mathematicians—are by every measure substantially more religious than their counterparts in the social sciences and humanities. It is only among anthropologists and non-clinical psychologists that we observe very high rates of disbelief and anti-religious sentiment. (2)

I refer the reader to the appendix of this article for the results of four major surveys of religious attitudes that support the view that science is not an antireligious discipline. More recent research completed in 2006, however, has concluded that the opposite is the case:

> Scientists in the social sciences are more likely to believe in God and attend religious services than are scientists in the natural sciences, according to a

survey of 1,646 faculty members at elite research universities by a Rice University sociologist. . . . [Elaine Howard Ecklund's] survey contained 36 questions on a variety of topics, including religious beliefs, participation in religious services, spiritual practices, and the intersection of spiritual beliefs and research ethics. (Murray)

The bulk of these results support the concordance of the practice of SAR, or are at least inconclusive. Concluding that science and religion conflict therefore requires different data.

An Argument for Common Sense

Since sociological research does not undermine the compatibility of science and religion, one might try a different approach: when science and religion conflict, can we avoid the problem on practical grounds? One might object to relegating the SAR debate to such an academic level and propose to look at it in a common-sense way. Let us consider this possibility. In situations where only religion has an answer to a question—for example, is Jesus the son of God?—it does not make sense to apply the scientific method. Similarly, religion has little to say about whether the boiling point of ethanol is 60 or 65 degrees. But where the two subjects intersect, people are faced with a kind of binomial choice; for example, you either believe in evolution or you do not. As for the counterexample of how sociologists have shown that scientists tend to be quite religious—the existence of religious scientists can be explained by noting that most religious beliefs are kinds of knowledge beyond the empirical grasp of science, such as moral or metaphysical. So, in the few situations when SAR conflict, scientists might give science precedence, but, overall, they can still be fairly described as religious. The example of religious scientists thus does not deal with the conflict of SAR; it simply points out that the conflict in belief might not be so glaring as to force an individual to choose between an entirely scientific or entirely religious world view.

Problems with Common Sense

The obvious response to this question is that of course we cannot avoid the problem on practical grounds since people are having debates about creationism and evolution on a daily basis. Why would one suggest that we can avoid the conflict of religion and science when clearly they already conflict? Here one simply has to point out that going from the fact that this conflict exists to the conclusion that it must exist does not logically follow. Rather, in order to show that a conflict does exist one has to show that it must exist. Showing that a conflict must arise is not an empirical question but instead a logical one—for one can believe that one is observing a causal connection between phenomena where there is in reality only correlation. This observation requires us to return to the theme of looking at the principles of the debate, for at that level logical inconsistencies might arise between the scientific and religious world views that offer a priori evidence for their incompatibility.

Properly addressing this question is a largely technical matter, and I refer 20 the interested reader to Bertrand Russell and Alfred North Whitehead's famous set paradox in philosophy (http://burks.bton.ac.uk/burks/foldoc/ 59/101.htm) or David Hilbert's well-known address to the International Congress of Mathematicians (http://aleph0.clarku.edu/~djoyce/hilbert/ problems.html) for a cursory overview of some of the big theoretical problems an exploration of the compatibility of two principles must overcome. There is, of course, no room here to address these theoretical questions properly.

Audi's Philosophy of Religion—Fusing Theory with Common Sense

So if comparing the culture of science and religion is not a fair comparison, what should the individual do? How does one compare epistemic principles without looking at the effects of those principles? We have already concluded that we ought to consider not the culture that arises out of both principles, but the principles themselves. Some would argue that this approach cannot be fruitful because we need a standard by which to judge a way of acquiring beliefs. After accepting a scientific or religious world view, we can't fairly judge other world views because we will be biased by the one we have adopted. This dynamic, it could be argued, leads to the unavoidable polarization of religious and scientific debates.

The answer to this question might lie in finding a third, broader epistemic criterion to evaluate the other two. This is what Robert Audi does in his forthcoming book *Rationality and Religious Commitment*, and I refer the reader to the later chapters of this work for a deeper discussion of how to begin to resolve the SAR debate at the most fundamental level. Audi builds an epistemic theory out of many common-sense epistemic principles. I will use a quintessentially Audian example to illustrate how he accommodates both scientific and religious world views: Audi shows how people constantly rely on the testimony of others as evidence in everyday interaction. If one goes to the supermarket and asks for a price check on a pack of gum, we assume the cashier is telling us the truth. Granted this trust in others is not absolute—when President George W. Bush claimed that Iraq had weapons of mass destruction, many were skeptical. Still, if people brought up in a religious tradition have no reason to believe that their parents and other members of the community are deceiving them and they trust the word of these individuals in nonreligious matters, there is no a priori reason to believe they are being tricked in religious matters. Similarly, if older members of the community have been brought up such that they held similar assumptions, a chain of testimony can be traced back indefinitely. Although this might appear as an overly simplistic, even childish theory— many children are, of course, tricked about the existence of Santa Claus—it simultaneously forces us to ask fundamental questions about the ultimate root of knowledge.

Testimony is a basis of both scientific and religious education since both rely on trusting teachers and peers. Some might object that science does not require such trust since any experiment can be replicated and proved by an individual scientist. But note that although an individual could theoretically replicate every scientific experiment if she had infinite time, the inevitability of human mortality implies that a certain amount of trust must be a foundation of an individual's perspective of science. Even if an individual scientist is considering a peer-reviewed study, he is still faced with the same problem, for, instead of trusting only the experimenter, one must also trust the reviewers. From an individual perspective, then, an understanding of when testimony can and cannot serve as the basis of knowledge is certainly relevant to clarifying the SAR debate.

Final Thoughts

We explored empirical (e.g., sociology), philosophical (e.g., compatibility of principles approach), and common-sense epistemic means to discuss the SAR debate. An overview of the difficulties and advantages of each approach were listed. Finally, Audi's position was defended as a common-sense approach to empirically evaluate the epistemic principles of SAR. SAR are not mutually opposed. Both systems arise from the application of universal human faculties that use similar epistemic principles—like testimony. Resolving the debate is accordingly a matter of understanding how Audi's broader principles support basic scientific and religious propositions like the scientific method or the existence of God. Wordsworth's poetry can be relevant if it addresses science and religion as two world views to be accepted or rejected based on a third criterion; but it will be dismissed when assessment of SAR precludes acceptance of either one.

As Audi emphasizes in his book, the diverse experiences of different 25 individuals lead to varying assessments of SAR through the broad epistemic principles he describes. The differing experiences of individuals thus calls for a certain amount of tolerance and humility in debating these sensitive questions. Attacking the character of the other party in the debate is not fair—or necessary—because many valid means exist for SAR to find common ground. For all the aforementioned reasons, the ad hominem fallacy does not advance the SAR debate. For all the above cited reasons, individuals participating in the SAR debate have legitimate means to engage the other party. ◎/◎

Works Cited

Audi, Robert. Rationality and Religious Commitment. *Oxford UP, forthcoming. Manuscript dated 1 Feb. 2002 to 28 Mar. 2004.*

Chang, Kenneth. *"Anti-evolution petition doubted: Review of petition's signers show many are evangelicals who may have a built-in bias."* Detroit News 2 March 2006. Detnews.com 2 Mar. 2006. http://www.detnews.com/apps/pbcs.dll/article?AID=/ 20060302/LIFESTYLE04/ 603020345/1020/NATION.

Google.com. *"Intelligent Design and Evolution."* 2 March 2006. http://news.google.com/ news?h1=en&ned=us&ie=UTF-8&q=intelligent+design+and+evolution&scoring= d&sa=N&start=190.

Hilbert, David. *"Mathematical Problems: Lecture delivered before the International Congress of Mathematicians at Paris in 1900."* Ed. David Joyce. 19 Mar. 2006. http://aleph0.clarku.edu/ ~djoyce/hilbert/problems.html.

McKown, Delos B. *"Science vs. Religion in Future Constitutional Conflicts."* The Well-Crafted Argument: A Guide and Reader, 1st Ed. Fred D. White and Simone J. Billings (Boston: Houghton Mifflin, 2005) 586–591.

Muhle, Rebecca, Stephanie Trentacoste, and Isabelle Rapin. *"The Genetics of Autism."* Pediatrics 113.5 (2004): 472–486.

Murray, Bob. *"Do Scientists Believe In God?"* Uplift Program Newsletter 1 Nov. 2005. 19 Mar. 2006. http://www.upliftprogram.com/healthupdates.html.

"Russell's Paradox." The Free Online Dictionary of Computing. Ed. Denis Howe. 1 Nov. 2000. 17 Mar. 2006. http://burks.bton.ac.uk/burks/foldoc/59/101.htm.

Iannaccone, Laurence, Rodney Stark and Roger Finke. *"Rationality and the 'Religious Mind.'"* Economic Inquiry 36 (1998): 373–89.

Weinberg, Steven. *"A Designer Universe?"* The Well-Crafted Argument: A Guide and Reader, 3rd Ed., Ed. Fred D. White and Simone J. Billings (Boston: Houghton Mifflin, 2008) 533–541.

Wordsworth, William. *"Where Lies the Truth? Has Man, In Wisdom's Creed."* 1846. Bartleby.com 6 Mar. 2006. http://www.bartleby.com/145/ww989.html.

Reflections and Inquiries

1. According to Raad, "Galileo's astronomical discoveries in the sixteenth century marked the first real conflict between science and religion." Do you agree, and if so, why would this be the case? (You might wish to review the selection by Galileo, and the commentary preceding it, in Chapter 2, pages 75–76.)

2. Raad distinguishes between working in science and adopting a scientific world view. How important is this distinction, in your view? How does the distinction relate to Raad's thesis?

3. Comment on Raad's organizational strategy for his term paper. Why does he begin by explaining what he will *not* discuss? How useful are his subheadings? How would you describe the logical progression of his argument?

Reading to Write

After conducting research on scientists' religious experiences (or lack of them), write an essay in which you discuss the possibilities of practicing one's religion and at the same time pursuing a scientific career.

Issues for Further Research: Teaching Human Origins in the Public Schools

Dorothy, It's Really Oz | Stephen Jay Gould

One of the best-loved science writers of the late twentieth century, Stephen Jay Gould (1941–2002) was a professor of geology at Harvard and the author of numerous books on science, such as The Panda's Thumb *(winner of the 1981 American Book Award for science),* Dinosaur in a Haystack: Reflections in Natural History *(1995), and* Rocks of Ages: Science and Religion in the Fullness of Life *(1999). In the following essay, Gould explains why the 1999 Kansas Board of Education ruling to remove basic scientific theories from the state schools' science curricula was not such a good idea.*

The Kansas Board of Education voted 6 to 4 to remove evolution, and the Big Bang theory as well, from the state's science curriculum. In so doing, the board transported its jurisdiction to a never-never land where a Dorothy of the new millennium might exclaim, "They still call it Kansas, but I don't think we're in the real world anymore." The new standards do not forbid the teaching of evolution, but the subject will no longer be included in statewide tests for evaluating students—a virtual guarantee, given the realities of education, that this central concept of biology will be diluted or eliminated, thus reducing courses to something like chemistry without the periodic table, or American history without Lincoln.

The Kansas skirmish marks the latest episode of a long struggle by religious Fundamentalists and their allies to restrict or eliminate the teaching of evolution in public schools—a misguided effort that our courts have quashed at each stage, and that saddens both scientists and most theologians. No scientific theory, including evolution, can pose any threat to religion—for these two great tools of human understanding operate in complementary (not contrary) fashion in their totally separate realms: science as an inquiry about the factual state of the natural world, religion as a search for spiritual meaning and ethical values.

In the early 1920s, several states simply forbade the teaching of evolution outright, opening an epoch that inspired the infamous 1925 Scopes trial (leading to the conviction of a Tennessee high school teacher) and that ended only in 1968, when the Supreme Court declared such laws unconstitutional on First Amendment grounds. In a second round in the late 1970s, Arkansas and Louisiana required that if evolution be taught, equal time must be given to Genesis literalism, masquerading as oxymoronic "creation science." The Supreme Court likewise rejected those laws in 1987.

The Kansas decision represents creationism's first—and surely temporary—success with a third strategy for subverting a constitutional imperative: that by simply deleting, but not formally banning, evolution, and by not demanding instruction in a biblically literalist "alternative," their narrowly partisan religious motivations might not derail their goals.

Given this protracted struggle, Americans of goodwill might be excused 5 for supposing that some genuine scientific or philosophical dispute motivates this issue: Is evolution speculative and ill founded? Does evolution threaten our ethical values or our sense of life's meaning? As a paleontologist by training, and with abiding respect for religious traditions, I would raise three points to alleviate these worries:

First, no other Western nation has endured any similar movement, with any political clout, against evolution—a subject taught as fundamental, and without dispute, in all other countries that share our major sociocultural traditions.

Second, evolution is as well documented as any phenomenon in science, as strongly as the earth's revolution around the sun rather than vice versa. In this sense, we can call evolution a "fact." (Science does not deal in certainty, so "fact" can only mean a proposition affirmed to such a high degree that it would be perverse to withhold one's provisional assent.)

The major argument advanced by the school board—that large-scale evolution must be dubious because the process has not been directly observed—smacks of absurdity and only reveals ignorance about the nature of science. Good science integrates observation with inference. No process that unfolds over such long stretches of time (mostly, in this case, before humans appeared), or at an infinitude beneath our powers of direct visualization (subatomic particles, for example), can be seen directly. If justification required eyewitness testimony, we would have no sciences of deep time—no geology, no ancient human history either. (Should I believe Julius Caesar ever existed? The hard bony evidence for human evolution . . . surely exceeds our reliable documentation of Caesar's life.)

Third, no factual discovery of science (statements about how nature "is") can, in principle, lead us to ethical conclusions (how we "ought" to behave) or to convictions about intrinsic meaning (the "purpose" of our lives). These last two questions—and what more important inquiries could we make?—lie firmly in the domains of religion, philosophy and humanistic study. Science and religion should be equal, mutually respecting partners, each the master of its own domain, and with each domain vital to human life in a different way.

Why get excited over this latest episode in the long, sad history of 10 American anti-intellectualism? Let me suggest that, as patriotic Americans, we should cringe in embarrassment that, at the dawn of a new, technological millennium, a jurisdiction in our heartland has opted to suppress one of the greatest triumphs of human discovery. Evolution is not a peripheral subject but the central organizing principle of all biological science. No one who has not read the Bible or the Bard can be considered educated in Western traditions; so no one ignorant of evolution can understand science.

Dorothy followed her yellow brick road as it spiraled outward toward redemption and homecoming (to the true Kansas of our dreams and possibilities). The road of the newly adopted Kansas curriculum can only spiral inward toward restriction and ignorance. ◎/◎

Reflections and Inquiries

1. Why does Gould allude to Dorothy from *The Wizard of Oz* as a framing device for his essay?

2. Gould examines three possible questions Americans might have about evolution, given the fact that evolution caused so much contention since the 1920s. How representative are these questions, and how satisfactorily, in your opinion, does Gould answer them?

3. Gould sees antievolution movements as an example of American anti-intellectualism. Is this an accurate characterization? Explain your response.

Reading to Write

Study the rationales behind various school board antievolution rulings since the 1970s. Then, in an essay, discuss what you consider to be the common features of these rationales. How valid or invalid are they? What seems to you to be the most common reasons for their wanting to remove evolution from the science classrooms in their respective states?

Teaching Evolution at a Christian College | David Ludden

Like Stephen Jay Gould, David Ludden is a science teacher (an assistant professor of psychology at Lindsey Wilson College in Columbia, Kentucky); and because this college is church affiliated, many of his students, as he points out, voice objections to evolution. The manner in which he and other science teachers handle the evolution issue in such an environment is the subject of this essay.

I teach psychology at a church-affiliated liberal-arts college in rural Kentucky. Because I take a strong cognitive-neuroscience approach to psychology, the

---

Source: David Ludden, "Teaching Evolution at a Christian College." Copyright © 2006 by the Council for Secular Humanism (CSH). This article originally appeared in *Free Inquiry* magazine, volume 26, number 3 (April–May 2006), published by the CSH in Amherst, New York.

topic of human evolution inevitably comes up. Also inevitably, there are students who object to the theory on religious grounds.

I have a standard set of responses to these objections: First, I remind these students of the fact that mainstream Christian denominations (Catholic, Lutheran, Presbyterian, Episcopal, and so on) accept divinely guided evolution as part of their faiths. Second, I point out that many biologists working within the Darwinian framework are also Christians. And, finally, I inform them that the official position of the college is that evolutionary theory does not contradict the teachings of Christianity. Generally speaking, arguments for the compatibility of Darwinism and Christian faith fail to convince these students; and, I must admit, they fail to convince me as well.

Many science educators argue that there need not be a conflict between the acceptance of evolutionary theory and the maintenance of religious beliefs. For example, *Science* magazine publisher Alan Leshner notes that "Many scientists are deeply religious and see scientific investigation and religious faith as complementary components of a well-rounded life." This observation is true, but it does not address the issue of whether the Darwinian worldview and Christian faith are logically compatible. Rather, what this observation speaks to is the ability of human beings to simultaneously hold contradictory beliefs.

Another way to argue for the compatibility of evolution and religion is to maintain—like Eugenie Scott, the executive director of the National Center for Science Education—that science "in and of itself is neutral toward religion" and that it is "neither antireligious nor pro-religious." Even if these claims are true, the fact remains that at least some forms of religion are hostile to science, and it is invariably the student that adheres to such a science-unfriendly faith who challenges evolutionary theory when it is presented in class. Hence, this argument fails to convince those who do not accept Darwinism and is unnecessary for those who do accept it.

The compatibility argument can be made even more subtle by distinguishing between methodological and philosophical materialism. Methodological materialists assume no supernatural causes for the purposes of doing science. However, only the philosophical materialist takes that skepticism of the supernatural home from the lab. Thus, Scott reassures her religious students that "There are many scientists who use methodological materialism in their work, but who are theists and therefore not philosophical materialists." Again, this line of reasoning is unconvincing to the pious student, who demands to know why the scientist who accepts God outside the lab refuses to accept him inside the lab. I wonder the same thing myself.

Other science educators extend an olive branch to theistic students by claiming that science and religion are simply different ways of arriving at

JUST DIFFERENT PATHS TO THE TRUTH

truth. Arguing along this line, Kansas State University professor of secondary education Lawrence Scharmann cautions that "It is very important for teachers and students to be aware when they are using science and when they are using religion as their basis for explanation." This approach would be reasonable if both science and religion led to similar worldviews, but in fact they do not always do so. The student has already learned "truths" about the world through religious instruction. If the teachings of science and religion conflict, the student is quite reasonable in insisting that one is right and that one is wrong. When presented with a scientific worldview that contradicts what his or her religion has taught him or her, this student sees the different-paths argument as patently false.

I agree with the religious student's logic; yet, to paraphrase geneticist Theodosius Dobzhansky, nothing in psychology makes sense except in the light of evolution. And so, if religion and science lead to contradictory "truths," I must, as a scientist, accept the scientific worldview. On the other hand, the devout student, immersed in religious dogma and not at all interested in a career in which evolutionary theory is relevant, is just as reasonable to reject science and accept the revealed "truth" of his religion.

It is disingenuous for science teachers to ease their students into a discussion of evolutionary theory by assuring them that there will be no challenge to their cherished beliefs. This approach is like that of the drug pusher who gives away the drug for free until the client is hooked and then demands payment in full. But this tack will not work in the science classroom, because science, for most people, does not produce the high that religion does. As science educators, we must teach our field without apology or equivocation, leaving it up to our students to decide how, or whether, they can accommodate science with their faiths. ◎/◎

Reflections and Inquiries

1. Why does the college's official position on the compatibility of evolution and Christian faith fail to convince most of Ludden's students, even Ludden himself?

2. What distinction does Ludden draw between methodological and philosophical materialism, and why is the distinction important in the context of thinking about ways to reconcile science with religion?

3. Some science educators, according to Ludden, appease their religious students by asserting that "science and religion are simply different ways of arriving at truth." Do you agree or disagree with this approach, and why?

Reading to Write

Interview two science professors and two religious studies professors on the ways in which they reconcile (if at all) science with faith in their respective disciplines. Report your findings and draw your conclusions in an essay.

Issues for Further Research: Religion in Public Schools

The Real Message of Creationism | Charles Krauthammer

According to creationists, the theory of evolution has no more solid grounding in undisputed fact than the Biblical story of creation, which at least is the word of God (and therefore beyond disputation). Thus, being on equal footing with evolution, creationism has a rightful place in the science classroom as an alternative theory of human origin. Biologists, however, argue that creationism cannot possibly be on equal footing with science because creationism accepts as a precondition of inquiry the fact that God created the earth and all life on it. There can be no preconditions in scientific inquiry, scientists argue. In the following essay, Charles Krauthammer, an eminent journalist and contributing writer for Time, *argues for a middle ground: While creationism may not qualify as science, it still deserves inclusion in the schools.*

W hen the Kansas Board of Education voted recently to eliminate evolution from the state science curriculum, the sophisticates had quite a yuk. One editorial cartoon had an ape reclining in a tree telling his mate, "We are descended from the Kansas School Board." The decision has been widely

---

Source: Charles Krauthammer, "The Real Message of Creationism," *Time,* Nov 22, 1999: 120. © *Time Inc.* Reprinted by permission. *Time* is a registered trademark of Time Inc. All rights reserved.

*At the 1925 Scopes Trial in Dayton, Tennessee, Clarence
Darrow (left) defended John Scopes, the teacher arrested for
teaching theories of evolution in a public school. He is seen
here with William Jennings Bryan who represented the State
of Tennessee in defense of Biblical Creationism.*

derided as a sign of resurgent Middle American obscurantism, a throwback to
the Scopes "monkey trial."

Well, to begin with, the Scopes trial is not the great fable the rather fic-
tional *Inherit the Wind* made it out to be. The instigators of the trial were not
bluenosed know-nothings wanting to persecute some poor teacher for teaching evolution. They were officials of the American Civil Liberties Union so
eager for a test case to overturn a new Tennessee law prohibiting the teaching
of evolution that they promised to pay the expenses of the prosecution! The
A.C.L.U. advertised for a volunteer and found one John Scopes, football coach
and science teacher, willing to take the rap. He later said he was not sure
whether he'd ever even taught any evolution.

Son of Scopes is not quite what it seems either. The twist in the modern
saga is the injection of creationism as the scientific alternative to evolution. So,
let's be plain. Creationism, which presents *Genesis* as literally and historically
true, is not science. It is faith crudely disguised as science.

It is not science because it violates the central scientific canon that a
theory must, at least in principle, be disprovable. Creationism is not. Any
evidence that might be brought—fossil, geological, astronomical—to contradict the idea that the universe is no more than 6,000 years old is simply
explained away as false clues deliberately created by God at the very
beginning.

Why? To test our faith? To make fools of modern science? This is hardly 5
even good religion. God may be mysterious, but he is certainly not malicious.
And who but a malicious deity would have peppered the universe with endless phony artifacts designed to confound human reason?

Creationism has no part in the serious curriculum of any serious country.
Still, I see no reason why biblical creation could not be taught in the schools—
not as science, of course, but for its mythic grandeur and moral dimensions.
If we can assign the *Iliad* and the *Odyssey*, we certainly ought to be able to
assign *Genesis*.

But can we? There's the rub. It is very risky to assign *Genesis* today. The
A.C.L.U. might sue. Ever since the Supreme Court decision of 1963 barring
prayer from the public schools, any attempt to import not just prayer but
biblical studies, religious tenets and the like into the schools is liable to end
up in court.

That is why the Kansas school board decision on evolution is so significant. Not because Kansas is the beginning of a creationist wave—as
science, creationism is too fundamentally frivolous and evolution too intellectually powerful—but because the Kansas decision is an important
cultural indicator.

It represents the reaction of people of faith to the fact that all legitimate
expressions of that faith in their children's public schooling are blocked by the
new secular ethos. In a society in which it is unconstitutional to post the Ten
Commandments in school, creationism is a back door to religion, brought in
under the guise—the absurd yet constitutionally permitted guise—of science.

This pedagogic sleight of hand, by the way, did not originate with reli- 10
gious folk. Secularists have for years been using biology instruction as a back
door for inculcating their values. A sex-ed class on the proper placement of a
condom is more than instruction in reproductive mechanics. It is a seminar—
unacknowledged and tacit but nonetheless powerful—on permissible sexual
mores.

Religion—invaluable in America's founding, forming and flowering—
deserves a place in the schools. Indeed, it had that place for almost 200 years.
A healthy country would teach its children evolution and the Ten
Commandments. The reason that Kansas is going to have precisely the
opposite—the worst of both worlds—is not because Kansans are primitives,
but because a religious people has tried to bring the fruits of faith, the teachings and higher values of religion, into the schools and been stymied.

The result is a kind of perverse Law of Conservation of Faith. Block all
teaching of religious ideas? O.K., we'll sneak them in through biology.

This is nutty. It has kids looking for God in all the wrong places. For the
purposes of a pluralist society, the Bible is not about fact. It is about values.
If we were a bit more tolerant about allowing the teaching of biblical values
as ethics, we'd find far less pressure for the teaching of biblical fables as
science. ◎╱◎

Reflections and Inquiries

1. What is Krauthammer's reason for saying that "creationism . . . is not science"? Do you agree or disagree? How might David Ludden respond?

2. What does it mean that a theory "must be disprovable" to qualify as science?

3. Krauthammer interprets the Kansas Board of Education's decision to eliminate evolution from the state's public school curriculum to be a public reaction against the "new secular ethos" that seems to be blocking expressions of faith in the schools. Do you agree that such secular resistance to faith exists? Explain.

4. Religion, asserts Krauthammer, "deserves . . . a place in the schools." Do you agree or disagree? If the former, how would you reconcile it with the separation of church and state?

Reading to Write

In a short essay, defend or challenge Krauthammer's claim that "the Bible is not about fact. It is about values." How convincingly does Krauthammer support this claim? How should *fact* and *values* be defined in this context?

Student Essay

The Battle over Creationism | Patrick Green

In the following essay, Patrick Green, a Santa Clara University graduate who majored in religious studies, defends creationism, asserting that fundamentalist criticism of evolution "falls nothing short of an act of worship." Nevertheless, Green takes issue with Biblical literalism. "Creation stories," he writes, "are symbols of God's transcendent power." Decide whether Green makes his case convincingly.

Today we find the battle over creationism staged on many fronts. Christians of many sorts conflict over its basis as a theory. Educators butt heads over how it will influence children. Often this argument seems like a tennis match between two equally competitive players, statements and theories flying across the court without either giving a point to the other. Advocates of both science and religion argue so adamantly for their cause because it symbolizes their deep dedication. For a fundamentalist, the argument against evolution falls nothing short of an act of worship; for a scientist, the defense of the natural world is a struggle against dogmatism. Despite the passion of both sides, perhaps there is a way both scientists and creationists could speak without disrespecting the other. The outcome of a mutual respect for each other appears less like an argument and more like a discussion. For creationists, discussing evolution would make present the Bible's emphasis on loving the other. For scientists, dogma would be objectified and studied rather than seen as an irrational belief. This discussion facilitates a spiritual analysis of the Christian debate and nullifies the competition over the Bible's interpretation. Ultimately, Christians must reconcile through the acceptance of certain spiritual truths that remain the same no matter how readers interpret the Bible.

If either group were to begin speaking of creationism, it would be best to examine its theological context due to its Biblical foundation. Readers approach the creation stories in two different theological frameworks. The first perspective claims a fundamental/literal perspective of scriptural analysis, which makes the creation stories the exact account of the world's birth. The second theological approach to the creation stories takes place through a metaphorical lens. This form of interpretation does not believe that the world was created the way the Bible says, but rather believes the stories hold a symbolic significance. These frameworks shape how people read the Bible and, therefore, how people apply their faith to the rest of the world.

These two theological lenses differ in nature, but those who follow them share two inherent truths. The first truth regards the Bible and our spirituality: we turn to the Bible for spiritual guidance. It offers a wealth of enriching, spiritual knowledge. Many Christians consider it God's word, hailing directly from the mouth of the Almighty. Most notably, those who rely on the Bible for assistance are those who need it the most. Trust in the Bible intensifies when men and women meet the challenges of life in the most painful of circumstances. The Bible becomes the refuge from the calamities of life. Therefore, those who suffer often associate the Bible and religion directly with God. This process manifests itself often in our society. Members of Alcoholics Anonymous turn to a "higher power" in their steps to recovery. For Catholics, one of many allusions to this tendency is the "Prayers of the Faithful," a time set aside in mass for people to pray together about problems they consider pertinent to their faith. For those who suffer, the Bible is a strong foundation on which to stand, declaring wisdom of the deepest of all mysteries: God.

We read the Bible in harsh times because we need comfort in our troubles and insight into why they happen. Why must I suffer? What have I done? An understanding of our struggles entices those searching for refuge and security; however, does the Bible fully address the search to know God? This question must become of the utmost importance to the Christian. Can God, the most infinite and ultimate force that transcends the cosmos, be understood through the Bible? How we interpret the Bible may answer this question, but how we read the Bible, whether metaphorically or literally, determines theological implications.

While we already agree that all Christians turn to the Bible for spiritual help, we also share a belief central to our spirituality: God is all powerful. The subject of God's nature is the common ground among all believers. As elements of creation, we inherently cannot understand the infinite nature of the all-powerful God. The true nature of God will eternally mystify us. In order to respect God's authority as the Creator of the universe, we implicitly acknowledge this truth. Sadly, it also implies that we can only have insight into God, but not fully know God. For example, we do not love the way God loves because we sin, something God cannot do. This truth speaks of the relationship between God and humanity, but also respects the Almighty's transcendent power. This means we cannot say we love the way God does because that would be disrespectful. To assert that we did have the power to comprehend God would claim that we had a quality unique to God, and would therefore be blasphemous.[1]

In light of our separation from God, we occasionally feel God's presence through experiences we have. Maybe those experiences occur through the Bible, or science, or our families, nature, artwork, the list goes on. God's infinity cannot be limited, and so all things possibly manifest God. In themselves, these things are not God, but they point to a reality deeper than themselves. This is the nature of a symbol,[2] and through symbols we know God. The ultimate cannot be understood purely, again, to do so would make us God.

The creation stories are symbols of God's transcendent power. The word *symbol* is not a bad one. Creation stories symbolize something deeper that cannot be known perfectly through human knowledge. Symbols are incredibly important, and religions use them often. For example, Christianity uses the crucifix as a symbol for Christ's sacrifice. Water becomes the symbol for cleansing, as practiced through baptism. The symbol serves as the key which unlocks the door to a deeper meaning.[3] Can physical things fully encompass all that is God? No, but we have things that point to a deeper reality that we can understand. At best, what we know of God is symbolic.

The finite, physical symbols we have of God partially make present the infinite truths that can only be attributed to God. These symbols become deeply important to us because of their powerful ability to communicate the power of love, forgiveness, and creation itself. Since God graces us through symbols, does it matter that creation occurred the way the Bible says? This question becomes especially important within of the context of Christians who demonize those who believe contrary to them, an act which undermines God's call to love one another.

As stated previously, we know God through experiences, scriptures, people, and many other wonderful but finite things. However, we cannot fully comprehend God through them, so we believe in symbols that help us become closer to God. And so when Christians fight over the creation stories, do they fight over what the stories symbolize? They symbolize something all Christians know, no matter how they interpret the Bible. Christians cannot

---

[1]Tillich, Paul. *Dynamics of Faith*. New York: Perennial Classics, 2001: 13.
[2]Ibid., 48.
[3]Ibid., 48.

fight over the nature of the creation stories. What Christians fight over is the symbol itself, a finite thing.

The creation stories provide something deeper than empirical evidence. 10 They make present a transcendent reality. For example, an object of creation is the Red Knot, a miraculous little bird that flies the length of the Americas each year. We can say that this bird has wings, eats approximately 135,000 horseshoe crab eggs in a few weeks, and then flies 18,000 miles.[4] These are empirical facts supported by science. However, just because we can measure the Red Knot's wing span, weigh it, and study its habits does not mean that we know the miracle of the bird's creation. Only our sense of awe and genuine care for the Knot's creation enlightens us to the power of God, something science cannot study. The same is true with the creation stories. The same is true of creation. We cannot study the transcendence that takes place in the creation stories.

Whether we believe creation occurred the way the Bible says or we do not, does not matter. Whichever way we do, we must be careful to not objectify God's creative act. The creation is more than a story; it is a symbol, something that surpasses our knowledge.

We Christians read the Bible differently, but our differences are not irreconcilable. God unites us through creation, a symbol of God's all-powerful transcendence. To truly respect the nature of God in this creative act, we must acknowledge that there are parts of it we cannot comprehend, and all that we know of it stands only as a symbol of its meaning. These truths reconcile Christians rather than tear them apart. ◎⁄◎

Reflections and Inquiries

1. How accurately does Green represent the views of creationists or the theological contexts for creationism?

2. Green argues that the word *symbol* is not a bad one. What does he mean by this?

3. Why is it important for Christians to acknowledge that there are parts of God's nature that cannot be comprehended? How does this relate to Green's thesis?

Reading to Write

Read the story of creation in the Book of Genesis, and then read three or four theological interpretations of the story. What are the similarities and differences in these interpretations. What conclusions do you draw from these differences?

---

[4]Raymo, Chet. "Miracles and Explanations." *The Well-Crafted Argument*, 3rd Ed., Ed. Fred D. White and Simone J. Billings, Boston: Houghlin Mifflin, 2008: 554.

Connections Among the Clusters

1. What issues in multicultural learning (see Cluster 4) might involve matters relating to religion-science interconnections?

2. To what extent is the creation-evolution debate a censorship issue? (See Cluster 3, Media Regulation.)

3. What connections can you make between stem cell or therapeutic cloning research and intellectual property issues? (See Cluster 2.)

Writing Projects

1. Write a detailed evaluation of the "argument from design" debate, starting, perhaps, with its originator William Paley (see his *Natural Theology* [1802]). Give equal attention to both sides of the argument. In your conclusion, decide which side offers the most compelling argument and explain why.

2. Using Classical, Toulmin, or Rogerian strategies, argue on behalf of the usefulness—or uselessness—of attempting to reconcile one's religious beliefs with scientific understanding.

Suggestions for Further Reading

Behe, Michael J. "Design for Living" [a defense of Intelligent Design]. *New York Times* 7 Feb. 2005: A27.

Bowler, Peter J. *Reconciling Science and Religion: The Debate in Early-Twentieth-Century Britain.* Chicago: U of Chicago P, 2001.

Coyne, Jerry. "The Faith That Dare Not Speak Its Name: The Case against Intelligent Design. *New Republic* 22 & 29 August 2005: 21–33.

Davies, Paul. *God and the New Physics.* New York: Simon, 1983.

Gould, Stephen Jay. "Evolution as Fact and Theory." *Hen's Teeth and Horse's Toes.* New York: Norton, 1983. 253–62.

———. *Rocks of Ages: Science and Religion in the Fullness of Life.* New York: Ballantine, 1999.

Gyatso, Tenzin, "Our Faith in Science." *New York Times* 12 Nov. 2005: A27.

Larson, Edward J. *Trial and Error: The American Controversy over Creation and Evolution.* New York: Oxford UP, 1985.

Miller, Kenneth R. *Finding Darwin's God: A Scientist's Search for Common Ground Between God and Evolution.* New York: Cliff Street, 1999.

Pennock, Robert T., ed. *Intelligent Design Theory and Its Critics.* Cambridge: MIT, 2001.

Polkinghorne, John. *One World: The Interaction of Science and Theology.* Princeton: Princeton UP, 1988.

Quammen, David. "Darwin's Big Idea." *National Geographic* Nov. 2004: 2–30.

Raymo, Chet. *Skeptics and True Believers: The Exhilarating Connection Between Science and Religion.* New York: Walker, 1998.

Rennie, John. "15 Answers to Creationist Nonsense." *Scientific American* July 2002: 78–85.

Ruse, Michael. "Answering the Creationists: Where They Go Wrong and What They're Afraid Of." *Free Inquiry* 18 (Spring 1998): 28–33.

Sullivan, Charles, and Cameron McPherson Smith. "Getting the Monkey Off Darwin's Back: Four Common Myths about Evolution." *Skeptical Inquirer* May/June 2005: 43–48.

Teilhard de Chardin, Pierre. *Science and Christ.* Trans. Rene Hague. New York: Harper, 1965.

Weiss, Rick. "The Stem Cell Divide." *National Geographic* July 2005: 2–27.

7 Biomedical Research: What Role Should Ethics Play?

Introduction

The human genome has been mapped. A mother can test her unborn child for genetic defects. Implantation of embryonic stem cells (and perhaps other types of stem cells) may someday reverse the effects of paralysis, Alzheimer's, and neuromuscular diseases. Consciousness has now become a subject of scientific scrutiny. "Questions once confined to theological speculations and late-night dorm-room bull sessions," writes Harvard psychologist Steven Pinker in his article "The Mystery of Consciousness" (part of *Time*'s January 29, 2007 special issue on the human brain), "are now at the forefront of cognitive neuroscience" (60). Exciting? Frightening? Yes to both, many would agree.

Others would insist that we are going too far: certain aspects of our being—like our cellular beginnings or the domain of the soul (where consciousness is traditionally located)—should not be anatomized by the icy rationality of science. To delve into what many consider to be the sacred mysteries of life is to risk dehumanization through eugenics, mind control, and transforming human beings (or their organs) into marketable commodities. Many insist, to put it more bluntly, such research is flat-out immoral, despite the arguments that such research is profoundly moral because it can alleviate suffering and help us to better know ourselves.

As the following cluster of articles suggest, the debate is far from resolved. As with any controversy, it is important to examine all points of view with care, understanding, and objectivity, no matter how tempting it is to dismiss those views with which we disagree. When it comes to issues of a scientific nature, there's an additional challenge: lack of familiarity with the scientific topic in question. This does not mean that one has to be a biochemist or neurologist to be able to pass judgment on the ethics of stem cell or brain research; but it does mean that before agreeing or disagreeing, say, that destroying embryonic stem cells is tantamount to destroying living human beings, one needs to have at least a grounding in prenatal biology as well as a grounding in bioethics. Pursuing one without the other is to risk flawed, biased judgment.

Can Biomedical Issues Be Separated from Politics?

Political Science/Politicized Science | Dave Coverly

A good editorial cartoon can, through exaggeration and word play, bring out aspects of a controversy that would otherwise be difficult to articulate. In the case of Dave Coverly's cartoon, reproduced here, the cause in question is the blurring of the distinctions between politics and science that commonly occur in the popular media. Dave Coverly is the creator of the successful, syndicated cartoon series Speed Bump, *which appears in over two hundred periodicals. He has twice received a Reuben Award (in 1995 and 2003) for the best newspaper panel by the National Cartoonists Society. Coverly's website is http://www.speedbump.com.*

Reflections and Inquiries

1. What is the basis of the humor in this cartoon?

2. How would you distinguish between "political science" and "politicized science"? Why do you suppose political science is so named, instead of,

say, "political studies"? How does the idea of science change from political science to the so-called hard sciences, such as chemistry or physics?

3. Comment on the "books" on the rack. In what ways have stem cell research, contraception, global warming, and air pollution been politicized?

4. What other "books" of politicized science would you be willing to place on the rack?

Reading to Write

Write an essay on whether you believe a particular science should be "politicized." If so, what kinds of legislation would you consider appropriate for the scientific research, and why? If not, what would be your reasons for keeping the science insulated from, say, governmental control?

Who Should Read Your Mind? | Francine Russo

What if it were possible for neurologists to scan people's brains for signs of racism—not necessarily to eliminate it through the use of psychoactive (mind-altering) drugs, similar to the way certain drugs are currently being used to fight depression—see Russo's sidebar, "How to Change a Personality," but at least to enable law enforcement agencies to identify it in those, say, arrested on suspicion of committing a hate crime? Would such a procedure be ethical? At New York University, as Francine Russo reports in the following article, experiments of this kind are being conducted, resulting in a new branch of bioethics known as neuroethics. Francine Russo is a staff writer for Time.

Brain scanners are becoming more powerful all the time—and privacy experts are worried

Neuroscientists usually scan people's brains looking for tumors or aneurysms or to localize the extent of physical trauma. But in a series of experiments performed at New York University a few years ago, scientists went looking for racism. When they showed subjects pictures of unfamiliar white and black faces and scanned their brains with functional MRI machines, they could see heightened activity in the amygdala, a part of the brain that corresponds with emotional arousal. Moreover, the brain activity matched up with psychological tests designed to measure unconscious racism. "This technology is probably not ready for prime time yet," says University of Pennsylvania neuroscientist Martha Farah, but she can foresee a day when police academies, for example,

---

Illustrations for TIME *by Jonathon Rosen*

might scan prospective cadets to weed out racists. "If we could, in fact, define racism," Farah says, "this would be a potentially useful tool—but with very serious issues of privacy and informed consent."

Welcome to the exploding new field of neuroethics, the study of the ethical and philosophical dilemmas provoked by advances in brain science. It's only since a seminal conference in 2002 that the field has even existed; shortly thereafter, Penn and Stanford founded the first academic centers for neuroethics in the country. Last year a multidisciplinary group—including philosophers, lawyers and psychologists—created the Neuroethics Society to explore the issues in a formal way.

Just in time. As brain science becomes increasingly sophisticated, the moral and legal quandaries it poses threaten to proliferate into every part of our lives. And as the racism experiment makes clear, brain imaging has already started to do so. Even in their current state, brain scans may be able to reveal, without our consent, hidden things about who we are and what we think and feel. "I don't have a problem with looking into your brain," says Alan Leshner, former director of the National Institute on Drug Abuse and current head of the American Association for the Advancement of Science. "But I'm not so sure I want you looking into mine."

These technologies may become an intimate part of our lives sooner than we think. "It's not so futuristic," says Stanford neuropsychologist Judy Illes, "to imagine an employer able to test for who is a good team player, who a leader or a follower." Before such scans are used, neuroethicists warn, we must understand what they can and cannot do. A device that might be helpful in personnel testing, for example, might not be rigorous enough to be used in a criminal trial, where the standard of proof is higher. That's currently the case with the polygraph. But Farah is afraid that because of the high-tech aura of brain scans, people may put more faith in them than is warranted.

Perhaps even more critical is the question of who should be allowed to   5 peek into our brains. Employers? Schools? The government? The answers are far from clear. Employers, for example, already give psychological tests to job applicants, and schools test 3- and 4-year-olds to anticipate reading problems. Brain scans may actually give better results. But brain scans are also much more powerful and far more invasive, and the law is murky on whether they can be performed without our consent. We may feel instinctively that we have a right to brain privacy, but feelings have no legal standing.

The courts may soon be forced to address these questions. Columbia University psychiatry professor Paul Appelbaum points out that current criminal law allows government agencies to invade bodily privacy when, for example, it lets police draw blood after a suspected drunk driving accident. But not always. Americans, for example, can't currently be compelled to give a DNA sample. Nor can they be forced to submit to an MRI or have electrodes fixed to their skulls without consent or a court order, says Hank Greely, a Stanford law professor. But it's conceivable that prosecutors might become much more aggressive in demanding brain scans—"like a search warrant for the brain," he suggests. "There's little precedent, and we're moving into new and scary territory."

The technology also has national-security implications. At a Neuroethics Society–sponsored symposium at Tufts University last September, ethicists and policymakers debated the potential benefits and threats to individual liberty of brain imaging and stimulation during intelligence gathering, which may be just around the corner. Cephos Corp., a brain-imaging firm based in Pepperell, Mass., hopes to have a lie-detection scan with 90% accuracy ready for use by late 2007, according to CEO Steven Laken, who says the U.S. intelligence community is watching closely. "If someone says, 'I know where bin Laden is,'" Laken asserts, "the U.S. government could hire us to verify the intelligence."

Intelligence agencies aren't the only customers for such services. A growing number of firms now offer brain scans to companies and individuals, promising to measure such intangibles as the compatibility of prospective partners, the truthfulness of a spouse or even a subject's soft-drink preferences. "We try to identify these hot spots," Illes says, "and help researchers be aware of how their work may be used, even for nefarious purposes."

Some companies insist they are determined not to cross ethical lines. Human Bionics, a neuroimaging firm that sells cognitive-assessment and lie-detection services, has hired Illes as an adviser and come up with a 180-page ethics policy that places limits on what the company can extract from the scans and who can access them without a subpoena.

Such ethical questions will eventually invade the home, Greely predicts. 10 Suppose parents want to grill their teens about sex or drugs under a lie-detection MRI? Or try to make a rebellious kid docile? Ultimately, society will have to decide whether parents may do these things or whether child protective services should intervene. As brain science evolves, these questions will only get harder.

The answers, neuroethicists say, will come not from any pronouncements they might make but from the dialogue they are initiating with the public. "We need to keep this discussion rational," Leshner says, "so that science can advance and society can benefit from the tremendous potential of being able to look into the brain of a living, breathing, behaving individual and watch the mind in action."

HOW TO CHANGE A PERSONALITY

Drugs and implants can be used for more than treating brain disorders. But there are limits

Deep brain stimulation, or DBS, is a treatment given to Parkinson's patients who don't respond to medication. A neurosurgeon implants a set of electrodes deep into the victim's brain, where they give off little jolts of electricity to disrupt the involuntary tremors and other symptoms of the disease. But according to Martha Farah, a neuroscientist at the University of Pennsylvania, at least one patient routinely chooses which electrical contact to activate depending on how she wants to feel: calm for every day, more "revved up" for a party.

Devices like DBS and psychoactive drugs like Ritalin and Prozac are already manipulating brain function in millions of people. And future pharmaceuticals, Farah says, targeting very specific parts of the brain, will be even more effective and will have fewer side effects. These new brain-control tools open a Pandora's box of ethical and philosophical dilemmas, including what kind of society— and what kinds of selves— we want.

Indeed, where there once seemed to be a clear boundary between mental health and mental dysfunction, it's now clear that these states lie along a spectrum. "Thirty years ago," says Farah, "only seriously depressed people took antidepressants. But I'm sitting in a coffee shop now where probably half the people have taken them." Some ethicists argue that unless you're ill, you're not really yourself when you're on these drugs. On the other hand, says Farah, we change our brain chemistry no more with Prozac than with coffee or tea.

With that in mind, Farah is studying modafinil, a drug developed for narcolepsy that is prescribed off-label to patients with depression, ADHD or even jet lag. In the military, it's used to sharpen soldiers' alertness and cognition. Her research is attempting to determine how this chemical affects normal people. "Is there a trade-off," she wonders, "between focusing attention and reducing creativity? And if more workers use it to excel, will we have a workforce of narrow, rigid thinkers?"

Neuroethicists are also worried that these new cognitive technologies could widen the gap between those who can afford them and those who can't, eventually creating different classes of human beings. Just as problematic as unequal access, some say, is the prospect of people being forced, implicitly or explicitly, to take mind-altering medications. Some day we may all feel pressure to take—or give our kids—focus or memory-sharpening drugs to compete at school or work. In fact, says Richard Glen Boire, senior fellow on law and policy at the Center for Cognitive Liberty & Ethics in Davis, Calif. "some schools require kids—not diagnosed with ADHD by doctors—to take Ritalin to attend school."

Farah also imagines the day when we have what she calls a "neuro-correctional system" that could transform criminals into noncriminals. We already force sex offenders to take libido-dampening drugs or face denial of parole. A drug to dampen violent impulses might someday be similarly applied. That could, in theory, prevent crimes.

But so would the castration of rapists, and that is considered a nearly unthinkable invasion of a person's body, Do we have a comparable right, neuroethicists ask, to "freedom of mind"? The ethicists are raising the questions, but it will be up to the courts— and ultimately society at large— to decide when the benefits of this powerful but intrusive branch of brain science outweigh the dangers. ◎/◎

Reflections and Inquiries

1. If drugs are used to treat, say, attention-deficit disorders or depression, would it be equally valid to use drugs for treating sociopathic attitudes and behaviors such as racism, assault, theft, or acts of terrorism? What are your reasons for permitting or prohibiting such drug use?

2. If you agree to a limited use of drugs to control personality disorders, where would you draw the line, and why?

3. Russo asserts that brain scans are far more powerful and invasive than psychological tests. What are your reasons for agreeing or disagreeing?

4. Why is the intelligence community interested in brain-scan technology?

5. Comment on the rhetorical strategies Russo employs in her article (effectiveness of the opening paragraph, logical progression of ideas, transitions from one point to another, tone of voice, word choice, strength of the conclusion).

Reading to Write

Familiarize yourself with the activities and publications of neuroethics centers, the Neuroethics Society, and perhaps other bioethics societies as well. Then write an article in which you weigh the pros and cons of brain-scanning technology. In your conclusion take a stance on what, if anything, you consider to be unethical, and why.

Bioengineering and Self-Improvement | Arthur Caplan

Many people feel uncomfortable using modern-day technology for self-improvement, especially when such improvement involves enhancing one's physical appearance. In the following essay Arthur Caplan, professor of bioethics at the University of Pennsylvania and director of the university's Center for Bioethics, identifies the reasons behind people's associating self-improvement with unethical behavior, and explains why using biotechnology to enhance one's physical well-being is not unethical.

I walked by a laser-eye-surgery clinic in a shopping mall recently. There was a sign high up over the door. I could not read it, so I put on my glasses. The sign said, "Our latest techniques are safe, easy, painless and quick—you may see better than 20/20." Which got me to thinking—is there anything wrong with using medicine and biological engineering to modify our brains and bodies to improve or enhance them?

Very few people have 20/20 vision. Being able to see well is crucial to success in some sports. Those who have extraordinary vision, better than 20/20, turn out to be especially good at hitting a baseball or catching a lacrosse ball. On the whole, few of us see 20/20, and almost none of us sees better than that. The clinic was claiming that, in only a few hours in the mall, they could make those with lousy vision see as well as or better than most of humanity ever has! Is there anything immoral about doing that? Surprisingly, a lot of people think the answer to that question is yes.

There has been a lot of interest on the part of President George W. Bush's Council on Bioethics in the subject of human improvement. They have spent a

---

considerable amount of time in recent years pondering the question of whether it is right to improve or enhance ourselves using new biological knowledge.

Just over a year and a half ago, the council issued a report titled *Beyond Therapy* that wrestles with the question of what we are going to do with the explosion of knowledge about the brain—some biochemical (e.g., drugs that affect the brain), some technological (implants that might go into the brain), and some related to scanning and diagnostics (ways to see the brain and make forecasts about propensities or abilities). What should we do in the face of this new area of knowledge?

The Council isn't alone in having worries about the wisdom of whether it   5
is right to use bioengineering to try to improve ourselves. Writers such as Carl Elliott, Michael Sandel, Bill McKibben, and Francis Fukuyama are made quite nervous by the prospect of people choosing bioengineering to enlarge their breasts, smooth out their wrinkles, mellow out their moods, and pep up their memories. We might dub these people "anti-meliorists" and their doubts "anti-meliorism."

What the anti-meliorists argue is that, if we don't put a stop to things like laser surgery and liposuction, who knows where it will all end? Our children, or their children, will all have been slugging down chemical concoctions of who knows what in the incessant pursuit of perfection, concoctions fobbed off on them by a greedy pharmaceutical industry. Worse still, the chase for betterment is vain (as in narcissistic), unfair, and doomed to fail.

One aspect of improvement that seems to really gall anti-meliorists is their conviction that trying to improve yourself is vain. Accept yourself as you are, rather than letting Madison Avenue, Joan Rivers, *Town and Country*, or *Vogue* tell you how you ought to be. But it doesn't just have to be a matter of vanity. If it's really all vain, then why don't we just take off our clothes, throw away the makeup, get rid of the fashion industry, and reconcile ourselves to grubbing around in grass skirts? We know that, to some extent, part of what gives us pleasure is trying to control our appearance, to control how others see us. But it may be something in which we can overindulge. I would grant that the person who undergoes her or his twentieth cosmetic-surgery procedure (I have a certain aging pop singer in mind here) may be abusing the idea of improvement. But that doesn't show that it is vain if you want to remove a port-wine-stain blemish from your face, to see better through laser surgery, to wear contacts rather than glasses, or even to remove your wrinkles.

I'm not arguing that it's right for fourteen-year-olds to get breast-augmentation surgery. I think you should learn to decide whether you like your body or not, and you're not ready at that age to make such a decision. But, it is not self-evident that all pursuit of beauty or looks or appearance is vain in and of itself. And certainly, vanity has nothing to do with interest in trying to think faster or have more memory, or in the decision about whether one wants to be stronger or to be able to increase aptitudes and capabilities. That's not vanity; that's self-regard.

It is true that we in the developed world could find ourselves having access to biological engineering that poor people in poor nations do not. It's also true that we in rich countries could find ourselves with a lot of people unable to buy or purchase many of these things that might lead to improvement or enhancement.

I'm not in favor of inequity. But, if I said, "We're going to guarantee to any- 10 one who wants it access to a chip that can be put into somebody's head and improve his memory"—if, in other words, equity is taken off the table—then worries about equity evaporate. Inequity is bad. But it's not bad because it might be connected to biological engineering. Inequity is immoral because it is unfair.

Well, the anti-meliorists fret, can you really be happy through biological tinkering? If we wind up using biological knowledge to engineer ourselves so that we can think more quickly in solving a problem, have more memory, figure out problems better than we could before, because we've taken a drug, in what sense have we earned or do we merit these improvements?

If we swallow a cup of coffee or tea every morning as a stimulant, should those who do so all feel morally bad for a while? Cheap thrills may be cheap, but they can still be thrilling. Some people do think that the only way to get to the top of the mountain is to hike or bike up there. I don't have a problem with that. If they like doing that, that's fine. Me, I like a helicopter. View's the same. I don't care. I get to the top.

Not all forms of pleasure have to be earned to be pleasurable. There are plenty of things that you and I are all happy about that we have nothing to do with the creation or attainment of, that we don't struggle, practice, earn, fight for, or do anything to attain. They just happen, and we say, "Well, that's good fortune." It is only a bizarre form of puritanical, capitalistic hedonism, which seems to have infected the anti-meliorists, that supports the view that only earned happiness is authentic happiness.

The drive to improve ourselves using bioengineering is not immoral in principle. So, why shouldn't we try to improve ourselves both biologically and socially? I find no convincing arguments why, in principle, we shouldn't try to improve ourselves at all. I don't find it persuasive that to say you want to be stronger, faster, or smarter makes you vain, unfair, or doomed to be dissatisfied. I have yet to meet anyone who has had laser surgery with good results who says he or she feels unsatisfied because a laser did the work.

If we limit ourselves in the way that many anti-meliorists are suggesting 15 that we do now, then we will rob ourselves and our descendants of some of the most exciting opportunities that the biological revolution presents. ◎/◎

Reflections and Inquiries

1. How does Caplan refute the position of the anti-meliorists that enhancing ourselves through laser surgery, liposuction, and the like is vain and futile? How convincingly does he refute them?

2. Caplan admits that controlling our appearance "may be something in which we can over-indulge." What do you suppose he means by "over-indulge" in the context of his defense of self-improveent?

3. Do you agree or disagree with the anti-meliorists that only earned happiness is authentic happiness?

4. If you had an opportunity to enhance your memory through biotechnology, would you take advantage of it? Would your response be different if the enhancement were aimed at improving some aspect of your physical appearance? Explain.

5. What is Caplan's aim in his opening and concluding paragraphs? How well does the opening paragraph set the stage for what follows? How, specifically does the concluding paragraph serve to achieve closure?

Reading to Write

1. Use "Suggestions for Further Readings" at the end of this cluster to gain a wider understanding of the ethical issues involved in biotechnological applications for self-improvement; then conduct a survey to determine student attitudes toward the use of biotechnology for intellectual enhancement and for physical enhancement. Report on and interpret your findings in an essay.

2. Write an essay about self-improvement (through surgery or drugs) from a religious perspective. After obtaining theological or scriptural reasons either for or against it, argue for or against these reasons.

Ethics, Politics, and Genetic Knowledge | Robert P. George

Despite the "blessings" of genetic knowledge," Robert P. George explains in the following essay that ethicists are worried that (1) society might begin to compromise the way that individuals with severe disorders are treated in society and (2) procreation could become a kind of commodity whereby embryos are bought and sold in the scientific marketplace for eugenics purposes. George says these worries are "urgent," and calls attention to bioethicist Leon Kass's warning that the eugenic vision is "gaining strength." Robert P. George, professor of jurisprudence and director of the James Madison Program in American Ideals and Institutions at Princeton University, is the author of In Defense of Natural Law *(1999) and* Making Men Moral: Civil Liberties and Public Morality *(1993). For five years (1993–98), he served as a presidential appointee to the United States Commission on Civil Rights.*

Source: Robert P. George, "Ethics, Politics, and Genetic Knowledge," *Social Research* (73:3, Fall 2006): 1029–32. Reprinted by permission of *Social Research.*

The day may come when biotechnological science makes it possible for parents to custom design their offspring, manipulating genes to produce children with the "superior" traits—strength, intelligence, beauty—the parent or parents desire. But that day is still a long way off. The relationship between genes and qualities such as intelligence and athletic prowess turns out to be so complex that the dream or nightmare of "designer babies" may never become a reality. That does not mean we should not worry about the possibility. But, for now, we should not spend too much of our worry budget on it. There are far more urgent things to be concerned about today in the field of biotechnology.

Before discussing these things, however, we should pause to reflect on the blessings that genetic knowledge and the biotechnologies it makes possible have delivered or will deliver soon. Much generic knowledge has been generated by inquiry aimed at curing diseases, healing afflictions, and ameliorating suffering. Valuable biotechnologies have been developed for the purpose of advancing human health and well-being. This is to be applauded.

Moreover, genetic knowledge, like knowledge in other fields of intellectual inquiry, is intrinsically valuable. Even apart from its utility in medicine, such knowledge is humanly fulfilling and, indeed, fulfilling in a special way since much genetic knowledge is a species of self-knowledge. Advances in genetics help us to explore and understand more fully that greatest of mysteries, namely, the mystery of man himself. These advances, too, deserve our applause.

Now let us turn to the worries—the urgent ones.

The first worry is that we may compromise, or further compromise, in both science and politics, the principle that every human being, irrespective of age, size, mental or physical condition, stage of development, or condition of dependency, possesses inherent worth and dignity and a right to life. Proponents of research involving the destruction of human beings in the embryonic stage for biomedical research began by proposing only that "spare" embryos held in cryopreservation in IVF clinics be sacrificed. These microscopic humans would, they argued, likely die anyway, so nothing would be lost (and no wrong would be done) by destroying them to harvest stem cells. Soon, however, many of these people were calling for the mass production by cloning of human embryos precisely for use as disposable research material. For now, most insist that they desire to use only embryos in the blastocyst (5- to 6-day) stage, and are not proposing to implant and gestate embryos that would then be killed at later stages of development to harvest cells, tissues, or organ primordia. But this is bound to change. Having abandoned the moral norm against deliberately taking innocent human life, many will be carried by the logic of their position to the view that producing human beings to be killed in the fetal and even early infant stages is justified in the cause of regenerative medicine.

The second worry is closely related. It is that many people are coming to view procreation as akin to manufacture. They also regard children not as gifts

5

to be cherished and loved even when "imperfect," but rather as products that may legitimately be subjected to standards of quality control and discarded or killed in the embryonic, fetal, and even infant stages if they do not measure up. Pre-implantation genetic diagnosis (PGD) of embryos in the context of assisted reproduction is increasingly widely practiced. In IVF clinics in the United States, it is common for a larger number of embryos to be produced than can be safely implanted. So, people reason, why not choose the ones likely to be healthiest? Embryonic human beings are considered more or less worthy of life, and sometimes not worthy of life at all, depending on their "quality." And the eugenic ethic embodied in the practice of PGD is not confined to choosing among embryos for implantation. Eugenic abortion—and, in some cases, even infanticide—is regarded as perfectly legitimate by many in the United States and elsewhere. A child in the womb who has been diagnosed with Down's syndrome or dwarfism is likely to be aborted. A newborn may be deprived of a simple life-saving surgery and "allowed to die." Those responsible will, perhaps, tell themselves that they are doing it "for the good of the child." The reality, however, is that they are treating the mentally or physically handicapped child as a "life unworthy of life." And let no one suppose that such decisions, ghastly as they are even when chosen by parents, are or will remain a matter of unencumbered "choice." Social pressures exist and will build for parents to spare society the burdens of caring for, or even encountering, mentally or physically handicapped people. Some years ago, the geneticist Bentley Glass, envisaging a future in which genetic screening would become the routine thing it is today, proclaimed triumphantly that "no parent will . . . have a right to burden society with a malformed or a mentally incompetent child."

The great bioethicist Leon Kass has diagnosed the situation insightfully. Speaking at the United States Holocaust Museum, Kass warned:

> [The] eugenic vision and practice are gaining strength, all the more so because they grow out of sight behind the fig leaf of the doctrine of free choice. We are largely unaware that we have, as a society, already embraced the eugenic principle "Defectives shall not be born" because our practices are decentralized and they operate not by coercion but by private reproductive choice.

One should observe, of course, that many people continue to resist the eugenic ethic and struggle to reverse it; and despite the (sometimes amusing) boasting of the eugenicists, there is no good reason to think that it cannot be reversed in significant measure. Yet a sober assessment of the situation requires us to acknowledge that support for the eugenic killing of human beings in the fetal and infant stages is no longer a "fringe" position, and is particularly strong in elite sectors of the culture.

Groups dedicated to defending the dignity and rights of handicapped 10 persons (even when they take no official position on the ethics of abortion as such) have recognized the dire implications of the eugenic ethic for the people they serve. As Dr. Kass puts it, "persons who happen still to be born with these conditions, having somehow escaped the spreading net of detection and eugenic abortion, are increasingly regarded as 'mistakes,' as inferior human beings who should not have been born." This has produced an alliance between the pro-life movement and advocates of justice for the handicapped or disabled in a number of domains.

The glory of our political tradition is its affirmation of the profound, inherent, and equal dignity of all human beings. The history of our politics and social practice, our law and economics, and even our medicine is in significant measure the struggle to live up to the demands of this affirmation. The trouble, of course, is that individual and collective self-interest are often at war with it. All too often, people will have powerful motives to regard others as less than fully human, or to believe that humanity can be divided into classes—superiors and inferiors, "persons" and subpersonal or nonpersonal members of the human family. It was true in the days of slavery; it is true in the era of eugenic abortion and infanticide. Sometimes people say that the challenges of biotechnological science will require us to invent new principles of ethics and politics. At least when it comes to the immediate dangers we face, that is not true. What we need is fidelity to the principles of human equality and dignity that have always served us well when we have had the wisdom and fortitude to honor them. ◎◎

Reflections and Inquiries

1. What do you suppose George means when he states that "genetic knowledge . . . is intrinsically valuable"?

2. George is skeptical of those who insist they would restrict their research to blastocysts (embryos at the 5- or 6-day stage), saying "this is bound to change." On what grounds, if any, does he rest that claim? How convincing is it, in your opinion?

3. What is problematic about pre-implantation genetic diagnosis (PGD) of embryos, according to George? What if anything might be done to keep this practice from becoming exploitive?

4. How well does George support his assertions regarding genetic knowledge? That is, how compelling is his evidence? What other kinds of evidence, if any, might he have used to develop his argument?

Reading to Write

After reading about the history of eugenics programs (including those practiced by the Nazis during World War II), write an essay on the prospects of eugenics for the future, keeping in mind both the dangers of its getting out of hand and the prospects of its relieving humanity of dreaded diseases and deformities.

Designer Babies: One Step Closer | Samuel Hensley

Attaching the word "design" or "designer" to human beings frightens a lot of people—and with good reason, considering the shameful history of eugenics programs by totalitarian governments who thought they could artificially produce a "master race" or engage in "ethnic cleansing." Even with the most humane of intentions, like wanting to prevent diseases that result in a lifetime of suffering, serious ethical concerns are raised when embryos are subjected to a screening process called pre-implantation genetic diagnosis (PGP), as Samuel Hensley, a doctor, points out in the following article. Samuel Hensley, M.D., is a fellow of the Center for Bioethics and Human Dignity and a surgical pathologist at Mississippi Baptist Medical Center in Jackson, Mississippi.

A recent *USA Today* article describes the difficulties of Joe Fletcher and his family in Northern Ireland. Joe's son, Joshua, has Diamond-Blackfan anemia, a condition that usually occurs as a spontaneous genetic mutation.[1] If the affected individual reaches reproductive age, the trait is usually heritable as an autosomal dominant disease. Joshua must receive repeated blood transfusions to counteract his inability to produce red blood cells, which carry oxygen to various parts of the body. The only cure for this condition is a stem cell transplant from a compatible donor. Joshua's older brother is not a compatible donor and the chance of any other future siblings being compatible is one in four. The Fletchers hope to improve those odds significantly by using a technique known as *pre-implantation genetic diagnosis* (PGD). The process requires in vitro fertilization. Eggs and sperm from the parents are mixed in a petri dish, and the resulting embryos undergo DNA analysis. Embryos compatible with Joshua could be inserted into the mother's womb to produce compatible siblings. Alternatively, if only a few embryos are compatible, they could be cloned to produce additional embryos in case the first attempt fails to result in implantation and fetal development.

This procedure is illegal in Great Britain and is regarded as unethical. Why? Before exploring the British objection, let me add an additional concern from a Christian perspective that regards these embryos as early human life, made in the image of God, possessing unique genes and the capability of continued human development. An important question for Christians is what will happen to the healthy embryos that are incompatible with Joshua. Will they be implanted later and given an equal chance at continued life or will they be discarded? Embryos not selected may be destroyed directly or by destructive embryo research, which is contrary to an understanding of human

---

Source: Samuel Hensley, "Designer Babies: One Step Closer," *The Center for Bioethics and Human Dignity,* Commentary, July 1, 2004. Reprinted by permission of the author.

life being sacred. The *USA Today* article does not mention what plans the parents have for these other offspring.

The British concern expressed previously by the Human Fertilization and Embryology Authority (HFEA) is that human life would be created for the purpose of benefiting others, in this case a brother and the parents. This is a serious ethical concern. Should a child be created specifically to save another person's life, or should a child be welcomed and loved unconditionally regardless of his or her instrumental value in helping someone else? This is important not just from a Christian perspective. Immanuel Kant, the prominent philosopher of rationalism, felt that human beings should always be treated as ends in themselves and not as the means for another person to attain his or her ends. In the Fletcher case, it does not seem that the embryos would be screened to test for known genetic defects. If Diamond-Blackfan anemia is a spontaneous mutation, and no known genetic anomalies are detectable in the parents (such as a mutation for RPS 19 on chromosome 19), then genetic screening is not a helpful option.[2] The decision on life or death then would be made solely on whether a particular embryo, at a later stage of life, might be useful in helping Joshua. This pushes the issue of creating life to serve our needs and wants to a new level, and raises the issue of designer babies.

Prenatal genetic testing allows scientists to test established pregnancies for genetic defects that then could be avoided by aborting the pregnancy. Pre-implantation genetic diagnosis allows multiple embryos to be tested and inserted into the mother only if certain *desirable* traits are present. This possibility was recently discussed by Dr. Francis Collins, director of the National Human Genome Research Institute, when he noted that the time may soon arrive when pre-implantation screening will be used to pick desirable traits even in the absence of particular genetic disorders.[3] In the coming years, human genome research will delineate gene clusters associated with increased intelligence, athletic ability, and musicality to name a few. The temptation to redefine parenthood to include choosing particular characteristics in their children, as opposed to unconditionally accepting offspring as a gift of God, seems fraught with perils beyond the scope of this article. For the sake of reflection, let us briefly consider a few issues.

Blastomere biopsy, the process by which a single cell is taken from the embryo for genetic testing, seems safe, but no long-term studies are available to exclude later problems from the procedure itself. In medical research, when new therapies are tested on human subjects, the welfare of the patient is a paramount concern. However, with in vitro fertilization, blastomere biopsy, and genetic screening, the embryos are not considered human subjects even though they are the earliest forms of childhood development and the beginning of lives whose health and well-being will later be a concern to all. Safety for the embryo must be a vital concern.

Our culture has generally considered parents to be the best judges of the welfare of their offspring, but even this has limits. Children are weak and vulnerable; they require protection from abuse and negligence. The ability for parents to choose which offspring die and which live and what traits they will manifest is an awesome responsibility. The President's Council of Bioethics recently noted that

> With genetic screening, procreation begins to take on certain aspects of the *idea*—if not the practice—of manufacture, the making of a product to a specified standard. The parent—in partnership with the IVF doctor or genetic counselor—becomes in some measure the master of the child's fate, in ways that are without precedent . . . Today, parents using PGD take responsibility for selecting for birth children who will not be chronically sick or severely disabled; in the future, they might also bear responsibility for picking and choosing which "advantages" their children shall enjoy. Such an enlarged degree of parental control over the genetic endowments of their children cannot fail to alter the parent-child relationship. Selecting against disease merely relieves the parents of the fear of specific ailments afflicting their child; selecting for desired traits inevitably plants specific hopes and expectations as to how their child might excel. More than any child does now, the "better" child may bear the burden of living up to the standards he was "designed" to meet. The oppressive weight of his parents' expectations—resting in this case on what they believe to be undeniable biological facts—may impinge upon the child's freedom to make his own way in the world.[4]

These concerns for tomorrow begin with Joshua's parents today. The proposal is to select purposefully a child solely for his ability to provide a donor source for another child.[5] Creating life primarily to serve someone else, especially when the other life may be rejected and destroyed for the simple reason that it did not meet the parents' needs, is an action that should always be condemned. ◎∕◎

Notes

1. Wickramasinghe S. N., McCullough J. *Blood and Bone Marrow Pathology.* Churchill-Livingstone, 2003.
2. See Willig T. N., Gazda H., Sieff C. A. "Diamond Blackfan Anemia." *Curr Opin Hematol.* 2000 Mar; 7(2): 85–94. Da Costa L, Willig TN, Fixler J, Mohandas N, Tchernia G: Diamond Blackfan Anemia *Curr Opin Pediatr.* 2001 Feb; 13(1): 10. Dianzani I, Garelli E, Ramenghi U: Diamond Blackfan Anemia. *Paediatr Drugs* 2000 Sep-Oct; 2(5): 345–55.
3. Collins F. *Genetic Enhancements: Current and Future Prospects.* Presentation at the December 2002 meeting of the President's Council on Bioethics, Washington, D.C. Transcript available on Council's web site at www.bioethics.gov.
4. President's Council on Bioethics: *Beyond Therapy—Biotechnology and the Pursuit of Happiness.* Available at Council web site at www.bioethics.gov.
5. Verlinsky Y., Rechitsky S., Sharapove T., Kuliev A., et al. "Preimplantation Genetic Testing." *JAMA* 2004 May 5; 291(17): 2125–6.

Reflections and Inquiries

1. What is the basis for the controversy behind PGD embryo screening? Do you agree or disagree that the procedure should be illegal? Why?

2. According to Hensley, the British find it unethical that human life be created for the purpose of benefiting others. How valid is this view, in your opinion?

3. Do you agree with the President's Council of Bioethics that "with genetic screening, procreation begins to take on certain aspects of . . . manufacture? Explain your reasoning.

Reading to Write

Hensley asserts that in medical research embryos are not considered human subjects. Conduct your own research into biomedical practices and write an essay in which you agree or disagree with Hensley's claim. If you agree, how should medical research be constrained? If you disagree, what further direction should it take?

Issues for Further Research: The Stem Cell Debate

The Stem Cell Debate | John W. Donohue

One of the most divisive issues of the twenty-first century is whether embryonic stem cells should be cultivated and used for medical research and, potentially, for curing devastating diseases like Alzheimer's, neuromuscular disorders, and Down's Syndrome—and possibly even for spinal cord regeneration that would restore movement to paralyzed people. The problem, of course, is that embryos are considered by some to be human, every bit as sacred as postembryonic human life. Who has the authority to say that this is, or is not, the case?

In the following article, John W. Donohue, S. J., a priest and the associate editor of America *magazine, gives a succinct overview of the controversy, revealing his own position in the process.*

Why is there an irreconcilable division between two groups of thoughtful and sympathetic people?

Orrin Hatch, Utah's Republican senior senator, is a firm opponent of abortion. He is also a firm supporter of research on embryonic stem cells,

---

Source: John W. Donohue, "The Stem Cell Debate," reprinted from *America*, Nov. 13, 2006 with permission of America Press Inc. © 2006. All rights reserved. For subscription information visit www.americamagazine.org.

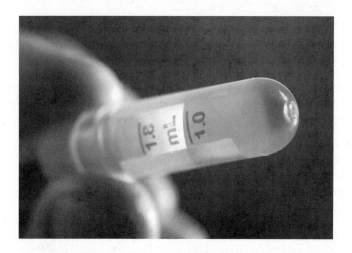

even though this involves destruction of the embryos. The senator's reasons for this latter position are mainly two. He believes, as he has said, that life starts in the womb, "not in a petri dish," and he believes this research on embryos has promise of developing regenerative therapies for such devastating afflictions as Alzheimer's and Parkinson's diseases and for the injuries that produce paraplegics. On July 18, Mr. Hatch was one of the 63 senators who voted for substantial increases in federal funding for embryonic stem cell research.

On the other hand, President George W. Bush and the 37 senators who voted against that bill, along with the members of the U.S. Conference of Catholic Bishops and millions of other citizens, are opposed to enlarging federal grants for research on embryonic stem cells. They are just as compassionate as Senator Hatch and just as hopeful that scientific inquiries will find cures for crippling sicknesses. All the same, they oppose research even on 5- or 6-day-old embryos, because it regularly destroys human life in its earliest stages. On this account, President Bush on July 19 vetoed that bill, which would have removed the restrictions he imposed in 2001 when he limited embryonic stem cell research to the 22 authorized stem cell colonies already in existence.

How does it happen that on this issue there is an irreconcilable division between two groups of thoughtful and sympathetic people? No doubt the answer is complex, but it includes the difference between those whose thinking is dominated by the imagination and those who think more abstractly. Publicists for embryonic stem cell research often point out that the embryos used for this research are no larger than the dot at the end of this sentence. Not only do they not look like a fetus; they cannot be imagined as looking like anything at all and cannot be fancied as human.

On the other hand, opponents of stem cell research can detach themselves from fancy. They know, as a wise scientist once said, that if 100 first-rate biologists were gathered together, they would all agree that even an eight-cell embryo is living. They might not agree on the definition of life, but they would agree that if this embryo were to nest in a womb, it would normally grow into a baby ready for birth. Those who view the question from this perspective have formed an intellectual judgment that science itself has established. They also argue that research on embryonic stem cells should not be federally funded because it offends the consciences of many Americans.

President Bush made the right decision when he vetoed the stem cell bill. 5 Nevertheless, as Representative Mike Pence, Republican of Indiana, remarked at the signing of the veto, he and other opponents of embryonic stem cell research are losing the argument with the American people. Where does that argument stand today? At this point in history, a few conclusions are reasonably certain.

By now, the question of funds for embryonic stem cell research is practically moot. This research is already amply supported by such private sources as university institutes and biotechnology companies, along with monies from some states. It is worth noting, however, that so far none of this research has produced those miraculous therapies that have been predicted. Speaking of these promises, the best that Douglas A. Melton, director of the Harvard Stem Cell Institute could say not long ago was, "We haven't learned anything that makes us think this won't work."

It is known, however, that research on adult stem cells has produced some therapeutic experiments that do work. For instance, the Sept. 21 issue of the *New England Journal of Medicine* reported a study that found that adult stem cells from patients' own bone marrow had improved those patients' cardiac function after a heart attack. Research on these adult stem cells is morally unobjectionable, because they are derived without harm to the donor. The National Institutes of Health currently supports this adult stem cell research and take the position that government funding for it should be substantially increased.

The success of work with adult stem cells will not, however, satisfy those who think no boundaries should be imposed on scientists and their research. This was pointed out by Robert George, a professor of jurisprudence at Princeton University, who is also a member of the President's Council on Bioethics. On the July 17 broadcast of the "NewsHour with Jim Lehrer," Mr. George called the Senate debate about stem cells a sideshow. The real debate now, he said, is about the next step in embryonic stem cell research—a debate about the creation of cloned human embryos that are a match for a particular patient and will be destroyed once their stem cells have been harvested for regenerative medicine. A law that banned federal funding for this "fetal farming" would clearly represent a choice of life over death. ◎∕◎

Reflections and Inquiries

1. What is Donohue's thesis? How does he convey it?

2. Why do you suppose Donohue begins his article with Utah Senator Orin Hatch's supportive stance on stem cell research?

3. What are Donohue's reasons for supporting President Bush's veto of the bill that would have supported stem cell research? Explain why you agree or disagree with the veto.

Reading to Write

Donohue alludes to the possibility of using adult stem cells instead of embryonic stem cells. How promising are adult stem cells according to the latest research? Write an essay on your findings.

The Morality of Killing Human Embryos | Bonnie Steinbock

In the following scholarly article, Bonnie Steinbock, a professor of philosophy at the State University of New York at Albany and a specialist in human reproduction and genetics, conducts an in-depth analysis of the physiological nature of embryos and their status, from a biological as well as philosophical perspective, as living entities. As you read this challenging but lucid article, note the meticulous attention Steinbock gives to matters that are either ignored or glossed over in more journalistic pieces.

Embryonic stem cell research is morally and politically controversial because the process of deriving the embryonic stem (ES) cells kills embryos. If embryos are, as some would claim, human beings like you and me, then ES cell research is clearly impermissible. If, on the other hand, the blastocysts from which embryonic stem cells are derived are not yet human beings, but rather microscopic balls of undifferentiated cells, as others maintain, then ES cell research is probably morally permissible. Whether the research can be justified depends on such issues as its cost, chance of success, and numbers likely to benefit. But this is an issue for any research project, not just ES cell research. What makes the debate over ES cell research controversial is that it, like the debate over abortion, raises "questions that politicians cannot settle: when does human life begin, and what is the moral status of the human embryo?"[1] This paper looks at several theories of moral status and their implications for embryo research.

When we ask whether a being has moral status, we are asking whether it counts or matters from the moral point of view; whether it must be considered in our moral deliberations. It seems obvious that not everything has moral status. We are not required to consider the impact of our moral decisions on mere things—for example, ordinary rocks. It seems equally obvious that paradigmatic people—people like you and me—do have moral status. In fact, most

---

Source: Bonnie Steinbock, "The Morality of Killing Human Embryos," *Journal of Law, Medicine and Ethics,* Spring 2006: 26–34. Reprinted by permission of Blackwell Publishing.

people take it for granted that even if moral status isn't limited to people (that animals count, for example) human beings count for more. To express this in Kantian terms, humanity has a dignity and worth which separates humankind from the rest of creation. Because this view is commonplace in moral thinking and in the law, we can call it the common-sense view of moral status.

The Common-Sense View: The Biological Humanity Criterion

The common-sense view of moral status is derived from the Judeo-Christian tradition which teaches that only human beings are created in God's image, and therefore human beings alone have this special moral status. In addition, this special moral status belongs to all human beings, regardless of race, ethnicity, nationality, or gender. We are all God's children. Compared to views that limit moral status to members of one's own group or tribe, the Judeo-Christian view is quite progressive. Theoretically (though often not in reality), it prohibits the enslaving or killing of other human beings, simply because they are "outsiders." The secular version of this view bases the unique moral status of humanity on a biological category—membership in the species *Homo sapiens*.

The biological humanity criterion of moral status states that all and only human beings, members of our species, have full moral status. But even those who agree on the criterion may differ on this question: when does a human being come into existence? Sometimes this is put in a different way: when does human *life* begin? But this question, familiar from the abortion debate, poses the issue in a misleading way, because every cell in your body is both human (possessed of a human genome) and alive. Human gametes (ova and sperm) are alive, and sperm even swim. So the question, "when does human life begin?" is better understood as asking, "when does an individual human organism come into existence?"

One answer is that a human organism comes into existence at conception. 5 Those who hold the conception view adopt the biological humanity criterion of moral status, which says that all and only human organisms have full moral status. In addition, they believe that a human organism exists at the moment of conception. Indeed, they usually hold that this is a plain matter of biological fact.

However, this is dubious, as there are biological reasons to think that the unique human organism begins to exist only some time after the beginning of fertilization. Fertilization or conception does not occur at a precise moment. It is a process taking place over hours, even days. The process of conception is not completed until syngamy, when the chromosomes from the egg and the sperm have merged, some time after the sperm has penetrated the egg. However, even syngamy may not mark the beginning of a human organism. Ron Green points out, biologists usually describe the cells of an organism has having the full range of cellular structure including a single cell nucleus that contains DNA within its own nuclear membrane. But at syngamy the zygote has no definitive nuclear membrane . . . A distinctive diploid cell nucleus does not make its appearance until the two-cell stage, after the zygote undergoes its first cell division . . .[2]

Moreover, in the early stages of an embryo's life, many of its cells, or blastomeres, remain "totipotent." This means that each blastomere is undifferentiated and remains capable, if properly manipulated, of developing into a full human being. One kind of cloning—called embryo splitting or blastomere separation—is accomplished in this way. Embryo splitting also occurs naturally in the case of identical twins (or triplets). Green comments, "if biological humanness starts with the appearance of a unique diploid genome, twins and triplets are living evidence that the early embryo is not yet one human being, but a community of possibly different individuals held together by a gelatinous membrane."[3] He goes on to quote an embryology text as saying, "a genetically unique but non-individuated embryo has yet to acquire determinate individuality, a stable human identity."[4] In this view, a genuine human organism begins to exist only after twinning is no longer possible: at the beginning of gastrulation when the primitive streak (the precursor of the nervous system) forms. In a pregnancy, gastrulation coincides with implantation, the imbedding of the embryo in the uterus, which occurs about fourteen days after fertilization.

The debate over when a human organism comes into existence occurs within the context of the biological humanity criterion. However, the criterion itself has been challenged.

The Person View

In her classic article, "On the Moral and Legal Status of Abortion,"[5] Mary Anne Warren argues that the conservative view on abortion rests on a confusion between two distinct senses of "human being." One sense is biological or genetic. It refers to the species to which an entity belongs. Human fetuses are unquestionably human in the biological sense. However, it does not follow from their genetic humanity that they are human in the other sense, the moral sense, which refers to their moral status and rights. Why should a biological category confer a special moral status? The belief that humanness does imply such a status and rights (human rights) stems from a failure to distinguish between the two senses. To avoid this confusion, Warren suggests that we reserve the term "human" for the biological or genetic sense, and use the term "person" to refer to beings who are full-fledged members of the moral community, possessed of moral rights—in particular, the right to life. This enables us to avoid begging the question in the abortion debate, for it remains an open question whether a human fetus is a person with a right to life.

Why not base moral status and moral rights on species membership? 10
After all, all the persons we know are, in fact, members of the species *Homo sapiens*. Why not use species membership as a marker for moral personhood? The reason is the arbitrariness of limiting moral status to genetic human beings. This can be seen if we imagine coming across an extraterrestrial like the eponymous character in the movie, *E.T.* If we were deciding what it would be morally permissible to do to him—say, put him in a zoo, or make him into hamburger—surely the question would not be decided by the number of chromosomes in his cells (if he even had chromosomes). His not being a member of the species *Homo sapiens* would not determine his moral status. It seems likely that we would regard him as a person—a non-human person—with all the rights of any one of us.

The example of *E.T.* is meant to show that biological humanity isn't a necessary condition of full moral status. Instead, moral status is based on certain psychological characteristics, such as sentience, consciousness, self-consciousness, the ability to use language, rationality, and moral agency. These characteristics are typical of members of our species, but not necessarily limited to them, as the example of *E.T.* is intended to show. Moreover, there seem to be members of our species who lack these person-making characteristics, such as anencephalic babies and patients in persistent vegetative states. They are biologically human, but not persons, and thus do not have the moral status reserved to persons.

An objection made to the person view is that, without an account of the moral relevance of person-making characteristics, it is as arbitrary as a theory based on species membership. Why should moral status and moral rights be limited to sentient, self-conscious, language-using, rational agents? Moreover, depending on how many person-making characteristics are needed for full moral status and rights, the person view appears to exclude those human beings who, due to severe developmental disabilities or mental illness or senility, or even infancy, do not have the capacity to reason or use language. It is hard to accept that human beings in these categories—who are often members of our own families—are not moral persons, with the same moral status and rights as the rest of us. Advocates of the biological humanity criterion maintain that any criterion other than genetic humanity will have this fatal flaw.

The challenge, then, is to construct a theory of moral status that is neither arbitrary (like the biological humanity criterion) nor unduly restrictive (like the person view). Moreover, the view should explain the moral relevance of its criterion for moral status.

The Interest View[6]

The interest view bases moral status on the possession of interests. The view derives from Joel Feinberg's "interest principle,"[7] which was intended to answer the question, what kinds of beings can logically have rights? Feinberg suggests that the answer comes from the purpose or function of rights, which is to protect, the interests of the being alleged to have the rights. He usefully analogizes having an interest in something to having a "stake" in it. I am better off if the things in which I have a stake, such as my health, my career, my assets, my family, flourish or prosper. Their flourishing is in my interest. Feinberg writes:

> One's interests, then, taken as a miscellaneous collection, consist of all those things in which one has a stake, whereas one's interest in the singular, one's personal interest or self-interest, consists in the harmonious advancement of all of one's interests in the plural. These interests . . . are distinguishable components of a person's well-being: he flourishes or languishes as they flourish or languish. What promotes them is to his advantage or *in his interest;* what thwarts them is to his detriment or *against his interest.*[8]

This is not to claim a one-to-one connection between what a person desires   15 and what is in his self-interest. I can take an interest in something (like junk food) that is not in my interest; and something can be in my interest but not be something I take an interest in (like exercise). But the reason exercise is in my interest, and junk food is not, is that exercise promotes other goals and desires of mine, such as staying healthy and alive, and eating junk food does not. If I had no desires, goals, or preferences at all, nothing would be in my interest.

Unless a being has interests and a welfare of its own, it makes no sense to ascribe rights to it. Feinberg's insight about the logical conditions of having rights can be applied, more generally to having moral status. To have moral status is to count or matter, from the moral point of view. If a being has moral status, then its interests must be considered when we engage in moral deliberation. If a being has no interests, its interests cannot be considered. So the possession of interests is a necessary condition of having moral status, and I would argue that it is also a sufficient condition. That is, if a being has interests, there is no justification for ignoring those interests when making moral decisions. (It is a separate question how much weight to accord to the interests of different beings, that is, whether there are other factors that give some beings a higher moral status than others.)

The Feinbergian account of having interests as having stakes in things suggests a conceptual link between interests and consciousness. Only conscious beings—beings with some sort of mental life, however rudimentary—can have wants; only beings with wants can have a stake in anything; only beings that can have a stake in something can have interests of their own. Non-conscious beings, whether mere things (like cars and rocks and works of art) or living things without nervous systems (like plants), have no interests of their own. This is not to say that they cannot be cared for or neglected; repaired or destroyed; nourished or killed. It is rather to say that it does not matter to non-conscious beings what we do to them. We can preserve their existence, and even promote their welfare in the sense of making them better entities of a certain kind. For example, we can fertilize the roses so that they grow vigorously and bloom; we can bring in the car for regular service so that it runs beautifully. However, we cannot do these things out of concern for what matters to them, because nothing matters to them. They do not have a stake in anything, including their own existence. For this reason, I maintain that they, unlike conscious beings, do not have a welfare or sake of their own.

Some will object that we cannot base moral status on consciousness unless we have a definition of consciousness, but there does not seem to be any satisfactory, non-circular definition. Acknowledging the problem, David Boonin says, "It is tempting to say that to be conscious is to be aware of something, for example, but then awareness will surely have to be defined in terms of being in a conscious state."[9] What follows from the absence of a definition of consciousness? Not much, Boonin argues. It is not as if we had no idea what consciousness is. He writes:

> As Nagel famously put it, using an expression that has since become ubiquitous in discussions of the subject, "an organism has conscious mental states if and only if there is something that it is like to *be* that organism— something it is like for the organism." Even if this does not constitute a definition of consciousness, you do know what I am talking about when I refer to the fact that there is something that it is like to be you when you see a clear blue sky, hear a shrill scream, feel a sharp prick, or a cold wind, or a burning itch. And this is enough to make clear what is meant by the claim that there is a morally relevant difference between an organism that is conscious in this sense and an organism that is not.[10]

The morally relevant difference between conscious and non-consciousness beings is that conscious beings have interests and a welfare of their own, compounded out of those interests. Non-conscious beings do not have either of these things.

Sentience is only one form of conscious awareness, but it is a very important one. If a being is sentient, that is, it can experience treatment as painful, it has at least one interest: the interest in not experiencing pain. The fact that a being can suffer gives us a reason to treat it in certain ways, and not in other ways. It matters to sentient beings what one does to them, and this is why they have moral claims on us. To take a homely example, it is fine if a child plucks the petals off a daisy while saying "He loves me, he loves me not." It is not fine if the child recites the rhyme while pulling the legs off an insect, or the feathers off a (trapped) bird.

Implications of the Interest View for Embryos
Embryos are not mere things. They are alive and, under certain conditions, have the potential to become beings with interests—indeed, to become people, like you and me. But their potential to become persons does not give

them the moral status or the rights of actual persons. Early embryos, indeed early-gestation fetuses, have no consciousness, no awareness, no experiences of any kind, even the most rudimentary. Without even the precursor of a nervous system, pre-implantation embryos cannot possibly have any kind of consciousness. Without consciousness, they cannot have desires; without desires, they cannot have interests. It is not wrong to kill embryos because it doesn't matter to an embryo whether it is killed or goes on living. Its continued existence is clearly not something an embryo takes an interest in, because it is impossible for a non-conscious, non-sentient being to take an interest in anything. More importantly, the interest view maintains that continued existence is not in the interest of a non-sentient fetus. For continued existence to be in its interest, it would have to have a welfare of its own, compounded out of all of its interests taken together. Lacking interests, embryos do not have a welfare of their own. In this respect, they are like gametes. Gametes are alive and human, but this is not sufficient for moral status. To have moral status is to be the kind of being whose interests and welfare we moral agents are required to consider. Without interests, there is nothing to consider. This is not to say that there might not be other reasons, including moral reasons, to protect non-interested beings. It is to say that these reasons cannot stem from their own interests or welfare, since they have none. Indeed, on a plausible conception of harming as setting back a being's interests, it follows that killing non-interested beings does not harm them.[11] If this sounds odd, it is because, for *us*, being killed is ordinarily the greatest of harms. But that is because we have interests, and in particular, an interest in continuing to exist. However, if a being has no interests, death is not a harm to it, any more than being destroyed is a harm to an automobile.

Of course, embryos differ from automobiles in one very significant way: embryos are living beings with the potential to develop into human persons, just like you or me, if they are not killed. In a now-classic article, Don Marquis argues that it is wrong to kill fetuses for the very same reason that it is wrong to kill you or me: because doing so deprives them (and us) of our valuable futures. In the next section, I will assess the Valuable Futures argument and its implications for the morality of killing embryos.

Marquis and the Valuable Futures Argument

According to Marquis, both sides of the abortion debate have insurmountable problems. What is needed is a fresh start, an account of why killing is wrong in the paradigm cases in which everyone would agree that it is wrong—namely, the killing of adult human beings, like you or me. Killing adult human beings is *prima facie* wrong because killing them deprives them of their future. Marquis writes:

> The loss of one's life is one of the greatest losses one can suffer. The loss of one's life deprives one of all the experiences, activities, projects, and enjoyments that

would otherwise have constituted one's future. Therefore, killing someone is wrong, primarily because the killing inflicts (one of) the greatest possible losses on the victim. . . . When I am killed, I am deprived both of what I now value which would have been part of my future personal life, but also what I would come to value. Therefore, when I die, I am deprived of all of the value of my future. Inflicting this loss on me is ultimately what makes killing me wrong. This being the case, it would seem that what makes killing *any* adult human being *prima facie* seriously wrong is the loss of his or her future.[12]

But exactly the same is true of killing a human fetus, and so abortion is, *prima facie*, wrong. *Prima facie* because killing is wrong only if it deprives the one killed of a "valuable future" or a "future-like-ours" (FLO, as it has come to be referred to). Thus, the valuable futures argument does not imply that it is wrong to kill someone in a persistent vegetative state (PVS) because someone in PVS no longer has a valuable future. It's also consistent with voluntary euthanasia, because persons who are severely and incurably ill and who face a future of pain and despair and who wish to die will not have suffered a loss if they are killed, because the future of which they are deprived is not considered by them to be a valuable one. Equally, the aborting of fetuses with defects so severe as to prevent them having FLO might be justifiable on Marquis's account. How severe would the disabling condition have to be to make abortion morally permissible? Is it only lethal conditions (such as Tay-Sachs disease) which deprive fetuses of FLO? Or could non-lethal conditions, such as mental retardation, deprive a fetus of FLO, and thus justify abortion? Marquis does not address these sorts of questions, indeed, does not provide an account of "just what it is about my future or the futures of other adult human beings which make it wrong to kill us."[13] His aim is, rather, to show that abortion is in general a grave wrong. For most fetuses clearly do have valuable futures. If they are not aborted, they will come to have lives they will value and enjoy, just as you and I value and enjoy our lives. Therefore, abortion is seriously wrong for the same reason that killing an innocent adult human being is seriously wrong: it deprives the victim of his or her valuable future.

On the interest view, the killing of non-sentient beings is not seriously 25 wrong because non-sentient beings are not deprived of anything they want or have a stake in by being killed. Marquis thinks that this reveals a fundamental flaw in the interest view, or indeed in any sentience- or desire-based view. First, it seems to imply that it is not wrong to kill someone in a reversible coma or even in deep and dreamless sleep. Such a person is not now conscious or sentient. If we explain the wrongness of killing him by appealing to his future conscious states, then it seems that it is equally wrong to kill a pre-conscious fetus, who will become conscious and sentient in the natural course of events, if it is not aborted. Either the interest view entails that it is morally permissible to kill temporarily comatose adults, in which case it cannot be the right view of moral status, or it must concede that it is wrong to kill fetuses, in which case it cannot be the basis for a defense of abortion. By contrast, the FLO account can explain the wrongness of killing temporarily unconscious adults; this deprives them of their valuable futures.

Second, Marquis argues, the interest view cannot explain why it is wrong to kill someone who is conscious and sentient, but who does not want to go on living. If it is the desire to go on living that makes killing someone seriously wrong, then presumably it is not wrong to kill someone who does not have the desire to go on living, due to (treatable) depression. But of course, Marquis argues, it *is* wrong, and the FLO account can explain why. A person can have a valuable future, even if, due to depression, he does not now have the desire to go on living. It would be seriously wrong to kill him and thereby to deprive him of that valuable future. (Presumably it would not be wrong to kill someone whose depression was untreatable and who faced "a future of pain and despair." At least, it would not wrong the person killed, though Marquis leaves it open that there might be other reasons why killing him would be wrong.)

The interest view is not vulnerable to these alleged counter-examples. The difference between a fetus and a temporarily comatose adult (TCA) is that a TCA has desires, including a desire to go on living, that make it seriously wrong to kill him. The same is not true of an embryo or first-trimester fetus, which has no desires at all.[14] Admittedly, a TCA does not have any conscious desires. But even while he is unconscious, he still has desires, just as he still has beliefs. David Boonin points out that not all of our beliefs are ones of which we are consciously aware: they are not all occurrent beliefs. To illustrate the dispositional nature of many of our beliefs, Boonin gives the following example. Ten minutes ago you probably were not consciously aware of believing that a triangle has three sides. Yet if I were to ask you, "how many sides does a triangle have?" you would be disposed to answer, "three." That is why it is a dispositional belief. Nevertheless, it is one of your beliefs, a belief you already have. As Boonin puts it, "you do not lose all of your beliefs each time you go to bed and then acquire a new and identical set of beliefs each time you wake up. You retain your beliefs as dispositional beliefs and occasionally have some or others as occurrent beliefs."[15]

Similarly, if you desire not to be killed, you continue to have that desire dispositionally while you are in a reversible coma. On the basis of this desire, we can ascribe to you an interest in continued existence, an interest that exerts a moral claim on the rest of us not to kill you while you are temporarily comatose. But the same cannot be said of a being, like an embryo, that has never been conscious and so has no desires, occurrent or dispositional, and hence no interests.

In a forthcoming article, "Abortion Revisited," Marquis writes, "Boonin's account of and defense of a dispositional desire strategy for dealing with the alleged temporarily unconscious adult counterexample to the present desire view seems reasonable."[16] I take this to mean that Marquis now agrees that the alleged counterexample of the temporarily comatose adult is not a problem for desire- or sentience-based accounts. But what about someone who has no desire, occurrent or dispositional, to go on living, due to severe but temporary depression? Can the interest view explain why it would be seriously wrong to kill such a person without at the same time implying that it would be seriously wrong to kill a fetus?

Boonin responds by arguing that sometimes we need to correct a person's actual desires because, due to various distorting conditions, they do not represent what the individual really wants. He writes, ". . . in many cases in which we believe that the present desires of others are morally significant, we distinguish between the actual content of the desire that a person has given her actual circumstances and the content the desire she actually has *would* have had if the actual desire had been formed under more ideal circumstances."[17] In the case of the depressed person who does not want to live, it is the depression that makes him unable to think clearly and unable to enjoy his life. When he comes out of the depression, life will seem to him to be worth living again. So of course it would be seriously wrong to kill him while he is in the depressed state. As Boonin puts it, ". . . when someone's desires are such that they would very strongly desire that you not do something to them were they able to reflect more clearly on the question, then that counts as a very strong moral reason not to do it."[18]

Marquis thinks that the case of the depressed person ("Hans" in Boonin's example) and the fetus are analogous. If what makes killing Hans seriously wrong is that Hans would want to go on living if he were able to think clearly, then why can't we say that what makes killing the fetus wrong is that it would want to go on living, if it could think about it. This is not like saying that a rock would want to go on living if it could think about it, because unlike a rock, a fetus has a future of value, that is, a life that it will value in the future. In this respect, the fetus is just like Hans. And so Marquis writes, "Fetuses are quite different. Hypothetical desires can be attributed as easily to fetuses as to Hans."[19] However, fetuses do not have distorted desires, which need correcting in order to perceive what they really want. Preconscious fetuses do not have desires at all. It seems to me one thing to ascribe an ideal or hypothetical desire to a person whose desires have been distorted, and quite another to ascribe hypothetical desires to a being incapable of having any desires. In any event, I am not sure how much Marquis wants or needs to base his argument on the ascription of hypothetical desires to fetuses, as he has a different argument, which is not dependent on the existence of such desires. He suggests that we can ". . . attribute interests to a presently insentient being in virtue of its well-being at some future sentient stage of its natural history."[20] In other words, although the fetus is now unconscious and has no desires, it can still have an interest in its future, in the sense that its future is *in* its interest. The motivation for this claim is the view of the fetus as just one stage in a person's natural history. If my life and my future existence are something I value, then it is rational for me to be glad that I was not killed at an earlier stage, for example, when I was a fetus. My valuable future is its valuable future. Having that future (that is, not being killed) is as much in its interest as it is in mine. Or rather, not being killed is as much in my interest when I was a fetus as it is in my interest now.

McMahan's Mind Essentialism

So the next question is, was I ever a fetus? That may seem indisputable, given the biological facts. Everyone, surely, started life as a zygote, which developed into an embryo, which became a fetus, and then was born as a baby. However, this is exactly what Jeff McMahan wants to deny. He writes,

> . . . even if we grant that a new human organism begins to exist at conception, it follows from this fact that we began to exist at conception only if we are human organisms. . . . if I am a human organism, I began to exist when this organism did. But the assumption that I am numerically identical with the organism with which (to put it as neutrally as possible) I coexist is hardly uncontroversial.[21]

McMahan thinks that the most plausible account of what I essentially am is an embodied consciousness. And if that's the case, then I never existed as a nonconscious fetus. I came into existence when my organism began to be conscious—sometime between 20 and 28 weeks of gestation.[22] Summarizing McMahan's position, David DeGrazia writes,

> . . . the thesis of mind essentialism implies that early fetuses, lacking minds, cannot become minded beings, since it asserts that anything that is ever minded is always minded. Thus, early abortions do not kill beings with significant moral status, making these abortions "relevantly like contraception and wholly unlike the killing of a person." The Valuable Futures Argument therefore trips on the mistaken assumption that the early fetus will develop into a minded being. Because it will not, the early fetus does not *have* a valuable future.[23]

McMahan's theory provides a neat response to Marquis—but only if one accepts his mind essentialism, and the idea that the preconscious fetus cannot develop into a conscious fetus, much less a person like you or me. That seems to me to fly in the face of the facts. It seems much more plausible to say that I was once a child, and before that an infant, and before that a fetus. Boonin, commenting on the pictures in his office of his son, Eli, at various stages after birth, says, "through all of the remarkable changes that these pictures preserve, he remains unmistakably the same little boy." He also has another picture of Eli taken 24 weeks before his birth. Boonin writes, "there is no doubt in my mind that this picture, too, shows that same little boy at a very early stage in his physical development."[24] McMahan would have to say that the sonogram is a picture of Eli's organism at a very early stage, but it is not a picture of Eli. I would say (and I assume Boonin would agree) that I am my organism, although this is not all that I am. However, to posit a "me" that is distinct from my physical self seems implausible, and the wrong way to defend abortion. Rather, I would say that when I was a fetus, it would have been permissible to abort me, because had I been aborted before I became conscious and sentient, it would not have mattered to me. It would have made no more difference to me than preventing my conception. So while I agree with Marquis that I was once a fetus, I deny that when I was a fetus, I had an interest or a stake in my valuable future. I think that when I was a mindless fetus, I had no interests at all.

Implications for Blastocysts

I began this paper with the question whether it is seriously wrong to kill 35 embryos at the blastocyst stage. I want to suggest now that even if Marquis is right about the morality of abortion—that it's wrong to kill fetuses because they have valuable futures it is not plausible to claim that pre-implantation embryos do. For unlike a fetus, an extracorporeal embryo is not developing into someone with a valuable future. Left alone (that is, not aborted), the fetus will (most likely) develop into someone with a valuable future. But the same is just not true of an embryo, whether left-over from IVF or deliberately created for research. Left alone, an extracorporeal embryo will just die. That's not much of a valuable future.

It might be argued that the blastocyst *could* be implanted into a uterus, where it too would develop into a baby, and thus it has, hypothetically, a valuable future. Of course, this is true only of viable embryos. Non-viable embryos— embryos incapable of further development—cannot have valuable futures. Presumably, even on Marquis's view, it would be morally permissible to use non-viable embryos left over from infertility treatment in embryo research (although I do not know if the stem cells derived from non-viable embryos could be used in treating disease, should ES cell therapies ever be developed).

Most opponents of ES cell research make no distinction between embryos created by IVF and embryos created by cloning. However, on the Valuable Futures approach, there might be a considerable difference. We know that it is possible, under some set of conditions, for an IVF embryo to develop into a baby. Over 35,000 babies were born in the United States alone in 2000 (ASRM/SART Registry 2004). By contrast, biologist Rudof Jaenisch maintains that "a cloned embryo has little, if any, potential to develop into a normal human being." He explains:

> By circumventing the normal processes of gametogenesis and fertilization, nuclear cloning prevents the proper reprogramming of the clone's genome . . . which is a prerequisite for the development of an embryo into a normal organism. It is unlikely that these biologic barriers to normal development can be overcome in the foreseeable future.[25]

Jaenisch hastens to point out that the embryonic stem cells derived from a cloned embryo are functionally indistinguishable from those derived from IVF embryos, making them equally useful as a source for ES cells in research or therapy.

The chance a human embryo has of developing into a normal human being is irrelevant from the perspective of the biological humanity criterion. What matters for moral status is that the embryo is a human organism (although, as we have seen, there is considerable debate about when a human organism comes into existence). On this criterion, the moral status of the embryo is determined by its genetic humanity, not what it can or cannot develop into. Marquis, however, explicitly rejects the genetic humanity criterion, because it is hard to see why a merely biological category should make a moral difference. Clearly, he is sympathetic to this objection expressed by pro-choicers: "why, it is asked, is it any more reasonable to base a moral conclusion on the number of chromosomes in one's cells than on the color of one's skin?"[26] By contrast, on the Valuable Futures approach, the developmental potential of an embryo makes all the difference in the world, since if a cloned embryo cannot develop into someone like you or me, it cannot have FLO. Killing it does not deprive it of its valuable future, and therefore, presumably, is not seriously wrong.

This has interesting implications for the "created/spare" distinction, 40 appealed to by the National Bioethics Advisory Commission (NBAC) in its report, *Cloning Human Beings.* According to NBAC, it would be wrong to create embryos solely for the purpose of research; to do so would be inconsistent with the respect due to embryos as a form of human life. However, it would be ethically permissible to use embryos created for reproductive purposes, which are no longer needed (so-called "spare" embryos), since these embryos would be discarded anyway. President Bush considered this argument in his August 6, 2001 address to the nation, but ultimately rejected it. He maintained that it was impermissible to kill any embryos, even those that would be discarded anyway. On the valuable futures approach, it appears that the created/spare distinction has moral relevance, though precisely opposite to that claimed by NBAC. Whereas NBAC argued that only spare embryos can be ethically used (and destroyed) in research, in the valuable futures approach, it would be morally acceptable to use cloned human embryos as sources of stem cells since they lack FLO, but unacceptable to use embryos discarded after fertility treatment, since they have FLO. They have FLO because they could be used to make babies, even if their creators do not wish to use them for this purpose. This is a rather startling implication of the Valuable Futures argument. The claim that it is morally better to use cloned embryos rather than embryos left over from infertility treatment is not one that I have seen anywhere in the Valuable Futures literature.

My own view is that we should reject the created/spare distinction, although not for the reason President Bush gave. I think that it is permissible to use human embryos in research that kills them because embryos lack moral status. In my view, it makes no difference what the source of the embryos is, whether they are created by IVF or cloned; whether they are created specifically for research purposes or are left over from infertility treatment. However, I do not think it is permissible to use embryos for frivolous or trivial purposes. I maintain that respect for human life requires that human embryos be used for morally important purposes, but that is a topic for another paper.[27] ◎/◎

References

1. S. G. Stolberg, "Controversy Reignites Over Stem Cells and Clones," *New York Times,* December 18,2001, at F1.
2. R. M. Green, *The Human Embryo Research Debates* (New York: Oxford University Press, 2001): at 28.
3. *Id.,* at 29.
4. See also J. A. Robertson, *Children of Choice: Freedom and the New Reproductive Technologies* (Princeton: Princeton University Press, 1994): at 251, note 13: ". . . recent studies suggest that a new genome is not expressed until the four- to eight-cell stage of development." See Braude, Bolton, and Moore, "Human Gene Expression First Occurs Between the Four and Eight-Cell Stages of Preimplantation Development," *Nature* 332 (1988): at 459, 460.
5. M. Warren, "On the Moral and Legal Status of Abortion," *The Monist* 57, no. 1, (1973): 43–61. Warren's views have changed since 1973, and her current views on moral status are given in her book, *Moral Status.* Nevertheless, her earlier article is an excellent statement of the person view, a view that many people continue to hold.
6. I develop the interest view in chapter 1 of my book, *Life Before Birth: The Moral and Legal Status of Embryos and Fetuses* (New York: Oxford University Press, 1992).
7. J. Feinberg, "The Rights of Animals and Unborn Generations," in William T. Blackstone, ed., *Philosophy & Environmental Crisis* (Athens: University of Georgia Press, 1974).
8. J. Feinberg, *Harm to Others* (New York: Oxford University Press, 1984): at 34.
9. D. Boonin, *A Defense of Abortion* (Cambridge: Cambridge University Press, 2003): at 102.
10. *Id.,* at 102–103, citing T. Nagel, "What Is It Like to Be a Bat?" in T. Nagel, *Mortal Questions* (Cambridge: Cambridge University Press, 1979): at 166.
11. Some philosophers apparently reject the idea that harming involves the setting back or thwarting of a being's interests. See, for example, E. Harman, "The Potentiality Problem," *Philosophical Studies* 114 (2003): 173–198. Harman thinks that it is obvious that beings without moral status can be harmed, and gives the following example: The deprivation of light harms a weed. However, the reason why I maintain that a weed is not harmed when it is killed is not that weeds lack moral status. Rather, it is that I agree with Feinberg that harming involves the setting back or thwarting of interests. Since weeds (or prize orchids, for that matter) do not have interests, they cannot be harmed, though they can be killed. To show that this is wrong, one would need to give an alternate account of harming, something Harman does not do.
12. D. Marquis, "Why Abortion Is Immoral," *The Journal of Philosophy* 86, no. 4 (1989): 183–202, at 189–190.
13. *Id.,* at 191.
14. In *Life Before Birth*, I argued that sentience was unlikely until well into the second trimester. "Pain perception requires more than brain waves. It involves the development of neural pathways and particular cortical and subcortical centers, as well as neurochemical systems associated with pain transmission. In light of this, it seems extremely unlikely that a first-trimester fetus could be sentient," B. Steinbock, *supra* note 6, at 189. This is consistent with moral recent findings of researchers on fetal pain. Vivette Glover and Nicholas Fisk write, "To experience anything, including pain, the subject needs to be conscious, and current evidence suggests that this involves activity in the cerebral cortex and

possibly the thalamus. We do not know for sure when or even if the fetus becomes conscious. However, temporary thalamocortical connections start to form at about 17 weeks and become established from 26 weeks. It seems very likely that a fetus can feel pain from that stage." V. Glover and N. Fisk, *British Medical Journal* 313 (1996): 796. For this reason, Glover and Fisk suggest that more attention should be paid to pain relief during labor and delivery for the baby as well as the mother, and that safe methods of administering analgesia to the fetus in late terminations (after 20 weeks) should be developed. At the same time, in an interview with the BBC, Dr. Glover stressed that it is incredibly unlikely that a first-trimester fetus can feel pain because there is no linking to the brain at all. Editor, "Abortion Causes Foetal Pain," *BBC. News*, at http://news.bbc.co.uk/1/hi/health/900848.stm (last visited December 6, 2005).

15. D. Boonin, *A Defense of Abortion.* (Cambridge: Cambridge University Press, 2003): at 65–66.
16. D. Marquis, "Abortion Revisited," in B. Steinbock, ed., *The Oxford Handbook of Bioethics.* (Oxford: Oxford University Press, forthcoming).
17. Boonin, *supra* note 15, at 70.
18. *Id.*, at 76.
19. Marquis, *supra* note 16.
20. D. Marquis, "Justifying the Rights of Pregnancy: The Interest View," Review of Bonnie Steinbock, "Life Before Birth," *Criminal Justice Ethics* 13, no. 1 (1994): 67–81, at 72.
21. J. McMahan, *The Ethics of Killing: Problems at the Margins of Life* (New York: Oxford University Press, 2002): at 4.
22. Or as early as 17 weeks, if Glover and Fisk are right, *supra* note 14.
23. D. DeGrazia, "Identity, Killing, and the Boundaries of Our Existence," *Philosophy & Public Affairs* 31, no. 4 (2003): 413–442, at 427.
24. Boonin, *supra* note 15, at xiv.
25. R. Jaenisch, "Human Cloning—The Science and Ethics of Nuclear Transplantation," *New England Journal of Medicine* 351, no. 27(2004): 2787–2791.
26. D. Marquis, *supra* note 12, at 186.
27. See B. Steinbock, "Respect for Human Embryos," in P. Lauritzen, ed., *Cloning and the Future of Human Embryo Research* (New York: Oxford University Press, 2001). See also B. Steinbock, "Moral Status, Moral Value, and Human Embryos: Implications for Stem Cell Research," in B. Steinbock, ed., The *Oxford Handbook of Bioethics* (Oxford: Oxford University Press, forthcoming).

Reflections and Inquiries

1. What is meant by moral status, and how does it apply to the stem cell controversy?

2. According to Steinbock, what are the biological challenges to the view that life begins at conception (fertilization)? How valid are these challenges, in your opinion?

3. How, exactly, does the "person view" of human life differ from the biological view? How do both of these views differ from the "interest view"?

4. What is the "valuable futures" argument? How, if at all, does it influence your stance on the moral status of embryos?

5. How compelling an argument is McMahan's theory of "mind essentialism" in the context of determining the status of embryos?

6. What is Steinbock's thesis in this article?

7. Compare this article to other articles in the stem cell debate section. What are the specific elements, in addition to footnotes, that make it a scholarly article? Regarding the footnotes, what do they contribute to the scholarly nature of the article?

Reading to Write

1. Do an in-depth analysis of one of the theorists whose arguments Steinbock discusses in her article. For example, read Don Marquis's article, "Why Abortion Is Immoral" (see Steinbock's footnote 12) and analyze the strengths and/or weaknesses of his argument.

2. Read Steinbock's book, *Life Before Birth* (see footnote 14); then write an essay supporting or defending her argument regarding the beginning of human life.

A Middle Ground for Stem Cells | Yuval Levin

What really lies at the heart of the stem cell debate? Is it when life first begins? About ethical limits to scientific research? In the following op-ed piece, Yuval Levin, the former executive director of the President's Council on Bioethics and a fellow at the Ethics and Public Policy Center, asserts that it is about neither, but rather about whether every human life, including embryonic life, is equal.

With each new round of argument, the ethical questions at the heart of the embryonic stem cell debate get buried under more layers of hype and confusion.

Backers of a House bill, approved last week, that would loosen the limits on federal support for the research argue that there is now a "ban" on financing, that embryonic stem cells will cure tens of millions and that current federal policy sets American scientists behind their foreign counterparts. But the Bush administration has spent more than $100 million on embryonic stem cell research in the past six years; the research, while promising, remains purely speculative; and American scientists hold a huge and steady lead that no other country comes close to challenging.

Defenders of the president's policy, meanwhile, too often get caught up in comparing adult and embryonic stem cell research. This leads them to deny the utility of embryonic cells, which scientists clearly do find useful, rather than articulating the moral justification for a policy that avoids the destruction of developing life.

Source: Yuval Levin, "A Middle Ground for Stem Cells," *New York Times,* Jan. 19, 2007.

All of this leaves us confused over just what the debate is about. It is, to begin with, not about stem cell research, any more than an argument about the lethal extraction of livers from Chinese political prisoners would be a debate about organ transplantation. There are ethical and unethical ways to transplant organs, and there are ethical and unethical ways to conduct stem cell research. The question is to which category a particular technique—the destruction of living embryos for their cells—belongs.

The debate is also not about whether there ought to be ethical limits on 5 science. Everyone agrees there should be strict limits when research involves human subjects. The question is whether embryos destroyed for their cells are such human subjects.

But that does not mean the stem cell debate is about when human life begins. It is a simple and uncontroversial biological fact that a human life begins when an embryo is created. That embryo is human, and it is alive; its human life will last until its death, whether that comes days after conception or many decades later surrounded by children and grandchildren.

But the biological fact that a human life begins at conception does not by itself settle the ethical debate. The human embryo is a human organism, but is this being—microscopically small, with no self-awareness and little resemblance to us—a person, with a right to life?

Many advocates of federal financing for embryo-destructive research begin from a negative answer to that question. They argue that the human embryo is just too small, too unlike us in appearance, or too lacking in consciousness or sensitivity to pain or other critical mental capacity to be granted a place in the human family. But surely America has learned the hard way not to assign human worth by appearances. And surely we would not deny those who have lost some mental faculties the right to be regarded with respect and protected from harm. Why should we deny it to those whose faculties are still developing?

At its heart, then, when the biology and politics have been stipulated away, the stem cell debate is not about when human life begins but about whether every human life is equal. The circumstances of the embryo outside the body of a mother put that question in perhaps the most exaggerated form imaginable, but they do not change the question.

America's birth charter, the Declaration of Independence, asserts a positive 10 answer to the question, and in lieu of an argument offers another assertion: that our equality is self-evident. But it is not. Indeed, the evidence of nature sometimes makes it very hard to believe that all human beings are equal. It takes a profound moral case to defend the proposition that the youngest and the oldest, the weakest and the strongest, all of us, simply by virtue of our common humanity, are in some basic and inalienable way equals.

Our faith in that essential liberal proposition is under attack by our own humanitarian impulses in the stem cell debate, and it will be under further attack as biotechnology progresses. But the stem cell debate, our first real test, should also be the easiest. We do not, at least in this instance, face a choice between science and the liberal society. We face the challenge of championing both.

President Bush's stem cell policy seeks to meet that challenge. It encourages scientists to pursue the cells they seek without destroying life. Scientific advances in the past two years have suggested that this can be done: that "pluripotent" cells could be developed without harming human embryos; that stem cell science and ethics can be reconciled. But some members of Congress nonetheless insist on a policy that sets the two at odds.

If we cannot pass this first and simplest test of our devotion to human equality and dignity in the age of biotechnology, we will have little chance of meeting the far more difficult challenges to come. Biomedical science can offer us tremendous benefits, but only if we make sure they do not come at the cost of our highest ideals. ◎／◎

Reflections and Inquiries

1. What, exactly, is Levin's "middle ground" in the stem cell debate?

2. According to Levin, our very faith in the claim by the Declaration of Independence that all human beings are created equal is "under attack by our own humanitarian impulses in the stem cell debate." What does he mean by that? How would you defend or refute Levin's claim?

3. Defend or challenge Levin's assertion that the challenge we face is "not between science and the liberal society," but "the challenge of championing both." Suggest how it would be possible to champion both.

Reading to Write

For Levin "strict limitations" are beyond dispute when it comes to human subjects. After reviewing the pros and cons regarding the human status of embryos (see, for example, Bonnie Steinbock's article on page 606), write an essay defending or challenging the assumption that stem cells quality as human subjects.

Stem Cell Spin | Editors of *The New Atlantis*

The United States, according to the editors of The New Atlantis, *"is falling behind other countries in human embryonic stem cell research." Their article reflects on why this is the case and how the Bush administration's policy on stem cell research, contrary to public opinion, is not to blame, but rather the administration's critics are.*

Source: "Stem Cell Spin," *The New Atlantis,* Spring 2006. Reprinted with permission. For more information see www.TheNewAtlantis.com.

The Bush Policy and Its Unreasonable Critics

For connoisseurs of stem cell spin, recent weeks have offered a feast. In its April 2006 issue, the journal *Nature Biotechnology* published a short paper entitled "An international gap in human ES [embryonic stem] cell research." The authors, Jason Owen-Smith of the University of Michigan and Jennifer McCormick of Stanford, carefully reviewed all scientific publications involving the use or derivation of human embryonic stem cells, starting with the very first paper in 1998 and ending just over a year ago.

Their aim, very clear in the tone and tenor of the text, was to show that American stem cell scientists were falling behind their counterparts abroad, and that the Bush administration's funding policy was to blame. "Expanding the purview of federal [human embryonic stem] cell funding can still prevent the United States from slipping off the leading edge of developments in this vital field," the authors write. A press release accompanying the article breathlessly proclaims that "the fear that United States researchers might lose ground to their international counterparts in human embryonic stem cell research now appears to have become a fact."

Coverage of the study took much the same tone. "The United States is falling behind other countries in human embryonic stem cell research," reported UPI. The *Washington Post* began its brief report on the study by telling its readers "American scientists are falling behind researchers elsewhere in stem cell discoveries because of U.S. limits on the use of federal funding, a study has found."

The study itself, however, tells a very different story. Owen-Smith and McCormick reviewed the 132 human embryonic stem cell articles published in 55 scientific journals since 1998. Far from showing the United States lagging behind in the field, they found that American scientists had by far the most publications—46 percent of the total, while the other 54 percent were divided among scientists from 17 other countries. They also found that the number of papers in the field published by Americans has increased each year, with a particularly notable growth spurt beginning in 2002.

How, then, to support the image of Americans "falling behind"? The best 5
the authors could do was to note that, as their accompanying press release claims, "human embryonic stem cell research has been accelerating at a faster pace internationally." They point out that while in 2002 a third of the papers published in the world came from the U.S., in 2004 only a quarter did. Their data also show, however, that in 2002 there were only 10 papers published on human embryonic stem cells (of which 3 were American), while in 2004 there were 77 papers, of which 20 were American. So the number of American publications in the field was nearly seven times greater in 2004 than it was in 2002—a trend that hardly supports the image of research stifled or held back by government policy.

To advance the perception of American science in crisis, Owen-Smith and McCormick compare the output of American scientists to that of their counterparts in the rest of the world combined, hoping to obscure the inconvenient fact that no single country comes close to challenging America's dominance of embryonic stem cell research.

Another recent study, highlighted by *The Scientist* magazine in March 2006, found the same to be the case in the larger field of stem cell research. Between 2000 and 2004, 42 percent of all scientific publications in stem cell research were by Americans. Our nearest competitor was Germany, far behind with only 10 percent of the total.

But the most extraordinary aspect of the Owen-Smith and McCormick study—which the authors conveniently and deliberately fail to highlight— was what it said about the use of those embryonic stem cell lines approved for federal funding under President Bush's 2001 policy. Besides claiming that America is falling behind, critics of the Bush policy have argued relentlessly that the presidentially-approved lines are inadequate or even useless. But this claim is also severely undermined by the study.

Grudgingly, and almost in passing, Owen-Smith and McCormick note that "Only 14.4% (19) of publications described the use or derivation of lines not approved by the NIH." In other words, more than 85 percent of all the published embryonic stem cell research in the world has used the lines approved for funding under the Bush policy. Since this is almost twice the number of papers published by Americans, it is clear that a great deal of the work done abroad has also involved these lines, even though most of it could not have been funded by the NIH. The lines are used, in other words, because they are useful, not only because they are eligible for federal support.

Many critics of the Bush policy claim that the Bush lines are useless because 10 they are contaminated with mouse-feeder cells. This claim also seems largely specious. Two recent studies have shown methods of culturing the NIH-funded lines that leave them free of all trace of animal materials. Discussing his company's use of the Bush-approved lines, Geron CEO Tom Okarma recently told *Wired News*, "the stuff you hear published that all of those lines are irrevocably contaminated with mouse materials and could never be used in people— hogwash. If you know how to grow them, they're fine."

In early April, the *Wall Street Journal* reported similar sentiments from other researchers in the field. While scientists would always welcome more funding for their work (who wouldn't?), those reached by the *Journal* seem not to see Bush's policy as the intolerable impediment his political opponents suggest it is. "There is a lot going on in the U.S.," said Renee Reijo-Pera, co-director of the Human Embryonic Stem Cell Center at the University of California, San Francisco. "The official story [of stem-cell advocates] is how we are falling behind in tragedy and dismay. And I don't think that is the case."

Of course, the argument for the Bush administration's funding policy does not finally rest on scientific utility but on moral and democratic principle. As the President has put it: "We should not use public money to support the further destruction of human life." This means that some types of research, even if beneficial, should never be conducted with federal dollars.

The current limit would not move—and the moral principle it upholds would not change—even if it were true that it "crippled" American stem cell science. And supporters of the Bush policy should be up-front about the fact that some useful research may not advance as quickly or at all, at least in America, because of such limits. Surely more could be done, and more quickly, if more public dollars were spent on more lines—that is, if the profound ethical dilemmas involved were simply ignored.

That said, it is dishonest to obscure the useful research that the Bush policy has indeed facilitated, and disingenuous to claim that America is "falling behind" when it remains, by far, the world's leader in stem cell science. Rather than make the narrow case for funding embryo-destructive research, many opponents of the Bush policy zealously claim that the Bush policy "stops" all useful research. In doing so, they wrongly suggest that scientific advance and ethical boundaries are fundamentally opposed to one another, or they ignore the moral issue entirely, treating stem cell policy as if it were entirely a scientific question to be settled by scientific data.

The point of the Bush policy, for all its many limitations and drawbacks, is to show that science can proceed without violating human dignity or destroying nascent human life, even if it cannot proceed as quickly and by as many simultaneous routes. The choice it offers is not between science and ethics, but between a devotion to science and health so total that it abandons all ethical limits, and a devotion to science and health balanced and constrained by a respect for human equality and dignity, and committed to a culture of life largely understood.

Opponents of the policy usually avoid taking on that basic ethical principle, 15 and so they have offered up various practical arguments against the scientific utility of the policy: the lines are contaminated, there are not enough to support research, they are causing American researchers to fall behind their foreign counterparts. Being practical arguments, these assertions must stand up to factual scrutiny. And so far, the evidence suggests they mostly do not.

One can make reasonable arguments for a more permissive funding policy; one cannot reasonably claim that the policy is wreaking havoc on American science, or that America is becoming backward because only private dollars or state funds are available for the derivation of stem cells from destroyed human embryos. To make such a claim is not science or even the rational defense of science; it is fundamentalism in the name of science, employing the most unscientific means imaginable: playing with the data to advance one's cause.

All things considered, the Bush policy still looks reasonable as it approaches its five-year anniversary. It is helping useful science advance without making embryo destruction a national project and without trampling on the deepest values of those citizens who believe (with good rational arguments) that embryo destruction is a grave wrong. The fight over the policy has also shown, sadly, that the self-proclaimed defenders of reason cannot always be counted on to be reasonable themselves. ◎/◎

Reflections and Inquiries

1. What does this article suggest about the role of politics in establishing stem cell research policies?

2. How convincingly do the authors make their case that the Bush policy enables stem cell research to proceed without violating human dignity?

Reading to Write

Stem cell research policies are continuously being modified. Visit the National Institutes of Health Stem Cell Information website, http:// stemcells.nih.gov, and study the latest information on research policies. Write an essay in which you argue the ethical aspects of these policies.

Issues for Further Research: Transgenic Animals

Genetically Engineered Animals and the New "Pharm" Animal Factories | Michael W. Fox

In 1980 an American scientist received a patent for an oil-eating bacterium that she engineered, and in the nearly thirty years since then many animal species from mice to livestock have been genetically enhanced for commercial purposes. At least one cancer researcher has genetically engineered a mouse containing 1 percent human brain tissue. Cows and chickens are manipulated to yield higher muscle-mass to body fat ratios.

As one might expect, many individuals and agencies have campaigned against genetically manipulating animals. Greenpeace, for example, has issued a position statement, "Say no to genetic engineering" (www.greenpeace.org/international/ campaigns/genetic-engineering). Similarly, Dr. Michael W. Fox, in his book Killer Foods, *addresses the dangers of this rapidly proliferating biotechnology. In the following selection from his book, Fox considers the ethics and the dangers of attempting to make farm animals more productive through genetic manipulation. Michael W. Fox is a member of the Royal College of Veterinary Surgeons and Chief Consultant/Veterinarian for the India Project for Animals and Nature. In his Universal Bill of Rights for Animals and Nature (http://tedeboy.tripod.com/ drmichaelwfox/id54.html), Fox writes,*

Source: "Genetically Engineered Animals and the New 'Pharm' Animal Factories," from *Killer Foods* by Michael W. Fox, copyright © 1999 by Michael W. Fox, used by permission of The Lyons Press, Guilford, CT.

The humane treatment of animals and the consideration of their needs not only safe-guards these living, feeling earth-relatives of ours from harm and suffering, but also elevates and refines the human spirit.

A cow is nothing but cells on the hoof.
—Dr. Thomas Wagner

Transgenic Animals

Animals carrying genes from other species that have been inserted during early embryonic development are referred to as *transgenic*. Transgenic organisms carry genetic information not normally present in the species. This genetic information has been deliberately amplified, spread, or disseminated in the species at a much faster rate than occurs naturally. In many instances these new genes will be passed on to offspring, so they become permanently incorporated into the germ line, or hereditary makeup of the animal.

Thousands of varieties of transgenic animals have been created, and in many instances mortality is high and suffering considerable. The first transgenic animal to be patented was a mouse that was bioengineered by Harvard University scientists with funding from DuPont Chemical Company to be extremely susceptible to cancer-causing chemicals and to succumb at an early age to breast cancer. The first transgenic farm animals were developed with public funds by scientists of the U.S. Department of Agriculture, who spliced human growth genes into pigs. These pigs experienced considerable suffering, physical deformities, and high mortalities at an early age.

The genetic engineering of animals produces a number of questionable consequences. These include physical suffering; psychological distress; behavioral impairment; developmental, reproductive, and immunological disorders; metabolic and regulatory disturbances; different nutritional and other physiological requirements; and new diseases that will be difficult to diagnose and treat. There are also moral concerns such as the sanctity of life and the integrity of species, and ecological concerns, as with the potentially adverse environmental impact and harm to wild plant and animal species and communities if deliberately or accidentally released transgenic animals, especially insects and fish, become established and multiply. This threat to natural biodiversity is compounded by the increasing loss of genetic diversity in domesticated plant and animal varieties as a shrinking genetic pool is utilized in conventional agriculture. Contrary to the claims of genetic-engineering advocates, this technology will not increase genetic diversity. It will more likely result in unforeseen genetic anomalies and increased susceptibility to environmental stress and diseases because of the inherent genetic uniformity of existing commercial plant and animal breeding stocks that are now being genetically engineered.

"Pharm" Animal Bioreactors*

The results of various genetic engineering experiments reviewed by Vernon G. Pursel, Ph.D., a USDA employee and one of the creators of the crippled transgenic "Beltsville pigs," make dubious a future in which biotechnology is used to make farm animals more productive. Pursel states, "At present, the transgenic approach for improvement of farm animals for production purposes remains only a hope for the future." As for engineering farm animals to produce new-generation healthcare products, he cautions:

> Even though several human therapeutical proteins have now been successful- 5
> ly produced in milk and blood of transgenic animals, some difficult problems
> must be solved before these products are approved for use. Product safety is
> a large issue. These products will require the same rigorous scrutiny as the
> products extracted from animal tissue produced by tissue culture or synthe-
> sized by recombinant organisms. Products from transgenic animals must be
> purified to remove all non-human proteins that might cause allergic reactions.
> In addition, it is still not known whether these complex human proteins are
> sufficiently similar in structure and biological activity to the natural proteins
> produced by the human body so that antibodies are not produced. While
> scientists are confident that these technical and regulatory obstacles can be
> overcome, few people are willing to predict how long it will take to work out
> these problems and complete the clinical testing that will be required to obtain
> approval of regulatory authorities for marketing to the public.

Scientists of the U.S. company Genzyme Transgenics Corporation reported a "biopharming" breakthrough in January 1998 with the creation of transgenic mice that produce human growth hormone from urinary bladder cells. This is seen as offering an alternative to the mammary gland as a bioreactor for producing pharmaceuticals, since milk, unlike urine, contains much protein and fat, making purification more difficult and costly. Plus with a bladder bioreactor, products could be harvested shortly after birth from both sexes. Also, milk may contain more viruses and other potential pathogens. Since plants, unlike goats and cows, have few diseases that are transmissible to humans, creating transgenic plants to produce vaccines and various pharmaceuticals would seem safer and less costly, and the plants would be easier to distribute in developing countries, as by growing transgenic bananas and spinach locally to produce rabies, hepatitis B, and other oral vaccines for humans and animals.** The creation of such transgenic plants, provided they do not cause genetic pollution

---

Bioreactor is the term used by the industry for an animal or animal's organ that produces pharmaceutical products.

**The first successful trials of an edible vaccine (to prevent *E. coli* travelers' diarrhea) in genetically engineered raw potatoes was announced in April 1998 by the Boyce Thompson Institute for Plant Research, Inc., an affiliate of Cornell University, in collaboration with the University of Maryland School of Medicine's Center for Vaccine Development in Baltimore.

and are protected from nontarget species, is one area of genetic engineering I would endorse in these times of plagues and pestilence.

One ethical issue concerns the ever intensifying commercial exploitation of animals as bioreactors or "biomachines" and as a source of replacement body fluids and parts for humans, from blood and bones to livers and hearts. These valuable, patented human creations—"manimals"—of the new industrial biofarms of the next century will serve a wealthy elite. Their existence may deter some extremely wealthy people from having themselves cloned as a source of organ parts. Manimals instead will provide replacement parts as needed. But will their products be safe?

Transgenic animals do produce relatively higher concentrations of mono-clonal antibodies and other health care products in their milk, such as lactofer-rin, than can be achieved using cell cultures and transgenic plants. But this advantage of higher production efficiency must be weighed against the greater risks of disease (zoonosis) from animals to humans, from retroviruses to prions, a bovine variant of which has caused an epidemic of a human brain disease in the U.K. called Creutzfeldt-Jakob disease. A major advantage of using transgenic plants rather than "pharm" animals to produce pharmacological proteins is that the likelihood of cross-contamination or rejection by the human immune system is lower with plant proteins. Regardless, European-based Pharming B.V is devel-oping transgenic animals to produce the following biomedical proteins in their milk: human lactoferrin/lysozyme, human collagen, and human serum albu-min. PPL Therapeutics (in Blacksburg, Virginia, and Edinburgh, Scotland) is developing animals to produce the human protein alpha lactalbumin.

Organ Parts

According to the *London Times* (October 26, 1997), while pig xenotransplants (genetically engineered pig organs designed to be put into humans) are banned in the U.K., three hospitals in the United States are connecting patients with hepatic failure to transgenic pigs' livers.*

The August 1998 issue of the British medical journal *Lancet* carries a cau-   10
tionary word in its "Early Reports" section, "Expression of pig endogenous retrovirus [PERV] by primary porcine endothelial cells and infection of human cells," in which Ulrich Martin and his coauthors state that pigs pose "a serious risk of retrovirus transfer after xenotransplantation" (retroviruses are a type of virus that lives in animals' cells and can be inherited). In three breeds of pig from twelve sites in Denmark, Russia, Germany, and France, these investigators detected PERV in every sample of skin, liver, lung, and aortic endothelial cells. Co-cultivation of the aortic cells with human embryonic kidney cells "led to productive infection of the human cells and expression of PERV," they wrote.

*Controversy was sparked in May 1998 when Imutran, the U.K. company that has developed organ-donor pigs, shipped some to the Netherlands to a primate research facility where macaque monkeys would be experimented upon as recipients of pigs' organs.

In a review in *Nature Magazine* (vol. 391, 1998, p. 322), further concerns about the hazards of human infection with pig viruses from infected organs was underscored by the finding that ten diabetic patients who received pancreatic islet cells from pigs had antibodies to porcine influenza virus, five to parvovirus, and five to other pig viruses.

Genetically Engineered Poultry

Because chickens breed quickly and their embryos beneath the shell are easier to manipulate than mammalian embryos, it is surprising that so little transgenic research has been done on them. Engineered eggs could give new meaning to nutraceuticals (nutrients with medical benefits) and provide human pharmaceuticals such as immunoglobulins and blood proteins. Currently, modified avian leukemia and reticulo-endothelial cancer are used as vectors to transmit genes, many being human, into developing chick embryos and adult birds. According to chicken engineer Dr. F. Abel Ponce de Leon, head of the Department of Animal Science at the University of Minnesota, Minneapolis, whose work is supported by a grant from Sima Biotechnology, a subsidiary of Avian Farms:

> Chickens produce sugar moieties [types] more similar to those produced by humans than those made by cattle. There may be a large number of pharmaceuticals that are better to produce in the chicken—for instance, thrombosis drugs and blood thinners. Because there is no biological cross-reactivity, overexpression of these drugs won't harm the chicken. These are theoretical advantages. We won't know for sure until we have a finished product.

Creating chicken and egg bioreactors to produce useful health care products may be preferable if Dr. Ponce de Leon is correct that transgenic mammals can be harmed by overproduction of these drugs in their bodies.

The problem of "overexpression" of transgenic traits in animals is a serious animal health and welfare concern. Excessively high levels of growth hormones in transgenic sheep developed by Australian government scientists, for example, induced a diabetic condition that led to ketosis and death; while in pigs, serious joint problems, stomach ulcers, and infertility were reported by U.S. government scientists. The diagnosis and treatment of these new kinds of disease in transgenic animals will be a difficult and costly challenge.

Engineering More Meat

One of the most disturbing areas of transgenic animal research is aimed at creating massively muscled farm animals that are essentially crippled monstrosities, many of which have to be delivered by Caesarian section because they are already so enormous at birth. A mutation in the myostatin gene causes double muscles in Belgian blue cattle. When this muscle-growth–regulating gene was "knocked out" in engineered mice, their muscles grew huge. Research into this technique is proceeding in the hope of making farm animals like these mice, 15 with the rationale being that "extra helpings of tasty meat at essentially no cost could prove hard to resist," according to reporter Steven Dickman.

Following another transgenic-mouse model that resulted in enlarged muscles and reduced body fat when the chicken cSKI gene was transferred (a system developed by bioengineers at USDA and patented by the U.S. Chamber of Commerce), pigs and calves were similarly engineered. The results were catastrophic for the animals—abnormal, crippling muscle growth, muscle atrophy, weakness, and degeneration.

The *London Times* of May 14, 1995, reported that Israeli scientists have bioengineered broiler chickens with 40 percent fewer feathers, which eat more because they are cold and hence grow faster and go for slaughter sooner; that Australian scientists have developed a "self-shearing" sheep that sheds its wool; and that USDA's second-generation Beltsville, Maryland, "Schwarzenegger pigs"—made to grow massive muscles following transgenic insertion of a suspected chicken cancer gene—became sickly cripples by three months of age.

We now have the technology to clone beef, chicken, and pork cells and to make nutritious biological analogs of hamburgers and pork sausages without causing animals any harm. So why don't we use this technology instead of raising billions of animals in bio concentration camps—the factory sheds and feedlots that blight the countryside?

The animal factories of agribusiness operate under the economics of bioconcentration, coupled with centralization of production and product uniformity. Ecologists and forensic scientists recognize bioconcentration, the overpopulation of various species, as an indicator of population imbalance and disease. This can mean the demise of biodiversity and healthy ecosystems. Imbalance creates disease, and this is why farm animals become sicker and suffer the more we subject them to bioconcentration in factory production systems and extensive rangeland conditions of overgrazing. The state of mind that embraces such bioconcentration as necessary and even progressive must submit to nature's wisdom, or suffer the consequences.

Turn from the pig, chicken, cow, and bullock concentration camps to the 20 bioconcentrated and chemical-dependent fields and plantations where genetically "improved" biomass commodity crops, such as wheat, rice, corn, cotton, tomato, tobacco, and potato—our life's staples—are now being planted. These new "supercrops," because of bioconcentration and biological uniformity, will be subject to a host of new diseases, fungal blights, viral wilts, and insect invasions. The same fateful consequences of bioconcentration, coupled with an accelerating loss of biodiversity and cultural diversity, will afflict us ever more severely. Thus, the less choice we will have in the marketplace for natural, wholesome food.

Had her forests not gone to beef and lumber, Honduras would not have been so devastated by the 1998 hurricane. Nor would millions continue to sicken and even die from eating the products of bioconcentrated industrial fields and animal bioconcentration camps, which are often contaminated chemically, bacterially, and in other ways.

And it is cause for concern that China, whose rapidly industrializing human biomass is over one billion, with India close behind, should now begin to worsen the bioconcentration and biodiversity situations by adopting Western systems of livestock and crop production. China now has millions of acres of genetically engineered crops, especially tobacco, for export. More Chinese are eating chicken and hamburgers and are already experiencing the rush of Western appetites and disease. Humanity should be advised that until all living beings under our control are seen as subjects to be served rather than as objects to be exploited, we and they will never be well. ◎/◎

Reflections and Inquiries

1. According to Fox, genetic manipulation of animals produces several negative consequences. Which seem to you to be the most serious, and why?

2. Genetic engineering of animals shows promise of providing "replacement body fluids and parts for humans, from blood and bones to livers and hearts." Do you agree or disagree that this should be considered an ethical problem? Explain.

3. Discuss the implications behind Fox's claim "that until all living beings under our control are seen as subjects to be served rather than as objects to be exploited, we and they will never be well."

Reading to Write

Fox published his book in 1999. How have policies and practices regarding the genetic engineering of animals changed since the book was published? Write an essay on what you consider to be a continuing or newly developed concern with either animal patenting or the genetic altering of animals.

Patenting Life | Michael Crichton

Patenting genetically altered animals for laboratory research may seem like a good idea from an intellectual property point of view. After all, if a scientist creates a microorganism capable of, let us say, absorbing pesticide traces that have been absorbed into harvested crops or traces of mercury that have been absorbed by fish, shouldn't that scientist's right of ownership (and the remuneration resulting from it) be protected? No, insists Michael Crichton, for the reasons he explains in the following op-ed piece. Michael Crichton, the creator of the television series ER *and famous for his blockbuster science fiction novels* The Andromeda Strain, Jurassic Park, *and* Next, *is a graduate of Harvard Medical School, and served as a postdoctoral fellow at the Salk Institute.*

Source: Michael Crichton, "Patenting Life," *New York Times*, Feb. 13, 2007. © 2007, The New York Times. Reprinted by permission.

You, or someone you love, may die because of a gene patent that should never have been granted in the first place. Sound far-fetched? Unfortunately, it's only too real.

Gene patents are now used to halt research, prevent medical testing and keep vital information from you and your doctor. Gene patents slow the pace of medical advance on deadly diseases. And they raise costs exorbitantly: a test for breast cancer that could be done for $1,000 now costs $3,000.

Why? Because the holder of the gene patent can charge whatever he wants, and does. Couldn't somebody make a cheaper test? Sure, but the patent holder blocks any competitor's test. He owns the gene. Nobody else can test for it. In fact, you can't even donate your own breast cancer gene to another scientist without permission. The gene may exist in your body, but it's now private property.

This bizarre situation has come to pass because of a mistake by an under-financed and understaffed government agency. The United States Patent Office misinterpreted previous Supreme Court rulings and some years ago began—to the surprise of everyone, including scientists decoding the genome—to issue patents on genes.

Humans share mostly the same genes. The same genes are found in other   5
animals as well. Our genetic makeup represents the common heritage of all life on earth. You can't patent snow, eagles or gravity, and you shouldn't be able to patent genes, either. Yet by now one-fifth of the genes in your body are privately owned.

The results have been disastrous. Ordinarily, we imagine patents promote innovation, but that's because most patents are granted for human inventions. Genes aren't human inventions, they are features of the natural world. As a result these patents can be used to block innovation, and hurt patient care.

For example, Canavan disease is an inherited disorder that affects children starting at 3 months; they cannot crawl or walk, they suffer seizures and eventually become paralyzed and die by adolescence. Formerly there was no test to tell parents if they were at risk. Families enduring the heartbreak of caring for these children engaged a researcher to identify the gene and produce a test. Canavan families around the world donated tissue and money to help this cause.

When the gene was identified in 1993, the families got the commitment of a New York hospital to offer a free test to anyone who wanted it. But the researcher's employer, Miami Children's Hospital Research Institute, patented the gene and refused to allow any health care provider to offer the test without paying a royalty. The parents did not believe genes should be patented and so did not put their names on the patent. Consequently, they had no control over the outcome.

In addition, a gene's owner can in some instances also own the mutations of that gene, and these mutations can be markers for disease. Countries that don't have gene patents actually offer better gene testing than we do, because when multiple labs are allowed to do testing, more mutations are discovered, leading to higher-quality tests.

Apologists for gene patents argue that the issue is a tempest in a teapot, that 10 patent licenses are readily available at minimal cost. That's simply untrue. The owner of the genome for Hepatitis C is paid millions by researchers to study this disease. Not surprisingly, many other researchers choose to study something less expensive.

But forget the costs: why should people or companies own a disease in the first place? They didn't invent it. Yet today, more than 20 human pathogens are privately owned, including haemophilus influenza and Hepatitis C. And we've already mentioned that tests for the BRCA genes for breast cancer cost $3,000. Oh, one more thing: if you undergo the test, the company that owns the patent on the gene can keep your tissue and do research on it without asking your permission. Don't like it? Too bad.

The plain truth is that gene patents aren't benign and never will be. When SARS was spreading across the globe, medical researchers hesitated to study it—because of patent concerns. There is no clearer indication that gene patents block innovation, inhibit research and put us all at risk.

Even your doctor can't get relevant information. An asthma medication only works in certain patients. Yet its manufacturer has squelched efforts by others to develop genetic tests that would determine on whom it will and will not work. Such commercial considerations interfere with a great dream. For years we've been promised the coming era of personalized medicine—medicine suited to our particular body makeup. Gene patents destroy that dream.

Fortunately, two congressmen want to make the full benefit of the decoded genome available to us all. Last Friday, Xavier Becerra, a Democrat of California, and Dave Weldon, a Republican of Florida, sponsored the Genomic Research and Accessibility Act, to ban the practice of patenting genes found in nature. Mr. Becerra has been careful to say the bill does not hamper invention, but rather promotes it. He's right. This bill will fuel innovation, and return our common genetic heritage to us. It deserves our support. ◎/◎

Reflections and Inquires

1. According to Crichton, just as we "can't patent snow, eagles or gravity," we "shouldn't be able to patent genes, either." Comment on the soundness of this analogy.

2. Crichton argues that gene patenting could be used to block innovation and hurt patient care. What evidence does Crichton present to support his claim, and how convincing is it in your opinion?

3. What is the current status of the Genomic Research and Accessibility Act? Explain why you would support or challenge this congressional effort to make the benefits of the decoded genome accessible?

Reading to Write

1. In Crichton's view, the counterargument that patents are readily available at minimal cost is "simply untrue." After learning more about current costs involved in using patented organisms in biomedical research, write a position paper supporting or defending the practice of gene patenting.

2. Write an essay in which you consider the ethical implications of patenting genetically altered organisms.

A Question of Chimeras | Clare Kittredge

In the following report, Clare Kittredge calls attention to some of the more startling events in the history of animal patenting, such as the creation of "chimeras" (animals that have been modified by the insertion of genetic material from other species, including humans), and the filing by two antianimal patenting experts (one a cell biologist, the other a well-known activist against genetic engineering) of a "protest patent"— for a theoretical chimera never actually created, for the express aim of its being rejected so that the United States Patent and Trademark Office (USPTO) ruling would "prevent scientists and biotechs from obtaining similar patents." Clare Kittredge, a long-time correspondent for the Boston Globe, *writes extensively on medical and health-care issues.*

Scientists Say Ruling on Protest Patent Won't Have an Impact on Future Chimerac-Animal Patents

Looking to cure a host of neurodegenerative diseases, StemCells, a Palo Alto, Calif.-based company, has transplanted human neural stem cells into the brains of thousands of mice. The mice are technically chimeras, or is a mix of two or more species. (The word "chimera" refers to the Greek mythological creature that has a lion's head, a goat's body, and a serpent's tail.) President and CEO Martin McGlynn says his biotech company is now waiting for the FDA's permission to test human neural stem cells—the ones already tested in mice—in human patients.

Such animals, especially mice, have been used to search for ways to cure human diseases including Parkinson and Alzheimer disease. "Having the

---

Source: Clare Kittredge, "A Question of Chimeras," *The Scientist: A Magazine of the Life Sciences* 19.7 (11 April 2005). Reprinted by permission.

ability to evaluate human cells in a mouse or other animal is critical to translating scientific discoveries into therapeutic medicine," says McGlynn. "It's the key. It's the bridge to the clinic."

However, the use of such chimeric animals is the focus of a complicated patent case that is raising legal and ethical questions. In this case, opponents to the patenting of living things applied for a chimera patent. The US Patent and Trademark Office (USPTO) recently refused to issue a patent for the human-animal chimera in the application, on the grounds that it would have been too nearly human.

In the volatile debate over bioengineered life forms, many disagree about the ramifications of the recent case. The critics of the biotechnology industry who applied for the patent say the case has serious business and research implications. But some leading scientists and industry observers say the case is just another effort to grab attention in a field rife with more heat than rational discussion.

The Patent as a Form of Protest

Stuart Newman, a professor of cell biology and anatomy at New York Medical 5 College in Valhalla, says he opposes the patenting of living things. Newman, working with Washington, DC, activist Jeremy Rifkin, filed a patent application in 1997 for a theoretical creature he never actually made. For "tactical reasons," Newman says he eventually split his patent application into two: one involving primates and the other focused on other animals.

Using what he calls the "embryo chimera technique," Newman sought to patent a creature combining human embryo cells with cells from the embryo of a monkey, ape, or other animal to create a blend of both. Other scientists have used similar methods to create a "geep" (part goat, part sheep) says Newman, adding that his chimera could be used for drug testing and as a source of organs to transplant into humans.

After seven years and several rejections and appeals, the USPTO turned down both of Newman's patent applications in August 2004, saying, among other things, that his creatures would be too close to human. Newman and Rifkin let the six-month appeals period lapse and declared victory in February 2005. Both Rifkin and Newman say they expect the ruling to prevent scientists and biotechs from obtaining similar patents for 20 years, the time a patent is usually viable. Rifkin says crossing species boundaries is a form of animal abuse and a violation of nature and human dignity.

"The ruling has significant implications for the future of the biotech industry," says Rifkin, president of the nonprofit Foundation on Economic Trends, and one of the most vocal critics of biotechnology products such as genetically engineered organisms. "The implications for commercial interests are far-reaching. It means anyone applying for a patent for human-animal chimeras ought to be turned down."

Newman says he expects the ruling to affect stem cell researchers, too. "There are people who are producing or who express their intention to produce mixtures of humans and mice for research purposes in order to test the potential of human stem cells. This decision does not block their ability to do that in their labs," says Newman, "but if they wanted to patent and market these mixed human and animal organisms, it would be more difficult for them to commercialize it." However, some leading stem cell researchers say the case is unlikely to stop work on chimeric animals.

Can You Patent a Mouse with a Human Brain?

Twenty-five years ago, US scientist Ananda Chakrabarty, who worked for 10 General Electric at the time, obtained the first patent on a living organism, a genetically engineered bacterium that consumes oil spills. The patent office originally denied the application, believing it could not patent living organisms, according to Brigid Quinn, USPTO spokesperson. The case landed in the US Supreme Court, which in 1980 ruled that patents could be awarded on anything that was human-made.

Since then, some 436 transgenic or bioengineered animals have been patented, including 362 mice, 26 rats 19 rabbits, 17 sheep, 24 pigs, 2 chickens, 20 cows, 3 dogs, and many more. Many say the 1980 ruling led to the birth of biotechnology in the United States.

However, Quinn notes that US law clearly prohibits the patenting of people. "One reason we denied the case was the examiner believed one or more of the claims encompassed human beings." Asked whether the case will affect future patent applications for chimeric lab animals, Quinn says examiners always decide first if it is patentable subject matter. "Humans aren't. Anything found in nature is not patentable subject matter," says Quinn. "It has to be new, useful, nonobvious, and fully disclosed in writing."

Quinn wouldn't comment on whether the case will affect future chimera patent applications. "Each patent application is reviewed on its own merits." Irving L. Weissman, a professor of cancer biology, pathology, and developmental biology at Stanford University has created mice with brains that contain about 1 percent human tissue. Weissman says recent news reports that he plans to create a mouse with a 100 percent human brain are "inaccurate." A pioneer in the field of stem cell research, Weissman is credited as being the first scientist to identify and isolate hematopoietic stem cells from mice and humans. He says that the news reports were fueled by an academic inquiry he made to find out, in theory, what his university ethics panel thought of the idea. He says he has no current plans to create such a mouse.

The Newman/Rifkin patent is "a new attempt to block science," while the "use of human-mouse chimeras is old," Weissman says. In 1988, J. Michael McCune patented the SCID-hu mouse, "a severe combined immunodeficient mouse with human organs, bones, lymphoid tissue, thymus, and liver," says Weissman, who is also director of Stanford's Institute of Cancer/Stem Cell Biology and Medicine and a cofounder of Stem-Cells and other companies.

"The precedent is there, the discoveries are long published, and people's 15 lives have been affected by those discoveries. Would they take back all those discoveries and be happy if the therapies discovered through them were taken away?" Weissman dismisses the Newman/Rifkin case as "typical Rifkin," adding that "one example doesn't hold. It doesn't invalidate the others, so it's a hollow victory. The case is not the precedent they think."

Chimeras and Stem Cells

Austin Smith, director of the Institute for Stem Cell Research at the University of Edinburgh, agrees. The case is "irrelevant to mainstream stem cell research and the companies interested in this area. They're not interested in creating monsters. It's absurd. The idea of using them to create body parts is just ludicrous."

Smith notes that the point of much of stem cell research is to develop cells that can be transplanted into patients to cure disease. "You can only test the medication by injecting it into animal models—an already made animal, not an early embryo—which means part of the animal will be chimeric," he says. "Of necessity, it will have some human cells in it."

While there is a legitimate ethical discussion concerning the mixing of very early cells from a human embryo and an animal embryo, such as a chimpanzee, it's not an application anyone is pursuing, says Smith. "Nobody's ever proposed doing that. It's like some dark fantasy. No scientist would ever think of doing that because there's no reason to do that" he says.

"I can't see any business use of primary embryo chimeras," says Smith. "For late chimeras, yes, it's an important testing system to research and test therapies for degenerative diseases like Parkinson's or juvenile diabetes, so a company might want to use it, absolutely. To get it into the clinic, you need commercial involvement."

Robert Lanza, medical director at Advanced Cell Technology, Worcester, 20 Mass., says the patent case is most likely "a publicity stunt." Certain changes are acceptable, such as introducing a specific human gene into pigs to prevent transplant patients from rejecting pig organs, he says. However, he adds that it's "inhumane to create any chimeric animal that causes it distress or solely for entertainment purposes, such as glow-in-the-dark fish." In 2002, a Taiwanese company inserted DNA from jellyfish into zebrafish, creating glow-in-the-dark fish.

To address ethical issues, Canada passed the Assisted Human Reproduction Act last year, which bars the transfer of a nonhuman cell into a human embryo or of human cells into a nonhuman embryo. In the United States, the National Academy of Sciences is expected in the spring to issue voluntary guidelines for researchers who work with human embryonic stem cells.

Lila Feisee, director for intellectual property for the Biotechnology Industry Organization, a trade group, says companies are aiming to provide life-saving treatments, not patent people. "No one from our industry that I'm aware of has applied for a patent on a human being."

McGlynn says chimeric animals, and patents, are crucial to a biotech's ability to develop cures for human diseases. To protect its investment, for example, StemCells has more than 43 US patents on its stem cell technology, though none are on bioengineered mice. "If the private sector cannot receive a patent on all its work and invention," he says, "it's unlikely to engage in the work because it takes so much time and effort and money."

"The ability to retain a return on your investment is crucial," says McGlynn, adding: Mice are the backbone of biotechs, pharmaceuticals, and drug development." ⊚⁄◎

Reflections and Inquiries

1. What are your views on the use of the term "chimera," with its origins in Greek mythology, to describe transgenic organisms?

2. Reflect on Stuart Newman's and Jeremy Rifkin's strategy for filing a "protest patent." What recent (post-2005) evidence can you find that their strategy has been serving its purpose?

3. On what grounds does cancer biologist Irving Weissman dismiss the Newman/Rifkin protest patent? What are your reasons for agreeing or disagreeing with Weissman?

Reading to Write

Prepare a research paper in which you examine the reasons for and against the insertion of human brain tissue into the brains of mice—a procedure pioneered by Stanford biology professor Irving Weissman. What is the aim of this kind of genetic modification? What are the reasons for and against it? Where do you stand on the issue?

Student Essay

Priorities of Gene Therapy | Nikolay Balbyshev

Two obstacles have been facing researchers in gene therapy (the process of treating diseases at the genetic level, for example, by enabling diseased cells to produce healthy cellular material): producing sufficient quantities of genetic material to use in therapy and obtaining sufficient funding (federal and private). In the following paper, Nikolay Balbyshev, a student at North Dakota State University at the time of writing, examines what he identifies as the priorities for gene therapy research.

Source: Nikolay Balbyshev, "Priorities of Gene Therapy." Reprinted by permission of the author.

Introduction

Gene therapy is a relatively new area of medicine that attempts to apply recent advances in molecular biology, genetics and biotechnology to the treatment of human diseases. Gene therapy uses a set of approaches to the treatment of human disease based on the transfer of genetic material (DNA) into an individual. Gene delivery can be achieved either by direct administration of gene-containing viruses or DNA to blood or tissues, or indirectly through the introduction of cells manipulated in the laboratory to harbor foreign DNA. As a sophisticated extension of conventional medical therapy, gene therapy attempts to treat disease in an individual patient by the administration of DNA rather than a drug. (1)

Genetic manipulations, such as replacing defective or missing genes with healthy ones, can be used to alter germ cells (egg or sperm) and somatic cells. Theoretically germ-line gene therapy appears to have more advantages since it aims at preventing a genetic defect from being transmitted to future generations. However, the prospects of germ-line gene therapy look more remote due to many unresolved ethical and social problems as well as technical obstacles. (2) What is presently understood as gene therapy is, mostly, somatic cell gene therapy. By altering the genetic material of somatic cells onetime cures of devastating, inherited disorders may be potentially achieved. But, "in principle, gene therapy should be applicable to many diseases for which current therapeutic approaches are ineffective or where the prospects of effective treatment appear exceedingly low." (1) However, gene therapy is still extremely new and highly experimental. The number of approved clinical trials is small, and relatively few patients have been treated to date.

Early Progress

In 1991, Dr. H. French Anderson and his colleagues at the National Institutes of Health initiated the first clinical experiment in human gene therapy. Their successful creation and introduction of an artificial human gene into the T cells of a young girl suffering from adenosine deaminase deficiency have brought to life many hopes for treating other genetic diseases. Among the first in that list were sickle-cell anemia, hemophilia, cystic fibrosis, muscular dystrophy, familial hypercholesterolemia (high serum cholesterol), and some cancers (melanoma, neuroblastoma, and brain tumors). The idea seemed simple and eloquent. Many inherited diseases are caused by a single faulty gene, and gene therapy would deliver the needed gene to a person's cells, which would then begin producing the missing essential substance. By 1995, there were 106 clinical trials (studies in humans) approved to test gene therapy for some of these diseases, and AIDS in the United States. (1) A number of impressive applications of the new recombinant DNA technology and the molecular pathology of single-gene disorders have been introduced.

The U.S. Government was providing annually about $200 million in research grants for gene therapy projects. To evaluate the effect of these investments, a special panel was set up by the National Institutes of Health. Report and recommendations of the panel released in December 1995 summarized the recent progress of research in gene therapy. It also stated that the importance of this research for clinical medicine has been greatly overestimated by the scientists and industry, and further exaggerated by scientific press and mass media. According to the report, scientific evidence of consistent improvement in patients was lacking, although some patients have reported gains. There were too many poorly coordinated research projects. Recommendations included a strict control over selection of gene therapy projects through peer review. Among other things, the report brought attention to the possibilities of applying gene therapy to the treatment of other diseases, including those that are infectious.

Recent Progress and Major Problems

The major problem with gene therapy so far is that researchers have not been   5
able to deliver the genes in large enough quantities to the proper cells, or to have the genes expressed to produce the required protein for a sufficient length of time. Ideally, a vector (agents that carry or deliver DNA to target cells) should accommodate an unlimited amount of inserted DNA, lack the ability of autonomous replication of its own DNA, be easily manufactured, and be available in concentrated form. Secondly, it should have the ability to target specific cell types or to limit its gene expression to specific cell types, and to achieve sustained gene expression in the long term or in a controlled fashion. Finally, it should not be toxic or immunogenic. Such a vector does not exist and none of the DNA delivery systems currently available for in vivo gene transfer is perfect with respect to any of these points. Gene therapy and the means to promote it depend heavily on the development and improvement of new gene vector systems. (3) Most approaches to gene therapy use viruses as vectors. The virus's harmful genes are removed, and a therapeutic gene is inserted in their place.

Retroviruses are the first and most used vectors in human gene therapy. They can infect important cellular types of diverse animals and humans with a high efficacy of infection. Retroviruses, particularly a disabled mouse virus, are proven to integrate and replicate the genetic material of interest in the genome of the host cell. Their disadvantage is that the integration of the viral genome only occurs during cell division, and they are not effective in tissues in which cells are not dividing. The integration of the viral genome into the cell creates an insertional mutation, and there is a possibility that a gene controlling cellular division may be affected leading to a cancerous growth.

Another well-developed vector is adenovirus that can be used to insert new genes into many kinds of human cells and provide effective gene expression. But the duration of gene expression is limited to about 8 weeks, because by that time the host immune system develops antibodies against the cells harboring the adenovirus. It was recently reported that a patient died while undergoing adenovirus-mediated gene therapy against ornithine transcar-bamylase deficiency at the University of Pennsylvania in Philadelphia. If it is proven that adenovirus is the cause of death, the future use of this vector may be problematic. (4, 5)

The body's immune system is a factor of concern in all cases of gene replacement because antibodies are formed against any substance that is new to it. The normal protein produced by the correct gene may nevertheless be treated as foreign by the patient's immune system.

One of the possible dangers is that a virus with correct gene might inad-vertently get into the patient's eggs or sperm. The virus could insert itself cor-rectly, remedying a genetic disease in the patient's descendants, or the inser-tion could occur in the middle of a gene, disrupting the gene's function and causing an inherited defect.

In order to limit the body's immune defenses, the work is in progress on a   10 new delivery system based on a small virus, so called adeno-associated virus. It has only two genes, both of which can be removed, leaving just its head and tail as a shell to carry therapeutic genes into target cells. It has been used to improve the condition of dogs with hemophilia B. Following a single injection of the gene for Factor IX, the missing blood clotting protein lasted for 20 weeks. Human tri-als with this gene therapy are due to begin this year. Adeno-associated virus has been also used on monkeys to insert the gene for hormone erythropoetin, which stimulates production of red blood cells in bone marrow. The construct includes a two-part switch activating the gene only in the presence of the drug rapamycin. Vectors based on adeno-associated viruses appear safe and reason-ably effective, but they are limited in the size of the genes they can carry.

Lentiviral vectors gained attention because they can integrate into nondivid-ing host-cell genomes, evade the body's immune defenses and carry large genes. They are widely used as effective gene delivery tools in cells from liver, retina, skeletal muscle and the central nervous system. Recently a number of efficient lentiviral vector systems were introduced that use human immunodeficiency virus type 1 (HIV-1) in combination with a packaging and transducing vectors, and an envelope-encoding plasmid. These may be used in both dividing and nondividing cells at similar efficiencies. New potentially less pathogenic HIV-2 based vectors have been described also. (6, 7)

Viral-based, infectious vectors have significant limitations in their expres-sion characteristics, lack specificity in targeting tumor cells for gene transfer, and pose safety concerns regarding induction of secondary malignancies and recombination to form replication-competent virus. To avoid these problems, researchers turn to nonviral DNA-mediated gene transfer techniques such as liposomes. Although generally not as efficient as viral vectors, such nonviral systems have the potential advantages of being less toxic, nonrestrictive in cargo DNA size, potentially targetable, and easy to produce in relatively large amounts. More important, lipidic vectors generally lack immunogenicity, allowing repeated in vivo transfection using the same vector. Three types of lipidic gene transfer vectors have been described: 1) DNA/cationic liposome complexes, 2) DNA encapsulated in neutral or anionic liposomes, and 3) liposome-entrapped, polycation-condensed DNA (LPDI and LPDII). (8)

A major obstacle to successful gene therapy is the relative inefficiency of the targeting process in mammalian cells. Gene targeting may be accomplished by two different mechanisms: homologous recombination and mismatch correction of DNA heteroduplexes. The second mechanism has been improved by using the recombinogenic activity of oligonucleotides and, especially, specifically designed chimeric RNA/DNA oligonucleotides. The use of proteins like active recombinase to stimulate searching for homology and forming stable DNA heteroduplexes between oligonucleotides and chromosomal DNA may improve the gene targeting events. (9) The chimeric molecules have been demonstrated to be effective in the alteration of single nucleotides in episomal and genomic DNA in cell culture, as well as genomic DNA of cells in situ. This is a potentially powerful strategy for gene repair for the multitude of hepatic genetic diseases caused by point mutations. (10)

A new area is In Utero Gene Therapy (IUGT) using stem cells technology. Stem cells are multi-purpose embryonic cells from which each organ is originally formed. Inserting corrective genes into these cells, once they are identified could prove more effective than using viruses and other vectors for DNA insertion. A number of genetic disorders result in irreversible damage to the fetus before birth. In these cases, as well as when patients may benefit from therapy before symptoms are manifested, in utero gene therapy could be beneficial. Some successes with in utero gene transfer have been reported in animals. But stem cell technology is in its infancy, and a number of technical and ethical questions need to be answered before any clinical tests are allowed. (11)

Shift in Priorities

Even as significant technology hurdles are being overcome, other issues— 15 business ones—may keep gene therapy from helping people. The promise of a powerful therapy remains unrealized because "the whole concept of gene therapy for genetic diseases doesn't fit the business model." Most companies, particularly the new ones that are doing most of the gene therapy work, say they cannot afford to spend money on treatments for rare diseases because of the limited potential for payback.

The focus of gene therapy has shifted from inherited diseases toward more common ailments like cancer, AIDS, and heart disease—all areas that could prove more profitable. Many genetic disorders, and there are about four thousand of them, affect anywhere from a handful to a few thousand people worldwide, hardly a commercially promising prospect for pharmaceutical companies. Genes for conditions like obesity and baldness have much more support for further investigation than rare disorders. Of the 244 gene therapy trials registered since 1989 with the Recombinant DNA Advisory Committee at the National Institutes of Health, about 150 are for cancer and another 23 are for HIV. Only 33 are for diseases caused by a defect in a single gene, and

16 of those are for cystic fibrosis, the most common inherited disease. Seventeen tests cover 12 other genetic diseases. Among trials registered since the beginning of 1997 the balance is even more lopsided—53 for cancer and 8 for hereditary diseases. (12)

Funding problems leave many scientists only a hope that their work on cancer and other widespread diseases will eventually produce more effective technologies, and they will revisit their research projects on single gene defects armed with better knowledge. It appears to be a popular option under present U.S. Government's policy of selective support and regulation of gene therapy based on the 1995 Panel Report and recommendations. (1)

Personal Opinion

Even a brief account of recent advances in the area of gene therapy gives an idea of intensive search for a technology which is both effective and ethically acceptable. Considerable amounts of public finances have been and continue to be invested in gene therapy research. Understandably, concentration of this research funding in a few major areas can be more productive nationally. And it looks democratic to give priority to the treatment of heritable diseases and conditions that affect a large part of the society. The U.S. Government's shift in policy is based on political, technical, and economic considerations. But the ethics of this choice deserve some criticism.

I agree that cancer is a tragedy that can strike anyone, and there is a great public interest in effective treatment of this disease. There are people with inherited heart conditions and there are innocent victims of HIV infection and Alzheimer's disease who need society's help. Giving priority to gene therapy of these diseases is quite appropriate. But whatever is the aggregate distress of millions of old and obese people, it is not comparable to sufferings of one child having cystic fibrosis or other potentially fatal genetic diseases. And it sounds like the Government tells these people: "You have to wait." It would be better, in my view, to leave totally the development of gene therapy for not life-threatening conditions to private industries. Also, for some of the wide-spread diseases with a genetic component such as diabetes and some heart problems there are reasonably effective conventional therapies and surgical procedures which makes them lower priority areas for gene therapy.

Some people have reservations about the prospect of big private companies 20 monopolizing and profiteering on gene therapy using the results of publicly funded research. But the shift in Government's policy towards gene therapy is, in a way, recognition of the enormity of the problem and government's inability to tackle it on its own. Attracting private investments is of crucial importance to the success of this endeavor, and it is the law of the land that private capital is invested for profit. If public is well informed, and there is political will, the Government could introduce some controls to avoid a hike in costs of gene therapy or apply antitrust laws to stimulate competition among smaller companies and disrupt creation of monopolies providing gene therapy for specific diseases. I also think that when industry's involvement in gene therapy is sufficient, the government funding priorities should be reversed so that the people suffering from rare genetic disorders get more attention.

Conclusion

Gene therapy is one of the youngest and most promising fields of medicine. In the course of one decade, the basic research in recombinant DNA has been translated into a number of applied projects aiming at curing the disease at its root—the gene. Though no clinically acceptable protocols have yet been developed, the researchers' ability to solve many technical problems of gene therapy has greatly improved. After 1995 the funding priorities have changed in favor of major diseases (cancer, HIV) so that the results of publicly funded research could spur involvement of private industry. ◎／◎

References

1. Orkin, S.H., A.G. Motulsky. 1995. "Report and Recommendations of the Panel to Assess the NIH Investment in Research on Gene Therapy."
2. National Institutes of Health. 1993. *Questions and Answers About Gene Therapy.*
3. Dani, S.U. 1999. "The challenge of vector development in gene therapy." *Braz J Med Biol Res* 32(2):133–45.
4. Batshaw, M.L., J.M. Wilson, S. Raper, M. Yudkoff, M.B. Robinson. 1999. "Recombinant adenovirus gene transfer in adults with partial ornithine transcarbamylase deficiency." *Hum Gene Ther* 10(14):2419–37.
5. Lehrman, S. 1999. "Virus treatment questioned after gene therapy death." *Nature* 401(6753):517–8.
6. Federico, M. 1999. "Lentiviruses as gene delivery vectors." *Curr Opin Biotechnol* 10(5):448–453.
7. Iwakuma, T, Y. Cui, L.J. Chang. 1999. "Self-inactivating lentiviral vectors with U3 and U5 modifications." *Virology* 15; 261(1):120–32.
8. Ropert, C. 1999. "Liposomes as a gene delivery system." *Braz J Med Biol Res* 32(2):163–9.
9. Lanzov, V.A. 1999. "Gene Targeting for Gene Therapy: Prospects." *Mol Genet Metab* 68(2):276–282.
10. Kren, B.T., R. Metz, R. Kumar, C.J. Steer. 1999. "Gene repair using chimeric RNA/DNA oligonucleotides." *Semin Liver Dis* 19(1): 93–104.
11. Zanjani, D., W. French Anderson. 1999. "Prospects for in Utero Human Gene Therapy." *Science* 285(5436) p.2084–8.
12. *New York Times,* August 4, 1998.

Reflections and Inquiries

1. What is Balbyshev's thesis? Explain why you agree or disagree with it.

2. What lies behind the inability of researchers to deliver genes in large enough quantities to the proper cells, according to Balbyshev? In the several years since Balbyshev wrote his paper, how has this problem been resolved, if at all?

3. Critique Balbyshev's rhetorical strategies: his explanation of technical concepts, his organizational scheme, his use of sources.

Reading to Write

Write an essay on the success and/or problems associated with gene therapy today.

Connections Among the Clusters

1. How do issues in bioethics relate to the conflicts between science and religion (see Cluster 6)?

2. Suggest ways in which genetic engineering or stem cell research could become an issue of national security (see Cluster 5).

3. How might issues in biotechnology relate to issues in intellectual property rights? (see Cluster 2).

Writing Projects

1. Write an essay in which you weigh the potential benefits and potential liabilities of gene therapy, genetic engineering, animal patenting, or stem cell research; then present your own position on the issue in light of your examination of both sides.

2. How do the essays in this cluster affect your views of biomedical research? Should such research be restricted? If so, how, and by whom?

Suggestions for Further Reading

Federal Coordinating Council for Science, Engineering & Technology (FCCSET), Committee on Life Sciences and Health. *Biotechnology for the 21st Century.* Washington, DC: U. S. GPO, 1992.

Holland, Suzanne, Karen Lebacqz, and Laurie Zoloth, eds. *The Human Embryonic Stem Cell Debate.* Cambridge: MIT Press, 2001.

Kalb, Claudia. "Ethics, Eggs and Embryos." *Newsweek* 145; June 20, 2005: 52–53.

Kenney, Martin. *Biotechnology: The University-Industrial Complex.* New Haven: Yale University P, 1986.

Lauritzen, P., ed. *Cloning and the Future of Human Embryo Research.* New York: Oxford UP, 2001.

Robertson, J. A. *Children of Choice: Freedom and the New Reproductive Technologies.* Princeton: Princeton UP, 1994.

Ruse, Michael, and Christopher A. Pynes, eds. *The Stem Cell Controversy: Debating the Issues.* Amherst, NY: Prometheus, 2003.

Wolfson, Elissa. "Animal Patenting." *E Magazine: The Environmental Magazine* 5.2; March/April 1994: 25–26.

8 Masterpieces of Argument: What Do They Teach Us About the Art of Persuasion?

Introduction

Many of the greatest works ever written or spoken are arguments. They have appeared in all disciplines: philosophy (Plato's "Allegory of the Cave"), theology (Jonathan Edwards's "Sinners in the Hands of an Angry God"), literature (Andrew Marvell's "To His Coy Mistress"), sociology/politics (Frederick Douglass's "I Hear the Mournful Wail of Millions"), Swift's "A Modest Proposal," and Stanton's keynote address at the first woman's rights convention, photojournalism (Nick Ut's photograph of the terrified and wounded Vietnamese children fleeing their napalmed village), psychology (the unsettling Stanley Milgram experiment), and even chemistry (Rachel Carson's account, from *Silent Spring*, of the environmental damage caused by insecticides).

What do these masterpieces of argument have in common? They all illuminate a dark corner of human or physical nature or of the relationship between the two, a corner that needs resolution. They combine clarity with subtlety, eloquence with forcefulness. As you read each of this cluster's selections, ask yourself three questions:

1. What is most effective or distinctive about the author's approach to the subject matter?

2. How has he or she combined objective factual information with subjective persuasive power?

3. Why do these arguments still make for valuable reading, even though some of them are centuries old?

The Tragedy of Vietnam | Nick Ut

On June 8, 1972, Associated Press photographer Nick Ut was accompanying a troop of South Vietnamese soldiers assigned to engage enemy troops in order to reopen a road leading from Saigon to isolated areas of combat. As they drew near the enemy-seized village of Trang Bang, the South Vietnamese field commander called for air-combat assistance. Shortly thereafter, two South Vietnamese air force planes attacked the village with a combination of explosive and incendiary (napalm) bombs. Moments later wounded, terrified civilians, many of them children, came fleeing out of the village. One of them, a nine-year-old girl named Kim Phuc, severely burned by napalm, had torn off her clothes and began running toward Ut, who instinctively took the photograph that would epitomize the tragic horror of the Vietnam War, if not all wars. Immediately after taking the photograph, Ut and several soldiers gave Kim Phuc and others of the wounded emergency first aid and then rushed them to a nearby hospital. Ut's photograph earned him the Pulitzer Prize. He currently resides in Los Angeles.

Reflections and Inquiries

1. What particulars of Ut's photograph do you find most disturbing, and why?

2. What argument does Ut's photograph seem to make about the Vietnam War, perhaps about any war? How convincingly does it do so?

Source: AP Images/Nick Ut.

3. A powerful photograph such as this affects us on many levels: psychological, emotional, aesthetic, spiritual, historical, political, sociological. On what level does the photograph speak to you most clearly? Why?

Reading to Write

"The Tragedy of Vietnam" is one of several photographs that Ut took near the bombed village of Trang Bang on June 8, 1972. Examine these other photographs by visiting http://www.digitaljournalist.org/issue0008/ng2 .htm and write an essay in which you discuss the role that photography plays in conveying the experience of the Vietnam War.

Allegory of the Cave | Plato

In his masterful dialogue, The Republic, *Plato (428–347 B.C.E.) attempts to show that a rational relationship exists among the cosmos, the human soul, and the state. Qualities such as justice, good, and beautiful must coexist harmoniously in life. Politics, law, education, art, and literature are the means by which we come to perfect these qualities of the good life. In Book Seven of the dialogue, Socrates argues his case for the potential of educators to lead humanity out of the darkness of deceptions and superficial appearances into the light of higher truth. This "Allegory of the Cave," as it has come to be known, is one of the most powerful meditations on the relationship between appearance and reality and of the importance of education in society.*

SOCRATES, GLAUCON.
The den, the prisoners:
the light at a distance.

And now, I said, let me show in a figure how far our nature is enlightened or unenlightened:—Behold! human beings living in an underground den, which has a mouth open towards the light and reaching all along the den; here they have been from their childhood, and have their legs and necks chained so that they cannot move, and can only see before them, being prevented by the chains from turning round their heads. Above and behind them a fire is blazing at a distance, and between the fire and the prisoners there is a raised way; and you will see, if you look, a low wall built along the way, like the screen which marionette players have in front of them, over which they show the puppets.

I see.

Source: Plato, "Allegory of the Cave," *The Republic*, trans. Benjamin Javett and Lewis Campbell (Oxford: Clarendon, 1894) 293–99. Book VII, 514–518.

The low wall, and the moving figures of which the shadows are seen on the opposite wall of the den.

And do you see, I said, men passing along the wall carrying all sorts of vessels, and statues and figures of animals made of wood and stone and various materials, which appear over the wall? Some of them are talking, others silent.

You have shown me a strange image, and they are strange prisoners.

Like ourselves, I replied; and they see only their own 5 shadows, or the shadows of one another, which the fire throws on the opposite wall of the cave?

True, he said; how could they see anything but the shadows if they were never allowed to move their heads?

And of the objects which are being carried in like manner they would only see the shadows?

Yes, he said.

The prisoners would mistake the shadows for realities.

And if they were able to converse with one another, would they not suppose that they were naming what was actually before them?

Very true.   10

And suppose further that the prison had an echo which came from the other side, would they not be sure to fancy when one of the passers-by spoke that the voice which they heard came from the passing shadow?

No question, he replied.

To them, I said, the truth would be literally nothing but the shadows of the images.

That is certain.

And now look again, and see what will naturally follow if 15 the prisoners are released and disabused of their error. At first, when any of them is liberated and compelled suddenly to stand up and turn his neck round and walk and look towards the light, he will suffer sharp pains; the glare will distress him, and he will be unable to see the realities of which in his former state he had seen the shadows; and then conceive some one saying to him, that what he saw before was an illusion, but that now, when he is approaching nearer to being and his eye is turned towards more real existence, he has a clearer vision—what will be his reply? And you may further imagine that his instructor is pointing to the objects as they pass and requiring him to name them,—will he not be perplexed? Will he not fancy that the shadows which he formerly saw are truer than the objects which are now shown to him?

And when released, they would still persist in maintaining the superior truth of the shadows.

Far truer.

And if he is compelled to look straight at the light, will he not have a pain in his eyes which will make him turn away to take refuge in the objects of vision which he can see, and which he will conceive to be in reality clearer than the things which are now being shown to him?

True, he said.

And suppose once more, that he is reluctantly dragged on a steep and rugged ascent, and held fast until he is forced into the presence of the sun himself, is he not likely to be pained and irritated? When he approaches the light his eyes will be dazzled, and he will not be able to see anything at all of what are now called realities.

When dragged upwards, they would be dazzled by excess of light.

Not all in a moment, he said.   20

He will require to grow accustomed to the sight of the upper world. And first he will see the shadows best, next the reflections of men and other objects in the water, and then the objects themselves; then he will gaze upon the light of the moon and the stars and the spangled heaven; and he will see the sky and the stars by night better than the sun or the light of the sun by day?

Certainly.

At length they will see the sun and under- stand his nature.

Last of all he will be able to see the sun, and not mere reflections of him in the water, but he will see him in his own proper place, and not in another; and he will contemplate him as he is.

Certainly.

He will then proceed to argue that this is he who gives 25 the season and the years, and is the guardian of all that is in the visible world, and in a certain way the cause of all things which he and his fellows have been accustomed to behold?

Clearly, he said, he would first see the sun and then reason about him.

They would then pity their old companions of the den.

And when he remembered his old habitation, and the wisdom of the den and his fellow prisoners, do you not suppose that he would felicitate himself on the change, and pity them?

Certainly, he would.

And if they were in the habit of conferring honors among themselves on those who were quickest to observe the passing shadows and to remark which of them went before, and which followed after, and which were together; and who were therefore best able to draw conclusions as to the future, do you think that he would care for such honors and glories, or envy the possessors of them? Would he not say with Homer,

Better to be the poor servant of a poor master and to endure anything, rather than think as they do and live after their manner?

Yes, he said, I think that he would rather suffer anything 30 than entertain these false notions and live in this miserable manner.

Imagine once more, I said, such an one coming suddenly out of the sun to be replaced in his old situation; would he not be certain to have his eyes full of darkness?

To be sure, he said.

And if there were a contest, and he had to compete in measuring the shadows with the prisoners who had never moved out of the den, while his sight was still weak, and before his eyes had become steady (and the time which would be needed to acquire this new habit of sight might be very considerable), would he not be ridiculous? Men would say of him that up he went and down he came without his eyes; and that it was better not even to think of ascending; and if any one tried to loose another and lead him up to the light, let them only catch the offender, and they would put him to death.

No question, he said.

This entire allegory, I said, you may now append, dear 35 Glaucon, to the previous argument; the prison house is the world of sight, the light of the fire is the sun, and you will not misapprehend me if you interpret the journey upwards to be the ascent of the soul into the intellectual world according to my poor belief, which, at your desire, I have expressed—whether rightly or wrongly God knows. But, whether true or false, my opinion is that in the world of knowledge the idea of good appears last of all, and is seen only with an effort; and, when seen, is also inferred to be the universal author of all things beautiful and right, parent of light and of the lord of light in this visible world, and the immediate source of reason and truth in the intellectual; and that this is the power upon which he who would act rationally either in public or private life must have his eye fixed.

I agree, he said, as far as I am able to understand you.

Moreover, I said, you must not wonder that those who attain to this beatific vision are unwilling to descend to human affairs; for their souls are ever hastening into the upper world where they desire to dwell; which desire of theirs is very natural, if our allegory may be trusted.

Yes, very natural.

But when they returned to the den they would see much worse than those who had never left it.

The prison is the world of sight, the light of the fire is the sun.

Nothing extraordinary in the philosopher being unable to see in the dark.

And is there anything surprising in one who passes from divine contemplations to the evil state of man, misbehaving himself in a ridiculous manner; if, while his eyes are blinking and before he has become accustomed to the surrounding darkness, he is compelled to fight in courts of law, or in other places, about the images or the shadows of images of justice, and is endeavoring to meet the conceptions of those who have never yet seen absolute justice?

Anything but surprising, he replied.   40

Anyone who has common sense will remember that the bewilderments of the eyes are of two kinds, and arise from two causes, either from coming out of the light or from going into the light, which is true of the mind's eye, quite as much as of the bodily eye; and he who remembers this when he sees anyone whose vision is perplexed and weak, will not be too ready to laugh; he will first ask whether that soul of man has come out of the brighter life, and is unable to see because unaccustomed to the dark, or having turned from darkness to the day is dazzled by excess of light. And he will count the one happy in his condition and state of being, and he will pity the other; or, if he have a mind to laugh at the soul which comes from below into the light, there will be more reason in this than in the laugh which greets him who returns from above out of the light into the den.

> The eyes may be blinded in two ways, by excess or by defect of light.

That, he said, is a very just distinction.

But then, if I am right, certain professors of education must be wrong when they say that they can put a knowledge into the soul which was not there before, like sight into blind eyes.

> The conversion of the soul is the turning round the eye from darkness to light.

They undoubtedly say this, he replied.

Whereas, our argument shows that the power and   45 capacity of learning exists in the soul already; and that just as the eye was unable to turn from darkness to light without the whole body, so too the instrument of knowledge can only by the movement of the whole soul be turned from the world of becoming into that of being, and learn by degrees to endure the sight of being, and of the brightest and best of being, or in other words, of the good.

Very true.

And must there not be some art which will effect conversion in the easiest and quickest manner; not implanting the faculty of sight, for that exists already, but has been turned in the wrong direction, and is looking away from the truth?

Yes, he said, such an art may be presumed.

The virtue of wisdom
has a divine power
which may be turned
either towards good or
towards evil.

And whereas the other so-called virtues of the soul seem to be akin to bodily qualities, for even when they are not originally innate they can be implanted later by habit and exercise, the virtue of wisdom more than anything else contains a divine element which always remains, and by this conversion is rendered useful and profitable; or, on the other hand, hurtful and useless. Did you never observe the narrow intelligence flashing from the keen eye of a clever rogue—how eager he is, how clearly his paltry soul sees the way to his end; he is the reverse of blind, but his keen eyesight is forced into the service of evil, and he is mischievous in proportion to his cleverness?

Very true, he said.   50

But what if there had been a circumcision of such natures in the days of their youth; and they had been severed from those sensual pleasures, such as eating and drinking, which, like leaden weights, were attached to them at their birth, and which drag them down and turn the vision of their souls upon the things that are below—if, I say, they had been released from these impediments and turned in the opposite direction, the very same faculty in them would have seen the truth as keenly as they see what their eyes are turned to now.

Very likely.

Neither the uneducated
nor the overeducated
will be good servants
of the State.

Yes, I said; and there is another thing which is likely, or rather a necessary inference from what has preceded, that neither the uneducated and uninformed of the truth, nor yet those who never make an end of their education, will be able ministers of State; not the former, because they have no single aim of duty which is the rule of all their actions, private as well as public; nor the latter, because they will not act at all except upon compulsion, fancying that they are already dwelling apart in the islands of the blessed.

Very true, he replied.

Then, I said, the business of us who are the founders of 55
the State will be to compel the best minds to attain that knowledge which we have already shown to be the greatest of all—they must continue to ascend until they arrive at the good; but when they have ascended and seen enough we must not allow them to do as they do now.

What do you mean?

Men should ascend to
the upper world, but
they should also return
to the lower.

I mean that they remain in the upper world: but this must not be allowed; they must be made to descend again among the prisoners in the den, and partake of their labors and honors, whether they are worth having or not.

But is not this unjust? he said; ought we to give them a worse life, when they might have a better?

You have again forgotten, my friend, I said, the intention of the legislator, who did not aim at making any one class in the State happy above the rest; the happiness was to be in the whole State, and he held the citizens together by persuasion and necessity, making them benefactors of the State, and therefore benefactors of one another; to this end he created them, not to please themselves, but to be his instruments in binding up the State.

True, he said, I had forgotten.   60

The duties of philosophers.

Observe, Glaucon, that there will be no injustice in compelling our philosophers to have a care and providence of others; we shall explain to them that in other States, men of their class are not obliged to share in the toils of politics: and this is reasonable, for they grow up at their own sweet will, and the government would rather not have them. Being self-taught, they cannot be expected to show any gratitude for a culture which they have never received. But we have brought you into the world to be rulers of the hive, kings of yourselves and of the other citizens, and have educated you far better and more perfectly than they have been educated, and you are better able to share in the double duty.

Their obligations to their country will induce them to take part in her government.

Wherefore each of you, when his turn comes, must go down to the general underground abode, and get the habit of seeing in the dark. When you have acquired the habit, you will see ten thousand times better than the inhabitants of the den, and you will know what the several images are, and what they represent, because you have seen the beautiful and just and good in their truth. And thus our State, which is also yours, will be reality, and not a dream only, and will be administered in a spirit unlike that of other States, in which men fight with one another about shadows only and are distracted in the struggle for power, which in their eyes is a great good. Whereas the truth is that the State in which the rulers are most reluctant to govern is always the best and most quietly governed, and the State in which they are most eager, the worst.

Quite true, he replied.

And will our pupils, when they hear this, refuse to take their turn at the toils of State, when they are allowed to spend the greater part of their time with one another in the heavenly light?

They will be willing but not anxious to rule.

Impossible, he answered; for they are just men, and the commands which we impose upon them are just; there can be no doubt that every one of them will take office as a stern necessity, and not after the fashion of our present rulers of State.

The statesman must be provided with a better life than that of a ruler; and then he will not covet office.

Yes, my friend, I said; and there lies the point. You must 65 contrive for your future rulers another and a better life than that of a ruler, and then you may have a well-ordered State; for only in the State which offers this, will they rule who are truly rich, not in silver and gold, but in virtue and wisdom, which are the true blessings of life. Whereas if they go to the administration of public affairs, poor and hungering after their own private advantage, thinking that hence they are to snatch the chief good, order there can never be; for they will be fighting about office, and the civil and domestic broils which thus arise will be the ruin of the rulers themselves and of the whole State.

Most true, he replied.

And the only life which looks down upon the life of political ambition is that of true philosophy. Do you know of any other?

Indeed, I do not, he said.

Reflections and Inquiries

1. What is Plato's thesis in this allegory?

2. Why do you suppose Plato presents his argument as a dialogue? How does this approach contribute to the persuasive force of Plato's argument?

3. What physiological limitations of human vision does Plato use as an analogy to flawed understanding of reality? How accurate an analogy is it, in your opinion?

4. What criticism of education is Plato presenting to Glaucon?

5. How does Plato characterize the ideal legislator? How realistic a characterization is this, from your perspective?

Reading to Write

1. Reread the "Allegory of the Cave" and then present your own mini-dialogue between yourself (as a modern-day Plato) and a high school student. Topic: Why a liberal arts education is more valuable than mere training for a specific occupation.

2. Write an essay on Plato's conception of the soul, based on his discussion of it in this dialogue.

To His Coy Mistress | Andrew Marvell

Arguments can be presented poetically, as in the case of this famous late-seventeenth-century "carpe diem" poem, "To His Coy Mistress" ("mistress" meaning here "a woman of stature and authority"). Andrew Marvell (1621–1678) liked to debate difficult philosophical, political and—in the case of the following poem—moral issues poetically but without resolving them.

> Had we but world enough, and time,
> This coyness, lady, were no crime.
> We would sit down, and think which way
> To walk, and pass our long love's day.   5
> Thou by the Indian Ganges' side
> Should'st rubies find; I by the tide
> *sing melancholy songs   Of Humber would complain*. I would
> Love you ten years before the Flood,
> And you should, if you please, refuse
> Till the conversion of the Jews.   10
> *fertile, ample   My vegetable* love should grow
> Vaster than empires, and more slow;
> An hundred years should go to praise
> Thine eyes, and on thy forehead gaze;
> Two hundred to adore each breast,   15
> But thirty thousand to the rest;
> An age at least to every part,
> And the last age should show your heart.
> For, lady, you deserve this state,
> Nor would I love at lower rate.   20
>   But at my back I always hear
> Time's winged chariot hurrying near;
> And yonder all before us lie
> Deserts of vast eternity.
> Thy beauty shall no more be found,   25
> Nor, in thy marble vault, shall sound
> My echoing song, then worms shall try
> That long preserved virginity:
> And your quaint honor turn to dust,
> And into ashes all my lust.   30
> The grave's fine and private place,
> But none, I think, do there embrace.

Source: Andrew Marvell, "To His Coy Mistress," *Andrew Marvell: The Complete English Poems* (New York: St. Martin's, 1974) 50–51.

Now therefore, while the youthful hue

glow,   Sits on thy skin like morning glew
luminescence   And while thy willing soul transpires   35
               At every pore with instant fires,
               Now let us sport us while we may,
               And now, like amorous birds of prey,
               Rather at once our time devour,
               Than languish in his slow-chapped power.   40
               Let us roll all our strength and all
               Our sweetness up into one ball,
               And tear our pleasures with rough strife,
               Through the iron gates of life.
               Thus, though we cannot make our sun   45
               Stand still, yet we will make him run. ◎/◎

Reflections and Inquiries

1. Summarize the speaker's argument. How valid is it? How would you refute it?

2. Many consider this poem to be a satire. If so, what is it satirizing?

3. The poem uses a literary device called hyperbole (exaggeration). Where do you see examples of it? Why does the speaker use it?

4. Why does Marvell present his argument as a poem? Why not a prose manifesto instead?

5. The poem presents only one side of the argument. Why doesn't Marvell include the woman's counterresponse?

Reading to Write

1. Analyze the speaker's argument in terms of introduction, body of evidence, and conclusion.

2. Write a point-by-point counterargument (in verse or prose) from the woman's point of view.

A Modest Proposal | Jonathan Swift

Originally published as a pamphlet in 1729 with the title "A Modest Proposal for Preventing the Children of Poor People in Ireland from Being a Burden to Their Parents or Country, and for Making Them Beneficial to the Public," this bitterly satiric

---

Source: Jonathan Swift, "A Modest Proposal," *Gulliver's Travels and Other Writings,* ed. Lois A. Landa (Boston: Houghton, 1960) 429–36.

*proposal for alleviating the famine in Ireland was sparked by Jonathan Swift's intoler-
ance of the hypocrisy of his native Ireland that preached the joys of parenthood and the
sacredness of life while at the same time permitting economic corruption and famine.
Swift (1667–1745), a political journalist and the author of* Gulliver's Travels *(1726),
was also an ordained priest and Dean of St. Patrick's Cathedral, Dublin.*

It is a melancholy object to those who walk through this great town or travel in the country, when they see the streets, the roads, and cabin doors, crowded with beggars of the female sex, followed by three, four, or six children, all in rags and importuning every passenger for an alms. These mothers, instead of being able to work for their honest livelihood, are forced to employ all their time in strolling to beg sustenance for their helpless infants, who, as they grow up, either turn thieves for want of work, or leave their dear native country to fight for the Pretender in Spain, or sell themselves to the Barbadoes.

I think it is agreed by all parties that this prodigious number of children in the arms, or on the backs, or at the heels of their mothers and frequently of their fathers, is in the present deplorable state of the kingdom a very great additional grievance; and therefore whoever could find out a fair, cheap, and easy method of making these children sound useful members of the commonwealth would deserve so well of the public as to have his statue set up for a preserver of the nation.

But my intention is very far from being confined to provide only for the children of professed beggars; it is of a much greater extent, and shall take in the whole number of infants at a certain age who are born of parents in effect as little able to support them as those who demand our charity in the streets.

As to my own part, having turned my thoughts for many years upon this important subject, and maturely weighed the several schemes of other projectors, I have always found them grossly mistaken in their computation. It is true, a child just dropped from its dam may be supported by her milk for a solar year, with little other nourishment; at most not above the value of two shillings, which the mother may certainly get, or the value in scraps, by her lawful occupation of begging; and it is exactly at one year old that I propose to provide for them in such a manner as instead of being a charge upon their parents or the parish, or wanting food and raiment for the rest of their lives, they shall on the contrary contribute to the feeding, and partly to the clothing, of many thousands.

There is likewise another great advantage in my scheme, that it will prevent those voluntary abortions, and that horrid practice of women murdering 5 their bastard children, alas, too frequent among us, sacrificing the poor innocent babes, I doubt, more to avoid the expense than the shame, which would move tears and pity in the most savage and inhuman breast.

The number of souls in this kingdom being usually reckoned one million and a half, of these I calculate there may be about two hundred thousand couples whose wives are breeders, from which number I subtract thirty thousand couples who are able to maintain their own children, although I apprehend there cannot be so many under the present distress of the kingdom; but this being granted, there will remain an hundred and seventy thousand breeders. I again subtract fifty thousand for those women who miscarry, or whose children die by accident or disease within the year. There only remain an hundred and twenty thousand children of poor parents actually born. The question therefore is, how this number shall be reared and provided for, which, as I have already said, under the present situation of affairs, is utterly impossible by all the methods hitherto proposed. For we can neither employ them in handicraft or agriculture; we neither build houses (I mean in the country) nor cultivate land. They can very seldom pick up a livelihood by stealing till they arrive at six years old, except where they are of towardly parts; although I confess they learn the rudiments much earlier, during which time they can however be looked upon only as probationers, as I have been informed by a principal gentleman in the country of Cavan, who protested to me that he never knew above one or two instances under the age of six, even in a part of the kingdom so renowned for the quickest proficiency in that art.

I am assured by our merchants that a boy or a girl before twelve years old is no salable commodity, and even when they come to this age they will not yield above three pounds, or three pounds and half a crown at most on the Exchange; which cannot turn to account either to the parents or the kingdom, the charge of nutriment and rags having been at least four times that value.

I shall now therefore humbly propose my own thoughts, which I hope will not be liable to the least objection.

I have been assured by a very knowing American of my acquaintance in London, that a young healthy child well nursed is at a year old a most delicious, nourishing, and wholesome food, whether stewed, roasted, baked, or boiled, and I make no doubt that it will equally serve in a fricassee or a ragout.

I do therefore humbly offer it to public consideration that of the hundred 10 and twenty thousand children, already computed, twenty thousand may be reserved for breed, whereof only one fourth part to be males, which is more than we allow to sheep, black cattle, or swine; and my reason is that these children are seldom the fruits of marriage, a circumstance not much regarded by our savages, therefore one male will be sufficient to serve four females. That the remaining hundred thousand may at a year old be offered in sale to the persons of quality and fortune through the kingdom, always advising the mother to let them suck plentifully in the last month, so as to render them plump and fat for a good table. A child will make two dishes at an entertainment for friends; and when the family dines alone, the fore or hind quarter will make a reasonable dish, and seasoned with a little pepper or salt will be very good boiled on the fourth day, especially in the winter.

I have reckoned upon a medium that a child just born will weigh twelve pounds, and in a solar year if tolerably nursed increaseth to twenty-eight pounds.

I grant this food will be somewhat dear, and therefore very proper for landlords, who, as they have already devoured most of the parents, seem to have the best title to the children.

Infant's flesh will be in season throughout the year, but more plentiful in March, and a little before and after. For we are told by a grave author, an eminent French physician, that fish being a prolific diet, there are more children born in Roman Catholic countries about nine months after Lent than at any other season, therefore, reckoning a year after Lent, the markets will be more glutted than usual, because the number of popish infants is at least three to one in this kingdom; and therefore it will have one other collateral advantage, by lessening the number of Papists among us.

I have already computed the charge of nursing a beggar's child (in which list I reckon all cottagers, laborers, and four fifths of the farmers) to be about two shillings per annum, rags included; and I believe no gentleman would repine to give ten shillings for the carcass of a good fat child, which, as I have said, will make four dishes of excellent nutritive meat, when he hath only some particular friend or his own family to dine with him. Thus the squire will learn to be a good landlord, and grow popular among the tenants; the mother will have eight shillings net profit, and be fit for work till she produces another child.

Those who are more thrifty (as I must confess the times require) may flay 15 the carcass; the skin of which artificially dressed will make admirable gloves for ladies, and summer boots for fine gentlemen.

As to our city of Dublin, shambles may be appointed for this purpose in the most convenient parts of it, and butchers we may be assured will not be wanting; although I rather recommend buying the children alive, and dressing them hot from the knife as we do roasting pigs.

A very worthy person, a true lover of his country, and whose virtues I highly esteem, was lately pleased in discoursing on this matter to offer a refinement upon my scheme. He said that many gentlemen of his kingdom, having of late destroyed their deer, he conceived that the want of venison might be well supplied by the bodies of young lads and maidens, not exceeding fourteen years of age nor under twelve, so great a number of both sexes in every county being now ready to starve for want of work and service; and these to be disposed of by their parents, if alive, or otherwise by their nearest relations. But with due deference to so excellent a friend and so deserving a patriot, I cannot be altogether in his sentiments; for as to the males, my American acquaintance assured me from frequent experience that their flesh was generally tough and lean, like that of our schoolboys, by continual exercise, and their taste disagreeable; and to fatten them would not answer the charge. Then as to the females, it would, I think with humble submission, be a loss to the public, because they soon would become breeders themselves: and besides, it is not improbable that some scrupulous people might be apt to censure such a practice (although indeed very unjustly) as a little bordering upon cruelty; which, I confess, hath always been with me the strongest objection against any project, how well soever intended.

But in order to justify my friend, he confessed that this expedient was put into his head by the famous Psalmanazar, a native of the island Formosa, who came from thence to London about twenty years ago, and in conversation told my friend that in his country when any young person happened to be put to death, the executioner sold the carcass to persons of quality as a prime dainty; and that in his time the body of a plump girl of fifteen, who was crucified for an attempt to poison the emperor, was sold to his Imperial Majesty's prime minister of state, and other great mandarins of the court, in joints from the gibbet, at four hundred crowns. Neither indeed can I deny that if the same use were made of several plump young girls in this town, who without one single groat to their fortunes cannot stir abroad without a chair, and appear at the playhouse and assemblies in foreign fineries which they never will pay for, the kingdom would not be the worse.

Some persons of a desponding spirit are in great concern about that vast number of poor people who are aged, diseased, or maimed, and I have been desired to employ my thoughts what course may be taken to ease the nation of so grievous an encumbrance. But I am not in the least pain upon that matter, because it is very well known that they are every day dying and rotting by cold and famine, and filth and vermin, as fast as can be reasonably expected. And as to the younger laborers, they are now in almost as hopeful a condition. They cannot get work, and consequently pine away for want of nourishment to a degree that if at any time they are accidentally hired to common labor, they have not strength to perform it; and thus the country and themselves are happily delivered from the evils to come.

I have too long digressed, and therefore shall return to my subject. I think 20 the advantages by the proposal which I have made are obvious and many, as well as of the highest importance.

For first, as I have already observed, it would greatly lessen the number of Papists, with whom we are yearly overrun, being the principal breeders of the nation as well as our most dangerous enemies; and who stay at home on purpose to deliver the kingdom to the Pretender, hoping to take their advantage by the absence of so many good Protestants, who have chosen rather to leave their country than to stay at home and pay tithes against their conscience to an Episcopal curate.

Secondly, the poorer tenants will have something valuable of their own, which by law may be made liable to distress, and help to pay their landlord's rent, their corn and cattle being already seized and money a thing unknown.

Thirdly, whereas the maintenance of a hundred thousand children, from two years old and upwards, cannot be computed at less than ten shillings a piece per annum, the nation's stock will be thereby increased fifty thousand pounds per annum, besides the profit of a new dish introduced to the tables of all gentlemen of fortune in the kingdom who have any refinement in taste. And the money will circulate among ourselves, the goods being entirely of our own growth and manufacture.

Fourthly, the constant breeders, besides the gain of eight shillings sterling per annum by the sale of their children, will be rid of the charge of maintaining them after the first year.

Fifthly, this food would likewise bring great custom to taverns, where the vintners will certainly be so prudent as to procure the best receipts for dressing it to perfection, and consequently have their houses frequented by all the fine gentlemen, who justly value themselves upon their knowledge in good eating; and a skillful cook, who understands how to oblige his guests, will contrive to make it as expensive as they please.

Sixthly, this would be a great inducement to marriage, which all wise nations have either encouraged by rewards or enforced by laws and penalties. It would increase the care and tenderness of mothers toward their children, when they were sure of a settlement for life to the poor babes, provided in some sort by the public, to their annual profit instead of expense. We should see an honest emulation among the married women, which of them could bring the fattest child to the market. Men would become as fond of their wives during the time of their pregnancy as they are now of their mares in foal, their cows in calf, or sows when they are ready to farrow; nor offer to beat or kick them (as is too frequent a practice) for fear of a miscarriage.

Many other advantages might be enumerated. For instance, the addition of some thousand carcasses in our exportation of barreled beef, the propagation of swine's flesh, and improvements in the art of making good bacon, so much wanted among us by the great destruction of pigs, too frequent at our tables, which are no way comparable in taste or magnificence to a well-grown, fat, yearling child, which roasted whole will make a considerable figure at a lord mayor's feast or any other public entertainment. But this and many others I omit, being studious of brevity.

Supposing that one thousand families in this city would be constant customers for infants' flesh, besides others who might have it at merry meetings, particularly weddings and christenings, I compute that Dublin would take off annually about twenty thousand carcasses, and the rest of the kingdom (where probably they will be sold somewhat cheaper) the remaining eighty thousand.

I can think of no one objection that will possibly be raised against this proposal, unless it should be urged that the number of people will be thereby much lessened in the kingdom. This I freely own, and it was indeed one principal design in offering it to the world. I desire the reader will observe, that I calculate my remedy for this one individual kingdom of Ireland and for no other that ever was, is, or I think ever can be upon earth. Therefore let no man talk to me of other expedients: of taxing our absentees at five shillings a pound: of using neither clothes nor household furniture except what is of our own growth and manufacture; of utterly rejecting the materials and instruments that promote foreign luxury: of curing the expensiveness of pride, vanity, idleness, and gaming in our women: of introducing a vein of parsimony, prudence, and temperance: of learning to love our country, in the want of which we differ even from Laplanders and the inhabitants of Topinamboo: of quitting our animosities and factions, nor acting any longer like the Jews, who were murdering one anther at the very moment their city was taken: of being a little cautious not to sell our country and conscience for nothing: of teaching landlords to have at least one degree of mercy toward their tenants: lastly, of putting a spirit of honesty, industry, and skill into our shopkeepers; who, if a resolution could now be taken to buy only our native goods, would immediately unite to cheat and exact upon us in the price, the measure, and the goodness, nor could ever yet be brought to make one fair proposal of just dealing, though often and earnestly invited to it.

Therefore, I repeat, let no man talk to me of these and the like expedients, 30 till he hath at least some glimpse of hope that there will ever be some hearty and sincere attempt to put them in practice.

But as to myself, having been wearied out for many years with offering vain, idle, visionary thoughts, and at length utterly despairing of success, I fortunately fell upon this proposal, which, as it is wholly new, so it hath something solid and real, of no expense and little trouble, full in our own power, and whereby we can incur no danger in disobliging England. For this kind of commodity will not bear exportation, the flesh being of too tender a consistence to admit a long continuance in salt, although perhaps I could name a country which would be glad to eat up our whole nation without it.

After all, I am not so violently bent upon my own opinions as to reject any offer proposed by wise men, which shall be found equally innocent, cheap, easy, and effectual. But before something of that kind shall be advanced in contradiction to my scheme, and offering a better, I desire the author or authors will be pleased maturely to consider two points. First, as things now stand, how they will be able to find food and raiment for an hundred thousand useless mouths and backs. And secondly, there being a round million of creatures in human figure throughout this kingdom, whose sole subsistence put into a common stock would leave them in debt two millions of pounds sterling, adding those who are beggars by profession to the bulk of farmers, cottagers, and laborers, with their wives and children who are beggars in effect; I desire those politicians who dislike my overture, and may perhaps be so bold to attempt an answer, that they will first ask the parents of these mortals whether they would not at this day think it a great happiness to have been sold for food at a year old in this manner I prescribe, and thereby have avoided such a perpetual scene of misfortunes as they have since gone through by the oppression of landlords, the impossibility of paying rent without money or trade, the want of common sustenance, with neither house nor clothes to cover them from the inclemencies of the weather, and the most inevitable prospect of entailing the like or greater miseries upon their breed forever.

I profess, in the sincerity of my heart, that I have not the least personal interest in endeavoring to promote this necessary work, having no other motive than the public good of my country, by advancing our trade, providing for infants, relieving the poor, and giving some pleasure to the rich. I have no children by which I can propose to get a single penny; the youngest being nine years old, and my wife past childbearing. ◉◎

Reflections and Inquiries

1. Why do you suppose Swift chooses to express his views satirically? What advantage does satire have over a straightforward approach to the problem?

2. What social ills does Swift call attention to in his proposal?

3. Why does Swift refer to childbearing women as *breeders*?

4. How does Swift attempt to speak to the moral consciousness of his largely Catholic readership? What exactly is he saying to them via his proposal?

Reading to Write

Write an analysis of Swift's use of satire in this proposal. How, exactly, does it come across so powerfully?

Sinners in the Hands of an Angry God | Jonathan Edwards

One of the greatest of American theologians, Jonathan Edwards (1703–1758) is associated with a major religious revival in New England known as the Great Awakening. Edwards wished to propagate his idea of freedom of the will, based not only on Calvinist theology but also on his profound understanding of human psychology, largely influenced by the philosopher John Locke. In the following sermon, preached in Connecticut on Sunday, July 8, 1741, to an enthralled congregation, Edwards deploys his extraordinary literary and rhetorical skills to dramatize how utterly slender is the thread that holds us back from damnation.

Their foot shall slide in due time.

In this verse is threatened the vengeance of God on the wicked unbelieving Israelites, who were God's visible people, and who lived under the means

---

Source: Jonathan Edwards, "Sinners in the Hands of an Angry God," *Jonathan Edwards: Representative Selections*, rev. ed., ed. with Introduction, Bibliography, and Notes by Clarence H. Faust and Thomas H. Johnson (New York: Hill, 1935; 1962) 155–72.

of grace; but who, notwithstanding all God's wonderful works towards them, remained (as ver. 28.) void of counsel, having no understanding in them. Under all the cultivations of heaven, they brought forth bitter and poisonous fruit; as in the two verses next preceding the text.—The expression I have chosen for my text, *Their foot shall slide in due time,* seems to imply the following things, relating to the punishment and destruction to which these wicked Israelites were exposed.

1. That they were always exposed to *destruction;* as one that stands or walks in slippery places is always exposed to fall. This is implied in the manner of their destruction coming upon them, being represented by their foot sliding. The same is expressed, Psalm lxxiii. 18. "Surely thou didst set them in slippery places; thou castedst them down into destruction."

2. It implies, that they were always exposed to sudden unexpected destruction. As he that walks in slippery places is every moment liable to fall, he cannot foresee one moment whether he shall stand or fall the next; and when he does fall, he falls at once without warning: Which is also expressed in Psalm lxxiii. 18, 19. "Surely thou didst set them in slippery places; thou castedst them down into destruction: How are they brought into desolation as in a moment!"

3. Another thing implied is, that they are liable to fall *of themselves,* without being thrown down by the hand of another; as he that stands or walks on slippery ground needs nothing but his own weight to throw him down.

4. That the reason why they are not fallen already, and do not fall now, is   5
only that God's appointed time is not come. For it is said, that when that due time, or appointed time comes, *their foot shall slide.* Then they shall be left to fall, as they are inclined by their own weight. God will not hold them up in these slippery places any longer, but will let them go; and then, at that very instant, they shall fall into destruction; as he that stands on such slippery declining ground, on the edge of a pit, he cannot stand alone, when he is let go he immediately falls and is lost.

The observation from the words that I would now insist upon is this.— "There is nothing that keeps wicked men at any one moment out of hell, but the mere pleasure of God"—By the *mere* pleasure of God, I mean his *sovereign* pleasure, his arbitrary will, restrained by no obligation, hindered by no manner of difficulty, any more than if nothing else but God's mere will had in the least degree, or in any respect whatsoever, any hand in the preservation of wicked men one moment.—The truth of this observation may appear by the following considerations.

1. There is no want of *power* in God to cast wicked men into hell at any moment. Men's hands cannot be strong when God rises up. The strongest have no power to resist him, nor can any deliver out of his hands.—He is not only able to cast wicked men into hell, but he can most easily do it. Sometimes an earthly prince meets with a great deal of difficulty to subdue a rebel, who has found means to fortify himself, and has made himself strong by the numbers

of his followers. But it is not so with God. There is no fortress that is any defence from the power of God. Though hand join in hand, and vast multitudes of God's enemies combine and associate themselves, they are easily broken in pieces. They are as great heaps of light chaff before the whirlwind; or large quantities of dry stubble before devouring flames. We find it easy to tread on and crush a worm that we see crawling on the earth; so it is easy for us to cut or singe a slender thread that any thing hangs by: thus easy is it for God, when he pleases, to cast his enemies down to hell. What are we, that we should think to stand before him, at whose rebuke the earth trembles, and before whom the rocks are thrown down?

2. They *deserve* to be cast into hell; so that divine justice never stands in the way, it makes no objection against God's using his power at any moment to destroy them. Yea, on the contrary, justice calls aloud for an infinite punishment of their sins. Divine justice says of the tree that brings forth such grapes of Sodom, "Cut it down, why cumbereth it the ground?" Luke xiii. 7. The sword of divine justice is every moment brandished over their heads, and it is nothing but the hand of arbitrary mercy, and God's mere will, that holds it back.

3. They are already under a sentence of *condemnation* to hell. They do not only justly deserve to be cast down thither, but the sentence of the law of God, that eternal and immutable rule of righteousness that God has fixed between him and mankind, is gone out against them, and stands against them; so that they are bound over already to hell. John iii. 18. "He that believeth not is condemned already." So that every uncoverted man properly belongs to hell; that is his place; from thence he is, John viii. 23. "Ye are from beneath:" And thither he is bound; it is the place that justice, and God's word, and the sentence of his unchangeable law assign to him.

4. They are now the objects of that very same *anger* and wrath of God, 10 that is expressed in the torments of hell. And the reason why they do not go down to hell at each moment, is not because God, in whose power they are, is not then very angry with them; as he is with many miserable creatures now tormented in hell, who there feel and bear the fierceness of his wrath. Yea, God is a great deal more angry with great numbers that are now on earth: yea, doubtless, with many that are now in this congregation, who it may be are at ease, than he is with many of those who are now in the flames of hell.

So that it is not because God is unmindful of their wickedness, and does not resent it, that he does not let loose his hand and cut them off. God is not altogether such an one as themselves, though they may imagine him to be so. The wrath of God burns against them, their damnation does not slumber; the pit is prepared, the fire is made ready, the furnace is now hot, ready to receive them; the flames do now rage and glow. The glittering sword is whet, and held over them, and the pit hath opened its mouth under them.

5. The *devil* stands ready to fall upon them, and seize them as his own, at what moment God shall permit him. They belong to him; he has their souls in

his possession, and under his dominion. The scripture represents them as his goods, Luke xi. 12. The devils watch them; they are ever by them at their right hand; they stand waiting for them, like greedy hungry lions that see their prey, and expect to have it, but are for the present kept back. If God should withdraw his hand, by which they are restrained, they would in one moment fly upon their poor souls. The old serpent is gaping for them; hell opens its mouth wide to receive them; and if God should permit it, they would be hastily swallowed up and lost.

6. There are in the souls of wicked men those hellish *principles* reigning, that would presently kindle and flame out into hell fire, if it were not for God's restraints. There is laid in the very nature of carnal men, a foundation for the torments of hell. There are those corrupt principles, in reigning power in them, and in full possession of them, that are seeds of hell fire. These principles are active and powerful, exceeding violent in their nature, and if it were not for the restraining hand of God upon them, they would soon break out, they would flame out after the same manner as the same corruptions, the same enmity does in the hearts of damned souls, and would beget the same torments as they do in them. The souls of the wicked are in scripture compared to the troubled sea, Isa. lvii. 20. For the present, God restrains their wickedness by his mighty power, as he does the raging waves of the troubled sea, saying, "Hitherto shalt thou come, but no further;" but if God should withdraw that restraining power, it would soon carry all before it. Sin is the ruin and misery of the soul; it is destructive in its nature; and if God should leave it without restraint, there would need nothing else to make the soul perfectly miserable. The corruption of the heart of man is immoderate and boundless in its fury; and while wicked men live here, it is like fire pent up by God's restraints, whereas if it were let loose, it would set on fire the course of nature; and as the heart is now a sink of sin, so if sin was not restrained, it would immediately turn the soul into a fiery oven, or a furnace of fire and brimstone.

7. It is no security to wicked men for one moment, that there are no visible means of death at hand. It is no security to a natural man, that he is now in health, and that he does not see which way he should now immediately go out of the world by any accident, and that there is no visible danger in any respect in his circumstances. The manifold and continual experience of the world in all ages, shows this is no evidence, that a man is not on the very brink of eternity, and that the next step will not be into another world. The unseen, unthought-of ways and means of persons going suddenly out of the world are innumerable and inconceivable. Unconverted men walk over the pit of hell on a rotten covering, and there are innumerable places in this covering so weak that they will not bear their weight, and these places are not seen. The arrows of death fly unseen at noon-day; the sharpest sight cannot discern them. God has so many different unsearchable ways of taking wicked men out of the world and sending them to hell, that there is nothing to make it appear, that

God had need to be at the expence of a miracle, or go out of the ordinary course of his providence, to destroy any wicked man, at any moment. All the means that there are of sinners going out of the world, are so in God's hands, and so universally and absolutely subject to his power and determination, that it does not depend at all the less on the mere will of God, whether sinners shall at any moment go to hell, than if means were never made use of, or at all concerned in the case.

8. Natural men's prudence and care to preserve their own lives, or the care of others to preserve them, do not secure them a moment. To this, divine providence and universal experience do also bear testimony. There is this clear evidence that men's own wisdom is no security to them from death; that if it were otherwise we should see some difference between the wise and politic men of the world, and others, with regard to their liableness to early and unexpected death: but how is it in fact? Eccles. ii. 16. "How dieth the wise man? even as the fool."

9. All wicked men's pains and *contrivance* which they use to escape hell, while they continue to reject Christ, and so remain wicked men, do not secure them from hell one moment. Almost every natural man that hears of hell, flatters himself that he shall escape it; he depends upon himself for his own security; he flatters himself in what he has done, in what he is now doing, or what he intends to do. Every one lays out matters in his own mind how he shall avoid damnation, and flatters himself that he contrives well for himself, and that his schemes will not fail. They hear indeed that there are but few saved, and that the greater part of men that have died heretofore are gone to hell; but each one imagines that he lays out matters better for his own escape than others have done. He does not intend to come to that place of torment; he says within himself, that he intends to take effectual care, and to order matters so for himself as not to fail.

But the foolish children of men miserably delude themselves in their own schemes, and in confidence in their own strength and wisdom; they trust to nothing but a shadow. The greater part of those who heretofore have lived under the same means of grace, and are now dead, are undoubtedly gone to hell; and it was not because they were not as wise as those who are now alive: it was not because they did not lay out matters as well for themselves to secure their own escape. If we could speak with them, and inquire of them, one by one, whether they expected, when alive, and when they used to hear about hell, ever to be the subjects of that misery: we doubtless, should hear one and another reply, "No, I never intended to come here: I had laid out matters otherwise in my mind; I thought I should contrive well for myself: I thought my scheme good. I intended to take effectual care; but it came upon me unexpected; I did not look for it at that time, and in that manner; it came as a thief: Death outwitted me: God's wrath was too quick for me. Oh, my cursed foolishness! I was flattering myself, and pleasing myself with vain dreams of what I would do hereafter; and when I was saying, Peace and safety, then suddenly destruction came upon me."

10. God has laid himself under *no obligation*, by any promise to keep any natural man out of hell one moment. God certainly has made no promises either of eternal life, or of any deliverance or preservation from eternal death, but what are contained in the covenant of grace, the promises that are given in Christ, in whom all the promises are yea and amen. But surely they have no interest in the promises of the covenant of grace who are not the children of the covenant, who do not believe in any of the promises, and have no interest in the Mediator of the covenant.

So that, whatever some have imagined and pretended about promises made to natural men's earnest seeking and knocking, it is plain and manifest, that whatever pains a natural man takes in religion, whatever prayers he makes, till he believes in Christ, God is under no manner of obligation to keep him a moment from eternal destruction.

So that, thus it is that natural men are held in the hand of God, over the pit of hell; they have deserved the fiery pit, and are already sentenced to it; and God is dreadfully provoked, his anger is as great towards them as to those that are actually suffering the executions of the fierceness of his wrath in hell, and they have done nothing in the least to appease or abate that anger, neither is God in the least bound by any promise to hold them up one moment; the devil is waiting for them, hell is gaping for them, the flames gather and flash about them, and would fain lay hold on them, and swallow them up; the fire pent up in their own hearts is struggling to break out: and they have no interest in any Mediator, there are no means within reach that can be any security to them. In short, they have no refuge, nothing to take hold of; all that preserves them every moment is the mere arbitrary will, and uncovenanted, unobliged forbearance of an incensed God.

Application
The use of this awful subject may be for awakening unconverted persons in this congregation. This that you have heard is the case of every one of you that are out of Christ.—That world of misery, that lake of burning brimstone, is extended abroad under you. There is the dreadful pit of the glowing flames of the wrath of God; there is hell's wide gaping mouth open; and you have nothing to stand upon, nor any thing to take hold of; there is nothing between you and hell but the air; it is only the power and mere pleasure of God that holds you up.

You probably are not sensible of this; you find you are kept out of hell, but do not see the hand of God in it; but look at other things, as the good state of your bodily constitution, your care of your own life, and the means you use for your own preservation. But indeed these things are nothing; if God should withdraw his hand, they would avail no more to keep you from falling, than the thin air to hold up a person that is suspended in it.

Your wickedness makes you as it were heavy as lead, and to tend downwards with great weight and pressure towards hell; and if God should let you go, you would immediately sink and swiftly descend and plunge into the bottomless gulf, and your healthy constitution, and your own care and prudence, and best contrivance, and all your righteousness, would have no more influence to uphold you and keep you out of hell, than a spider's web would have to stop a fallen rock. Were it not for the sovereign pleasure of God, the earth would not bear you one moment; for you are a burden to it; the creation groans with you; the creature is made subject to the bondage of your corruption, not willingly; the sun does not willingly shine upon you to give you light to serve sin and Satan; the earth does not willingly yield her increase to satisfy your lusts; nor is it willingly a stage for your wickedness to be acted upon; the air does not willingly serve you for breath to maintain the flame of life in your vitals, while you spend your life in the service of God's enemies. God's creatures are good, and were made for men to serve God with, and do not willingly subserve to any other purpose, and groan when they are abused to purposes so directly contrary to their nature and end. And the world would spew you out, were it not for the sovereign hand of him who hath subjected it in hope. There are black clouds of God's wrath now hanging directly over your heads, full of the dreadful storm, and big with thunder; and were it not for the restraining hand of God, it would immediately burst forth upon you. The sovereign pleasure of God, for the present, stays his rough wind; otherwise it would come with fury, and your destruction would come like a whirlwind, and you would be like the chaff of the summer threshing floor.

The wrath of God is like great waters that are dammed for the present; they increase more and more, and rise higher and higher, till an outlet is given; and the longer the stream is stopped, the more rapid and mighty is its course, when once it is let loose. It is true, that judgment against your evil works has not been executed hitherto; the floods of God's vengeance have been withheld; but your guilt in the mean time is constantly increasing, and you are every day treasuring up more wrath; the waters are constantly rising, and waxing more and more mighty; and there is nothing but the mere pleasure of God, that holds the waters back, that are unwilling to be stopped, and press hard to go forward. If God should only withdraw his hand from the flood-gate, it would immediately fly open, and the fiery floods of the fierceness and wrath of God, would rush forth with inconceivable fury, and would come upon you with omnipotent power; and if your strength were ten thousand times greater than it is, yea, ten thousand times greater than the strength of the stoutest, sturdiest devil in hell, it would be nothing to withstand or endure it.

The bow of God's wrath is bent, and the arrow made ready on the string, 25 and justice bends the arrow at your heart, and strains the bow, and it is nothing but the mere pleasure of God, and that of an angry God, without any promise or obligation at all, that keeps the arrow one moment from being made drunk with your blood. Thus all you that never passed under a great change of heart, by the mighty power of the Spirit of God upon your souls;

all you that were never born again, and made new creatures, and raised from being dead in sin, to a state of new, and before altogether unexperienced light and life, are in the hands of an angry God. However you may have reformed your life in many things, and may have had religious affections, and may keep up a form of religion in your families and closets, and in the house of God, it is nothing but his mere pleasure that keeps you from being this moment swallowed up in everlasting destruction. However unconvinced you may now be of the truth of what you hear, by and by you will be fully convinced of it. Those that are gone from being in the like circumstances with you, see that it was so with them; for destruction came suddenly upon most of them; when they expected nothing of it, and while they were saying, Peace and safety: now they see, that those things on which they depended for peace and safety, were nothing but thin air and empty shadows.

The God that holds you over the pit of hell, much as one holds a spider, or some loathsome insect over the fire, abhors you, and is dreadfully provoked: his wrath towards you burns like fire; he looks upon you as worthy of nothing else, but to be cast into the fire; he is of purer eyes than to bear to have you in his sight; you are ten thousand times more abominable in his eyes, than the most hateful venomous serpent is in ours. You have offended him infinitely more than ever a stubborn rebel did his prince; and yet it is nothing but his hand that holds you from falling into the fire every moment. It is to be ascribed to nothing else, that you did not go to hell the last night; that you was suffered to awake again in this world, after you closed your eyes to sleep. And there is no other reason to be given, why you have not dropped into hell since you arose in the morning, but that God's hand has held you up. There is no other reason to be given why you have not gone to hell, since you have sat here in the house of God, provoking his pure eyes by your sinful wicked manner of attending his solemn worship. Yea, there is nothing else that is to be given as a reason why you do not this very moment drop down into hell.

O sinner! Consider the fearful danger you are in: it is a great furnace of wrath, a wide and bottomless pit, full of the fire of wrath, that you are held over in the hand of that God, whose wrath is provoked and incensed as much against you, as against many of the damned in hell. You hang by a slender thread, with the flames of divine wrath flashing about it, and ready every moment to singe it, and burn it asunder; and you have no interest in any Mediator, and nothing to lay hold of to save yourself, nothing to keep off the flames of wrath, nothing of your own, nothing that you ever have done, nothing that you can do, to induce God to spare you one moment.—And consider here more particularly,

1. *Whose* wrath it is: it is the wrath of the infinite God. If it were only the wrath of man, though it were of the most potent prince, it would be comparatively little to be regarded. The wrath of kings is very much dreaded, especially of absolute monarchs, who have the possessions and lives of their subjects

wholly in their power, to be disposed of at their mere will. Prov. xx. 2. "The fear of a king is as the roaring of a lion: Whoso provoketh him to anger, sinneth against his own soul." The subject that very much enrages an arbitrary prince, is liable to suffer the most extreme torments that human art can invent, or human power can inflict. But the greatest earthly potentates in their greatest majesty and strength, and when clothed in their greatest terrors, are but feeble, despicable worms of the dust, in comparison of the great and almighty Creator and King of heaven and earth. It is but little that they can do, when most enraged, and when they have exerted the utmost of their fury. All the kings of the earth, before God, are as grasshoppers; they are nothing, and less than nothing: both their love and their hatred is to be despised. The wrath of the great King of kings, is as much more terrible than theirs, as his majesty is greater. Luke xii. 4, 5. "And I say unto you, my friends, Be not afraid of them that kill the body, and after that, have no more that they can do. But I will forewarn you whom you shall fear: fear him, which after he hath killed, hath power to cast into hell: yea, I say unto you, Fear him."

2. It is the *fierceness* of his wrath that you are exposed to. We often read of the fury of God; as in Isaiah lix. 18. "According to their deeds, accordingly he will repay fury to his adversaries." So Isaiah lxvi. 15. "For behold, the Lord will come with fire, and with his chariots like a whirlwind, to render his anger with fury, and his rebuke with flames of fire." And in many other places. So, Rev. xix. 15. we read of "the wine press of the fierceness and wrath of Almighty God." The words are exceeding terrible. If it had only been said, "the wrath of God," the words would have implied that which is infinitely dreadful: but it is "the fierceness and wrath of God." The fury of God! the fierceness of Jehovah! Oh, how dreadful must that be! Who can utter or conceive what such expressions carry in them! But it is also "the fierceness and wrath of *Almighty* God." As though there would be a very great manifestation of his almighty power in what the fierceness of his wrath should inflict, as though omnipotence should be as it were enraged, and exerted, as men are wont to exert their strength in the fierceness of their wrath. Oh! then, what will be the consequence! What will become of the poor worms that shall suffer it! Whose hands can be strong? And whose heart can endure? To what a dreadful, inexpressible, inconceivable depth of misery must the poor creature be sunk who shall be the subject of this!

Consider this, you that are here present, that yet remain in an unregenerate state. That God will execute the fierceness of his anger, implies, that he will inflict wrath without any pity. When God beholds the ineffable extremity of your case, and sees your torment to be so vastly disproportioned to your strength, and sees how your poor soul is crushed, and sinks down, as it were, into an infinite gloom; he will have no compassion upon you, he will not forbear the executions of his wrath, or in the least lighten his hand; there shall be no moderation or mercy, nor will God then at all stay his rough wind; he will have no regard to your welfare, nor be at all careful lest you should suffer too much in any other sense, than only that you shall *not suffer beyond what strict justice requires.* Nothing shall be withheld, because it is so hard for you to bear. Ezek. viii. 18. "Therefore will I also deal in fury: mine eye shall not spare, neither will I have pity; and though they cry in mine ears with a loud voice, yet I will not hear them." Now God stands ready to pity you; this is a day of mercy; you may cry now with some encouragement of obtaining mercy. But when once the day of mercy is past, your most lamentable and dolorous cries and shrieks will be in vain; you will be wholly lost and thrown away of God, as to any regard to your welfare. God will have no other use to put you to, but to suffer misery; you shall be continued in being to no other end; for you will be a vessel of wrath fitted to destruction; and there will be no other use of this vessel, but to be filled full of wrath. God will be so far from pitying you when you cry to him, that it is said he will only "laugh and mock," Prov. i. 25, 26, &c.

How awful are those words, Isa. lxiii. 3, which are the words of the great God. "I will tread them in mine anger, and will trample them in my fury, and their blood shall be sprinkled upon my garments, and I will stain all my raiment." It is perhaps impossible to conceive of words that carry in them greater manifestations of these three things, *viz.* contempt, and hatred, and fierceness of indignation. If you cry to God to pity you, he will be so far from pitying you in your doleful case, or showing you the least regard or favour, that instead of that, he will only tread you under foot. And though he will know that you cannot bear the weight of omnipotence treading upon you, yet he will not regard that, but he will crush you under his feet without mercy; he will crush out your blood, and make it fly, and it shall be sprinkled on his garments, so as to stain all his raiment. He will not only hate you, but he will have you, in the utmost contempt: no place shall be thought fit for you, but under his feet to be trodden down as the mire of the streets.

3. The *misery* you are exposed to is that which God will inflict to that end, that he might show what that wrath of Jehovah is. God hath had it on his heart to show to angels and men, both how excellent his love is, and also how terrible his wrath is. Sometimes earthly kings have a mind to show how terrible their wrath is, by the extreme punishments they would execute on those that would provoke them. Nebuchadnezzar, that mighty and haughty monarch of the Chaldean empire, was willing to show his wrath when enraged with Shadrach, Meshech, and Abednego; and accordingly gave orders that the burning fiery furnace should be heated seven times hotter than it was before; doubtless, it was raised to the utmost degree of fierceness that human art could raise it. But the great God is also willing to show his wrath, and magnify his awful majesty and mighty power in the extreme sufferings of his enemies. Rom. ix. 22. "What if God, willing to show his wrath, and to make his power known, endure with much long-suffering the vessels of wrath fitted to destruction?" And seeing this is his design, and what he has determined, even to show how terrible the unrestrained wrath, the fury and fierceness of

Jehovah is, he will do it to effect. There will be something accomplished and brought to pass that will be dreadful with a witness. When the great and angry God hath risen up and executed his awful vengeance on the poor sinner, and the wretch is actually suffering the infinite weight and power of his indignation, then will God call upon the whole universe to behold that awful majesty and mighty power that is to be seen in it. Isa. xxxiii. 12–14. "And the people shall be as the burnings of lime, as thorns cut up shall they be burnt in the fire. Hear ye that are far off, what I have done; and ye that are near, acknowledge my might. The sinners in Zion are afraid; fearfulness hath surprised the hypocrites," &c.

Thus it will be with you that are in an unconverted state, if you continue in it; the infinite might, and majesty, and terribleness of the omnipotent God shall be magnified upon you, in the ineffable strength of your torments. You shall be tormented in the presence of the holy angels, and in the presence of the Lamb; and when you shall be in this state of suffering, the glorious inhabitants of heaven shall go forth and look on the awful spectacle, that they may see what the wrath and fierceness of the Almighty is; and when they have seen it, they will fall down and adore that great power and majesty. Isa. lxvi. 23, 24. "And it shall come to pass, that from one new moon to another, and from one sabbath to another, shall all flesh come to worship before me, saith the Lord. And they shall go forth and look upon the carcasses of the men that have transgressed against me; for their worm shall not die, neither shall their fire be quenched, and they shall be an abhorring unto all flesh."

4. It is *everlasting* wrath. It would be dreadful to suffer this fierceness and wrath of Almighty God one moment; but you must suffer it to all eternity. There will be no end to this exquisite horrible misery. When you look forward, you shall see a long for ever, a boundless duration before you, which will swallow up your thoughts and amaze your soul; and you will absolutely despair of ever having any deliverance, any end, any mitigation, any rest at all. You will know certainly that you must wear out long ages, millions of millions of ages, in wrestling, and conflicting with this almighty merciless vengeance; and then when you have so done, when so many ages have actually been spent by you in this manner, you will know that all is but a point to what remains. So that your punishment will indeed be infinite. Oh, who can express what the state of a soul in such circumstances is! All that we can possibly say about it, gives but a very feeble, faint representation of it; it is inexpressible and inconceivable: For "who knows the power of God's anger?"

How dreadful is the state of those that are daily and hourly in the danger ³⁵ of this great wrath and infinite misery! But this is the dismal case of every soul in this congregation that has not been born again, however moral and strict, sober and religious, they may otherwise be. Oh that you would consider it, whether you be young or old! There is reason to think, that there are many in this congregation now hearing this discourse, that will actually be the subjects of this very misery to all eternity. We know not who they are, or in what seats they sit, or what thoughts they now have. It may be they are now at ease, and hear all these things without much disturbance, and are now flattering themselves that they are not the persons, promising themselves that they shall escape. If we knew that there as one person, and but one, in the whole congregation, that was to be the subject of this misery, what an awful thing would it be to think of! If we knew who it was, what an awful sight would it be to see such a person! How might all the rest of the congregation lift up a lamentable and bitter cry over him! But, alas! instead of one, how many is it likely will remember this discourse in hell? And it would be a wonder, if some that are now present should not be in hell in a very short time, even before this year is out. And it would be no wonder if some persons, that now sit here, in some seats of this meeting-house, in health, quiet and secure, should be there before tomorrow morning. Those of you that finally continue in a natural condition, that shall keep out of hell longest will be there in a little time! your damnation does not slumber; it will come swiftly, and, in all probability, very suddenly upon many of you. You have reason to wonder that you are not already in hell. It is doubtless the case of some whom you have seen and known, that never deserved hell more than you, and that heretofore appeared as likely to have been now alive as you. Their case is past all hope; they are crying in extreme misery and perfect despair; but here you are in the land of the living and in the house of God, and have an opportunity to obtain salvation. What would not those poor damned hopeless souls give for one day's opportunity such as you now enjoy!

And now you have an extraordinary opportunity, a day wherein Christ has thrown the door of mercy wide open, and stands in calling and crying with a loud voice to poor sinners; a day wherein many are flocking to him, and pressing into the kingdom of God. Many are daily coming from the east, west, north and south; many that were very lately in the same miserable condition that you are in, are now in a happy state, with their hearts filled with love to him who has loved them, and washed them from their sins in his own blood, and rejoicing in hope of the glory of God. How awful is it to be left behind at such a day! To see so many others feasting, while you are pining and perishing! To see so many rejoicing and singing for joy of heart, while you have cause to mourn for sorrow of heart, and howl for vexation of spirit! How can you rest one moment in such a condition? Are not your souls as precious as the souls of the people at Suffield,* where they are flocking from day to day to Christ?

Are there not many here who have lived long in the world, and are not to this day born again? and so are aliens from the commonwealth of Israel, and have done nothing ever since they have lived, but treasure up wrath against the day of wrath? Oh, sirs, your case, in an especial manner, is extremely dangerous. Your guilt and hardness of heart is extremely great. Do you not see

*A town in the neighbourhood. [Edwards's note.]

how generally persons of your years are passed over and left, in the present remarkable and wonderful dispensation of God's mercy? You had need to consider yourselves, and awake thoroughly out of sleep. You cannot bear the fierceness and wrath of the infinite God.—And you, young men, and young women, will you neglect this precious season which you now enjoy, when so many others of your age are renouncing all youthful vanities, and flocking to Christ? You especially have now an extraordinary opportunity; but if you neglect it, it will soon be with you as with those persons who spent all the precious days of youth in sin, and are now come to such a dreadful pass in blindness and hardness.—And you, children, who are unconverted, do not you know that you are going down to hell, to bear the dreadful wrath of that God, who is now angry with you every day and every night? Will you be content to be the children of the devil, when so many other children in the land are converted, and are become the holy and happy children of the King of kings?

And let every one that is yet of Christ, and hanging over the pit of hell, whether they be old men and women, or middle aged, or young people, or little children, now hearken to the loud calls of God's word and providence. This acceptable year of the Lord, a day of such great favours to some, will doubtless be a day of as remarkable vengeance to others. Men's hearts harden, and their guilt increases apace at such a day as this, if they neglect their souls; and never was there so great danger of such persons being given up to hardness of heart and blindness of mind. God seems now to be hastily gathering in his elect in all parts of the land; and probably the greater part of adult persons that ever shall be saved, will be brought in now in a little time, and that it will be as it was on the great out-pouring of the Spirit upon the Jews in the apostles' days; the election will obtain, and the rest will be blinded. If this should be the case with you, you will eternally curse this day, and will curse the day that ever you was born, to see such a season of the pouring out of God's Spirit, and will wish that you had died and gone to hell before you had seen it. Now undoubtedly it is, as it was in the days of John the Baptist, the axe is in an extraordinary manner laid at the root of the trees, that every tree which brings not forth good fruit, may be hewn down and cast into the fire.

Therefore, let every one that is out of Christ, now awake and fly from the wrath to come. The wrath of Almighty God is now undoubtedly hanging over a great part of this congregation: Let every one fly out of Sodom: "Haste and escape for your lives, look not behind you, escape to the mountain, lest you be consumed." ◎∕◎

Reflections and Inquiries

1. What, according to Edwards, keeps God from allowing sinners to descend into hell?

2. What recourse do sinners have to prevent their own eternal destruction?

3. Why does Edwards begin his sermon with a reference to Deuteronomy 32:35?

4. Why do you suppose Edwards gives such dramatic emphasis to God's anger?

Reading to Write

Do a stylistic analysis of this sermon. How does Edwards's use of certain kinds of sentence structure, metaphor, analogy, dramatization, word choice, repetition, and so on contribute to the emotional impact of his premise?

Keynote Address at the First Woman's Rights Convention | Elizabeth Cady Stanton

Barred from a world antislavery convention in London because she was a woman, Elizabeth Cady Stanton (1815–1902), an abolitionist and cofounder (with Susan B. Anthony) of the National Woman Suffrage Association (1869), teamed up with Lucretia Coffin Mott, founder of the Female Anti-Slavery Society in Philadelphia (1833), to organize the first Woman's Rights Convention in the United States in 1848. The following is an abridgment of Stanton's keynote address.

"Man cannot fulfill his destiny alone, he cannot redeem his race unaided."

We have met here today to discuss our rights and wrongs, civil and political, and not, as some have supposed, to go into the detail of social life alone. We do not propose to petition the legislature to make our husbands just, generous, and courteous, to seat every man at the head of a cradle, and to clothe every woman in male attire. None of these points, however important they may be considered by leading men, will be touched in this convention. As to their costume, the gentlemen need feel no fear of our imitating that, for we think it in violation of every principle of taste, beauty, and dignity; notwithstanding all the contempt cast upon our loose, flowing garments, we still admire the graceful folds, and consider our costume far more artistic than theirs. Many of the nobler sex seem to agree with us in this opinion, for the bishops, priests, judges, barristers, and lord mayors of the first nation on the globe, and the Pope of Rome, with his cardinals, too, all wear the loose flowing robes, thus tacitly acknowledging that the male attire is neither dignified

---

Source: Elizabeth Cady Stanton, "Keynote Address at the First Woman's Rights Convention, July 19, 1848," *A Treasury of the World's Greatest Speeches,* ed. Houston Peterson (New York: Simon, 1965) 389–92.

Elizabeth Cady Stanton, left (1815–1902), and Susan B. Anthony (1820–1906) were two early champions of woman's rights.

nor imposing. No, we shall not molest you in your philosophical experiments with stocks, pants, high-heeled boots, and Russian belts. Yours be the glory to discover, by personal experience, how long the kneepan can resist the terrible strapping down which you impose, in how short time the well-developed muscles of the throat can be reduced to mere threads by the constant pressure of the stock, how high the heel of a boot must be to make a short man tall, and how tight the Russian belt may be drawn and yet have wind enough left to sustain life.

But we are assembled to protest against a form of government existing without the consent of the governed—to declare our right to be free as man is free, to be represented in the government which we are taxed to support, to have such disgraceful laws as give man the power to chastise and imprison his wife, to take the wages which she earns, the property which she inherits, and, in case of separation, the children of her love; laws which make her the mere dependent on his bounty. It is to protest against such unjust laws as these that we are assembled today, and to have them, if possible, forever erased from our statute books, deeming them a shame and a disgrace to a Christian republic in the nineteenth century. We have met

To uplift woman's fallen divinity
Upon an even pedestal with man's.

And, strange as it may seem to many, we now demand our right to vote according to the declaration of the government under which we live. This right no one pretends to deny. We need not prove ourselves equal to Daniel Webster to enjoy this privilege, for the ignorant Irishman in the ditch has all the civil rights he has. We need not prove our muscular power equal to this same Irishman to enjoy this privilege, for the most tiny, weak, ill-shaped stripling of twenty-one has all the civil rights of the Irishman. We have no objection to discuss the question of equality, for we feel that the weight of argument lies wholly with us, but we wish the question of equality kept distinct from the question of rights, for the proof of the one does not determine the truth of the other. All white men in this country have the same rights, however they may differ in mind, body, or estate.

The right is ours. The question now is: how shall we get possession of what rightfully belongs to us? We should not feel so sorely grieved if no man who had not attained the full stature of a Webster, Clay, Van Buren, or Gerrit Smith could claim the right of the elective franchise. But to have drunkards, idiots, horse-racing, rum-selling rowdies, ignorant foreigners, and silly boys fully recognized, while we ourselves are thrust out from all the rights that belong to citizens, it is too grossly insulting to the dignity of woman to be longer quietly submitted to. The right is ours. Have it, we must. Use it, we will. The pens, the tongues, the fortunes, the indomitable wills of many women are already pledged to secure this right. The great truth that no just government can be formed without the consent of the governed we shall echo and re-echo in the ears of the unjust judge, until by continual coming we shall weary him. . . .

There seems now to be a kind of moral stagnation in our midst. Philanthropists have done their utmost to rouse the nation to a sense of its sins. War, slavery, drunkenness, licentiousness, gluttony, have been dragged naked before the people, and all their abominations and deformities fully brought to light, yet with idiotic laugh we hug those monsters to our breasts and rush on to destruction. Our churches are multiplying on all sides, our missionary societies, Sunday schools, and prayer meetings and innumerable charitable and reform organizations are all in operation, but still the tide of vice is swelling, and threatens the destruction of everything, and the battlements of righteousness are weak against the raging elements of sin and death. Verily, the world waits the coming of some new element, some purifying power, some spirit of mercy and love. The voice of woman has been silenced in the state, the church, and the home, but man cannot fulfill his destiny alone, he cannot redeem his race unaided. There are deep and tender chords of sympathy and love in the hearts of the downfallen and oppressed that woman can touch more skillfully than man.

The world has never yet seen a truly great and virtuous nation, because in the degradation of woman the very fountains of life are poisoned at their source. It is vain to look for silver and gold from mines of copper and lead.

5

It is the wise mother that has the wise son. So long as your women are slaves you may throw your colleges and churches to the winds. You can't have scholars and saints so long as your mothers are ground to powder between the upper and nether millstone of tyranny and lust. How seldom, now, is a father's pride gratified, his fond hopes realized, in the budding genius of his son! The wife is degraded, made the mere creature of caprice, and the foolish son is heaviness to his heart. Truly are the sins of the fathers visited upon the children to the third and fourth generation. God, in His wisdom, has so linked the whole human family together that any violence done at one end of the chain is felt throughout its length, and there, too, is the law of restoration, as in woman all have fallen, so in her elevation shall the race be recreated.

"Voices" were the visitors and advisers of Joan of Arc. Do not "voices" come to us daily from the haunts of poverty, sorrow, degradation, and despair, already too long unheeded. Now is the time for the women of this country, if they would save our free institutions, to defend the right, to buckle on the armor that can best resist the keenest weapons of the enemy—contempt and ridicule. The same religious enthusiasm that nerved Joan of Arc to her work nerves us to ours. In every generation God calls some men and women for the utterance of truth, a heroic action, and our work today is the fulfilling of what has long since been foretold by the Prophet—Joel 2:28: "And it shall come to pass afterward, that I will pour out my spirit upon all flesh; and your sons and your daughters shall prophesy." We do not expect our path will be strewn with the flowers of popular applause, but over the thorns of bigotry and prejudice will be our way, and on our banners will beat the dark storm clouds of opposition from those who have entrenched themselves behind the stormy bulwarks of custom and authority, and who have fortified their position by every means, holy and unholy. But we will steadfastly abide the result. Unmoved we will bear it aloft. Undauntedly we will unfurl it to the gale, for we know that the storm cannot rend from it a shred, that the electric flash will but more clearly show to us the glorious words inscribed upon it, "Equality of Rights.". . . ◎/◎

Reflections and Inquiries

1. Why does Stanton open with a reference to male and female modes of dress? What point does she make with her witty reference to the apparel of certain members of the clergy?

2. What laws does Stanton consider to be "a disgrace to a Christian republic"? Why?

3. What is the purpose of Stanton's allusion to Joan of Arc?

4. What consequences of female degradation does Stanton articulate?

Reading to Write

Examine Stanton's argument from an organizational perspective. Outline the sequence of points she makes, and then suggest a rationale for this sequence in relation to her thesis. How well does her opening prepare for what follows?

I Hear the Mournful Wail of Millions | Frederick Douglass

On July 4, 1852, Frederick Douglass (1817–1895), a former slave (he escaped to New England in his twenties) and member of the Massachusetts Antislavery Society who one day would discuss slavery with President Lincoln, was invited to commemorate Independence Day in Rochester, New York, with the following speech.

Fellow citizens, pardon me, allow me to ask, why am I called upon to speak here today? What have I, or those I represent, to do with your national independence? Are the great principles of political freedom and of natural justice, embodied in that Declaration of Independence, extended to us? and am I, therefore, called upon to bring our humble offering to the national altar, and to confess the benefits and express devout gratitude for the blessings resulting from your independence to us?

Would to God, both for your sakes and ours, that an affirmative answer could be truthfully returned to these questions! Then would my task be light, and my burden easy and delightful. For who is there so cold that a nation's sympathy could not warm him? Who so obdurate and dead to the claims of gratitude that would not thankfully acknowledge such priceless benefits? Who so stolid and selfish that would not give his voice to swell the hallelujahs of a nation's jubilee, when the chains of servitude had been torn from his limbs? I am not that man. In a case like that the dumb might eloquently speak and the "lame man leap as an hart."

But such is not the state of the case. I say it with a sad sense of the disparity between us. I am not included within the pale of this glorious anniversary! Your high independence only reveals the immeasurable distance between us. The blessings in which you, this day, rejoice are not enjoyed in common. The rich inheritance of justice, liberty, prosperity, and independence bequeathed by your fathers is shared by you, not by me. The sunlight that brought light and healing to you has brought stripes and death to me. This Fourth of July is yours, not mine. You may rejoice, I must mourn. To drag a man in fetters into the grand illuminated temple of liberty, and call upon him to join you in joyous anthems, were inhuman mockery and sacrilegious irony. Do you mean, citizens, to mock me by asking me to speak today? If so, there is a parallel to

---

Source: Frederick Douglass, "I Hear the Mournful Wail of Millions," *A Treasury of the World's Greatest Speeches,* ed. Houston Peterson (New York: Simon, 1965) 478–82.

your conduct. And let me warn you that it is dangerous to copy the example of a nation whose crimes, towering up to heaven, were thrown down by the breath of the Almighty, burying that nation in irrevocable ruin! I can today take up the plaintive lament of a peeled and woe-smitten people!

"By the rivers of Babylon, there we sat down. Yea! we wept when we remembered Zion. We hanged our harps upon the willows in the midst thereof. For there, they that carried us away captive, required of us a song; and they who wasted us required of us mirth, saying, Sing us one of the songs of Zion. How can we sing the Lord's song in a strange land? If I forget thee, O Jerusalem, let my right hand forget her cunning. If I do not remember thee, let my tongue cleave to the roof of my mouth."

Fellow citizens, above your national, tumultuous joy, I hear the mournful   5 wail of millions! whose chains, heavy and grievous yesterday, are, today, rendered more intolerable by the jubilee shouts that reach them. If I do forget, if I do not faithfully remember those bleeding children of sorrow this day, "may my right hand forget her cunning, and may my tongue cleave to the roof of my mouth"! To forget them, to pass lightly over their wrongs, and to chime in with the popular theme would be treason most scandalous and shocking, and would make me a reproach before God and the world. My subject, then, fellow citizens, is *American slavery*. I shall see this day and its popular characteristics from the slave's point of view. Standing there identified with the American bondman, making his wrongs mine. I do not hesitate to declare with all my soul that the character and conduct of this nation never looked blacker to me than on this Fourth of July! Whether we turn to the declarations of the past or to the professions of the present, the conduct of the nation seems equally hideous and revolting. America is false to the past, false to the present, and solemnly binds herself to be false to the future. Standing with God and the crushed and bleeding slave on this occasion, I will, in the name of humanity which is outraged, in the name of liberty which is fettered, in the name of the Constitution and the Bible which are disregarded and trampled upon, dare to call in question and to denounce, with all the emphasis I can command, everything that serves to perpetuate slavery—the great sin and shame of America! "I will not equivocate; I will not excuse;" I will use the severest language I can command; and yet not one word shall escape me that any man, whose judgment is not blinded by prejudice, or who is not at heart a slaveholder, shall not confess to be right and just.

But I fancy I hear someone of my audience say, "It is just in this circumstance that you and your brother abolitionists fail to make a favorable impression on the public mind. Would you argue more and denounce less, would you persuade more and rebuke less, your cause would be much more likely to succeed." But, I submit, where all is plain, there is nothing to be argued. What point in the antislavery creed would you have me argue? On what branch of the subject do the people of this country need light? Must I undertake to prove that the slave is a man? That point is conceded already. Nobody doubts it. The slaveholders themselves acknowledge it in the enactment of

*Frederick Douglass (1817–1895)
was a self-educated former slave
who discussed the evils of slavery
with Abraham Lincoln and served
as a U.S. minister to Haiti.*

laws for their government. They acknowledge it when they punish disobedience on the part of the slave. There are seventy-two crimes in the state of Virginia which, if committed by a black man (no matter how ignorant he be), subject him to the punishment of death; while only two of the same crimes will subject a white man to the like punishment. What is this but the acknowledgment that the slave is a moral, intellectual, and responsible being? The manhood of the slave is conceded. It is admitted in the fact that Southern statute books are covered with enactments forbidding, under severe fines and penalties, the teaching of the slave to read or to write. When you can point to any such laws in reference to the beasts of the field, then I may consent to argue the manhood of the slave. When the dogs in your streets, when the fowls of the air, when the cattle on your hills, when the fish of the sea and the reptiles that crawl shall be unable to distinguish the slave from the brute, then will I argue with you that the slave is a man!

For the present, it is enough to affirm the equal manhood of the Negro race. Is it not astonishing that, while we are plowing, planting, and reaping, using all kinds of mechanical tools, erecting houses, constructing bridges, building ships, working in metals of brass, iron, copper, silver, and gold; that, while we are reading, writing, and ciphering, acting as clerks, merchants, and secretaries, having among us lawyers, doctors, ministers, poets, authors, editors, orators, and teachers; that, while we are engaged in all manner of enterprises common to other men, digging gold in California, capturing the whale in the Pacific, feeding sheep and cattle on the hillside, living, moving, acting, thinking, planning, living in families as husbands, wives, and children, and, above all, confessing and worshiping the Christian's God, and looking hopefully for life and immortality beyond the grave, we are called upon to prove that we are men!

Would you have me argue that man is entitled to liberty? that he is the rightful owner of his own body? You have already declared it. Must I argue the wrongfulness of slavery? Is that a question for republicans? Is it to be settled by the rules of logic and argumentation, as a matter beset with great difficulty, involving a doubtful application of the principle of justice, hard to be understood? How should I look today, in the presence of Americans, dividing and subdividing a discourse, to show that men have a natural right to freedom? speaking of it relatively and positively, negatively and affirmatively? To do so would be to make myself ridiculous and to offer an insult to your understanding. There is not a man beneath the canopy of heaven that does not know that slavery is wrong for him.

What, am I to argue that it is wrong to make men brutes, to rob them of their liberty, to work them without wages, to keep them ignorant of their relations to their fellow men, to beat them with sticks, to flay their flesh with the lash, to load their limbs with irons, to hunt them with dogs, to sell them at auction, to sunder their families, to knock out their teeth, to burn their flesh, to starve them into obedience and submission to their masters? Must I argue that a system thus marked with blood, and stained with pollution, is wrong? No! I will not. I have better employment for my time and strength than such arguments would imply.

What, then, remains to be argued? Is it that slavery is not divine; that God   10 did not establish it; that our doctors of divinity are mistaken? There is blasphemy in the thought. That which is inhuman cannot be divine! Who can reason on such a proposition? They that can may; I cannot. The time for such argument is past.

At a time like this, scorching iron, not convincing argument, is needed. O! had I the ability, and could I reach the nation's ear, I would today pour out a fiery stream of biting ridicule, blasting reproach, withering sarcasm, and stern rebuke. For it is not light that is needed, but fire; it is not the gentle shower, but thunder. We need the storm, the whirlwind, and the earthquake. The feeling of the nation must be quickened; the conscience of the nation must be roused; the propriety of the nation must be startled; the hypocrisy of the nation must be exposed; and its crimes against God and man must be proclaimed and denounced.

What, to the American slave, is your Fourth of July? I answer: a day that reveals to him, more than all other days in the year, the gross injustice and cruelty to which he is the constant victim. To him, your celebration is a sham; your boasted liberty, an unholy license; your national greatness, swelling vanity; your sounds of rejoicing are empty and heartless; your denunciation of tyrants, brass-fronted impudence; your shouts of liberty and equality, hollow mockery; your prayers and hymns, your sermons and thanksgivings, with all your religious parade and solemnity, are, to Him, mere bombast, fraud, deception, impiety, and hypocrisy—a thin veil to cover up crimes which would disgrace a nation of savages. There is not a nation of savages. There is not a nation on the earth guilty of practices more shocking and bloody than are the people of the United States at this very hour.

Go where you may, search where you will, roam through all the monarchies and despotisms of the Old World, travel through South America, search out every abuse, and when you have found the last, lay your facts by the side of the everyday practices of this nation, and you will say with me that, for revolting barbarity and shameless hypocrisy, America reigns without a rival. ◎/◎

Reflections and Inquiries

1. How does Douglass use the special occasion of Independence Day as a foundation for his address? How effectively does it come across?

2. What is significant about the first two words of his speech from an historical/political perspective? From a rhetorical one?

3. At one point, Douglass asserts, regarding the abolition of slavery, that "there is nothing to be argued." Why does he say this?

4. How does Douglass characterize the Fourth of July from the perspective of a slave?

Reading to Write

Write a comparative analysis of Douglass's speech with Martin Luther King's "Letter from Birmingham Jail," on pages 143–156. In what ways are they similar? Different? Include a discussion of their respective rhetorical strategies.

The Obligation to Endure | Rachel Carson

In 1962, marine biologist Rachel Carson (1907–1964), known for her beautifully written sea trilogy (Under the Sea Wind, 1941; The Sea Around Us, 1951; The Edge of the Sea, 1954), published her most famous work, Silent Spring. *Her book almost single-handedly launched the modern environmental movement in the United States. It describes the devastating effects of pesticides on the environment. The title makes an ominous reference to the absence of birdsong as the result of massive bird deaths caused by DDT spraying. The book persuaded President John F. Kennedy to set up an office of environmental affairs, which eventually became the Environmental Protection Agency. In the following excerpt from* Silent Spring, *Carson introduces her case against the use of pesticides.*

The history of life on earth has been a history of interaction between living things and their surroundings. To a large extent, the physical form and the habits of the earth's vegetation and its animal life have been molded by the environment. Considering the whole span of earthly time, the opposite effect, in which life actually modifies its surroundings, has been relatively slight. Only within the moment of time represented by the present century has one species—man—acquired significant power to alter the nature of his world.

During the past quarter century this power has not only increased to one of disturbing magnitude but it has changed in character. The most alarming of all man's assaults upon the environment is the contamination of air, earth, rivers, and sea with dangerous and even lethal materials. This pollution is for the most part irrecoverable; the chain of evil it initiates not only in the world that must support life but in living tissues is for the most part irreversible. In this now universal contamination of the environment, chemicals are the sinister and little recognized partners of radiation in changing the very nature of the world—the very nature of this life. Strontium 90, released through nuclear explosions into the air, comes to earth in rain or drifts down as fallout, lodges in soil, enters into the grass or corn or wheat grown there, and in time takes up its abode in the bones of a human being, there to remain until his death. Similarly, chemicals sprayed on croplands or forests or gardens lie long in soil, entering into living organisms, passing from one to another in a chain of poisoning and death. Or they pass mysteriously by underground streams until they emerge and, through the alchemy of air and sunlight, combine into new forms that kill vegetation, sicken cattle, and work unknown harm on those who drink from once-pure wells. As Albert Schweitzer has said, "Man can hardly even recognize the devils of his own creation."

It took hundreds of millions of years to produce the life that now inhabits the earth—eons of time in which that developing and evolving the diversifying life reached a state of adjustment and balance with its surroundings. The environment, rigorously shaping and directing the life it supported, contained elements that were hostile as well as supporting. Certain rocks gave out dangerous radiation: even within the light of the sun, from which all life draws its energy, there were short-wave radiations with power to injure. Given time—time not in years but in millennia—life adjusts, and a balance has been reached. For time is the essential ingredient; but in the modern world there is no time.

The rapidity of change and the speed with which new situations are created follow the impetuous and heedless pace of man rather than the deliberate pace of nature. Radiation is no longer merely the background radiation of rocks, the bombardment of cosmic rays, the ultraviolet of the sun that have existed before there was any life on earth; radiation is now the unnatural creation of man's tampering with the atom. The chemicals to which life is asked to make its adjustment are no longer merely the calcium and silica and copper and all the rest of the minerals washed out of the rocks and carried in rivers to the sea; they are the synthetic creations of man's inventive mind, brewed in his laboratories, and having no counterparts in nature.

To adjust to these chemicals would require time on the scale that is nature's; it would require not merely the years of a man's life but the life of generations. And even this, were it by some miracle possible, would be futile, for the new chemicals come from our laboratories in an endless stream; almost five hundred annually find their way into actual use in the United States alone. The figure is staggering and its implications are not easily grasped—500 new chemicals to which the bodies of men and animals are required somehow to adapt each year, chemicals totally outside the limits of biologic experience.

Among them are many that are used in man's war against nature. Since the mid-1940's over 200 basic chemicals have been created for use in killing insects, weeds, rodents, and other organisms described in the modern vernacular as "pests"; and they are sold under several thousand different brand names.

These sprays, dusts, and aerosols are now applied almost universally to farms, gardens, forests, and homes—nonselective chemicals that have the power to kill every insect, the "good" and the "bad," to still the song of birds and the leaping of fish in the streams, to coat the leaves with a deadly film, and to linger on in soil—all this though the intended target may be only a few weeds or insects. Can anyone believe it is possible to lay down such a barrage of poisons on the surface of the earth without making it unfit for all life? They should not be called "insecticides," but "biocides."

The whole process of spraying seems caught up in an endless spiral. Since DDT was released for civilian use, a process of escalation has been going on in which ever more toxic materials must be found. This has happened because insects, in a triumphant vindication of Darwin's principle of the survival of the fittest, have evolved super races immune to the particular insecticide used, hence a deadlier one has always to be developed—and then a deadlier one than that. It has happened also because, for reasons to be described later, destructive insects often undergo a "flareback," or resurgence, after spraying, in numbers greater than before. Thus the chemical war is never won, and all life is caught in its violent crossfire.

Along with the possibility of the extinction of mankind by nuclear war, the central problem of our age has therefore become the contamination of man's total environment with such substances of incredible potential for harm—substances that accumulate in the tissues of plants and animals and even penetrate the germ cells to shatter or alter the very material of heredity upon which the shape of the future depends.

Some would-be architects of our future look toward a time when it will be possible to alter the human germ plasm by design. But we may easily be doing so now by inadvertence, for many chemicals, like radiation, bring about gene mutations. It is ironic to think that man might determine his own future by something so seemingly trivial as the choice of an insect spray.

All this has been risked—for what? Future historians may well be amazed by our distorted sense of proportion. How could intelligent beings seek to control a few unwanted species by a method that contaminated the entire environment and brought the threat of disease and death even to their own kind? Yet this is precisely what we have done. We have done it, more-over, for reasons that collapse the moment we examine them. We are told that the enormous and expanding use of pesticides is necessary to maintain farm production. Yet is our real problem not one of *overproduction*? Our farms, despite measures to remove acreages from production and to pay farmers *not* to produce, have yielded such a staggering excess of crops that the American taxpayer in 1962 is paying out more than one billion dollars a year as the total carrying cost of the surplus-food storage program. And is the situation helped when one branch of the Agriculture Department tries to reduce pro-duction while another states, as it did in 1958, "It is believed generally that reduction of crop acreages under provisions of the Soil Bank will stimulate interest in use of chemicals to obtain maximum production on the land retained in crops."

All this is not to say there is no insect problem and no need of control. I am saying, rather, that control must be geared to realities, not to mythical sit-uations, and that the methods employed must be such that they do not destroy us along with the insects. ◎/◎

Reflections and Inquiries

1. Why does Carson begin by emphasizing the interaction of living things on earth?

2. Why is much of the damage done to the environment by poisonous materi-als irreversible, according to Carson?

3. Despite massive use of deadly insecticides, harmful insects still prevail. Why?

4. Why is crop overproduction an environmental problem?

Reading to Write

Critique Carson's persuasive strategy. Does she make her case against the use of pesticides a convincing one, based on this excerpt? Why or why not? Read *Silent Spring* in its entirety to see if you find the additional information you were looking for here.

The Perils of Obedience | Stanley Milgram

In 1963, Stanley Milgram (1933–1984), a Yale University psychologist, conducted what was to become one of the most disturbing and controversial psychological experiments ever devised. To what degree, the experiment asked, will people follow orders from individuals whose authority in the activity involved seemed unquestionable? The "activity involved," the test subjects were told, was a scientific experiment in which they served as the assistants. The experiment, the subjects believed, was designed to measure the effects of punishment on learning. Toward that end, the test subjects were ordered to administer electric shocks to individuals who, in reality, were Milgram's assistants—actors pretending they were the test subjects. Before the experiment, Dr. Milgram and his team recorded their predictions for the outcome, but those predictions proved to be alarmingly short of the actual results. The following selection from Milgram's book, Obedience to Authority, *presents the details of the experiment, profiles the individuals who had been selected to participate, and reflects on the outcome.*

Obedience is as basic an element in the structure of social life as one can point to. Some system of authority is a requirement of all communal living, and it is only the person dwelling in isolation who is not forced to respond, with defiance or submission, to the commands of others. For many people, obedience is a deeply ingrained behavior tendency, indeed a potent impulse overriding training in ethics, sympathy, and moral conduct.

The dilemma inherent in submission to authority is ancient, as old as the story of Abraham, and the question of whether one should obey when commands conflict with conscience has been argued by Plato, dramatized in *Antigone*, and treated to philosophic analysis in almost every historical epoch. Conservative philosophers argue that the very fabric of society is threatened by disobedience, while humanists stress the primacy of the individual conscience.

The legal and philosophic aspects of obedience are of enormous import, but they say very little about how most people behave in concrete situations. I set up a simple experiment at Yale University to test how much pain an ordinary citizen would inflict on another person simply because he was ordered to by an experimental scientist. Stark authority was pitted against the subjects' strongest moral imperatives against hurting others, and, with the subjects' ears ringing with the screams of the victims, authority won more often than not. The extreme willingness of adults to go to almost any lengths on the command of an authority constitutes the chief finding of the study and the fact most urgently demanding explanation.

In the basic experimental design, two people come to a psychology laboratory to take part in a study of memory and learning. One of them is designated as a "teacher" and the other a "learner." The experimenter explains that the study is concerned with the effects of punishment on learning. The learner is conducted into a room, seated in a kind of miniature electric chair; his arms are strapped to prevent excessive movement, and an electrode is attached to his wrist. He is told that he will be read lists of simple word pairs, and that he will then be tested on his ability to remember the second word of a pair when he hears the first one again. Whenever he makes an error, he will receive electric shocks of increasing intensity.

The real focus of the experiment is the teacher. After watching the learner 5 being strapped into place, he is seated before an impressive shock generator. The instrument panel consists of thirty lever switches set in a horizontal line. Each switch is clearly labeled with a voltage designation ranging from 15 to 450 volts. The following designations are clearly indicated for groups of four switches, going from left to right: Slight Shock, Moderate Shock, Strong Shock, Very Strong Shock, Intense Shock, Extreme Intensity Shock, Danger: Severe Shock. (Two switches after this last designation are simply marked XXX.)

When a switch is depressed, a pilot light corresponding to each switch is illuminated in bright red; an electric buzzing is heard; a blue light, labeled "voltage energizer," flashes; the dial on the voltage meter swings to the right; and various relay clicks sound off.

The upper left-hand corner of the generator is labeled SHOCK GENERATOR, TYPE ZLB, DYSON INSTRUMENT COMPANY, WALTHAM, MASS. OUTPUT 15 VOLTS–450 VOLTS.

Each subject is given a sample 45-volt shock from the generator before his run as teacher, and the jolt strengthens his belief in the authenticity of the machine.

The teacher is a genuinely naïve subject who has come to the laboratory for the experiment. The learner, or victim, is actually an actor who receives no shock at all. The point of the experiment is to see how far a person will proceed in a concrete and measurable situation in which he is ordered to inflict increasing pain on a protesting victim.

Conflict arises when the man receiving the shock begins to show that he 10 is experiencing discomfort. At 75 volts, he grunts; at 120 volts, he complains loudly; at 150, he demands to be released from the experiment. As the voltage increases, his protests become more vehement and emotional. At 285 volts, his response can be described only as an agonized scream. Soon thereafter, he makes no sound at all.

For the teacher, the situation quickly becomes one of gripping tension. It is not a game for him; conflict is intense and obvious. The manifest suffering of the learner presses him to quit; but each time he hesitates to administer a shock, the experimenter orders him to continue. To extricate himself from this plight, the subject must make a clear break with authority.

The subject, Gretchen Brandt, is an attractive thirty-one-year-old medical technician who works at the Yale Medical School. She had emigrated from Germany five years before.[1]

On several occasions when the learner complains, she [Brandt] turns to the experimenter coolly and inquires, "Shall I continue?" She promptly returns to her task when the experimenter asks her to do so. At the administration of 210 volts, she turns to the experimenter, remarking firmly, "Well, I'm sorry, I don't think we should continue."

Experimenter: The experiment requires that you go on until he has learned all the word pairs correctly.

Brandt: He has a heart condition, I'm sorry. He told you that before.   15

Experimenter: The shocks may be painful but they are not dangerous.

Brandt: Well, I'm sorry, I think when shocks continue like this, they *are* dangerous. You ask him if he wants to get out. It's his free will.

Experimenter: It is absolutely essential that we continue. . . .

Brandt: I'd like you to ask him. We came here of our free will. If he wants to continue I'll go ahead. He told you he had a heart condition. I'm sorry. I don't want to be responsible for anything happening to him. I wouldn't like it for me either.

Experimenter: You have no other choice.   20

Brandt: I think we are here on our own free will. I don't want to be responsible if anything happens to him. Please understand that.

She refuses to go further and the experiment is terminated.

The woman is firm and resolute throughout. She indicates in the interview that she was in no way tense or nervous, and this corresponds to her controlled appearance during the experiment. She feels that the last shock she administered to the learner was extremely painful and reiterates that she "did not want to be responsible for any harm to him."

The woman's straightforward, courteous behavior in the experiment, lack of tension, and total control of her own action seem to make disobedience a simple and rational deed. Her behavior is the very embodiment of what I envisioned would be true for almost all subjects.

An Unexpected Outcome

Before the experiments, I sought predictions about the outcome from 25 various   25
kinds of people—psychiatrists, college sophomores, middle-class adults, graduate students, and faculty in the behavioral sciences. With remarkable similarity, they predicted that virtually all subjects would refuse to obey the experimenter. The psychiatrists, specifically, predicted that most subjects would not go beyond 150 volts, when the victim makes his first explicit demand to be freed. They expected that only 4 percent would reach 300 volts, and that only a

---

[1]Names of subjects described in this piece have been changed. [Milgram's note.]

pathological fringe of about one in a thousand would administer the highest shock on the board.

These predictions were unequivocally wrong. Of the forty subjects in the first experiment, twenty-five obeyed the orders of the experimenter to the end, punishing the victim until they reached the most potent shock available on the generator. After 450 volts were administered three times, the experimenter called a halt to the session. Many obedient subjects then heaved sighs of relief, mopped their brows, rubbed their fingers over their eyes, or nervously fumbled cigarettes. Others displayed only minimal signs of tension from beginning to end.

When the very first experiments were carried out, Yale undergraduates were used as subjects, and about 60 percent of them were fully obedient. A colleague of mine immediately dismissed these findings as having no relevance to "ordinary" people, asserting that Yale undergraduates are a highly aggressive, competitive bunch who step on each other's necks on the slightest provocation. He assured me that when "ordinary" people were tested, the results would be quite different. As we moved from the pilot studies to the regular experimental series, people drawn from every stratum of New Haven life came to be employed in the experiment: professionals, white-collar workers, unemployed persons, and industrial workers. *The experiment's total outcome was the same as we had observed among the students.*

Moreover, when the experiments were repeated in Princeton, Munich, Rome, South Africa, and Australia, the level of obedience was invariably somewhat *higher* than found in the investigation reported in this article. Thus one scientist in Munich found 85 percent of his subjects obedient.

Fred Prozi's reactions, if more dramatic than most, illuminate the conflicts experienced by others in less visible form. About fifty years old and unemployed at the time of the experiment, he has a good-natured, if slightly dissolute, appearance, and he strikes people as a rather ordinary fellow. He begins the session calmly but becomes tense as it proceeds. After delivering the 180-volt shock, he pivots around in his chair and, shaking his head, addresses the experimenter in agitated tones:

Prozi: I can't stand it. I'm not going to kill that man in there. You hear him hollering?

Experimenter: As I told you before, the shocks may be painful, but . . .

Prozi: But he's hollering. He can't stand it. What's going to happen to him?

Experimenter (his voice is patient, matter-of-fact): The experiment requires that you continue, Teacher.

Prozi: Aaah, but, unh, I'm not going to get that man sick in there—know what I mean?

Experimenter: Whether the learner likes it or not, we must go on, through all the word pairs. 35

Prozi: I refuse to take the responsibility. He's in there hollering!

Experimenter: It's absolutely essential that you continue, Prozi.

Prozi (indicating the unused questions): There's too many left here, I mean, Jeez, if he gets them wrong, there's too many of them left. I mean, who's going to take the responsibility if anything happens to that gentleman?

Experimenter: I'm responsible for anything that happens to him. Continue, please.

Prozi: All right. (Consults list of words.) The next one's "Slow—walk, truck, dance, music." Answer, please. (A buzzing sound indicates the learner has signaled his answer.) Wrong. A hundred and ninety-five volts. "Dance." (Zzumph!)

Learner (yelling): Let me out of here! My heart's bothering me! (Teacher looks at experimenter.)

Experimenter: Continue, please.

Learner (screaming): Let me out of here! You have no right to keep me here! Let me out of here, my heart's bothering me, let me out!

Prozi (shakes head, pats the table nervously): You see, he's hollering. Hear that? Gee, I don't know.

Experimenter: The experiment requires . . .

Prozi (interrupting): I know it does, sir, but I mean—hunh! He don't know what he's getting in for. He's up to 195 volts! (Experiment continues, through 210 volts, 225 volts, 240 volts, 255 volts, 270 volts, at which point Prozi, with evident relief, runs out of word-pair questions.)

Experimenter: You'll have to go back to the beginning of that page and go through them again until he's learned them all correctly.

Prozi: Aw, no. I'm not going to kill that man. You mean I've got to keep going up with the scale? No sir. He's hollering in there. I'm not going to give him 450 volts.

Experimenter: The experiment requires that you go on.

Learner: Ohhh. I absolutely refuse to answer anymore. (Shouting urgently now.) Let me out of here! You can't hold me here! Get me out. Get-me-out-of-here!

Experimenter: Continue. The next word is "Green," please.

Prozi: "Green—grass, hat, ink, apple." (Nothing happens. No answering buzz. Just gloomy silence.)

Prozi: I don't think he is going to answer.

Experimenter: If the learner doesn't answer in a reasonable time, about four or five seconds, consider the answer wrong. And follow the same procedures you have been doing for wrong answers. Say, "Wrong," tell him the number of volts, give him the punishment, read him the correct answer. Continue, please.

Prozi: "Green—grass, hat, ink, apple." Answer, please. (More silence. Subject just sits there.)

Experimenter: Go on with the procedure, please.

Prozi: Three hundred and fifteen volts. The answer is "ink." (Zzumph!)

Learner: Ohh. Ooohh.

Prozi (relieved to hear response): Next one . . .

Learner: I absolutely refuse to answer.   60

Prozi: You got to. You get a shock if you don't answer. (Experiment contin-
     ues with learner refusing to answer, and, finally, failing even to grunt
     or groan. At 375 volts, the subject stands up.)

Prozi: I think something's happened to that fellow in there. I don't get no
     answer. He was hollering at less voltage. Can't you check in and see if
     he's all right, please?

Experimenter (with same detached calm): Not once we've started. Please
     continue, Teacher.

Prozi (sits down, sighs deeply): "Cool—day, shade, water, paint." Answer,
     please. Are you all right in there? Are you all right?

Experimenter: Please continue, Teacher. Continue, please. (Subject pushes   65
     lever. Zzumph!)

Prozi (swiveling around in his chair): Something's happened to that man in
     there. (Swiveling back.) Next one. "Low—dollar, necklace, moon,
     paint." (Turning around again.) Something's happened to that man in
     there. You better check in on him, sir. He won't answer or nothing.

Experimenter: Continue. Go on, please.

Prozi: You accept all responsibility?

Experimenter: The responsibility is mine. Correct. Please go on. (Subject
     returns to his list, starts running through words as rapidly as he can
     read them, works through to 450 volts.)

Prozi: That's that.   70

Experimenter: Continue using the 450 switch for each wrong answer.
     Continue, please.

Prozi: But I don't get anything!

Experimenter: Please continue. The next word is "white."

Prozi: Don't you think you should look in on him, please?

Experimenter: Not once we've started the experiment.   75

Prozi: What if he's dead in there? (Gestures toward the room with the elec-
     tric chair.) I mean, he told me he can't stand the shock, sir. I don't mean
     to be rude, but I think you should look in on him. All you have to do is
     look in on him. All you have to do is look in the door. I don't get no
     answer, no noise. Something might have happened to the gentleman in
     there, sir.

Experimenter: We must continue. Go on, please.

Prozi: You mean keep giving him what? Four-hundred-fifty volts, what he's
     got now?

Experimenter: That's correct. Continue. The next word is "white."

Prozi (now at a furious pace): "White—cloud, horse, rock, house." Answer,   80
     please. The answer is "horse." Four hundred and fifty volts. (Zzumph!)

Next word, "Bag—paint, music, clown, girl." The answer is "paint." Four hundred and fifty volts. (Zzumph!) Next word is "Short—sentence, movie . . ."

Experimenter: Excuse me, Teacher. We'll have to discontinue the experiment.

Peculiar Reactions

Morris Braverman, another subject, is a thirty-nine-year-old social worker. He looks older than his years because of his bald head and serious demeanor. His brow is furrowed, as if all the world's burdens were carried on his face. He appears intelligent and concerned.

When the learner refuses to answer and the experimenter instructs Braverman to treat the absence of an answer as equivalent to a wrong answer, he takes his instruction to heart. Before administering 300 volts he asserts officiously to the victim, "Mr. Wallace, your silence has to be considered as a wrong answer." Then he administers the shock. He offers, half-heartedly to change places with the learner, then asks the experimenter, "Do I have to follow these instructions literally?" He is satisfied with the experimenter's answer that he does. His very refined and authoritative manner of speaking is increasingly broken up by wheezing laughter.

The experimenter's notes on Mr. Braverman at the last few shocks are:

- Almost breaking up now each time gives shock. Rubbing face to hide laughter.
- Squinting, trying to hide face with hand, still laughing.
- Cannot control his laughter at this point no matter what he does.
- Clenching fist, pushing it onto table.

In an interview after the session, Mr. Braverman summarizes the experiment 85 with impressive fluency and intelligence. He feels the experiment may have been designed also to "test the effects on the teacher of being in an essentially sadistic role, as well as the reactions of a student to a learning situation that was authoritative and punitive." When asked how painful the last few shocks administered to the learner were, he indicates that the most extreme category on the scale is not adequate (it read EXTREMELY PAINFUL) and places his mark at the edge of the scale with an arrow carrying it beyond the scale.

It is almost impossible to convey the greatly relaxed, sedate quality of his conversation in the interview. In the most relaxed terms, he speaks about his severe inner tension.

Experimenter: At what point were you most tense or nervous?

Mr. Braverman: Well, when he first began to cry out in pain, and I realized this was hurting him. This got worse when he just blocked and refused to answer. There was I. I'm a nice person, I think, hurting somebody, and caught up in what seemed a mad situation . . . and in the interest of science, one goes through with it.

When the interviewer pursues the general question of tension, Mr. Braverman spontaneously mentions his laughter.

"My reactions were awfully peculiar. I don't know if you were watching me, but my reactions were giggly, and trying to stifle laughter. This isn't the way I usually am. This was a sheer reaction to a totally impossible situation. And my reaction was to the situation of having to hurt somebody. And being totally helpless and caught up in a set of circumstances where I just couldn't deviate and I couldn't try to help. This is what got me."

Mr. Braverman, like all subjects, was told the actual nature and purpose of the experiment, and a year later he affirmed in a questionnaire that he had learned something of personal importance: "What appalled me was that I could possess this capacity for obedience and compliance to a central idea, i.e., the value of a memory experiment, even after it became clear that continued adherence to this value was at the expense of violation of another value, i.e., don't hurt someone who is helpless and not hurting you. As my wife said, 'You can call yourself Eichmann.' I hope I deal more effectively with any future conflicts of values I encounter."

The Etiquette of Submission

One theoretical interpretation of this behavior holds that all people harbor deeply aggressive instincts continually pressing for expression, and that the experiment provides institutional justification for the release of these impulses. According to this view, if a person is placed in a situation in which he has complete power over another individual, whom he may punish as much as he likes, all that is sadistic and bestial in man comes to the fore. The impulse to shock the victim is seen to flow from the potent aggressive tendencies, which are part of the motivational life of the individual, and the experiment, because it provides social legitimacy, simply opens the door to their expression.

It becomes vital, therefore, to compare the subject's performance when he is under orders and when he is allowed to choose the shock level.

The procedure was identical to our standard experiment, except that the teacher was told that he was free to select any shock level on any of the trials. (The experimenter took pains to point out that the teacher could use the highest levels on the generator, the lowest, any in between, or any combination of levels.) Each subject proceeded for thirty critical trials. The learner's protests were coordinated to standard shock levels, his first grunt coming at 75 volts, his first vehement protest at 150 volts.

The average shock used during the thirty critical trials was less than 60 volts—lower than the point at which the victim showed the first signs of discomfort. Three of the forty subjects did not go beyond the very lowest level on the board, twenty-eight went no higher than 75 volts, and thirty-eight did not go beyond the first loud protest at 150 volts. Two subjects provided the exception, administering up to 325 and 450 volts, but the overall result was that the great majority of people delivered very low, usually painless, shocks when the choice was explicitly up to them.

This condition of the experiment undermines another commonly offered explanation of the subjects' behavior—that those who shocked the victim at the most severe levels came only from the sadistic fringe of society. If one considers that almost two-thirds of the participants fall into the category of "obedient" subjects, and that they represented ordinary people drawn from working, managerial, and professional classes, the argument becomes very shaky. Indeed, it is highly reminiscent of the issue that arose in connection with Hannah Arendt's 1963 book, *Eichmann in Jerusalem.* Arendt contended that the prosecution's effort to depict Eichmann as a sadistic monster was fundamentally wrong, that he came closer to being an uninspired bureaucrat who simply sat at his desk and did his job. For asserting her views, Arendt became the object of considerable scorn, even calumny. Somehow, it was felt that the monstrous deeds carried out by Eichmann required a brutal twisted personality, evil incarnate. After witnessing hundreds of ordinary persons submit to the authority in our own experiments, I must conclude that Arendt's conception of the banality of evil comes closer to the truth than one might dare imagine. The ordinary person who shocked the victim did so out of a sense of obligation—an impression of his duties as a subject—and not from any peculiarly aggressive tendencies.

This is, perhaps, the most fundamental lesson of our study: Ordinary people, simply doing their jobs, and without any particular hostility on their part, can become agents in a terrible destructive process. Moreover, even when the destructive effects of their work become patently clear, and they are asked to carry out actions incompatible with fundamental standards of morality, relatively few people have the resources needed to resist authority.

Many of the people were in some sense against what they did to the learner, and many protested even while they obeyed. Some were totally convinced of the wrongness of their actions but could not bring themselves to make an open break with authority. They often derived satisfaction from their thoughts and felt that—within themselves, at least—they had been on the side of the angels. They tried to reduce strain by obeying the experimenter but "only slightly," encouraging the learner, touching the generator switches gingerly. When interviewed, such a subject would stress that he had "asserted my humanity" by administering the briefest shock possible. Handling the conflict in this manner was easier than defiance.

The situation is constructed so that there is no way the subject can stop shocking the learner without violating the experimenter's definitions of his own competence. The subject fears that he will appear arrogant, untoward, and rude if he breaks off. Although these inhibiting emotions appear small in scope alongside the violence being done to the learner, they suffuse the mind and feelings of the subject who is miserable at the prospect of having to repudiate the authority to his face. (When the experiment was altered so that the experimenter gave his instructions by telephone instead of in person, only a third as many people were fully obedient through 450 volts.) It is a curious thing that a measure of compassion on the part of the subject—an unwillingness to "hurt" the experimenter's feelings—is part of those binding forces inhibiting his disobedience. The withdrawal of such deference may be as painful to the subject as to the authority he defies.

Duty Without Conflict

The subjects do not derive satisfaction from inflicting pain, but they often like 100 the feeling they get from pleasing the experimenter. They are proud of doing a good job, obeying the experimenter under difficult circumstances. While the subjects administered only mild shocks on their own initiative, one experimental variation showed that, under orders, 30 percent of them were willing to deliver 450 volts even when they had to forcibly push the learner's hand down on the electrode.

Bruno Batta is a thirty-seven-year-old welder who took part in the variation requiring the use of force. He was born in New Haven, his parents in Italy. He has a rough-hewn face that conveys a conspicuous lack of alertness. He has some difficulty in mastering the experimental procedure and needs to be corrected by the experimenter several times. He shows appreciation for the help and willingness to do what is required. After the 150-volt level, Batta has to force the learner's hand down on the shock plate, since the learner himself refuses to touch it.

When the learner first complains, Mr. Batta pays no attention to him. His face remains impassive, as if to dissociate himself from the learner's disruptive behavior. When the experimenter instructs him to force the learner's hand down, he adopts a rigid, mechanical procedure. He tests the generator switch. When it fails to function, he immediately forces the learner's hand onto the shock plate. All the while he maintains the same rigid mask. The learner, seated alongside him, begs him to stop, but with robotic impassivity he continues the procedure.

What is extraordinary is his apparent total indifference to the learner; he hardly takes cognizance of him as a human being. Meanwhile, he relates to the experimenter in a submissive and courteous fashion.

At the 330-volt level, the learner refuses not only to touch the shock plate but also to provide any answers. Annoyed, Batta turns to him, and chastises him: "You better answer and get it over with. We can't stay here all night." These are the only words he directs to the learner in the course of an hour. Never again does he speak to him. The scene is brutal and depressing, his hard, impassive face showing total indifference as he subdues the screaming learner and gives him shocks. He seems to derive no pleasure from the act itself, only quiet satisfaction at doing his job properly.

When he administers 450 volts, he turns to the experimenter and asks, 105 "Where do we go from here, Professor?" His tone is deferential and expresses his willingness to be a cooperative subject, in contrast to the learner's obstinacy.

At the end of the session he tells the experimenter how honored he has been to help him, and in a moment of contrition, remarks, "Sir, sorry it couldn't have been a full experiment."

He has done his honest best. It is only the deficient behavior of the learner that has denied the experimenter full satisfaction.

The essence of obedience is that a person comes to view himself as the instrument for carrying out another person's wishes, and he therefore no longer regards himself as responsible for his actions. Once this critical shift of viewpoint has occurred, all of the essential features of obedience follow. The most far-reaching consequence is that the person feels responsible *to* the authority directing him but feels no responsibility *for* the content of the actions that the authority prescribes. Morality does not disappear—it acquires a radically different focus: The subordinate person feels shame or pride depending on how adequately he has performed the actions called for by authority.

Language provides numerous terms to pinpoint this type of morality: *Loyalty, duty, discipline* all are terms heavily saturated with moral meaning and refer to the degree to which a person fulfills his obligations to authority. They refer not to the "goodness" of the person per se but to the adequacy with which a subordinate fulfills his socially defined role. The most frequent defense of the individual who has performed a heinous act under command of authority is that he has simply done his duty. In asserting this defense, the individual is not introducing an alibi concocted for the moment but is reporting honestly on the psychological attitude induced by submission to authority.

For a person to feel responsible for his actions, he must sense that the behavior has flowed from "the self." In the situation we have studied, subjects 110 have precisely the opposite view of their actions—namely, they see them as originating in the motives of some other person. Subjects in the experiment frequently said, "If it were up to me, I would not have administered shocks to the learner."

Once authority has been isolated as the cause of the subject's behavior, it is legitimate to inquire into the necessary elements of authority and how it must be perceived in order to gain his compliance. We conducted some investigations into the kinds of changes that would cause the experimenter to lose his power and to be disobeyed by the subject. Some of the variations revealed that

- *The experimenter's physical presence has a marked impact on his authority.* As cited earlier, obedience dropped off sharply when orders were given by telephone. The experimenter could often induce a disobedient subject to go on by returning to the laboratory.

- *Conflicting authority severely paralyzes action.* When two experimenters of equal status, both seated at the command desk, gave incompatible orders, no shocks were delivered past the point of their disagreement.

- *The rebellious action of others severely undermines authority.* In one variation, three teachers (two actors and a real subject) administered a test and shocks. When the two actors disobeyed the experimenter and refused to go beyond a certain shock level, thirty-six of forty subjects joined their disobedient peers and refused as well.

Although the experimenter's authority was fragile in some respects, it is also true that he had almost none of the tools used in ordinary command structures. For example, the experimenter did not threaten the subjects with punishment—such as loss of income, community ostracism, or jail—for failure to obey. Neither could he offer incentives. Indeed, we should expect the experimenter's authority to be much less than that of someone like a general, since the experimenter has no power to enforce his imperatives, and since participation in a psychological experiment scarcely evokes the sense of urgency and dedication found in warfare. Despite these limitations, he still managed to command a dismaying degree of obedience.

I will cite one final variation of the experiment that depicts a dilemma that is more common in everyday life. The subject was not ordered to pull the lever that shocked the victim, but merely to perform a subsidiary task (administering the word-pair test) while another person administered the shock. In this situation, thirty-seven of forty adults continued to the highest level on the shock generator. Predictably, they excused their behavior by saying that the responsibility belonged to the man who actually pulled the switch. This may illustrate a dangerously typical arrangement in a complex society: It is easy to ignore responsibility when one is only an intermediate link in a chain of action.

The problem of obedience is not wholly psychological. The form and shape of society and the way it is developing have much to do with it. There was a time, perhaps, when people were able to give a fully human response to any situation because they were fully absorbed in it as human beings. But as soon as there was a division of labor things changed. Beyond a certain point, the breaking up of society into people carrying out narrow and very special jobs takes away from the human quality of work and life. A person does not get to see the whole situation but only a small part of it, and is thus unable to act without some kind of overall direction. He yields to authority but in doing so is alienated from his own actions.

Even Eichmann was sickened when he toured the concentration camps, 115 but he had only to sit at a desk and shuffle papers. At the same time the man in the camp who actually dropped Cyclon-b into the gas chambers was able to justify *his* behavior on the ground that he was only following orders from above. Thus there is a fragmentation of the total human act; no one is confronted with the consequences of his decision to carry out the evil act. The person who assumes responsibility has evaporated. Perhaps this is the most common characteristic of socially organized evil in modern society. ☺/☺

Reflections and Inquiries

1. An inevitable reaction to reading about this experiment is to imagine how you might have responded as one of the unknowing test subjects. Would you have administered what you assumed were painful, perhaps even crippling electric shocks because you'd been ordered to do so by a presumed authority figure? Try to answer this question as objectively as you can, explaining why you would have resisted to the end or given in.

2. Comment on the ethical basis for this experiment. Should the experiment, or any part of it, have been conducted differently? Why or why not? Keep in mind that the Milgram experiments led the United States to establish the Human Subjects Act, which all researchers who use human subjects in any of their experiments must adhere to. If the research is psychological, then the protocol must include plans and procedures for debriefing.

3. What were the specific factors that influenced the behavior of the test subjects?

4. Do you agree with Milgram's conclusions? Provide a well-detailed defense or rebuttal.

5. What lessons, if any, do we learn from the Milgram experiment?

Reading to Write

Do some background reading on the Milgram experiment, including reading additional material from Milgram's book. Then write an essay assessing its importance as a contribution to the study of human behavior and its implications for society.

The Character of Hamlet's Mother | Carolyn G. Heilbrun

In the following gem of literary criticism, Carolyn G. Heilbrun cleverly demonstrates that Queen Gertrude, Hamlet's mother, is far from being the dim-witted, passive, weak, and sentimental woman that even the most distinguished (and male) Shakespearean scholars of the past have interpreted her as being—on the contrary, she is a shrewd and strong-willed (if lustful) woman. The essay is a fine example of the way a hitherto unacknowledged critical perspective (in this case a feminist one) can shed new light on even the most famous, most written-about play of all time. Heilbrun (1926–2003) was the Avalon Foundation Professor in the Humanities Emerita at Columbia University. She is the author of Reinventing Womanhood *(1979),* Writing a Woman's Life *(1989),* The Education of a Woman: The Life of*

Gloria Steinem *(1995), and many other books, including the internationally known Kate Fansler mysteries (under her nom de plume, Amanda Cross).*

If you have not read Shakespeare's Hamlet *recently, it would be a good idea to do so first. Pay particular attention to the character of Gertrude and draw your own conclusions about her before evaluating the strengths or shortcomings of Heilbrun's argument.*

The character of Hamlet's mother has not received the specific critical attention it deserves. Moreover, the traditional account of her personality as rendered by the critics will not stand up under close scrutiny of Shakespeare's play.

None of the critics of course has failed to see Gertrude as vital to the action of the play; not only is she the mother of the hero, the widow of the Ghost, and the wife of the current King of Denmark, but the fact of her hasty and, to the Elizabethans, incestuous marriage, the whole question of her "falling off," occupies a position of barely secondary importance in the mind of her son, and of the Ghost. Indeed, Freud and Jones see her, the object of Hamlet's Oedipus complex, as central to the motivation of the play.[1] But the critics, with no exception that I have been able to find, have accepted Hamlet's word "frailty" as applying to her whole personality, and have seen in her not one weakness, or passion in the Elizabethan sense, but a character of which weakness and lack of depth and vigorous intelligence are the entire explanation. Of her can it truly be said that carrying the "stamp of one defect," she did "in the general censure take corruption from that particular fault" (I.iv.35–36).

The critics are agreed that Gertrude was not a party to the late King's murder and indeed knew nothing of it, a point which, on the clear evidence of the play, is indisputable. They have also discussed whether or not Gertrude, guilty of more than an "o'er-hasty marriage," had committed adultery with Claudius before her husband's death. I will return to this point later on. Beyond discussing these two points, those critics who have dealt specifically with the Queen have traditionally seen her as well-meaning but shallow and feminine, in the pejorative sense of the word: incapable of any sustained rational process, superficial and flighty. It is this tradition which a closer reading of the play will show to be erroneous.

Professor Bradley describes the traditional Gertrude thus:

> The Queen was not a bad-hearted woman, not at all the woman to think little of murder. But she had a soft animal nature and was very dull and very shallow. She loved to be happy, like a sheep in the sun, and to do her justice, it pleased her to see others happy, like more sheep in the sun. . . . It was pleasant to sit upon her throne and see smiling faces around her, and foolish and unkind in Hamlet to persist in grieving for his father instead of marrying Ophelia and making everything comfortable. . . . The belief at the bottom of her heart was that the world is a place constructed simply that people may be happy in it in a good-humored sensual fashion.[2]

Later on, Bradley says of her that when affliction comes to her "the good in her nature struggles to the surface through the heavy mass of sloth."

Granville-Barker is not quite so extreme. Shakespeare, he says,

> gives us in Gertrude the woman who does not mature, who clings to her youth and all that belongs to it, whose charm will not change but at last fade and wither; a pretty creature, as we see her, desperately refusing to grow old. . . . She is drawn for us with unemphatic strokes, and she has but a passive part in the play's action. She moves throughout in Claudius' shadow; he holds her as he won her, by the witchcraft of his wit.[3]

Elsewhere Granville-Barker says, "Gertrude, who will certainly never see forty-five again, might better be 'old.' [That is, portrayed by an older, mature actress.] But that would make her relations with Claudius—and *their* likelihood is vital to the play—quite incredible" (p. 226). Granville-Barker is saying here that a woman about forty-five years of age cannot feel any sexual passion nor arouse it. This is one of the mistakes which lie at the heart of the misunderstanding about Gertrude.

Professor Dover Wilson sees Gertrude as more forceful than either of these two critics will admit, but even he finds the Ghost's unwillingness to shock her with knowledge of his murder to be one of the basic motivations of the play, and he says of her, "Gertrude is always hoping for the best."[4]

Now whether Claudius won Gertrude before or after her husband's death, it was certainly not, as Granville-Barker implies, with "the witchcraft of his wit" alone. Granville-Barker would have us believe that Claudius won her simply by the force of his persuasive tongue. "It is plain," he writes, that the Queen "does little except echo his [Claudius'] wishes; sometimes—as in the welcome to Rosencrantz and Guildenstern—she repeats his very words" (p. 227), though Wilson must admit later that Gertrude does not tell Claudius everything. Without dwelling here on the psychology of the Ghost, or the greater burden borne by the Elizabethan words "witchcraft" and "wit," we can plainly see, for the Ghost tells us, how Claudius won the Queen: the Ghost considers his brother to be garbage, and "lust," the Ghost says, "will sate itself in a celestial bed and prey on garbage" (I.v.54–55). "Lust"—in a woman of forty-five or more—is the key word here. Bradley, Granville-Barker, and to a lesser extent Professor Dover Wilson, misunderstand Gertrude largely because they are unable to see lust, the desire for sexual relations, as the passion, in the Elizabethan sense of the word, the flaw, the weakness which drives Gertrude to an incestuous marriage, appalls her son, and keeps him from the throne. Unable to explain her marriage to Claudius as the act of any but a weak-minded vacillating woman, they fail to see Gertrude for the strong-minded, intelligent, succinct, and, apart from this passion, sensible woman that she is.

To understand Gertrude properly, it is only necessary to examine the lines Shakespeare has chosen for her to say. She is, except for her description of

Ophelia's death, concise and pithy in speech, with a talent for seeing the essence of every situation presented before her eyes. If she is not profound, she is certainly never silly. We first hear her asking Hamlet to stop wearing black, to stop walking about with his eyes downcast, and to realize that death is an inevitable part of life. She is, in short, asking him not to give way to the passion of grief, a passion of whose force and dangers the Elizabethans are aware, as Miss Campbell has shown.[5] Claudius echoes her with a well-reasoned argument against grief which was, in its philosophy if not in its language, a piece of commonplace Elizabethan lore. After Claudius' speech, Gertrude asks Hamlet to remain in Denmark, where he is rightly loved. Her speeches have been short, however warm and loving, and conciseness of statement is not the mark of a dull and shallow woman.

We next hear her, as Queen and gracious hostess, welcoming Rosencrantz 10 and Guildenstern to the court, hoping, with the King, that they may cheer Hamlet and discover what is depressing him. Claudius then tells Gertrude, when they are alone, that Polonius believes he knows what is upsetting Hamlet. The Queen answers:

I doubt it is no other than the main,
His father's death and our o'er-hasty marriage. (II.ii.56–57)

This statement is concise, remarkably to the point, and not a little courageous. It is not the statement of a dull, slothful woman who can only echo her husband's words. Next, Polonius enters with his most unbrief apotheosis to brevity. The Queen interrupts him with five words: "More matter with less art" (II.ii.95). It would be difficult to find a phrase more applicable to Polonius. When this gentleman, in no way deterred from his loquacity, after purveying the startling news that he has a daughter, begins to read a letter, the Queen asks pointedly "Came this from Hamlet to her?" (II.ii.114).

We see Gertrude next in Act III, asking Rosencrantz and Guildenstern, with her usual directness, if Hamlet received them well, and if they were able to tempt him to any pastime. But before leaving the room, she stops for a word of kindness to Ophelia. It is a humane gesture, for she is unwilling to leave Ophelia, the unhappy tool of the King and Polonius, without some kindly and intelligent appreciation of her help:

And for your part, Ophelia, I do wish
That your good beauties be the happy cause
Of Hamlet's wildness. So shall I hope your virtues
Will bring him to his wonted way again,
To both your honors. (III.i.38–42)

It is difficult to see in this speech, as Bradley apparently does, the gushing shallow wish of a sentimental woman that class distinctions shall not stand in the way of true love.

At the play, the Queen asks Hamlet to sit near her. She is clearly trying to make him feel he has a place in the court of Denmark. She does not speak again until Hamlet asks her how she likes the play. "The lady doth protest too much, methinks" (III.ii.240) is her immortal comment on the player queen. The scene gives her four more words: when Claudius leaps to his feet, she asks "How fares my Lord?" (III.ii.278).

I will for the moment pass over the scene in the Queen's closet, to follow 15 her quickly through the remainder of the play. After the closet scene, the Queen comes to speak to Claudius. She tells him, as Hamlet has asked her to, that he, Hamlet, is mad, and has killed Polonius. She adds, however, that he now weeps for what he has done. She does not wish Claudius to know what she now knows, how wild and fearsome Hamlet has become. Later, she does not wish to see Ophelia, but hearing how distracted she is, consents. When Laertes bursts in ready to attack Claudius, she immediately steps between Claudius and Laertes to protect the King, and tells Laertes it is not Claudius who has killed his father. Laertes will of course soon learn this, but it is Gertrude who manages to tell him before he can do any meaningless damage. She leaves Laertes and the King together, and then returns to tell Laertes that his sister is drowned. She gives her news directly, realizing that suspense will increase the pain of it, but this is the one time in the play when her usual pointed conciseness would be the mark neither of intelligence nor kindness, and so, gently, and at some length, she tells Laertes of his sister's death, giving him time to recover from the shock of grief, and to absorb the meaning of her words. At Ophelia's funeral the Queen scatters flowers over the grave.

Sweets to the sweet; farewell!
I hop'd thou shouldst have been my Hamlet's wife.
I thought thy bride-bed to have deck'd, sweet maid,
And not t' have strew'd thy grave. (V.i.266–269)

She is the only one present decently mourning the death of someone young, and not heated in the fire of some personal passion.

At the match between Hamlet and Laertes, the Queen believes that Hamlet is out of training, but glad to see him at some sport, she gives him her handkerchief to wipe his brow, and drinks to his success. The drink is poisoned and she dies. But before she dies she does not waste time on vituperation; she warns Hamlet that the drink is poisoned to prevent his drinking it. They are her last words. Those critics who have thought her stupid admire her death; they call it uncharacteristic.

In Act III, when Hamlet goes to his mother in her closet his nerves are pitched at the very height of tension; he is on the edge of hysteria. The possibility of murdering his mother has in fact entered his mind, and he has just met and refused an opportunity to kill Claudius. His mother, meanwhile, waiting for him, has told Polonius not to fear for her, but she knows when she sees Hamlet that he may be violently mad. Hamlet quips with her, insults her, tells her he wishes she were not his mother, and when she, still retaining dignity, attempts to end the interview, Hamlet seizes her and she cries for help. The important thing to note is that the Queen's cry "Thou wilt not murder me" (III.iv.21) is not foolish. She has seen from Hamlet's demeanor that he is capable of murder, as indeed in the next instant he proves himself to be.

We next learn from the Queen's startled "As kill a king" (III.iv.30) that she has no knowledge of the murder, though of course there is only confirmation here of what we already know. Then the Queen asks Hamlet why he is so hysterical:

What have I done, that thou dar'st wag thy tongue
In noise so rude against me? (III.iv.39–40)

Hamlet tells her: it is her lust, the need of sexual passion, which has driven her 20
from the arms and memory of her husband to the incomparably cruder charms of his brother. He cries out that she has not even the excuse of youth for her lust:

O Shame! where is thy blush? Rebellious hell,
If thou canst mutine in a matron's bones,
To flaming youth let virtue be as wax
And melt in her own fire. Proclaim no shame
When the compulsive ardor gives the charge,
Since frost itself as actively doth burn,
And reason panders will. (III.iv.82–87)

This is not only a lust, but a lust which throws out of joint all the structure of human mortality and relationships. And the Queen admits it. If there is one quality that has characterized, and will characterize, every speech of Gertrude's in the play, it is the ability to see reality clearly, and to express it. This talent is not lost when turned upon herself:

O Hamlet, speak no more!
Thou turn'st mine eyes into my very soul,
And there I see such black and grained spots
As will not leave their tinct. (III.iv.88–91)

She knows that lust has driven her, that this is her sin, and she admits it. Not that she wishes to linger in the contemplation of her sin. No more, she cries, no more. And then the Ghost appears to Hamlet. The Queen thinks him mad again—as well she might—but she promises Hamlet that she will not betray him—and she does not.

Where, in all that we have seen of Gertrude, is there the picture of "a soft animal nature, very dull and very shallow"? She may indeed be "animal" in the sense of "lustful." But it does not follow that because she wishes to continue a life of sexual experience, her brain is soft or her wit unperceptive.

Some critics, having accepted Gertrude as a weak and vacillating woman, see no reason to suppose that she did not fall victim to Claudius' charms before the death of her husband and commit adultery with him. These critics,

Professor Bradley among them (p. 166), claim that the elder Hamlet clearly tells his son that Gertrude has committed adultery with Claudius in the speech beginning "Ay that incestuous, that adulterate beast" (I.v.41ff). Professor Dover Wilson presents the argument:

> Is the Ghost speaking here of the o'er-hasty marriage of Claudius and Gertrude? Assuredly not. His "certain term" is drawing rapidly to an end, and he is already beginning to "scent the morning air." Hamlet knew of the marriage, and his whole soul was filled with nausea at the thought of the speedy hasting to "incestuous sheets." Why then should the Ghost waste precious moments in telling Hamlet what he was fully cognizant of before? . . . Moreover, though the word "incestuous" was applicable to the marriage, the rest of the passage is entirely inapplicable to it. Expressions like "witch-craft", "traitorous gifts", "seduce", "shameful lust", and "seeming virtuous" may be noted in passing. But the rest of the quotation leaves no doubt upon the matter. (p. 293)

Professor Dover Wilson and other critics have accepted the Ghost's word "adulterate" in its modern meaning. The Elizabethan word "adultery," however, was not restricted to its modern meaning, but was used to define any sexual relationship which could be called unchaste, including of course an incestuous one.[6] Certainly the elder Hamlet considered the marriage of Claudius and Gertrude to be unchaste and unseemly, and while his use of the word "adulterate" indicates his very strong feelings about the marriage, it would not to an Elizabethan audience necessarily mean that he believed Gertrude to have been false to him before his death. It is important to notice, too, that the Ghost does not apply the term "adulterate" to Gertrude, and he may well have considered the term a just description of Claudius' entire sexual life.

But even if the Ghost used the word "adulterate" in full awareness of its modern restricted meaning, it is not necessary to assume on the basis of this single speech (and it is the only shadow of evidence we have for such a conclusion) that Gertrude was unfaithful to him while he lived. It is quite probable that the elder Hamlet still considered himself married to Gertrude, and he is moreover revolted that her lust for him ("why she would hang on him as if increase of appetite had grown by what it fed on") should have so easily transferred itself to another. This is why he uses the expressions "seduce," "shameful lust," and others. Professor Dover Wilson has himself said "Hamlet knew of the marriage, and his whole soul was filled with nausea at the thought of the speedy hasting to incestuous sheets"; the soul of the elder Hamlet was undoubtedly filled with nausea too, and this could well explain his using such strong language, as well as his taking the time to mention the matter at all. It is not necessary to consider Gertrude an adulteress to account for the speech of the Ghost.

Gertrude's lust was, of course, more important to the plot than we may at first perceive. Charlton Lewis, among others, has shown how Shakespeare kept many of the facts of the plots from which he borrowed without maintaining the structures which explained them. In the original Belleforest story, Gertrude (substituting Shakespeare's more familiar names) was daughter of the king; to become king, it was necessary to marry her. The elder Hamlet, in marrying Gertrude, ousted Claudius from the throne.[7] Shakespeare retained the shell of this in his play. When she no longer has a husband, the form of election would be followed to declare the next king, in this case undoubtedly her son Hamlet. By marrying Gertrude, Claudius "popp'd in between th' election and my hopes" (V.ii.65), that is, kept young Hamlet from the throne. Gertrude's flaw of lust made Claudius' ambition possible, for without taking advantage of the Queen's desire still to be married, he could not have been king.

But Gertrude, if she is lustful, is also intelligent, penetrating, and gifted with a remarkable talent for concise and pithy speech. In all the play, the person whose language hers most closely resembles is Horatio. "Sweets to the sweet," she has said at Ophelia's grave. "Good night sweet prince," Horatio says at the end. They are neither of them dull, or shallow, or slothful, though one of them is passion's slave. ◎/◎

Notes

1. William Shakespeare, *Hamlet*, with a psychoanalytical study by Ernest Jones, M.D. (London: Vision Press, 1947), pp. 7–42.
2. A. C. Bradley, *Shakespearean Tragedy* (New York: Macmillan, 1949), p. 167.
3. Harley Granville-Barker, *Prefaces to Shakespeare* (Princeton: Princeton University Press, 1946), 1:227.
4. J. Dover Wilson, *What Happens in Hamlet* (Cambridge: Cambridge University Press, 1951), p. 125.
5. Lily B. Campbell, *Shakespeare's Tragic Heroes* (New York: Barnes & Noble, 1952), pp. 112–113.
6. See Bertram Joseph, *Conscience and the King* (London: Chatto & Windus, 1953), pp. 16–19.
7. Charlton M. Lewis, *The Genesis of Hamlet* (New York: Henry Holt, 1907), p. 36.

Reflections and Inquiries

1. Heilbrun, unlike other Shakespearean critics before her, sees Gertrude as strong instead of frail. How convincingly does Heilbrun support this view? Why do you suppose the other critics—among the greatest in Shakespearean scholarship—would take the opposite view?

2. As part of her argumentative strategy, Heilbrun pays close attention to Elizabethan usage. Why is this important? What word in particular may have been misunderstood by earlier critics, and why?

3. What are, to you, the most compelling examples of Gertrude's independent mindedness, her ability to decide things on her own? Do you find yourself disagreeing with Heilbrun's characterization of Gertrude anywhere? Explain.

4. Heilbrun agrees that Gertrude is a slave to passion. Does this assertion contradict her claim that Gertrude is strong-willed? Why or why not?

Reading to Write

Read two or three additional contemporary critics' assessments of Gertrude. Look for commentary by both feminist and nonfeminist critics. Then write a comparative analysis of critical interpretations of Gertrude, concluding with the assessment you consider to be most insightful, and why.

Connections Among the Clusters

1. If Swift's "A Modest Proposal" were made into a TV drama, it is conceivable that many would try to ban it on the basis of excessive violence. Defend or challenge this view. (See Cluster 3, Media Regulation.)

2. Discuss Frederick Douglass's and Elizabeth Cady Stanton's speeches in the context of multicultural learning. (See Cluster 4.)

3. How might Plato's "Allegory of the Cave" be used to resolve religious versus scientific ways of perceiving truth? (See Cluster 6.)

4. Assume that a school principal refuses to allow Andrew Marvell's "To His Coy Mistress" to be taught to sixth-grade students. Defend or challenge that principal's decision. (See Cluster 3, Media Regulation.)

5. What possible light might the Milgram experiment shed on issues of national security vs. individual freedom? (See Cluster 5.)

Writing Projects

1. Analyze the way Plato's allegory and Jonathan Edwards's sermon deal with spiritual truths. How would you describe their respective approaches to spirituality? What is most significant about each approach, in your opinion?

2. Write an essay that satirizes a social injustice. Use Swift's "A Modest Proposal" as a possible model.

3. Write a speech that calls attention to a current injustice in civil rights. Use Douglass's or Stanton's speech as a possible model.

4. Write an essay on the nature of free will in light of the findings of behavior psychologists such as Stanley Milgram and B. F. Skinner—the latter being one who argues forcefully, in his book *Beyond Freedom and Dignity* (1971), that there is no such thing as free will.

Suggestions for Further Reading

Speeches and Sermons

Bryan, William Jennings. "Cross of Gold" (1896). *A Treasury of the World's Great Speeches.* Ed. Houston Peterson. New York: Grolier, 1964.

Emerson, Ralph Waldo. "Divinity School Address" (1837). *Selected Writings of Ralph Waldo Emerson.* Ed. William H. Gilman. New York: Signet, 2003.

Jesus. "The Sermon on the Mount," Matthew 5–7.

Lincoln, Abraham. "The Gettysburg Address" (1863). *A Treasury of the World's Great Speeches.* Ed. Houston Peterson. New York: Grolier, 1964.

Trials

Barrett, W. P. *The Trial of Jeanne d'Arc* (1431). Trans. Coley Taylor and Ruth H. Kerr. New York: Gotham, 1932.

Hyde, H. Montgomery. *The Trials of Oscar Wilde* (1895). London: Hodge, 1948. *The World's Most Famous Court Trial: The Tennessee Evolution Case* (Transcript of the Scopes Trial, 1925). Cincinnati: National, 1925.

Rashke, Richard. *The Killing of Karen Silkwood: The Story Behind the Kerr-McGee Plutonium Case* (1979). Boston: Houghton, 1981.

Roe v. Wade, 410 U.S. 133 (U.S. Sup. Ct. 1973)

Smolla, Rodney A. *Jerry Falwell v. Larry Flynt: The First Amendment on Trial* (1981). New York: St. Martin's, 1988.

Steuart, A. Francis. *Trial of Mary Queen of Scots* (1586). London: Hodge, 1923.

Stone, I. F. *The Trial of Socrates* (399 B.C.E.). Boston: Little, 1988.

Tusa, Ann and John Tusa. *The Nuremberg Trial* (1946). New York: Atheneum, 1986.

Essays, Manifestoes, and Treatises

Darwin, Charles. *On the Origin of Species* (1859). New York: Bantam, 1999.

de Beauvoir, Simone. *The Second Sex.* Trans. H. M. Parshley. New York: Knopf, 1953.

Freud, Sigmund. *Civilization and Its Discontents* (1930). Trans. James Strachey. New York: Norton, 1962.

Machiavelli, Niccolo. *The Prince* (1532). Trans. George Bull. New York: Penguin, 1961.

Mead, Margaret, and James Baldwin. *A Rap on Race.* New York: Lippincott, 1971.

Orwell, George. "Politics and the English Language" (1946). *Selected Essays.* New York: Penguin, 1960.

Skinner, B. F. *Beyond Freedom and Dignity.* New York: Knopf, 1971.

Snow, C. P. *The Two Cultures & A Second Look.* Cambridge: Cambridge UP, 1959.

Thoreau, Henry David. "Civil Disobedience" (1849). *The Portable Thoreau.* Ed. Carl Bode. New York: Penguin, 1977.

Veblen, Thorstein. *The Theory of the Leisure Class* (1899). Boston: Houghton, 1973.

Glossary of Rhetorical Terms

Ad hominem fallacy.   Literally, argument directed against the person. An error of reasoning in which the arguer attacks an individual's character or person as a way of attacking his or her ideas or performance, as in "Adam Stone does not deserve an Oscar for Best Film Editing; he has been diagnosed as psychotic."

Affirming the consequent fallacy.   In order for the outcome of a hypothetical statement ("If x, then y") to be valid, the antecedent (the "if" clause) must be affirmed or the consequent (the "then" clause) denied. It is a fallacy, however, to say that if the consequent is affirmed, then the antecedent must be denied. Consider this hypothetical statement: "If taxes are raised, the economy will prosper." To affirm the consequent—that is, to say "the economy is indeed prospering; therefore, taxes were raised"—is a fallacy (the economy, given the framework of the statement, could have prospered for other reasons). One can only deny the consequent: "The economy did not prosper; therefore, taxes were not raised."

Analogy.   Comparison made, for purpose of clarification, between two ideas sharing similar characteristics.

Analysis.   Breakdown of an idea into its constituent elements to facilitate comprehension.

Appeals.   The three means of persuasion described by Aristotle: *ethos* (referring to persuasion through character, ethics, values); *pathos* (referring to persuasion through emotions, feelings); and *logos* (referring to persuasion through logical reasoning). The three appeals often overlap in an argument.

Apples and oranges.   An error of reasoning in which a comparison is made between two things that are not comparable (because they are not part of the same category).

Argument.   A discussion in which a claim is challenged or supported with evidence. *See also* Persuasion.

Backing.   In Toulmin argument, support for the *warrant*, which is not, in itself, self-validating. The more substantial the backing, the more compelling the warrant.

Bandwagon fallacy.   The assumption that if an opinion is shared by a majority, the opinion must be correct.

Begging the question fallacy.   (1) An error of reasoning in which the "evidence" used to support a claim is merely a rephrasing of the problem, as in "Imprisonment does not deter crime because it does nothing to discourage criminal activity"; (2) Presenting a disputable claim in a manner that suggests it is beyond dispute, as in "Her whimsical ideas should not be taken seriously."

713

Brainstorming.   A form of prewriting in which one spontaneously records or utters ideas for a topic.

Categorization.   Arrangement or classification according to shared similarities.

Claim.   The idea or thesis that forms the basis of an argument.

Classical (or Aristotelian) argument.   A model of argument that follows a pre-established structure consisting of an introduction to the problem, a statement of the thesis or claim, a discussion of the evidence in support of the thesis, a refutation of opposing views, and a conclusion.

Clustering.   A form of prewriting in which one spontaneously writes down similar ideas and examples in circled groupings or clusters, in order to generate content for an essay.

Composing process.   A reference to the multiple (but not necessarily sequential or otherwise orderly) activities of a writer in the act of completing a writing task. These activities typically involve such prewriting activities as brainstorming, freewriting, listing, and clustering; drafting activities such as preparing a first draft, revising, re-revising, and copyediting; and proofreading.

Data.   Another word for *evidence*. It can also refer to statistical evidence as opposed to testimonial, mathematical, or observational evidence.

Database.   An electronic list of references grouped by subject matter.

Deduction.   A mode of reasoning that begins with what is known to be true, and seeks to determine the elements or premises that demonstrate the validity of that truth. *See also* Induction.

Definition.   In argumentative writing, definitions of technical terms are often necessary when the claim involves a specialized topic in law, the sciences, technology, business, and industry. A definition often includes reference to a word or expression's origin (etymology), and usage history, as well as a standard lexical meaning.

Denying the antecedent fallacy.   *See* Affirming the consequent fallacy.

Development.   Examining an idea in depth, using illustrations, cases in point, analysis, statistics, and other means of supporting assertions.

Discourse.   Sustained communication through oral or written language. There are three modes of discourse: (1) expository (or referential), which refers to explanation and analysis; (2) expressive, which refers to descriptive and dramatic writing; and (3) persuasive, which refers to the use of the Aristotelian appeals to change readers' minds about something. *See also* Appeals.

Either/or fallacy.   An error of reasoning in which a many-sided argument is presented as having only two sides. Also known as the *false dichotomy*.

Enthymeme.   In deductive reasoning, a syllogism in which one of the premises goes unstated because it is assumed to be understood. In the enthymeme, "Socrates is mortal because he is a human being," the omitted-because-understood premise is "All human beings are mortal." *See also* Syllogism.

Ethos.   *See* Appeals.

Evidence.   Support for a claim. Evidence may be direct (data from surveys, experiments, research studies, and so on) or indirect (mathematical or logical reasoning). *See also* Proof.

Fallacy.   An error or flaw in logical reasoning.

False analogy or faulty analogy.   An error of reasoning that assumes the accuracy of an inaccurate (false) or inappropriate (faulty) comparison.

False dichotomy.   *See* Either/or fallacy.

Fourth-term fallacy.   An error of reasoning in which one term is carelessly or deceptively substituted for another in order to force the assumption that both terms mean the same thing (thereby adding a "fourth term" to a syllogism, which can contain only three terms in their respective premises: major, middle, and minor). *See also* Syllogism.

Freewriting.   A form of prewriting in which one writes spontaneously and swiftly without regard to organization, development, usage, or mechanics.

Generalization.   A nonspecific, summative statement about an idea or situation. If a generalization does not account for some situations it is said to be *hasty* or *premature*. If a generalization is not accompanied by particular examples, it is said to be *unsupported*.

Glosses.   Notes, such as comments or cross-references, in the margins of texts that enhance understanding as well as help to develop a critical stance on the ideas presented.

Hasty generalization.   *See* Generalization.

In-depth reading.   In critical reading, the stage of reading involving close attention to complexities of the topic, to subtle meanings and inferences; follows Previewing. *See also* Previewing.

Induction.   Form of reasoning whereby one attempts a generalization or hypothesis after considering particular cases or samples, not before. *See also* Deduction.

Linking.   In critical reading, the connecting of one part of a sentence with another in order to determine meaning and continuity of idea.

Listserv.   An online discussion group, acquired through subscription.

Mediation.   A form of argument that attempts to fairly present an objective discussion of opposing views before attempting to reach a conclusion.

Newsgroup.   An electronic bulletin board or forum. Also known as *usenet*.

Non sequitur fallacy.   Error in reasoning in which an assertion cannot logically be tied to the premise it attempts to demonstrate.

Paraphrase.   *See* Quotation.

Persuasion.   A form of argument that relies on using emotional appeals more than logical analysis to get readers or listeners to change their minds about something.

Plagiarism.   The use of others' ideas as if they were one's own. Plagiarism is a violation of international copyright law and therefore illegal.

Poisoning the well fallacy.   Attempting to corrupt an argument before the argument begins.

Post hoc fallacy.   Shortened form of *post hoc ergo propter hoc* ("after the fact, therefore because of the fact"). An error of reasoning in which one attaches a causal relationship to a sequential one.

Premature conclusion.   *See* Generalization.

Previewing.   The initial stage of critical reading consisting of prereading, skim-reading, and postreading. *See also* In-depth reading.

Prove.   To provide evidence involving mathematical deduction or the presentation of indisputable facts.

Proofreading.   Reading semifinal draft copy for errors in grammar, spelling, punctuation, capitalization, and the like.

Qualifier.   In Toulmin argument, a limitation imposed on a claim that makes it valid only under some or most circumstances, but not all. *See also* Toulmin argument.

Quotation.   The words of an authority used in argumentative writing to reinforce one's own views on a given topic. Direct quotation refers to verbatim citation of the author's words, which are placed in quotation marks. Indirect quotation or paraphrase refers to the author's idea without quoting verbatim. Both forms of quotation must be properly documented.

Red herring fallacy.   An error of reasoning in which one throws in an unrelated but similar seeming bit of information to throw one off the track of the issue being argued.

Refutation.   The technique of representing fairly and then demonstrating the shortcomings of assertions that challenge your own.

Research.   The process of searching, retrieving, and integrating information from outside sources to authenticate or reinforce one's argument.

Review.   A critical evaluation of an artistic work, a new product, or a restaurant.

Revising.   Substantive development or restructuring of a draft. *Cf.* Proofreading.

Rhetoric.   The art of or the techniques used in writing or speaking effectively. Aristotle defined rhetoric as the art of finding the best available means of persuasion in a given case.

Rhetorical rhombus.   A schematic for showing the elements involved in written or oral communication: Purpose, Audience, Writer, Subject.

Rogerian argument.   A mode of argument established by Carl Rogers in which arguers are urged to cooperate, to seek a common ground on which to negotiate their differences.

Serendipity.   In research, a fortunate coming-together of ideas through unexpected discovery.

Slippery slope fallacy. An error of reasoning in which one alludes to a sequence of highly unlikely consequences resulting from an observed or proposed situation.

Summary. A highly condensed version of a work using or paraphrasing only the work's key points.

Suspect authority. An error of authorization in which an authority's credentials do not prove his or her expertise on the topic.

Syllogism. A form of logical argument consisting of a major premise ("All stars are suns"), a minor premise ("Sirius is a star"), and a conclusion ("Therefore, Sirius is a sun").

Thesis. The claim or main idea or premise of an argument.

Topic. The specific subject of a paper.

Toulmin argument. A strategy of argument developed by philosopher Stephen A. Toulmin, in which it is understood that any claim is arguable because it is based on personal ethical values or warrants as well as on outside evidence or data.

Tracking. In critical reading, shifting the perspective of meaning from sentence to word or from sentence to paragraph or from paragraph to whole essay.

Tu quoque **fallacy.** Literally "you too." An error of reasoning whereby one asserts that an action (or refusal to take action) is validated by the fact that the other person acted or refused to act. "Why should I obey the rules when you're always breaking them?"

Unsupported generalization. *See* Generalization.

Vague authority. An error of authorization in which an ambiguous entity, such as a concept or discipline, is cited as a figure of authority.

Warrant. *See* Toulmin argument.

Index of Authors and Titles

Index of Terms